MAGILL'S CINEMA ANNUAL

MAGILL'S CINEMA ANNUAL 1993

A Survey of the Films of 1992

Edited by

FRANK N. MAGILL

SALEM PRESS

Pasadena, California Englewood Cliffs, New Jersey

∞ The paper used in these volumes conforms to the American National Standard for Permanence of Paper for Printed Library Materials, Z39.48-1984.

LIBRARY OF CONGRESS CATALOG CARD NO. 83-644357
ISBN 0-89356-412-5
ISSN 0739-2141

First Printing

PRINTED IN THE UNITED STATES OF AMERICA

PUBLISHER'S NOTE

Magill's Cinema Annual, 1993, is the twelfth annual volume in a series that developed from the twenty-one-volume core set, *Magill's Survey of Cinema*. Each annual covers the preceding year and follows a similar format in reviewing the films of the year. This format consists of four general sections: two essays of general interest, the films of 1992, lists of obituaries and awards, and the indexes.

In the first section, the first article reviews the career and accomplishments of the recipient of the Life Achievement Award, which is presented by the American Film Institute. In 1992, this award was given to the distinguished actor Sidney Poitier. Following this initial essay, the reader will find an essay that lists selected film books published in 1992. Briefly annotated, the list provides a valuable guide to the current literature about the film industry and its leaders.

The largest section of the annual, "Selected Films of 1992," is devoted to essay-reviews of one hundred significant films released in the United States in 1992. The reviews are arranged alphabetically by the title under which the film was released in the United States. Original and alternate titles are cross-referenced to the American-release title in the Title Index.

Each article begins with selected credits for the film. Credit categories include: Production, Direction, Screenplay, Cinematography, Editing, Art direction, and Music. Also included are the MPAA rating, the running time, and a list of the principal characters with the corresponding actors. This introductory information on a film not released originally in the United States also includes the country of origin and the year the film was released there. If the information for any of the standard categories was unavailable, the heading is followed by the phrase "no listing." Additional headings such as Special effects, Costume design, and Song have been included in an article's introductory top matter when appropriate. Also, the symbol (AA) in the top matter identifies those artists who have received an Academy Award for their contribution to the film from the Academy of Motion Picture Arts and Sciences.

The section of the annual labeled "More Films of 1992" supplies the reader with an alphabetical listing of an additional 209 feature films released in the United States during the year. Included are brief credits and short descriptions of the films. These films can be located, along with any cross-references, in the indexes.

Two further lists conclude the text of the volume. The first of these is the Obituaries, which provides useful information about the careers of motion-picture professionals who died in 1992. The second list is of the awards presented by ten different international associations, from the Academy of Motion Picture Arts and Sciences to the Cannes International Film Festival and the British Academy Awards.

The final section of this volume includes nine indexes that cover the films reviewed in *Magill's Cinema Annual*, 1993. Arranged in the order established in the introductory matter of the essay-reviews, the indexes are as follows: Title Index, Director Index, Screenwriter Index, Cinematographer Index, Editor Index, Art Director Index, Music Index, and Performer Index. A Subject Index is also provided. To assist the reader further, pseudonyms, foreign titles, and alternate titles are all cross-referenced. Titles of foreign films and retrospective films are followed by the year, in brackets, of their original release.

The Title Index includes all the titles of films covered in individual articles, in "More Films of 1992," and also those discussed at some length in the general essays. The next seven indexes are arranged according to artists, each of whose names is followed by a list of the films on which they worked and the titles of the essays (such as "Life Achievement Award" or "Obituaries") in which they are mentioned at length. The final listing is the Subject Index, in which any one film can be categorized under several headings. Thus, a reader can effectively use all these indexes to approach a film from any one of several directions, including not only its credits but also its subject matter.

CONTRIBUTING REVIEWERS

McCrea Adams
Free-lance Reviewer

Michael Adams
Fairleigh Dickinson University

JoAnn Balingit
University of Delaware

Mary E. Belles
Free-lance Reviewer

Cynthia K. Breckenridge
Free-lance Reviewer

Beverley Bare Buehrer
Free-lance Reviewer

Ethan Casey
Free-lance Reviewer

Greg Changnon
Free-lance Reviewer

Robert F. Chicatelli
Free-lance Reviewer

Richard G. Cormack
Free-lance Reviewer

George Delalis
Free-lance Reviewer

Bill Delaney
Free-lance Reviewer

Susan Doll
Free-lance Reviewer

Thomas L. Erskine
Salisbury State University

Dan Georgakas
Editor, Cineaste

Douglas Gomery
University of Maryland

Roberta F. Green
Virginia Polytechnic Institute and State University

Glenn Hopp
Howard Payne University

Eleah Horwitz
Free-lance Reviewer

Anahid Kassabian
Stanford University

Jim Kline
Free-lance Reviewer

Cher Langdell
Free-lance Reviewer

Leon Lewis
Appalachian State University

Blake Lucas
Free-lance Reviewer

Cono Robert Marcazzo
Upsala College

Robert Mitchell
University of Arizona

Debra Picker
Free-lance Reviewer

Francis Poole
University of Delaware

Stephen Soitos
University of Massachusetts

Catherine R. Springer
Free-lance Reviewer

Gaylyn Studlar
Emory University

Terry Theodore
University of North Carolina at Wilmington

James M. Welsh
Salisbury State University

CONTENTS

Life Achievement Award
Sidney Poitier

In the twentieth presentation of its Life Achievement Award, the American Film Institute honored an actor and director whose success within the Hollywood film industry in the 1950's and 1960's was unprecedented simply because of his race. Sidney Poitier's emergence as a leading man, as a major box-office power, and later as a successful director was groundbreaking for an African-American man in mainstream American cinema. The brilliance of the first phase of his career as a film actor can only be appreciated within the context of how Hollywood—both before, during, and after Poitier's arrival from the New York theater scene in 1950—relegated African Americans (and people of color from other nations as well) to stereotyped roles. Poitier himself has noted of his own film-going experience: "When I saw a Negro on the screen, I always left the theater feeling embarrassment and uneasiness."

Hollywood's racial stereotyping was as solidly in place by the time Poitier arrived in Hollywood as the techniques of editing, camera work, and storytelling that distinguished American films. In 1915, the so-called father of cinema, D. W. Griffith, created *The Birth of a Nation*, the first full-scale American film epic that simultaneously served as an affirmation of white supremacy through its celebration of the Ku Klux Klan as the heroes of Reconstruction. Ironically, Griffith cast white actors and extras in the roles of African Americans because he did not believe blacks capable of depicting their own "true" natures. To Griffith, that nature fell into two categories: sentimental and childlike former slaves or frenzied, miscegenation-minded subhumans. Although many critics reacted with loathing to Griffith's racial politics, *The Birth of a Nation* was an unprecedented box-office success.

Hollywood seemed to have learned little in the way of racial sensitivity and its own power to feed prejudice by 1927, the year that sound arrived in full force to American film. In *The Jazz Singer*, the Warner Bros. hit that sealed the transition to sound, it was still deemed acceptable for a white performer such as Al Jolson to don "blackface" and imitate African-American minstrel conventions. In the 1930's, African Americans were depicted in severely limited stereotypes, often as comic relief in the form of shiftless, superstitious servants epitomized in the performances of actor Stepin Fetchit (the stage name of Lincoln Perry). African-American actress Hattie McDaniel supposedly remarked that it was better to play a maid than to be one. Nevertheless, some commentators wondered how this type of character portrayal, even an Academy Award-winning one such as McDaniel's Mammy in *Gone with the Wind* (1939), could do more than reinforce the prejudice that kept African-American film viewers in racially segregated sections of film theaters throughout much of the country.

While musical performers and dancers such as Cab Calloway, the Nicholas Brothers, Lena Horne, Bill Robinson, and others might find their niche in Hollywood as specialty performers or in the cast of the occasional "all-Negro" musical, no African or African American had ever broken into the ranks of full-fledged, mainstream stardom. In particular, the idea of a black man becoming a leading man seemed virtually unthinkable. In the 1930's, former Rhodes scholar Paul Robeson portrayed Shakespeare's Othello on the London stage as a complex, sexualized human being; in Hollywood, however, Robeson could only play Eugene O'Neill's debased protagonist Emperor Jones or be frozen into the racial symbolism associated with the song "Ole Man River" in the 1936 film version of the Jerome Kern and Oscar Hammerstein musical *Show Boat*. It is no wonder, then, that the emerging career of Sidney Poitier during Hollywood's post-World War II era must be regarded, in many ways, as a miracle because of the entrenched audience prejudice and institutionalized stereotyping that he faced.

Born in the Bahamas, Poitier, the son of farmers, dropped out of school at the age of thirteen and immigrated to the United States to join his brother. As a delivery boy in Miami, he encountered what he later referred to as the "lacerating" effect of prejudice that demanded that he "go to the back door." Still a teenager, he joined the Army, only to be discharged within a year. Finding himself in New York City, he had few prospects beyond dishwashing because he was unable to read and write and was hindered by his thick Caribbean accent. Yet, undeterred by apparently overwhelming odds, he responded to an advertisement for an audition at a Harlem theater. He failed the audition, but his interest in acting led him to return to the theater to study in exchange for janitorial work. He learned "proper" English diction by listening to the radio.

His second audition in 1945 with the American Negro Theater Playhouse landed him the role of understudy to Harry Belafonte in *Days of Our Youth*. As luck would have it, one night Poitier had to assume the part. His theater career took off. Soon he acquired his first film role, as a doctor facing prejudice in *No Way Out* (1950), a Joseph L. Mankiewicz production that provoked critical controversy, as many Poitier films would later do because of their "racial politics." Within the political-cultural context of intolerance exacerbated by Joseph McCarthy and the House Committee on Un-American Activities hearings, it is no surprise that the film was accused of being "Red-inspired propaganda." *No Way Out* was also the first among many films in which Sidney Poitier would break with Hollywood's traditional depiction of African Americans. He would appear not as a comic foil or entertainer but as a sensitive and competent professional—as a doctor, lawyer, teacher, or police officer.

In 1951, Poitier traveled to South Africa for Zoltan Korda's production of *Cry the Beloved Country*, but in Hollywood, his breakthrough film came with *Blackboard Jungle* in 1955. In this film, he portrayed a juvenile delinquent who is finally influenced for the better by a schoolteacher played by Glenn Ford. Ironically, in 1967, Poitier would play a similar kind of teacher in James Clavell's *To Sir with Love*. This film would become a huge box-office hit, one of many successful films in the 1960's that elevated Poitier, perhaps Hollywood's unlikeliest of leading men in the racially tense 1960's, into the pantheon of box-office attractions.

Before hitting this pinnacle of popular success, Poitier turned in a number of quietly intense performances in films such as *Edge of the City* (1957) and Richard Brooks's heartfelt plea for civil rights, *Something of Value* (1957), which garnered for Poitier the Venice Film Festival's award for Best Actor. Unfortunately, for every step forward in revising Hollywood cinema's depiction of blacks, even Poitier sometimes had steps backward. In 1957, he was also cast as an ambitious former slave in *Band of Angels* (1957), a lurid Civil War melodrama starring Clark Gable and Yvonne DeCarlo. In 1959, Poitier accepted a role in the film version of *Porgy and Bess*. Of this experience he would later say: "I hated doing it, but pressure was brought . . . and there were threats of my career stopping dead." Between these two racially regressive films, Poitier costarred with Tony Curtis in Stanley Kramer's controversial story of the friendship that develops between black and white prisoners who are literally chained together. *The Defiant Ones* (1958), like a number of other Poitier films, was not screened in some Southern theater venues, but Poitier's performance nevertheless earned for him an Academy Award nomination for Best Actor, the first ever for a black man.

Intervening films would cement the critical consensus that Poitier was among the most talented actors in Hollywood. He provided one of his most moving performances of this period of his career in the film adaptation of Lorraine Hansberry's stage play *A Raisin in the Sun* (1961). In this film, Poitier essayed the role of Walter Lee Johnson, a role that, in spite of the passage of time, has lost none of its power to speak poignantly to the problematic place of young African-American males within American society at every level—including within their own families. Revealing a complexity that is still rare for films that deal with race in the United States, *A Raisin in the Sun* suggests that the place of African-American males is made problematic not by strong-minded African-American women but by a bigoted society that undermines their sense of self and frustrates their dreams of success at every turn.

In spite of Poitier's success in bringing more complex depictions of African-American men to the screen, some criticized his roles for failing to break a pattern: Hollywood's oscillation between desexualizing the African-American male and sexualizing him in wildly racist terms that harkened back to when Griffith showed Gus chasing after Little Sister in *The Birth of a Nation*. While Poitier's role as a jazz musician in *Paris Blues* (1961) was the first film to turn on his ability to play a romantic leading man (to Diahann Carroll), he was not the film's sole romantic male lead: Paul Newman costarred to romance Joanne Woodward's character. Some critics would find Poitier's next film the kind of safe role that was palatable to white audiences at the expense of the complex humanity of African-American men as sexual beings. In *Lilies of the Field* (1963), Poitier plays a handyman who comes to the aid of Austrian nuns who are trying to make a living on a farm. Nevertheless, in spite of some disgruntled reactions to Poitier's "asexual" role as Homer, *Lilies of the Field* proved that Poitier could carry a film as a star, and it would be notable too in providing the vehicle for his winning of the Academy Award for Best Actor, a feat never before achieved by a black man.

A string of critically and financially successful films would follow, capped by Poitier's memorable portrayal of Virgil Tibbs in *In the Heat of the Night*, winner of the Best Picture Oscar for 1967. This suspense thriller, directed by Norman Jewison, focuses on an African-American police officer's confrontation with the open bigotry of a small Southern town. As he quietly waits at the Sparta, Mississippi, train station, Tibbs is arrested. He hears the words, "On your feet, boy." A deputy (Warren Oates) assumes that because he is black and a stranger, Tibbs must be guilty of the murder of a local industrialist that has occurred that night. Sheriff Bill Gillespie (Rod Steiger) savagely ridicules Tibbs until Tibbs announces that he is a police officer. It soon becomes apparent that, as a homicide expert, Tibbs is needed to solve the murder of which he was formerly accused, but the town and the sheriff cannot tolerate the presence of a self-confident, independent African-American male. In spite of this fact, Tibbs is retained because Mrs. Colbert (Lee Grant), the rich widow of the murder victim, believes that Gillespie merely wants to use a cover-up arrest to solve her husband's murder.

As do a number of other Poitier films, *In the Heat of the Night* relies on a strategy of counterpointing Poitier as an attractive, rational, and dignified professional with ignorant, irrational, and unattractive racists. As in so many other of his roles during this period, Poitier's Virgil Tibbs exercises an almost superhuman control over his emotions in the face of ongoing racial abuse until finally exploding verbally in a moment of righteous anger. In the end, Tibbs solves the murder and accomplishes more, as the basically decent sheriff reaches beyond the limits of his own ingrained racism and is brought to a recognition of their shared interests and humanity.

Poitier's last major role of this period was in a film that has become a kind of bellwether of Hollywood's fitful attempt in the 1960's to deal with racial issues: Stanley Kramer's controversial hit *Guess Who's Coming to Dinner?* (1967). The film is a star-studded and stultifyingly self-conscious exploration of the impact of interracial romance on the families of those involved. Poitier plays the doctor and fiancé whose only "flaw" is his color. His saintly role in the film was overshadowed by the pairing of Katharine Hepburn and Spencer Tracy as the parents of the woman (played by Katharine Houghton) with whom Poitier's character has fallen in love.

After this film, Poitier began to turn to motion pictures that were more centered on African Americans, both in terms of the performers put in front of the camera and the crew behind it. He formed his own production company in 1972 and made his directorial debut with *Buck and the Preacher*, coproduced by his E and R Productions and Belafonte Enterprises. In 1973, Poitier joined a rarefied league of superstars by forming the First Artists Production Company with Paul Newman, Barbra Streisand, and Steve McQueen. In 1974, Poitier began directing a series of successful comedies, starting with *Uptown Saturday Night*, many of which would be smash box-office hits. For a few years, he continued to move between acting and directing, but by the end of the 1970's, he was solidly into direction. He began the 1980's by directing the biggest box-office hit of the year, the Richard Pryor-Gene Wilder comedy *Stir Crazy* (1980).

After a ten-year hiatus from acting, Poitier returned to the screen in *Little Nikita* (1988), but made his most impressive acting appearance of these later years in a television miniseries sensitively directed by George Stevens, Jr., entitled *Separate but Equal*. The miniseries' beginning is set in the early 1950's in Clarendon, South Carolina. A black minister and principal and a pupil's father decide that they want to buy a used school bus because African-American children must walk miles to their segregated "doghouse" school. This modestly conceived struggle for equality ultimately leads them to the Supreme Court of the United States. A beautifully photographed and finely nuanced drama, the miniseries' ostensible hero is National Association for the Advancement of Colored People (NAACP) lawyer Thurgood Marshall (Poitier), who argues the case against segregation before the courts. In addition to portraying many riveting scenes of courtroom drama involving Marshall, a future justice of the United States Supreme Court, the miniseries was unusually ambitious in illuminating the roles of unsung African Americans who risked their peace of mind, their homes, their livelihoods, and their lives by challenging the customs naturalized in their time and place as "right and proper" yet so obviously wrong. *Separate but Equal* revealed not only the potential power of television drama to deal with sensitive and important issues without trivializing them but also the continuing power of Poitier's acting talent.

By the 1990's, Sidney Poitier was no longer the young man whose success in Hollywood defied every unwritten law of the land concerning the requirements of film stardom. As a dramatic actor in such films as *Sneakers* (1992) and as a director of such films as *Ghost Dad* (1990), Poitier has continued to work within an industry that, metaphorically, still seems to ask black actors to "go to the back door." With the presentation of the American Film Institute's Life Achievement Award, Poitier's distinguished accomplishments as an individual artist and as a leader in changing the industry's racial attitudes were appropriately honored. While the success of the American feature film may have begun with the racism of D. W. Griffith, Sidney Poitier's triumph provides hope that this culturally powerful form of storytelling has progressed, or soon will progress, to a different and better place than the one where it began.

Gaylyn Studlar

SELECTED FILM BOOKS OF 1992

Altman, Dana. *Hollywood East: Louis B. Mayer and the Origins of the Studio System*. New York: Birch Lane Press, 1992. A study of the rise of the American studio system, including a stout effort to rehabilitate the reputation of mogul Louis B. Mayer.

Arkoff, Sam. *Flying Through Hollywood by the Seat of My Pants*. New York: Birch Lane Press, 1992. The cofounder of American International Pictures offers behind-the-scenes anecdotes from his career as the producer of popular low-budget films in the 1950's and 1960's.

Aumont, Jacques, Alain Bergala, Michel Marie, and Marc Vernet. *Aesthetics of Film*. Austin: University of Texas Press, 1992. Four prominent French film critics offer a comprehensive theory of film in this revised version of a work that was originally published in France in 1983.

Bawer, Bruce. *The Screenplay's the Thing*. Hamden, Conn.: Archon Books, 1992. Literary critic Bawer reviewed films for *The American Spectator* from 1986 to 1990. This book compiles eighty-five reviews plus several additional essays on cinema in general.

Beauchamp, Cari, and Henri Behar. *Hollywood on the Riviera: The Inside Story of the Cannes Film Festival*. New York: William Morrow, 1992. An entertaining history of the world's most famous film festival, offering details on the complex workings of the international film marketplace.

Berg, Charles Ramirez. *Cinema of Solitude: A Critical Study of Mexican Films, 1967-1983*. Austin: University of Texas Press, 1992. Berg analyzes the major films and filmmakers of Mexico's New Cinema movement in this first book-length study of Mexican cinema written in English.

Billips, Connie. *Janet Gaynor: A Bio-Bibliography*. New York: Greenwood Press, 1992. Gaynor was a prominent leading lady in the 1920's and 1930's; this work offers a summary of her career, along with a filmography and bibliography.

Bondanella, Peter. *The Cinema of Federico Fellini*. Princeton, N.J.: Princeton University Press, 1992. A scholarly analysis of the life and work of the Italian director, noting the influence of psychologist Carl Jung's writings on Fellini's films.

Bowman, Barbara. *Master Space: Film Images of Capra, Lubitsch, Sternberg, and Wyler*. New York: Greenwood Press, 1992. Bowman analyzes the use of screen space in the films of four master filmmakers.

Brown, Peter Harry, and Patte B. Barham. *Marilyn: The Last Take*. New York: Dutton, 1992. This account of the last fourteen weeks of Monroe's life offers details about the studio politics that led to the collapse of her final film and about the mysterious circumstances of her death.

Burton, Philip. *Richard and Philip: The Burtons, a Book of Memories*. London: Peter Owen, 1992. Playwright and director Philip Burton was Richard Burton's teacher, mentor, and adoptive father. This is the story of their four decades of friendship.

Champlin, Charles. *George Lucas: The Creative Impulse*. New York: Harry N.

Abrams, 1992. Champlin offers a profusely illustrated appreciation of the career of one of the most successful producer/directors of the 1980's.

Chesher, R. Donna. *"The End."* Jefferson, N.C.: McFarland, 1992. This volume compiles the closing lines of more than three thousand American films, listing the character who delivered the line and the actor who played the character.

Clover, Carol J. *Men, Women, and Chain Saws: Gender in the Modern Horror Film.* Princeton, N.J.: Princeton University Press, 1992. In this scholarly feminist study, Clover argues that audience identification with the women who ultimately defeat their attackers mitigates the misogynistic themes of contemporary "slasher" films.

Corey, Melinda, and George Ochoa. *Movies and TV: The New York Public Library's Book of Answers.* New York: Simon & Schuster, 1992. Arranged by category, this entertaining compilation of facts and trivia comes from the Telephone Reference Service of the New York Public Library.

Crawford, Peter Ian, and David Turton, eds. *Film as Ethnography.* New York: Manchester University Press, 1992. The nineteen scholarly essays in this collection examine documentary studies of other cultures. Compares the filmed versus the written representations of non-Western ways of life.

Custen, George F. *Bio/Pics: How Hollywood Constructed Public History.* New Brunswick, N.J.: Rutgers University Press, 1992. In this valuable addition to the literature, Custen offers a history of the American biographical film, analyzing three hundred films released between 1927 and 1960.

Dalle Vache, Angela. *The Body in the Mirror: Shapes of History in Italian Cinema.* Princeton, N.J.: Princeton University Press, 1992. A scholarly examination of Italian culture as expressed in Italian film.

Del Vecchio, Deborah, and Tom Johnson. *Peter Cushing: The Gentle Man of Horror and His Ninety-one Films.* Jefferson, N.C.: McFarland, 1992. This volume offers a detailed analysis of the actor's career. Entries for each film include cast and credits, a plot synopsis, and a commentary on the film and its reception.

Diawara, Manthia. *African Cinema: Politics and Culture.* Bloomington: Indiana University Press, 1992. A good overview of the state of film production and distribution in sub-Saharan Africa, tracing the history of and current developments in different countries in the region.

Dick, Bernard F., ed. *Columbia Pictures: Portrait of a Studio.* Lexington: University Press of Kentucky, 1992. A collection of thirteen essays on the Hollywood studio, including one historical overview and a dozen essays on important actors, directors, and films associated with Columbia. Also contains a filmography of the studio's output from 1920 to 1991.

Ehrenstein, David. *The Scorsese Picture: The Art and Life of Martin Scorsese.* New York: Birch Lane Press, 1992. Less a biography than an analysis of the work of an important filmmaker. Notes the influences on Scorsese's career and offers examples of his creative decision-making processes.

Endres, Stacey, and Robert Cushman. *Hollywood at Your Feet: The Story of the World-Famous Chinese Theatre.* Los Angeles: Pomegranate Press, 1992. An illustrated history of perhaps the most-famous film theater in the United States, Sid Grauman's Chinese Theatre.

Erickson, Hal. *Baseball in the Movies: A Comprehensive Reference, 1915-1991.* Jefferson, N.C.: McFarland, 1992. Covering eighty-one films, this reference volume provides information on cast and credits along with a plot summary and critical analysis for each film.

Everson, William K. *The Hollywood Western.* Secaucus, N.J.: Citadel Press, 1992. A revision of the author's 1971 *The Pictorial History of the Western Film*, this is an illustrated survey of the Western genre, with an emphasis on the classical, pre-1950 period.

Fetrow, Alan G. *Sound Films, 1927-1939: A United States Filmography.* Jefferson, N.C.: McFarland, 1992. A comprehensive filmography of the first thirteen years of American feature-length sound film production, including low-budget films as well as major studio productions. Each entry contains information on cast and credits, as well as a one-sentence plot synopsis.

Fowles, Jib. *Starstruck.* Washington, D.C.: Smithsonian Institution Press, 1992. Fowles examines the role of the celebrity in American culture, basing his conclusions on the lives of one hundred performers from a variety of entertainment media.

Fragola, Anthony N., and Roch C. Smith. *The Erotic Dream Machine.* Carbondale: Southern Illinois University Press, 1992. A series of interviews with writer-filmmaker Alain Robbe-Grillet, in which the director offers his views on literature and philosophy as well as on cinema.

Froug, William. *The New Screenwriter Looks at the New Screenwriter.* Los Angeles: Silman-James Press, 1992. Fifteen contemporary screenwriters analyze their craft and their careers in this compilation of interviews.

Fuller, Elizabeth. *Me and Jezebel: When Bette Davis Came for Dinner and Stayed.* New York: Berkley Publishing Group, 1992. Davis was the author's house guest for a month in 1985; this is a humorous account of that visit.

Goldman, Herbert G. *Fanny Brice: The Original Funny Girl.* New York: Oxford University Press, 1992. The definitive biography of the stage and screen star; it includes a complete filmography.

Grant, Barry Keith. *Voyages of Discovery: The Cinema of Frederick Wiseman.* Urbana: University of Illinois Press, 1992. A study of the work of the documentary filmmaker best known for his controversial *Titicut Follies.*

Grey, Rudolph. *Nightmare of Ecstasy: The Life and Art of Edward D. Wood, Jr.* Los Angeles: Feral House, 1992. Wood made such cult or camp classics as *Glen or Glenda?* (1953) and *Plan Nine from Outer Space* (1959); this is an oral history of the eccentric filmmaker.

Hamon, Herve, and Patrick Rotman. *You See, I Haven't Forgotten: Yves Montand.* New York: Alfred A. Knopf, 1992. A compelling biography of the French actor and entertainer, written in collaboration with Montand.

Helt, Richard C., and Marie E. Helt. *West German Cinema, 1985-1990: A Reference*

Handbook. Metuchen, N.J.: Scarecrow Press, 1992. This volume updates the authors' earlier work through the German reunification and the end of West Germany. It provides filmographies with information on cast and credits, as well as one-sentence plot synopses.

Hill, Geoffrey. *Illuminating Shadows: The Mythic Power of Film*. Boston: Shambala, 1992. Hill analyzes seventeen films in a collection of essays seeking to identify classic mythical archetypes in film.

Hirano, Kyoko. *Mr. Smith Goes to Tokyo*. Washington, D.C.: Smithsonian Institution Press, 1992. A scholarly study of Japanese cinema in the aftermath of World War II (from 1945 to 1952), when American occupation forces dictated the content of the films.

Imperato, Pascal James, and Eleanor M. Imperato. *They Married Adventure: The Wandering Lives of Martin and Osa Johnson*. New Brunswick, N.J.: Rutgers University Press, 1992. The Johnsons were documentary filmmakers in the early twentieth century; this work chronicles their career.

Jacobs, Diane. *Christmas in July: The Life and Art of Preston Sturges*. Berkeley: University of California Press, 1992. Jacobs chronicles Sturges' feast-or-famine career, from his successful comedies of the 1940's to his death in obscurity a decade later. One of two important works on this significant director published in 1992.

Jarvie, Ian. *Hollywood's Overseas Campaign: The North Atlantic Movie Trade, 1920-1950*. New York: Cambridge University Press, 1992. A scholarly examination of the growth, structure, and direction of the import and export of films between the United States, Canada, and Great Britain from 1920 to 1950.

Jenkins, Henry. *What Made Pistachio Nuts?* New York: Columbia University Press, 1992. This scholarly work, which examines the anarchic film comedies of the early sound era, traces vaudeville traditions in the cinematic work of the Marx Brothers, W. C. Fields, and their contemporaries.

Jewish Film Directory. Westport, Conn.: Greenwood Press, 1992. This alphabetical list of more than 1,200 films "of Jewish interest" is international in scope and covers eight decades of film. Each entry contains a one-sentence plot synopsis and a reference to reviews in *Variety* where such information exists.

Kaleta, Kenneth C. *David Lynch*. New York: Twayne, 1992. An enthusiastic survey of the quirky director's film career, including an analysis of the *Twin Peaks* television series.

Kalinak, Kathryn. *Settling the Score: Music and the Classical Hollywood Film*. Madison: University of Wisconsin Press, 1992. This scholarly study of film scoring emphasizes the valuable contribution that music makes to the overall impact of a film.

Kapsis, Robert E. *Hitchcock: The Making of a Reputation*. Chicago: University of Chicago Press, 1992. This addition to the long list of works about Alfred Hitchcock concentrates on the director's efforts to win respect from audiences and critics for the suspense and horror genres in which he worked.

Kenez, Peter. *Cinema and Soviet Society, 1917-1953*. New York: Cambridge University Press, 1992. Kenez examines Soviet film as propaganda and the ways in which the leaders of the Russian Revolution influenced Soviet society through cinema.

Kirihara, Donald. *Patterns of Time: Mizoguchi and the 1930's*. Madison: University of Wisconsin Press, 1992. A detailed and scholarly study of the early films of this major Japanese filmmaker.

Kisch, John, and Edward Mapp. *A Separate Cinema: Fifty Years of Black-Cast Posters*. New York: Farrar, Straus & Giroux, 1992. This compilation of publicity posters from films featuring black performers sheds light on an underexamined genre.

Kline, T. Jefferson. *Screening the Text*. Baltimore: The Johns Hopkins University Press, 1992. A scholarly analysis of French New Wave Cinema.

Knight, Julia. *Women and the New German Cinema*. London: Verso, 1992. Knight offers an in-depth study of the role of women filmmakers in the New German Cinema movement of the 1970's and 1980's.

Lawton, Anna, ed. *The Red Screen: Politics, Society, Art in Soviet Cinema*. London: Routledge, 1992. A collection of twenty scholarly essays on the role of film in Soviet society.

Leaming, Barbara. *Bette Davis: A Biography*. New York: Simon & Schuster, 1992. This biography of the late star contrasts the actress' on-screen talent with her messy personal life.

LoBrutto, Vincent. *By Design: Interviews with Film Production Designers*. Westport, Conn.: Praeger, 1992. These twenty interviews provide useful information on the art of production design for film.

Lorentz, Pare. *FDR's Moviemaker*. Reno: University of Nevada Press, 1992. Lorentz was a documentary filmmaker whose work so impressed Franklin Delano Roosevelt that the president made Lorentz head of the U.S. Film Service. This autobiography includes scripts from four films.

McBride, Joseph. *Frank Capra: The Catastrophe of Success*. New York: Simon & Schuster, 1992. One of two major biographies of Capra published in 1992, McBride's work tends to focus on the contradictions between the director's public image as a friend of the little man and his private life.

McCaffrey, Donald W. *Assault on Society: Satirical Literature to Film*. Metuchen, N.J.: Scarecrow Press, 1992. McCaffrey examines a wide variety of satirical or darkly comic films, primarily from the 1960's and 1970's, which were translated from literature to the screen.

McClelland, Doug. *Forties Film Talk*. Jefferson, N.C.: McFarland, 1992. An entertaining oral history of Hollywood in the 1940's, featuring interviews with actors and others involved with filmmaking. Illustrated with 120 lobby posters from the period.

Medved, Michael. *Hollywood vs. America*. New York: HarperCollins, 1992. Medved argues that popular films and television have consistently exhibited values that are contrary to those of mainstream America as regards religion, violence, sex, and the family.

Miller, Frank. *"Casablanca": As Time Goes By*. Atlanta: Turner, 1992. One of two commemorations of the fiftieth anniversary of this classic film, this volume offers extensive information on the cast and crew, as well as rare stills and other illustrations.

Molyneaux, Gerard. *James Stewart: A Bio-Bibliography*. New York: Greenwood Press, 1992. This work provides a brief biographical essay on the actor's career, as well as an extensive filmography, bibliography, discography, and list of radio and television appearances.

Morris, L. Robert, and Lawrence Raskin. *"Lawrence of Arabia": The Official Thirtieth Anniversary Pictorial History*. New York: Doubleday, 1992. A coffee-table book that salutes David Lean's rereleased epic.

Munn, Michael. *Hollywood Rogues*. New York: St. Martin's Press, 1992. A relatively standard compilation of film star gossip from Hollywood's golden age through modern times.

Nolletti, Arthur, Jr., and David Desser. *Reframing Japanese Cinema: Authorship, Genre, History*. Bloomington: Indiana University Press, 1992. A collection of fifteen scholarly essays, each of which examines some aspect of Japanese film from the silent era into the 1970's.

O'Donnell, Pierce, and Dennis McDougal. *Fatal Subtraction*. New York: Doubleday, 1992. The attorney of humorist Art Buchwald offers this account of Buchwald's lawsuit against Paramount over *Coming to America* (1988), offering insights on the "creative" accounting practices of major American studios.

Oldham, Gabriella. *First Cut: Conversations with Film Editors*. Los Angeles: University of California Press, 1992. A collection of interviews with twenty-two prominent film editors, illustrating the contribution made by their craft to the finished product on the screen.

Oshima, Nagisa. *Cinema, Censorship, and the State: The Writings of Nagisa Oshima, 1956-1978*. Cambridge, Mass.: MIT Press, 1992. One of Japan's most important filmmakers, Oshima has written extensively on the relationship of film and politics. This volume of his writings also includes a filmography.

Parenti, Michael. *Make-Believe Media: The Politics of Entertainment*. New York: St. Martin's Press, 1992. Parenti argues that contemporary films and television are militaristic, racist, sexist, and authoritarian.

Parish, James Robert. *Prostitution in Hollywood Films*. Jefferson, N.C.: McFarland, 1992. This work contains information on plots, cast, and credits, as well as brief critiques, for 389 American films that address the issue of prostitution.

Parish, James Robert, and Don Stanke. *Hollywood Baby Boomers*. New York: Garland, 1992. A biographical directory featuring extended and enthusiastic summaries of the careers of eighty American actors born between 1946 and 1964. For some of the less prominent actors profiled, this is the most extensive information available.

Parish, James Robert, and Michael R. Pitts. *The Great Hollywood Musical Pictures*. Metuchen, N.J.: Scarecrow Press, 1992. The authors continue their *Great Pictures* series with this volume on American musicals. They offer a plot synopsis; information on cast, credits, and critical reception; and commentary on nearly 350 films over six decades.

Pearson, Roberta E. *Eloquent Gestures*. Berkeley: University of California Press, 1992. Based on the author's dissertation, this study of acting in silent films focuses on D. W. Griffith's Biograph productions, in which exaggerated theatrical performances become more subtle and modern.

Ponti, James. *Hollywood East: Florida's Fabulous Flicks*. Orlando, Fla.: Tribune, 1992. Screenwriter and critic Ponti surveys every feature film shot in Florida up to 1992. This reference work also includes information on location sites in the state and other Florida film trivia.

Price, Theodore. *Hitchcock and Homosexuality*. Metuchen, N.J.: Scarecrow Press, 1992. Price argues that four interrelated themes were central to Hitchcock's career: homosexuality, Jack the Ripper (a murderer of prostitutes), the sex films of Weimar Germany, and the father-daughter theme. All these themes shed light on the director's ambivalence toward women.

Ragan, David. *Who's Who in Hollywood*. New York: Facts on File, 1992. This two-volume reference work contains biographical information on more than 35,000 actors. Most entries are brief, with filmographies comprising the bulk of the information.

Rainer, Peter, ed. *Love and Hisses: The National Society of Film Critics Sound Off on the Hottest Movie Controversies*. San Francisco: Mercury House, 1992. This compilation of arguments between prominent film critics offers back-to-back praise and condemnation of recent films.

Rainey, Buck. *Sweethearts of the Sage*. Jefferson, N.C.: McFarland, 1992. This handy reference work features biographical information and filmographies for 258 actresses—some prominent, some obscure—who worked in Western films.

Reimer, Robert C., and Carol J. Reimer. *Nazi-Retro Film: How German Narrative Cinema Remembers the Past*. New York: Twayne, 1992. The authors examine more than a hundred postwar German films that attempt to come to grips with the legacy of the Holocaust.

Richard, Alfred Charles, Jr. *The Hispanic Image on the Silver Screen*. New York: Greenwood Press, 1992. Richardson offers commentary on the portrayal of Hispanics in the early years of American cinema (from 1898 to 1935) in a filmography that emphasizes analysis rather than data.

Richardson, Carl. *Autopsy: An Element of Realism in Film Noir*. Metuchen, N.J.: Scarecrow Press, 1992. This study of *film noir* argues that locations were vital to the success of these films and that the element of fantasy introduced into later films led to the demise of the genre.

Rosenfield, Paul. *The Club Rules: Power, Money, Sex, and Fear—How It Works in Hollywood*. New York: Warner Books, 1992. Rosenfield analyzes the unwritten rules of filmmaking in Hollywood in this exposé of the film industry's power structure.

Ruddick, Nicholas, ed. *State of the Fantastic*. Westport, Conn.: Greenwood Press, 1992. This collection of twenty-one essays examines the theory and practice of the fantastic in literature and film.

Schutz, Wayne. *The Motion Picture Serial: An Annotated Bibliography*. Metuchen, N.J.: Scarecrow Press, 1992. A very comprehensive bibliography on film serials, with chapters devoted to the films as well as to production personnel and actors.

Segrave, Kerry. *Drive-In Theaters*. Jefferson, N.C.: McFarland, 1992. A history of the drive-in film theater, from its inception in 1933 through its current near extinction. Segrave examines the changes both in drive-in technology and in its audience as the medium moved from the family fare of the 1940's and 1950's to the exploitation films of later decades.

Senn, Bryan, and John Johnson. *Fantastic Cinema Subject Guide*. Jefferson, N.C.: McFarland, 1992. International in scope and with coverage extending from the silent era into the 1990's, this work provides a topical index to 2,500 horror, science-fiction, and fantasy films. Each entry contains information on cast and credits, as well as a plot synopsis.

Siegel, Jeff. *The "Casablanca" Companion: The Movie and More*. Dallas: Taylor, 1992. A brief compilation of facts and trivia on all aspects of this famous film.

Silverman, Stephen M. *David Lean*. New York: Harry N. Abrams, 1992. A well written and lavishly illustrated authorized biography of this celebrated British filmmaker.

Sklar, Robert. *City Boys: Cagney, Bogart, Garfield*. Princeton, N.J.: Princeton University Press, 1992. Sklar writes about the types of characters portrayed by these three actors in their most prominent films, arguing that they represented the urban values of rebellion and individualism.

Slater, Thomas J., ed. *Handbook of Soviet and East European Films and Filmmakers*. New York: Greenwood Press, 1992. Arranged by country, this useful reference volume provides biographical information on major Eastern European filmmakers, essays on the history of cinema in each country, as well as filmographies and bibliographies to aid further research.

Spignesi, Stephen J. *The Woody Allen Companion*. Kansas City: Andrews & McMeel, 1992. A giddy survey of this filmmaker's career, aimed at the uncritical Allen fan.

Spoto, Donald. *Blue Angel: The Life of Marlene Dietrich*. New York: Doubleday, 1992. The definitive biography of Dietrich, in which Spoto chronicles her sexual as well as her cinematic exploits.

_____________. *Lawrence Olivier: A Biography*. New York: HarperCollins, 1992. Striking a balance between the actor's personal and professional lives, veteran film biographer Spoto's most controversial claim is that Olivier carried on a ten-year love affair with actor and comedian Danny Kaye.

Staiger, Janet. *Interpreting Films*. Princeton, N.J.: Princeton University Press, 1992. Subtitled "Studies in the Historical Reception of American Cinema," this scholarly work analyzes the wide variety of approaches that critics and audiences bring to film.

Stam, Robert, Robert Burgoyne, and Sandy Flitterman-Lewis. *New Vocabularies in Film Semiotics*. London: Routledge, 1992. The subtitle of this work is "Structuralism, Post-Structuralism and Beyond." Offers a history of the application of semiology to film criticism.

Strasberg, Susan. *Marilyn and Me: Sisters, Rivals, Friends*. New York: Warner Books, 1992. In 1954, Marilyn Monroe, already a star but afforded little respect as an actress, began working with Lee Strasberg at Actor's Studio. Strasberg's actress daughter was a teenager at the time; this volume recounts the influence Monroe had on her and her family.

Thomajan, Dale. *From Cyd Charisse to "Psycho": A Book of Movie Bests*. New York: Walker, 1992. Thomajan offers an opinionated work, "written not to settle arguments but to start them," as he selects his personal cinematic "bests" in a variety of areas.

Thomson, David. *Showman: The Life of David O. Selznick*. New York: Alfred A. Knopf, 1992. Thomson chronicles the life of the famous producer in this well-researched and basically unsympathetic biography.

Thumim, Janet. *Celluloid Sisters: Women and Popular Cinema*. London: Macmillan, 1992. A British perspective on female characters in seventy-nine British and American films released between 1945 and 1965; as a feminist, the author deplores the absence of strong, autonomous women in these films.

Vidal, Gore. *Screening History*. Cambridge, Mass.: Harvard University Press, 1992. The popular author blends autobiography, political commentary, and film criticism as he describes his life and times in this slim but engaging volume.

Wapshott, Nicholas. *Rex Harrison: A Biography*. New York: Viking Press, 1992. This biography credits Harrison's acting talents but finds him personally unsympathetic, having been spoiled by a doting mother into insufferable egotism.

Weaver, Tom. *Poverty Row Horrors!* Jefferson, N.C.: McFarland, 1992. Weaver offers a detailed analysis of thirty-one films from Monogram, Republic, and PRC studios, which specialized in low-budget horror films in the early 1940's.

Weiser, Thomas. *Spaghetti Westerns: The Good, the Bad, and the Violent*. Jefferson, N.C.: McFarland, 1992. This reference work provides complete filmographies for 558 European-made Westerns, as well as additional information about personnel associated with these films.

Welles, Orson, and Peter Bogdanovich. *This Is Orson Welles*. Edited by Jonathan Rosenbaum. New York: HarperCollins, 1992. This compilation of interviews between Welles and director and critic Bogdanovich offers useful insights into Welles's career.

Wernblad, Annette. *Brooklyn Is Not Expanding: Woody Allen's Comic Universe*. Rutherford, N.J.: Fairleigh Dickinson University Press, 1992. Wernblad places Allen in the literary and cinematic tradition of artists such as Charlie Chaplin, Philip Roth, and Groucho Marx in this scholarly study.

Wetta, Frank J., and Stephen J. Curley. *Celluloid Wars*. New York: Greenwood Press, 1992. An exhaustive catalog, with commentary, of films about American wars; a useful reference work.

Williams, Alan. *Republic of Images: A History of French Filmmaking*. Cambridge, Mass.: Harvard University Press, 1992. Williams approaches French cinema via biographical studies of its filmmakers in this scholarly volume.

Youngblood, Denise J. *Movies for the Masses: Popular Cinema and Soviet Society in the 1920's*. New York: Cambridge University Press, 1992. A scholarly examination of the works of Iakov Protazanov, Boris Barnet, and Fridrikh Ermler, filmmakers whose work is little known today despite its popularity in the 1920's.

Yule, Andrew. *Sean Connery: From 007 to Hollywood Icon*. New York: Donald I. Fine, 1992. A well-researched biography of this Scottish actor.

Zinneman, Fred. *A Life in the Movies: An Autobiography*. New York: Charles Scribner's Sons, 1992. The heralded director of *High Noon* (1952) and *A Man for All Seasons* (1966) offers a solid, if reticent, account of his life and career.

SELECTED FILMS OF 1992

ALADDIN

Production: John Musker and Ron Clements for Walt Disney Pictures; released by Buena Vista
Direction: John Musker and Ron Clements
Screenplay: Ron Clements, John Musker, Ted Elliott, and Terry Rossio
Editing: H. Lee Peterson
Supervising animation: Glen Keane, Eric Goldberg, Mark Henn, Andreas Deja, Duncan Marjoribanks, Randy Cartwright, Will Finn, and David Pruiksma
Production design: R. S. Vander Wende
Art direction: Bill Perkins
Production management: Alice Dewey
Casting: Albert Tavares
Visual effects supervision: Don Paul
Computer graphics imagery supervision: Steve Goldberg
Artistic coordination: Dan Hansen
Sound: Terry Porter, Mel Metcalfe, and David J. Hudson
Music: Alan Menken (AA)
Songs: Howard Ashman (lyrics) and Alan Menken (music), "Arabian Nights," "Friend Like Me," and "Prince Ali"; Tim Rice (lyrics) and Alan Menken (music), "One Jump Ahead," "A Whole New World" (AA), and "Prince Ali Reprise"
MPAA rating: G
Running time: 90 minutes

Voices of principal characters:

Genie	Robin Williams
Aladdin	Scott Weinger (speaking voice)
Jasmine	Linda Larkin (speaking voice)
Jafar	Jonathan Freeman
Abu	Frank Welker
Iago	Gilbert Gottfried
Sultan	Douglas Seale
Aladdin	Brad Kane (singing voice)
Jasmine	Lea Salonga (singing voice)

Disney had yet another hit in its full-length animated feature *Aladdin*. The sixth animated adaptation of a classic fairy tale made by the Disney Studios, *Aladdin* followed in the wake of the extremely successful *The Little Mermaid* (1989) and *Beauty and the Beast* (1991). Not surprisingly, John Musker and Ron Clements, who directed and cowrote the screenplay for *Aladdin*, had also collaborated on *The Little Mermaid*. *Aladdin*, too, is a musical romance/adventure set in an exotic location. It centers on a poor street urchin, Aladdin (voice of Scott Weinger), in the mythic kingdom of Agrabah. Aladdin falls in love with a beautiful princess, Jasmine (voice of Linda Larkin), and finds a magic lamp with a genie (voice of Robin Williams), who Aladdin believes can make his dreams come true.

The film begins with an Arab storyteller. He tells of an evil sorcerer, Jafar (voice of Jonathan Freeman), who desires a magic lamp, which is buried deep in the mysterious Cave of Wonders, animated as a computer-enhanced tiger's head that rises out of the desert sands. This lamp has the power to make Jafar the most powerful person alive. He entices a man to enter the cave to get the lamp, with promises of rich rewards, only to watch the man be swallowed up because he is not the "diamond in the rough," the only one who can retrieve the lamp.

Following this sinister scene is a fast-paced, musical street sequence, featuring Aladdin and his monkey sidekick, Abu (voice of Frank Welker), during which Aladdin croons one of the many lively musical numbers in the film, "One Jump Ahead." Aladdin is chased through the marketplace by armed guards after he has stolen a loaf of bread. At last, he escapes, but before Aladdin or Abu can take a bite, they spy two hungry children looking through garbage pails for food, to whom kind-hearted Aladdin ends up giving his hard-earned bread. Aladdin is no ordinary boy. He has a dream, as he tells his friend: "Someday, Abu, things are going to change. We'll be rich, live in a palace, and never have any troubles at all."

The female lead, Jasmine, is a wealthy princess, but she too is unhappy. She feels trapped by the strictures of court life, one of them being that she must marry a prince by her next birthday, which is in three days. Being a very independent young woman, Jasmine wants to marry for love and so has refused all the prospective suitors who have come to claim her hand. With the help of her pet tiger, Rajah, Jasmine escapes the palace and wanders the marketplace. She, too, hands a starving child an apple, but she is caught by the shop owner and only narrowly escapes with the help of Aladdin. The two fall in love but are separated by Jafar's men, who seize Aladdin. Jafar, the grand vizier to Jasmine's father, the Sultan (voice of Douglas Seale), has discovered that Aladdin is the diamond in the rough whom he seeks to retrieve the lamp. When Jasmine protests Aladdin's capture, Jafar tells her that Aladdin has already been put to death. Jasmine's weak-willed father is under Jafar's influence and is powerless to help.

Jafar then lures Aladdin to the Cave of Wonders to retrieve the precious lamp. Aladdin descends into the bowels of the cave in one of the most visually exciting scenes in the film. Aladdin and Abu have been forewarned to pass up all the riches and touch only the lamp. Yet Abu is tricked and triggers a catastrophic series of events just as Aladdin grabs the lamp, and the two attempt to escape in a hair-raising scene reminiscent of the opening scenes of *Raiders of the Lost Ark* (1981). Although ultimately trapped by Jafar's trickery, Aladdin and Abu manage to retain the lamp.

By far the most outstanding feature of the film is the large, blue, hyperactive genie, with a voice provided by the comic genius of Robin Williams, who appears when Aladdin rubs the lamp. Through the dead-on, improvisational voice impersonations of popular figures, from Ed Sullivan to Harpo Marx to Arnold Schwarzenegger to Jack Nicholson to William F. Buckley and on and on, Williams provides a standout, show-stopping performance. The animators use the genie's wispy form to metamorphose him into a caricature of whomever Williams is parodying, and any scene featuring the genie is uproarious and guarantees to hold adults' interest. No subject is sacred, and Williams even pokes fun at Disney on several occasions, at one point asking Aladdin where he will celebrate now that he has won the princess' heart (with a few bars of "When You Wish upon a Star" playing on the soundtrack) in a sly reference to a widely used advertising campaign promoting the Disneyland and Disneyworld theme parks. With the help of the genie, and a puppy-like magic carpet that Aladdin befriended in the Cave of Wonders, Aladdin wins Jasmine's hand in marriage, foils the evil Jafar, and sets the genie free.

While *Aladdin* succeeds on many counts, its lead characters unfortunately are fairly generic. Aladdin is very similar in physical appearance to *The Little Mermaid*'s Prince Eric, and his rags-to-riches journey by way of the magic lamp is too easily accomplished. Jasmine may be feisty and strong-willed, but she dresses in nothing but a skimpy harem costume. Although she questions the law that states she must marry a prince by her next birthday, she never questions the idea that she must marry at all. Jafar is an evil, scheming figure—the male counterpart to the sea witch Ursula of *The Little Mermaid*. In fact, the final scene with Jafar becoming gargantuan in size and yelling "You little fools!" is straight out of that earlier film.

Nevertheless, Disney has taken the standard boy-meets-girl, boy-loses-girl, boy-gets-girl story and enlivened it with thrilling action sequences, a sound musical score, and a menagerie of sidekicks who insert much-needed comic relief when events become too serious or too scary. Jafar's ever-present parrot accomplice, Iago, has both a voice and a personality provided by comic Gilbert Gottfried, who provides many of the laughs in the film. Hilariously obnoxious, Iago provides running commentary on the events in the film and supports Jafar in some of his most evil plans. Aladdin's monkey, Abu, although he cannot speak intelligibly, does a great impersonation of Jasmine and, when turned into an elephant by the genie, does what any monkey would do under the circumstances—he climbs a tree. Wonderful too is the magic carpet, in both its animation and coloring. When first seen in the Cave of Wonders, this rug conveys a range of emotions, from playfulness, to fear, to shame, to affection. The talents of supervising animator Randy Cartwright must be acknowledged in this excellent anthropomorphization of a normally inanimate object.

Of the six musical numbers, three were written by the Academy Award-winning team of Howard Ashman, who provided the lyrics, and Alan Menken, who wrote the score, with Menken again winning the Academy Award for best score. The two had previously collaborated on both *Beauty and the Beast* and *The Little Mermaid.* "Arabian Nights," a tune with Middle Eastern overtones, is sung over the opening credits as a peddler on camel arrives at the city of Agrabah. "Friend Like Me," sung by Williams, and nominated for an Academy Award for best song, is a rousing 1940's show tune accompanied by a dazzling visual sequence, complete with flashing neon "Applause" sign when it is over. "Prince Ali" is a triumphant processional, sung again by Williams, that heralds Aladdin's entrance into the city on elephant in his new guise as Prince Ali, come to woo the princess. Unfortunately, Howard Ashman died before he was able to complete the film, and the lyrics of the three remaining songs were provided by Tony Award-winning songwriter Tim Rice. The Academy Award-winning "A Whole New World"—performed as a duet by Jasmine (sung by Lea Salonga) and Aladdin (sung by Brad Kane) as they fly at night through a starlit sky on the magic carpet—is very nice and provides a dreamy interlude to this fast-paced film. In addition, the rich, colorful backgrounds provided by production designer R. S. Vander Wende and art director Bill Perkins offer up a wealth of detail. Although *Aladdin* lacks the magic of *Beauty and the Beast*, it proved to be a strong and able contender for the 1992 holiday family-viewing crowd.

Cynthia K. Breckenridge

Reviews

Chicago Tribune. November 25, 1992, V, p. 1.
Entertainment Weekly. November 13, 1992, p. 88.
The Hollywood Reporter. November 4, 1992, p. 5.
Los Angeles Times. November 11, 1992, p. F1.
The New York Times. November 11, 1992, p. B1.
The New Yorker. LXVIII, November 30, 1992, p. 163.
Newsweek. CXX, November 23, 1992, p. 76.
Time. CXL, November 9, 1992, p. 74.
Variety. November 4, 1992, p. 2.
The Washington Post. November 25, 1992, p. E1.

ALIEN^3

Production: Gordon Carroll, David Giler, and Walter Hill for Brandywine; released by Twentieth Century-Fox
Direction: David Fincher
Screenplay: David Giler, Walter Hill, and Larry Ferguson; based on a story by Vincent Ward and on characters created by Dan O'Bannon and Ronald Shusett
Cinematography: Alex Thomson
Editing: Terry Rawlings
Production design: Norman Reynolds
Art direction: James Morahan
Set decoration: Belinda Edwards
Production supervision: Patricia Carr
Casting: Billy Hopkins (U.S.) and Priscilla John (U.K.)
Special effects supervision: George Gibbs
Visual effects production: Richard Edlund
Alien effects design: Alec Gillis and Tom Woodruff, Jr.
Sound: Tony Dawe
Makeup supervision: Peter Robb-King
Costume design: Bob Ringwood and David Perry
Music: Elliot Goldenthal
MPAA rating: R
Running time: 115 minutes

Principal characters:

Lieutenant Ellen Ripley	Sigourney Weaver
Dillon	Charles S. Dutton
Clemens	Charles Dance
Golic	Paul McGann
Andrews	Brian Glover
Aaron	Ralph Brown
Morse	Danny Webb
Rains	Christopher John Fields
Junior	Holt McCallany
Bishop II	Lance Henriksen
Murphy	Chris Fairbank
Frank	Carl Chase
Boggs	Leon Herbert
Jude	Vincenzo Nicoli
David	Pete Postlethwaite

Alien^3 is a sequel to a sequel. Returning to her role as Warrant Officer Ellen Ripley, first created in *Alien* (1979), Sigourney Weaver (now a coproducer as well) once again, after some blissful moments, battles to the death against her relentless alien foe. This time the warfare occurs on a remote prison planet inhabited by unarmed male ex-convicts who have nothing but their wits with which to fight. In the process, Ripley sacrifices her own life for the sake of her civilization.

Alien^3 cost an estimated $50 million to make, and, indeed, its sets are impressive. It was shot in the London Pinewood Studios in arduous fourteen-hour days and six-day weeks. Because of the complicated special effects, it became a constant struggle for the filmmakers to stay within the budget. As the dollars spent passed $40 million, Fox executives called the filmmakers home and ordered them to finish as cheaply as possible.

The cost came not from noted stars but from the apparatus spread across seven soundstages at Pinewood Studios in London. A mineral ore refinery, with its massive lead works and blast furnace, was built on the "James Bond" stage at Pinewood, the world's biggest (named for its recurring use in the James Bond films). The set took twelve weeks to build.

Alien^3 opened strongly, but grosses dropped off rapidly as word of mouth seemed to lessen the public's desire to see the film. *Alien*^{3} opened on the Friday of the 1992 Memorial Day weekend, heavily promoted as a big summer film. By and large, however, critics alerted the public to what they believed was an inferior effort. The film received lukewarm support at best from the reviewers.

Yet filmmakers, studio executives, critics, and the general public could agree on one thing: The heart of the film was its special visual effects, created by Boss Film Studios of Los Angeles in 65 millimeter and reduced to 35 millimeter for showing in theaters. In terms of decor, costume, and lighting, what appears on the screen is impressive.

First-time feature film director David Fincher and the producers sought to differentiate this effort from the previous two films in the series. There is no high-tech look in *Alien*^{3}; there are no state-of-the-art weapons. The world of the prison planet can be called nothing but stark; it is gray, black, and brown. White is totally absent.

Certainly the best sequence in *Alien*^{3} comes during the intercutting of the opening titles with the exposition of the story. The plot begins where *Aliens* (1986) left off, as Ripley's hibernation pod crash-lands on Fiorina 161, a barren, grim, all-male penal colony planet. It seems that the alien monster that audiences thought she had vanquished is still with her on the shuttle, and she and it alone survive on this "island" with a small group of converted convicts, led by Dillon (Charles S. Dutton), who have embraced a quasifundamentalist religion. This prison is a Middle Ages-inspired institution in which nothing works. Its inmates are gaunt-faced, almost monastic figures who walk through ever-dark, always oppressive corridors of foreboding doom. The world of *Alien*^{3} is all dank, all dreary.

Alien^3 is a science-fiction film with no emphasis on the glories of advanced technology, and thus it belongs to that subgenre populated by films such as *The Road Warrior* (1981), in which the past and the future clash disconcertingly. In *Alien*^{3}, Ripley must simply use fire and her wits—with a little help from old factory equipment—to vanquish her foe. Matters are not helped when she learns that she is carrying an alien monster inside her—a queen capable of producing thousands of eggs. The film only hints at how that little package got there, yet it precipitates the only surprise at the film's ending.

If complex decor, costume, and lighting are at the heart of *Alien*^{3}, then it seems surprising that the producers hired a director whose reputation was made with skilled editing rather than with the management of huge soundstage productions. Fincher cut his directorial teeth in the world of the blazing editing of music videos. Among the musical talents Fincher helped sell to the world were Madonna, George Michael, Billy Idol, Steve Winwood, Aerosmith, Don Henley, and Paula Abdul. Fincher also made a number of award-winning television commercials.

At its best, in the film's beginning, Fincher's rapid editing does dazzle, promising to make *Alien*^{3} a fascinating exercise in basic cinema. For its first few minutes, *Alien*^{3} entertains by flashing image after unconnected image before one's eyes. Thereafter, however, for two plodding hours, Fincher and his huge list of conspirators behind the camera seem only to be able to confuse the audience by never situating the viewer clearly in the story. One loses sight of who is chasing whom and of who is in conflict. Thus, in the end, one does not even really care that Ripley and her compatriots have seemingly killed the alien monster. The production team may have been so impressed with artful camera work and awesome sets that they forgot to produce a clear, gripping narrative.

Alien^3 is therefore a confused effort, containing sporadic moments of stark, stunning visual pleasure. Yet it also seemed oddly timely at its release, given the political climate in the United States in the spring of 1992. Thematically, *Alien*^{3} is about sacrifice in the face of an oppressive government that is not to be trusted. This seemed to fit into the political ethos of late May and early June of 1992, with the ascending presidential candidacy of H. Ross Perot. Most interesting is the initial part of the film, in which one sees Ripley faced with a world of men, foreshadowing a possible examination of sexual politics; the film then dodges that sensitive issue. For the record, Fincher stated that he tried to make an unusually ambitious horror film that would explore the five stages of dying, from denial to anger to bargaining to depression to acceptance.

Douglas Gomery

Reviews

Chicago Tribune. May 20, 1992, Take 2, p. 3.
Entertainment Weekly. May 29, 1992, p. 48.
Film Comment. XXVIII, July, 1992, p. 17.
The Hollywood Reporter. May 20, 1992, p. 5.
Los Angeles Times. May 22, 1992, p. F1.
The New York Times. May 22, 1992, p. B1.

The New Yorker. LXVIII, June 1, 1992, p. 61.
Newsweek. June 1, 1992, p. 73.
Variety. May 20, 1992, p. 2.
The Washington Post. May 22, 1992, p. D1.

ALL THE VERMEERS IN NEW YORK

Production: Henry S. Rosenthal for Complex Corporation, in association with American Playhouse Theatrical Films; released by Strand Releasing
Direction: Jon Jost
Screenplay: Jon Jost
Cinematography: Jon Jost
Editing: Jon Jost
Music: Jon A. English
MPAA rating: no listing
Running time: 87 minutes

Principal characters:

Anna	Emmanuelle Chaulet
Felicity	Grace Phillips
Mark	Stephen Lack
Nicole	Katherine Bean
Gordon	Gordon Joseph Weiss
Ariel Ainsworth	Laurel Lee Kiefer
Gracie Mansion	Herself
Max	Roger Ruffin

In this era of conservative Hollywood filmmaking, such commercially driven directors as Joel and Ethan Coen, Spike Lee, and Jim Jarmusch have been dubbed "independents" by the entertainment press. In comparison, Jon Jost's formally experimental, politically pointed films, including *All the Vermeers in New York*, seem radical. How then should Jost's work and career be labeled? Is he a "*very* independent filmmaker," as Jost chronicler Peter Hogue has called him? Is he an "anarchist outsider," as he once referred to himself? Questions of simple labeling aside, a look at Jost and his career is an examination of a director wholly outside the Hollywood system not only in terms of how his films are produced but also in their form and content.

In the late 1970's and early 1980's, several directors emerged who made their films outside Hollywood, more or less. These filmmakers, who were lauded as independents, included John Sayles, Wayne Wang, Jarmusch, and Lee, among others. As the decade progressed and financing was more difficult to obtain, the term "independent" became broader and began to refer to directors and filmmakers who made films that were merely "off-studio." Few independent films offered any discernible difference from their studio counterparts in terms of technique, structure, or narrative. Jost has written about this situation in various film journals, calling the independent label merely "subterfuge." According to Jost, the term "independent," as it has come to be used, claims a difference that does not really exist.

Given Jost's opinions on the state of independent filmmaking, it is not difficult to understand his films as being in opposition to Hollywood. With little interest in Hollywood films, or even respect for them, Jost makes use of devices that disrupt mainstream narrative and generic codes as well as of visual techniques that subvert the basic Hollywood style. For example, he eschews tightly constructed plots and the simple cause-and-effect story structures that are standard in commercial films. His formally experimental films deny viewers the pleasures associated with mainstream filmmaking techniques. His methods tend to distance viewers, placing them outside the narrative so that they can dismantle or analyze what is happening on the screen.

Contrasting Jost's work to Hollywood films is not the only context with which to understand him. Jost began his career in the early 1960's directing shorts in 16 millimeter. In the following decade, he began making 16-millimeter features, and his films exhibited some of the same modernist sensibilities as fine art of that era, most notably conceptualism and minimalism. Like modernist art, Jost's films, including *Speaking Directly, Slow Moves*, and *Rembrandt Laughing*, are reductive in content, letting form (techniques and structure) be as much the subject of his work as anything else.

Providing a considerable amount of context for understanding Jost's films is crucial for making them palatable to mainstream audiences. *All the Vermeers in New York* has been touted as Jost's most accessible film, in part because it is shot in 35 millimeter and features higher quality sound than his 16-millimeter work. Despite a larger budget and higher production values, the film is still off-putting because of its deliberately unconnected plot elements, unresolved story line, and unmotivated camera work.

The slight story line revolves around a romance between Anna (Emmanuelle Chaulet), a French actress living in New York City, and Mark (Stephen Lack), a financial broker. They meet in the Metropolitan Museum of Art in a room where five paintings by Dutch master Jan Vermeer are hung. Mark sees Anna for the first time while she is looking at Vermeer's *Head of a Young Woman*. He notices a resemblance between Anna and the woman in the painting and is immediately taken with her. When they meet later at a restaurant, Anna is there with her friend Felicity (Grace Phillips). The two women pretend that Anna does not speak English. Their manipulation of Mark with this little charade sets the tone for the romance. The smitten broker forms illusions about the opportunistic Anna. Near the end of the film, Mark generously gives her three thousand dollars to pay her rent. Anna uses the money for a return ticket to France.

The film concludes with a sequence that parallels Mark's emotional and physical breakdown with Anna preparing to leave the country. After a crisis at work, Mark telephones Anna, who just misses his call. From the distraught message that he leaves on her answering machine, Anna knows that Mark is heading for the Vermeer room at the Met. By the time that she gets there, however, she finds only his coat. She does not see his dead body slumped over in the telephone booth. A cryptic final scene consists of Anna reciting a vague monologue about mortality, Vermeer, and art while a shot of her head dissolves away, eventually revealing the painting *Head of a Young Woman.*

In addition to the romance between Anna and Mark, *All the Vermeers in New York* contains several unrelated subplots. Anna and Felicity quarrel with their roommate, Nicole (Katherine Bean), a classical singer whose vocal exercises are loud and irritating. Felicity argues with her wealthy father over the stocks that he purchased in her name. Gordon (Gordon Joseph Weiss), an artist, argues with the owner (Gracie Mansion) of the gallery that represents him. In the same sequence, wealthy art patron Ariel Ainsworth (Laurel Lee Kiefer) inquires about the sale of the paintings in the current exhibit. Little is resolved in these scenes, and they do not advance the central story line.

A thematic connection can be made among some of the diverse plot elements, which leads to a deeper appreciation of the film. The common thread running through many sequences and subplots is an opposition between art/culture and commerce/economics. Mark, for example, works as a financial broker who can only stand his fast-paced, rat-race job by escaping through the purity of art, particularly the five Vermeers at the Met and the three at the Frick Museum. Gordon the artist, on the other hand, screams at the gallery owner that he needs some cold, hard cash, probably to pay off a drug dealer. Ariel inquires about the sales record of the exhibit and is obviously prepared to pay an enormous price for a painting as an investment or a luxury; for Gordon, the paintings represent his livelihood. Anna decides to return to France because she fears that, if she stays, then she will become like all the other actresses in New York—acting only for money.

Yet the film does not encourage a precise reading of these events and scenes. Indeed, some are so sparse that no explanation for them is possible, including a sequence in which Felicity bursts into tears while reading on her bed. Aside from the not uncommon notion that art and commerce are diametrically opposed in a capitalist society, the narrative does not posit a singular message or interpretation.

Other readings of the film can be just as thought provoking. Several shots of Anna in the Vermeer room at the Met are framed and lighted so that her face is compared to the figure in Vermeer's *Head of a Young Woman.* Given these shots, in addition to the final scene, it is impossible not to compare the character of Anna to Vermeer's paintings. Vermeer's work contains figures, usually women, who are caught in a private moment of ordinary activity. Rendered with exact precision and in stable compositions, his subjects are calm, almost aloof. His ability to capture the qualities of light beaming through a window and reflecting on various surfaces conveys a solemn mood and emphasizes the impenetrability of his subjects. The viewer looks in on them during a few private moments but is not privy to their thoughts. So it is with the enigmatic Anna: The audience witnesses some fragments of her life—a few private moments—but cannot penetrate her calm, cool exterior.

More than narrative events, *All the Vermeers in New York* is unified through mood and tone, which is suggested in part through several unexpected digressions that are unrelated to the story line. Before the plot begins to unfold, Anna is shown opening the door to Felicity's bedroom in three different shots connected by jump cuts; each time Felicity appears in a different outfit. Logical time and space are suspended through this use of unconventional editing and these unrelated shots. Elsewhere, a slow, extended tracking shot moves across a marble floor, ending when the camera seems to peer over a railing. Later, in another tracking shot, the camera glides through a group of massive columns in the lobby of the Met as sunlight streams down from some offscreen source. More than once, the camera tracks across the floor of Anna and Felicity's apartment, drifting over various mainstream magazines, books, and postcards. These shots, which are not connected to any character's point of view or thoughts, offer an ambience of quiet and stillness that are reminiscent of Vermeer's paintings. Furthermore, these formal digressions act as distancing devices, placing viewers outside the narrative so that they can interpret and reinterpret the characters and events.

In order to understand Jost's films, viewers must be willing to bring something to them. They must interact with the film to derive any meaning from it in a process that is as frustrating as it is illuminating. This is the antithesis of the Hollywood film, which prizes entertainment above all else.

Susan Doll

Reviews

Chicago Tribune. May 1, 1992, VII, p. 44.
The Christian Science Monitor. May 1, 1992, p. 13.
Film Comment. XXVIII, March, 1992, p. 42.
Film Quarterly. XLV, Summer, 1992, p. 17.
The Hollywood Reporter. April 29, 1992, p. 5.
Interview. XXII, June, 1992, p. 30.
Los Angeles Times. May 1, 1992, p. F12.
The Nation. CCLII, January 28, 1991, p. 100.
The New York Times. May 2, 1992, p. 14.
Variety. CCCXL, September 24, 1990, p. 86.

AMERICAN DREAM

Production: Barbara Kopple and Arthur Cohn for Cabin Creek Films; released by Prestige
Direction: Barbara Kopple
Cinematography: Peter Gilbert, Kevin Keating, Hart Perry, Mark Petersson, and Mathieu Roberts
Editing: Cathy Caplan, Tom Haneke, and Lawrence Silk
Sound: Barbara Kopple
Music: Michael Small
MPAA rating: no listing
Running time: 100 minutes

Barbara Kopple's expansive embrace, which encompasses and gives ample voice to all sides of a conflict, is the most remarkable quality of her documentary film about a labor dispute at the Hormel meatpacking plant in Austin, Minnesota. The resulting strike lasted more than twenty-five weeks and garnered nationwide attention. Kopple's film begins with early, prestrike negotiations and takes the viewer through the harsh consequences of the local union's failure to achieve its objectives. Hers is the best kind of cinematic journalism in that, although she has made clear in interviews where her advocacy lies, she seems more intent on finding and representing the truth than in espousing a cause. Unless its viewers were participants in this mid-1980's struggle, or have been embroiled in some other labor dispute and bear the inevitable emotional scars that prevent objectivity, this film allows them to see the right and the wrong, the pure, driving purposes and the blemishes of more than one side.

The local meatpackers' union P-9, whose members resent a cut in their pay from $10.69 to $8.25 an hour, attempts to negotiate with management, which is adamant about the cut although Hormel's profits for the year were more than twenty-nine million dollars. The union enlists the help of a labor consultant, Ray Rogers, to get the hourly rate back to $10.69. His strategy—to embarrass the corporation through the media—eventually stirs up such animosity that management refuses to talk with him. Union members and their families, meanwhile, are articulating their plight with quiet dignity. One man expresses his concern at not being able to afford necessities such as medical care. His son had caught his finger in a closing car door and required three stitches; the doctor's bill was $125, half the worker's paycheck. Having to bear such hardship when the corporation is flourishing causes frustration and finally anger. Kopple's camera observes the transformation of these workers from earnest and eloquent advocates of their cause to members of a picket line shouting obscenities at scabs who dare to cross.

There are the dissenters who prefer not to strike or who, once the strike is in progress, eventually choose to go to work rather than to subject their families to further hardship. John Morrison, the leading spokesperson for this group, believes that Rogers and Jim Guyette, the president of the local union, have led unwisely, using tactics that will backfire and burn those that they are supposed to help. These dissenters find themselves in painfully difficult positions. For example, Ron Bergstrom sees his brother, who is loyal to the union, on television telling an interviewer that, if Ron crosses the picket line, then he would no longer be his brother. Another man, in one of the film's most moving segments, explains his personal conflict: Although he was reared to believe that crossing a picket line is immoral, he is nearing the point where he will be compelled to cross. His wife and children have jobs and have been virtually supporting the family while he sits around the house. His anguish and shame at not being able to fulfill his function as breadwinner causes him to weep; this is perhaps the one time when Kopple's lingering camera seems to be prying into a moment too painful and private for public display.

The spokespeople for management attempt to provide a rationale for the salary cut. Even though Hormel had a highly profitable year, they have decided to cut costs in order to remain competitive for the future. It will benefit all, they claim, if the corporation remains on solid fiscal ground. They argue rather passionlessly that they are concerned for the workers and would like to avoid the inevitable tragic outcome if the workers persist in their demands. While these corporate spokespeople speak in reasonable tones, their main concern seems to be the image of the company and of themselves. Kopple, merely by giving them time on camera, has allowed them to reveal a fundamental aloofness regarding the workers' concerns and tribulation.

A fourth major party in the unfolding story is the parent union, which advises against a strike because it would mean all-out war; if the union goes on strike and cannot do serious economic damage, then the employer will crush the union. At the advent of the strike, the Hormel Company simply shifts work to other plants. Negotiations continue but fail; Hormel's final offer of ten dollars an hour, frozen for three years, is rejected. Hormel starts to hire new workers, claiming that P-9 members will have the right to their places until those positions are filled by others. Lewie Anderson, the director of the meatpacking division for the parent International Union, fails in his attempts to persuade the local union to accept the company's offer. His warning that things will finish badly wins the contempt of the local union's leadership but the concurrence of Morrison and his followers, who are in the minority. In one of their later discussions, Anderson has an uncharacteristic fit of temper directed at Guyette and Rogers for their unreasonable encouragement of a suicidal course. Finally, in the twenty-fifth week of the strike, the parent union stops payments of forty dollars a week to the strikers. The local leadership is locked out, and the parent union negotiates for those workers who crossed the picket line, finally settling for $10.25 an hour. Those who honored the picket line are put on a waiting list, and eventually a mere 20 percent on that list are given jobs.

Kopple puts these events in the context of the 1980's, a hard decade for unions; President Ronald Reagan's successful battle with the airline traffic controllers set a course for the nation that affected the way in which many perceive labor disputes.

The question of whether the public still cares about unions grows out of the lack of response to a campaign, engineered by Rogers, attempting to communicate to citizens nationwide the plight of the meatpackers in Austin. Ultimately, Guyette and Rogers must have known that they were fighting a losing cause; at least once, toward the end of the battle, they seem to be persisting mostly to save face, despite the cost of many jobs. Yet one must admire their consistency and heroic defiance in the face of defeat.

Kopple tells this multifaceted story with her probing, occasionally prying, camera, which seems to want to be in the center of each significant moment, to find the quintessence of the sensibilities, mental processes, greed, self-interest, vulnerability, and pain that motivate principal players. For example, she often holds such extreme close-ups of various participants that their faces extend beyond the frame.

Her inquisitive spirit succeeds in providing a wealth of information—not only hard, numerical facts, of which she includes many, but also human details relating to the life-styles of the men and women of Austin, Minnesota. The camera pans through neighborhoods of modest, neat homes, takes a stop at the four-acre ranch of a worker who is fearful that he will lose his property if the strike continues, and spends some time at the union hall, which becomes an enjoyable place to unwind during the early days of the strike. She captures the marked contrast in facial expressions as the weeks pass, especially those of Guyette and Rogers; they are smiling, vigorous, and anticipating victory early on, disillusioned and grim later.

Generally, Kopple's style is straightforward, only occasionally heightened by deft creative touches, such as her repeated shots of pigs being decapitated, which serve as potent visual metaphors. Music in a minor key, composed by Michael Small, provides effectively bleak accompaniment to poignant segments, such as the anguished ride of those about to cross the picket line for the first time—individuals who hate to break with fellow workers and who include longtime friends and, in one case, a blood brother. As the vehicles pass, Kopple mutes the sound of the pickets, who are gesticulating and shouting angrily, and gives prominence to a descriptive voice-over.

Kopple won the Academy Award for Best Documentary Feature for *Harlan County, U.S.A.* (1977); she repeated that accomplishment for *American Dream*. This film collected many additional honors, including the Los Angeles Film Critics Award for best documentary and the Grand Jury Prize, the Audience Award, and the Filmmaker's Trophy at the 1991 Sundance Film Festival. Besides bestowing on Kopple fitting recognition, the awards are acknowledgment that, at a time when workers are under siege, it is appropriate that creative artists give them a strong voice.

Cono Robert Marcazzo

Reviews

Boxoffice. May, 1992, p. R-42.
Chicago Tribune. April 3, 1992, VII, p. 39.
Los Angeles Times. March 19, 1992, p. F1.
The Nation. CCLIV, March 30, 1992, p. 425.
The New York Times. October 6, 1990, p. A11.
The New Yorker. LXVIII, March 23, 1992, p. 88.
Newsweek. CXIX, April 13, 1992, p. 49.
Rolling Stone. April 16, 1992, p. 91.
Time. CXXXIX, April 6, 1992, p. 66.
Variety. CCCXL, October 8, 1990, p. 59.

AMERICAN ME

Production: Sean Daniel, Robert M. Young, and Edward James Olmos for Y.O.Y., in association with the Sean Daniel Company; released by Universal Pictures
Direction: Edward James Olmos
Screenplay: Floyd Mutrux and Desmond Nakano; based on a story by Mutrux
Cinematography: Reynaldo Villalobos
Editing: Arthur R. Coburn and Richard Candib
Production design: Joe Aubel
Art direction: Richard Yanez
Set design: Stephanie Gordon and Darrell Wight
Set decoration: Martin C. Price
Casting: Bob Morones
Sound: Dennis Jones
Costume design: Sylvia Vega-Vasquez
Music: Dennis Lambert and Claude Gaudette
MPAA rating: R
Running time: 126 minutes

Principal characters:

Santana	Edward James Olmos
J. D.	William Forsythe
Mundo	Pepe Serna
Puppet	Danny De La Paz
Julie	Evelina Fernandez
El Japo	Cary Hiroyuki Tagawa
Little Puppet	Daniel Villarreal
Pedro	Sal Lopez
Huero	Daniel A. Haro
Esperanza	Vira Montes
Pie Face	Domingo Ambriz
Cheetah	Vic Trevino
Dornan	Tom Bower
Santana (as an adolescent)	Panchito Gomez
J. D. (as an adolescent)	Steve Wilcox
Mundo (as an adolescent)	Richard Coca

"For all they that take the sword shall perish with the sword." That Biblical admonition appeared at the start of *Little Caesar* in 1930, but it could as easily have flashed on the screen as early as 1912 with D. W. Griffith's *The Musketeers of Pig Alley*. Gangster films became very popular in the 1930's, and *Little Caesar* was quickly followed by *Public Enemy* (1931) and *Scarface* (1932). Studios boasted that the hard-hitting newspaper headlines of the day suggested their plots. Gangster films had racy dialogue and plenty of action, with fast cars and blazing tommy guns. They featured the explosive performances of Edward G. Robinson, James Cagney, Paul Muni, Joan Blondell, Lee Tracy, and, in later years, Humphrey Bogart and George Raft.

The gangster genre eventually came to an end in 1940 following public protests. There have been periodic revivals since then, perhaps the most notable being the *Godfather* series that began in 1972. Yet another resurrection began in the late 1980's. In short, the gangster film has an honored place in film lore.

In the grand tradition of Hollywood—that is, seeking to capitalize on America's latest vogue—Universal Pictures has released *American Me*. Director Edward James Olmos has delivered a powerful film that focuses on gang violence, drug involvement, and the dehumanizing experience of prison life. It is a tough, no-nonsense picture about the Hispanic mafia and its "godfather," a character named Santana, played by Olmos himself.

The picture opens in 1972 with Santana being processed for prison life. Later the audience learns that he has already spent eighteen years, his whole adult life, behind bars. The convict begins narrating from a series of letters written to a girl he met on the outside. He attempts to explain, perhaps justify, his criminal existence. As Santana begins with his parents, the film cuts back in time. It is 1943 in Los Angeles during the time of the notorious Zoot Suit riots, in which World War II servicemen brawled with Mexican Americans. Santana's personality appears to have been formed from bad experiences during this time. His father was clubbed and his mother repeatedly raped. Neither of them forgot these violent acts.

Santana's narration then jumps sixteen years to 1959. Now, at age fifteen, he teams up with two pals, J. D. and Mundo, to form a gang. Tempting fate, the trio wanders into the barrio of a rival gang. The bloody aftermath leads to more violence, which precipitates the boys being sent to juvenile detention. The youngsters make no attempt to rehabilitate themselves, choosing instead to continue their downhill trek.

Santana is crudely raped by a prisoner wielding a knife. He, in turn, kills the perpetrator. His prison sentence at formidable Folsom Prison is extended, but Santana wins the respect of his fellow convicts. Years later he, J. D. (William Forsythe), and Mundo (Pepe Serna) are reunited. They decide to create their own prison mafia similar to those formed by African Americans and white supremacists. Their aim is to bring respect to Hispanics and protect them against rape, assault, and murder by other groups. Santana is chosen the leader. Over the years, his organization becomes extremely powerful, able to control Folsom Prison as well as the crime world beyond. J. D. says it best: "Control the inside—and you rule the outside."

Forgotten along the way are the founding ideals of protecting their Hispanic brothers. Santana's lust for power, his expansion of the Mexican mafia, the constant use of drugs, gambling, extortion, and the brutalization of prisoners are all graphically shown. To join his gang, now known as the EME, a prospective member must swear absolute allegiance to the "godfather." He may be ordered to commit the most heinous acts, even against loved ones. In fact, one of the film's most heart-rending scenes is a member killing his beloved brother and then crying in anguish and clasping the body in his arms. Failure to obey Santana's command is often followed by homosexual rape and death by multiple stab wounds in the abdomen. Getting out of the gang is impossible, since membership is for life; death is the only release.

Prisoners are disposed of in the same brutal fashion. In one example, Santana, while in his closed cell, passes some drugs to a prisoner several cells away. The process involves passing the package by hand, and one prisoner, an African American, removes some of the contents for himself. Several days later, while sitting quietly in his cell, the thief is doused with gasoline, set on fire, and burned to death. African American members of his gang demand a showdown with Santana. They get it. The racial divisions and the confrontation are vividly captured by Olmos in a charged atmosphere in which the convicts police themselves and the guards stay out of their way.

The day finally arrives when Santana is released from prison. His entry into the "civilized" world is less than successful. On the outside, he is like a fish out of water. His tribal codes of loyalty and vengeance seem oddly out of place, although he is still respected and feared. Ironically, Santana cannot even buy himself a decent pair of shoes.

Santana's pursuit of a macho code of ethics begins to shatter when he meets Julie (Evelina Fernandez). His brief relationship with her has a liberating effect on the gangleader's soul and leads to a reevaluation of his life and philosophy. His budding romance is cut short, however, when he becomes intimate with her (his first time with a woman) but cannot eliminate the violence from his soul. Olmos cleverly intercuts Santana's brutality toward a woman who loves him with scenes of his gang raping a prisoner. Julie, shocked, quickly drops him. A much disturbed Santana realizes not only that he cannot function on the outside world but also that his style of leadership is responsible for much of his people's misery and must be softened or changed.

Santana returns to prison following a wedding he attends for one of his gang members, the likeable Little Puppet (Daniel Villarreal). Although innocent of a crime that is committed by the drunken bridegroom, Santana takes the blame. Now the film comes full circle to its opening. Santana's growing social conscience and his failure to discipline his gang confuses and eventually alienates his followers. J. D. finally steps in, ordering his chief's execution, gangland style with many knife thrusts; Santana's body is dropped over the prison rail. Director Olmos closes the picture with shots of Hispanic children becoming involved with drugs and violence, culminating in random drive-by shootings.

The *American Me* script is by Floyd Mutrux, who wrote it in 1974, sold it for about $500,000, then saw it languish on the shelf for many years. An issue of *American Film* magazine hailed it as one of the best unmade films to date. Mutrux based it on real people and events. It is inspired by a Chicano gang leader named Cheyenne who was killed in prison in 1972.

Mutrux originally wrote the script for Al Pacino. When producer Sean Daniel acquired it, he decided he wanted Olmos to direct. It took him almost a decade to make. The wait was well worth it. Since his breakthrough Oscar-nominated performance as Jaime Escalante in *Stand and Deliver* (1987), Olmos has used his stature to focus on issues involving the Hispanic-American community. He serves as a mentor and role model to young people but is quick to tell them, "I'm your worst nightmare, because I know all the excuses."

The casting of *American Me* is superb. Olmos gives a mesmerizing, low-key performance as Santana. He has an effective physical stance, reminiscent of Humphrey Bogart in his early films; his squint and slouch convey much of the character's vitality and negativity. Equally effective is William Forsythe as the head-shaven J. D., the only white person allowed in EME, whose whole life is dedicated to crime. The two actors playing the brothers Puppet and Little Puppet, Danny De La Paz and Villarreal, are very touching in their portrayals of individuals who should never have become gang members. They share the screen's most poignant moments. Evelina Fernandez's performance as the widowed mother who sparks the only touch of decency in Santana should also be noted.

Controversy surrounded the making of the motion picture. Hispanic Americans in Los Angeles attacked *American Me*, fearing that the picture's heavy emphasis on drugs and violence would give the wrong signal to the outside world. The officials at Folsom Prison did not want the film to be shot there. The warden explained that the penal institution incarcerates more than 3,400 prisoners and that even fictitious scenes involving riots could be inflammatory. Olmos was first given only two days, but that stretched into three weeks. Actors mingled with inmates, and more than eight hundred prisoners were eventually used.

If good intentions were all, *American Me* would receive the highest marks. The film, however, suffers from several weaknesses. The first half, dealing with an imprisoned Santana, is more effective than when he is freed. Olmos paces and controls the prison-life segment well. Santana's return to the outside and his budding romance appear awkward. Olmos betrays his directorial inexperience by resorting to clichés. Also, some of his crude graphic images may strike some viewers as overly offensive. The director also lacks confidence in his material and begins to pontificate, slowing the picture's pace. The film drags to its conclusion because Olmos cannot overcome his moralistic impulse to sermonize, undercutting what is readily apparent in the visuals. All that said, Olmos has created a powerful work that should encourage and inspire other Latin filmmakers. It is a fascinating look at a subculture little seen on the screen.

Terry Theodore

Reviews

American Cinematographer. LXXIII, May, 1992, p. 26.
Chicago Tribune. March 13, 1992, VII, p. 42.

The Hollywood Reporter. March 9, 1992, p. 6.
Los Angeles Times. March 13, 1992, p. F1.
The New Republic. CVI, March 30, 1992, p. 26.
The New York Times. March 13, 1992, p. B9.
Newsweek. CXIX, March 30, 1992, p. 66.
Premiere. V, April, 1992, p. 38.
Variety. March 10, 1992, p. 2.

THE BABE

Production: John Fusco for Waterhorse/Finnegan-Pinchuk; released by Universal Pictures
Direction: Arthur Hiller
Screenplay: John Fusco
Cinematography: Haskell Wexler
Editing: Robert C. Jones
Production design: James D. Vance
Art direction: Gary Baugh
Set decoration: Les Bloom
Set design: Michael Merritt, Karen Fletcher-Trujillo, Linda Buchanan, and J. Christopher Phillips
Casting: Nancy Nayor and Valerie McCaffrey
Visual effects supervision: Chuck Comisky
Matte paintings: Illusion Arts, Inc., Syd Dutton, and Bill Taylor
Sound: Dennis Maitland
John Goodman's makeup/makeup supervision: Kevin Haney
Costume design: April Ferry
Stunt coordination: Rick LeFevour
Music: Elmer Bernstein
MPAA rating: PG
Running time: 113 minutes

Principal characters:

George Herman ("Babe") Ruth . . . . John Goodman
Claire Hodgeson Ruth . . . . Kelly McGillis
Helen Woodford Ruth . . . . Trini Alvarado
Jumpin' Joe Dugan . . . . Bruce Boxleitner
Harry Frazee . . . . Peter Donat
Brother Mathias . . . . James Cromwell
Jack Dunn . . . . J. C. Quinn
Miller Huggins . . . . Joe Ragno
Colonel Jacob Ruppert . . . . Bernard Kates
Lou Gehrig . . . . Michael McGrady
Young George Herman Ruth . . . . Andy Voils
Johnny Sylvester (age 10) . . . . Dylan Day
Johnny Sylvester (age 30) . . . . Stephen Caffrey
Guy Bush . . . . Richard Tyson
Ping . . . . Ralph Marrero
George Ruth, Sr. . . . . Bob Swan
Brother Paul . . . . Gene Ross
Carrigan . . . . Danny Goldring

The United States has produced some of the finest athletes in the world—the sport of baseball alone has boasted many courageous individuals—and George Herman "Babe" Ruth ranks as the finest baseball player and one of the most famous sports figures of all time. *The Babe* is a tribute to an all-American hero and the nation's most-loved game.

At the age of seven, young Ruth (Andy Voils) is sent to St. Mary's Industrial School for Boys, in Baltimore. Abandoned by his parents, he lives in the custody of the state. Brother Paul (Gene Ross), a baseball enthusiast, has the boys line up while he pitches baseballs at them. Ruth, a tubby little boy, misses the first few but then methodically hits all of the next balls out of the grounds. By the time that Ruth is a nineteen-year-old (now played by John Goodman), his playing ability is spotted by a professional Baltimore baseball scout. With little ceremony and no intervention from Ruth's father (Bob Swan)—his mother died many years before—Ruth is allowed to begin his professional career, signing to play with the Baltimore Orioles.

His sudden fame and wealth create problems for Ruth. On the baseball diamond, he can hit a home run at will; away from the sport, life proves a little more difficult. A newfound freedom that goes unchecked throws him into the life of partying, drinking, and women. Two women immediately figure in his life. The first is a petite waitress, named Helen Woodford (Trini Alvarado), at a local café. About the same time, Ruth also meets Claire Hodgeson (Kelly McGillis). Ruth was to marry both of these women during his checkered baseball career.

Ruth takes little time to prove that he is not only a master at hitting home runs but also a fine pitcher. While playing for the Orioles, he buys Helen a farm and they marry. Although Ruth wants everything for his new wife, he finds life on a farm to be very dull. Soon, Ruth is back in town drinking and partying, which causes friction within the marriage.

During Ruth's time with the Boston Red Sox, Harry Frazee (Peter Donat) became the owner of the baseball team. Recognizing the team's major asset, Frazee introduced Ruth to his circle of society people. This decision was a mistake on Frazee's part, as Ruth would tell lewd jokes and embarrass the club's owner. Suspensions and fines became the hallmark of Ruth's career as he continually argued with his managers and fellow players. Finally, financial difficulties forced Frazee to sell Ruth to the New York Yankees. Ruth loved the idea of playing in New York, although Helen loathed the company that he kept and remained on their farm in Massachusetts.

While hitting home runs was still Ruth's trademark, from the ranks of his own team came another hitter. Lou Gehrig (Michael McGrady) became the first player to challenge Ruth's domination on the field. During the 1927 season, Gehrig and Ruth matched each other for home runs. At one point, Gehrig was ahead of Ruth by three homers. Outraged that his supremacy as a hitter could be challenged, Ruth began to hit as many as three home runs per game. By season's end, Ruth had outstripped Gehrig and hit an unprecedented sixty home runs.

Success in baseball, however, does not translate into happiness in his home life.

Even after they adopt a child, Ruth's marriage to Helen ends in Helen walking out on him. Alone and unsure about his future, Ruth again meets Claire Hodgeson, now a Ziegfeld Follies showgirl and an avid follower of baseball. Ruth becomes more belligerent as a player, often arriving late for training practice and defying his coach's instructions. Recognizing that his career is nearing an end, Ruth approaches Colonel Jacob Ruppert (Bernard Kates) and asks if he will consider him as manager. Ruppert offers him a minor league team, to which Ruth responds by quitting the Yankees.

Ruth returns to Boston and takes a player-manager position with the Boston Braves. (After fifteen seasons with the Yankees, his old team had released him without much resistance.) Still driven by the need to stay in baseball after he retires, becoming a manager appears to be his only option. Yet this dream never materializes for Ruth, who cannot persuade the owners of the Braves that he would make a worthy manager. After hitting a home run for the last time, Ruth retires as one of the legends of baseball history.

The Babe uses the basic outline of Ruth's life and creates two passionate and stormy love stories around his unequalled career as a major league baseball player. Merely to catalog events as they happen would result in a lackluster film—and nearly every major event in Ruth's life has been documented in *The Babe*. Instead, the film must be judged on whether it manages to convey the spirit and feeling of this individual, rather than on whether it presents an accurate biography of his life. This balance between what actually happened and how these events are portrayed forces the viewer to discriminate between fact and fiction. Provided that the audience accepts that Ruth's character is based more on conjecture than on reality, *The Babe* offers telling insights into this baseball legend.

An interesting phenomenon occurs in films about famous personalities. Physical appearance is important for success when telling the story of a hero or heroine, but the actor must be able to embody the real-life person. John Goodman, while much heavier and broader than Ruth, acted as the inspiration for the retelling of Ruth's story. Goodman brings the same panache and sensitivity to his understanding of what this baseball player experienced as George C. Scott did to his portrayal of General George S. Patton.

Screenwriter John Fusco has bent Ruth's true story to make the film story work as a dramatic piece. In reality, Ruth was not completely abandoned by his parents at the age of seven. There were times when he went home, but because he was "incorrigible," his stays there became shorter and shorter. Ruth maintains in the film that his mother never saw him again and that she did not love him. Actually, his mother wanted him taken out of the school, and his father did celebrate with his son when Ruth joined the Boston Red Sox. As a boy, Ruth was a gangly child and only gained his paunch after he became a celebrity and took to heavy drinking and eating.

The Babe is far from being a documentary of the man who was nicknamed the "Bambino" and the "Sultan of Swat." What is authentic is that Ruth was never an easy person to manage. Although he played fifteen seasons with the New York

Yankees, there was continual fighting between Colonel Ruppert and Ruth. This inability to get along with people of power and position is shown throughout the film. Goodman's portrayal of a one-of-a-kind person is the strongest aspect of *The Babe*. He manages to convey the feeling of warmth and humanity that was also an acknowledged side of Ruth.

For much of the film, Ruth acts in a boorish manner. The premise of the film is that, as a consequence of being abandoned and unloved as a child, Ruth enjoyed living in whatever manner suited him in an attempt to counter his early deprivation. Unfortunately, the film makes no judgment on his more indulgent actions and even tends to endorse them. In real life, Ruth was self-centered and downright rude. *The Babe* manages to soften the impact of Ruth's undisciplined ways and even manages to make his personality weaknesses into on-screen virtues. There is no doubt that Ruth enjoyed all the attention and adoration that he received from his fans. Making the less palatable side of Ruth's life more acceptable may be what reduces the film to a very flimsy biography. *The Babe* brings together a number of fine supporting actors and actresses. Trini Alvarado and Kelly McGillis play Ruth's wives, and McGillis in particular brings to the role of Claire a sense of caring and concern for Ruth. To Ruth's credit, he did not immediately start dating Claire when Helen left him, waiting a few years before renewing their friendship. Bruce Boxleitner, as Jumpin' Joe Dugan, plays the perfect foil for Ruth. Although the part is a minor one, Ruth's kinder and gentler character is shown as Dugan tries to explain to Ruth about how to be a good roommate.

Taking a sports legend and dramatizing a story around the facts of that individual's life does not in itself guarantee success. *The Babe*, at the very least, offers a reminder that greatness is still a mystery. At times, facts become fiction in *The Babe*, but it gives a new generation of baseball enthusiasts a glimpse of a true baseball superstar.

Richard G. Cormack

Reviews

Boxoffice. June, 1992, p. R-46.
Chicago Tribune. April 17, 1992, VII, p. 33.
The Christian Science Monitor. April 17, 1992, p. 12.
Films in Review. XLIII, July, 1992, p. 260.
The Hollywood Reporter. April 13, 1992, p. 6.
Los Angeles Times. April 17, 1992, p. F1.
The New York Times. April 17, 1992, p. B7.
The New Yorker. LXVIII, May 4, 1992, p. 76.
Rolling Stone. May 14, 1992, p. 112.
Variety. April 13, 1992, p. 2.

BAD LIEUTENANT

Production: Edward R. Pressman and Mary Kane; released by Aries Film Releasing
Direction: Abel Ferrara
Screenplay: Zoe Lund and Abel Ferrara
Cinematography: Ken Kelsch
Editing: Anthony Redman
Production design: Charles Lagola
Set decoration: Stephanie Carroll
Casting: Meredith Jacobson
Sound: Michael Barosky
Makeup: Joe Cuervo
Costume design: David Sawaryn
Music: Joe Delia
MPAA rating: NC-17
Running time: 96 minutes

Principal characters:

Lieutenant .... Harvey Keitel
Nun .... Frankie Thorn
Zoe .... Zoe Lund
Jesus .... Paul Hipp
Lite .... Anthony Ruggiero
Jersey girl passenger .... Eddie Daniels
Jersey girl driver .... Bianca Bakija
Bowtay .... Victoria Bastell
Ariane .... Robin Burrows
Bet cop .... Victor Argo
Julio .... Fernando Velez
Paulo .... Joseph Michael Cruz
Lieutenant's son .... Brian McElroy
Lieutenant's son .... Frankie Acciario
Lieutenant's wife .... Peggy Gormley
Lieutenant's daughter .... Stella Keitel
Cop 1 .... Paul Calderone
Cop 2 .... Leonard Thomas
Detective Bo .... Bo Dietl
JC .... Vincent Laresca
Elderly woman .... Minnie Gentry
Momacita .... Iraida Polanco
Large .... Frank Adonis

Director Abel Ferrara has created one of the most brutal films in the history of American cinema. It is not violent in the way that countless slasher films are: There is little blood and gore. It is violent in a psychological sense, leaving the audience drained by the time the film has ended. The viewer continues to believe that the film cannot possibly delve any further into the sordid world of its protagonist, yet Ferrara repeatedly goes over the edge. He redefines the language and limits of independent filmmaking, much in the same way that George A. Romero did with the horror film in *Night of the Living Dead* (1968) and *Dawn of the Dead* (1979).

The film follows an unnamed character, known only as the Lieutenant (Harvey Keitel). He is bad when the film starts and becomes far worse as the film progresses. Like all great films dealing with brutal subject matter, *Bad Lieutenant* has a number of amusing scenes that act not only as comic relief but also as a contrast to the ferocity of the film. Without this use of humor, the film would be unbearable. This technique was perfected by Martin Scorsese, who used it brilliantly in *Taxi Driver* (1976) and *Raging Bull* (1980).

The opening scene is a marvelously comic sequence in which the Lieutenant drives his two sons to their parochial school because they are running late. He obviously resents having to drive them and interrogates them on the way, wanting to know why they were late. Even though this scene is played for laughs, it shows a skill at his job that the Lieutenant is unwilling to utilize through the rest of the film. Once he drops his kids off, the very first thing that he does, while still parked in front of the school, is snort cocaine.

Immediately following this scene, the Lieutenant arrives at a crime scene, where the bloody bodies of two young women sit lifeless in an automobile. The camera, taking the Lieutenant's point of view, focuses on one of the dead women's breasts. After ogling the corpse, the Lieutenant gets down to business, taking bets on the World Series from his fellow police officers.

In quick succession, the Lieutenant's three major vices have been exposed: drugs, sex, and gambling. He has an almost endless list of other vices and character flaws, but these are the main three. Although exhibiting admittedly unorthodox behavior for a police lieutenant, he still seems to be in control. This condition soon changes as he starts plummeting to the depths of damnation.

He is soon smoking crack in a filthy hallway, where he sells a bag of cocaine, with the evidence tag still on it, to a drug dealer. A short while later, he is staggering—drunk, drugged, and naked—as he parties with two prostitutes in a grimy apartment. The Lieutenant then arrives at the apartment of his mistress, Zoe (Zoe Lund). He sits down, battered and worn, but is still able to smoke heroin with Zoe. By this time, the audience is already wondering how much further he can freefall before hitting bottom. Ferrara and the Lieutenant are only getting warmed up.

At this point, Ferrara introduces religion into the equation. A nun (Frankie Thorn) is brutally raped on the altar of a church in Spanish Harlem. Jesus Christ (Paul Hipp) is shown wailing on the cross during the rape. Ferrara's compelling use of religious imagery adds to the power of this film. The Lieutenant is assigned to the case, but he could not be more indifferent or unsympathetic. This is a man who snorts cocaine off of the photographs of his daughter's first communion.

The Lieutenant is not only bad in the sense that he is a bad person, with all of his vices, he is also a bad lieutenant in the sense that he is bad at his job. His investigation consists of periodically wandering through the crime scene in a stupor. He is far more concerned with the World Series and his growing debt that results from its outcome. When he finally obtains useful information for the case, it is through no effort of his own. The information is given to him by an informant while the Lieutenant hallucinates in the church.

As with the plot element in *Taxi Driver* dealing with the rescue of the child prostitute, the solving of the nun's rape is not the subject matter of this film. Instead, *Bad Lieutenant* is a pure character study. The nun's rape is only important in the way in which it affects or does not affect the Lieutenant. There are also similarities between the Lieutenant and the character of Charlie that Harvey Keitel played in *Mean Streets* (1973). Both characters have a need for redemption and penance. While Charlie burned himself as penance, the Lieutenant destroys himself through self-abuse.

The Lieutenant is too far gone by the time that he seeks redemption. In his deluded, drug-ravaged mind, he sees himself as Christ. He will die for the sins of others. A crack house becomes the scene of his Last Supper, as he watches the final game of the World Series on television. The prisoners that he has captured and handcuffed become his disciples, with whom he smokes the last of his crack, his version of communion. He has learned forgiveness, but only for others, not for himself.

Harvey Keitel turns in an astonishing performance as the Lieutenant. Following up his bravura performance in *Reservoir Dogs* (1992; reviewed in this volume), Keitel showed himself to be back at the top of the acting profession. He had finally produced work surpassing his great early efforts in films such as *Mean Streets*, *Taxi Driver*, and *Blue Collar* (1978) after floundering for a decade in mediocre films. Keitel's performance as the Lieutenant was awarded the runner-up in the Best Actor category by the New York Film Critics.

It is a challenge to portray such a repugnant character while keeping the audience interested. Ferrara has correctly decided to avoid making the Lieutenant sympathetic in any way. Even when the Lieutenant lets out a series of long, anguished wails in a few scenes, it is difficult to feel any sympathy for him. These scenes are painful to watch, but they are vital in exploring the Lieutenant's character.

As the nun, whose character, like the Lieutenant's, is unnamed, Frankie Thorn brings a fresh-faced innocence to the role. A former model, Thorn convincingly makes the nun's all-forgiving character believable. Thorn does well with what is basically a one-character film. The only other character who appears in the film long enough to warrant mentioning is the Lieutenant's mistress, Zoe. Played by Zoe Lund, who also cowrote the film with Ferrara, Zoe is a junkie who provides the Lieutenant with heroin and injects it into him as well. At one point, her character mentions how lucky vampires are, to be able to feed on others, while addicts like the Lieutenant and herself have to feed on themselves. Unfortunately, the Lieutenant is too drugged to understand the truth of these words.

Lund's collaboration with Ferrara is a successful reunion, as it greatly improves on their previous work together. Known as Zoe Tamerlis at the time, she starred in Ferrara's *Ms. 45* (1981) as Thana, a mute rape victim. While *Ms. 45* was interesting in a number of ways, especially in Tamerlis' acting debut, it is a film that appears rather crude and amateurish in comparison to *Bad Lieutenant*.

There are many similarities between *Ms. 45* and *Bad Lieutenant*, yet they are basically opposites, almost as if *Bad Lieutenant* were a response, eleven years later, to *Ms. 45*. Unlike the absolutely forgiving nun in *Bad Lieutenant*, *Ms. 45*'s Thana becomes a crazed vigilante after being raped. In fact, during the bloody climax of *Ms. 45*, Thana is dressed as a nun. Both films feature a main character who has been driven over the edge. The difference is that in *Ms. 45* the audience is shown the event that leads to the character's breakdown, while in *Bad Lieutenant* it is not. The character's response, in this case the Lieutenant's, is more authentic when there is no motivation shown.

With *Bad Lieutenant*, Ferrara has finally delivered a film that is strong in every sense. It is well written, well acted, and well photographed. While his previous films, such as *Ms. 45* and *King of New York* (1990), showed promise, there was always something missing. As a result, Abel Ferrara was not a name that came to mind when great film directors were discussed. It may have taken Ferrara a long time to reach this level of competency, but he has arrived with *Bad Lieutenant*, which made many year-end Top Ten lists, including that of *Chicago Sun-Times* film critic Roger Ebert.

Helping Ferrara to achieve this cinematic success is a fine technical crew, including director of photography Ken Kelsch and production designer Charles Lagola. Working together, they have created a film that looks as gritty and brutal as the world it portrays. This is an important consideration, as a more antiseptic look would have greatly detracted from the power of the film. Praise is also due to editor Anthony Redman, one of the few people who know how to use a jump cut effectively and with some purpose in mind.

Bad Lieutenant is not a film for all tastes. Many people will find it excessive in a number of areas. The film's intention is to make the viewer uncomfortable, and it succeeds in doing this. It is able to deliver its message successfully because it refuses to pull any punches. Most important, *Bad Lieutenant* proves that there is a market and a need for adult-oriented films. In the late 1960's and early 1970's, adult-oriented films such as *Midnight Cowboy* (1969), *A Clockwork Orange* (1971), and *Last Tango in Paris* (1972) all carried X ratings, yet they were successful both critically and financially. All three were nominated for major Academy Awards, with *Midnight Cowboy* winning for Best Picture. In the 1990's, through the censorship efforts of many groups, including the major studios and large video outlets, the NC-17 rating carried the stigma of pornography that became associated with the X rating, even though NC-17 was created expressly to eliminate that particular stigma. Fortunately, an independent film movement developed that produced films that were not altered and reedited by studio executives and audience polls. *Bad Lieutenant* is a shining jewel in that independent crown.

George Delalis

Reviews

Chicago Tribune. January 22, 1993, VII, p. 21.
Entertainment Weekly. December 4, 1992, p. 44.
Film Comment. XXVIII, November, 1992, p. 6.
The Hollywood Reporter. September 16, 1992, p. 5.
Los Angeles Times. December 30, 1992, p. F7.
The New Republic. CCVII, November 23, 1992, p. 30.
The New York Times. November 20, 1992, p. B2.
Time. CXL, November 16, 1992, p. 95.
Variety. May 6, 1992, p. 2.
The Washington Post. January 29, 1993, p. C1.

BASIC INSTINCT

Production: Alan Marshall for Mario Kassar, Carolco, and Le Studio Canal Plus; released by TriStar
Direction: Paul Verhoeven
Screenplay: Joe Eszterhas
Cinematography: Jan De Bont
Editing: Frank J. Urioste
Production design: Terence Marsh
Art direction: Mark Billerman
Set design: Steve Berger and Barbara Mesney
Set decoration: Anne Kuljian
Casting: Howard Feuer and Judith Bouley
Special effects coordination: John Frazier
Sound: Fred Runner
Special makeup effects: Rob Bottin
Costume design: Ellen Mirojnick
Music: Jerry Goldsmith
MPAA rating: R
Running time: 127 minutes

Principal characters:

Detective Nick Curran	Michael Douglas
Catherine Tramell	Sharon Stone
Roxy	Leilani Sarelle
Dr. Beth Garner	Jeanne Tripplehorn
Gus Moran	George Dzundza
Lieutenant Walker	Denis Arndt
Andrews	Bruce A. Young
Captain Talbott	Chelcie Ross
Hazel Dobkins	Dorothy Malone
John Correli	Wayne Knight
Lieutenant Nilsen	Daniel Von Bargen
Dr. Lamott	Stephen Tobolowsky

Basic Instinct is a 1992 version of the classical psychological cat-and-mouse detective story, complicated by the fact that the prime suspect is a bisexual writer named Catherine Tramell (Sharon Stone) who has penned a novel that parallels the crime being investigated.

When a former rock star is found murdered—stabbed repeatedly with an ice pick while having sex—San Francisco police detective Nick Curran (Michael Douglas) questions the victim's girlfriend, the rich writer played by Stone. Tramell is quickly seen as a suspect; just as quickly, sexual sparks fly between her and Curran. Curran, the audience discovers, is a person prone to violence himself—he is being treated by a police psychiatrist and is nicknamed "Shooter" for his tendency to kill suspects and innocent bystanders in the line of duty.

The police psychiatrist, Beth Garner (Jeanne Tripplehorn), is also Curran's girlfriend; moreover, she is, like Tramell, bisexual, and she has violent secrets in her past. In fact, the film quickly becomes riddled with bisexuality, violent pasts, and suspicious motives. Even as she is flaunting her sexuality for Curran, for example, Tramell continues her affair with her jealous lover, Roxy (Leilani Sarelle).

More murders accrue, including a second gruesome ice-pick killing; Curran is even a suspect in one of the deaths. All the women characters in the film seem to have murdered someone at some time or other. Tramell passes a lie-detector test, yet she tells Curran that she is planning a new novel about a woman who kills a detective—to be based on him. By the time the film is over, the audience is reeling from liberal doses of violence and steamy sex, as well as from the plot's improbable convolutions.

Basic Instinct was controversial since its days as a screenplay. Months before anyone saw a release print, industry insiders gasped when told of the reported $3 million paid by Carolco Pictures to screenwriter Joe Eszterhas. This set a high-water mark for a fee to a screenwriter in Hollywood, and industry cynics whispered that "no script could be that good." Carolco simply sought with *Basic Instinct* a well-made, high-tension, and popular thriller like 1985's *Jagged Edge*, also penned by Eszterhas.

Bad publicity continued when gay activists disrupted location shooting. They objected to having the lesbian suspect portrayed as a wholly evil person. Group spokespersons repeatedly shouted their opposition to the film's depiction of lesbians as man-hating murderers wielding ice picks. They did not seek uniformly positive images, they said, only balanced, fair ones. They sought—for the first time—a gay hero in a major studio film; only then would they accept gay villains.

In the end, neither Eszterhas nor the protesters had much to do with the actual filming of *Basic Instinct*. After Paul Verhoeven was brought on board to direct (for a reported $5 million) and Michael Douglas was set to star (for a reported $10 million), screenwriter Eszterhas was forced out of the project, reportedly for "creative differences." Verhoeven stood his ground concerning the portrayal of sexuality in the film.

When *Basic Instinct* was finished and submitted to the Motion Picture Association of America for a rating, it received an NC-17, or what used to be an X. After a few cuts (reportedly less than a minute's worth) and some judicious substitution of words, the ratings board recanted and changed the film's rating to an "R."

Despite its inconsistencies and sensationalism, *Basic Instinct* transcends the ordinary. Director Verhoeven transfers his sense of Hitchcockian intrigue to mass-market filmmaking of the 1990's. The results at times can be visually powerful even if they frequently make little narrative sense. *Basic Instinct* contains frequent references to the films of Alfred Hitchcock. For example, when a kissing scene between

Douglas and Stone echoes the famous scene in *Notorious* (1946), film buffs cannot miss the reference.

The story of *Basic Instinct* is a variation on the overworked saga of the struggle between cops and killers that portrays them as "brothers" under the same skin. In this case, however, the cop is a man, while the potential killer is a woman. Thus the portraits of men and women are at the heart of the film. Sharon Stone, who played the deadly automaton in *Total Recall* (1990), here resembles the icy blond women (for example, Kim Novak and Grace Kelly) of many a famous Hitchcock thriller of the late 1950's and early 1960's. Yet there seems no trace of Hitchcock-type "class" here; one sees only a sinister, bisexual female who is sly, sultry, and uninhibited.

Thematically, the film's plot is tied to the mystery novels that Stone's character writes and to how this "real-life" case seems to resemble her written plots. Yet, on the level of narrative, *Basic Instinct* is a mess. The real power and complexity of the film come largely from the performance of Douglas, who plays the detective with a dark look and a fascination for remoteness. *Basic Instinct* may be Douglas' best performance; he holds the film together.

Basic Instinct's director, Paul Verhoeven, from The Netherlands, had a successful career in the 1980's with such films as *Robocop* (1987) and *Total Recall.* Like his previous work, *Basic Instinct* is a bleak, violent action thriller. Despite the wonderful, almost lush cinematography of fellow Dutchman Jan De Bont, *Basic Instinct* seems more of the same from Verhoeven.

Because of the controversy surrounding the film, however, few noticed. *Basic Instinct* was protested since its opening late in March of 1992, and many pointed out that all the publicity led to a huge success at the box office. Through its first few weeks in release in the United States, it finished among the top-grossing films, and by year's end had become the sixth-highest-earning film of the year. In the end, *Basic Instinct* received more publicity than it deserved. The film is simply a well-made, gripping pulp thriller. The controversy made more of less.

Douglas Gomery

Reviews

Chicago Tribune. March 20, 1992, VII, p. 33.
The Christian Science Monitor. March 30, 1992, p. 11.
Film Journal. April, 1992, p. 31.
The Hollywood Reporter. March 16, 1992, p. 9.
Los Angeles Times. March 20, 1992, p. F1.
The New York Times. March 20, 1992, p. B3.
Time. CXXXIX, March 23, 1992, p. 65.
Variety. March 16, 1992, p. 3.
The Wall Street Journal. March 19, 1992, p. A12.
The Washington Post. March 20, 1992, p. B1.

BATMAN RETURNS

Production: Denise Di Novi and Tim Burton; released by Warner Bros.
Direction: Tim Burton
Screenplay: Daniel Waters; based on a story by Waters and Sam Hamm and on the characters created by Bob Kane and published by DC Comics
Cinematography: Stefan Czapsky
Editing: Chris Lebenzon
Production design: Bo Welch
Art direction: Tom Duffield and Rick Heinrichs
Set design: Nick Navarro and Sally Thornton
Set decoration: Cheryl Carasik
Visual effects supervision: Michael Fink
Special effects supervision: Chuck Gaspar
Special Penguin makeup and effects: Stan Winston
Special visual effects: Boss Film Studios
Sound: Petur Hliddal
Sound effects: John Pospisil
Makeup: Ve Neill
Costume design: Bob Ringwood and Mary Vogt
Music: Danny Elfman
MPAA rating: PG-13
Running time: 126 minutes

Principal characters:

Batman/Bruce Wayne	Michael Keaton
Penguin/Oswald Cobblepot	Danny DeVito
Catwoman/Selina Kyle	Michelle Pfeiffer
Max Shreck	Christopher Walken
Alfred	Michael Gough
Mayor	Michael Murphy
Ice Princess	Cristi Conaway
Chip Shreck	Andrew Bryniarski
Commissioner Gordon	Pat Hingle
Organ grinder	Vincent Schiavelli
Josh	Steve Witting
Jen	Jan Hooks
Penguin's father	Paul Reubens
Penguin's mother	Diane Salinger

Expected to be the summer blockbuster of 1992, *Batman Returns* was launched amid all the hype, product tie-ins, and pop analysis that had accompanied *Batman* three years earlier. *Batman Returns* broke the box-office record for an opening weekend, just as the original had done, by grossing $45,687,711 during its first three days of release. A decline at the box office during the first few weeks of release caused near-sighted critics to question the film's box-office "legs." Industry expectations were borne out, however, as *Batman Returns* proved to be 1992's top-grossing film in the United States, eventually pulling in $162.8 million.

Tim Burton returned to direct this much-awaited follow-up to *Batman*, and Michael Keaton reprised his role as the Dark Knight and his alter ego, Bruce Wayne. This time around, Batman is pitted against three villains, the Penguin (Danny DeVito), Catwoman (Michelle Pfeiffer), and wealthy industrialist Max Shreck (Christopher Walken).

A pretitle sequence explains the origins of the Penguin, who was born Oswald Cobblepot, the deformed offspring of blue-blood parents (Paul Reubens and Diane Salinger). Unable to accept their grotesque son, the Cobblepots toss the baby into the small river that winds around and below Gotham City. Eventually ending up in the sewer system, the baby is rescued by a flock of penguins that live in the deserted Arctic World pavilion beneath the old Gotham Zoo. The sequence is set on a soft, snowy evening at Christmastime, making the act of abandoning a child even more heartless. The irony of the time and setting is underscored by the only line of dialogue spoken in the entire sequence—a "Merry Christmas" uttered by a passing couple to the guilty Cobblepots as they scurry to do their cowardly deed.

The film's main action takes place at Christmastime thirty-three years later, when the Penguin surfaces above ground to seek his true identity and reclaim his birthright as Oswald Cobblepot. Forming an unholy alliance with unscrupulous tycoon Max Shreck, the Penguin seeks the respect long denied him and launches a campaign to run for mayor. Shreck schemes to control Gotham City's power supply, a plan that will be possible only if the corruptible Penguin is in office. Shreck's oppressed and beleaguered assistant, Selina Kyle, discovers his plan, which results in her attempted murder by the ruthless tycoon. Resuscitated by a pack of alley cats, Selina is transformed into the vengeful and unstable Catwoman. The Penguin and Catwoman team up to destroy Batman, who threatens both of them in different ways.

Batman foils the interrelated plans of all three villains, and the inevitable large-scale conclusion finds the four in a showdown in the Penguin's lair in the old Arctic World. The Penguin is killed when his missile-laden penguin army misfires into his lair; Shreck is electrocuted in a fight to the finish with Catwoman. Catwoman's exact fate is left a mystery. The final sequence shows Bruce Wayne searching for her in an alley as he chases an elusive cat-shaped shadow. The last line of dialogue, in which Wayne wishes a solemn "Merry Christmas" to a violent, chaotic world, echoes the film's first line in word and tone.

Reviewers tended to relate the dark look and tone of *Batman Returns* to director Burton's quirky, sober personality. Some even attributed the initial decline in the film's box office to Burton and screenwriter Daniel Waters' grim interpretation of the material and the weakly structured narrative, though this cause-and-effect explanation proved incorrect.

Burton's films represent more than a personal inclination toward the dark side.

His work is clearly influenced by German expressionism; the emphasis on elaborate sets constructed in studio interiors, the extreme camera angles, the forced perspectives, and the low-key lighting combined with a heavy use of shadows are straight out of the expressionist canon. His use of mise-en-scène to evoke and carry meaning aligns him with those expressionist filmmakers who used visual distortion and exaggeration in sets and costumes to convey the physical world as a projection of a character's personality or inner self. Shreck's skyscraper office, for example, is located high atop Shreck's department store, emphasizing his exalted position as a wealthy tycoon who sees himself far above the simple masses he manipulates. His office interior features walls upholstered in a gray, satinlike material that is reminiscent of a coffin. Shreck's stark white hair, pale skin, and dark suits make him appear sinister, not unlike a vampire. The connotation fits the greedy industrialist, who plans to drain the power from Gotham City ("bleed" it dry) in order to sell it back at a profit. Completing the vampire metaphor is the name "Max Shreck," which is a homage to the classic vampire film *Nosferatu* (1922). The star of that German expressionist masterpiece by F. W. Murnau was a mysterious actor named Max Schreck. (*Schreck* is German for "fright" or "terror.")

Other sets offer a rich array of connotations and symbols that help define the characters. The first shot of Bruce Wayne depicts a brooding, reluctant hero sitting alone in his dark mansion. The stillness is disrupted by the bat signal, which has been projected high above Gotham City but is reflected through the skylight of Wayne Manor. A reflection of the signal is cast across Wayne's body as he stands up to heed the call. Then, a point-of-view shot from Wayne's perspective shows the barred skylight with the bat signal visible through it. The two images succinctly suggest that Batman may be Bruce Wayne's role in life, but it is also his prison. Unable to reconcile his dual identity as prominent citizen and violent vigilante, Wayne is trapped by his duty and obsession to be Batman.

Often, the mise-en-scène recalls specific sets from prominent films or other familiar imagery, and the connotations of these images add another layer of meaning. The large-scale architecture and massive statuary that make up Gotham Plaza, for example, are reminiscent of styles favored by totalitarian or fascist societies of the past, which glorified the industrial age and represented the human body as an idealized, machine-age form. The style and scale are dehumanizing and oppressive, suggesting the negative effects that industrialists such as Shreck have had on Gotham City. The statues also serve another function: Shots of the imposing figures are occasionally intercut with the action in order to comment on a scene. After Batman is framed by the Penguin for the murder of the Ice Princess (Cristi Conaway), a shot of one of the statues with its head bowed and shoulders stooped suggests grief over the situation. Another example of familiar imagery is the main living room of Wayne Manor, which features a huge stone fireplace. As Bruce Wayne stands in front of the fireplace, the shot recalls a similar scene in *Citizen Kane* (1941), allowing viewers to compare the loneliness and isolation of Wayne to that of Charles Foster Kane.

Burton has also borrowed another feature of German expressionism: the extensive use of the *Doppelgänger*, or double. Batman, the Penguin, and Catwoman are characterized by their dual identities. Each has a good side and a dark side. Even Max Shreck is two-faced in that his benevolent public persona differs greatly from his true, greedy self. On a more sophisticated level, the main characters can also be understood as mirror images of each other—a structuring device that flushes out all the nuances of the characters' personas. The key to understanding the *Doppelgänger* is that it implies an opposing double rather than a duplication. The Penguin is obviously Batman's *Doppelgänger*. Both are "lonely beast-men"—as Alfred the butler (Michael Gough) refers to them—whose alter egos emerged from the traumatic loss of their parents during childhood; both were the sons of wealthy, blue-blooded families; and both plan their strategy in cavelike lairs. The two are also in opposition: One seeks revenge by turning to crime; the other seeks justice by fighting crime.

Batman and Catwoman also constitute an intriguing pair, particularly because of the sexual interplay between the two. Though there are no love scenes, they "mate" by inflicting wounds on each other, which is an equally personal exchange. Batman's and Catwoman's motives are similar in that they both avenge victims of crime; he, however, seeks justice, while she seeks vengeance. Like Selina Kyle, Bruce Wayne has problems reconciling the less desirable character traits of his alter ego with his true identity, but her inability to control her dark side is more apparent. It is his empathy for her split personality that attracts him to her: He sees himself in her. By understanding Catwoman/Selina Kyle as Batman/Bruce Wayne's double, the viewer deduces that Wayne's hold over his dark side is almost as tenuous as hers. Thus, a much grimmer Batman emerges. The use of the *Doppelgänger* suggests that the criminal and the crimefighter are parts of the same whole, bound together in an endless dance of committing crimes and exacting justice. Without the Penguin, Max Shreck, Catwoman, or another mutant in a mask, Batman has no reason for existence.

Batman Returns offers countless examples of richly connotative sets as well as an interesting approach to character development, but it is at the expense of a fast-paced, well-structured narrative. The film is largely a contemplative experience, one in which the viewer must concentrate on the sophisticated mise-en-scène and study the complexities of the character pairings in order to decode the significance of the references and associations. It represents an unconventional and unexpected approach for an action film.

Susan Doll

Reviews

Chicago Tribune. June 19, 1992, VII, p. 39.
Entertainment Weekly. Summer double issue, 1992, p. 90.

Films in Review. XLIII, September, 1992, p. 337.
The Hollywood Reporter. June 15, 1992, p. 12.
Los Angeles Times. June 19, 1992, p. F1.
The New York Times. June 19, 1992, p. B1.
Newsweek. CXIX, June 22, 1992, p. 50.
Rolling Stone. July 9-23, 1992, p. 111.
Time. CXXXIX, June 22, 1992, p. 69.
Variety. June 15, 1992, p. 4.

BEETHOVEN

Production: Joe Medjuck and Michael C. Gross for Ivan Reitman; released by Universal Pictures
Direction: Brian Levant
Screenplay: Edmond Dantes and Amy Holden Jones
Cinematography: Victor J. Kemper
Editing: Sheldon Kahn and William D. Gordean
Production design: Alex Tavoularis
Art direction: Charles Breen
Set decoration: Gary Fettis
Set design: Stan Tropp and Gary Diamond
Casting: Steven Jacobs
Sound: Charles Wilborn
Costume design: Gloria Gresham
Animal action coordination: Karl Lewis Miller
Music: Randy Edelman
MPAA rating: PG
Running time: 88 minutes

Principal characters:

George Newton .... Charles Grodin
Alice Newton .... Bonnie Hunt
Dr. Varnick .... Dean Jones
Ryce .... Nicholle Tom
Ted .... Christopher Castile
Emily .... Sarah Rose Karr
Harvey .... Oliver Platt
Vernon .... Stanley Tucci
Brad .... David Duchovny
Brie .... Patricia Heaton
Devonia Peet .... Laurel Cronin

Beethoven appears, in many respects, to be a throwback to the family pictures from decades past, complete with children, animals, evil bad guys, and ultimately redeemable but uptight fathers. The stage is set early on for the battle between the forces of good and evil, all within the confines of a contemporary Rockwellian portrait of small-town America. The first heart-tugging "puppy-in-the-pet-shop-window" images of Beethoven are compounded as its fellow canines find homes, leaving the poor Saint Bernard behind as the proverbial underdog. Its fate seems slated to worsen when, on a dark and stormy night, the evil henchmen of a criminal animal testing laboratory break in and steal a shipment of puppies. Yet a wily stray dog that is also incarcerated engineers its own and Beethoven's great escape before the truck arrives at its terrible destination.

After its rescuer runs off into the sunset, the clumsy, exhausted puppy drifts off to sleep in the shelter of a cold garbage can. In the morning light, Beethoven finds itself in front of a spacious, neurotically tidy family home, which the dog enters. This idyllic dwelling, formerly run by "Daddy's rules," which include rising at 7:00 A.M. on a Saturday morning, is plunged into chaos when the youngest of the three children awakens to a pink puppy tongue licking her face. Repressed and materialist George Newton (Charles Grodin) tries desperately to explain to his family that they are people-people, goldfish-people, or antfarm-people at best. Soon, however, the Newtons are on their way to becoming dog-people—and their property value suffers accordingly.

Amid the love of the three children and their doting yet intelligent mother, the lost puppy grows to be the huge, smelly, muddy, and slobbering nemesis of George, a man whose career is developing air fresheners. Beethoven is a catalyst, exactly what is needed to humanize this tunnel-visioned pursuer of the American Dream. (The audience recognizes this fact well ahead of time, along with George's family.) Each family member forms a special, although clichéd, bond with the loyal giant, who turns out to be somewhat of a town character as well. Yet the story belongs predominantly to George, because he is the one who needs to grow the most in order to find his true self. Alice Newton (Bonnie Hunt) is much quicker than her husband to grasp the lessons that life, and Beethoven, have to offer in regard to her family. Unfortunately, hers is the most jolting episode of the film (and certain parts of it are indeed episodic). In an inversion of the old standard, the husband longs for his wife to return to work and join him in expanding the family air-freshener business to more competitive proportions. Although she is at first reluctant, she eventually does so, with near disastrous results save for the determined bravery of Beethoven. While the filmmakers set out to promote a return to the basics of family values, highlighting the different perspectives that each parent holds at this point in the film, this point is made in a heavy and insultingly archaic manner.

Interestingly, from a more stylistic point of view, this portion of the film employs the obligatory saving-the-little-girl sequence with the augmentation of an unusual camera trick. The close-up of Beethoven watching the endangered child mirrors a scene in *Jaws* (1975), in which that film's main character's horror is registered in the sudden receding of the background around him. This effect is achieved by simultaneously tracking the camera and changing the focal plane (or zooming) the lens in opposite directions and was developed by Alfred Hitchcock for the sickening sensation in his thriller *Vertigo* (1958). This relatively tame "animal picture" is informed by a variety of sources and other texts. Consequently, *Beethoven* is not exactly in the same class as the Disney-era examples of family entertainment that preceded it.

Although it has been informed by many more aspects of the cinema than *The Shaggy Dog* (1959), *Beethoven* is acceptable family fare, combining some simple laughs with some antimaterialist, down-home values. Small children can appreciate the sentimental, silly humor and slapstick gags, while their parents need not worry about the frenetic lingo or martial arts stunts that some other children's films unleash. Another bonus, from the adult perspective, is that the film tells a personal, identifiable story about the father's character in a basic, down-to-earth manner. Thus, *Beethoven* is a slightly reactionary, overtly manipulative, and humanizing tale of the triumph of middle-class values that could surprise some parents with its ability to hold their attention. Full of more good-natured mainstream exaggeration than the stylized indictment of *The Incredible Shrinking Woman* (1981), which also cast Grodin as a contemporary consumer-society Dad, the film depicts evil in accepted ways, thus alienating relatively few people who venture out to motion pictures merely to be entertained.

When the plot arrives at the climax, *Beethoven* introduces the blackly comic casting of Dean Jones as the corrupt veterinarian animal tester, who resurfaces to steal the full-grown Beethoven. Jones's early career was established by portraying good guys in children and animal films such as *That Darn Cat* (1965), *The Horse in the Gray Flannel Suit* (1968), and *The Shaggy D.A.* (1976). Adults will be sure to chuckle to themselves because of the irony.

Grodin's performance as George Newton may seem overly theatrical in his first sequences, but there is something to be said for the way in which he creates empathy in his later, more difficult moments. Deceived into believing that the enormous pet is a dangerous threat to society, George, a man whose deepest vulnerability lies in his ability to be worn down by his family, must stand alone in carrying out the messy work of what must be done. On their last fateful journey together, George, trapped in a no-win situation, looks quite differently into the forgiving animal's eyes and finds the understanding that many take for granted to be there. In such an exploitative and tear-jerking scene, it takes a certain presence to infuse a hint of dignity into a line of dialogue such as, "Y'know . . . you were my dog too." George is able to break out of himself after the scam is uncovered and become the maverick, middle-class hero that underdogs everywhere aspire to be.

Mary E. Belles

Reviews

Boxoffice. May, 1992, p. R-42.
Chicago Tribune. April 3, 1992, VII, p. 42.
Entertainment Weekly. April 3, 1992, p. 34.
The Hollywood Reporter. March 27, 1992, p. 6.
Los Angeles Times. April 3, 1992, p. F8.
The New York Times. April 3, 1992, p. B10.
The New Yorker. LXVIII, May 4, 1992, p. 75.
Variety. March 30, 1992, p. 2.
The Wall Street Journal. April 12, 1992, p. A12.
The Washington Post. April 3, 1992, p. D1.

THE BEST INTENTIONS (DEN GODA VILJAN)

Origin: Sweden
Released: 1992
Released in U.S.: 1992
Production: Lars Bjälkeskog for SVT1 Drama, in association with ZDF, Channel Four, RAIDUE, La Sept, DR, YLE 2, NRK, and RUV; released by the Samuel Goldwyn Company
Direction: Bille August
Screenplay: Ingmar Bergman
Cinematography: Jörgen Persson
Editing: Janus Billeskov Jansen
Production design: Anna Asp
Sound: Lennart Gentzel and Johnny Ljungberg
Makeup: Kjell Gustavsson
Costume design: Ann Mari Anttila
Music: Stefan Nilsson
MPAA rating: no listing
Running time: 180 minutes

Principal characters:

Henrik Bergman .... Samuel Fröler
Anna Bergman .... Pernilla August
Johan Akerblom .... Max von Sydow
Karin Akerblom .... Ghita Nørby
Nordenson .... Lennart Hjulstrom
Alma Bergman .... Mona Malm
Frida Strandberg .... Lena Endre
Ernst Akerblom .... Björn Kjellman
Carl Akerblom .... Borje Ahlstedt
Reverend Gransjo .... Hans Alfredson
Queen Viktoria .... Anita Bjork
Petrus .... Elias Ringquist
Elin Nordenson .... Marie Goranzon
Magda Sall .... Lena T. Hansson

Ingmar Bergman has boasted of making each film as if it were his last. Upon completing *Efter repetitionen* (1984; *After the Rehearsal*, 1984), he declared that that indeed was his last film and retired from directing for the screen in order to direct for the stage. Then, while writing his autobiography, *Laterna magica* (1987; *The Magic Lantern*, 1988), he was haunted and inspired by the story of his parents' difficult courtship and early marriage during the ten years immediately preceding his birth. As their lives did not belong in his autobiography, he imagined and embellished their tale in the screenplay of *The Best Intentions.*

Having been enthralled by the Oscar-winning *Pelle erobreren* (1988; *Pelle the Conqueror*, 1988), Bergman offered his script to its director, Danish-born Bille August, who enthusiastically accepted the assignment and welcomed collaboration with the legendary Bergman. The two spent months together, working and reworking the manuscript until they arrived at a mutual vision. Well matched, they both relish, as is clear in previous projects, the depiction of human vulnerability and the particular brutality of Scandinavian art and life.

Before relinquishing his script to August, Bergman made a significant directorial decision—that of casting Pernilla Ostergren as his mother. The actress, well known in Scandinavia and Great Britain for her work on stage and television, appeared as a maid in Bergman's autobiographical *Fanny och Alexander* (1982; *Fanny and Alexander*, 1983) and had since been directed by him in several stage plays. The choice turned out to be significant for the director too, as a real-life romance paralleled that of the script, and by the end of filming Pernilla Ostergren had become Pernilla August.

The recurring theme of emotional and moral rigidity is forcefully displayed in a pretitle sequence showing Henrik Bergman (Samuel Fröler) in a formal conference with his estranged grandfather, who offers to fund Henrik's education in theology and give him a monthly allowance only if Henrik will visit his dying grandmother and allow her to beg his forgiveness for some unnamed slight that occurred years ago. Henrik listens to the old man's appeals to his senses of compassion and mercy but is not able, and indeed makes no effort, to summon either.

In contrast to the bitter, stark introduction of Henrik, Anna Akerblom (Pernilla August) is met tiptoeing through her family's opulent mansion toward her sleeping father, Johan (the outstanding Oscar winner Max von Sydow), whom she awakens by gently blowing on his face. He rhapsodizes that this must be what it is like to be awakened by angels in paradise. Their affection for each other has an almost sexual quality.

Anna and Henrik meet when Anna's brother Ernst (Björn Kjellman) brings Henrik home from the university for dinner. Embarrassed because they are late, and overwhelmed by the Akerbloms' apparent wealth, Henrik is shy and almost runs away. Anna puts him at ease with a smile and introductions to the family and friends in attendance, one of whom she describes as "considered to be my intended," clearly revealing that it is not she who considers him to be so. As Henrik continues to be intimidated by the Akerblom manners and refinement, Anna continues to smile at him and he to gaze at her. One who notices these looks is Anna's mother, Karin (Ghita Nørby), and the disapproval is apparent in her face.

Brother Ernst has quite the opposite reaction to the interest between his sister and his schoolmate, and he endeavors to get them together as often and as privately as possible. After begging their mother to allow Anna to come to the city to look after him while in school, Ernst invites Henrik to their apartment and promptly leaves the two alone. Hardly shy, Anna all but throws herself at Henrik, then announces after their first kiss, "I supposed we're engaged now." She is corrected by Henrik, who has long been engaged to the beautiful and patient Frida (Lena Endre), whom Henrik continues to take food from and sleep with but remains reluctant to introduce to his mother or take any formal steps toward marrying. Given Anna's interest in him, Henrik offers to abandon Frida at once. Anna questions his fickleness and callousness until Henrik mentions that Frida is a waitress. At this, Anna turns up her snobbish nose, prompting Henrik's criticism of her upper-class values. This comparatively mild exchange foreshadows the more violent eruptions held in the future toward which they stubbornly move.

Mother Karin provides characteristic opposition so strong that it only inspires the headstrong Anna to defy her. Mrs. Akerblom invites Henrik to visit for a few days in the summer, only to confront him with proof of his continuing affair with Frida and the threat that, if he does not leave Anna himself, then she will pass the information on to Anna, causing the same outcome but with much more pain to him and to her daughter. What the mother does not know is that this visit has allowed Henrik and Anna to deepen their feelings and commitment to each other, become lovers, and plan a future together despite any opposition. Nevertheless, Anna comes home from a carriage ride with her brothers to find that the less resolute Henrik has gone. Anna confronts her mother, whom she knows to be the cause of Henrik's flight, and vows never to forgive. Mrs. Akerblom, confident in her belief that a marriage between her daughter and the future pastor would be a disaster, rhetorically asks, "Who will you never forgive? Me, or your friend, or life, or God?"

As winter falls, a series of seemingly insurmountable obstacles begins to unfold. Frida requests a meeting with Anna, in which she begs Anna to take Henrik back. With more grace and sophistication than the condescending Anna would ever have attributed to a waitress, Frida generously describes Henrik as an unfortunate wretch for whom things have never been right in his entire miserable life. She explains that he needs someone to love him so that he may not hate himself so much.

Shortly thereafter, while packing to go to nursing school, Anna contracts tuberculosis. While she recovers in a Swiss sanatorium, she writes to Henrik, but her letters are invariably intercepted by Mrs. Akerblom, who suffers some remorse and the disapproval of her husband and Anna's loving father, but not enough to sway her from her determination to prevent the union.

As soon as Anna is released from the sanatorium, Mrs. Akerblom spirits her away to Italy, ostensibly for additional needed recuperation. While they are away, the elderly and lonely Johan Akerblom dies. Mrs. Akerblom's regret over abandoning her husband to die alone meshes with her guilt over the deception she has used to control her daughter's life. Immediately upon her return to Uppsala, Anna rushes to the dormitory to find Henrik. They reconcile and plan to begin marriage arrangements the day after the funeral.

Henrik's mother, Alma (Mona Malm), is only slightly less discouraging than Mrs. Akerblom. Henrik takes Anna to meet her on their way to inspect the far north parsonage that they will acquire from its ailing priest. Mrs. Bergman feigns approval laced with left-handed compliments and self-pitying references to the Akerblom wealth. Then, in her bed at night, she prays to God to take Anna out of her son's life.

Although the Bergmans are destined to remain together, their life will be inundated with turmoil from beginning to end. Even before the wedding, they argue over the ramshackle home that they are given by the parish, whether to have the wedding there or in the Uppsala Cathedral, and ultimately whether to marry at all. Their prejudices over class conflict, politics, and their peculiar expectations of love serve to make the relationship volatile at best and violent in the extreme.

In a disturbing subplot, Anna and Henrik take in an abused and ghostly looking boy named Petrus (Elias Ringquist). When Henrik is offered a prestigious chaplaincy in Stockholm, Petrus' panic at the potential abandonment that this would mean for him, fueled by Anna's obvious excitement at the prospect of reentering the sort of life-style in which she was reared, causes Petrus to threaten the life of Anna and Henrik's infant son, Dag. Anna looks on in approval as Henrik beats Petrus severely, then, overwrought by the harshness of their life together, leaves Henrik for her family home in Uppsala. Henrik raises a violent hand to his wife (not for the first time), as he claims to have known all along that she would one day leave him. His anticipation of her betrayal may be what kept him from ever loving fully, thus causing the self-fulfillment of his prophecy of their failure.

Henrik eventually follows Anna to Uppsala where, even then, it is she who must do the work of patching up their bruised feelings. With Anna pregnant (with the child whom the audience knows will be Ingmar Bergman), the Bergmans decide to go to Stockholm and try to forgive each other, again.

Though *The Best Intentions* was awarded the prestigious Palme d'Or for best picture and best actress for Pernilla August at the 1992 Cannes Film Festival, it was declared ineligible for Oscar consideration as best foreign-language film by the Academy of Motion Picture Arts and Sciences. The film ran as a television miniseries in December 1991 in Sweden which, despite Bille August's arguments that the re-edited feature was an entirely separate artistic creation, defies Academy rules.

At ten million dollars, *The Best Intentions* had the biggest budget in the history of Swedish filmmaking. At three hours, it may set a record for the most thorough analysis of a relationship that barely changed in ten years.

Eleah Horwitz

Reviews

Boxoffice. August/September, 1992, p. R-65.
Chicago Tribune. August 14, 1992, VII, p. 20.
The Christian Science Monitor. July 10, 1992, p. 12.
Entertainment Weekly. July 24, 1992, p. 40.
The Hollywood Reporter. May 19, 1992, p. 7.

Los Angeles Times. July 17, 1992, p. F1.
The New York Times. July 10, 1992, p. B6.
Rolling Stone. August 6, 1992, p. 66.
Variety. May 15, 1992, p. 2.
The Village Voice. July 14, 1992, p. 60.

BOB ROBERTS

Production: Forrest Murray for Polygram/Working Title, in association with Barry Levinson, Mark Johnson, and Live Entertainment; released by Paramount Pictures and Miramax Films
Direction: Tim Robbins
Screenplay: Tim Robbins
Cinematography: Jean Lepine
Editing: Lisa Churgin
Production design: Richard Hoover
Art direction: Gary Kosko
Set decoration: Brian Kasch
Casting: Douglas Aibel and April Webster
Sound: Stephen Halbert
Costume design: Bridget Kelly
Music: David Robbins
Songs: David Robbins and Tim Robbins
MPAA rating: R
Running time: 105 minutes

Principal characters:

Bob Roberts . . . . Tim Robbins
Lukas Hart III . . . . Alan Rickman
Bugs Raplin . . . . Giancarlo Esposito
Chet MacGregor . . . . Ray Wise
Terry Manchester . . . . Brian Murray
Senator Brickley Paiste . . . . Gore Vidal
Delores Perrigrew . . . . Rebecca Jenkins
Franklin Shields . . . . Harry J. Lennix
Clark Anderson . . . . John Ottavino
Bart Macklerooney . . . . Robert Stanton
Clarissa Flan . . . . Kelly Willis
Mayor's wife . . . . Anita Gillette
Mayor's son . . . . Jack Black
Chuck Marlin . . . . James Spader
Tawna Titan . . . . Susan Sarandon
Chip Daley . . . . Fred Ward
Cutting Edge Live host . . . . John Cusack
Rose Pondell . . . . Helen Hunt
Dan Riley . . . . Peter Gallagher
Carol Cruise . . . . Pamela Reed
Mack Laflin . . . . David Strathairn
Michael Janes . . . . Bob Balaban

Ernesto Galleano .... Robert Hegyes
Rock Bork .... Fisher Stevens

The plot for *Bob Roberts* is a simple one: It is the story behind the campaign of a young, successful Yuppie (Tim Robbins) who is a candidate for one of Pennsylvania's senatorial seats. It is presented through the cinema verité lens of a British television documentary filmmaking crew led by Terry Manchester (Brian Murray) that follows Roberts everywhere. The result is a look behind the scenes (and behind the headlines) of current elections in the best mock-documentary style. *Bob Roberts* does for politicians what *This Is Spinal Tap* (1984) did for rock musicians.

Bob Roberts is the epitome of the American politician: charming (he flashes his dimpled smile easily), handsome (the television cameras love him), entertaining (his messages are encapsulated in hummable songs), and a self-made millionaire (the Yale MBA is typical of the American economic dream). Yet Bob Roberts is all image. He may appear humble and engaging, but in reality he is shrewd and powerful. He is a friendly fascist, the kind that is extremely difficult to recognize and harder still to dislike. His scary, oppressive, subterranean message does not seem to be getting across to the public. They are beguiled by his charisma, but they do not see the opportunism. He preys on society's worst fears and suspicions while seductively wrapping himself in popular values (and the American flag). He appeals to some of the best hopes and goals that people hold, but he subverts them to his own ends. Roberts is a "me-firster" who would (and does) do anything to get elected.

To tell this story, Robbins, who wrote the screenplay and directs the film, places his thirty-five-year-old Yuppie into a scathingly realistic milieu. Roberts travels in a campaign bus named "Pride" that has the purpose not of making campaigning easier but of keeping the millionaire constantly hooked into the worldwide economic information network. His schedule is crowded with personal appearances at beauty contests and television shows. Reporters follow the seductive candidate to all these appearances, their cameras ready in case something important happens. The crowds at each stop are carefully orchestrated so that they will be sending the correct message to the homes of the voters via the reporters' coverage. To these contrived images, Roberts provides an abundance of sound bites. He knows how to make the job easier for the airhead television anchors, contributing to the lack of information that they provide to the American electorate.

Perhaps it is this manipulation of information that is the real story behind *Bob Roberts*. People have come to rely on images for their information, not substance. As his opponent says, "Politics is about reality, not image." Unfortunately, as *Bob Roberts* proves, images are easy to manipulate. None of the giddy television anchors (played in wonderful cameos by Fred Ward, James Spader, Helen Hunt, Peter Gallagher, Pamela Reed, and even Robbins' wife, Susan Sarandon) is going to ask the hard questions.

The hard questions are going to have to come from other sources. Here they are posed by a writer for an underground newspaper, the appropriately named Bugs

Raplin (Giancarlo Esposito). Typical of the very strong supporting cast, Esposito plays a disheveled and seemingly paranoid African American investigative journalist for the *Troubled Times* who digs up the dirt on Roberts. He dogs the candidate's footsteps trying to ferret out answers to whether his "philanthropic" organization, the Broken Dove, supplied planes, guns, and drugs during the Iran-Contra affair, was directly involved in a failed savings and loan, and used housing authority funds illegally to buy the planes in the first place. As a result of his quest for truth, Bugs becomes entangled in the politician's fate in an unsuspected and disastrous way. It proves to be the ultimate dirty trick.

Other strong cast members include Alan Rickman playing Lukas Hart III, a sleazy former Central Intelligence Agency (CIA) operative who directs the Broken Dove operation and currently acts as Roberts' campaign manager, and Ray Wise (the actor who portrayed Laura Palmer's father on David Lynch's television series *Twin Peaks*) playing the unctuous public relations director Chet MacGregor. The best role, however, may be Gore Vidal's bow-tied incumbent Senator Brickley Paiste, who seems ineffectual when it comes to fighting such dirty tricks as the photograph of the senator with a sixteen-year-old friend of his daughter that was distributed to the media with the implication of prurient interest. For most of the film, Vidal delivers mostly liberal monologues (which were actually extemporaneous answers to questions that Robbins asked him off camera). Vidal is inspired casting because he is the epitome of the liberal intellectual. He even ran for and lost a seat in the House of Representatives from a staunchly Republican upstate New York district in 1960 and again ran unsuccessfully in 1982 in the California Democratic primary for the United States Senate. Vidal had his own fling with bashing the world of politics in his 1960 Broadway play *The Best Man*, which was made into a film in 1964.

Robbins' own background has its parallels in the Roberts' character. The fictional Roberts was reared on a commune by a hippie mother; Robbins was reared in Greenwich Village, the son of folksinger Gil Robbins of the Highwaymen ("Michael, Row the Boat Ashore"). Both have an affinity for music: Roberts' using his guitar and harmonica to dish out a startlingly unfolksy message, and Robbins using his skills to write the film's music and lyrics along with his brother David.

It is veritable culture shock to see Roberts, looking very much like Bob Dylan, singing the perverted lyrics to such songs as "Times Are Changin' Back," "Retake America," and "Drugs Stink." Most amusing of all may be Roberts' music video for "Wall Street Rap," which is a direct send-up of Dylan's film for "Subterranean Homesick Blues." The song's reactionary lyrics provide the images of liberal folksinger Woody Guthrie but the messages of conservative television evangelist Pat Buchanan. (Robbins had it written into his contract that no sound-track album could be made from the film because it might be used out of context by the right-wing extremists he is lampooning.)

Robbins has proved himself to be a versatile actor with performances ranging from the spacey pitcher in *Bull Durham* (1988) to the seemingly psychotic vet in *Jacob's Ladder* (1990) and the sleazy producer in *The Player* (1992; reviewed in this volume). Because, in addition to acting in and writing the music and lyrics for *Bob Roberts*, Tim Robbins also wrote the script and made his directorial debut with the film, it was no wonder that many began to call him the Orson Welles of the 1990's.

Robbins' directing debut won for him recognition as runner-up for best new director at the New York Film Critics' Circle Awards. His acting garnered him a nomination as best actor in a comedy at the Golden Globe Awards. Interestingly enough, at the Golden Globes, actor Robbins in *Bob Roberts* lost to his second nomination in the same category for his appearance in Robert Altman's scathing *The Player*.

Bob Roberts started out as a short film shown on *Saturday Night Live* in 1985. With a limited budget of $4 million, Robbins has produced a mockingly sardonic film that initially went into a limited release under the unusual distribution pairing of Paramount Pictures and Miramax Films. Although it received critical praise, keeping this small a film from wider distribution for so long caused it to become lost in the shuffle. That situation was unfortunate, especially because its release in the months before the 1992 presidential election made it all the more dead on target.

Bob Roberts is amusing, but not as much as *This Is Spinal Tap*. Its message, however, is much more important. It is a devastatingly cynical commentary on a subject that every American should examine. Leaving the theater, one is inclined to question whether Bob Roberts is already here.

Beverley Bare Buehrer

Reviews

Boxoffice. November, 1992, p. R-79.
Chicago Tribune. September 11, 1992, VII, p. 38.
The Christian Science Monitor. September 11, 1992, p. 13.
Entertainment Weekly. September 4, 1992, p. 50.
The Hollywood Reporter. May 13, 1992, p. 6.
Los Angeles Times. September 4, 1992, p. F1.
The New York Times. September 4, 1992, p. B1.
The New Yorker. LXVIII, September 7, 1992, p. 84.
Newsweek. CXX, September 7, 1992, p. 58.
Variety. May 13, 1992, p. 2.

THE BODYGUARD

Production: Lawrence Kasdan, Jim Wilson, and Kevin Costner for Tig, in association with Kasdan Pictures; released by Warner Bros.
Direction: Mick Jackson
Screenplay: Lawrence Kasdan
Cinematography: Andrew Dunn
Editing: Richard A. Harris and Donn Cambern
Production design: Jeffrey Beecroft
Art direction: William Ladd Skinner
Set decoration: Lisa Dean
Set design: Antoinette J. Gordon and Roy Barnes
Casting: Elisabeth Leustig
Sound: Richard Bryce Goodman
Costume design: Susan Nininger
Music: Alan Silvestri
Song: Dolly Parton, "I Will Always Love You"
MPAA rating: R
Running time: 130 minutes

Principal characters:

Frank Farmer . . . . Kevin Costner
Rachel Marron . . . . Whitney Houston
Sy Spector . . . . Gary Kemp
Devaney . . . . Bill Cobbs
Herb Farmer . . . . Ralph Waite
Nicki . . . . Michele Lamar Richards
Tony . . . . Mike Starr
Fletcher . . . . DeVaughn Nixon

A fit description for *The Bodyguard* is "slick," a word that connotes both the strength of its careful packaging and the weakness of its reliance on formula. The film is clearly a star vehicle for one of Hollywood's most popular leading men, Kevin Costner, and for one of the biggest names in popular music, Whitney Houston, for whom the film represents her screen debut. Both performers play characters who, like the film, show more style than complexity: He is the title character, a stoic bodyguard who craves order and control, and she is a flighty recording star who always gets her way. The premise brings these opposites together in order for him to protect her from an obsessed fan, and part of the audience's fun is anticipating the predictable attraction that results. The film also features a flashy cinematic style that borrows some of its effects from music videos. In addition, Houston sings "I Will Always Love You" over the closing credits in a performance that became a hit recording soon after the release of the film. Two other songs were nominated for

Academy Awards. With two major stars, clear-cut characters, a sure-fire premise, and a hit sound track, *The Bodyguard* succeeds more at following the recipe for a lightweight, escapist film than at working any original ingredients into the mix.

Lawrence Kasdan wrote the script in 1975 when he was working in Detroit for an advertising firm, and, like many writers' early work, the script is more derivative than original. Kevin Costner, who worked with Kasdan on *Silverado* (1985) and learned of the script, saw that the character of bodyguard Frank Farmer somewhat resembled Steve McQueen's character in *Bullitt* (1968). Kasdan acknowledged the influence: "In 1975, I wanted to write a part that would appeal to McQueen. The irony is that 17 years later I made this film starring someone else who idolized Steve—Kevin Costner." Costner's austere performance is likely intended as a homage to McQueen, as is his character's crew cut.

The plot centers on the two lead characters. Popular singer Rachel Marron (Houston) has been receiving threatening letters. After a bomb hidden in a doll destroys her dressing room, former Secret Service agent Frank Farmer (Costner) agrees reluctantly ("I don't do celebrities") to supervise Rachel's security. Frank exudes control and strictness, which contrasts with Rachel's fun-loving disposition. Seemingly always poised, Frank even heads off a little girl approaching Rachel for an autograph. In the changing room at a clothing store, Rachel baits Frank, who waits outside, chiding him for keeping his emotions smothered. She asks him to hand her another dress, and he delivers the perfect riposte: "I'm here to keep you alive, not help you shop." Rachel's reluctance to modify her public appearances leads to some close calls. Frank soon gives her a jeweled cross that she accepts as a token of affection. He brusquely explains his motives by showing her that it conceals a radio transmitter allowing her to summon him.

As expected, these opposites begin to attract. Because her security has become so strict, Rachel talks Frank into taking her to dinner. At first, she has difficulty getting him to unwind, but when she coyly invites him to dance ("So, is this a full-service date?"), a tentative romance soon develops. The threats to Rachel develop as well, even when it seems that the police are closing in on the culprit. The mixed emotions of the love plot and the growing tension of the stalker plot climax when Rachel attends the Academy Awards and Frank tries to maintain security.

Director Mick Jackson's reliance on close-ups and flash cutting serves some scenes better than others. The technique works nicely when Rachel insists on performing at a rowdy nightclub. As the enthusiastic crowd presses closer and begins to spill on stage, the jittery, hand-held close-ups establish the disorientation and danger. In another scene, Frank dryly informs Henry, Rachel's easygoing chauffeur, that his duties will now include being Frank's assistant. As Frank says this, he slaps a fresh ammunition clip into his revolver. Jackson crisply cuts from the close-up of the gun and the click of the clip to a tight shot of Henry's gulp of surprise. Such a quick, cause-effect edit conveys Frank's no-nonsense approach to his job and Henry's safety-first approach to his. During the climax at the Academy Awards, Jackson's style, as in the earlier scene at the nightclub, captures the subtext of growing suspense and danger in an unpredictable public setting. Costner, who co-produced the film, commented that "we wanted a rich style, a director with a distinct visual flair to make the most of a great script."

In other scenes, however, the close-ups become redundant and obtrusive. When Frank first drives up to Rachel's estate, for example, the intercom at the front gate is rusty and battered, a sign of Rachel's carelessness toward her security. By inserting tight shots of the frayed wires while Frank attempts to contact the house, Jackson risks belaboring the point. As another example, an early scene establishes Frank's skill at knife throwing; later, moments before he must defend himself in a fight, he sits in Rachel's kitchen slicing a peach. The extreme close-up of his knife blade not only telegraphs the imminent attack but also gives away Frank's method of defending himself.

Jackson's style also needlessly complicates some key conversations. Finally accepting the severity of the mysterious threats, Rachel must persuade Frank that she now desires to cooperate with him. One night, they talk alone on the balcony of the Fontainebleau Hotel in Miami. The camera frames both of them in one shot, but the soft-focus lens keeps only Frank clearly visible in the foreground. For some of her most important lines, Rachel's face remains a background blur. As an intended remedy, Jackson inserts selected close-ups of Rachel as the dialogue continues, but these images do not always correspond to her most dramatic moments in the scene. Moreover, these stabbing inserts disorient and distract from the emotions of the characters. The same inappropriate use of soft focus later hampers a tender scene when Frank overhears his father (Ralph Waite) tell Rachel at dinner about Frank as a boy. Such narrowness of style captures the excitement of the action scenes but impairs the intimacy of some of the film's quieter moments.

The type of finesse needed in these scenes does turn up somewhat unexpectedly in the final shot of the film. Though it lasts only about forty-five seconds, this shot succeeds at least as well as most of the previous film at conveying the mood of the bodyguard quietly maintaining order. After the threat to Rachel has been resolved, the film cuts to a new scene, and the camera slowly pans along rows of long tables toward the dais at the front of a banquet hall. A host prepares to introduce the evening's final speaker but first calls on a clergyman to pronounce the benediction. The camera, still panning in one unbroken shot, now moves to the right of the dais where the clergyman stands, extending while he prays a crucifix like the one that Frank gave Rachel. In the background of the frame, the film audience can barely discern Frank standing amid the curtains and looking out over the room. The fluid movement of the camera from the farthest to the nearest and the final framing hold the entire meaning of the scene: While hundreds bow their heads during the prayer, one man vigilantly keeps watch over the proceedings, his protection symbolized by the cross that the clergyman holds out prominently toward the camera.

The Bodyguard can be approached in two ways. Many will see it as an exciting illustration of Hollywood's ability to adhere to successful formulas, a film that mixes the right ingredients and works where comparable films have failed. Its popularity made it one of the highest-grossing films in the United States and Canada in 1992. This argument maintains that there is always room for the well-made, escapist film. Others, however, will carp over the many talented artists who chose to play it safe with this film rather than challenge themselves. This approach will see in *The Bodyguard* a good example of the theory that film studios have become more skilled at assembling and marketing a film package than in creating original motion pictures.

Glenn Hopp

Reviews

Chicago Tribune. November 27, 1992, VII, p. 25.
Entertainment Weekly. December 4, 1992, p. 42.
The Hollywood Reporter. November 20, 1992, p. 5.
Los Angeles Times. November 25, 1992, p. F1.
The New York Times. November 25, 1992, p. B1.
The New Yorker. LXVIII, December 14, 1992, p. 123.
Newsweek. CXX, November 30, 1992, p. 80.
Time. CXL, December 7, 1992, p. 71.
Variety. November 20, 1992, p. 2.
The Washington Post. November 25, 1992, p. E1.

BOOMERANG

Production: Brian Grazer and Warrington Hudlin for Eddie Murphy, in association with Imagine Films Entertainment; released by Paramount Pictures
Direction: Reginald Hudlin
Screenplay: Barry W. Blaustein and David Sheffield; based on a story by Eddie Murphy
Cinematography: Woody Omens
Editing: Earl Watson
Production design: Jane Musky
Art direction: William Barclay
Set decoration: Alan Hicks
Casting: Aleta Chappelle
Sound: Russell Williams II
Costume design: Francine Jamison-Tanchuck
Stunt coordination: Jery Hewitt
Music: Marcus Miller
MPAA rating: R
Running time: 118 minutes

Principal characters:

Marcus	Eddie Murphy
Jacqueline	Robin Givens
Angela	Halle Berry
Tyler	Martin Lawrence
Strangé	Grace Jones
Nelson	Geoffrey Holder
Lady Eloise	Eartha Kitt
Bony T	Chris Rock
Yvonne	Tisha Campbell
Christie	Lela Rochon
Mr. Jackson	John Witherspoon
Mrs. Jackson	Bebe Drake-Massey
Todd	John Canada Terrell
Chemist	Leonard Jackson

Eddie Murphy's much-publicized *Boomerang* has all the strengths and weaknesses of a typical star vehicle. Although it purports to be about male-female relationships in the 1990's, stylistically it is a throwback to the 1940's screwball comedies and has as one of its subtle intents the desire to modify Murphy's image, presenting him as a new Cary Grant. The plot revolves around Marcus (Murphy), a very successful, accomplished marketing director of a major cosmetics firm who is particularly attuned to making ads that sell his products. Marcus is an executive whose company is being acquired by another cosmetics company called Lady Eloise, presided over by Lady Eloise herself (Eartha Kitt). The fact that he is both the reason for his company's success and the resident sex symbol means that Marcus must straddle both roles—that of lady's man and creative director of the company. The dual roles come fully into play when his new boss is also the lady with whom he falls in love; thus as both lover and dutiful employee, Marcus is cast into the passive role in their relationship.

Most of the humor of *Boomerang* stems from the fact that Marcus cannot dominate the relationship although his natural tendency as a womanizer is to do exactly that. The tension between what he desires and what he is able to do creates many of the film's comic moments. Marcus is cast mostly in the traditionally female role in their relationship: always having to await her call, angry when she misses a date or comes home late because of a long meeting at work, or hurt when she does not notice the trouble he has taken to broil the perfect filet of salmon in rosemary butter sauce. This unfamiliar passivity, a sharp departure from Murphy's rascally persona in the *Beverly Hills Cop* films (1984 and 1987), inhibits action and tension in *Boomerang*, making the entire production less lively and comical than the films that Murphy usually makes. Nevertheless, it is not without its touches of ribald humor and even burlesque.

Marcus falls for the brash, assertive, highly competitive Jacqueline (Robin Givens), a woman who competes with Marcus, becomes his boss, and then puts her career before him. After she ends the relationship, he goes through a difficult time during which art director Angela (Halle Berry) tries to cheer him up; inevitably, the two find that they have more in common than they first realized. Angela is a talented painter who has the political and social consciousness to teach art to children in a New York ghetto once a week. When Jacqueline discovers their liaison, however, she decides to revive their original affair. Yet this act only forces Marcus to realize that he loves one woman for how she looks and another for who she is. The denouement is a rather surprising twist, with two characters doing about-faces.

With the exception of the bizarre Strangé (Grace Jones) and Lady Eloise, the manners of these high-powered executives are almost uniformly impeccable. In this film, the only violence is verbal, and sexual acts are discreetly concealed. The audience is clearly shown which African Americans have class (Marcus and his colleagues) and which are ignorant (the older generation, Marcus' spurned female neighbor, and the mailboy at the office). Almost no one shouts at anyone else. Classy, successful directors spar elegantly, if not always realistically, with one another, and only the déclassé Strangé is tawdry enough to make a real scene; significantly, she makes it when Marcus turns her down, but she does so with impunity because she is French. Yet, except for Strangé's temper tantrums and sexy exhibitionist outbursts, nothing shocking occurs. One is meant to see that the truly good and classy people are the black upper-middle or upper classes; they are New York's last surviving yuppies. Carefree, well-off, and healthy, these are beautiful people in a cultural time warp. The problems of male-female relationships, so central to this film, were concerns more relevant to the greedy 1980's rather than the leaner, more desperate 1990's; the question of who is in charge in a relationship palls by comparison to weightier and more pressing social concerns.

Some reviewers commented on the sharpness of the film's antiwhite remarks, which may have kept some of the film's potential white audience away. To understand the race relations in *Boomerang*, a viewer must realize that all race relations are totally reversed and that African American social structures are wholly separate from those of whites. This is not a film about integration or multiculturalism: It is purely and solely a film about relationships within the African American community, especially among young black men. Although the press pack coyly announces that this film is Murphy's gesture toward feminism and women's liberation—indeed it depicts successful African American women as well as men—the only true bonding in *Boomerang* takes place among Marcus and his male workmates. The film's feminist façade obscures the fact that this is still a film aimed at the male viewer, full of feminine near-nudity but no similar shots of Murphy, or any other men. Men are the observers and the most analytical speakers; the women, though sometimes in charge, rarely express their real motives or thoughts. The production and its action are created to be experienced and enjoyed chiefly by men: They are the watchers and the women are the watched. Murphy's gesture to appease the women is a sham: It is merely that—only a gesture.

Kenneth Turan, of the *Los Angeles Times*, noted that the most interesting aspect of *Boomerang* is not the film's story, which is pallid and too predictable, but "its racial composition, for this film takes pains to create a reverse world from which white people are invisible except when comic relief is called for." A fussy and cowardly shopkeeper, whom Turan calls a "bumbling racist store clerk," or a stupid waitress provide the same sort of comic relief as Butterfly McQueen's silly maid Prissy in *Gone with the Wind* (1939). Those white viewers not accustomed to laughing at themselves could be offended by this sharp-edged humor, but then in a sense they are proving Murphy's point and are themselves becoming part of what his humor seeks to debunk—the self-importance and sense of racial Manifest Destiny felt by many American whites.

Boomerang is a stagy, high-concept comedy of manners. It aims at being a screwball comedy with Marcus as a Cary Grant-like leading man, suave and debonair. Instead of succeeding in this goal, however, in the words of one African American film critic, Marcus comes off as a gigolo, pandering to ladies' wishes throughout and without direction or will of his own. The formerly quick-thinking, fast-talking trickster of Murphy's first successful films is absent. Although Murphy is a prominent celebrity, his keen interest in the actor's craft seems to have disappeared, as well as the spring in his step. Described by *The New York Times* reviewer Maureen Dowd as both at his happiest and gloomiest here, Murphy offers some stand-up comedy, thin and clichéd character development, and a plot that is beguiling but unoriginal. Although audiences may find it immensely entertaining in parts, the whole disintegrates into less than the sum of its parts, leaving the viewer with a sense of puzzlement, if not disappointment. Although not an important film in the span of Murphy's filmography, *Boomerang* is interesting for its reversal of racial roles and its lesson in how not to become a romantic hero. If, in this film, Murphy was seeking to repeat the successes of his previous popular films, then that dream boomeranged back in his face.

Cher Langdell

Reviews

Boxoffice. August/September, 1992, p. R-64.
Chicago Tribune. July 1, 1992, V, p. 3.
Films in Review. XLIII, September, 1992, p. 334.
Entertainment Weekly. July 10, 1992, p. 40.
The Hollywood Reporter. June 29, 1992, p. 5.
Los Angeles Times. July 1, 1992, p. F1.
The New York Times. June 28, 1992, p. H1.
Newsweek. CXX, July 6, 1992, p. 54.
Rolling Stone. August 6, 1992, p. 63.
Variety. June 29, 1992, p. 2.

BRAM STOKER'S DRACULA

Production: Francis Ford Coppola, Fred Fuchs, and Charles Mulvehill for American Zoetrope and Osiris Films; released by Columbia Pictures
Direction: Francis Ford Coppola
Screenplay: James V. Hart; based on the novel by Bram Stoker
Cinematography: Michael Ballhaus
Editing: Nicholas C. Smith, Glen Scantlebury, and Anne Goursaud
Production design: Thomas Sanders
Art direction: Andrew Precht
Set decoration: Garrett Lewis
Casting: Victoria Thomas
Visual effects: Roman Coppola
Sound: Robert Janiger
Sound effects editing: Tom C. McCarthy (AA) and David E. Stone (AA)
Makeup: Michele Burke (AA), Greg Cannom (AA), and Matthew W. Mungle (AA)
Costume design: Eiko Ishioka (AA)
Music: Wojciech Kilar
Song: Annie Lennox, "Love Song for a Vampire"
MPAA rating: R
Running time: 130 minutes
Also known as: Dracula

Principal characters:

Dracula	Gary Oldman
Mina Murray/Elisabeta	Winona Ryder
Professor Abraham Van Helsing	Anthony Hopkins
Jonathan Harker	Keanu Reeves
Dr. Jack Seward	Richard E. Grant
Lord Arthur Holmwood	Cary Elwes
Quincey P. Morris	Bill Campbell
Lucy Westenra	Sadie Frost
R. M. Renfield	Tom Waits
Dracula's bride	Monica Bellucci
	Michaela Bercu
	Florina Kendrick

In this unusually faithful adaptation of Bram Stoker's 1897 gothic novel, director Francis Ford Coppola has made a visually stunning, intense, and romantic fairy tale. In Coppola's version of *Dracula*, the love story between Dracula (Gary Oldman) and Elisabeta/Mina (Winona Ryder) is the centerpiece, and blood is the symbol of both betrayal and passion. Screenwriter James V. Hart, who wrote *Hook* (1991), translates the story into a sweeping epic romance, with the sexually charged Dracula a tragic figure who has lost his soul and who vainly searches for it by pursuing the love of a beautiful woman. Dracula destroys everything he touches, however, and thus in winning Mina's love he must sacrifice her life.

The film is structured in four acts, preceded by a prologue that illustrates how Dracula became a vampire. The prologue opens in Transylvania in the year 1462 with a shot of a battlefield. In a voice-over, Professor Abraham Van Helsing (Anthony Hopkins) recounts the history of the Moslem invasion of Europe and the attack on Christian Romania. He describes the rise of one particular king, Vlad the Impaler, known as Dracula, who took up the sword and fought valiantly in defense of Christendom. Dracula successfully led his army of seven thousand against thirty thousand Turks in a final heroic stand to save his country and the Church. In one of many interesting visual effects in *Bram Stoker's Dracula*, Coppola filmed the battle scenes in silhouette as the opposing troops clashed before a blood-red sunset. Only their moving shapes are visible to render the fury of battle. To heighten the sense of the merciless nature of the warrior king, the battlefield is punctuated with the outlines of Turkish soldiers impaled on lances.

While the battle rages, Dracula's young and beautiful bride, Elisabeta, receives a note from the Turks saying that her husband has been killed. Believing the message to be true and suffering unbearable anguish, Elisabeta throws herself from the battlements. When the victorious Dracula returns to his castle, he discovers the lifeless body of his beloved lying at the foot of the chapel altar, attended by monks. Because she has taken her own life, the monks tell him, Elisabeta's soul is damned.

Grief stricken by the loss of his bride and in a fit of rage at this cruel twist of fate, Dracula curses the god he has so valiantly defended and turns over the font of holy water, which spills across the floor and mixes with Elisabeta's blood. Plunging his sword into the altar cross, he fills a goblet with the bloody holy water and drinks, vowing, "The blood is the life. And it shall be mine." Thus Dracula, of the family order of Dracul, the dragon, is damned to an eternal life dependent upon infusions of human blood. His parodying of Christ's words gives the film a resonant undertone of the betrayal of the son (Dracula) by his father (God).

Act 1, "A Storm from the East," jumps ahead four hundred years to London and the Carfax asylum, where Dr. Jack Seward (Richard E. Grant) is examining the strange case of R. M. Renfield (Tom Waits), a solicitor for a real-estate firm who has recently returned from business in Transylvania in a state of mental collapse. Dr. Seward is puzzled at Renfield's odd display of symptoms, which include an appetite for spiders and other small creatures and ravings about the coming of his "master." The firm meanwhile plans to send Renfield's young assistant, Jonathan Harker (Keanu Reeves), back to Transylvania in his place to complete the business with Count Dracula. Harker is engaged to Wilhelmina "Mina" Murray (Winona Ryder), and reluctantly they decide to postpone their wedding until his return.

Harker's arrival in the Carpathian Mountains of Transylvania is accompanied by an unsettling sense of doom. Wolves even follow Harker's coach as it winds through the wild and mysterious landscape. Harker is greeted at Castle Dracula by the count, a grim, sad-faced old man sumptuously dressed in a long oriental gown. Despite Dracula's bizarre and threatening behavior toward him, Harker proceeds to close the deal for several properties around London. When Dracula sees Harker's photograph of Mina, the resemblance to his Elisabeta is so strong that he believes her to be his reincarnated love. Dracula insists that Harker remain in his castle with him while he makes arrangements for the journey to England.

Meanwhile, Mina is staying at Hillingham Estate, the home of her rich young friend Lucy Westenra (Sadie Frost). Lucy is being courted by several suitors, including Dr. Seward, the young Texan Quincey Morris (Bill Campbell), and Lord Arthur Holmwood (Cary Elwes). Back in Castle Dracula, Harker is seduced by Dracula's three voluptuous brides (Monica Bellucci, Michaela Bercu, and Florina Kendrick), who periodically drink his blood to keep him weak and under their spell. During successive days, Harker discovers Dracula's true demonic nature. After preparations are complete, Dracula, who is sealed in his coffin filled with Transylvanian soil, is placed aboard ship for the journey. As the ship approaches the English coast, it encounters a violent storm and Dracula escapes. Taking the form of a wolf, he makes his way to Hillingham. There he attacks Lucy in the garden, where he ravishes her and drinks her blood. The two puncture wounds left in Lucy's neck are Dracula's calling card, the mark of the vampire. Dracula's coffin and cargo of Transylvanian earth are deposited in the ruined chapel of Carfax Abbey.

The next act, "The Blood Is the Life," is set in London, where the four-hundred-year-old Dracula has been transformed into a youthful-looking count. There on a busy London street, Dracula meets and begins pursuing Mina. After an awkward start in which Mina is filled with vague apprehensions, their relationship begins to grow. The young count is morosely charming, and Mina finds it hard to resist his ardor. Lucy, now grown pale and weak from the earlier attack, is visited by Dr. Seward, who suspects that she is infected with a malevolent disease of the blood. Fearing that Lucy may be dying, Seward summons Dr. Van Helsing in a desperate plea for his advice and aid in treating Lucy.

Van Helsing arrives at Hillingham and, upon examining Lucy and seeing the two puncture wounds in her neck, realizes that she has been bitten by a mysterious creature. As a man of science, he immediately begins giving Lucy blood transfusions. Yet Van Helsing also mistrusts his own powers to explain the irrational, and he gives grudging respect to the supernatural. Van Helsing reveals to Seward, Quincey, and Holmwood his belief that Lucy is being drained of life by a vampire, Nosferatu, one of the undead.

Dracula continues his conquest of Mina, seducing her with absinthe, a powerful intoxicant, and tales of his land and the tragic story of his lost love. While Dracula and Mina grow closer, Harker finally manages to escape from the castle and finds refuge in a convent. When Mina receives word that he is safe, she immediately makes plans to join him there so that they can be married. Dracula receives a letter from Mina explaining her decision, and he is both heartbroken and enraged. In his sorrow, the pain and fury of his old loss are revived. On the night that Harker and

Mina are married, Dracula, taking the form of a batlike beast, enters Hillingham and ravages Lucy one last time, leaving her for dead.

In act 3, "She Is Vampyre," Mina and Jonathan Harker have arrived back in London after their reunion and marriage on the continent. Though Lucy has been buried in her family crypt, Van Helsing discovers that she has tragically become a vampire. One night, when Lucy returns to her coffin, Van Helsing directs that she be killed according to vampire lore, by driving a stake through her heart and beheading her. In the remainder of act 3, Dracula seduces Mina, consummating the unholy ritual in which the curse of everlasting life and bloodlust is passed from vampire to victim. Mina, now infected and under Van Helsing's care, grows steadily weaker. Meanwhile, Dracula begins a journey by sea back to his homeland.

Act 4, "Love Never Dies," is set in Transylvania as Van Helsing and his band of vampire killers—Harker, Seward, Holmwood, and Quincey—await Dracula's return. Before the final battle, however, Van Helsing manages to kill Dracula's brides and to fend off Mina's growing bloodlust. When the men at last confront the evil count, Quincey stabs Dracula in the heart with his Bowie knife. Mina then follows the dying count back inside his castle. With Dracula's death, he at last gains the peace he longed for and Mina is freed from his curse.

There have been a number of so-called vampire films since Stoker's compelling tale was first published in 1897. Perhaps the most chilling among them was F. W. Murnau's 1922 silent, *Nosferatu*. In it, Max Schreck as Count Orlok created a monster so foul that his image continues to evoke a sense of horror. No performer has been more associated with the role, however, than Bela Lugosi, who portrayed the vampire in Tod Browning's 1931 *Dracula*.

The film was actually adapted from a play based on Stoker's novel, which had had a successful run on Broadway in 1927. The play had starred the Hungarian-born Bela Lugosi and Browning cast him in the lead role in his film. Lugosi's cultivated charm, strange accent, and mysterious gaze created a stir among women in the audience, some of whom fainted during showings of the film. Lugosi's Dracula was a handsome seducer, and suggestions of his powers as a sexual predator were obvious. In fact, Universal, which released the film, had its publicity department advertise *Dracula* as "the story of the strangest passion the world has ever known."

Coppola's genius for taking risks in the exploration and manipulation of the film medium makes *Bram Stoker's Dracula* above all a director's film. Though Coppola's *Dracula* attempts to convey the richness and seriousness of the original tale, it is likely to be remembered mainly for its stunning cinematic style and special effects reminiscent of the experimental films of Jean Cocteau. The director's son, Roman Coppola, drew from his extensive knowledge of classic special effects in older films to give *Bram Stoker's Dracula* a period feel. The somewhat eccentric sets were all constructed on soundstages, for both budgetary and stylistic reasons. Costume designer Eiko Ishioka created costumes that were both beautiful and unique. Relying upon a wide range of influences for inspiration, Ishioka achieved a style in her costumes that used color, fabric type, and pattern to denote character. At the Academy Awards, *Dracula* won Oscars for sound effects editing, makeup, and costume design.

Winona Ryder is dutiful as Mina, and Anthony Hopkins gives the character of Van Helsing a more virile if loony reading than has been conveyed by other actors in the role. While Gary Oldman plays the lead with a studied and feverish energy, ultimately this *Dracula* does not give audiences any new understanding of the complexities of the creature. What is more, as several critics pointed out, *Bram Stoker's Dracula* is not even that scary. It seems that Dracula may be forever doomed to walk the earth either as a parody of himself, as in *Love at First Bite* (1979), or as a gallant, tormented, sometimes sentimental monomaniac.

Francis Poole

Reviews

Chicago Tribune. November 13, 1992, VII, p. 39.
Entertainment Weekly. November 13, 1992, p. 57.
Film Comment. XXIX, January, 1993, p. 27.
The Hollywood Reporter. November 9, 1992, p. 6.
Los Angeles Times. November 13, 1992, p. F1.
The New York Times. November 13, 1992, p. B1.
The New Yorker. November 30, 1992, p. 162.
Newsweek. November 23, 1992, p. 78.
Time. CXL, November 23, 1992, p. 71.
Variety. November 9, 1992, p. 4.

A BRIEF HISTORY OF TIME

Origin: Great Britain and United States
Released: 1992
Released in U.S.: 1992
Production: David Hickman for Anglia Television/Gordon Freedman, in association with NBC, Tokyo Broadcasting System, and Channel Four, UK; released by Triton Pictures
Direction: Errol Morris
Screenplay: Based on the book by Stephen Hawking
Cinematography: John Bailey and Stefan Czapsky
Editing: Brad Fuller
Production design: Ted Bafaloukos
Art direction: David Lee
Visual effects photography: Balsmeyer & Everett, Inc.
Computer animation: Rhythm & Hues
Sound: Randy Thom
Music: Philip Glass
MPAA rating: no listing
Running time: 80 minutes

Principal characters:

Stephen Hawking .... Himself
Isobel Hawking .... Herself
Janet Humphrey .... Herself
Mary Hawking .... Herself
Basil King .... Himself
Derek Powney .... Himself
Norman Dix .... Himself
Robert Berman .... Himself
Gordon Berry .... Himself
Roger Penrose .... Himself
Dennis Sciama .... Himself
John Wheeler .... Himself
Brandon Carter .... Himself
John Taylor .... Himself
Kip Thorne .... Himself
Don Page .... Himself
Christopher Isham .... Himself
Brian Whitt .... Himself
Raymond LaFlamme .... Himself

What does an individual do whose body has become a virtual vegetable yet whose mind is still alert? In the case of Stephen Hawking, one contemplates the universe. Hawking is a brilliant and popular professor of physics at the University of Cambridge and the author of the 1988 best-seller upon which the critically acclaimed documentary *A Brief History of Time* is based.

Whereas Hawking's book is primarily a physics text, the film instead combines elements of the book with reminiscences about Hawking's personal and professional life by family and friends, including such world-renowned scientists as Brandon Carter, Christopher Isham, and John Wheeler. Notably absent from the list of participants is Hawking's wife, Jane, from whom he had just separated prior to the start of production. What makes Hawking's discoveries, publications, and lectures all the more inspiring is the fact that he is almost completely crippled by ALS, or amyotrophic lateral sclerosis, a disease that takes center stage throughout the film. For a documentary with such weighty subject matter, however, *A Brief History of Time* is a surprisingly uplifting film. Rather than bemoan Hawking's disability, the film points up the fact that his disease gave focus and purpose to his life and work, and may even have shaped the path that his studies would eventually take.

Born in 1942, exactly three hundred years after the death of Galileo, as Hawking states, he was an admittedly lackadaisical student both as a boy and as a young man at the University of Oxford. He was preoccupied by games—the more complicated, the better. Ironically, he also enjoyed very physical activities. He especially liked dancing, and a family friend, Janet Humphrey, recalls how when he was living with her he organized Scottish dancing in the evenings. He came from a very eccentric, yet loving, family, as evidenced by the wonderful interviews with his mother, Isobel Hawking, and sister, Mary. Their opening comments help set the light, amused tone of the film, which is maintained consistently throughout by the entertaining anecdotes related by Hawking's friends and colleagues, as well as by Hawking himself. As Hawking relates following his final exam at Oxford: "I was on the borderline between a first and second class degree, and I had to be interviewed by the examiners to determine which I should get. In the interview, they asked me about my future plans. I replied I wanted to do research. If they gave me a first, I would go to Cambridge. If I only got a second, I would stay in Oxford. They gave me a first."

The filmmakers tease the viewer at first with only glimpses of Hawking. One hears a stiff, computer-generated voice speaking and sees Hawking only in pieces: his eyes, his hand on a computer control, his body turned toward a computer monitor. As the story of Hawking's life unfolds, the audience gradually sees Hawking in his motor-driven wheelchair, communicating via a special computer. When Hawking lost the use of his voice after contracting pneumonia, a California computer expert designed a special system with a voice synthesizer in order to provide him with a way of "speaking." This computer-generated voice is the one heard as Hawking's throughout the film. Given only two and a half years to live while he was a doctoral student at Cambridge, Hawking not only exceeded that time by decades but also made significant contributions to humankind's understanding of the universe. The gradual death of his body is thus constantly juxtaposed with the life of his mind.

Hawking's studies have concentrated on such broad topics as the origin of the universe and the nature of time, and, as a result, any discussion of his work seems more a mixture of philosophy and science fiction than pure science. Hawking himself says that he has always preferred theories to facts. The onset of ALS is credited with the direction Hawking's studies came to take. As he lost control of his motor functions, and it became more difficult to write things down, he began to think in pictures. Computer-generated pictures are interspersed throughout the documentary to illustrate Hawking's theories and discoveries. Fortunately for the general viewer, the film avoids equations and mathematics, favoring instead this more popular and visual approach. Much of Hawking's voice-over of his scientific theories in the film is actually from his best-selling book. A popular subject of discussion, and one that Hawking has studied extensively, is that of black holes, a term coined in 1969 by American scientist John Wheeler.

A black hole is a collapsed star that has become infinitely dense, with a gravitational field so strong that no light can escape from it—hence the name. One of the many anecdotes related by the participants is the one by Wheeler explaining how a black hole can be detected when it cannot be "seen." He compares black holes and stars to boys and girls at a ball. The boys wear black, the girls white, and the lights are turned down low. As the couples twirl, only the white of the girl's gown can be seen, yet one knows that there must be something dancing with her by the way she moves: "The girl is the ordinary star and the boy is the black hole." Such is the very visual way in which these extremely mind-boggling concepts are explained.

Hawking, in turn, gives an excellent description of some of the properties of a black hole. He states that, were an astronaut with a wristwatch to jump into a black hole, the second hand of the watch would appear to an outside observer to move slower and slower as the astronaut descended into the hole, until the last second would seem to last forever. From the astronaut's perspective, time on Earth would seem to pass so quickly that the astronaut would view all of its future, but too quickly to be comprehended. Unfortunately, the astronaut, in the process of being sucked into the black hole, would be turned into spaghetti, as Hawking so colorfully puts it.

A Brief History of Time was well appreciated at the Sundance Film Festival, winning the Grand Jury Prize for best documentary of 1992; in addition, director Errol Morris received the Filmmakers Trophy for the documentary division. Morris had previously established his reputation with his widely acclaimed documentary *The Thin Blue Line* (1988), which was credited with having led to the release of an innocent man from death row.

Although the people interviewed in *A Brief History of Time* appear to be sitting in homes and offices, in actuality this "realism" was achieved by production designer Ted Bafaloukos, who created twenty-nine separate sets for each of the participants. Even Hawking's office at Cambridge was re-created, complete with the various Marilyn Monroe posters on the walls. A distinct disadvantage of the film, but probably only a minor quibble for most viewers, is the fact that no identification of the various people interviewed appears until the end of the film. Listing their names and some identification when they first appear during the course of the film would have been helpful.

Nevertheless, *A Brief History of Time* will serve as an excellent and accessible introduction to the general public of the life and work of Stephen Hawking. More than that, Hawking's success story is an inspiration, showing as it does a man who overcame great odds in order to continue with his life's work and make a significant contribution to humankind's knowledge and understanding of the universe. The film ends as Hawking's book ended, with these inspiring words: "If we do discover a complete theory, it should in time be understandable in broad principle by everyone, not just a few scientists. Then we shall all, philosophers, scientists, and just ordinary people, be able to take part in the discussion of the question of why it is that we and the universe exist. If we find the answer to that, it would be the ultimate triumph of human reason—for then we would know the mind of God."

Cynthia K. Breckenridge

Reviews

Chicago Tribune. August 28, 1992, VII, P. 38.
The Christian Science Monitor. August 24, 1992, p. 14.
Entertainment Weekly. August 28, 1992, p. 42.
The Hollywood Reporter. August 18, 1992, p. 5.
Los Angeles Times. August 21, 1992, p. F1.
The New York Times. August 21, 1992, p. B1.
The New Yorker. LXVIII, September 7, 1992, p. 87.
Newsweek. August 31, 1992, p. 68.
Time. CXL, August 31, 1992, p. 66.
Variety. January 20, 1992, p. 2.

CHAPLIN

Production: Richard Attenborough and Mario Kassar for Carolco, Le Studio Canal Plus, and RCS Video; released by TriStar Pictures
Direction: Richard Attenborough
Screenplay: William Boyd, Bryan Forbes, and William Goldman; based on a story by Diana Hawkins, and on the books *My Autobiography*, by Charles Chaplin, and *Chaplin: His Life and Art*, by David Robinson
Cinematography: Sven Nykvist
Editing: Anne V. Coates
Production design: Stuart Craig
Art direction: Norman Dorme, Mark Mansbridge, and John King
Set decoration: Chris A. Butler and Stephenie McMillan
Casting: Mike Fenton, Valorie Massalas, and Susie Figgis
Sound: Edward Tise
Chaplin prosthetic makeup creation: John Caglione, Jr.
Costume design: John Mollo and Ellen Mirojnick
Music: John Barry
MPAA rating: PG-13
Running time: 144 minutes

Principal characters:

Charlie Chaplin .... Robert Downey, Jr.
Hannah Chaplin .... Geraldine Chaplin
George Hayden .... Anthony Hopkins
Sydney Chaplin .... Paul Rhys
Mack Sennett .... Dan Aykroyd
Douglas Fairbanks .... Kevin Kline
J. Edgar Hoover .... Kevin Dunn
Paulette Goddard .... Diane Lane
Hetty Kelly/Oona O'Neill .... Moira Kelly
Mabel Normand .... Marisa Tomei
Mary Pickford .... Maria Pitillo
Fred Karno .... John Thaw
Mildred Harris .... Milla Jovovich
Edna Purviance .... Penelope Ann Miller
Joan Barry .... Nancy Travis
Lawyer Scott .... James Woods

Richard Attenborough's film biography of Charlie Chaplin traces the life of the famous filmmaker from his beginnings in London music halls to his acceptance of an honorary Oscar at the age of eighty-three. The screenwriters, working from Chaplin's *My Autobiography* (1964) as well as David Robinson's *Chaplin: His Life and Art* (1985), have tied many of the episodes to the two recurring ideas of Chaplin's politics and his love life. Both caused scandal for Chaplin. The iconoclastic attitudes toward social institutions that turned up in his films and his fondness for young women clashed repeatedly with the conservatism of the United States, his adopted country.

The filmmakers attempt to create some unity in the narrative by introducing the fictional character of editor George Hayden (Anthony Hopkins), who visits Chaplin (Robert Downey, Jr.) in Switzerland during the star's extended exile from the United States. Hayden comes with a list of questions for Chaplin about the sections of his newly written autobiography that remain sketchy. Either in voice-over conversations or in short introductions to flashback sequences, Hayden prompts Chaplin to recall particular moments of his life and to provide needed explanations. Though a clichéd device, this premise works better than it sounds by permitting the filmmakers to target the areas of Chaplin's life that are of greatest dramatic interest and to try to establish a consistent viewpoint and interpretation.

Chaplin's life is probably one of the best known of any modern creative artist, and Attenborough's film follows the milestones of his career faithfully. Chaplin's success in London music halls leads him to Fred Karno (John Thaw) and a trip to the United States with Karno's stage comics and acrobats. While in Butte, Montana, Charlie wanders into a funeral parlor being used as a makeshift nickelodeon. He watches for the first time the "flickers," or silent films, and is intrigued by what he sees. Comedy filmmaker Mack Sennett (Dan Aykroyd) has heard of Chaplin's famous drunk act and invites him to Hollywood. After an apprenticeship with Sennett and Mabel Normand (Marisa Tomei), during which he receives his first taste of fame, Chaplin is encouraged by his brother Sydney (Paul Rhys) to split from Sennett and become an independent filmmaker. He then achieves an even greater success.

As his creative fortunes rise, however, Chaplin experiences personal setbacks. The image of his first love, fifteen-year-old Hetty Kelly (Moira Kelly), a girl from the London music halls, haunts him. In Hollywood, he encounters the willing, young Mildred Harris (Milla Jovovich), and he lingers in his seduction of her to have her rouge her lips in the fashion of Hetty. Chaplin and Mildred marry when she has a false pregnancy, but that first marriage and Chaplin's other early relationships are temporary.

To some extent, his political difficulties grow out of the social consciousness implied in his comedies. Loyally sympathizing with the have-nots, Chaplin often renders the institutions of society in an irreverent or negative light. Sydney notices in *The Immigrant* (1917) the ironic contrast between a shot depicting the squalid treatment of shipboard refugees and the following insert of the Statue of Liberty. He cautions his brother about the dangers of criticizing American values. Charlie nevertheless punctures the dignity of Federal Bureau of Investigation chief J. Edgar Hoover (Kevin Dunn) at a Hollywood dinner. Tired of hearing Hoover pontificate about American morality, Chaplin grabs two forks and begins performing his dance of the dinner rolls on the tabletop. The perplexed guests divide their attention between Hoover's remarks and Charlie's upstaging antics, their laughter increasing. Hoover's corresponding anger nourished a lifelong hatred of Chaplin that led to the actor's eventual exile from the United States in 1952.

The film's episodic structure is mostly redeemed by the effectiveness of the actors. Robert Downey, Jr., in an Academy Award-nominated performance, is uncanny. Downey excels in a role in which he not only must twirl a cane and saunter along as the Little Tramp but also must play the offscreen Chaplin who ages in the film from his teens to his eighties. He captures the innocence and curiosity of the young Chaplin who dressed backstage with chorus girls during his music hall days. He achieves the same blend of comic ballet and pantomime that can be found in Chaplin's two-reel comedies. He displays the crotchety reluctance of the aging artist-in-exile to answer questions that touch on old wounds. Watching a compilation of Chaplin footage at the 1972 Academy Awards, he reveals the tearful poignance of an old man who realizes that the industry that he helped to create has not forgotten him. Downey's preparation for the role included work with a mime to alter his posture, training with a dialect coach, a tour of London's East End with biographer David Robinson, and a thorough study of important Chaplinalia—films, books, and props. His diligence is not wasted. The greatest pleasure of the film is savoring Downey's matchless work.

Other performances enliven the film in different ways. Geraldine Chaplin, playing her own grandmother, conveys the madness that brought about Hannah Chaplin's incarceration in an asylum, yet she manages to preserve the character's fragility and dignity. Dan Aykroyd plays Mack Sennett with robust energy, while Anthony Hopkins brings a big name to the somewhat thinner part of the fictional editor George Hayden. More effectively, Kevin Kline portrays the athleticism and charm of matinee idol Douglas Fairbanks, but he also shows an underlying depth. Talking to Chaplin during the heyday of the 1920's, Fairbanks tries to warn Charlie about his negative publicity and the recklessness of his nonconformity. Chaplin answers naïvely: "It's a good country underneath." Fairbanks, who created and marketed an image of himself as the American hero, responds more knowingly: "No, it's a good country on top." One of Kline's best moments occurs in a scene set in the 1940's toward the end of Fairbanks' life. Nearly forgotten and dying from a heart condition, he leans over a mirrored bartop, catches a glimpse of his drawn appearance, and folds his hands wearily over his reflection.

The structure of the film is also buoyed by some memorable scenes. One of these is the music hall sequence in which Downey first appears as Chaplin. Playing a drunk in evening dress who arrives late to watch the show, Chaplin stumbles around his stage-side stall and interrupts the act in progress. To the growing laughter of the audience, the master of ceremonies tries to get the unruly drunk seated so that the show may proceed. After a series of daring pratfalls, Chaplin is ushered off the stage to the applause of even the trained seal that his clowning interrupted. His first appearance as the Little Tramp affords another example. After piecing together his costume from stray props, he barges into a wedding scene from a comedy Mack

Sennett is directing. As in the music hall sequence, Chaplin's spirited antics inject comic anarchy into a staid ritual. Sennett enjoys the improvisation and instructs the cameraman to continue cranking. While Sennett shouts direction to Chaplin and the others, the scene grows in comic ingenuity and chaos. As in nearly all of Sennett's comedies, this scene ends with a chase. Attenborough's film suggests correctly that Chaplin's reasons for separating from Sennett were tied to finances and his growing popularity, but it mistakenly leaves out some of Chaplin's instinctive knowledge about the personality of the Little Tramp. The real-life Chaplin sensed that his future lay less in the plot-centered comedy of Sennett's chase films than in a film-by-film exploration of this new-found character.

Chaplin's films themselves have often been faulted for their deficient narrative structure. The real Chaplin used on-the-set inspiration to spur his artistry. As part owner of his studio, he could tolerate his own great delays as a filmmaker, as in the protracted filming of *City Lights* (1931). Attenborough's film suffers from the same fragmentation, and it could also benefit from an additional focus on Chaplin at work on his films. Some of Chaplin's greatest achievements, such as *The Gold Rush* (1925), *The Circus* (1928), and *Monsieur Verdoux* (1947), are completely overlooked. Perhaps the sprawling material of the artist's long life overwhelmed the narrower format of the film biography. The best vehicle for such a subject might have been a high-prestige television miniseries. One can easily imagine an excellent seven-hour version of Chaplin's life that maintains the strengths of period detail, strong acting, and inspired scenes of *Chaplin* but that adds the needed development to complete the picture.

Glenn Hopp

Reviews

Chicago Tribune. January 8, 1993, VII, p. 19.
The Christian Science Monitor. December 31, 1992, p. 12.
Entertainment Weekly. January 8, 1993, p. 32.
The Hollywood Reporter. December 7, 1992, p. 6.
Los Angeles Times. December 25, 1992, p. F1.
The New York Times. December 25, 1992, p. B6.
The New Yorker. LXVIII, December 28, 1992, p. 202.
Newsweek. December 28, 1992, p. 57.
Time. CXL, December 28, 1992, p. 64.
Variety. December 7, 1992, p. 4.

CITY OF JOY

Origin: Great Britain and France
Released: 1992
Released in U.S.: 1992
Production: Jake Eberts and Roland Joffé for Lightmotive; released by TriStar Pictures
Direction: Roland Joffé
Screenplay: Mark Medoff; based on the book *Cité de la joie*, by Dominique Lapierre
Cinematography: Peter Biziou
Editing: Gerry Hambling
Production design: Roy Walker
Art direction: John Fenner and Asoke Bose
Set decoration: Rosalind Shingleton
Casting: Priscilla John
Sound: Daniel Brisseau
Costume design: Judy Moorcroft
Cultural consulting: Sunil Gangopadhyay
Music: Ennio Morricone
MPAA rating: PG-13
Running time: 134 minutes

Principal characters:

Character	Actor
Max Lowe	Patrick Swayze
Joan Bethel	Pauline Collins
Hasari Pal	Om Puri
Kamla Pal	Shabana Azmi
Ashoka	Art Malik
Amrita Pal	Ayesha Dharker
Shambu Pal	Santu Chowdhury
Manooj Pal	Imran Badsah Khan
Ram Chander	Debtosh Ghosh
Ghatak	Shyamanand Jalan
Poomina	Suneeta Sengupta

City of Joy is based on Dominique Lapierre's inspiring and emotional nonfiction work *Cité de la joie* (1985; *The City of Joy*, 1985). The book, which has sold six and a half million copies worldwide, depicts life among the determined, vibrant, and desperately poor residents of a *bustee*, or Calcutta slum. Fortunately, the film narrows down Lapierre's abundant number of characters to a relative few.

Director Roland Joffé focuses on two strong and emotionally volatile men whose lives become intertwined by chance. Their friendship provides a vital framework for the story because their ways of seeing the world are so different. This contrast between the two friends is what finally allows each to see his own strengths and weaknesses in a new light. Both learn how to face life's demands with renewed grace and courage.

Max Lowe (Patrick Swayze) is a young doctor from Texas disillusioned by the death of a child patient and his own uncertain purpose in life. He has quit his medical practice and come to India to find answers to his spiritual and moral dilemmas. Max's ill-defined search for meaning, however, has left him feeling even more empty than before. Traveling through Calcutta, he meets a farmer who has moved his family to the great city to escape famine and drought. Hasari Pal (Om Puri) becomes Max's friend after saving his life one night.

On that night, a young beautiful prostitute named Poomina (Suneeta Sengupta) has helped Max to become thoroughly drunk, as she was told to do. Waiting thieves jump him in the street as he leaves the tavern. Sleeping with his family on a nearby street, Hasari hears the brawl, and he alone comes to Max's aid. The thieves leave Max badly hurt and manage to escape with everything he had, including his passport and a cherished gold medallion.

Hasari transports Max to a busy makeshift free clinic in the City of Joy *bustee*. The clinic is run by a benevolent Irish woman named Joan Bethel (Pauline Collins). The City of Joy Self-Help School and Dispensary is one of the very few places providing medical care for some of Calcutta's poorest residents. Curious about Max's purpose in India and his background, Joan coaxes him into revealing that he is a nonpracticing physician. She scolds him for this waste of needed talent, as she sees it, and tells him there are only three choices in life: to run, to spectate, or to commit. She wants him to make a commitment by working for the dispensary, but Max flatly refuses. It is clear that he fears offering himself to a situation that might cause him more pain.

Having accompanied Max's rickshaw driver to the dispensary, Hasari decides that he could pull a rickshaw in order to support his family. He and his wife, Kamla (Shabana Azmi), his daughter, Amrita (Ayesha Dharker), and his sons, Shambu (Santu Chowdhury) and Manooj (Imran Badsah Khan), have been suffering the indignity and dangers of living on the streets. They have been conned out of the last of their money, and Hasari is desperate to find work. Reluctantly, the rickshaw driver takes Hasari to his employer's quarters.

In a half-dilapidated mansion, the Godfather, Ghatak (Shyamanand Jalan), presides in a thronelike chair. He is surrounded by assorted thugs and lackeys, including his own unsympathetic son, Ashoka (Art Malik). These are the men that beat up Max. The Godfather offers Hasari permission to pull one of his rickshaws and rents him a shack in the City of Joy. Despite Ghatak's obvious cunning and indifference, Hasari thanks the Godfather profusely and pledges his loyalty to him. It becomes clear in this scene that Ghatak virtually owns the residents of the City of Joy. Hasari's family is overjoyed with his perceived good fortune, and they celebrate by inviting Max to have dinner in their new home, a small shanty.

Max is awestruck by the suffering and resilience of the residents in the City of

Joy. Their spirit and courage move him. He is shocked by their living conditions and outraged by the way they are controlled by Ghatak's mafia. Yet, despite Max's sympathy for the people, Joan still cannot persuade him to resume medical work and to help her many patients at the dispensary. He is still wrestling with his own demons—a self-absorption that he cannot shake. In this way, he reflects the common Western trait of self-centeredness.

It takes a crisis to persuade Max that he can no longer be a bystander to the suffering around him. A leper comes to the dispensary to fetch help for his wife, who is in childbirth. Something is wrong, and both the mother and baby are in danger. Max accompanies Joan and an entourage to the leper village and takes charge. In an electrifying scene that records a real birth, Max saves the mother's and baby's lives by successfully delivering the breech baby. Kamla, Hasari's wife, expertly reassures the leper woman and calmly assists Max with the delivery. Both Max and Joan are terribly moved by the birth, but Max again rebuffs Joan's plea for him to come work with her. The child, he snaps, is simply another being unfortunate enough to have been born into suffering.

Yet Max's heart knows better, and he soon relents and joins the dispensary staff. Impressed with Kamla's skill, Max invites her to be his assistant. She is thankful, even overjoyed to be allowed "to be of use," but Hasari does not share her enthusiasm. Hasari knows that Kamla's work is important, but he cannot help feeling jealous about the time that she spends with the young doctor and about the pleasure that his children take in being with Max. He is doing well in his demanding job as a rickshaw puller and has gained regular clients, but the excruciating demands of the job exhaust him and his health is failing. He needs not only to support his family but also to save enough of his meager earnings to provide a dowry for his daughter, Amrita. More and more, he feels beaten down by life, and matters get worse.

Hasari learns that he has somehow incurred the wrath of Ghatak's brutal son, Ashoka. The tension between them spills over into a larger confrontation between the residents of the City of Joy (including Max and Joan) on the one side and Ghatak's gangsters on the other. Plans to expand the dispensary and treat lepers have brought a demand for more protection money, or "rent," from Ghatak. Max and Joan refuse to pay and decide to build a new clinic on another site.

This decision involves Max more heavily in a conflict that is becoming dangerous, and for his perceived allegiance to Max, Hasari is informed that he has lost his rickshaw privilege. This terrible blow to Hasari's pride seems insurmountable to him. Meanwhile, Max continues to encourage the city's residents to revolt against Ghatak's unfair demands. He also wants Hasari to run his own rickshaw without worrying about the Godfather's permission. He tries to teach the passive residents to take control of their own community and lives. Very few, however, are willing to take the chance. Their tradition and their religion have taught them to accept whatever hardships life brings, and Ghatak's men respond to Joan's resourcefulness by having the new clinic destroyed by a crowd protesting the treatment of lepers.

The thugs continually threaten those involved with the dispensary. The child-prostitute Poomina, whom Max and Joan have befriended and sent to school, is brutally attacked and has her face slashed by Ashoka, who intends to intimidate the City of Joy community. Even Joan agrees to their demand for the higher rent. Finally, after they attempt to kill his son Manooj, Hasari, sick with tuberculosis and tired of being singled out for intimidation, repudiates Max and demands that his wife, Kamla, leave the clinic. He accuses Max of being self-serving in his interests in the community. Since he is a foreigner, Hasari insists, Max can always leave Calcutta without any consequence. It is easy for a foreigner to come in and suggest how the poor might change their lives, he says. Many in the City of Joy remain fearful of what the Godfather can do to them.

The conflict between Max and Hasari illustrates one of Joffé's interests—how dissimilar traditions create in people different loyalties and different means of action. Both Hasari and Max are tied to the past, but Max's tradition is bound to success and striving for it, while Hasari's is bound to the caste system and its limitations. The two are lucky to have each other: Their differences illuminate these boundaries, which they learn can be arbitrary.

Max is deeply hurt by his friend's accusations, but the rift in their friendship is healed when Hasari saves Max from drowning in a monsoon-swollen river. Max has just saved the lives of the leper family whose baby he delivered when a tree falls and plunges him under water. The storm in this dark climactic scene metaphorically reflects the emotional storms that Hasari and Max have been trying to negotiate. Both find that their troubles are assuaged and begin to recede only after they have seized the chance to offer themselves to others. Recuperating at the clinic, Max tells Joan the boyhood story of his father's infidelity to his mother and his complicity in the coverup. He begins to understand the inner fears and old guilt that he has been harboring.

Hasari meanwhile begins to understand Max's insistence on standing up to Ashoka and his gang. The Godfather has died, leaving his son in power, and conditions have grown even worse. No matter how hard Hasari tries to please them, their unjust demands escalate. Hasari finally realizes that he must fight back when the Godfather's son threatens his daughter. His final battle with Ashoka ends with Hasari victorious and Ghatak's loyal thugs relieved to be free of Ashoka's greed and cruelty. With the new Godfather stripped of his power, a yoke has been lifted from the residents of the City of Joy. They rally round Hasari, recognizing in him a new leader. Hasari needed the interaction of someone like Max, a person with a completely different view of the world, to show him that he could take a stand.

The last scenes are a wonderful enactment of a traditional Hindu wedding. Amrita has finally been accepted by her boyfriend's family to become his wife because her dowry has been made complete. Max's medallion, recovered by Manooj after his father fought Ashoka, becomes the ounce of gold that seals the proposal. Max has also made a proposal: He tells Joan that he will stay at the clinic. Calcutta has helped Max find the strength to be reborn and to beat his personal devils. The film ends with a quote from Hasari Pal: "All that is not given is lost."

Roland Joffé has said that the city of Calcutta itself is his film's chief protagonist. The images that Joffé captured of this magnificent and shocking metropolis, with its teeming, milling crowds, convey both its human wealth and its incredible human burden. Of the eleven million people who inhabit Calcutta, the majority live in poverty far more bleak than many Westerners, especially Americans, can imagine. Yet Joffé has also tried to convey the palpable and heartwarming love so evident in the lives of even the poorest families. By concentrating often on the love and devotion of friends and family members for one another—for example the kindness and loyalty that the City of Joy residents show members of the leper colony—Joffé succeeds in capturing a sort of beauty that is heroic and energizing. Moreover, the energy of the Calcutta streets captured in this film makes it a visual masterpiece.

These qualities underscore both the strength of Joffé's creative vision and his formidable skill as a filmmaker. The great Indian director Satyajit Ray told Joffé that he would be unable to shoot in the streets of Calcutta. Joffé, however, a documentarian at heart, said that the unpredictability of the Calcutta streets lent excitement and immediacy to the footage. In fact, the film crew experienced serious problems and delays when, for several weeks, protesters attempted to stop the filming. The Calcutta political powers believed that the script overemphasized the city's poverty and crime and that it would paint an unbalanced portrait of the city's life. Yet Joffé's devotion to Calcutta and to the story he wished to tell resulted in a film with a well-balanced and even inspiring view of the legendary city. This devotion, coupled with outstanding performances from Patrick Swayze and the great Indian actors Om Puri and Shabana Azmi, makes *City of Joy* a remarkable and moving film.

JoAnn Balingit

Reviews

Boxoffice. May, 1992, p. R-36.
Chicago Tribune. April 17, 1992, VII, p. 32.
The Christian Science Monitor. April 24, 1992, p. 12.
Films in Review. XLIII, July, 1992, p. 261.
The Hollywood Reporter. April 8, 1992, p. 6.
Los Angeles Times. April 15, 1992, p. F6.
The New York Times. April 15, 1992, p. B4.
Premiere. March, 1992, p. 56.
Rolling Stone. April 30, 1992, p. 64.
Variety. April 8, 1992, p. 2.

THE CRYING GAME

Origin: Great Britain and Ireland
Released: 1992
Released in U.S.: 1992
Production: Stephen Woolley for Palace and Channel Four Films, in association with Eurotrustees, Nippon Film Development, and Finance, Inc., with the participation of British Screen; released by Miramax Films
Direction: Neil Jordan
Screenplay: Neil Jordan (AA)
Cinematography: Ian Wilson
Editing: Kant Pan
Production design: Jim Clay
Art direction: Chris Seagers
Set decoration: Martin Childs
Casting: Susie Figgis
Sound: Colin Nicolson
Makeup: Morag Ross
Costume design: Sandy Powell
Music: Anne Dudley
MPAA rating: R
Running time: 112 minutes

Principal characters:

Fergus	Stephen Rea
Jude	Miranda Richardson
Dil	Jaye Davidson
Jody	Forest Whitaker
Maguire	Adrian Dunbar
Col	Jim Broadbent
Dave	Ralph Brown

After making *The Company of Wolves* (1984), an aesthetically distinctive and idiosyncratic horror film, writer-director Neil Jordan followed with *Mona Lisa* (1986), a highly complex crime drama. The quality of Jordan's films fell drastically after *Mona Lisa*, however, the nadir being his ill-conceived, unwatchable 1989 remake of *We're No Angels. The Crying Game* returns Jordan to form with his most unusual and emotionally compelling film yet. Like *Mona Lisa*, *The Crying Game* deals with violence and interracial love but adds unexpected humor and highly original plot twists to Jordan's earlier formula.

The Crying Game opens with the kidnapping in Northern Ireland of a black British soldier by the Irish Republican Army (IRA). These terrorists promise to kill Jody (Forest Whitaker) unless an imprisoned colleague is released. No one, least of all Jody, expects this exchange of prisoners to take place. While Maguire (Adrian Dunbar) and Jude (Miranda Richardson), the leaders of the group, treat Jody like an animal, he is looked upon more gently by the kindhearted Fergus (Stephen Rea), who takes off the prisoner's hood, feeds him, and even helps him to urinate. Because Fergus treats him like a human being, Jody opens up to Fergus, begging him to look up his lover back in London. When the deadline for the release of the IRA member passes, Fergus is glad to be the one chosen to kill the soldier, because Jody deserves to be treated humanely even in such inhumane circumstances. As Jody tries to run away, Fergus is unable to shoot his friend in the back, but the soldier dies anyway when run over by the trucks of the arriving British forces. Fergus flees during the ensuing attack and makes his way to London, assuming the identity of a construction worker named Jimmy.

Fergus finds Dil (Jaye Davidson), Jody's lover, and timidly attempts to become acquainted with the attractive black hairdresser. Disturbed by Dil's relationship with Dave (Ralph Brown), a violent suitor, Fergus begins following Dil and eventually takes Dave's place by beating him. The growing love between the quiet, shy Fergus and the vivacious Dil, presided over by Col (Jim Broadbent), a paternal bartender, is interrupted when Jude and Maguire track down their former comrade and try to coerce him into assassinating an English judge.

The Crying Game is remarkable for presenting three equally engaging stories: the IRA activities, the developing relationship between Fergus and Dil, and the way that relationship changes after Fergus makes a startling discovery about Dil. In an age when even the best films offer few surprises, Jordan, equally adept as both screenwriter and director, challenges and entertains his audience by creating a film that constantly reinvents itself.

Like *Mona Lisa*, *The Crying Game* is a *film noir* exploring the emotional complexity of people living on the edge of society, whose lives could explode at any moment and who seem to thrive on this sense of danger. Despite feeling sure of themselves, Fergus and Dil are actually relative innocents in a world much more volatile than they expect. Jordan is aided in creating this dark moral miasma by the evocative cinematography of Ian Wilson and the production design of Jim Clay, who makes Dil's flat both garish and a credible summary of the character's life.

The Crying Game generated considerable publicity for its distributor's request that critics refrain from revealing Fergus' discovery, midway through the film, that Dil is a man dressed as a woman and for audiences' delight in also keeping what came to be known as "the secret." The cross-dressing theme and the conspiracy between journalists and viewers to keep it a secret from those who had not seen the film threatened to allow one element, although an important one, to dominate the perception of the film.

Dil's sexual identity does, however, illustrate the cleverness and complexity of Jordan's achievement, as many of the elements that preceded the revelation take on new meanings, including the film's opening with Percy Sledge's "When a Man Loves a Woman" playing in the background and Jody's saying that Jude is not his type. In describing his love of cricket to Fergus, Jody tells about learning how to bowl a googly (roughly the cricket equivalent to the screwball in baseball). When Fergus learns the truth about Dil, he imagines Jody's delighted face at having bowled him a googly.

Most important, Dil's transvestism underscores Jordan's point about overcoming barriers of nationality, politics, race, and sex. Fergus and Dil grow to love each other in a way that transcends sexual preference. The future of their relationship is left whimsically ambiguous at the film's conclusion.

A major factor in holding together the disparate elements of *The Crying Game* is the uniformly excellent performances. Adrian Dunbar makes Maguire a frightening villain, totally the opposite of his effervescent promoter in *Hear My Song* (1991). Ralph Brown's rodentlike Dave is memorably repellent. Jim Broadbent, one of the best English character actors of the previous decade for his performances in *The Good Father* (1987), *Life Is Sweet* (1991), and *Enchanted April* (1992; reviewed in this volume), avoids the clichés associated with all-knowing bartenders, presenting Col as compassionate toward but amused by his customers. Forest Whitaker, whose bumbling vulnerability has threatened to become a cliché as well, gives his best screen performance. Rather than portraying Jody as a whimpering victim, Whitaker invests the prisoner with a passion for life, especially as defined by Dil and cricket, to balance his unavoidable fear.

Miranda Richardson has displayed tremendous range with her jealous lover-turned-murderer in *Dance with a Stranger* (1984), blissfully childish Queen Elizabeth I in the television series *Blackadder*, neurotically murderous wife in *After Pilkington* (a 1986 television film by Simon Gray), mother relentlessly determined to recover her kidnapped children in the 1990 miniseries *Die Kinder*, and neglected, restless housewife in *Enchanted April*. Possessing a remarkable ability to be both plain and beautiful, Richardson makes each of her characters distinctive. Her Jude is a hauntingly erotic portrayal of political singlemindedness and evil. Making his principal villain a woman without a tinge of sexism is another of Jordan's remarkable achievements in *The Crying Game*.

Another such achievement is the performance Jordan elicits from Jaye Davidson, who had never acted prior to this film. Discovered by casting director Susie Figgis at a party celebrating the conclusion of filming for Derek Jarman's *Edward II* (1992), Davidson is one of those natural performers whom the camera loves. Employed in the fashion business before and after making *The Crying Game*, Davidson is at ease with the glamorous façade Dil erects and displays extremely well the character's mixture of strength and vulnerability, confidence and fear.

Most of all, however, *The Crying Game* is dominated by the quiet strength of Stephen Rea's portrayal of Fergus. Torn by conflicting feelings regarding friendship, love, and politics, Fergus is an Everyman caught up in a nightmare he has helped create. Unremarkable physically, Rea embodies Fergus' ordinariness while investing him with the passion to make sense of the unusual circumstances in which he finds himself. Rea's supporting parts in such films as *The Company of Wolves* and

Life Is Sweet give little indication of the star power he subtly generates here.

The Crying Game deserved its numerous awards. In addition to Jordan's Academy Award for best original screenplay, his script was honored by the New York Film Critics, the Boston Society of Film Critics, and the Writers' Guild. Rea was named best actor by the National Society of Film Critics and Richardson best supporting actress by the New York Film Critics. The film won the British Academy Award's Alexander Korda Award for best British film, was named best foreign film by the Los Angeles Film Critics, and received Academy Award nominations for best picture, director, actor, supporting actor (Davidson), and film editing. That it became an unanticipatedly large commercial hit after being released nationwide shows that viewers are willing to support intelligent, unusual films.

Recalling such masterpieces as Sir Carol Reed's *The Third Man* (1949), Roman Polanski's *Chinatown* (1974), and Francis Ford Coppola's *The Conversation* (1974), *The Crying Game* proves that Jordan's work is to be eagerly awaited. Few films have said so much about love and loneliness so remarkably.

Michael Adams

Reviews

Chicago Tribune. December 18, 1992, VII, p. 34.
Entertainment Weekly. December 11, 1992, p. 48.
Film Comment. XXVIII, November, 1992, p. 67.
The Hollywood Reporter. September 17, 1992, p. 7.
Los Angeles Times. November 25, 1992, p. F1.
The New York Times. September 26, 1992, p. 13.
The New Yorker. LXVIII, November 16, 1992, p. 127.
Time. CXL, November 30, 1992, p. 79.
Variety. September 11, 1992, p. 2.
The Washington Post. December 18, 1992, p. D1.

DAMAGE

Origin: Great Britain and France
Released: 1992
Released in U.S.: 1992
Production: Louis Malle for Skreba, NEF, and Le Studio Canal Plus; released by New Line Cinema
Direction: Louis Malle
Screenplay: David Hare; based on the novel by Josephine Hart
Cinematography: Peter Biziou
Editing: John Bloom
Production design: Brian Morris
Art direction: Richard Earl
Set decoration: Jill Quertier
Casting: Patsy Pollock
Sound: Jean-Claude Laureux
Costume design: Milena Canonero
Music: Zbigniew Preisner
MPAA rating: R
Running time: 112 minutes

Principal characters:

Dr. Stephen Fleming	Jeremy Irons
Anna Barton	Juliette Binoche
Ingrid	Miranda Richardson
Martyn	Rupert Graves
Edward Lloyd	Ian Bannen
Elizabeth Prideaux	Leslie Caron
Peter Wetzler	Peter Stormare
Sally	Gemma Clark

Whether one believes anything in Louis Malle's *Damage* depends on one's tolerance for the foolish nature of sexual obsession. Accepting the possibility of two people falling instantly in love, or perhaps merely in lust, simply by catching eyes across a room is a requirement for becoming involved in the film's narrative. Yet another questionable scenario that Malle and screenwriter David Hare ask viewers to accept—this one harder to swallow—is the notion that two successful, upper-class people would quickly risk everything for an extramarital affair made up of a few frantic moments of nonverbal passion. These stretches in credibility notwithstanding, *Damage* is a finely crafted and competently acted sexual thriller which, because of a most peculiar European approach to sex, is capable of eliciting more than a few giggles.

Tales of erotic obsession run rampant through the history of European cinema;

American filmgoers can always count on foreign films to give them a healthy dose of nudity and sex. Louis Malle, always one of the more accessible of the French New Wave directors, and his *The Lovers* (1958), with its lyrical love scenes and adoring camera, outraged many American viewers but paved the way for the import of many more explicit foreign films. Despite their appeal, these saucy European films are often dismissed as silly and overwrought. In freer cultures, two people falling over each other may be perceived as beautiful, but in American culture, intense sexual expression has become almost taboo. *Damage* demands to be taken seriously, but with scenes requiring its lovers to make love on the sly in church doorways, in alleys, and on kitchen tables, it not only risks offending an American viewer's sense of propriety but may very well incite uncomfortable laughter as well.

Dr. Stephen Fleming (Jeremy Irons), gray-haired and respectable, is one of the more ambitious members of Parliament. His aggressiveness and passion are reserved, however, only for his office; Fleming's domestic life consists of a cold, somber wife, Ingrid (Miranda Richardson), and a gawky teenage daughter, Sally (Gemma Clark). Stephen's son, Martyn (Rupert Graves), a journalist on the rise, is the only member of the family who appears to be having any fun; he drives around in a sleek sports car and enjoys a love affair with the voluptuous Anna Barton (Juliette Binoche). Ingrid disapproves of her son's choice of girlfriend, but when Stephen meets her at a political cocktail party, he is instantly enraptured. Stephen and Anna stare wordlessly at each other, but when Martyn brings Anna to meet his family a few days later, they pretend never to have met. Anna calls Stephen afterward and gives him her address. He rushes over, and the two make love without saying a word.

Martyn announces to his father that he has been promoted at his newspaper and wants to celebrate with a dinner party. At the dinner, Stephen steals glances at Anna, who reveals to all that her only brother killed himself years earlier. After the dinner, Ingrid expresses her disapproval of Anna, but Stephen feigns disinterest and excuses himself. He retreats to Anna's apartment, where he waits for Martyn to leave and then makes love to Anna. During the night, Anna tells Stephen that she is "damaged": Her teenage brother, passionately in love with her, killed himself when he discovered her in a boyfriend's embrace.

When Martyn takes Anna to Paris for a romantic weekend, Stephen follows. He entices Anna out of her hotel room, makes love to her in the entryway to a church, and later watches her flirt with his son through a hotel room window. Back in England, Stephen considers leaving his wife for Anna; he feels that his newfound passion is spinning out of control and desires to transform it into something more manageable. Anna, unwilling to let Stephen change the dynamics of their affair, refuses to let him consider legitimizing their love. She even lets Stephen know that she suspects that Martyn, with his new job giving him an exciting future, will ask her to marry him: By accepting, Anna hopes she will forever be in Stephen's life. Stephen, completely baffled about how to live with such unbridled passion, struggles to remain calm at his job and at home.

Ingrid begrudgingly invites Anna to spend a weekend at her family's country home, where Martyn announces his engagement to Anna. Later, after Ingrid gets over her initial shock, Martyn asks his father why he does not seem enthused. Martyn, a litte perturbed, tells his father that he has always found him to be a cold, passionless man. Back in England, Stephen meets Anna's friend Peter (Peter Stormare), who Anna later reveals is the boyfriend who indirectly caused her brother's suicide. Later, the Flemings entertain Anna's mother, Elizabeth (Leslie Caron), and over a discussion of wedding plans, Anna's mother describes the similarity between Martyn and Anna's dead brother. Such talk disturbs Anna; consequently, Elizabeth, accompanied by Stephen, is quickly sent to her hotel. On the way, Elizabeth warns Stephen to stay away from her daughter. Apparently, Stephen's pained looks and aversion to Anna in public give him away. Deciding that it is the best move for everyone, Stephen breaks off his affair with Anna and, in a discussion with Martyn, apologizes for being such an unemotional father.

Days later, Anna sends a key and an address to Stephen and pleads with him to meet her at a newly leased apartment. Once there, Anna persuades Stephen to continue their affair by meeting her every Friday afternoon at the apartment. Stephen is unable to resist, and the couple consummates the new arrangement with an afternoon of rough sex. Martyn, responding to a call for Anna from a strange landlord, comes to the apartment and finds Stephen and Anna. Shocked, Martyn slips on the landing and falls several stories to his death. A naked Stephen runs to his side, and Anna slips away. That evening, Ingrid, completely distraught, berates Stephen for his betrayal. Stephen, in the midst of a horrific scandal, retires from Parliament. After Martyn's funeral, he searches out Anna, who now will have nothing to do with him. Years later, Anna has started a family with her old friend Peter, and Stephen has moved to a Middle Eastern country, where he lives life as a hermit—occupying his days by staring at a large photograph of Anna, Martyn, and himself.

David Hare's screenplay for *Damage* is based on Josephine Hart's 1991 bestseller of the same name, a slim potboiler that delighted readers but annoyed critics. Hart's purple prose, masquerading as fine literature, is faithfully and expertly adapted by Hare. Motivations behind Anna and Stephen's affair are vaguely described in Hart's book, but Hare wisely spends more time focusing on and illuminating both characters' sexual psyches. Stephen, distressed that his life has been devoid of any kind of feeling, embarks on an affair that will not only provide passion but give his life new meaning as well. It is only when he tries to control his passion, by following Anna's lead and setting a time constraint, that he is finally punished. Jeremy Irons, cool and restrained as usual, seems perfectly cast as Stephen, but unfortunately the most striking thing about his performance is the lithe, overly toned body he displays in the many sex scenes.

The damaged Anna, on the other hand, is destined to repeat the same destructive pattern of loving two men and forcing the weakest to self-destruct. Martyn and her dead brother are linked in terms of their appearance and their ultimate fate, while

Peter and Stephen are linked by their existence as Anna's true lovers. This motivational scheme is certainly less believable than the one that incites Stephen, and what complicates its effectiveness is the bland, flat performance by Juliette Binoche. The actress, who played the fragile, naïve lover in Philip Kaufmann's *The Unbearable Lightness of Being* (1988), relies more on her physical appearance than her emotions to suggest the severe sensuousness of her character. When she first appears at the Flemings' house, stepping out of Martyn's sports car, her outrageous leather outfit and lacquered hair make her look more like a space creature than a forbidden lover.

Zbigniew Preisner's music provides a somber, dangerous mood to the film, and Brian Morris' production design effectively duplicates the world of the English elite. Perhaps the most memorable aspect of *Damage*, though, is Miranda Richardson's Academy Award-nominated turn as Ingrid Fleming. Putting twenty years on her actual age to portray the betrayed wife, Richardson implodes with emotion in the scenes following Martyn's death. In her final moments on screen, Ingrid lashes out at her husband's indifference to her, and Richardson, stripping off her nightgown, expertly offers a glimpse into her character's obliterated soul. Richardson's performance gives *Damage* a final kick of emotion but ultimately fails to save the film from sinking into high-class soap opera.

Greg Changnon

Reviews

Chicago Tribune. January 22, 1993, VII, p. 20.
Entertainment Weekly. CLV, January 29, 1993, p. 38.
The Hollywood Reporter. CCCXXIV, December 4, 1992, p. 6.
Los Angeles Times. December 23, 1992, p. F1.
The New York Times. December 23, 1992, CXLII, p. B3.
The New Yorker. January 25, 1993, p. 95.
Newsweek. January 4, 1993, p. 50.
Time. CXLI, January 11, 1993, p. 50.
Variety. CCXXXVII, December 4, 1993, p. 3.
The Washington Post. January 22, 1993, p. C1.

DEATH BECOMES HER

Production: Robert Zemeckis and Steve Starkey; released by Universal Pictures
Direction: Robert Zemeckis
Screenplay: Martin Donovan and David Koepp
Cinematography: Dean Cundey
Editing: Arthur Schmidt
Production design: Rick Carter
Art direction: Jim Teegarden
Set decoration: Jackie Carr
Set design: Lauren Polizzi, Elizabeth Lapp, Masako Masuda, and John Berger
Casting: Karen Rea
Visual effects: Ken Ralston (AA), Doug Chiang (AA), Doug Smythe (AA), and Tom Woodruff (AA)
Special visual effects: Industrial Light and Magic
Sound: William B. Kaplan
Makeup design: Dick Smith
Prosthetics makeup supervision: Kevin Haney
Costume design: Joanna Johnston
Music: Alan Silvestri
MPAA rating: PG-13
Running time: 103 minutes

Principal characters:

Madeline Ashton .... Meryl Streep
Dr. Ernest Menville .... Bruce Willis
Helen Sharp .... Goldie Hawn
Lisle von Rhumans .... Isabella Rossellini
Chagall .... Ian Ogilvy
Dakota .... Adam Storke
Rose .... Nancy Fish
Psychologist .... Alaina Reed Hall
Anna .... Michelle Johnson
Vivian Adams .... Mary Ellen Trainor
Mr. Franklin .... William Frankfather
Eulogist .... John Ingle
Doctor .... Sydney Pollack

Death Becomes Her, which relies almost more heavily on special effects than did *Terminator II: Judgment Day* (1991), is far from satisfactory as a piece of drama. At its release, however, the film had a novelty that intrigued youthful audiences and that promised to influence the course of Hollywood filmmaking. Its three stars were rich and famous enough to do anything they wanted, and in *Death Becomes Her* that is exactly what they do. It is like a costume party in which everyone is invited to come as the person he or she would like to be. It is high camp: The three stars are not really acting but "acting"—or acting as if they are acting.

Over the years, Meryl Streep, Goldie Hawn, and Bruce Willis have acquired very definite images from the films in which they have had their greatest successes. Streep is thought of as cool, cerebral, and reserved, the way she appeared in such films as *The Deer Hunter* (1978), *Kramer vs. Kramer* (1979), and *Out of Africa* (1985). Hawn has built an image as the stereotypical "dumb blonde" from films such as *Private Benjamin* (1980) and *Housesitter* (1992; reviewed in this volume). Willis made a fortune playing the indestructible detective John McClane in *Die Hard* (1988) and *Die Hard II: Die Harder* (1990) and then appeared as a tough gangster with Dustin Hoffman in *Billy Bathgate* (1991).

In *Death Becomes Her*, Streep, the iceberg, appears as the headliner in a Broadway musical wearing as little as possible and cavorting with a host of male dancers in a manner reminiscent of Betty Grable, Marilyn Monroe, and the Marlene Dietrich of *The Blue Angel* (1930). Hawn wears slinky gowns, dyes her hair, plasters on makeup, and plays a femme fatale. Willis plays a Caspar Milquetoast, absent-minded-professor type who is so unlike his usual screen persona that it takes the audience some time to figure out that it is really him hiding behind the mustache and eyeglasses.

Madeline Ashton (Streep) and Helen Sharp (Hawn) have been friendly enemies for many years. During this time, Helen has lost all of her boyfriends to the irresistible Madeline. When Madeline steals Helen's fiancé Ernest Menville (Willis), a wealthy plastic surgeon, and marries him, it is the last straw: Helen goes insane and must be locked up. When she is finally released, she has only one thought in her deranged mind: to get revenge on Madeline.

Madeline encounters Helen at a big Beverly Hills party and is flabbergasted by Helen's youthful appearance. Madeline herself is beginning to show her age in both her face and figure (effects achieved by the makeup and wardrobe departments, respectively). Madeline is feeling desperate as her career seems to be fading away with her fading looks. Seeking the secret of eternal youth, Madeline demands a radical beauty treatment and is given a card bearing the address of the world's most exclusive beautician, Lisle von Rhumans (Isabella Rossellini).

Behind Madeline's back, Helen makes heated overtures to Ernest, who is susceptible because he has become thoroughly disillusioned with Madeline. Their loveless marriage has turned him into an alcoholic, and in order to make more money to meet her insatiable demands for luxuries, he has specialized as the mortician for the stars at an exclusive funeral parlor. Madeline treats Ernest with contempt and is totally faithless. When she discovers that her latest young lover despises her because he considers her to be old, too, she runs to the sinister-looking gothic mansion that is the headquarters of the exotic Lisle, agreeing to pay an exorbitant price for the treatment that will give her back her youth.

The secret is a luminous pink potion in a crystal vial. When Madeline drinks it, the age spots disappear from her hands, the wrinkles vanish from her face, and her body takes on the svelte contours of an eighteen-year-old starlet. Unfortunately, by this time Helen has persuaded Ernest to murder Madeline, and he ends up pushing his bitchy wife down a long flight of marble stairs.

This is where the special effects begin and the story starts to fall apart. Madeline should be dead, but she comes back to life while Ernest is on the phone reporting the fatal "accident" to the police. The potion has not only restored Madeline's youthful appearance but has made her immortal. The magical mixture, however, is far from perfect: It cannot fix her broken neck or make her heart start beating again. When Ernest rushes her to the hospital, he causes pandemonium by asking the medical staff (including an uncredited Sydney Pollack) to treat a patient who is alert and talkative but legally dead.

Madeline's broken neck will not support the weight of her head. Through the use of special effects, her body is twisted into various crazy shapes, and the film relies heavily on these contortions for its comedy. When she finds out that Helen was responsible for Ernest's uncharacteristic behavior, she uses a shotgun to blow an enormous hole through her rival's midsection. As might have been suspected, however, Helen too has drunk the magic potion and comes back to "life," although she has a porthole in her stomach.

Death Becomes Her might have been entitled "Three Characters in Search of an Author." The plot hangs from a slender thread of feminine rivalry to begin with, and when that thread breaks halfway through the film, the three principals are stranded in midair like those cartoon characters who run straight out from the edge of a cliff without realizing there is nothing underneath them but empty space. After causing each other's deaths, the two erstwhile enemies inexplicably become bosom friends, and there is really nothing left to keep the film going until the end. They are fortunate that the script writers have provided them with a special relationship with a plastic surgeon who knows everything there is to know about restoring corpses.

With the aid of paint and other radical procedures, Ernest keeps them both looking superficially youthful until, through their vanity, they try to force him to drink the potion. He refuses, abandons them, and lives a full and happy life, dying of old age many years later. Madeline and Helen are condemned to immortality but relentless deterioration, illustrating the thesis of the film: Humans should not tamper with Mother Nature.

A film such as *Death Becomes Her* stands or falls on the charisma of its stars. Streep, Hawn, and Willis have accumulated much of what might be called "charismatic capital" and squander it recklessly on this venture. It is questionable whether they could go on repeating such stunts. Streep is the only one who truly benefits from the film, as it shows her as more human, more versatile, and certainly sexier than most people suspected. She received a Golden Globe nomination in the category of best actress in a comedy or musical for her performance. Willis benefits the least or may even be injured by his performance as a henpecked milksop. Goldie Hawn still seems like Goldie Hawn, whatever she does, just as Lucille Ball remained Lucille Ball regardless of the outrageous disguises that she chose to assume.

Death Becomes Her illustrates Hollywood's biggest problem: the dearth of good dramatic stories and the resultant attempt to compensate with guns, explosives, aerial photography, various mechanical contrivances, and nudity. Robert Altman's brilliant film *The Player* (1992; reviewed in this volume) shows the deadly way in which stories are manufactured in Hollywood by committees of hacks and plagiarists. John Huston once said that the three most important ingredients of a good motion picture are story, story, and story. Yet it appears that many Hollywood filmmakers consider the three most important ingredients to be superstars, a heavily budgeted art department, and a creative director as auteur. The auteur in this case is producer-director Robert Zemeckis, who has become the leading exponent of special-effects features with *Who Framed Roger Rabbit* (1988) and the *Back to the Future* trilogy (1985, 1989, 1990), four films that altogether grossed more than a billion dollars in worldwide distribution.

With the ongoing application of computerization to filmmaking, a spinoff of space-age technology, nervous filmgoers should brace themselves for films that are more and more like animated cartoons. Villains who are blown to bits will put themselves back together with the insouciance of Wile E. Coyote of the Road Runner films. Although these gimmicks may appeal to younger mentalities, thoughtful adults may deplore them as another step in the dehumanization of art that characterized the twentieth century.

Bill Delaney

Reviews

Boxoffice. October, 1992, p. R-69.
Chicago Tribune. July 31, 1992, VII, p. 35.
Entertainment Weekly. August 14, 1992, p. 39.
Films in Review. XLIII, September, 1992, p. 339.
The Hollywood Reporter. July 27, 1992, p. 5.
Los Angeles Times. July 31, 1992, p. F1.
The New York Times. July 31, 1992, p. B1.
Newsweek. September 3, 1992, p. 56.
Rolling Stone. August 20, 1992, p. 57.
Variety. July 27, 1992, p. 2.

THE DISTINGUISHED GENTLEMAN

Production: Leonard Goldberg and Michael Peyser for Hollywood Pictures, in association with Touchwood Pacific Partners I; released by Buena Vista
Direction: Jonathan Lynn
Screenplay: Marty Kaplan; based on a story by Kaplan and Jonathan Reynolds
Cinematography: Gabriel Beristain
Editing: Tony Lombardo and Barry B. Leirer
Production design: Leslie Dilley
Art direction: Ed Verreaux
Set decoration: Dorree Cooper
Casting: Mary Goldberg
Sound: Russell Williams II
Costume design: Francine Jamison-Tanchuck
Music: Randy Edelman
MPAA rating: R
Running time: 111 minutes

Principal characters:

Thomas Jefferson Johnson .... Eddie Murphy
Dick Dodge .... Lane Smith
Celia Kirby .... Victoria Rowell
Miss Loretta .... Sheryl Lee Ralph
Olaf Andersen .... Joe Don Baker
Arthur Reinhardt .... Grant Shaud
Terry Corrigan .... Kevin McCarthy
Elijah Hawkins .... Charles S. Dutton
Van Dyke .... Sonny Jim Gaines
Armando .... Victor Rivers

Often when an actor has established and developed a striking screen presence and used it successfully in several films, there is a temptation to continue to refine the basic conception in additional films, as well as a desire to work beyond the confines of the familiar character. In films such as *48 HRS.* (1982), *Trading Places* (1983), and *Beverly Hills Cop* (1984), Eddie Murphy rocketed to stardom with an ingenious portrayal of a hip outsider whose street wit, solid intelligence, and exuberant spirit enabled him to undermine the pretensions of the arrogant, powerful, and ruthless masters of the modern world. Yet in variations of this character in *The Golden Child* (1986) and in *Harlem Nights* (1989), the latter of which he also wrote and directed, Murphy's attempts to extend his range were only partially successful. In an effort to maintain his position in the industry, he reverted to his original role in the sequels *Beverly Hills Cop II* (1987) and *Another 48 HRS.* (1990). In these films, Murphy was a mixture of the character he played in the originals and the one in *Harlem*

Nights, in which he attempted to combine comedy with a kind of insolent macho bravado that depended on profanity, violence, and preening in order to captivate the audience.

In 1992, Murphy made an effort to explore both possibilities, toning down his character in *Boomerang* (reviewed in this volume) and letting its brighter, more energetically dazzling elements have free rein in *The Distinguished Gentleman*. In the final year of his first decade in motion pictures, Murphy solidified a comic persona that recalls the ones fashioned by the great film comedians of the silent era: Buster Keaton's dour, determined, and inquisitive athlete; Harold Lloyd's eager innocent; and Charlie Chaplin's archetypal "little tramp." Murphy's work may not equal theirs, but his creation of a recognizable, singular comic stance reflecting some basic attitudes of American life gives him the opportunity to comment perceptively on his times. Murphy's brilliant wariness, his beguiling charm, and his chameleonic versatility produce an electricity that makes him the audience's natural focus of attention. The filmmakers who created *The Distinguished Gentleman* have built a motion picture around his talents, setting up as targets for satire the smug, self-satisfied, hypocritical insiders who are the natural subjects of Murphy's most scathing disdain.

Making a film about corruption in government in 1992, an election year in which all candidates tried to position themselves as outsiders working for reform and change, is a fairly safe marketing strategy, as well as an invitation to dullness and predictability. In order to overcome the numbing familiarity of stories about Washington, D.C., as a festering magnet for influence peddling, legislative manipulation, and outright thievery, Marty Kaplan's screenplay presents Murphy as Thomas Jefferson Johnson, the leader of a group of genial con artists who wins an election because his name is similar to that of recently deceased incumbent Jefferson Davis Johnson. Congressman Johnson—played by James Garner in a superb cameo that perfectly captures the bogus bonhomie and practiced sincerity of the professional politician—dies while exercising one of the perks of his office: the sexual availability of an attractive legislative assistant. Murphy's Jeff Johnson leaps at the opportunity to move his venue of operations to the biggest con game in the country. The invention and enthusiasm he brings to the "campaign"—forging an alliance with a loveable club of elderly Jewish activists, creating an appropriate voice-image from a sound truck for each ethnic neighborhood of the district, and running the race with his con team from a pay phone—gives the early sequences of the film a zest that is infectious, pulling the audience into the project. Jonathan Lynn's direction is fast-paced and his timing sure here as he uses quick-cutting in the manner of contemporary political advertisements, incorporating sound bites as public statements and ironic private comments on the clichés of received political wisdom. Lynn's *My Cousin Vinny* (1992; reviewed in this volume) demonstrated his competence, but his extensive work in British television (such as the *Yes, Minister* series) gave him the background that he utilizes in making the stunning election result seem plausible.

The film carries the idea of an outsider untainted by political experience arriving in Washington, D.C., with a fresh perspective on government from the more innocent times of Jimmy Stewart's Jefferson Smith of *Mr. Smith Goes to Washington* (1939) in the late 1930's to the less naïve 1990's. Jeff Johnson not only seems bereft of Smith's idealism but also is ready to challenge the criminals of Congress at their own game. Described by Kaplan as a kind of reverse of Voltaire's *Candide* (1759) in which a corrupt young man finds a conscience, the first part of the film gleefully introduces Johnson and his entourage to the enticing splendor of the corridors of power, maintaining the momentum of the campaign in a series of revelations about the operations of government. The idea of a conversion is kept in reserve as Johnson meets and fits in among the power brokers and sleazemongers. His team—with the addition of Arthur Reinhardt (Grant Shaud, in a turn on his role in the television series *Murphy Brown*), a fumbling clerical character who aspires to Machiavellian careerism—is like a shadow culture that parallels the dominant culture of self-advancement. In one of the strongest features of the film, the principal figures of the congressional establishment are played by perfectly cast, experienced professionals. As the smooth lobbyist Terry Corrigan, Kevin McCarthy has the right touch of self-congratulatory complicity; Joe Don Baker exudes confidence and heartiness as Olaf Andersen, the CEO of an electric utility in Johnson's district; and Lane Smith, as Dick Dodge, the chair of the House committee with the greatest opportunities for graft, is uncanny in his resemblance to several political celebrities. Smith portrayed Richard Nixon in the miniseries *The Final Days* and uses some of Nixon's vocal and physical mannerisms to make Dodge a hilarious but sinister caricature. The comic style is very broad and is definitely designed for an audience that is not particularly fond of Nixon, but vocal parodies of Jesse Jackson and even Martin Luther King, Jr. (which Murphy delivers in a phone call) expand the scope of the satire.

To show Johnson outwitting the Capitol criminals might be sufficient for a *Saturday Night Live* sketch, but it is hard to maintain sympathy over the course of two hours for a protagonist who is only out for himself. Johnson's latent decency emerges when he meets public interest lawyer Celia Kirby, played by Victoria Rowell (who has a suggestive resemblance to Anita Hill), and instantly aspires to a romantic relationship. His interest in her convictions is enhanced by Johnson's contacts with her uncle, Elijah Hawkins (Charles S. Dutton, of the television show *ROC*), a congressman and minister who delivers a hilarious sermon using an Internal Revenue Service audit as a metaphor for God's judgment and whose principles are an example of a true representative of the American people. To instigate Johnson's transformation, one of his constituents whose daughter is suffering from cancer demands that he investigate the potential carcinogenic hazards of electrical transmission lines, throwing Johnson into a direct conflict with Olaf Andersen's electric company.

The well-known monuments of the Washington, D.C., landscape tend to serve, as they did for Stewart's Jefferson Smith, as symbolic reminders of the inspiring ideas of the founders of the Republic. The cinematography by Gabriel Beristain presents the city in an exceptionally attractive light, with the glow of late spring and early summer serving as a contrast to the darkness of the machinations inside the buildings. The shots at night, which Beristain managed by the use of huge cranes with powerful xenon lights in order to overcome the prohibition against placing any equipment on the grounds of the Capitol, offer a vista of spectacular possibility.

As a degree of conscience appears beneath the protective veneer of the con man, Johnson tries to balance his acquisitive tactics with a modicum of concern for good government, but an exploration of that type of compromise is beyond the scope of the film. Instead, he discovers that, contrary to the code of his old accomplices, there is no loyalty among political thieves. This is a rather dubious distinction, but it leads to a cabal of corrupters offering him a Faustian bargain to the accompaniment of a thunderstorm. Johnson seems to accept their offer but actually launches a sting operation to expose them all. The arrangement of the plan, its apparent success, its apparent failure in a classic reverse, and then its real success in a double reverse of expectations culminates in the public humiliation of all the criminals, the tendency toward vindictive pleasure characteristic of the edge that gives Murphy's humor its nasty kick. Celia's morality does not seem to have moved Johnson as much as the opportunity to destroy his adversaries, but because the narrative force of the film is based on Johnson's zest for combat with the power structure, the conclusion is quite satisfying. In the film's last scene, Johnson tells Celia that even the presidency is not out of reach, his audacity ratifying a personal triumph rather than any significant advance in governmental procedures. The rapid movement of the camera in the committee room leads to a mood of chaos common to slapstick silent comedy, and its effect is liberating and exhilarating.

Murphy has been most effective in films directed by experienced craftsmen such as John Landis (*Trading Places*) or Walter Hill (*48 HRS*). *The Distinguished Gentleman* continues Murphy's engaging work in this format, but like those films, it does not leave much of an impression beyond Murphy's comic style. The film consists of skillfully mounted comic sequences that fail to coalesce into a form larger than the separate sections. The comments that the script makes about governmental power and corruption are timely but not revelatory. The film is unlikely to please anyone not previously disposed to Murphy's abilities or to the film's political perspective.

Even though the People's Choice Awards conducted by the Gallup Organization placed Murphy with Steve Martin and Robin Williams as one of the top three actors in Comedy Motion Picture and ranked *The Distinguished Gentleman* third in the same category, the film's receipts were disappointing, particularly in comparison with some of Murphy's more successful vehicles. For Murphy to develop his comic vision, something more ambitious is required. Otherwise, even the superb production values and technical mastery this film offers—including the use of public buildings in Pennsylvania and Maryland to stand in for Congress and meticulously detailed interiors that provide a compelling sense of authenticity—will remain part of a surface that essentially covers a void.

Leon Lewis

Reviews

Chicago Tribune. December 4, 1992, VII, p. 47.
The Christian Science Monitor. December 24, 1992, p. 12.
Entertainment Weekly. December 11, 1992, p. 45.
The Hollywood Reporter. December 4, 1992, p. 6.
Los Angeles Times. December 4, 1992, p. F1.
The New York Times. December 4, 1992, p. B1.
Newsweek. CXX, December 14, 1992, p. 78.
People Weekly. December 14, 1992, p. 17.
Variety. December 4, 1992, p. 2.
The Washington Post. December 4, 1992, p. D1.

ENCHANTED APRIL

Origin: Great Britain
Released: 1992
Released in U.S.: 1992
Production: Ann Scott for BBC Films, in association with Miramax Films and Greenpoint Films; released by Miramax
Direction: Mike Newell
Screenplay: Peter Barnes; based on the novel by Elizabeth von Arnim
Cinematography: Rex Maidment
Editing: Dick Allen
Production design: Malcolm Thorton
Casting: Susie Figgis
Sound: John Pritchard
Costume design: Sheena Napier
Music: Richard Rodney Bennett
MPAA rating: PG
Running time: 101 minutes

Principal characters:

Rose Arbuthnot	Miranda Richardson
Mrs. Fisher	Joan Plowright
Lottie Wilkins	Josie Lawrence
Lady Caroline Dester	Polly Walker
Mellersh Wilkins	Alfred Molina
Frederick Arbuthnot	Jim Broadbent
George Briggs	Michael Kitchen

As Lottie Wilkins (Josie Lawrence) rides the cramped and steamy train, being jostled by rude travelers and feeling damp from London's incessant spring rain, she spies an advertisement on the back of the newspaper being read by the passenger opposite her. It offers: "To those who appreciate wisteria and sunshine. Small medieval Italian castle on the shores of the Mediterranean to be let furnished for the month of April. Servants remain." Suddenly presented with an escape from her achingly dreary life, Lottie rushes from the train station to the women's club and throws herself at the feet of her shocked and embarrassed neighbor, Rose Arbuthnot (Miranda Richardson).

Rose and Lottie do not really know each other; they merely recall having nodded to each other at church. Nevertheless, Lottie sees a kindred spirit in Rose, calling her beautiful and sad. She proposes that they rent the castle together. Rose, quite reasonably thinking Lottie a madwoman, extricates herself from Lottie's grasp and flees. Lottie follows her, not knowing why she is confessing her unhappiness with her husband and her life to this virtual stranger. At the mention of husbands, Rose begins to consider Lottie's suggestion.

Rose's husband, Frederick (Jim Broadbent), is a loving man who misses the affection of his wife. Rose does not know whether it is Frederick or love itself that she can no longer bear, and she turns her energies instead to religious works. Struck by her combination of pale beauty and coldness, Frederick compares his wife to a "disappointed Madonna." He works off his frustrations by publishing novels that Rose finds scandalous, further distancing them. The marketing of these books brings him into contact with such exciting society ladies as Lady Caroline Dester (Polly Walker), whom he does not know his wife will soon meet.

Lottie's husband, Mellersh Wilkins (Alfred Molina), is a stereotypical solicitor, concerned with money above all else. To Mellersh, Lottie is merely a cook, housekeeper, and a proper companion to show off at business parties. Lottie's spirit and love of beauty are stifled by this man who considers flowers "an extravagance of the most blatant kind" and forces her to report every penny that she gives to wounded soldiers in the street. Whereas Frederick kindly agrees to Rose's spending April in Italy, it is Mellersh's forbidding Lottie to go on the basis of cost that moves her to defy him for the first time in her life.

Rose and Lottie visit George Briggs (Michael Kitchen), who placed the advertisement in *The Times*, and put a cash deposit on the castle, called San Salvatore. George assumes that, because the ladies are going alone, that they are war widows. He tells Rose that she will be very comfortable at the castle because there are several portraits of her on the walls. By this he means the Madonnas; Rose asks if they are disappointed.

The money for the deposit being all they had, Rose and Lottie place an advertisement of their own for two women to come along and share expenses. In response, they interview two very different and difficult women. The first is Lady Caroline Dester, a beautiful, young, spoiled socialite who is suffering from an overabundance of boredom, privilege, and men. The second is Mrs. Fisher (Joan Plowright), a grand dame who is not as elderly as she pretends to be, although most of her friends and family are deceased and she has become isolated and lonely. Her initial meeting with Rose and Lottie is a comic one: She drops names of famous artists and writers with whom she has been associated, behaves as if she is interviewing them and not the other way around, and swings her cane lethally around the room with every gesture, causing her dignified guests to duck for their lives.

The journey to San Salvatore is harrowing for Rose and Lottie. At sea they are seasick, there is no one to meet them at the train station, Lottie must use her umbrella to beat off a man who would steal their luggage, and, adding insult to injury, it is raining. They finally arrive at the castle in the pitch blackness of night and are let in by men who they fear might as well be murderers as the household staff. When they awake in the morning, however, it is all brilliant sunlight, shining sea, singing birds, and countless flowers whose colors and scents defy description. Lottie and Rose hold hands as they explore the grounds, wondering aloud if it is all real and if they have ever been so happy.

They get down to the business of running a household, divvying up the rooms and instructing the staff, only to find that Mrs. Fisher and Lady Caroline have already arrived and beaten them to it. The best rooms have been claimed, the staff is hopping, and the hostesses are left to their own devices, if a little confused.

Lottie is the first to succumb to the castle's magic, and she soon invites Mellersh despite the fact that getting away from him was the whole purpose of this adventure. Lady Caroline wants nothing to do with men; the one man she loved was killed in the war, and she perceives the rest of them as "grabbers." Rose tearfully fears that Frederick would not come if invited. Mrs. Fisher, tragically, has few friends left to invite.

Though the women argue, Lottie remains resolute and Mellersh does come. His purpose at first is to meet Mrs. Fisher and Lady Caroline and to establish them as business contacts (an ambition that seems vulgar within the context of San Salvatore's hypnotic gardens), but even Mellersh is transformed by the place and is soon swimming with Lottie, combing her hair, and marveling that he did not realize long ago how attractive his wife is.

When the agonized Rose finally sends for Frederick, he arrives in less time than it should take the letter to have made it to England. In fact, Frederick had ferreted out the whereabouts of Lady Caroline and, despite her complete lack of interest in him, come all this way to see her. Rose, having allowed the indescribably lovely surroundings to strip her of her fears and inhibitions, greets Frederick with a passion that neither of them have known since the earliest days of their marriage. Never having fallen out of love with his wife, only grieving that the sensual part of her had seemed to vanish, Frederick responds fully and joyfully. The discreet Lady Caroline gladly keeps Frederick's secret.

A surprise visit is made by George Briggs, who had hoped to woo Rose and who is greatly saddened to find that she is not a war widow. Lady Caroline sighs at the arrival of yet another male, judging this one to be a "grabber" for sure. It is she who is surprised to find that George's nearsightedness makes him immune to her beauty—and thus a challenge to her. When George almost topples over a cliff, Lady Caroline grabs him and hangs on.

Though Mrs. Fisher laments that all the others have paired off, she is determined not only to remember departed friends but also to make new ones. Lottie, the self-appointed leader of this Italian Enlightenment, and her much-softened Mellersh take Mrs. Fisher under their wings, and she is not alone.

Even the most enchanted April must end, and soon the group returns to England. As they leave, there is some concern that the feelings that flourished in San Salvatore may not survive in London, but there is little doubt that they will return to replenish the supply as often as necessary.

Though a small film by Hollywood standards, *Enchanted April* received the highest American accolades. Miranda Richardson was honored by the New York Film Critics Circle and the Golden Globe Awards. Joan Plowright was also nominated for a Golden Globe as well as for an Oscar for her supporting role. Additional

Academy Award nominations went to Peter Barnes for best screenplay based on previously published material and to Sheena Napier for achievement in costume design.

Joan Plowright, who had long wanted to adapt this novel to film (she and Maggie Smith had once hoped to play Lottie and Rose), is a revered actress of stage, screen, and television. Her more recent film performances known in the United States include *Drowning by Numbers* (1988), *Avalon* (1990), and *I Love You to Death* (1990). Acclaimed British actress Miranda Richardson is best known to Americans for her performances in *Dance with a Stranger* (1984), which was also directed by Mike Newell, and *Empire of the Sun* (1987). Josie Lawrence and Polly Walker are both relatively new to the screen, with Lawrence having a history as a nightclub singer and successful television comedienne and Walker having studied ballet and theater arts.

Enchanted April was filmed in the very villa in which the 1922 novel, by Elizabeth von Arnim, was written. Although the setting is authentically Italian, the story, with its amusing and liberated characters, is decidedly British and in the tradition of E. M. Forster's novels *A Room with a View* (1908) and *Howards End* (1910), which were adapted into films in 1986 and 1992, respectively. (*Howards End* is reviewed in this volume.) This is no coincidence, as the author and Forster were acquainted when he tutored her son and four daughters.

After writing the macabre but cathartic *Vera*, about her disastrous marriage to Francis, the second Earl Russell (brother of Bertrand Russell), celebrated novelist Elizabeth von Arnim was determined to write a "happy book." To this end, she rented the sunny, flower-filled castle in Portofino, Italy, allowed herself to be transformed by its romance and charm, and then imagined four wildly disparate characters thrown into the same circumstance. The result was the comic and sweetly hopeful novel *The Enchanted April*. In 1935, RKO produced a version of the story; the film failed miserably. Fortunately, this 1992 adaptation is, as its title promises, enchanting.

Eleah Horwitz

Reviews

Boxoffice. October, 1992, p. R-76.
Chicago Tribune. August 7, 1992, VII, p. 36.
The Christian Science Monitor. July 31, 1992, p. 12.
Entertainment Weekly. August 21, 1992, p. 40.
The Hollywood Reporter. January 10, 1992, p. 9.
Los Angeles Times. July 31, 1992, p. F8.
The New York Times. July 31, 1992, p. B5.
Newsweek. CXX, August 17, 1992, p. 56.
Rolling Stone. August 20, 1992, p. 60.
Variety. November 8, 1991, p. 2.

ENCINO MAN

Production: George Zaloom for Touchwood Pacific Partners I and Hollywood Pictures; released by Buena Vista
Direction: Les Mayfield
Screenplay: Shawn Schepps; based on a story by George Zaloom and Schepps *Cinematography:* Robert Brinkmann
Editing: Eric Sears
Production design: James Allen
Set decoration: Cheryal Kearney
Makeup: Gandhi Bob Arrollo
Costume design: Marie France
Choreography: Peggy Holmes
Music: J. Peter Robinson
MPAA rating: PG
Running time: 89 minutes

Principal characters:

Dave Morgan	Sean Astin
Link (Linkovitch Chomofsky)	Brendan Fraser
Stoney Brown	Pauly Shore
Robyn Sweeney	Megan Ward
Ella	Robin Tunney
Matt	Michael DeLuise
Phil	Patrick Van Horn
Will	Dalton James
Mrs. Morgan	Mariette Hartley
Mr. Morgan	Richard Masur

In *Encino Man*, best friends Dave Morgan (Sean Astin) and Stoney Brown (Pauly Shore) are at the end of their senior year in high school. Dave wants nothing more than to be cool, but the duo is referred to as the Dork Squad by those whom they wish to join. To help their cause, Dave is hand-digging a pool in his backyard; he hopes to have the ultimate post-prom pool party, which will guarantee his popularity.

When an earthquake dislodges a chunk of ice in Dave's excavation, the boys discover a caveman (Brendan Fraser) embedded in it. Their new plan is to become famous for their archaeological discovery. To their surprise, however, when the ice melts, their ice man is alive. Still with dreams of popularity, they clean him up, tame him down, and name him Link, as in "missing link." Improbably explained away as an exchange student from Estonia, Link quickly becomes the most popular male at Encino High School.

While the most interesting part of the film's plot revolves around teaching Link "stuff" such as basic communication and survival in a convenience store, there is also a weak subplot involving Dave's infatuation with popular Robyn Sweeney (Megan Ward), the steady girlfriend of the class bully, Matt (Michael DeLuise). Matt is the real Neanderthal in the plot, and he spends most of his time making Dave's life miserable. By the time Robyn realizes how primitive Matt's behavior is and dumps him, it is not Dave her interest turns toward but Link. This drives a wedge between the two, but obviously, in this kind of formula film, Robyn will eventually end up with Dave, Link and Dave will remain friends, and Matt will receive his just desserts.

While the film's "be yourself" theme is a tried and true one for younger audiences, it seems hollow within this setting, in which popularity is gained amid a sea of suburban conformity. A larger problem for the film is the pairing of Shore and Astin. Astin, who did a superb job in *Memphis Belle* (1990), is boyishly normal here, and his friendship with the bizarre Shore character strains credulity. While the filmmakers were obviously trying to capitalize on the success of such teen film duos as Bill and Ted (1989's *Bill and Ted's Excellent Adventure* and 1991's *Bill and Ted's Bogus Journey*) and Wayne and Garth (1992's *Wayne's World*; reviewed in this volume), Stoney and Dave are simply too opposite to mesh.

While MTV personality Shore might provide the film with a built-in audience, a little of him goes a long way. His speech is often indecipherable, and his laid-back attempts at lovableness are cloying at best. His success on the MTV program "Totally Pauly" made him so well known that he signed a three-picture deal with Hollywood Pictures.

Since the Astin character is so normal, it falls to relative newcomer Fraser as Link to give the film what energy and watchability it does have. Playing the Cro-Magnon as an unselfconscious, mischievous innocent, Fraser's humor (while not often rising above that involving food) is highly physical and imitative.

Although the film does have problems, it did manage to become a box-office success story earning $40 million as of December 31, 1992. Some of this success may be attributable to Pauly Shore's popularity on MTV, some to the obvious audience appetite for comic teenage duos as was seen in the "Bill and Ted" and "Wayne and Garth" epics, but it is more likely that it was because of the spirited and entertaining antics provided by Brendan Fraser's Link, which were wisely highlighted in the film's promotions. A fish out of water like Link proved to be a real attraction for the targeted audience in their teens and twenties.

The basic story of *Encino Man*, however, is weak, and certainly does not bear much scrutiny. While a viewer might, for entertainment's sake, suspend disbelief that someone could be frozen in ice and thawed out alive (that idea made 1984's *Iceman* fascinating), such fanciful events are compounded again and again so as to stretch believability. Who would dig their own swimming pool, for example? (Admittedly, the production notes for the film indicate that producer George Zaloom, who also conceived the story idea, actually did try to do this.) As if this were the type of film that needed it, Zaloom maintained that he attempted to research the film to make it historically correct. When he discovered that underground glaciers never advanced as far south as Encino, however, Zaloom was reported to have said, "Go ahead and fudge a little."

Actually, producer/story source Zaloom and director Les Mayfield do have a distinguished career, but not in feature filmmaking. *Encino Man* is their banal debut in that area. They are primarily known for their promotional documentaries based on the making of films, such as *Empire of the Sun* (1987) and *Who Framed Roger Rabbit?* (1988), and television anniversary specials, such as those for *The Honeymooners* and *The Bob Newhart Show*. Their greatest success was with the powerful documentary *Hearts of Darkness: A Filmmaker's Apocalypse* (1992), about Francis Ford Coppola and the making of *Apocalypse Now* in 1979.

There is no power in *Encino Man*, however; in fact, there are no surprises, no originality, no creativity, and worst of all, few laughs. It insultingly paints teenagers as making prom kings out of nonverbal cavemen and reconfirms typical racial stereotypes, such as Asian computer nerds and macho Hispanics. It is a low-budget film (shot in thirty-three days with a budget of $7 million), a no-brainer genre formula.

Beverley Bare Buehrer

Reviews

Boxoffice. July, 1992, p. R-55.
Entertainment Weekly. May 29, 1992, p. 48.
The Hollywood Reporter. May 22, 1992, p. 5.
Los Angeles Times. May 22, 1992, p. F12.
The New York Times. May 22, 1992, p. B3.
People Weekly. June 1, 1992, p. 17.
Rolling Stone. June 25, 1992, p. 48.
Time. CXXXIX, June 8, 1992, p. 95.
Variety. May 22, 1992, p. 2.
The Washington Post. May 22, 1992, p. D7.

FAR AND AWAY

Production: Brian Grazer and Ron Howard for Imagine Films Entertainment; released by Universal Studios
Direction: Ron Howard
Screenplay: Bob Dolman; based on a story by Dolman and Ron Howard
Cinematography: Mikael Salomon
Editing: Michael Hill and Daniel Hanley
Production design: Allan Cameron and Jack T. Collis
Art direction: Jack Senter
Set design: Joseph Hubbard and Robert M. Beall
Set decoration: Richard Goddard
Casting: Karen Rea, Ros Hubbard, and John Hubbard
Sound: Ivan Sharrock
Costume design: Joanna Johnston
Music: John Williams
MPAA rating: PG-13
Running time: 140 minutes

Principal characters:

Joseph Donelly	Tom Cruise
Shannon Christie	Nicole Kidman
Stephen Chase	Thomas Gibson
Christie	Robert Prosky
Nora Christie	Barbara Babcock
Danty Duff	Cyril Cusack
Molly Kay	Eileen Pollock
Kelly	Colm Meaney
Dermody	Douglas Gillison
Grace	Michelle Johnson
Bourke	Wayne Grace
Joe	Niall Toibin
McGuire	Barry McGovern
Gordon	Gary Lee Davis
Paddy	Jared Harris

In western Ireland of 1892, where *Far and Away* begins, the dying father of Joseph Donelly (Tom Cruise) leaves him with this advice: "Without land, a man is nothing. Land is a man's very own soul." As a tenant farmer under the tyrannical rule of their landlord's overseer, Stephen Chase (Thomas Gibson), Joseph plans on heeding his father's advice, but not before exacting revenge on their landlord, Christie (Robert Prosky). At the landlord's estate, however, while hiding in the stable, Joseph is stabbed in the thigh with a pitchfork wielded by the landlord's beautiful and spirited daughter, Shannon (Nicole Kidman). (She is not a typically prim Victorian daughter; she rides horses at an unladylike gallop and plays jazzy tunes on the piano.) Undaunted, Joseph tries to carry out his mission. Unfortunately, he is victimized by his own exploding shotgun, and the bewildered Christies take the unconscious Joseph into their home. While convalescing under their roof, he is challenged to a duel by the arrogant overseer, who will surely defeat the twice-wounded Joseph.

Shannon, however, has a plan. With Joseph as her protector and servant, she will pay their passage to the United States, where they will trade her set of silver spoons for a chance to participate in the Oklahoma land rush and the hundred acres of free land promised to those who can stake a claim. At first, Joseph refuses to run away with her, but while dueling with Chase on a very foggy morning, practicality overcomes his honor, and he escapes with Shannon at the last minute.

In Boston, however, things do not go smoothly. The spoons are stolen, and the two are forced by circumstances to pose as brother and sister and share a room above a brothel. They take jobs in a chicken-processing plant, but Joseph quickly trades his position in the sweatshop for the more lucrative winnings he earns as a bare-knuckles boxer—a pastime he learned at the hands of his feisty brothers and which he takes up now to subdue his sexual frustration at living so close to the seemingly unobtainable Shannon.

Their dreams of moving on to Oklahoma are derailed first by Joseph's success, then by his running afoul of ward boss Kelly (Colm Meaney). When the Christies and the arrogant Chase, who plans to marry Shannon, come to Boston looking for her, Shannon and Joseph are penniless and living on the streets. While finding a moment's respite from Boston's biting winter, the two share a small meal in a house where no one is home. When the owner returns, Shannon is wounded by gunfire; Joseph is forced to take her to her parents. Believing he has nothing to offer her and that she is better off with them, Joseph runs away. The two will not be apart for long, however, for they will meet again—in Oklahoma.

If there is one word to describe *Far and Away*, it is old-fashioned. The predictable characters are from the 1930's (any film starring Errol Flynn or Tyrone Power), the familiar plot is from the 1940's and 1950's (it is particularly reminiscent of *The Quiet Man* of 1952), while the cinematography is straight out of the epics of the 1960's and 1970's. That last comparison is especially appropriate, because *Far and Away* is the first film since *Ryan's Daughter* (1970) and *TRON* (1982) to be shot on 65 millimeter stock and shown in 70 millimeter (the other 5 millimeters are for the soundtrack). While the older, similarly named Super Panavision provided a wider image, this Panavision Super 70 is in the normal aspect ratio. As a result, seeing the film in one of the theaters equipped to show it in this format provides viewers with brilliant and crisp images which are truly the highlights of the film.

Far and Away is a handsomely mounted film, and its lavish $70 million budget is easily apparent on the screen. The gorgeous blues and greens of western Ireland, the grittiness of old Boston (actually filmed in Dublin's historic Temple Bar district), and the wide-open blue and gold of Oklahoma (actually Montana) are breathtaking to see. Yet they are not quite enough to overcome the clichéd dialogue and contrived plot in which nearly every obstacle imaginable is put in the path of the two potential lovers—who the audience knows will get together by the final reel, despite an attempt by Howard to throw viewers off with a penultimate red-herring ending.

Cruise and Kidman do an admirable job with their characters and accents, and there is no doubt that their on-screen chemistry reflects that of their off-screen marriage. Kidman, who made an impressive appearance in 1989's *Dead Calm*, is very much the headstrong rebel, the liberated woman seeking her own life; Cruise is all boyish hero, cocky and competent by turns. The film is also populated by a delightful collection of secondary characters, from Eileen Pollock as coquettish Molly Kay to Cyril Cusack's leprechaun-like Danty Duff.

Unfortunately, *Far and Away* is also old-fashioned in that it relies heavily on what Hollywood has always presented as stereotypical Irish behavior. Within minutes of the film's start, there is fighting and drinking, which occur again and again throughout the film. One can only wonder why an Irish antidefamation league does not protest this persistent negative image. Another reliance on tried-and-true film formulas is the use of the obvious class conflict between rich and poor as a plot device to keep the lovers apart. Nothing is ever made, however, of the more interesting (and potentially more explosive) problem that Shannon is an English-ancestored Protestant, while Joseph is undoubtedly a Catholic. Surely this would be a more insurmountable obstacle than class and wealth differences, even in the late nineteenth century.

While this type of film must have its lovers united, it also calls for the defeat of the villain. While Chase is indeed beaten in the end, one wishes that the Christies, who cheat during the land rush, would also get their comeuppance. Even though the film has tried to make Christie a likable character, it is dramatically unsatisfying to have the Christies so unfairly win their prized piece of land in the end.

These shortcomings aside, however, it is obvious that for Howard, this film was a labor of love. The film was a long time in coming, having its beginnings when he first saw Ireland as a boy. Howard, screenwriter Bob Dolman, and producer Brian Grazer worked on *Far and Away* for eight years, with inspiration coming from Howard's own immigrant past and the fact that three of his great-grandparents took part in the 1893 Cherokee Strip Land Race in Oklahoma.

The result of their efforts is not a typical film of the 1990's. It takes its time in telling the story and provides little in the way of dramatic urgency. Yet, for audiences tired of high-tech action pictures and of a sometimes overwhelming emphasis on profanity and violence in films, *Far and Away* is vintage family filmmaking made luminous in 70 millimeter.

Beverley Bare Buehrer

Reviews

Boxoffice. July, 1992, p. R-56.
Chicago Tribune. June 5, 1992, VII, p. 44.
The Christian Science Monitor. May 29, 1992, p. 12.
Entertainment Weekly. May 22, 1992, p. 51.
The Hollywood Reporter. May 11, 1992, p. 9.
Los Angeles Times. May 22, 1992, p. F1.
The New York Times. May 22, 1992, p. B3.
The New Yorker. May 25, 1992, p. 75.
Time. CXXXIX, May 25, 1992, p. 67.
Variety. CCCXLVII, May 11, 1992.

A FEW GOOD MEN

Production: David Brown, Rob Reiner, and Andrew Scheinman for Castle Rock Entertainment; released by Columbia Pictures
Direction: Rob Reiner
Screenplay: Aaron Sorkin; based on his play
Cinematography: Robert Richardson
Editing: Robert Leighton
Production design: J. Michael Riva
Art direction: David Frederick Klassen
Set decoration: Michael Taylor
Casting: Jane Jenkins and Janet Hirshenson
Sound: Bob Eber
Costume design: Gloria Gresham
Music: Marc Shaiman
MPAA rating: R
Running time: 138 minutes

Principal characters:

Lieutenant (jg) Daniel Kaffee . . . . Tom Cruise
Colonel Nathan R. Jessep . . . . Jack Nicholson
Lieutenant Commander JoAnne Galloway . Demi Moore
Captain Jack Ross . . . . Kevin Bacon
Lieutenant Jonathan Kendrick . . . . Kiefer Sutherland
Lieutenant Sam Weinberg . . . . Kevin Pollak
Private Louden Downey . . . . James Marshall
Lieutenant Colonel Matthew Markinson . . . . . J. T. Walsh
Lance Corporal Harold Dawson . . . . . Wolfgang Bodison

Prior to *A Few Good Men*, Rob Reiner had only directed hit films, such as *Stand by Me* (1986), *The Princess Bride* (1987), *When Harry Met Sally* (1989), and *Misery* (1990). With $16 million in its opening weekend (and $64.2 million by year's end), *A Few Good Men* continued this streak. Crafted in the image of such military courtroom greats as *The Caine Mutiny* (1954) and studded with stars such as Jack Nicholson and Tom Cruise, *A Few Good Men* made the transition from stage to screen ably.

The premise of the film is that Lieutenant (jg) Kaffee (Cruise) is assigned to represent two young marines, Private Louden Downey (James Marshall) and Lance Corporal Harold W. Dawson (Wolfgang Bodison), charged with the murder of a fellow soldier. In what looks to be an old-style hazing incident, termed a "code red," a marine private dies when a rag is stuffed into his throat, prior to his mouth being taped. A slick young Harvard graduate and softball enthusiast, Kaffee has earned for himself a reputation for negotiation and settlement. When the film begins, however, he has yet to have seen the inside of a courtroom. Teamed with ace investigator Lieutenant Commander JoAnne Galloway (Demi Moore) and litigator Lieutenant Sam Weinberg (Kevin Pollak), Kaffee must choose between the quick fix that the military desires and the truth. Also, he is the son of a famous attorney whose reputation haunts Kaffee throughout the course of the film.

A Few Good Men is a film of words and performances, not action. The ample dialogue is drawn by Aaron Sorkin from his hit Broadway play of the same name that opened in November, 1989, ran for 449 performances, and became Broadway's longest-running drama. Before the play even made it to Broadway, the film rights were bought by David Brown, the producer of *The Sting* (1973), *Jaws* (1975), *The Verdict* (1982), and *Driving Miss Daisy* (1989). Subsequently, Brown made a deal with Castle Rock Entertainment, and once Reiner saw the play, he was on board for the film.

Working almost daily with Reiner for more than five months of script conferences, Sorkin reconsidered much of the motivation of his characters and much of the staging of the story. For example, the relationship between Kaffee and his father was only hinted at in the stage play, while it becomes a prime motivation for Kaffee in the film. Also, in the play, Kaffee goes into court with much more of a smoking gun, while in the film he is, in the words of director Reiner, "in there flying by the seat of his pants, using all of his intelligence to take on this big case, not sure whether or not he would win." Much of the press surrounding the film has detailed these script conferences, not only to showcase Reiner's fabled push for perfection and bearlike personality but also to show the attention given to each word, each speech—from the large, showstopping, Queeg-like speeches of Colonel Nathan R. Jessep (Jack Nicholson) to the venomous invectives of the minor characters, such as the denouncement of the dead marine by Lieutenant Jonathan Kendrick (Kiefer Sutherland): "He had no code, and God was watching." Sorkin was reported to be so pleased with the resulting screenplay that he subsequently revised his play to bring it in line with the film.

Performances are the other component of this courtroom drama, and while the three main stars (Nicholson, Cruise, and Moore) received much attention for their strong representations, perhaps the real power of the film comes from the supporting roles. For example, the character of Captain Jack Ross (Kevin Bacon) combines the right amount of officiousness and casual camaraderie to make it clear that, while officially the government has no comment, off the record it has everything to lose with this case. While Bacon has comparatively little screen time, his performance is believable and solid. Also exceptional are Kevin Pollak's Weinberg, a thoughtful, ethical, no-flash attorney, and the menacing Kiefer Sutherland as a fundamentalist junior officer. As for the young marines who stand accused of the murder, their precision (such as their posture and demeanor) and their dedication to honor (as they understand the concept) provide strong support for the idea that what is on trial is the system as much as the act of murder itself. Behind the credit sequence performs a precision drill team, symbolizing the uniformity and teamwork that makes the military work. It is a fitting beginning and perhaps the clearest example of foreshadowing in the film. Once the background is set by strong support performances, the audience is ready to believe the powerhouse work of the stars.

Much of what the stars produce is quite fine. Perhaps the most noteworthy performance comes from Nicholson, who captures some of the same maniacal belief in precision, and in the system, that made Humphrey Bogart's Captain Queeg so memorable in *The Caine Mutiny*. Nicholson has three major scenes as Jessep, and while he is poisonous in each, he is able to vary that venom from sarcasm to full-bore anger. When the investigative team first encounters Jessep, he is obsequious, congratulating Kaffee on his good fortune in having such a fine father. Soon, however, the team sees a very different side of Jessep. After an outdoor lunch, as Kaffee and Galloway use different methods of questioning him, Jessep's response simmers through several emotions, ending finally in a vituperative explosion. The final courtroom sequence also provides an arena for the subtleties that Nicholson brings to Jessep.

Tom Cruise plays a variation of a role that he has played before—the slick young man who takes nothing seriously until he has no choice. Maverick Mitchell in *Top Gun* (1986), Charlie Babbitt in *Rain Man* (1988), Brian Flanagan in *Cocktail* (1988), Cole Trickle in *Days of Thunder* (1990), and Joseph Donelly in *Far and Away* (1992; reviewed in this volume) all belong to this category. Yet it is a role he succeeds in bringing to life. Kaffee is uncommitted; he slides by with his charm. Early in the film, the audience sees Kaffee on a baseball diamond settling a court case and hitting fly balls at the same time. Neither action breaks—or even slows—his stride, his affable good sportsmanship. Life and its challenges have always come easily to him. The trial of these two marines becomes a challenge for Kaffee, not only an intellectual challenge but also a challenge to how he lives his life. The case forces him to choose between the status quo and a rough road that may carry him away from everything that he has known. While Cruise breaks little new ground for himself here, he is smooth, winning, and believable.

Demi Moore's JoAnne Galloway may be one of the most wasted performances in the film. In repeated interviews, Moore discussed how she tried to bring some humanity to a role written as controlling and precision-driven. Whatever humanity she has tried to bring is largely lost, however, and the humanity that she does show earns for her rebukes from those around her. When the viewer first encounters Galloway, she is practicing asking to represent the two young marines. The audience sees her turned down and learns that her supervisors believe she is overly concerned with detail. When she tries to investigate what she thinks is a key point with Jessep, he attacks her personally and appears clearly the more powerful person. In court, she speaks only in error, and in one truly amazing scene, she asks Kaffee for a date, during which she reveals all of her personal fears. The character of JoAnne Galloway has a hard time in this film, perhaps because she bounces only between the extremes of professional control and self-doubt, or perhaps because she is trying to communicate in a world in which people adhere to their own codes or to those of the system. Either way, she is all alone. Although several Hollywood actresses were considered for the part—including Julie Warner, Penelope Ann Miller, Elizabeth Perkins, Nancy Travis, Linda Hamilton, Helen Hunt, and Michelle Pfeiffer—Reiner was quoted as saying that he chose Demi Moore for her "directness, a don't-even-flirt-with-me attitude." Said Reiner, "JoAnne is everything that Kaffee isn't. She's got the passion and is the force that really drives him."

Much effort was expended to make such a dialogue-driven film visually interesting. For example, each of the four walls of the courtroom is significantly different, so that each provides a very different backdrop to the characters. The plan was to avoid having a rotating series of speakers in front of the same brown wall. Also, although the military courtrooms explored by the production personnel were more like administrative offices, the design personnel fudged this reality and delivered a lavishly traditional court. According to production designer J. Michael Riva, "We suggested an old courtroom from a grander time in which the military in this country was born. We created an environment in which there was a time and a place for time-honored tradition. We found a building in Washington which dated back to 1915 that suggested a palatial size inside. The courtroom itself is very detailed with wooden panels, columns, French doors and ornate-paintings."

In working to unify the film, Riva also incorporated the color of brass into many of the locations, particularly Kaffee's apartment and Jessep's office. For Cuba, the key tones were hot yellow, while military settings in Washington were almost monochromatic. Blue accents were used to distinguish the navy (Kaffee) from the marines (Jessep).

The shots of the naval base at Guantánamo Bay, Cuba, were actually shot in Southern California. For example, the fenceline site that plays a key role in the film is actually two miles of chain link and barb wire constructed at the Crystal Cove State Park near Laguna. Portions of the film were shot at Fort McArthur and Point Mugu Naval Air Station, and hundreds of marines were used as extras.

Since its release, *A Few Good Men* has been a contender in a variety of award arenas. The film received five Golden Globe nominations, including one for best dramatic motion picture: The other Golden Globe nominations were Tom Cruise for actor in a drama; Jack Nicholson for supporting actor; Rob Reiner for director; and Aaron Sorkin for the screenplay. While nominated for four Academy Awards, *A Few Good Men* was passed over on Oscar night. Rob Reiner was nominated for the Director's Guild of America's DGA 1992 Outstanding Director award, although that award was eventually given to Clint Eastwood for his film *Unforgiven* (1992; reviewed in this volume).

Additional recognition of the film came from the National Board of Review (NBR), which awarded its D. W. Griffith Award to Jack Nicholson for best supporting actor for his portrayal of Jessep. NBR ranked the film fourth for the year, and while Tom Cruise was nominated for best actor kudos, that award went to Jack Lemmon for his role in *Glengarry Glen Ross* (1992; reviewed in this volume). In the People's Choice Awards, the film and its performers received six mentions within the top three favorites as judged by a Gallup poll of five thousand people nationwide. *A Few Good Men* also received recognition for its editing, when Robert Leighton was nominated for the American Cinema Editors' ACE Eddie award.

In many ways, *A Few Good Men* is one of the large productions that make Hollywood the phenomenon that it is. There are few surprises; in fact, the ending may seem too pat to some viewers. Yet, without question, the film is entertaining and engaging to watch for the precision of the storytelling, the filmmaking, and the performances.

Roberta F. Green

Reviews

Boxoffice. December, 1992, p. R-86.
Chicago Tribune. December 11, 1992, VII, p. 33.
The Christian Science Monitor. December 11, 1992, p. 13.
Entertainment Weekly. December 18, 1992, p. 40.
The Hollywood Reporter. November 13, 1992, p. 6.
Los Angeles Times. December 11, 1992, p. F1.
The New York Times. December 11, 1992, p. B1.
Time. CXL, December 14, 1992, p. 70.
Variety. November 13, 1992, p. 2.
The Washington Post. December 11, 1992, p. B1.

FINAL ANALYSIS

Production: Charles Roven, Paul Junger Witt, and Tony Thomas, in association with Roven-Cavallo Entertainment; released by Warner Bros.
Direction: Phil Joanou
Screenplay: Wesley Strick; based on a story by Robert Berger and Strick
Cinematography: Jordan Cronenweth
Editing: Thom Noble
Production design: Dean Tavoularis
Art direction: Angelo Graham
Set decoration: Bob Nelson
Casting: David Rubin
Special visual effects: Dream Quest Images
Visual effects supervision: Hoyt Yeatman
Sound: Lee Orloff
Costume design: Aude Bronson-Howard
Music: George Fenton
MPAA rating: R
Running time: 124 minutes

Principal characters:

Isaac Barr	Richard Gere
Heather Evans	Kim Basinger
Diana Baylor	Uma Thurman
Jimmy Evans	Eric Roberts
Mike O'Brien	Paul Guilfoyle
Detective Huggins	Keith David
Alan Lowenthal	Robert Harper
Pepe Carrero	Agustin Rodriguez
District Attorney Brakhage	Harris Yulin

Films clearly imitative of the psychological thrillers of Alfred Hitchcock became plentiful even before the director's death in 1980. These homages have ranged from crude melodramas, as with Brian DePalma's *Dressed to Kill* (1980), to unamusing spoofs, as with Mel Brooks's *High Anxiety* (1977). Phil Joanou's *Final Analysis* is one of the few effective and entertaining Hitchcock pastiches. Borrowing heavily from *Vertigo* (1958), the master's greatest film, *Final Analysis* is playful with its Hitchcockian elements without insulting its source of inspiration.

Isaac Barr (Richard Gere), a San Francisco psychiatrist, is treating Diana Baylor (Uma Thurman) for neuroses rooted in events from her past. Diana suggests that Isaac may be helped in his analysis by speaking to her sister, Heather Evans (Kim Basinger). Heather quickly seduces Isaac and turns his attention from Diana's problems to her own condition as the terrified wife of a brutal Greek-American gangster, Jimmy Evans (Eric Roberts).

Even before finding himself in this dangerous situation, Isaac has the attention of Huggins (Keith David), a police detective who resents that the psychiatrist's expert testimony helps criminals to succeed in their pleas of temporary insanity. Meanwhile, Heather displays several neuroses of her own, especially her rages after drinking only a small amount of alcohol. She embarrasses her husband with one such violent fit in a posh restaurant, and Jimmy threatens to kill her if she does so again.

During one outburst, Heather grabs a dumbbell and strikes Jimmy in the head, leading to his drowning in a nearby sunken bathtub. The murder weapon mysteriously disappears afterward. Isaac persuades his best friend, attorney Mike O'Brien (Paul Guilfoyle), to defend Heather and his colleague Alan Lowenthal (Robert Harper) to give expert testimony about the condition called pathological intoxication.

Following a tense courtroom victory, Heather goes to a psychiatric facility to await release after the formality of a routine examination. Before he can arrange his lover's discharge, Isaac accidentally learns that Heather has attended several court cases in which he testified. Other clues cumulate to persuade Isaac that Heather has used him to get away with murder. When he confronts her, she reveals that his fingerprints are on the fatal dumbbell. Isaac gets his revenge by tricking Heather into an emotional outburst at a sanity hearing. Heather and Diana then switch clothing so that Heather can escape and turn the dumbbell over to Huggins. Events lead to a confrontation between Isaac, Heather, and Huggins atop a lighthouse near San Francisco Bay.

Final Analysis shares the headlong, visceral qualities exhibited by Wesley Strick's three earlier screenplays: *True Believer* (1989), *Arachnophobia* (1990), and *Cape Fear* (1991). Like these films, *Final Analysis* draws more upon the cinema for ideas than upon real life. A smart woman choosing a gullible professional man to manipulate through a legal technicality comes from *Body Heat* (1981). A beautiful woman who loses control when she drinks is borrowed from *Blind Date* (1987), in which the part is also played by Basinger. The borrowings from *Vertigo* include the San Francisco setting, false secrets hidden in a character's past (such as Heather's claim that Diana, sexually abused by their father, killed him in a fire), a man tricked through his weaknesses into offering an alibi for a murder, and the climax with the lighthouse substituting for the Spanish mission tower from which Kim Novak's character falls to her death.

Joanou contributes to the Hitchcock homage with his staging of several scenes, especially the lighthouse finale, which also echoes similar scenes in *Saboteur* (1942) and *North by Northwest* (1959). Joanou's version, however, set amid a violent storm, is decidedly more gothic. After the unwatchable *Three O'Clock High* (1987) and the pompous rock documentary *U2: Rattle and Hum* (1988), Joanou made the surprisingly powerful and adept *State of Grace* (1990). In that gangster film and in *Final Analysis* as well, he exhibits a kinetic, often hysterical, style reminiscent of Sam Peckinpah's.

Contributing to the technical polish of *Final Analysis* are the cinematography of Jordan Cronenweth, particularly in the night scenes, and the production design of the great Dean Tavoularis, whose credits include *Bonnie and Clyde* (1967) and the three *Godfather* films (1972, 1974, and 1990). Cronenweth and Tavoularis combine their skills to create the impression that a lighthouse actually fifty miles south of San Francisco is just beneath the Golden Gate Bridge.

Basinger, given the rare opportunity to portray a thinking woman, gives one of her best performances. Thurman continues to grow as an actress, showing that the magnetic performance she gives in *Henry and June* (1990) is not a fluke. Roberts, whose overacting in the past has known no limits, finally has a role in which his mannerisms are appropriate. His Jimmy Evans is a memorably idiosyncratic villain struggling to control his rages. Excellent supporting performances are also given by Guilfoyle as the cocky attorney and Harper as the exceedingly nervous psychiatrist. Even though Gere is one of the film's executive producers, he simply walks through *Final Analysis.* A forceful actor when playing disreputable characters, as in *American Gigolo* (1980) and *Internal Affairs* (1990), Gere barely registers here.

The neutrality of Gere's characters adds to the major weakness of *Final Analysis.* The audience is supposed to root for the good Isaac in his battle with the evil Heather, but the psychiatrist is more foolish than good and Heather gives her cruel husband what he deserves. Hitchcock's films always place innocent protagonists in situations of great danger. By making Isaac naïve rather than innocent, *Final Analysis* fails to justify his revenge or to make the audience care about his fate. Arbitrarily making Heather the villain leaves the film open to charges of sexism. Also bothersome is Isaac's lack of qualms over having an affair with a relative of a patient, though this matter of medical ethics is not as flagrant as in *The Prince of Tides* (1991).

Strick and Joanou never clear up a few confusing plot elements: Was Diana raped by her father? Did Diana or Heather kill him? Does Heather suffer from pathological intoxication, or is she merely putting on an act? Other examples of careless filmmaking include Isaac's habit of never locking the doors of his office or house even when working alone at night; Heather casually strolls in whenever she visits him. Heather's escape from the hospital also stretches credibility. *Final Analysis* is thus a schizophrenic film: stylish entertainment flawed by frequent examples of schlock.

Michael Adams

Reviews

Boxoffice. March, 1992, p. R-21.
Chicago Tribune. February 7, 1992, VII, p. 27.
The Christian Science Monitor. LXXXIV, February 7, 1992, p. 14.
Entertainment Weekly. February 14, 1992, p. 34.
The Hollywood Reporter. February 6, 1992, p. 9.

Los Angeles Times. February 7, 1992, p. F1.
The New York Times. February 7, 1992, p. B5.
Time. CXXXIX, March 9, 1992, p. 11.
Variety. CCCXLVI, February 4, 1992, p. 2.
The Washington Post. February 7, 1992, p. B7.

FOREVER YOUNG

Production: Bruce Davey for Icon, in association with Edward S. Feldman; released by Warner Bros.
Direction: Steve Miner
Screenplay: Jeffrey Abrams
Cinematography: Russell Boyd
Editing: Jon Poll
Production design: Gregg Fonseca
Art direction: Bruce Miller
Set decoration: Jay R. Hart
Casting: Marion Dougherty
Sound: Jim Tanenbaum
Creative makeup design: Dick Smith
Special makeup: Greg Cannom
Costume design: Aggie Guerard Rodgers
Music: Jerry Goldsmith
MPAA rating: R
Running time: 138 minutes

Principal characters:

Daniel	Mel Gibson
Claire	Jamie Lee Curtis
Nat	Elijah Wood
Helen	Isabel Glasser
Harry	George Wendt
Cameron	Joe Morton
John	Nicolas Surovy
Wilcox	David Marshall Grant
Felix	Robert Hy Gorman
Susan Finley	Millie Slavin
Steven	Michael Goorjian

Nostalgia has traditionally brought many an audience to the cinema. Moreover, writers and directors have been quick to capitalize on the fact that filmgoers enjoy seeing their leading men and women in roles that are not only heroic but also romantic. Set during World War II, *Forever Young* fulfills these criteria.

In 1939, Daniel McCormick (Mel Gibson) is asked to become a test pilot for the newly formed Air Corps flying the B-25, the latest strategic Air Force bomber. Despite the courage required in his new job, however, Daniel lacks the fortitude to make a long-term commitment to his childhood sweetheart, Helen (Isabel Glasser). One afternoon, Daniel tries to propose marriage at their favorite diner. For some reason, words fail him, and Helen leaves for her appointment. Moments later, Helen is struck by a produce truck while crossing the street in front of the diner. Daniel sits by Helen's bed while she remains in a coma, but she does not awaken. He soon loses all interest in his life.

When nearly a year has passed, Daniel's friend Harry Finley (George Wendt), an aircraft designer, urges Daniel to reenter mainstream society. Daniel, realizing that he has nothing to live for with Helen still in a coma, insists that he be frozen as part of a top-secret cryogenics experiment. He is supposed to be unfrozen after a year, but a bureaucratic mishap causes Daniel to be forgotten until 1992.

Two young friends, Nat (Elijah Wood) and Felix (Robert Hy Gorman), discover Daniel's survival chamber inside a military compound. A make-believe game of submarine begins, and within moments, the boys accidentally unseal the chamber. Daniel's arm lunges upward, terrifying the young boys. The next day, Daniel returns Nat's jacket after finding the boy's address label inside the coat. Daniel has nowhere to stay for the night, so Nat offers him his treehouse as temporary refuge. That evening, an old boyfriend visits Nat's mother, Claire (Jamie Lee Curtis), and soon begins to hit her during a fiery altercation. Before the boyfriend has time to turn around, Daniel knocks him to the floor and chases him from the house. Thankful for this stranger's help, Claire invites Daniel to stay the night.

Daniel believes that, by locating his former colleague Harry Finley, he will somehow make sense of all that has happened to him. Through a chance telephone call, he is able to meet Harry's daughter, Susan (Millie Slavin). She tells Daniel that, although her father died a number of years ago, Helen emerged from her coma and is still alive.

When Daniel tries to tell some military personnel that he was frozen as part of a top-secret experiment, they assume that he is lying. The chamber that housed Daniel's frozen body is discovered, however, and after a number of phone calls, they are told that such an experiment took place at this particular military base. Before long, a number of high-ranking officials from the government arrive in town.

Meanwhile Nat, who has a vivid imagination, manages to replicate the cockpit of a B-25 with wire and cardboard. Seated side by side with Nat, Daniel pretends that they are flying a real B-25. At the end of this make-believe session, Daniel suddenly collapses and falls out of the treehouse. Nat arranges for Daniel to be taken to the hospital.

Daniel has begun to age rapidly as an aftereffect of his cryogenic state. The government officials want to find Daniel in order to learn more about the experiment. Claire arranges for him to escape from the hospital before they arrive. Daniel returns to Harry's house to search all the old journals that documented his research. Daniel feverishly looks through the many volumes until he discovers a page stating that the aging process is irreversible.

Knowing his fate, Daniel asks Claire to drive him to his old home town to see Helen for possibly the last time. As they are driving, the aging process continues to accelerate. In a desperate act to see Helen, Daniel commandeers a restored B-25 at a local airshow. During the flight, Daniel goes into seizures. Fortunately, Nat has managed to stow away on the plane, and he is able to land the aircraft near Helen's home. Daniel and Helen embrace, hardly able to comprehend what has occurred.

Forever Young manages to evoke nostalgia for the late 1930's using period settings, but there is little to disguise the fact that the film, at heart, is a straightforward romance. What becomes difficult to explain, and where the thrust of the story fails, is the rather convoluted way in which Daniel passes from the 1930's to the 1990's. The scientific element of *Forever Young* is undoubtedly the weakest aspect of the film. It is difficult to accept the premise that a man can be frozen for fifty years and then return to life and accept his present circumstances with little trouble. *Forever Young* tries to make the experiment a credible part of the plot, but there is so little build-up to the freezing of Daniel's body that his reawakening carries little dramatic effect. Indeed, for the most part, any serious drama in the film is often wrapped up in some kind of comedy, undermining the message that is meant to be conveyed.

What *Forever Young* tries to provide is an atmosphere in which the most enduring romance can be created. Yet the early establishing scenes between Daniel and Helen try overly hard to prove that this couple's love is unique. Time and again, the story falls into formula. When Helen is struck by a produce truck moments after Daniel tries but fails to propose marriage, he continues to hope that somehow they will be reunited. As a result of his enduring passion for Helen, Daniel volunteers for a somewhat bizarre military experiment and asks to be woken up should his true love ever recover from the coma. Daniel appears to volunteer for the experiment without any doubt that he will come back to life easily after his freezing. This laissez-faire attitude tends to make light of what is supposed to be a traumatic event in his life. This happy-go-lucky approach is also evident when Daniel finds himself in the 1990's. His reactions to this bewildering situation always border on the comedic, rather than exploring the deeper implications of what has happened. *Forever Young* uses its time-lapse theme merely as a vehicle to prove that love is the strongest of all emotions.

In addition, much of the film actually concentrates on Daniel's relationship with Nat. Elijah Wood brings a naturalness to his acting that at times is completely disarming. Perhaps Mel Gibson should have paid more attention to the familiar adage that actors should never work with animals or children because they are likely to be upstaged. As he did in *Radio Flyer* (1992), Wood manages to evoke all the right emotions, furthering the story as a result. His performance is in direct contrast to the rather uneven acting of Gibson, who treats some of the more dramatic moments with inappropriate lightness. Since Wood can clearly hold his own with such a seasoned professional as Gibson, Wood's career as an actor is now assured.

Many times in the film, the events occurring on-screen seem to exist only to serve the finale in which Daniel and Helen are reunited. A successful film flows naturally from one event to the next with undetectable shifts, but nearly all the transitions in *Forever Young* are rather forced. For example, when Daniel meets Claire, Nat's mother, the circumstance allows a scene in which Nat and his friend Felix can show total surprise at seeing their friend in the house. When Daniel begins to age suddenly, he immediately becomes a wanted man who must run desperately from pursuing government officials. The stock chase scene only further emphasizes the overwhelming direction of the film to reunite Daniel and Helen.

Forever Young tries to be a classic romance in the style of *Romeo and Juliet* while creating a vehicle that is equal to the talent and appeal of Mel Gibson. Unfortunately, even with all these elements in the right place, *Forever Young* cannot rise above its limitations.

Richard G. Cormack

Reviews

Chicago Tribune. December 16, 1992, V, p. 3.
The Hollywood Reporter. December 7, 1992, p. 6.
Los Angeles. XXXVII, December, 1992, p. 144.
Los Angeles Times. December 16, 1992, p. F1.
The New York Times. December 16, 1992, p. C17.
Newsweek. CXX, December 28, 1992, p. 58.
Rolling Stone. January 7, 1993, p. 51.
Time. CXL, December 28, 1992, p. 64.
Variety. December 7, 1992, p. 5.
Washingtonian. XXVIII, January, 1993, p. 28.

GAS FOOD LODGING

Production: Daniel Hassid, Seth M. Willenson, and William Ewert for Cineville; released by I.R.S.
Direction: Allison Anders
Screenplay: Allison Anders; based on the novel *Don't Look and It Won't Hurt*, by Richard Peck
Cinematography: Dean Lent
Editing: Tracy S. Granger
Production design: Jane Ann Stewart
Art direction: Lisa Denker and Carla Weber
Set decoration: Mary Meeks
Sound: Clifford "Kip" Gynn
Music: J. Mascis
MPAA rating: R
Running time: 100 minutes

Principal characters:

Nora .... Brooke Adams
Trudi .... Ione Skye
Shade .... Fairuza Balk
John Evans .... James Brolin
Dank .... Robert Knepper
Hamlet .... David Lansbury
Javier .... Jacob Vargas
Darius .... Donovan Leitch
Raymond .... Chris Mulkey
Elvia Rivero .... Nina Belanger

"If it weren't for Elvia Rivero (Nina Belanger), this story wouldn't even be worth telling," narrates teenage Shade (Fairuza Balk), who spends her afternoons in Laramie, New Mexico's local Spanish cinema, enraptured by the beautiful and strong serial heroine who celebrates her womanhood with such lines as "My giving comes from my strength, not weakness." Alone in the darkened theater, Shade gets the idea that what is missing in her life is a man—not for herself, but for her mother.

Nora (Brooke Adams) gave birth to Shade's sister Trudi (Ione Skye) when she was eighteen. The girls' father left a few years later, shortly after Shade was born. Left to rear her daughters alone, Nora rushes between her trailer home, where there is no respite from the crises common to young women, and her job as a waitress in the Pull-Off Plaza truck stop. After what seems like a lifetime of falling in love with men who leave or, as in the case of her most recent lover, are married and therefore never truly there to begin with, the last thing that Nora wants is a man to disrupt what she imagines is a lull in her family's life.

The lull does not last long. Seventeen-year-old Trudi is becoming increasingly belligerent. She and Nora cannot be in the same room for a minute without fighting, usually about the late hours that Trudi keeps and the possibility that she will end up pregnant and alone the way her mother did. The only thing that troubles Shade more than their screaming is Trudi's threat to move out, but even she is running out of patience with Trudi.

At the truck stop where Nora works, Trudi embarrasses Shade by being rude to the busboy, Javier (Jacob Vargas)—calling him a wetback, even though the Mexican families in Laramie have been there far longer than the so-called Americans. Trudi then leaves for a date with a local boy who uses her for sex, then ridicules her in front of his friends. By the time that Trudi returns to the Pull-Off Plaza, Nora has left to meet her married lover Raymond (Chris Mulkey). Trying for the umpteenth time to break off with this unavailable man, Nora rationalizes that she must set a good example for her daughters. Raymond suggests that, if he makes her feel good, then she could not be setting a better example. Confused, Nora kisses him and drives off.

At the truck stop, an English geologist named Dank (Robert Knepper) is touched by Trudi's sorrow. He invites her to accompany him into the desert in search of rocks. Enchanted by the colorful world that he shows her with his ultraviolet light, as well as by his gentleness, especially in comparison with the other boys she has known, Trudi makes love to the shy but very willing Dank. She then confesses her history of promiscuity to him with the explanation that her first sexual experience was rape, and that, ever since then, she has been purposely aggressive so that what she assumes is inevitable will at least be perceived as her idea. This, Trudi whispers, was the first time she really wanted to make love, the first time she felt anything. The next morning, when Dank tells her that he must leave for a few days on business, Trudi fears he is leaving her but eventually believes his promise to return to Laramie and to her. Dank drives off, and Trudi happily waltzes into her trailer home, only to find Nora hysterical that Trudi was out all night. They fight, and Nora gives Trudi one month to find a new place to live.

Nora, however, does not practice what she preaches. Awakened at five in the morning by the noise of construction, Nora exits her trailer and finds Hamlet Humphrey (David Lansbury) installing a satellite dish next door. Nora insults, Hamlet comforts, they flirt, and soon Hamlet recommends something more personal than cable television to improve Nora's disposition.

Meanwhile, innocent Shade is beginning to learn too much, too quickly about the men in her life. At the Spanish cinema, she encounters Javier. After storming out of the Pull-Off Plaza because of Trudi's rudeness, he was hired as the projectionist of the Elvia Rivero films. When Javier assumes that Shade holds the same opinions of Mexicans as does her sister, Shade shows that, though sweet and innocent, she can take care of herself. Javier notices that, like Elvia Rivero, Shade's strength makes her even more beautiful. Armed with that confidence, Shade endeavors to transform her androgynous friend Darius (Donovan Leitch) into a boyfriend. She accosts him, dressed as his heroine: 1970's pop star Olivia Newton-John. Unfortunately, what

Shade has failed to realize is that Darius wants not to love a woman like Olivia but to be a woman like Olivia.

Still on the trail of a man for her mother, Shade meets and mistakes Raymond for an eligible suitor, as Nora once did. So as not to hurt Shade, Raymond and Nora suffer through a candle-lit dinner without revealing their secret past. Finally, as if men have not caused enough trouble in these women's lives, Shade discovers that a friendly newcomer to Laramie is actually her long-departed father, John Evans (James Brolin). He now has a new wife and a new life, but he is nevertheless won over by his beautiful and good-hearted younger daughter.

Trudi, on the other hand, has no such triumphs. Dank has not come back from the trip that he said would only take a few days, and in her misery, Trudi discovers that she is pregnant. She leaves for Dallas to have her baby and give it up for adoption. Nora and Shade meet her there for the birth, and on the way back, fate intervenes to let Shade know that Dank did not desert her sister intentionally. This revelation, combined with her first love affair with Javier, gives Shade a sense of hope and optimism that her mother and sister may once have had but have lost long ago. Perhaps Shade, like her fictional heroine Elvia Rivero, is woman enough to give it back to them.

Brooke Adams is credible and sympathetic as the exhausted, struggling, abandoned mother. After her film debut in *Days of Heaven* (1978), Adams appeared in the remake of *Invasion of the Body Snatchers* (1978), *A Man, a Woman, and a Bank* (1979), *Cuba* (1979), and *The Dead Zone* (1983).

Despite a love scene inside a cave (which is difficult to find erotic for worrying that the actors must be in terrible pain perched on the jagged rocks) and despite her incessant whining (or maybe because of it), Ione Skye is perfectly cast as the troubled and troublesome Trudi. Skye's first film was the controversial *River's Edge* (1987). She was then seen in *A Night in the Life of Jimmie Reardon* (1988), *Say Anything* (1989), *The Rachel Papers* (1989), and in a brief role as the daughter of Liv Ullman's character in *Mindwalk* (1990).

Simultaneously precocious and naïve, Fairuza Balk brings tremendous depth to the role of Shade. *Gas Food Lodging* represents Balk's most realistic role to date. Previously, she reprised the role of Dorothy in the macabre pseudo-sequel *Return to Oz* (1985) and also starred as the aristocratic young bride in Miloš Forman's *Valmont* (1989).

Though the men serve as little more than backdrops in *Gas Food Lodging*, they must be talented and exciting backdrops in order to win the attentions of the audience and of the female leads. James Brolin's early career includes such films as *Fantastic Voyage* (1966), but he is far better known for his role in television's Emmy-winning *Marcus Welby, M.D.* and in the dramatic series *Hotel*. Robert Knepper, an Ohio native who used a British accent for this role, appeared in the films *That's Life!* (1986) and *Made in Heaven* (1987), but he was also at home on the small screen in such series as *L.A. Law*, *Civil Wars*, and *Star Trek: The Next Generation*. David Lansbury came to motion pictures from the stage; *Gas Food Lodging* is his second feature film, and *Gorillas in the Mist* (1988) was his first. Donovan Leitch, who is the real-life brother of Ione Skye, starred in *And God Created Woman* (1988), the remake of *The Blob* (1988), and *Glory* (1989), and he appeared in several television films and series. Jacob Vargas, deeply romantic for such a young age, is an accomplished singer and dancer and earned a role in *Little Nikita* (1988).

For this, her directorial debut, Allison Anders was voted best new director of 1992 by the New York Film Critics Circle. In adapting Richard Peck's novel *Don't Look and It Won't Hurt* (1972), she made it very personal, herself being a fatherless daughter and a single mother of teenagers. Anders was a protégé of German director Wim Wenders and assisted on the set of his American film *Paris, Texas* (1984).

Gas Food Lodging is perhaps the female version of Gus Van Zant's *My Own Private Idaho* (1991) in its shots of never-ending highways that, no matter how faithfully the characters follow, always lead them back to where they started, hopefully a bit wiser than when they left.

Eleah Horwitz

Reviews

Boxoffice. July, 1992, p. R-57.
Chicago Tribune. November 6, 1992, VII, p. 40.
The Christian Science Monitor. August 14, 1992, p. 12.
Entertainment Weekly. August 21, 1992, p. 39.
The Hollywood Reporter. January 21, 1992, p. 12.
Los Angeles Times. August 14, 1992, p. F8.
The New York Times. August 1, 1992, p. 13.
Time. CXL, August 17, 1992, p. 63.
Variety. January 21, 1992, p. 20.
The Village Voice. August 4, 1992, p. 56.

GLENGARRY GLEN ROSS

Production: Jerry Tokofsky and Stanley R. Zupnik for Zupnik Enterprises; released by New Line Cinema
Direction: James Foley
Screenplay: David Mamet; based on his play
Cinematography: Juan Ruiz Anchia
Editing: Howard Smith
Production design: Jane Musky
Art direction: Bill Barclay
Set decoration: Robert J. Franco
Casting: Bonnie Timmermann
Sound: Danny Michael
Costume design: Jane Greenwood
Music: James Newton Howard
MPAA rating: R
Running time: 100 minutes

Principal characters:

Ricky Roma .... Al Pacino
Shelley Levene .... Jack Lemmon
Dave Moss .... Ed Harris
George Aaronow .... Alan Arkin
John Williamson .... Kevin Spacey
Blake .... Alec Baldwin
James Lingk .... Jonathan Pryce
Mr. Spannel .... Bruce Altman
Detective .... Jude Ciccolella

On the stage, *Glengarry Glen Ross*, David Mamet's 1984 Pulitzer Prize-winning play about the desperation of real-estate salesmen, resembled the sadness of Arthur Miller's *Death of a Salesman* (1949) combined with the frenetic comic pace of Ben Hecht and Charles MacArthur's *The Front Page* (1928), the dark humor of a Harold Pinter play such as *The Birthday Party* (1958), and Mamet's particular genius for profane vernacular. In reimagining *Glengarry Glen Ross* as a film, Mamet, who adapted his play, and director James Foley have slowed the pace, subdued the humor, and emphasized the pathos.

Mamet's dying salesmen are Shelley Levene (Jack Lemmon), aging yet full of energy, hopeful yet unable to make a sale; George Aaronow (Alan Arkin), also past his prime and losing the will to make the effort; Dave Moss (Ed Harris), younger but also unsuccessful, desperate to try anything to survive; and Ricky Roma (Al Pacino), slick and confident, a born con man, seemingly able to sell anything to anyone. The four salesmen operate out of a seedy Chicago office supervised by the inept John Williamson (Kevin Spacey).

Their business is selling suspect land in Arizona and Florida to suckers responding to junk-mail promises of prizes for listening to sales pitches. The salesmen lie to their prospective customers, known as leads, claiming to be executives of fictional firms who just happen to be making a Chicago stopover and can spare a few hours to offer the chance of a lifetime. Because fewer people are falling for this line, the home office, in the person of the belligerent Blake (Alec Baldwin), threatens to fire all but the top two salesmen at the end of the month. Instead of giving them fresh leads, Williamson offers the names of those who have been approached numerous times without success. Only those who convince these unlikely prospects to hand over thousands of dollars will receive the new leads and survive.

Moss, realizing that he has been given an impossible task, decides that one of them should break into Williamson's office, steal the list of leads, and sell it to a rival firm. He attempts to coerce Aaronow into committing the crime, but the timid George refuses. The film's final scene finds each of the four being interrogated by police, Levene joyous at making an apparently lucrative sale, and Roma confronted by an upset customer. Roma has met a pathetic soul, James Lingk (Jonathan Pryce), in a bar and convinced him that a plot of Florida land is the answer to his problems. Lingk arrives apologetically during the investigation to say that his wife has demanded he get his check back and that she has contacted the state's consumer-protection agency.

The stage version of *Glengarry Glen Ross* bombards its audience with the spectacle of angry men whose dreams have failed as an earthy, obscene comedy as much about language and how people use it as a weapon for survival as about the emptiness of the salesmen's lives. Several of the film's scenes retain the rapid-fire humor for which Mamet is famous: Blake's degrading lecture, a conversation between Moss and Aaronow in which they resemble vaudeville comedians, and, most impressive of all, the ploys improvised by Roma and Levene to attempt to stall Lingk. For the most part, however, Foley slows down the pace to a more realistic level and employs perhaps an excessive use of close-ups to make his audience confront the agonizing uncertainty of these lives. Juan Ruiz Anchia's cinematography creates the sense of dusty, claustrophobic interiors and dark, damp, and threatening exteriors: Chicago as hell on earth. These qualities make *Glengarry Glen Ross* an excruciatingly painful portrait of an American society without values, willing to try anything to avoid the abyss of despair.

The unusual combination of humor and desperation at the center of *Glengarry Glen Ross* is conveyed well by the actors. Kevin Spacey presents Williamson as an incompetent bumbler who survives because of luck and a willingness to step all over those who work under him. Just as Roma has worked himself out of the Lingk dilemma, Williamson blurts out something to ruin matters. Spacey conveys very effectively Williamson's embarrassment, merged with his anger at those who have confronted him with his mistake. Alec Baldwin's Blake, a character added for the film, is a cocky opportunist indifferent to the humanity of others. Blake is an angrier, slimier version of the Jimmy Swaggart that he portrayed in *Great Balls of Fire!* (1989).

Ed Harris and Alan Arkin do well with comparatively underwritten roles. Like Blake, Harris' Moss is opportunistic and manipulative, yet he lacks the killer instinct. He cannot go as far as he needs to be a successful salesman not because of any inherent humanity but because of uncertainty about himself. Harris can easily portray cocky characters, but here he shows the weakness underlying superficial confidence. Normally prone to exaggerated mannerisms, Arkin gives one of his most subtle performances as a salesman too tired to be as desperate as success seemingly requires.

Like Arkin, Jack Lemmon has specialized in playing "everymen" downtrodden by society. Also like Arkin, Lemmon gives a somewhat less mannered performance than he might have in the past, but it is still showy and sentimental. As in *The Apartment* (1960) and *Save the Tiger* (1973), Lemmon strains to display his character's humanity, never letting the audience forget that this is Jack Lemmon giving a powerhouse performance as a weakling. At his best when not forcing the viewer to like or feel sorry for his character, Lemmon comes alive when Levene assists Roma in avoiding Lingk, as Levene instantly transforms himself into a worldly, confident executive.

The most impressive performers in *Glengarry Glen Ross* are Jonathan Pryce and Al Pacino. While most self-consciously mannered performances are irritating, sometimes such extremes are justified. Pryce's Lingk is given few lines to describe the shallow sadness of his life and is too inarticulate to do so anyway. Pryce conveys Lingk's desperation by mumbling, stammering, gesturing wildly, hunching his lanky body as if to try to hide inside himself. Pacino, like Dustin Hoffman and Robert De Niro, is one of those rare actors who is equally powerful playing quiet, subtle characters, as with Michael Corleone in the three *Godfather* films, and exuberant neurotics, as in *Serpico* (1973), *Dog Day Afternoon* (1975), and *Sea of Love* (1989). His Ricky Roma is one of the latter and one of Pacino's most powerful performances. Unlike the other salesmen, Roma is bursting with confidence, but despite his high energy, he has the patience to take the necessary time to make a sale. With Lingk, he talks for hours about all sorts of subjects before closing in for the kill. Pacino is equally adept at showing the ease with which Roma manipulates people, the pride that he takes in this skill, and the sincere compassion that he displays when he realizes how frazzled Lingk has become as a result of believing in Roma. The talent for listening that is essential for stage actors is rarely necessary for any length of time in a film, but Foley shoots the scene in which Roma listens to Levene decribe his sale so that the emphasis is on the listener and the genuine pleasure Roma experiences in hearing of a colleague's triumph. Pacino is superb throughout the film, but in this scene he is particularly good. He well deserved his Academy Award nomination and should have won for this performance rather than for his more obvious acting in *Scent of a Woman* (1992; reviewed in this volume).

Glengarry Glen Ross has perhaps been overpraised because so few American films have dealt with the despair of modern life so unflinchingly. Yet Foley's execution of this theme is too often obvious and pedestrian. In the three films that he has both written and directed, Mamet himself has proven to have more cinematic skill than Foley demonstrates here. While Mamet's *Homicide* (1991) is depressing yet exhilarating, Foley's *Glengarry Glen Ross* is merely sad.

Michael Adams

Reviews

Boxoffice. November, 1992, p. R-78.
Chicago Tribune. October 2, 1992, VII, p. 19.
The Christian Science Monitor. September 29, 1992, p. 11.
Entertainment Weekly. October 9, 1992, p. 40.
The Hollywood Reporter. September 30, 1992, p. 6.
Los Angeles Times. September 30, 1992, p. F1.
The New York Times. September 30, 1992, p. B1.
The New Yorker. LXVIII, October 5, 1992, p. 162.
Variety. August 31, 1992, p. 4.
The Washington Post. October 2, 1992, p. C1.

THE HAIRDRESSER'S HUSBAND

Origin: France
Released: 1992
Released in U.S.: 1992
Production: Thierry de Ganay; released by Triton Pictures
Direction: Patrice Leconte
Screenplay: Claude Klotz and Patrice Leconte; based on a story by Leconte
Cinematography: Eduardo Serra
Editing: Joëlle Hache
Art direction: Ivan Maussion
Production management: Frédéric Sauvagnac
Sound: Pierre Lenoir
Costume design: Cécile Magnan
Music: Michael Nyman
MPAA rating: no listing
Running time: 82 minutes

Principal characters:

Antoine	Jean Rochefort
Mathilde	Anna Galiena
Twelve-year-old Antoine	Henry Hocking
Madame Shaeffer	Anne-Marie Pisani
Antoine's father	Roland Bertin
Agopian	Maurice Chevit
Gay customer	Claude Aufaure
Adopted child's mother	Michele Laroque
Gloomy man	Julien Bukowski
Tunisian customer	Youssef Hamid
Antoine's sister-in-law	Arlette Tephany
Twelve-year-old Antoine's brother	Christophe Pichon
Little Edouard	Thomas Rochefort

With regard to his inspiration to script and direct *The Hairdresser's Husband*, Patrice Leconte has written, "Ever since I was little, I've always enjoyed going to the hairdresser. When I was about twelve or thirteen, my enjoyment became even more intense. This was when I started going to a woman hairdresser. More than anything, I loved the way this woman tended to me. She smelled good, she was gentle and her voice was very calm. I figured that whoever lived with her must be the happiest man in the world. From then on, I swore to myself that one day I'd marry a hairdresser. Fate had other plans for me. It was doubtless my failure to marry a hairdresser that gave me the urge to write this film, this story that might have been about me. *The Hairdresser's Husband* is a love story. It is not autobiographical, although it really ought to have been."

The film begins with twelve-year-old Antoine (Henry Hocking) alone on a patio at a small French seaside resort, wearing a pith helmet and flowing scarf to match, and performing a comic yet strangely sensual dance to a popular Arab tune played on his tape recorder. Adult Antoine (Jean Rochefort) narrates the memory of his childhood summers by the sea, the clearest image being that of the red wool, pom-pommed bathing suits his mother had crocheted for Antoine and his brother (Christophe Pichon), which itched and sagged and never fully dried. The peculiar sensations caused by the wet, often sand-filled suit coincided with the sensations of the adolescent's first sexual awareness.

It was about the same time that Antoine, sent by his mother for a haircut—an assignment usually met with whines and complaints and contrivances to postpone the perceived indignity—encountered a new hairdresser at his regular salon. Madame Shaeffer (Anne-Marie Pisani), a smiling, zaftig woman with auburn hair and a perpetually unbuttoned blouse, unknowingly and most innocently turned the dreaded experience of a haircut into a sensual, sexual encounter that would haunt the boy for life. Soon Antoine was voluntarily going to the hairdresser every three weeks. He relished the ritual tying-on of the smock. He luxuriated in the feel of her massaging and rinsing his scalp. He drank in her strong smell, a combination of lotions, shampoos, and Madame Shaeffer's own need to bathe. Through adult Antoine's voice and little Antoine's face is conveyed the transformation of the mundane to the blissful.

At supper one night, Antoine's father (Roland Bertin) inquired of his sons what they planned to do when they grew up. After his brother listed some acceptable choices of profession, Antoine stated proudly that he would marry a hairdresser. His father impulsively slapped Antoine, causing Antoine to run from the table and lock himself in his bedroom for hours. No amount of coaxing and apologizing from his stunned and confused parents drew him out. As the adult Antoine narrates, he had already won: He would marry a hairdresser.

This conviction was further burned into Antoine's psyche when, upon his next visit to the salon, he found Madame Shaeffer unconscious on the floor. Antoine was childishly less concerned with the cause of the hairdresser's position than with the opportunity it offered him to look up her dress. Suddenly, the police arrived with an ambulance, and Madame Shaeffer was pronounced dead of an overdose of barbiturates. As they took her body away, Antoine tiptoed over broken glass into the shop, to sit in Madame Shaeffer's chair one more time.

Decades later, a middle-aged Antoine, the events of his life between that surreal past and the present unknown, is still in search of the lady barber to fulfill his fantasy. He finds her at a salon called Isadore's, where the elderly proprietor has bequeathed the business to his beautiful young assistant, Mathilde (Anna Galiena). When Antoine walks into the empty shop requesting a shampoo, Mathilde tells him he must come back in half an hour. He leaves but spies on the shop and sees that no one else enters or leaves during the thirty minutes Mathilde has made him wait.

Antoine is aroused by what he perceives as a torturous flirtation and reminiscent of his father's slap at the mere mention of his desire.

As Mathilde finishes shampooing Antoine, he impulsively proposes marriage. Understandably confused, Mathilde pretends not to have heard. The embarrassed Antoine pays for the shampoo, apologizes, and departs. That night, he sits under the window above the salon, Mathilde's apartment, and wonders what she does all night. Antoine remembers his father's admonition that failure was proof that one was not truly deserving. Antoine narrates this memory over scenes of the seaside where, while the other children hurried futilely with buckets full of sand, young Antoine enlisted the aid of a bulldozer to create a dam to protect his sandcastle.

Three weeks later, Antoine returns to Isadore's. At first, Mathilde acts as though she has never seen him before. Just as Antoine is about to leave, however, Mathilde tells him that, if he was serious and if the offer still stands, she accepts his proposal of marriage. Antoine imagines that he sees his twelve-year-old self beaming at him from the salon window.

Antoine and Mathilde spend the next ten years in idyllic isolation. Their wedding and reception are in the salon. They live above the salon. Antoine assists Mathilde with the salon's customers and sits watching her or doing crossword puzzles when his help is not required. Antoine is proud of the fact that they do not socialize with other couples, stating that the love of those couples who need outside interests is obviously inferior to that of his and Mathilde's. The members of their family are the salon's regular patrons, about whose health and welfare they worry and in whose arguments they intervene. They work as a team: When an uninterested mother brings her adopted son, kicking and screaming, into the salon for a much needed haircut, Antoine coaxes the hysterical boy out from under the chair and mesmerizes him with his Arabian undulations until Mathilde has successfully and painlessly finished the boy's hair. After hours, or even during the day if the mood strikes them, Antoine and Mathilde close up shop and unabashedly make love in full view of the glass door to the rarely visited outside. In one stirringly sensual scene, Antoine goes so far as to make love to Mathilde while she shampoos a dozing and oblivious customer.

Although Mathilde is open and giving of her love to her husband, she bears many secrets. When she accepts his marriage proposal, an amazing phenomenon, Antoine merely celebrates the fulfillment of his fantasy. He has been searching for Mathilde or someone like her his entire life, but he never questions what she sees in him or how she arrived at being the accepting creature that she is. Foreshadowed throughout the film are Mathilde's thoughts and fears, which threaten the couple's happiness. Her reluctance to discuss her childhood, her tears at Antoine's talk of what their life might be like years into the future, and her extreme anxiety at visiting the retired Isadore (to whom she owes her livelihood and her and Antoine's sanctuary) all lead frantically to the chilling climax, which will leave Antoine stuck in time, alone, but eternally the hairdresser's husband.

Jean Rochefort, a delight as he improvises his Arabian dances to entertain his wife and the occasional unruly customer, is considered a mainstay of French cinema and has worked extensively with such respected directors as Luis Buñuel, Philippe de Broca, and Yves Robert. Anna Galiena is a native Italian who studied acting and performed all over the world before returning to settle in Rome. She had been moved by Leconte's previous films and longed to work with him one day. Within moments of meeting her, Leconte knew she would make exactly the Mathilde he had in mind.

Composer Michael Nyman also created the score for Leconte's *Monsieur Hire* (1989). His other film work includes more than a dozen Peter Greenaway films, such as *A Zed and Two Noughts* (1985), *The Cook, the Thief, His Wife, and Her Lover* (1989), and *Prospero's Books* (1991). Leconte chose Portuguese cinematographer Eduardo Serra to provide a warm, optimistic feeling to the images which Leconte freely manipulates, serving as his own camera operator.

Following nine comedy features, as well as a career in television advertising, Leconte attracted international acclaim for his first drama, the erotically suspenseful *Monsieur Hire*. Like *Monsieur Hire*, *The Hairdresser's Husband* draws its strength from the psychology of its characters, their needs, and their moods. Although *The Hairdresser's Husband* contains the whimsical delights of a comedy, its unrevealed secrets and dramatic conclusion render it as dark and disturbing as its predecessor.

Eleah Horwitz

Reviews

Boxoffice. June, 1992, p. R-51.
Chicago Tribune. August 7, 1992, VII, p. 35.
The Hollywood Reporter. February 26, 1992, p. 19.
Los Angeles Times. July 10, 1992, p. F16.
National Review. XLIV, August 31, 1992, p. 71.
The New Republic. CCVII, July 27, 1992, p. 46.
The New York Times. June 19, 1992, p. C11.
Rolling Stone. June 25, 1992, p. 49.
Time. CXXXIX, June 29, 1992, p. 85.
The Village Voice. June 23, 1992, p. 55.

THE HAND THAT ROCKS THE CRADLE

Production: David Madden for Hollywood Pictures and Interscope Communications, in association with Nomura Babcock & Brown; released by Buena Vista
Direction: Curtis Hanson
Screenplay: Amanda Silver
Cinematography: Robert Elswit
Editing: John F. Link
Production design: Edward Pisoni
Art direction: Mark Zuelzke
Set decoration: Sandy Reynolds Wasco
Set design: Gilbert Wong
Casting: Junie Lowry-Johnson
Visual consulting: Carol Fenelon
Sound: James Pilcher
Costume design: Jennifer von Mayrhauser
Music: Graeme Revell
MPAA rating: R
Running time: 110 minutes

Principal characters:

Claire Bartel	Annabella Sciorra
Peyton Flanders	Rebecca De Mornay
Michael Bartel	Matt McCoy
Solomon	Ernie Hudson
Marlene	Julianne Moore
Emma Bartel	Madeline Zima
Dr. Mott	John de Lancie
Marty	Kevin Skousen

This domestic suspense film was shot in Seattle and nearby Tacoma, an area that resembles the more frequently photographed San Francisco with its steep hills, encircling water, and picturesque old houses. Most of the action takes place in and around a big, white, frame house that the hero and heroine have recently acquired and are devoting much time and money to renovating. Michael Bartel (Matt McCoy) works as a genetic biologist, and Claire Bartel (Annabella Sciorra) is expecting their second child. They are the epitome of the happy, affluent yuppie family.

The plot thickens very quickly when Claire visits her new gynecologist, Dr. Mott (John de Lancie), who subjects Claire to intense embarrassment by examining her body in an flagrantly unprofessional manner. Claire is so outraged that she reports him to the authorities. Once her accusation becomes hot local media news, four other women come forward with similar charges. Unable to bear the disgrace, Mott shoots himself in the head. His wife, Peyton (Rebecca De Mornay), who is expecting their first child, is left to bear the whole burden of the tragedy. She is wiped out financially, loses her beautiful house, and suffers a miscarriage brought on by emotional distress. She blames everything on Claire and lies in her hospital bed plotting revenge.

Six months later, Claire has a baby boy and is advertising for a live-in nanny. Serious trouble is in the offing when Peyton arrives to apply for the job. Outwardly, she is smiling, pleasant, kind, and considerate; inwardly, she is seething with insane jealousy and hatred and watching like a wicked witch for opportunities to wreak havoc.

Here, the viewer's credulity is sorely tested. Few women would be as open and vulnerable as Claire, and she is almost too glaring a foil to the svelte, smooth-talking Peyton, who would seem more in place as an executive secretary than a nanny. Most employers would not want to hire anyone so obviously overqualified and would be suspicious about her motives in applying for such a menial job in the first place. The average housewife would certainly not want such a sexy young blonde living under the same roof as a potential competitor for her young husband's affections. Yet Claire hires Peyton without references, without verification of her identity, and on the basis of a rudimentary interview.

Peyton moves into a little room in the basement—quite a comedown for a woman who was once married to a prominent physician and lived in a hillside house worth almost a million dollars. There is an ongoing contrast between the Bartels' happiness and Peyton's misery that helps to establish the forlorn widow as a believable and not altogether unsympathetic character.

Since her miscarriage, Peyton has evidently been using a breast pump in order to keep her milk from drying up, and one of the first things that she does is to begin breast-feeding Claire's new baby in the dead of night. There are overtones of *Rosemary's Baby* (1968): The infant continues to gain weight even though, to Claire's dismay, he refuses to suckle from her own breasts. He is bonding to Peyton and not to his own mother. When Peyton also begins making strong advances toward Michael, the viewer realizes that her intention is to steal Claire's home and her entire family to replace the home and family that she lost.

The plot is rather ingenious in some of its psychological aspects. When Peyton begins to seek the affections of Claire's five-year-old daughter, Emma (Madeline Zima), the little girl is susceptible to the new nanny's blandishments because of her natural resentment of her mother's interest in the new baby.

Whatever sympathies the viewer might have had for Peyton evaporate as it becomes apparent that she is utterly unscrupulous. The Bartels have hired a retarded black handyman named Solomon (Ernie Hudson). He becomes devoted to the family and intuitively suspicious of Peyton. Like the Fool in William Shakespeare's *King Lear*, Solomon has been so badly mistreated all of his life that he has learned to see through people's hypocritical masks. While up on a ladder, he happens to catch sight of Peyton nursing Claire's baby; Peyton looks up in time to see Solomon's horrified face at the window. She immediately defuses this potential threat by accusing Solomon of molesting little Emma and by planting evidence to support her accusation. Poor Solomon, who is too tongue-tied to explain his suspicions about Peyton, is sent back to institutional custody.

Peyton tries to drive a wedge between Claire and her husband by scheming to make it appear that Michael is having an affair with an old flame named Marlene (Julianne Moore). Marlene, a shrewd, hard-boiled residential real-estate broker, becomes suspicious and goes to the library to look up the stories about Dr. Mott's suicide. In a back issue of a Seattle newspaper, she finds a photograph of Peyton as the bereaved Mrs. Mott.

Stephen King developed a plot twist that might be termed the "false denouement." A character who seems to be coming to the rescue is brutally murdered, which puts the hero or heroine in even worse straits. In *The Shining* (1980), the black cook rushes all the way from Florida to Colorado to save the little boy from his murderous father, only to be killed with an ax as soon as he steps inside the big hotel. In *Misery* (1990), the local sheriff nearly rescues the imprisoned writer but is killed by the deranged female fan who is holding the poor man captive. In *The Hand That Rocks the Cradle*, the audience fully expects Marlene to save the day by exposing Peyton, but in a King-like twist Marlene is killed when she is showered with broken glass in the greenhouse death trap that Peyton had just rigged to eliminate Claire.

After this grisly scene, the plot quickly unravels. Claire goes to Marlene's office to discover why the dead woman had come to see her and had left a message that she must talk to her immediately. On Marlene's desk, Claire finds a listing for the Mott's $900,000 hillside house, which has remained unsold. Guided by intuition, Claire goes to the house and looks through the empty rooms. In a room intended to have been a nursery, she finds an abandoned breast pump, and this clue makes her suddenly realize that Marlene's death was not a freak accident but a murder.

The final scene closely parallels the hair-raising conclusion of *Fatal Attraction* (1987). Peyton goes berserk when she is exposed and tries to kill Michael and Claire. Solomon, who has been secretly watching over the family, arrives and tries to help but is badly wounded. The feckless Michael is helpless after being hit over the head with a shovel and breaking both legs in falling down the basement stairs. Emma, who now understands that Peyton is not her friend but a menace to the entire family, is hiding in the closet. Claire is lying on the floor overcome by an asthma attack, an affliction to which she is susceptible when emotionally aroused. Just when it appears that Peyton has won the battle royal and will run off with both the children, Claire makes a supreme effort of the will and charges at her tormentor, knocking her through a second-story window to her death.

The film is part of a wave of Hollywood productions—such as *Thelma and Louise* (1991), *The Silence of the Lambs* (1991), and many others, beginning with *Jagged Edge* (1985)—in which the heroines take an aggressive role in solving their own problems rather than waiting for a knight in shining armor to ride up and save them. The remarkable proliferation of films featuring women and dealing with women's problems probably does not reflect an emergence of social conscience in

Hollywood but a pragmatic recognition of the fact that more and more women are in a position to buy their own theater tickets and are demanding entertainment that they find edifying.

Unfortunately, *The Hand That Rocks the Cradle* has an ambiguous and slow-moving story line because there is no real antagonist to counter Peyton's machinations. Claire cannot be considered the antagonist because she is totally unsuspecting until the last ten minutes of the film. Michael cannot be considered the antagonist because he has no sexual involvement with Peyton and is even more gullible, if possible, than his gullible wife. In attempting to shore up this plot deficiency, scriptwriter Amanda Silver has thrown Solomon and then Marlene into the breach. Minor characters, however, rarely furnish sufficient opposition to create a logically escalating dramatic conflict that will lead to an emotionally satisfying conclusion. *The Hand That Rocks the Cradle* holds the audience's attention but fails to achieve the powerful impact of *Fatal Attraction*, the film to which it has been compared by viewers and critics alike.

Bill Delaney

Reviews

Chicago Tribune. January 10, 1992, V, p. 2.
The Hollywood Reporter. January 3, 1992, p. 6.
Los Angeles Times. January 10, 1992, p. F1.
The New Republic. CCVI, February 24, 1992, p. 22.
The New York Times. January 10, 1992, p. C8.
Newsweek. CXIX, January 20, 1992, p. 60.
Rolling Stone. February 6, 1992, p. 88.
Time. CXXXIX, January 20, 1992, p. 58.
Variety. CCCXLV, January 6, 1992, p. 17.
The Washington Post. January 10, 1992, p. D1.

HERO

Production: Laura Ziskin; released by Columbia Pictures
Direction: Stephen Frears
Screenplay: David Webb Peoples; based on a story by Laura Ziskin, Alvin Sargent, and Peoples
Cinematography: Oliver Stapleton
Editing: Mick Audsley
Production design: Dennis Gassner
Art direction: Leslie McDonald
Set decoration: Nancy Haigh
Casting: Howard Feuer and Juliet Taylor
Sound: Ronald Judkins
Costume design: Richard Hornung
Music: George Fenton
MPAA rating: PG-13
Running time: 112 minutes

Principal characters:

Bernie LaPlante .... Dustin Hoffman
Gale Gayley .... Geena Davis
John Bubber .... Andy Garcia
Evelyn .... Joan Cusack
Chucky .... Kevin J. O'Connor
Winston .... Maury Chaykin
Wallace .... Stephen Tobolowsky
Conklin .... Christian Clemenson
Chick .... Tom Arnold
Donna O'Day .... Susie Cusack
Joey .... James Madio
News director .... Chevy Chase (uncredited)

One of the biggest laughs in Stephen Frears's *Hero* takes place in the hotel suite of newly crowned savior John Bubber (Andy Garcia) after he is awarded a million dollars for saving the lives of fifty-four passengers of a crashed jetliner. Bubber, amazed, looks around the penthouse at the many gifts and floral arrangements sent by admirers. The message attached to one particularly impressive flower basket reads, "To John Bubber, from Barbra Streisand." This flippant reference to contemporary pop culture, one of many in the director's valiant effort to re-create the social comedies of the 1930's and 1940's, detracts from the nostalgic pull of the rest of the film. Frears is attempting here to duplicate the frenetic, farcical style of Frank Capra and Preston Sturges but also, in broad comedic brushstrokes, to satirize the current state of television news. Unlike his superb thriller *The Grifters* (1990), in which Frears infused modern-day Los Angeles with the dark paranoia of 1950's *film noir*, *Hero* fails to establish a consistent tone; the various influences within the film do battle but never come together to create a unique and timeless film world.

Bernie LaPlante (Dustin Hoffman) is a cynical minor-league crook facing a prison term for dealing in stolen goods. His marriage to Evelyn (Joan Cusack) failed years ago, and his relationship with his son, Joey (James Madio), consists merely of random visits. On the way to pick up Joey, LaPlante, in the middle of a blinding thunderstorm, witnesses a plane crash and reluctantly heeds a passenger's plea for help. Removing his hundred-dollar shoes, Bernie wades through a muddy stream to open the plane's door, then adheres to his life's motto—"keep a low profile"—and tries to disappear. A small boy, however, pleads for him to go into the fuselage to rescue his injured father. Bernie, for reasons of which even he is not sure, returns to the plane and saves all the injured passengers. Before he carries Gale Gayley (Geena Davis), a Chicago television reporter, to safety, Bernie steals her purse. When rescue crews arrive, Bernie takes off, missing one shoe. His car breaks down, and he is picked up by John Bubber, a homeless Vietnam veteran. Bernie tells John his story, gives him his useless shoe to sell, and goes on with his seedy life.

Gale, who complains to her station manager (Chevy Chase, in an uncredited role) about their tendency to dwell on depressing stories, later learns that her savior disappeared into the night. Apparently, no other survivor saw the hero's face, and Gale, sensing a brilliant and inspirational news story, begins a search for the "Angel of Flight 104." The missing shoe turns up, and the station offers a million-dollar reward for the hero who has the other one. Bernie, however, is nabbed by the police for trying to sell Gale's credit cards and is thrown into jail. Meanwhile, Bubber comes forward with Bernie's shoe and claims the reward.

The station grooms the homeless man into a smooth, clean-cut hero, and Bubber, with his self-effacing words about the heroism inside everyone, is an instant media star. The public loves him, asking for autographs and applauding him in restaurants. Gale, chaperoning Bubber around town, begins to fall in love with him. Bubber, unaware that his scam would attract this much attention, struggles with his guilt. At the same time, Bernie, sprung from jail by his rookie attorney (Susie Cusack), tries to debunk Bubber, but no one believes that a bum such as Bernie could be a hero.

The police approach Gale with the news that they have recovered her purse and nabbed the culprit. Bubber witnesses this scene and panics. Gale, sniffing a possible twist in the story, takes cameraperson Chucky (Kevin J. O'Connor) to find Bernie. At Bernie's apartment, news comes that Bubber has walked out onto the ledge of Chicago's Drake Hotel and is preparing to jump. The media surrounds the Drake, and Bubber tells them that he will only talk to reporter Gale Gayley. On the way to the Drake, Gale berates Bernie for forcing Bubber onto the ledge. She believes that Bubber borrowed her purse while rescuing her, sold it to Bernie for some badly needed spare change, and then was blackmailed by Bernie after Bubber became a millionaire.

At the Drake, Bubber has written Gale a suicide note revealing the truth, but Gale tells him that she already has everything figured out. Bernie fights his way out onto the ledge with a plan that would help Bubber and himself. He persuades Bubber to continue masquerading as the hero but asks for a share of the million-dollar reward; Bernie knows that the American public would not accept him as a hero, but he needs money to get himself out of jail. The arrangement is agreed upon, but when the two crawl off the ledge, Bernie slips. Bubber pulls him to safety and is again hailed as a hero for saving Bernie. Later, Gale, recognizing the haggard face of her true hero, advises Bernie to tell his son just how heroic he really is. As the film comes to a close, Bernie tells Joey the truth and is promptly called on to rescue another life at the local zoo.

The essential story of *Hero* recalls the populist hero tales of Capra's *Meet John Doe* (1941) and Sturges' *Hail the Conquering Hero* (1944) and the mistaken sainthood narrative of William A. Wellman's *Nothing Sacred* (1937). Geena Davis' Gale Gayley is a contemporary version of both the Barbara Stanwyck and Fredric March roles in *Meet John Doe* and *Nothing Sacred*, respectively; all three, searching for a more humanistic and popular approach to news, discover inspirational scoops that lead them to ease their grip on their journalistic standards. Andy Garcia's John Bubber, like the Eddie Bracken character in *Hail the Conquering Hero*, struggles to stop the intense media attention, but the sheer momentum of the successful scam prevents him from coming clean. The twist that *Hero* adds to the genre is the introduction of and focus on a third character: the true hero unable to get the credit for his heroism. Hoffman's Bernie does not act like a hero, and with his perpetual five-o'clock shadow, his rumpled clothes, and his caustic personality, he certainly fails to fit the image. If a lowlife such as Bernie LaPlante could be prone to honorable acts, then surely everyone has the potential to be a hero. The concept of universal heroism is the special thread that makes the story of *Hero* so appealing.

Screenwriter David Webb Peoples, fresh from Clint Eastwood's revisionist Western *Unforgiven* (1992; reviewed in this volume), and British director Stephen Frears seem to be a perfect team to create a memorable piece of film out of a high-potential story. What results from this unique partnership, however, is a film that never quite catches a rhythm. The part of *Hero* that provides a cynical, satirical look at the state of television news collides with its more sentimental, melodramatic side. Peoples' script reaches too desperately for broad comedy; most of the slapstick humor dulls the sharp, witty edge that the writer creates when rendering the moral insanity of the contemporary news media. With dolls made in John Bubber's image and a station logo that includes a crashing plane, the film becomes increasingly difficult to take seriously; a tearjerker of an ending that teaches a lesson, however, demands that the viewer do that very thing.

Director Frears, whose three fine films *Prick Up Your Ears* (1987), *Dangerous Liaisons* (1988), and *The Grifters* are powerful and grim tales of human destruction, displays a lighter touch here and is considerably less successful. To his credit, Frears attempts something that other directors may have not had the gumption to try. In order to emphasize the film's Capraesque qualities, he forces into *Hero* a 1930's filmic sensibility. George and Ira Gershwin's "The Man I Love" drifts through the more romantic sequences. Spinning newspaper headlines are used to advance the plot, and the line of lowlifes that claim to be the "Angel of Flight 104″ bear a striking resemblance to the bums who claim to be John Doe in Capra's 1941 classic. These nostalgic touches, however, do little to strengthen the satire and serve more to disrupt the film than to pull it together.

Hero boasts lead performances by three Hollywood stars who have all proven their box-office strength. Dustin Hoffman has the hits *Rain Man* (1988) and *Hook* (1991) under his belt and is currently one of the few film actors who can simultaneously win awards and sell tickets. Andy Garcia, although not quite a certified box-office star, has a résumé that includes Francis Ford Coppola's most recent success, *The Godfather, Part III* (1990), and Brian De Palma's last hit, *The Untouchables* (1987). Geena Davis, slowly emerging as one of a mere handful of women who can push a film's box-office take past $50 million, is fresh from the controversial success of *Thelma and Louise* (1991) and the summer blockbuster *A League of Their Own* (1992; reviewed in this volume). The mix of three popular actors with eight Academy Award nominations and three Academy Awards among them certainly should have made the film a box-office hit, let alone one full of brilliant acting. The failure of *Hero* to generate much viewer interest or any critical kudos, however, certainly proves that nothing in Hollywood is a guarantee.

Hoffman's performance, an amalgamation of his roles as Ratso Rizzo in *Midnight Cowboy* (1969), Ted Kramer in *Kramer vs. Kramer* (1979), and Raymond Babbitt in *Rain Man* (1988), is impressive but a tad too familiar. Geena Davis, tall and striking, displays some of the same comedic panache that made Barbara Stanwyck a legend. Andy Garcia, all dark eyes and stubble, whispers his lines with his usual quiet magnetism. The look of the film is slick and seamless; the crucial plane crash sequence is as realistic a disaster as any seen before. Despite these highlights, however, the film produced little at the box office; after four weeks, *Hero*'s gross receipts totalled little more than sixteen million dollars. Perhaps the film's failure at the box office suggests that modern audiences, like Bernie LaPlante, are much too cynical to embrace the idea of universal heroism.

Greg Changnon

Reviews

Boxoffice. December, 1992, p. R-86.
Chicago Tribune. October 2, 1992, VII, p. 20.
The Christian Science Monitor. October 2, 1992, p. 12.
Entertainment Weekly. CXXXVIII, October 2, 1992, p. 38.
The Hollywood Reporter. CCCXXIII, September 22, 1992, p. 10.
Los Angeles Times. October 2, 1992, p. F1.

The New York Times. CXLII, October 2, 1992, p. B1.
The New Yorker. LXVIII, October 5, 1992, p. 161.
Time. CXL, October 12, 1992, p. 91.
Variety. CCXXXVII, September 22, 1992, p. 2.

HOFFA

Production: Edward R. Pressman, Danny DeVito, and Caldecot Chubb, in association with Jersey Films; released by Twentieth Century-Fox
Direction: Danny DeVito
Screenplay: David Mamet
Cinematography: Stephen H. Burum
Editing: Lynzee Klingman and Ronald Roose
Production design: Ida Random
Art direction: Gary Wissner
Set decoration: Brian Savegar
Set design: Charles Daboub, Jr., and Robert Fechtman
Casting: David Rubin and Debra Zane
Visual consulting: Harold Michelson
Sound: Thomas D. Causey
Makeup: Ve Neill
Special makeup effects: Greg Cannom
Costume design: Deborah L. Scott
Music: David Newman
MPAA rating: R
Running time: 140 minutes

Principal characters:

James R. Hoffa	Jack Nicholson
Bobby Ciaro	Danny DeVito
Carol D'Allesandro	Armand Assante
Frank Fitzsimmons	J. T. Walsh
Pete Connelly	John C. Reilly
Young kid	Frank Whaley
Robert F. Kennedy	Kevin Anderson
Red Bennett	John P. Ryan
Billy Flynn	Robert Prosky
Jo Hoffa	Natalija Nogulich
Hoffa's attorney	Nicholas Pryor
Ted Harmon	Paul Guilfoyle
Solly Stein	Cliff Gorman
Father Doyle	Dale Young

This biography of the controversial labor leader James R. Hoffa (Jack Nicholson) follows the life of this modern legend through four decades, from his rise to power and his struggles with the United States federal government to his prison term and supposed murder by union compatriots. *Hoffa* seems to be a careful documentary, but in reality it is more myth than fact. The film plays fast and loose with interpretations of what happened during Hoffa's career. In this version, Hoffa the corrupt union leader becomes Hoffa the working-class hero fighting for his fellow union members, and only incidentally receiving help from organized crime.

In fact, the real Jimmy Hoffa did make the working world better for his men. In the 1930's, truck drivers were paid to make a schedule, not to sleep. This demand meant grueling work and sometimes death. Wages were low, overtime was nonexistent, and firings were common. To his credit, Hoffa changed all that. His International Brotherhood of Teamsters brought higher wages, job security, benefits, and safer conditions—but all at a price.

Hoffa offers a world of thugs, struggle, and violence. This version of Hoffa presents a man who was a firebrand, who made speech after speech, who was faithful to his wife, and who was done in by his allies. Indeed, the first section of director Danny DeVito's dark look at the American business world consists almost entirely of Hoffa building his Teamsters Union through effective speech making.

To make a tighter narrative, many compromises were made. Indeed, characters were invented. For example, DeVito plays Hoffa's ever-present trusted ally, Bobby Ciaro. This composite character (with no reference in reality) represents Everyman, Hoffa's sounding board. The only person who played that role in Hoffa's life was his wife. The script by playwright David Mamet also skips over illegal union activities and focuses on Hoffa's tough character and his considerable organizing skills. Mamet fashions clever dialogue that, at times, is rich and fascinating, but the script is not consistent enough to make the almost two-and-a-half-hour film either riveting or spellbinding. The real Hoffa was far more interesting. His wife, for example, played a major role as adviser and helpmate in his rise to power, but Mamet hardly involves Jo Hoffa in the story. Hoffa's ties to the Mafia were far more complex than the simple allusions hinted at in *Hoffa*. The result is not a faithful documentary about a major player in the rise and fall of unionism in the United States. Instead, the film is far closer to the traditional, biased 1930's Hollywood biography.

Yet, even as a simplistic biography, *Hoffa* suffers. For example, no psychological motivations are provided. In the second half of the film, Hoffa infrequently deals with the Mafia, but only in the cause of the "working man." The ever-vexing questions of corrupt ethics are simply never raised. It seems that the filmmakers all came to admire their character of "Jimmy Hoffa" too much. Perhaps more distance would have given the film several dimensions, instead of only one.

Mamet's script was ready in 1989. The head of Twentieth Century-Fox, Joe Roth, then hired Danny DeVito as actor and director. Both then focused on signing Jack Nicholson to become Hoffa. Nicholson quickly agreed, but the actual production did not begin for two years. Nicholson's prior commitments and DeVito's own busy schedule necessitated a lengthy delay. That gave DeVito, Nicholson, and Mamet endless time to revise the initial script. By 1991, they had fashioned a conventional structural recrafting of a classic gangster film. The central character works with religious fervor, ascending to the acme of power—here the presidency of the union. Yet the means of his rise are corrupt. The audience knows that the gangster must die at the end of the film, as dictated by the formula.

It is the rise to power that proves fascinating. In *Hoffa*, the dramatic climax of this rise comes with Hoffa's confrontation with Attorney General Robert F. Kennedy (Kevin Anderson) in public hearings. Hoffa calls Kennedy a "punk," while Kennedy promises that he will convict the labor leader. In time, Kennedy does send Hoffa to jail; he is eventually pardoned by President Richard M. Nixon. Thereafter, however, Hoffa cannot hold office in the union and is betrayed by younger, more ambitious labor leaders. The film's ending is intriguing. Intercut with this classic rise-to-power tale are scenes of an aged Hoffa and Ciaro sitting at a roadside cafe waiting for unknown associates. With his boss waiting in a parked car, Bobby Ciaro chats with a young fellow (Frank Whaley), and the audience knows that their deaths are inevitable.

To its credit, *Hoffa* does convey convincingly the hard and dangerous world of truck driving of the 1930's. The film's production unit spent five weeks in Pittsburgh, Pennsylvania, at the Teamster Hall in the Troy Hill section of that labor city. Additional scenes were shot at the Pennsylvania State Correctional Institute and the campus of Carnegie-Mellon University, both found in the Pittsburgh area. The look of the film is gritty, and the filmmakers also make effective use of locations in Detroit and Chicago.

Yet it is Nicholson's performance that makes *Hoffa* special, as this Academy Award-winning actor pulls out all the stops to fashion a tough-talking Teamsters Union boss. Eyes glazed behind a carefully crafted, Hoffa-like nose, Nicholson suggests a larger-than-life, legendary figure. He is a pleasure to watch, in particular during the congressional hearings and at the Teamsters' 1957 Miami convention at which Hoffa was elected president of the union. Even though most filmgoers in 1992 chose to see Nicholson's performance in *A Few Good Men* (reviewed in this volume), which opened a few weeks before *Hoffa* and eclipsed it as the serious film of the Christmas season, *Hoffa* offers yet another glorious performance by one of Hollywood's great actors, one surprisingly not honored by the Oscar.

Douglas Gomery

Reviews

Chicago Tribune. December 25, 1992, VII, p. 15.
Entertainment Weekly. January 8, 1993, p. 32.
The Hollywood Reporter. December 21, 1992, p. 6.
Los Angeles Times. December 25, 1992, p. F1.
The New York Times. December 25, 1992, p. B1.
The New Yorker. LXVIII, December 28, 1992, p. 198.
Newsweek. CXX, December 28, 1992, p. 56.
Time. CXL, December 28, 1992, p. 64.
Variety. December 21, 1992, p. 4.
The Washington Post. December 25, 1992, p. B1.

HOME ALONE II
Lost in New York

Production: John Hughes; released by Twentieth Century-Fox
Direction: Chris Columbus
Screenplay: John Hughes; based on characters created by Hughes
Cinematography: Julio Macat
Editing: Raja Gosnell
Production design: Sandy Veneziano
Art direction: Gary Lee
Set decoration: Marvin March
Set design: Stephen Berger
Casting: Janet Hirshenson and Jane Jenkins
Visual effects supervision: Craig Barron
Sound: Jim Alexander
Costume design: Jay Hurley
Stunt coordination: Freddie Hice
Music: John Williams
MPAA rating: PG
Running time: 120 minutes

Principal characters:

Kevin McCallister .... Macaulay Culkin
Harry .... Joe Pesci
Marv .... Daniel Stern
Kate McCallister .... Catherine O'Hara
Peter McCallister .... John Heard
Buzz .... Devin Ratray
Megan .... Hillary Wolf
Linnie .... Maureen Elisabeth Shay
Jeff .... Michael C. Maronna
Uncle Frank .... Gary Bamman
Aunt Leslie .... Terrie Snell
Rod .... Jedidiah Cohen
Tracy .... Senta Moses
Sondra .... Daiana Campeanu
Fuller .... Kieran Culkin
Brooke .... Anna Slotky
Concierge .... Tim Curry
Pigeon lady .... Brenda Fricker
Mr. Duncan .... Eddie Bracken
Bellman .... Rob Schneider
Desk clerk .... Dana Ivey

In this sequel to what had become the most successful comedy in movie box-office history, and one of the highest earning films of 1992, the ever-resourceful Kevin (Macaulay Culkin) is stranded in Manhattan, finds a way to live in style, and in the end fends off assaults on his "home" (here an under-renovation brownstone belonging to his aunt and uncle). In the process, Kevin again bonds with an outsider, a Central Park homeless woman who feeds the pigeons.

Because Kevin is now in the big city—not home alone in the suburbs—the sequel's setup offers more possibilities of fun than the 1990 original. Reassuringly, everybody from the original returns, and Tim Curry, as the hotel concierge, is the new victim of Kevin's many schemes. Brenda Fricker adds a touch of class as the "pigeon lady." Yet *Home Alone II: Lost in New York* cannot avoid a curious contradiction. It is as if producer-writer John Hughes and director Chris Columbus could not decide between a sentimental image of lovable beggars in the Big Apple and a portrait of the gritty despair that really described New York City in 1992.

Home Alone II, with these additions and confusions, offers a safe sequel. The formula proved to be successful: In its first ten days, the film grossed in excess of seventy-five million dollars, generating revenues at twice the rate of the original. This fact astonished Hollywood, as children under twelve attended *Home Alone II* at discounted fees. Despite this strong opening, however, the film hardly impressed the critics. Newspaper pundits found little to praise in this synthesized version of the original comedy. Nevertheless, Twentieth Century-Fox's exit polls found that the filmgoing public liked the sequel better than the first outing.

In *Variety*'s review of the opinions of critics from New York City, Chicago, Los Angeles, and Washington, D.C., twice as many reviewers panned the film as praised it. Cynically, they viewed *Home Alone II* as a most obvious sequel. In particular, these critics were put off by the excesses in promotion for the film. There were the usual towels and T-shirts, but for *Home Alone II*, *The New York Times* ran a photograph of Macaulay Culkin somewhere in the newspaper and asked readers to find it, fill in a coupon, and send it in—all to win a weekend for four at the Plaza Hotel or a gift certificate for Bloomingdale's department store. This contest, long common with tabloids, was a first for this august newspaper.

Producer and writer Hughes surely played it safe. He assembled the same cast and crew, down to last gaffer and grip. Culkin reprises the cute central character, Joe Pesci and Daniel Stern play the bandits to excess, and Catherine O'Hara replays her role as Kevin's hysterical mother.

Director Columbus skillfully choreographs the blond, wide-eyed Culkin to emote the cutely precocious, all the while remaining vulnerable to childish whims such as running up whopping room service tabs at the Plaza Hotel. The action sequences are thoroughly well choreographed but mean-spirited. Harry (Pesci) has his hair set afire, and Kevin shoots Marv (Stern) in the face with a staple gun. Columbus freeze-frames the latter ghastly moment.

Hughes and Columbus have made *Home Alone II*, like its predecessor, a live-action cartoon, and one wonders if children can appreciate the difference. At the climax of the film, Kevin, a midget Marquis de Sade, unleashes a ten-minute blast of bashing in ever cruder and crueler fashion.

Home Alone II is far more than a simple comedy sequel that is twenty minutes longer than the original. The film still represents the ultimate child's fantasy about outsmarting adults. The grown-ups here, from the criminal cartoon pair to the not-to-be-believed parents, are so cartoonish that the film seems to be an attack on the adult audience. The filmmakers distract these viewers, however, with the nostalgic Christmas songs of rock-and-roll legend Darlene Love, country star Alan Jackson, and classicists Johnny Mathis, Andy Williams, and Bobby Helms.

Surely the plot complications of *Home Alone II* would not challenge any adult mind. Once again Kevin, provoked by his older brother, finds himself in the doghouse in the days before the annual family vacation. This time, Kevin accidently boards the wrong plane and ends up in New York City as his family flies off to Florida. Surprisingly, his parents (O'Hara and John Heard) do not realize that their son is missing until they reach the baggage-claim counter in the Miami airport.

Meanwhile, Harry and Marv, the inept thieves from the first film, have escaped from prison and caught a truck that arrives in New York City just when Kevin does. Using his father's credit cards and an envelope full of money, Kevin checks into the ritzy Plaza Hotel, where he finds more adults to outwit, in this case a snooty concierge (Curry) and the rest of the haughty staff of this fine hotel. Ironically, Kevin's family, left without money, must check into a sleazy hotel in Florida.

Ultimately, however, the sequel boils down to Kevin versus the two escaped thieves, with the ingenious child setting traps at his aunt and uncle's reconstructed Manhattan brownstone—the aunt and uncle naturally being out of town for the holidays. Kevin eventually thwarts the criminal duo. It is not surprising that, at the end of the film, he is "rescued" by his family.

At its best, *Home Alone II* does present a simple travelogue in which the true cinematic stars are familiar New York City landmarks—Central Park, the World Trade Center, Rockefeller Center, Radio City Music Hall, and the Plaza Hotel. The motion picture offers no filmic challenge, only a setup for future sequels and future profits for Twentieth Century-Fox, John Hughes, and Chris Columbus.

Douglas Gomery

Reviews

Chicago Tribune. November 20, 1992, VII, p. 39.
The Christian Science Monitor. December 11, 1992, p. 12.
Entertainment Weekly. November 27, 1992, p. 54.
The Hollywood Reporter. November 16, 1992, p. 5.
Los Angeles Times. November 20, 1992, p. F1.
The New York Times. November 20, 1992, p. B1.

The New Yorker. LXVIII, November 30, 1992, p. 164.
Time. CXL, November 30, 1992, p. 75.
Variety. November 16, 1992, p. 2.
The Washington Post. November 20, 1992, p. C1.

HONEY, I BLEW UP THE KID

Production: Dawn Steel and Edward S. Feldman for Walt Disney Pictures, in association with Touchwood Pacific Partners I; released by Buena Vista
Direction: Randal Kleiser
Screenplay: Thom Eberhardt, Peter Elbling, and Garry Goodrow; based on a story by Goodrow and on characters created by Stuart Gordon, Brian Yuzna, and Ed Naha
Cinematography: John Hora
Editing: Michael A. Stevenson
Production design: Leslie Dilley
Art direction: Ed Verreaux
Set decoration: Dorree Cooper
Set design: Antoinette J. Gordon
Casting: Renee Rousselot
Visual effects supervision: Harrison Ellenshaw
Visual effects production: Thomas G. Smith
Visual effects coordination: Michael Muscal
Mechanical effects design/coordination: Peter M. Chesney
Sound: Roger Pietschmann
Special makeup effects: Kevin Yagher
Costume design: Tom Bronson
Stunt coordination: Bobby J. Foxworth
Music: Bruce Broughton
MPAA rating: PG
Running time: 89 minutes

Principal characters:

Wayne Szalinski .... Rick Moranis
Diane Szalinski .... Marcia Strassman
Nick Szalinski .... Robert Oliveri
Clifford Sterling .... Lloyd Bridges
Adam Szalinski .... Joshua Shalikar
Daniel Shalikar
Charles Hendrickson .... John Shea
Mandy Park .... Keri Russell
Marshall Brooks .... Ron Canada
Amy Szalinski .... Amy O'Neill
Smitty .... Ken Tobin
Captain Ed Myerson .... Michael Milhoan
Terence Wheeler .... Gregory Sierra
Constance Winters .... Leslie Neale

When a studio has a hit as big as 1989's *Honey, I Shrunk the Kids*, it is expected that there will be a sequel. By the summer of 1992, absent-minded inventor and lovable father Wayne Szalinski (Rick Moranis) was back. This time, however, Wayne and his wife, Diane (Marcia Strassman), have moved to Vista Del Mar, an upscale suburb of Las Vegas, Nevada. Their daughter, Amy (Amy O'Neill), has been sent to college, and son Nick (Robert Oliveri) has grown into that awkward stage where his interest in girls is threatened by his perceived appearance as a nebbishy nerd, exactly like his father. The family's new addition is two-and-a-half-year-old baby Adam (Daniel and Joshua Shalikar).

Also changed is that Wayne no longer tinkers with his inventions in his attic. He has been hired by Sterling Labs, a corporation more interested in his invention than in the inventor. Its day-to-day operations are run by the ruthless Charles Hendrickson (John Shea), who would like to rid himself of Wayne and Clifford Sterling (Lloyd Bridges) in order to run the company his way.

Wayne is experimenting with his laser ray, which shrank the kids in the earlier film, to see if it can be used to make things much larger. Everything keeps exploding, however, until Wayne discovers the solution. Because Hendrickson is virtually keeping Wayne from his own invention, Wayne must sneak into the laboratory on a weekend while he is babysitting Adam and Nick in order to test his new theory. Wayne and Nick try to manipulate the computer but are thwarted by security codes that no one has ever given to Wayne. Not one to be defeated so easily, Wayne jury-rigs the laser with a coke bottle and proceeds to experiment on Adam's favorite stuffed animal, Big Bunny.

As the switches are thrown, Adam runs for Big Bunny and both are zapped, unbeknownst to Wayne and Nick. (Unlike the first film, the effects are not immediately apparent.) They are soon discovered by a security guard, and Wayne, Nick, and a slightly larger Adam escape. At home, Adam begins to grow larger every time he is near an electrical current, such as a microwave oven or a television set. He has soon overgrown his own house and begins to rampage the neighborhood, eventually escaping into the desert where a high-tension wire leaves him 112 feet tall. Adam heads to Las Vegas, where the electromagnetic flux generated by the neon signs is assured to make him even larger.

The problem becomes how to capture Adam. Hendrickson, sensing a guinea pig on which to experiment, wants to shoot him with a tranquilizer shell from a helicopter. Wayne suggests using Big Bunny, which is now as large as Adam, and luring him out of town with the bells from an ice cream truck. Eventually, Wayne must use his own invention to shrink Adam back to his normal size, but not before thwarting the evil Hendrickson and "blowing up" another member of his household.

Honey, I Blew Up the Kid is an evenly paced film with moments of brightness, but it fails to deliver the wit, the sparkle, or even the surprise of the first film. Rick Moranis, still endearing as the nice but nerdy Wayne, manages to do a credible job as the befuddled father. He works well with his pint-size stars, the Shalikar brothers, using his own improvisational skills to enhance a script that is dependent on these toddlers. Unfortunately, the script may be the film's main problem. It is strictly lightweight and often relies on fitting the story to the baby's action instead of the virtual impossibility of trying to have a baby follow the script.

Randal Kleiser, who made his directorial debut in 1978 with *Grease*, has an eye for films that appeal to children. Also in his résumé are *Flight of the Navigator* (1986), *Big Top Pee-Wee* (1988), and *White Fang* (1991). *Honey, I Blew Up the Kid* is such a simple film, however, that it appeals only to very small children. The sequel has neither the suspense nor the charm of its predecessor: It was easier for a viewer to worry about finding shrunken children lost in the hostile environment of a backyard, apprehension that is missing from the second film. A 112-foot baby never really seems to be in any jeopardy, not even from the cardboard villain Hendrickson. Moreover, while clever means had to be employed to find the ant-sized children of the first film, clumsy means are used to corral the monster Adam. Also sadly missing from the second film are the humor and unintentional sarcasm provided by next-door neighbor "Big" Russ Thompson (Matt Frewer) in *Honey, I Shrunk the Kids*.

The film relies heavily on special effects that are adequate but not impressive by contemporary standards. It did, however, provide one family film for the summer of 1992, which was welcome news to those beleaguered parents who were upset with the violence in *Batman Returns* (reviewed in this volume). As is typical for a Disney film, no matter how deep the trouble the Szalinski family gets into, it will always pull together to find a solution. There is nothing in the film to offend anyone.

The idea of a two-year-old running amok in Las Vegas like a cranky but benign Godzilla is an amusing idea, but this interesting premise is underutilized by the script. Perhaps part of the problem is that it is very difficult for a two-year-old to comment on his situation. As far as Adam is concerned, growing to 112 feet must be all in a day's growing up: He never seems to react in any way to what is happening to him.

Honey, I Blew Up the Kid had an impressive $11.5 million in box-office grosses in its first weekend, but it was not the hit that its prequel was. At the film's release, however, it was rumored that the moguls at Disney were already working on ideas for a third installment in the adventures of the Szalinski family.

As with *Honey, I Shrunk the Kids*, this film is also preceded by a cartoon. This time, however, it does not feature the fast-paced, wacky Roger Rabbit of "Tummy Trouble." Instead, it is a partially computer-generated cartoon called "Off His Rockers" about a young boy who forsakes his old-fashioned rocking horse for video games. It took seventy-three artists and technicians two years to combine story and technology for this cartoon, with the young boy being animated in traditional style while the horse and the room are the results of computer graphics. The cartoon is very slow, however, and will probably only appeal to animation buffs and the young children who will be amused by the feature that follows it.

Beverley Bare Buehrer

Reviews

Boxoffice. October, 1992, p. R-70.
Chicago Tribune. July 17, 1992, VII, p. 37.
Entertainment Weekly. July 24, 1992, p. 68.
The Hollywood Reporter. July 17, 1992, p. 10.
Los Angeles Times. July 17, 1992, p. F10.
The New York Times. July 17, 1992, p. B1.
Newsweek. July 27, 1992, p. 42.
Time. CXL, July 27, 1992, p. 69.
Variety. July 17, 1992, p. 2.
The Washington Post. July 17, 1992, p. C7.

HONEYMOON IN VEGAS

Production: Mike Lobell for Castle Rock Entertainment, in association with New Line Cinema; released by Columbia Pictures
Direction: Andrew Bergman
Screenplay: Andrew Bergman
Cinematography: William A. Fraker
Editing: Barry Malkin
Production design: William A. Elliott
Art direction: John Warnke
Set decoration: Linda De Scenna
Casting: Michael Fenton and Valorie Massalas
Sound: David MacMillan, Tom Fleischman, Steve Maslow, and Robert Beemer
Costume design: Julie Weiss
Stunt coordination: Rick Barker
Music: David Newman
MPAA rating: PG-13
Running time: 95 minutes

Principal characters:

Tommy Korman	James Caan
Jack Singer	Nicholas Cage
Betsy Nolan/Donna	Sarah Jessica Parker
Mahi	Pat Morita
Johnny Sandwich	Johnny Williams
Sally Molars	John Capodice
Sidney Tomashefsky	Robert Costanzo
Bea Singer	Anne Bancroft
Chief Orman	Peter Boyle
Roy	Burton Gilliam
Sid Feder	Jerry Tarkanian

From the oddball lunacy of *Wayne's World* (1992; reviewed in this volume), in which two average teenagers revel in their geeky ordinariness, to Hollywood's send-up of itself in *The Player* (1992; reviewed in this volume), to the morose timing of Woody Allen's art-imitating-life film *Husbands and Wives* (1992; reviewed in this volume), mainstream American film in 1992 seemed almost to drip with self-reflexive irony. There seemed to be no better time for *Honeymoon in Vegas*, which parodies modern American popular culture and serves as a comic self-reflexive vision of what the country has become. In the simplest terms, *Honeymoon in Vegas* is a love story. Looked at more closely, however, the film is a shrewdly crafted farce that has no limitations and knows no shame. *Honeymoon in Vegas* centers its comedy in the modern American psyche's obsessions and fears.

Honeymoon in Vegas opens with a simple enough premise. Jack Singer (Nicholas Cage) is forced to make a promise to his dying mother (Anne Bancroft) that he will never marry. Five years later, the story finds Jack in New York City, self-employed as a private investigator and happily but noncommittedly involved with his girlfriend, Betsy (Sarah Jessica Parker). He is perfectly content in his life, with a beautiful and loving girlfriend, a steady income, and a reliable bookie who satisfies his penchant for gambling. There is only one problem: Betsy wants to get married. Having waited patiently for five years in the hopes that Jack will eventually overcome his crippling fear of marriage, Betsy realizes that Jack is no closer to making a commitment now than he was when he met her, so she confronts him with an ultimatum. Up against the wall, Jack agrees. Fully committed, for the moment, Jack decides to get married as soon as possible, before he changes his mind. They head for Las Vegas.

The otherwise bland story line of *Honeymoon in Vegas* derives its central charm from Jack's well-drawn character. Jack is nearly suffocated by more than just the modern American male's fear of commitment: He has a curious Oedipus complex that reaches out from beyond the grave and haunts him late into his adulthood. Director Andrew Bergman captures the psychological trauma in which Jack navigates throughout the course of the story, and Cage plays him with the perfect paranoid edge. This is no average romantic Hollywood hero, which is why Nicholas Cage is the perfect choice for Jack. Because Cage was known for his offbeat character portrayals in such films as *Valley Girl* (1983), *Raising Arizona* (1987), *Moonstruck* (1987), and *Wild at Heart* (1990), he was considered a risk to play a romantic lead such as Jack Singer. Yet Cage possesses a strange charisma that allows him to play a range of characters, while also being able to play an average Joe—an Everyman—with great success. Jack is likable but not wholly sympathetic, not too handsome and not too smart. Cage's varied performance earned for him a Golden Globe nomination for best actor (in a comedy or musical).

Once in Las Vegas, Jack goes all out and books the "Ali Baba suite" in Bally's Hotel and Casino. While Jack and Betsy are checking into the hotel, the other key player in the story, Tommy Korman (James Caan), is introduced. Korman is a legendary gangster who is feared and revered by everyone in the gambling world. A quirky yet powerful presence, Tommy walks the casino floor with a strut, like an alleycat protecting its turf. Yet, at the same time, Tommy has a sensitive side. He bemoans the hazards of lying in the sun as he walks by the pool in the blazing afternoon heat, as his wife, Donna, recently died of skin cancer, a victim of too many rays. Tommy's soft spot and his ego collide as he catches a glimpse of Betsy as she and Jack check into the hotel. Betsy is a dead ringer for Tommy's dead wife, and he vows then and there to have her for himself. He sets up a poker game and has Jack invited. Jack, a gambling addict, takes the bait as he joins the game while Betsy relaxes by the pool. Jack has promised that they will get married after the game.

It is at this point in the story that *Honeymoon in Vegas* begins to hit its stride as an offbeat but charming comedy. While Betsy and Jack are at Bally's, a convention of Elvis Presley impersonators is staying at the hotel. Therefore, throughout the course of the film there is a constant stream of assorted "Elvises" in the background, as well as Elvis tunes floating on the soundtrack, oftentimes in comic timing with the action. The film utilizes the setting of Las Vegas to the utmost as it serves as the embodiment of excess in every imaginable way, a perfect setting for the beginning of the bizarre string of events that takes place in Jack Singer's life.

In the poker game, Tommy plays Jack like a fiddle, and Jack loses $65,000 to him. Devastated and panicked, Jack frantically tries to figure out how to escape the situation alive. Perfectly aware that he is not in an enviable position, owing $65,000 to a famous gangster, Jack pleads with Tommy for some way to minimize the pain. Tommy makes Jack an offer that he cannot refuse, simply because it is an offer that he cannot refuse. Tommy offers to erase the debt if he can have Betsy's company for the weekend. Stunned, Jack weighs his options and realizes that he does not have any. Betsy has no choice but to consent to the agreement, realizing that $65,000 is a debt too large for either of them to pay. After meeting Tommy for drinks, Betsy consents to Tommy's offer of accompanying him to Hawaii for the rest of the weekend. Still furious over the situation in which Jack put her, she decides to get back at him by sitting back and enjoying the royal treatment that Tommy provides. After all, he is the perfect gentleman.

As Betsy and Tommy relax and play in and around Tommy's gorgeous hideaway palace on Kauai, Jack fumes in New York, visualizing the things that Betsy and Tommy may be doing in Hawaii. Unable to stand it and angry at himself, Jack decides to take things into his own hands and retrieve Betsy, debt and all. As Tommy finds out that Jack is on his way to Kauai, he orders his men to stall him. Tommy proposes marriage to Betsy after a whirlwind few days of sunset strolls and skin diving, while Jack finds himself on a wild goose chase around Kauai led by a loony cabbie, Mahi (Pat Morita), who is on Tommy's payroll.

Although Tommy offers Betsy a gargantuan diamond engagement ring, she is reluctant to say yes. She still loves Jack, after all, despite his faults. Sensing that he will not be able to coax an agreement from Betsy, Tommy lies and tells her that Jack put her up in the game and that he only lost $3,000, not $65,000. Angry and confused, Betsy agrees to marry Tommy, desperate to get on with her life and feeling betrayed by Jack. Meanwhile, Tommy has Jack thrown in jail, and as Jack is being booked, Tommy and Betsy fly off to—where else—Las Vegas to say their vows. Betsy, still reluctant but heartbroken, desperately tries to contact Jack in New York, unaware that Jack is trying everything he can to get to her. Unable to reach him, Betsy becomes more and more doubtful of her decision to marry Tommy.

Jack, meanwhile, encounters more obstacles set by Tommy and cannot book a flight to Las Vegas. He finally gets a ride with a group of Elvis impersonators who happen to be flying to Las Vegas that night. Grateful for the ride and in a hurry, Jack fails to notice that he has hitched a ride with skydivers and that the only way he will get to Las Vegas is with a parachute on his back. Meanwhile, down at Bally's, Betsy tells Tommy that she is not ready to marry him yet; it is too soon. Tommy, sensing that he is losing control of the situation, offers Betsy a half million dollars if she will marry him immediately. She refuses, so Tommy offers a million. When she refuses again, he threatens her. Finally realizing the gangster that Tommy is, Betsy escapes into the lobby crowd and follows the flow outside. The Flying Elvises are about to land, Jack included. Jack makes the jump and successfully lands at Bally's just in time to take Betsy in his arms and whisk her off to the nearest wedding chapel.

Although *Honeymoon in Vegas*, which garnered a Golden Globe nomination for best picture (comedy or musical), is a straight-out comedy, it is a significant reflection of American culture. The locations of New York City, Hawaii, and Las Vegas represent three particular extremes of what the United States has to offer—culture and attitude included. The settings often have more to do with the story than the dialogue, as the seductive quality of Hawaii and the intoxicating gambling atmosphere of Las Vegas bring out innate instincts in human beings. There are also the obvious obsessions played out within the characters: Jack's fear of fidelity and obsessive attachment to gambling and his mother, Tommy's obsession with his dead wife and control, and Betsy's desire to avenge five years of patience. Everything in *Honeymoon in Vegas* is done to excess, but the film is a subtle yet powerful comment on a country in which one could watch this film and easily say, "only in America."

Catherine R. Springer

Reviews

Chicago Tribune. August 28, 1992, VII, p. 32.
Entertainment Weekly. August 28, 1992, p. 42.
The Hollywood Reporter. August 20, 1992, p. 6.
Los Angeles Times. August 28, 1992, p. F1.
The New York Times. August 28, 1992, p. B1.
Newsweek. CXX, August 31, 1992, p. 68.
Rolling Stone. September 17, 1992, p. 102.
Time. CXL, September 14, 1992, p. 77.
Variety. August 20, 1992, p. 2.
The Washington Post. August 28, 1992, p. C1.

HOUSESITTER

Production: Brian Grazer for Imagine Films Entertainment; released by Universal Pictures
Direction: Frank Oz
Screenplay: Mark Stein; based on a story by Stein and Brian Grazer
Cinematography: John A. Alonzo
Editing: John Jympson
Production design: Ida Random
Art direction: Jack Blackman and Jeff Sage
Set design: Philip Messina
Set decoration: Tracey A. Doyle
Casting: John Lyons
Sound: Martin Raymond Bolger
Costume design: Betsy Cox
Music: Miles Goodman
MPAA rating: PG
Running time: 100 minutes

Principal characters:

Newton Davis .... Steve Martin
Gwen .... Goldie Hawn
Becky .... Dana Delany
Edna Davis .... Julie Harris
George Davis .... Donald Moffat
Marty .... Peter MacNicol
Ralph .... Richard B. Shull
Mary .... Laurel Cronin
Moseby .... Roy Cooper
Reverend Lipton .... Christopher Durang

New England architect Newton Davis (Steve Martin) has been in love with Becky (Dana Delany) since the ninth grade. He secretly has designed and built his dream house, in which he hopes they will live happily ever after. Unfortunately, when he takes her to see it, complete with a giant red ribbon and bow, and to propose to her, Becky refuses.

Three months later, a very depressed Davis is working in a lackluster job for a large, bland Boston architectural company. His dream house, in his hometown of Dobbs Mill, sits vacant, the red ribbons tattering in the wind. Then, one day at a business party at the Budapest restaurant, Davis makes a play for a Hungarian waitress who seems to understand no English. Unknown to him, however, this is only the first deception that the waitress, Gwen (Goldie Hawn), will perpetrate on the staid and heartbroken Newton. The two spend the night together, but Davis slips away early the next morning. The free-spirited Gwen, armed with the cocktail napkin on which Davis drunkenly drew his dream house, takes the bus to Dobbs Mill and proceeds to move into Davis' house and, indirectly, into his life.

Needing provisions, Gwen buys groceries at the local store not with money but with an active imagination and Davis' credit account. She weaves a story of matrimony that soon reaches Davis' parents, Edna (Julie Harris) and George (Donald Moffat). The Davises are initially surprised and then delighted that their son has finally settled down. They immediately take to the chameleon-like Gwen, who spins any story needed to be liked by those she needs to con. It is not long before Gwen's deception is discovered by Davis. His first reaction is to expose her hoax, but he quickly discovers that an unforeseen result of their phony marriage is that his beloved Becky has become somewhat jealous and now finds Davis more attractive than she had thought. Davis agrees to go along with Gwen's deceit in exchange for her help in winning Becky's affections.

Soon, Davis, who initially could not even tell a white lie to curry favor with his boss, is corroborating Gwen's lies and even compounding them. While Gwen is playing her part, she does more for Davis than spark Becky's interest in the man she had spurned: She also manages to repair the strained relations between Newton and his parents and even obtains a long-awaited promotion for him by winning over his boss with the coincidence of how her "father" had served on the U.S.S. *Pennsylvania* during World War II—the same ship on which Davis' boss served.

Their fantasies about their problems as newlyweds grow and entwine them until the lines between invention and actuality blur. When Newton's parents want to have a reception for them, they suddenly find themselves having to pick a china pattern. When they actually agree on one—"That's us!"—it is as if they really were a couple. No one is more surprised than Davis. Perhaps he has discovered that Gwen's fabrications are much more interesting than his normal life, and he likes it.

It will come as no surprise to anyone that by the end of the film, Davis has forgotten about Becky and comes close to losing Gwen, the woman he really wants to marry. While the ending may be predictable, the actors make the journey to it worthwhile; a host of secondary characters are played to perfection by an able cast. *Housesitter* obviously is out to revive the screwball comedy (shades of Cary Grant and Irene Dunne in 1940's *My Favorite Wife*) and has many of its predictable plot devices: two women who are opposites (the eccentric but lovable Gwen versus the preppie, conservative Becky), a man who would seem destined to love one but ends up loving the other, lies that compound themselves until they must be made real (Gwen has to produce that phony veteran father for Davis' boss), and all of this seasoned with a little bit of sophisticated slapstick.

Perhaps no contemporary actor can provide that final element as well as Martin. He is the master of reactions (falling over sofas while people's backs are turned and ending upright as if nothing had happened when they turn around). He provides an off-beat combination of handsome leading man and comic physical responses to situations that conjures up Cary Grant at his best. He can just as effortlessly set up and deliver punch lines with expert timing. On top of these comedic skills, Martin manages to bring a high level of endearment to his characters and provides someone with whom audiences can identify easily.

While some of the more elaborate and entertaining fabrications provide the best moments in the film, it is their delivery by Martin and Hawn that makes them memorable. Although there may be a few too many close-ups of her posterior, Hawn's kookiness helps her to weave great yarns. The best of these is arguably her recounting to Becky of how she and Davis met in a hospital and were married while bandages were being unwrapped from her face—which Davis had never seen. Yet perhaps Hawn is a bit too adorable for the character. She does not really seem devious enough to be someone for whom lying and conning has become a life-style. Her innate lovableness provides an ambiguity of character that is perplexing. Perhaps Gwen is a true con woman; perhaps she is a scorned lover. She may be mentally unstable, fabricating lies because she cannot help it. Perhaps she has been in love with Davis from the beginning.

In the end it may not matter. Director and former Muppeteer Frank Oz (who also directed Martin in 1988'S *Dirty Rotten Scoundrels*) has created a film that is more ingratiating than intense and certainly more slight than substantive, but *Housesitter* is nevertheless a pleasant and successful romantic comedy.

Beverley Bare Buehrer

Reviews

Boxoffice. July, 1992, p. R-55.
Chicago Tribune. June 12, 1992, VII, p. 41.
Entertainment Weekly. June 12, 1992, p. 36.
The Hollywood Reporter. June 5, 1992, p. 9.
Los Angeles Times. June 12, 1992, p. F1.
The New York Times. June 12, 1992, p. B3.
The New Yorker. LXVIII, June 29, 1992, p. 73.
Newsweek. CXIX, June 15, 1992, p. 53.
Time. CXXXIX, June 22, 1992, p. 73.
Variety. June 5, 1992, p. 2.

HOWARDS END

Origin: Great Britain
Released: 1992
Released in U.S.: 1992
Production: Ismail Merchant for Merchant Ivory Productions, in association with Nippon Film Development Finance and Film Four International; released by Sony Pictures Classics
Direction: James Ivory
Screenplay: Ruth Prawer Jhabvala (AA); based on the novel by E. M. Forster
Cinematography: Tony Pierce-Roberts
Editing: Andrew Marcus
Production design: Luciana Arrighi (AA)
Art direction: John Ralph
Set decoration: Ian Whittaker (AA)
Casting: Celestia Fox
Sound: Mike Shoring
Costume design: Jenny Beavan and John Bright
Music: Richard Robbins
MPAA rating: PG
Running time: 140 minutes

Principal characters:

Henry Wilcox .... Anthony Hopkins
Ruth Wilcox .... Vanessa Redgrave
Margaret Schlegel .... Emma Thompson (AA)
Helen Schlegel .... Helena Bonham Carter
Charles Wilcox .... James Wilby
Leonard Bast .... Sam West
Jacky Bast .... Nicola Duffett
Evie Wilcox .... Jemma Redgrave
Aunt Juley .... Prunella Scales
Dolly Wilcox .... Susan Lindeman
Tibby Schlegel .... Adrian Ross Magenty
Miss Avery .... Barbara Hicks
Paul Wilcox .... Joseph Bennett
Annie .... Jo Kendall
Percy Cahill .... Mark Payton
Music lecturer .... Simon Callow

Howards End is the fifth of E. M. Forster's six novels to be brought to the screen. *A Room with a View* (1986) was lauded as a masterpiece from the skillful hands of director James Ivory and producer Ismail Merchant, as was *Maurice* (1987).

Howards End completes a trio of films that stand as some of the finest adaptations in cinematic work. Much of this success rests on the screenplays of Ruth Prawer Jhabvala. As a writer, Jhabvala has the ability to draw on the most important elements of the story, giving the entire film an air of authenticity. This collaboration between writer, producer, and director revealed itself for the first time in the making of *Shakespeare Wallah* (1965). Their subsequent films include *The Europeans* (1979), *Heat and Dust* (1982), and *The Bostonians* (1984). Yet it was not until *A Room with a View* was made that the Ivory/Merchant team became a recognizable force in filmmaking.

Howards End deals with the problems facing all levels of English society at the beginning of the twentieth century. Forster had little time for the power struggle that was so apparent during his lifetime. As a journalist who once wrote for *The Independent Review*, his views were liberal, with a strong anti-imperialist stance. Even so, *Howards End* manages to remain human and not become lost in class bickering.

Howards End is an English country house that has no particularly outstanding feature other than being a safe haven for Ruth Wilcox (Vanessa Redgrave) and her family. Helen Schlegel (Helena Bonham Carter) has been invited down from London for the weekend. A misunderstanding between herself and her companion, Paul Wilcox (Joseph Bennett) results in Helen returning to London and Paul deciding to travel to India. This occasion should have been the last time that the Schlegel and Wilcox families would ever meet. By chance, however, Paul's brother, Charles, moves with his new bride into an apartment directly across from the Schlegel residence.

Before long, Helen's sister, Margaret Schlegel (Emma Thompson), and Ruth have become companions. Ruth is not in good health, which prompts Margaret to suggest that they go Christmas shopping together. A warm friendship results from their continual meetings. Ruth desperately wants Margaret to come and see Howards End. On the very afternoon that the two companions are ready to board the train to the country, her husband, Henry Wilcox (Anthony Hopkins), meets them coincidentally on the platform. The trip is postponed. Ruth's health deteriorates, and she dies quite soon after an operation. Yet, before Ruth dies, she wills Howards End over to Margaret. The family is outraged and burns the questionable, pencil-written request without telling Margaret.

While at a concert one evening, Helen accidentally picks up an umbrella belonging to a lowly clerk named Leonard Bast (Sam West). This chance encounter causes the Schlegel sisters to take an active interest in the career of Leonard. Through a number of chance meetings and arranged dinner dates, Henry Wilcox unexpectedly proposes marriage to Margaret. When Helen approaches Henry to consider Leonard for a position in his company, Henry politely refuses to help. On hearing where Leonard works, he suggests that they tell their friend that this particular company is going to collapse and that Leonard should seek alternative employment.

Henry and Margaret continue to make arrangements for their wedding. Margaret's London apartment is soon to be pulled down, so she makes arrangements to store her furniture at Howards End. Helen cares little for Henry and blames him for the fact that Leonard is no longer employed. During a family wedding, Helen brings Leonard and his wife, Jacky (Nicola Duffett), to confront Henry. The Basts are now destitute, and Helen wants her sister's help in persuading Henry to give Leonard a job. While strolling in the garden, Jacky recognizes Henry. Shocked at seeing his former mistress, Henry runs away, shouting to Margaret that their engagement is off.

Once the wedding guests have gone, Henry explains to Margaret that he had met Jacky in Cyprus when she was only sixteen. At about the same time, Helen is also told of how Leonard married Jacky because she seemed so destitute. Helen's affections for Leonard express themselves in her giving him a kiss while boating on the nearby river.

Outraged with both her sister and Henry, Helen leaves for a stay on the Continent. Margaret is naturally anxious about Helen's state of mind. Through a series of telegrams, Helen arranges to pick up some books from Howards End. When the two sisters next meet, Helen is pregnant. The child belongs to Leonard Bast, whom she has not seen since their boating trip. Helen remains one further night at the house and prepares to leave in the morning, but Leonard comes down from London to see her. When Leonard enters the house, Charles Wilcox, outraged that Leonard should show his face to Helen again, begins to beat him about his body with an old army sword. In the struggle, a large heavy bookcase falls on Leonard, killing him instantly. The resulting inquest charges Charles with manslaughter.

The trauma is too much for Margaret, and she wishes to break off her engagement. Henry sits down on the lawn and weeps, asking for her help. Gathered together in the sitting room, the Wilcox family and Margaret discuss Henry's will. Howards End will belong to Margaret and to her nephew after her.

In many ways, *Howards End* begins where *A Room with a View* ends. For example, there are close similarities between Lucy Honeychurch and Helen Schlegel. In *A Room with a View*, Lucy is kissed by George Emerson—a kiss that opens up Lucy's deeper feelings. This one incident drives the entire story to a happy ending. Helen Schlegel receives a kiss from Paul Wilcox under a tree at Howards End and thinks that they will marry soon. Unfortunately, Helen has misunderstood Paul's advances. This incident propels the story to a very different ending.

Howards End takes a long, ponderous look at how English society molds the way people speak, think, and feel about one another. Forster explores these relationships using all three levels of English society. The Wilcox family stands for those who are upper class and who have gained the most from the British Empire. Henry Wilcox is a man with very little feeling or compassion. The Schlegel sisters, while of German descent, live the life of the middle-class intelligentsia. Margaret and Helen show compassion toward their fellow creatures. Leonard and Jacky Bast represent the downtrodden working class, rising only when those above them allow any such progress. To live in such a culture becomes restrictive and desperate.

From this background comes the opportunity to realize life through romance and meaningful relationships. Margaret and Ruth are the first to discover companionship. In fact, every character in Howards End is looking for some kind of meaningful relationship, and only upbringing, breeding, and good manners keep each of them from fully expressing their deepest emotions. Forster strove to show that men and women could transcend their class and find true happiness with another person.

Characterization is one of the fundamental bases of Forster's work. To adapt one of his stories successfully requires that the acting be of a similar caliber. Emma Thompson brings a wonderful vivaciousness to the part of Margaret Schlegel. She seems to be a continual chatterbox, but beneath the laughter and joy, Thompson gives Margaret a warmth and feeling of dependability. This fine portrayal of an Edwardian spinster earned for Thompson an Academy Award for best actress. Helena Bonham Carter manages to reflect the same simplicity that she did as Lucy Honeychurch but to add more fire to Helen. As sisters, they contrast very well with the stiff-collared family of the Wilcoxes and the quiet desperation of the Basts.

What is remarkable about *Howards End* is the way in which the film moves incrementally toward its conclusion. This is not a story in which satisfaction comes from an elaborately worked out ending, as in a Hitchcock thriller. Rather, the opposite takes place. Fate plays its hand time and time again, and it is how each person responds to life at the moment that gives *Howards End* a classic quality. Following the fortunes of three families, and how each individual within these families has a direct or indirect bearing on the film's outcome, builds a relationship between the fictional world and the viewer. Forster's characters take on the same qualities in the film as they do in the novel, which results in one of the closest approximations possible of experiencing one medium (literature) expressed in another medium (film).

Richard G. Cormack

Reviews

Boxoffice. May, 1992, p. R-40.
Chicago Tribune. May 1, 1992, VII, p. 39.
The Christian Science Monitor. March 20, 1992, p. 12.
The Hollywood Reporter. March 13, 1992, p. 9.
Los Angeles Times. April 15, 1992, p. F1.
The New Republic. March 23, 1992, p. 26.
The New York Times. March 13, 1992, p. B1.
The New Yorker. May 4, 1992, p. 74.
Time. CXXXIX, March 16, 1992, p. 72.
Variety. February 24, 1992, p. 4.

HUSBANDS AND WIVES

Production: Robert Greenhut for Jack Rollins and Charles H. Joffe; released by TriStar Pictures
Direction: Woody Allen
Screenplay: Woody Allen
Cinematography: Carlo Di Palma
Editing: Susan E. Morse
Production design: Santo Loquasto
Art direction: Speed Hopkins
Set decoration: Susan Bode
Casting: Juliet Taylor
Sound: James Sabat
Makeup: Fern Buchner
Costume design: Jeffrey Kurland
MPAA rating: R
Running time: 107 minutes

Principal characters:

Gabe Roth	Woody Allen
Judy Roth	Mia Farrow
Sally	Judy Davis
Jack	Sydney Pollack
Rain	Juliette Lewis
Michael	Liam Neeson
Sam	Lysette Anthony
Rain's mother	Blythe Danner
Rain's father	Brian McConnachie
Interviewer/narrator	Jeffrey Kurland

The standard Woody Allen film is accompanied by minimum publicity and a modest advertising campaign; Allen and his cast typically duck reporters and critics, and the film exits the theater as quietly as it entered—notwithstanding an ongoing scrutiny from film critics who demand genius from Allen when they will settle for much less from others. This film, however, decorated gossip columns a month prior to its release because the subject matter—husbands and wives carrying on affairs and splitting up—hinted strongly at the real-life deterioration of Allen and costar Mia Farrow's long-term relationship and at the middle-aged Allen's affair with Farrow's twenty-one-year-old adopted daughter. The eerie similarities between the on-screen drama and the reality cause the film to strike the viewer at such a personal level that one cannot help but respect it for its honesty of emotion and complexity of plot.

Among Allen's repertoire, *Husbands and Wives*—the twenty-second film that he has both written and directed—stands out both as one of the most satisfying and most disturbing. Allen candidly reexplores numerous themes that have come to be associated with his film career: love, marriage, the consequences of personal growth and change within a relationship, and the anguished existence that confines a self-conscious artist.

The film opens with Gabe and Judy Roth (Allen and Farrow) anticipating the arrival of their closest friends, Jack and Sally (Sydney Pollack and Judy Davis), and preparing to have their restaurant suggestion for dinner shot down by their guests. When Jack and Sally finally arrive, however, they announce news much more threatening than their disdain for Gabe and Judy's favorite restaurant. They explain coolly that they are splitting up—news that sends Judy to a crisis point and forces her to question and reassess her own marriage. In this opening scene, Allen entraps the audience in all the angst and discomfort of his characters by employing unsteady, headache-inducing camera shots and uneven sound that registers yelling as unbearable shrieks.

Judy, shocked that she and Gabe were blind to the warning signs of Jack and Sally's lackluster marriage and impending breakup, discusses with Gabe problems in their own marriage, but Gabe assures her that everything is fine with their union. In the meantime, however, Gabe, a critically acclaimed novelist and creative writing professor at Columbia University, begins to shower one of his young, gifted, and aspiring students with attention. Rain (Juliette Lewis), named for the poet Rainer Maria Rilke, and her parents (Blythe Danner and Brian McConnachie) idolize Gabe for his literary output. They claim to be some of his biggest fans; so when he expresses more than just an academic interest in Rain's writing about love and relationships, she tries to warm up to him as well. In fact, at her request, Gabe entrusts her with reading the manuscript of his latest novel, which has been tormenting him. Though Judy had offered to read her husband's manuscript and make comments and suggestions, Gabe would not consider divulging its contents to her. When Judy later finds out that Rain has had the privilege of reading the novel, she is hurt and frustrated.

The relationship that develops between Gabe and Rain is very curious, as is the relationship that develops between Jack and his aerobics instructor, Sam (Lysette Anthony), who is nearly thirty years his junior. When Jack and Sam move in together, Jack at first feels that he has found the love that he desired all along. The health-conscious Sam has whipped Jack into shape: They jog together, eat health food, and best of all for Jack, enjoy watching sports together—an activity that Jack could never share with Sally because of her dislike for sports in favor of such activities as opera and theater.

Though Gabe tries to counsel Jack in the matter, telling him that he is acting irrationally and criticizing Sam by referring to her repeatedly as a "cocktail waitress," Jack will hear none of it. Inevitably, however, Jack loses all interest in Sam when he feels embarrassed by her at a party where she preaches astrology to his erudite friends. Jack grows to despise Sam. Ironically, he finds her to be juvenile while he is the one who handles himself like a child in his breakups with both Sally and Sam.

While Gabe and Jack are traipsing about with their young lovers (Gabe sharing an intimate, romantic moment kissing Rain at her twenty-first birthday party), Judy sets up Sally with one of her coworkers, Michael (Liam Neeson), who immediately falls in love with the opinionated Sally. Although Sally had fantasized about being single again and looks forward to putting her years of experience to work in developing a new relationship, she feels awkward with Michael. Though she adores him, she cannot relax in his company; during a potentially intimate sexual experience with him, her mind concentrates only on classifying all the people she knows as either foxes or hedgehogs, making for a truly hilarious scene.

It is Judy who really feels for Michael. She finds everything about him charming, especially that he quotes William Butler Yeats in his drunkenness. She feels confident enough with Michael to share some of her poetry with him, whereas she fears sharing it with Gabe because she thinks that he would find it silly. The relationship between Michael and Judy begins as a friendship—Judy looks out for Michael at work and helps him deal with Sally's rejection—but it grows into love, and eventually Judy leaves Gabe to marry Michael.

Thus, Judy ends up with Michael, and Jack and Sally reunite after discovering that they were perfect for each other all along, but Gabe ends up alone. He was one in a string of older men with whom Rain had had affairs, and he knew, rationally, that he could not have a long-term relationship with her.

This film is reminiscent of Allen's *A Midsummer Night's Sex Comedy* (1982), the first film in which he worked with Farrow, for all the partner switching that takes place. Each of the characters finds hidden meaning in his or her marriage (or relationship) after exploring different possibilities with a new (or temporary) partner. In the end, it is Gabe and Judy, the ones who had not stopped along the way to question, who find that their marriage is doomed; whereas Jack and Sally, who had struggled throughout and found gaping holes that they assumed were irreparable, redefine their true wants and needs and realize why they got married in the first place.

The plot unravels with the aid of an unseen interviewer/narrator (the voice of costume designer Jeffrey Kurland) who encourages the characters to discuss and decipher the meaning within their varied relationships and to track their evolving thoughts and concerns. Although the device creates a choppy progression, it does lead to honest first-person confessions that the audience could not gain from the action alone.

Allen, as usual, pulls stellar performances from his cast. Despite the current affairs that accompanied the film's opening, Allen and Farrow's acting appears effortless; they seem intimately familiar with the subject matter. Pollack, one of Hollywood's accomplished directors (he won an Oscar for *Out of Africa* in 1985), gives a brilliant performance that earned for him the position of runner-up for best supporting actor from the Los Angeles Critics Association. Judy Davis, however, steals the spotlight. She delivers Sally to the brink of hysteria, then reels her back in safely and securely. The audience may wonder why Michael becomes so enamored with Sally, whose self-righteous comments can grow annoying; the attraction must have something to do with the magnetism generated by her effervescent character.

For this memorable performance, Davis garnered best supporting actress awards from the Los Angeles Film Critics Association, the National Society of Film Critics, the National Board of Review's annual D. W. Griffith Awards, and the Boston Society of Film Critics. In addition, the Academy of Motion Picture Arts and Sciences and the British Academy of Film and Television Arts honored her with nominations for best supporting actress. These two prestigious organizations also recognized Woody Allen by nominating *Husbands and Wives* for best original screenplay of the year.

Debra Picker

Reviews

Boxoffice. November, 1992, p. R-78.
Chicago Tribune. September 18, 1992, VII, p. 39.
The Christian Science Monitor. September 18, 1992, p. 12.
Entertainment Weekly. September 18, 1992, p. 50.
The Hollywood Reporter. August 26, 1992, p. 5.
Los Angeles Times. September 18, 1992, p. F1.
The New York Times. September 18, 1992, p. B1.
Newsweek. September 21, 1992, p. 76.
Time. CXL, September 21, 1992, p. 64.
Variety. August 26, 1992, p. 2.

IN THE SOUP

Production: Jim Stark and Hank Blumenthal for Cacous Films, in association with Will Alliance, Pandora Films, Why Not Prods., Odessa Films, Alta Films, and Mikado Films; released by Triton Pictures
Direction: Alexandre Rockwell
Screenplay: Alexandre Rockwell and Tim Kissell
Cinematography: Phil Parmet
Editing: Dana Congdon
Production design: Mark Friedberg
Art direction: Ginger Tougas
Casting: Georgianne Walken and Sheila Jaffe
Sound: Pavel Wdowczak
Costume design: Elizabeth Bracco
Music: Mader
MPAA rating: no listing
Running time: 93 minutes

Principal characters:

Aldolpho	Steve Buscemi
Joe	Seymour Cassel
Angelica	Jennifer Beals
Dang	Pat Moya
Skippy	Will Patton
Old man	Sully Boyer
Louis Bafardi	Steven Randazzo
Frank Bafardi	Francesco Messina
Monty	Jim Jarmusch
Barbara	Carol Kane
Gregoire	Stanley Tucci

Independent films have a certain luxury. They have few requirements or expectations placed on them by a studio and are oftentimes made strictly for the sake of artistry and form. *In the Soup* is a typical example of modern independent filmmaking. While still operating within a standard narrative structure, the film offers a true study in character, with little attention to plot. Filmed in black and white, *In the Soup* is an engaging slice-of-life piece about an aspiring filmmaker who will do anything and trust anyone in order to get his masterpiece filmed. It is a tale of idealism and dreams and what happens when reality marches in to diminish both. Even more than that, however, *In the Soup* is about friendship and what it takes to awaken a dormant spirit.

The film relies on the quirky. The lead character, Aldolpho (Steve Buscemi), lives in a broken-down tenement in New York run by two singing gangster landlords who belt out show tunes while threatening to break their delinquent renter's legs. From there the audience meets Aldolpho's neighbors, a somewhat bizarre clan of misfits, immigrants, and one stunningly beautiful woman named Angelica (Jennifer Beals). Aldolpho is in love with Angelica, although they have never met. He wants her to star in his film that he is confident will someday be produced. Aldolpho's film—in fact only a lengthy, tattered script—is the inspiration that gets him through the long days and lonely nights. A personification of the starving artist, Aldolpho finds solace in his poverty and bizarre surroundings, as he is sure that it will make for a better biography when he does, in fact, become famous. Aldolpho is a literary dreamer who fantasizes of being the next François Truffaut. For example, his script is a five-hundred-page epic that features legendary author/philosophers Friedrich Nietzsche and Fyodor Dostoevski exchanging dialogue during a ping-pong match. Aldolpho's reality is less grand, however, as he works odd jobs, doing anything that he can to scrape enough money together to pay the rent. When his bumbling landlords come calling and demand their rent money, Aldolpho is forced to sell his one material possession of any worth—his script.

He puts an advertisement in the paper offering his masterpiece to any interested buyer. When only one person answers, a guy named Joe (Seymour Cassel), Aldolpho arranges to meet him to give him the script. Yet Joe, a kindly but off-center small-time gangster, has other things in mind. Joe tells Aldolpho that he likes his look and that he wants to make his film. Although Joe does not show the slightest bit of interest in the plot or even the subject matter of Aldolpho's masterpiece, he does give Aldolpho a roll of cash as a sign of good faith. Though curious as to who this trusting stranger is, Aldolpho is nevertheless thrilled with the prospect of having found a producer. He is able to pay his rent and daydream about fulfilling his hopes for fame.

Joe, however, has other plans for his partnership with Aldolpho. He brings Aldolpho along on a series of petty crimes, from stealing a Porsche to breaking and entering, assuring him along the way that producing the film is the top priority. Yet Joe has a passion for living the high life, and Aldolpho eventually realizes that they spend as much as they make. Aldolpho, so in awe of Joe's energy and a gullible victim of his promises, does not realize until it is too late that his film is never going to be made. Joe's life is itself a film, and Aldolpho finally understands that he has been the unknowing star.

Even though Aldolpho realizes that Joe has been using him from the beginning, he also realizes that Joe's intoxicating personality and friendship has been a constant source of companionship—a companionship the type of which Aldolpho has never known. Although Aldolpho is angry, Joe is still the only person who ever lent any validation to his dream and someone who makes Aldolpho feel alive. Joe's encouragement also gives Aldolpho the strength that he needs to approach Angelica. Although she is suspicious of Aldolpho, she is intrigued at the thought of starring in his film. Her icy exterior slowly begins to thaw as she realizes Aldolpho's honest intentions. Even Angelica cannot help but be affected by Joe's wacky and endearing ways. She releases her hostilities and suspicions and allows Aldolpho into her life.

In the Soup is a curious blend of tragedy and romance. The film is tragic because of the total trust that Aldolpho places in Joe and the betrayal that Aldolpho suffers at his hands. More than tragic, however, *In the Soup* is romantic—not only in the sense of traditional love but also for the spirit that Joe awakens in both Aldolpho and Angelica, spirit that they never knew they had. Aldolpho's and Angelica's souls had become blunt and weather-beaten from the constant blows of the harsh reality that they had to suffer until Joe entered their lives and invigorated them with renewed senses of passion and love for life. Joe's optimism and energy are contagious. Although Aldolpho lived with a dream of making his film, he lived without passion or desire, passively waiting for his dream to happen to him instead of actively seeking it out. Joe teaches Aldolpho to take risks, to live life on the edge, and to tempt fate; that is the only way to be an artist.

Seymour Cassel's performance as Joe was widely spoken of as one of the year's best because of the energy that he brings to the role, a role that could so easily have been done with convention and little effort. Yet Cassel demonstrates a complexity of character little seen in American cinema, as Joe is vibrant and moving, yet quietly manipulative and devilish. It is difficult even for the audience to believe that this kind-hearted, fun-loving man has been taking the hero Aldolpho for a ride. Cassel is no less than superb.

Steve Buscemi's Aldolpho is similarly laden with subtleties, a character with hidden passions and a dormant spirit. An artist in his own mind, Aldolpho is a person no one would ever notice on the street. His striking features offer a brilliant contrast to Aldolpho's bland outward existence but serve notice of the character's myriad deep thoughts and fantasies. Buscemi never goes over the top and never strays from Aldolpho's cautious but keenly curious nature. Aldolpho is Everyman, anonymous and ordinary on the surface, but complex and full of passion and dreams. Buscemi is perfect in the role, as he brings out Aldolpho's desires and feelings in a slow-paced, low-key way.

Jennifer Beals, who had not made much of a splash with audiences since her famous role in *Flashdance* (1983), is surprisingly strong in this dramatic role, as she masters a Latina accent and plays Angelica with a deep-seated anger. Director Alexandre Rockwell, who is Beals's husband, does well to create the air of mystery that surrounds Aldolpho's beautiful neighbor. Her multidimensional character exudes an angry vulnerability that makes her utterly believable as Aldolpho's fantasy leading lady.

Rounding out the cast of quirky characters are Joe's brother, Skippy (Will Patton), a hemophiliac drug dealer who never trusts Aldolpho, and Gregoire (Stanley Tucci), Angelica's French husband of convenience. Skippy, like the other characters featured in the film, lives on the fringe of reality. He is suspicious of nearly everyone, and Patton plays the part with violent subtlety, never revealing if Skippy is slightly off-balance or completely insane. Gregoire, on the other hand, fits in perfectly with the odd surroundings that characterize Aldolpho's manic existence.

When Gregoire, a total stranger, knocks on Aldolpho's door and asks to use his fire escape to get to his apartment next door, Aldolpho is curious and confused, intrigued by this soft-spoken stranger in his apartment. Gregoire believes that he has found a confidant in Aldolpho, however, as he pours out his soul and reveals that he is Angelica's husband, a Frenchman who needed American citizenship. Although neither Skippy nor Gregoire are intricately involved in the plot of *In the Soup*, they are fitting pieces in the unfolding puzzle that Aldolpho's life has become.

In the Soup is, in the end, a story of character, of the effects that people can have on one another's lives. It is a study of human nature, of dreams and weaknesses. Aldolpho is quick to trust Joe, a stranger, with his life's passion because the weight of his dreams far surpasses the cautions of reality. Aldolpho is the ultimate romantic. He is a passionate character who chooses to believe and trust Joe even when his conscience would suggest otherwise. Human nature tends to trust more than it does to suspect, which is one of its greatest strengths and its greatest weakness.

In the Soup is a touching story of passion and friendship. A result of a collaboration between six countries (Japan, Germany, France, Spain, Italy, and the United States), the film is a classic example of modern independent filmmaking, with a purity of character and a simplicity of purpose.

Catherine R. Springer

Reviews

Chicago Tribune. January 29, 1993, VII, p. 28.
The Christian Science Monitor. October 29, 1992, p. 13.
The Hollywood Reporter. January 27, 1992, p. 6.
Interview. XXII, November, 1992, p. 71.
Los Angeles Times. November 6, 1992, p. F1.
The New York Times. October 3, 1992, p. 13.
Time. CXL, November 16, 1992, p. 103.
Variety. January 24, 1992, p. 2.
The Village Voice. September 29, 1992, p. 62.
The Wall Street Journal. November 5, 1992, p. A15.

INDOCHINE

Origin: France
Released: 1992
Released in U.S.: 1992
Production: Eric Heumann (AA) for Paradis Films et la Générale D'Images, Bac Films, Orly Films, and Ciné Cinq; released by Sony Pictures Classics
Direction: Régis Wargnier
Screenplay: Erik Orsenna, Louis Gardel, Catherine Cohen, and Régis Wargnier
Cinematography: François Catonné
Production design: Jacques Bunoir
Casting: Pierre Amzallag
Sound: Geneviève Winding
Costume design: Gabriella Pescucci and Pierre-Yves Gayraud
Music: Patrick Doyle
MPAA rating: PG-13
Running time: 155 minutes

Principal characters:

Éliane .... Catherine Deneuve
Camille .... Linh Dan Pham
Jean-Baptiste Le Guen .... Vincent Pérez
Guy Asselin .... Jean Yanne
Yvette .... Dominique Blanc
Tanh .... Eric Nguyen

How enigmatic is the existential sleight of hand that lifts French sentiment above American schmaltz. It helps immensely to have cast as your central figure the queen of enigma, Catherine Deneuve, the star of *Repulsion* (1965) and *Le Dernier Métro* (1980; *The Last Métro*). Régis Wargnier's *Indochine*, which won the Academy Award for Best Foreign-language film, deftly plays its doomed characters against the epic tides of events surrounding the country that Americans know as Vietnam, and the colony that the French called Indochina, with a narrative voice that is at once more mature and less all-knowing than in many Hollywood productions. The film is ultimately satisfying on levels that American directors such as Oliver Stone have yet to explore.

Indochine is about the demise of colonialism. From the melancholy opening shot of the funeral barge, as the beautiful blond European woman clasps the tiny princess' hand, the viewer is already in the midst of death. Éliane (Catherine Deneuve), who adopts Camille (Linh Dan Pham) after the death of her parents, considers the land her rightful home. She adores her daughter and rules over her rubber plantation with a firm, pragmatic hand. The filmmakers have made an interesting choice in using a strong woman to represent the mixed motives of patriarchal imperial society. Éliane even places bets on her own natives in a sporting event against the navy from

France, a country that she has never even seen.

Yet this woman, who dances a playful tango with her innocent teen-aged daughter—while in another room her own father exploits his concubine, a plantation girl of the same age—is missing a significant element. Though she has had many lovers, never has she truly been in love. This condition changes when she meets the brash, arrogant Jean-Baptiste Le Guen (Vincent Pérez), an angry young officer suffocating in Indochina and carrying out the bidding of the crown.

Éliane shows Jean-Baptiste the entrenched realities of the land and the magical spoils of its occupation. These two might have continued a lengthy affair had it not been for the first seemingly random event that throws Jean-Baptiste and Camille together. As the political forces surge forward to take over the narrative, Éliane struggles to hold onto her position of control. Yet, while Jean-Baptiste is able to change in the presence of the awakening young woman/nation, Éliane cannot. In defiance of the mother who betrayed her by trying to control her destiny, young Camille sets out in search of true love and discovers her true identity—and it is with the revolution. The Joan of Arc metaphors are obvious, but the enactment is captivating nevertheless.

Except for the long last third of the film, which honorably plays out the necessary chain of events, *Indochine* is quite successful in presenting its themes. Each of the three major characters bears symbolic responsibility for the epic weight of the motion picture. They embody the traits, characteristics, and impulses of the place known as Indochina.

These characters act out the film's conflicting motives as only partly autonomous forces, not quite as the usual three-dimensional protagonists. They are prisoners of symbolism, each sketched with a particular element exaggerated in its lacking. Perhaps even more significant, however, is the sense that the audience is not privy to the decision-making process that is often a hallmark of character identification, particularly in American cinema. In *Indochine*, the audience often learns only after the fact what a character has decided offscreen. Thus the actions wash over the viewer with an unstoppable flow, mirroring the inevitability of history. This effect is further augmented by the use of a voice-over in the past tense.

Still, the audience is moved by the larger-than-life sufferings of the three protagonists, all of whom are forced to change radically over the course of the story. The engagement lies in the filmmaker's efforts to strike a tenuous balance between making the characters real in their own right and making them parts of a more important context. Wargnier's notion of character contrasts the more chauvinistic American definition, which offers a character with a higher degree of control over his or her circumstances. Such a variance is at the center of what differentiates American cinema from the films of most other countries.

This premise is further articulated by a stylized sequence from the middle of the film. After violence and fear have broken out, the workers, and even Éliane's foreman, will not enter the factory. Éliane and her aged father attempt to rally them and lead the way to reopen the production line. The editing pace and the soaring sound track would seem to indicate that the production line will continue, the serfs will fall in line, and Éliane's cause will triumph because of her sheer will. Yet it is not to be. As the music fades, her old father's strength ebbs, and Éliane too halts in recognition of the futility of her situation. This scene undercuts character and colonialism in the same process.

The European approach is a more mature one when it comes to the relatively new art form of film. Much motion-picture history has come long after the age of colonialism and the painful lessons it brought to bear on so many of the countries of Asia and Africa. The United States, however, has come into its own peculiar brand of military imperialism relatively recently—coinciding with the evolution of American cinema. Such aspects of national character help to explain the differences in cultural approach to such a subject as Vietnam/Indochina: While many Americans are still trying to come to grips with their loss, the French have, in many ways, gotten beyond theirs. One of the first lessons of film scholarship is recognizing that any period piece reveals less about the era covered within the story line than about the culture that produces the film. American films about the Vietnam War illustrate this tenet. The brilliant, though flawed, *Apocalypse Now* (1979) was followed by a backlash of Vietnam War macho fantasy films. Oliver Stone's noble efforts toward articulating the Vietnam War experience, such as in *Platoon* (1986) and *Born on the Fourth of July* (1989), invariably fall victim to a heavy-handed structure that undercuts the ambiguity of the subject matter. In Wargnier's work, however, the expected clear-cut catharsis is exchanged for a more dense, troubling experience.

The reviews for *Indochine* were mixed. Many critics hailed the film and bestowed awards upon it, while others expressed disdain for its blatant melodrama. Noting the story's dual tendencies, some skewered it for being neither "trashy" enough for a full-blown romance scenario nor elevated enough to be regarded as a historical piece of significance. Such a reduction may miss the point of this particular work. Gone are the days when such film genres as the "women's picture" or the "historical masterpiece" were mutually exclusive. It is possible, with changing sensibilities, to incorporate the female perspective into one's view of history. *Indochine* deals with political themes, and Éliane and Camille make up a two-thirds majority of how the audience is given access to these themes. War is shown to be not merely a story of men with guns and the loss of lands, but rather of the losses of mothers and how they are integral to culture as a whole. This feminization of legitimate, shared history should be considered not as a radical concept but as merely a phenomenon that is long overdue, in some countries particularly more than in others.

Mary E. Belles

Reviews

Chicago Tribune. February 5, 1993, VII, p. 42.
The Hollywood Reporter. December 23, 1992, p. 6.

Los Angeles Times. December 25, 1992, p. F4.
The New York Times. December 24, 1992, p. B1.
Newsweek. CXX, August 24, 1992, p. 52.
Time. CXL, December 21, 1992, p. 72.
Vanity Fair. LV, December, 1992, p. 171.
Variety. CCCXLVII, May 1, 1992.
The Wall Street Journal. December 12, 1992, p. A12.
The Washington Post. February 5, 1993, p. B1.

JUICE

Production: David Heyman, Neal H. Moritz, and Peter Frankfurt, in association with Island World; released by Paramount Pictures
Direction: Ernest R. Dickerson
Screenplay: Gerard Brown and Ernest R. Dickerson; based on a story by Dickerson
Cinematography: Larry Banks
Editing: Sam Pollard and Brunilda Torres
Production design: Lester Cohen
Set decoration: Alyssa Winter
Casting: Jaki Brown
Sound: Franklin D. Stettner
Costume design: Donna Berwick
Music supervision: Kathy Nelson
Music: Hank Shocklee and the Bomb Squad
MPAA rating: R
Running time: 96 minutes

Principal characters:

Q	Omar Epps
Bishop	Tupac Shakur
Steel	Jermaine Hopkins
Raheem	Khalil Kain
Yolanda	Cindy Herron
Radames	Vincent Laresca
Trip	Samuel L. Jackson
Brian	George O. Gore
Ruffhouse M. C.	Queen Latifah

Director Ernest Dickerson, who was the youngest member of the American Society of Cinematographers at the time of this film's release, rose to prominence as cinematographer for director Spike Lee, working on such films as *Do the Right Thing* (1989) and *Malcolm X* (1992; reviewed in this volume). Dickerson also filmed John Sayles's *The Brother from Another Planet* (1984), Robert Townsend's *Eddie Murphy Raw* (1987), and music videos for Miles Davis, Anita Baker, Branford Marsalis, Patti LaBelle, and Bruce Springsteen. *Juice* marks Dickerson's directorial debut on a feature film, working from a screenplay that he coauthored and that was based on his original story. Although Dickerson admits that his main interest in film has always been cinematography, he also admits that directing has been a temptation: "There were stories I wanted to tell, stories that weren't being told, and I think that's the main reason I got interested in wanting to direct."

Surrounded by a landslide of press regarding violence at the film's openings across the country, controversy over weapons pictured in the film's poster (and the removal of those weapons), and excitement over the rap and rhythm-and-blues soundtrack, the film itself became only a small part of a larger *Juice* phenomenon, perhaps because films by African American directors continued to draw attention simply for their rarity. In 1991, twelve feature films by African American directors were released. While admittedly this was a small percentage of the nearly four hundred films released that year, fewer than twelve were released in the preceding decade.

Chronicling the coming-of-age of four young men, *Juice* was shot on location in New York. The story begins with each of the teenagers waking and dressing, presumably for school. Quickly, the audience learns about the families, the homes, and the personalities of each young man. These students do not spend their days at school, however, but on the streets, finding adventures, misadventures, and tests of their skills and bravery.

One of the continuing themes in the film is the search for respect, or, using its street name, "juice." One of the teens, Q (Omar Epps), dreams of being a disc jockey and spends equal amounts of time dreaming and practicing. Another, Bishop (Tupac Shakur), dreams of a different kind of respect, that earned by violence. His "practice" is watching such old gangster films as James Cagney's *White Heat* (1949), a clip of which appears in the film. To Bishop, the choices look easy: to get juice, one needs the power—superior fire power. Bishop glorifies violence, supposing it to be a sign of courage. Raheem (Khalil Kain) has a child by his former girlfriend, signifying another kind of respect that the young men pursue on the street. Steel (Jermaine Hopkins) worries the most and seems to be the youngest of the group. For him, the process of growing from a teenager to an adult seems nearly incomprehensible.

Much of the early part of *Juice* follows the foursome as they spend their day narrowly escaping trouble: police officers, a Puerto Rican gang, angry shop clerks, and crimes in progress. Very quickly, however, the teen pranks become real crimes, and before the film ends this rite of passage will leave two of the youths dead and two wary survivors.

In developing these characters, Dickerson has used two main devices: their dreams and their various selves. Each of the characters has a dream, an idea of how to succeed on the streets or how to escape them. Q has the interest and the talent to be a disc jockey, here termed "mixmaster." His motivation to succeed is his own personal juice—yet the film questions what it takes to keep dreams alive with little encouragement and huge opposition. In one particular scene, Q must choose between competing in a contest that would mean exposure and opportunities and helping his friends commit a crime. Clearly, he wants to compete, yet just as clearly he is unable to disappoint his friends, to admit that their priorities are no longer his own.

In addition, the characters become three dimensional when they are shown interacting with the people around them. Probably the clearest example of this transformation is the difference in the young men when they are with their families:

Bishop's loving grandmother and catatonic father; Steel's gruff father and supportive mother; Raheem's loving and gentle mother and hardworking sister; and Q's little adoring brother. These are the people who have great expectations for the young men and lament the passing of their dreams. It is interesting to note that the streetwise young men become polite and soft-spoken around their families. Their street names disappear and their hip talk drops away and is replaced by respectful conversation.

Juice shows a tug-of-war between perseverance and escape. Dickerson shows talented, motivated young people who cannot shake the chaos around them and succeed. They have families and dreams, but in the end that is not enough. *Juice* offers no simple answers, if it can be seen as offering any answers at all.

Certainly part of the continuing lore in filmmaking is that great directors are made, acquiring their "eye" through working in other capacities on other productions. Whether it is literally true that one of the roads to cinematic greatness is to acquire an appreciation for the strengths and weaknesses of the form in a more hands-on capacity, it is certainly true that Dickerson brings a keen visual sense to his film.

Film production texts speak of a design principle popularly referred to as the Rule of Thirds. Specifically, the concept is as follows: The frame remains constant, literally a stationary window. The changing pictures within the frame, however, form designs that, as they change, modify the feel of the film. For example, in the classic *The Third Man* (1949), much of the film is shot at tilted angles. Something is awry in that world, and the film visually reflects the problem. The audience consciously or unconsciously reads the visual clues and responds. Classically, one of the most visually pleasing of these frame divisions is into thirds, therefore the name Rule of Thirds. Instead of filming a horizon so that it bisects the frame, it is more interesting and visually pleasing, the theory goes, to have the line break the frame one-third or two-thirds of the way up or down the frame. The same holds true for vertical breaks. Dickerson relies on this design principle throughout his film. For example, when Bishop chases Q down the dark and empty streets of Harlem, the picture is literally of chaos and violence, but the design of the frame is pure classical balance, pleasing and calming. One runner is closer and sharply in focus. He runs toward the camera, maintaining a position one-third of the way vertically into the frame. The other youth follows a half block behind, two-thirds of the way into the frame, creating a perfect balance. Dickerson's film is thematically iconoclastic, yet it is a product of classic film techniques.

Many of the shots in the film are so individual and so clearly art that careful viewers may remember shots long after the story fades. The opening credits are high-speed aerial shots of New York traffic at night, and while thematically the footage works to achieve a backdrop for what follows, it also is visually beautiful and mesmerizing to watch. The last scene of the film is an extreme close-up, showing a boy-made-man, forged in this hell. It is a chilling shot—and a brave and exciting directorial choice. Another distinctive feature is camera motion: The camera flies up and over fences with the runners and artfully watches the action from behind a garbage can and between the ears of a cat. The attention to detail, the color, the crowd scenes, and the lighting are all technically expert. While any discussion of film technique can quickly become tedious, technique can work to enhance plot. For a film about violence and loss, *Juice* is a visual ballet. The effect on the viewer is oddly exhilarating yet tranquilizing, naturalizing the urban jungle.

Much of the press on the film centered on *Juice*'s dark message, as the violence that it portrays quickly spawned copycat violence at the theaters. It would be unrealistic to gloss over the scenes of pure brutality, but to see this film as simply another epic of street violence is to miss the point altogether. Exciting and artistic, *Juice* is a serious film that enthusiasts will not want to miss.

Roberta F. Green

Reviews

Boxoffice. March, 1992, p. R-24.
Chicago Tribune. January 17, 1992, VII, p. 33.
The Hollywood Reporter. January 17, 1992, p. 9.
Los Angeles Times. January 17, 1992, p. F1.
The New York Times. January 17, 1992, p. B4.
San Francisco Chronicle. January 17, 1992, p. D1.
USA Today. January 17, 1992, p. 4D.
Variety. January 17, 1992, p. 2.
The Village Voice. January 28, 1992, p. 56.
The Washington Post. January 17, 1992, p. C1.

THE LAST OF THE MOHICANS

Production: Michael Mann and Hunt Lowry; released by Twentieth Century-Fox
Direction: Michael Mann
Screenplay: Michael Mann and Christopher Crowe; based on the novel by James Fenimore Cooper and on the screenplay by Philip Dunne, adaptation by John L. Balderson, Paul Perez, and Daniel Moore
Cinematography: Dante Spinotti
Editing: Dov Hoenig and Arthur Schmidt
Production design: Wolf Kroeger
Art direction: Richard Holland and Robert Guerra
Set decoration: Jim Erickson and James V. Kent
Sound: Chris Jenkins (AA), Doug Hemphill (AA), Mark Smith (AA), and Simon Kaye (AA)
Costume design: Elsa Zamparelli
Music: Trevor Jones and Randy Edelman
MPAA rating: R
Running time: 110 minutes

Principal characters:

Hawkeye	Daniel Day-Lewis
Cora	Madeleine Stowe
Chingachgook	Russell Means
Uncas	Eric Schweig
Alice	Jodhi May
Magua	Wes Studi
Heyward	Steven Waddington
Colonel Munro	Maurice Roëves
General Montcalm	Patrice Chéreau
John Cameron	Terry Kinney

Michael Mann's film *The Last of the Mohicans*, based on James Fenimore Cooper's 1826 novel of the same name from the Leatherstocking Tales, revolves around the friendship between Hawkeye (Daniel Day-Lewis) and the Mohican chief Chingachgook (Russell Means) and his son, Uncas (Eric Schweig). Hawkeye, the son of white settlers, was reared by Mohicans after becoming orphaned as a child. Having lived among them for so long, he has learned many of the skills and adopted many of the ways of the tribe. Hawkeye and his Native American friends live a kind of idealized natural existence in their forest home. Of course, this story takes place during a time when there were still virginal forests in America and indigenous peoples living free in them.

The film attempts a faithful realization of the natural paradise, both ravishing in its beauty and fearsome in its savageness, that was the American wilderness. Situated along the frontier near present-day Albany, New York, the forest primeval where Hawkeye and his Native American brothers move as surely and quietly as the deer that they pursue is becoming scarred by the encroachment of the Europeans and their frontier settlements. Along with the destruction of the forests, the advance of civilization brings with it turmoil and violence.

Cooper's tale is set in prerevolutionary America against the backdrop of the French and Indian Wars. In 1757, British Fort William Henry, commanded by Colonel George Munro (Maurice Roëves), was surrounded and besieged by French commander General Montcalm (Patrice Chéreau) and his Native American allies. Early in the film, a detachment of British troops led by Major Duncan Heyward (Steven Waddington) is escorting Colonel Munro's two young daughters, Cora (Madeleine Stowe) and Alice (Jodhi May), to this fort near Lake Champlain. Accompanying Heyward is Magua (Wes Studi), a Mohawk scout who is secretly planning to kill Munro and his daughters in revenge for the killing of his own family by Munro's forces.

Traveling on foot through the depths of an unfamiliar forest realm, the expedition is ambushed by a Huron war party. Hawkeye, Chingachgook, and Uncas, who are passing nearby on their way to Kentucky, swoop down upon the Huron raiders and rescue Heyward and Munro's daughters. Magua, who set up the ambush, escapes. Hawkeye offers to lead the dazed survivors to the fort, though it means passing through enemy lines. The violence has escalated so rapidly that many of the settlers are becoming caught in the crossfire. Along the way, the party encounters the still-smoldering remains of a frontier cabin. The Huron warriors who have attacked the settlements are so cunning and stealthy that Hawkeye and his companions do not even stop to bury the dead. As Hawkeye explains to an unbelieving Cora, even the slightest disturbance of the site would betray their presence to the Hurons, exposing them to further danger.

Along the way, Hawkeye and Cora are drawn to each other and Uncas is attracted to Alice. Cora, the older of the two sisters, is an intelligent and independent woman who is surprised by the way such outdoor adventure stirs her blood. For Cora, Hawkeye becomes the embodiment of the mysterious force that animates this strange new land. Alice, though less assertive, is a young woman of resilience and quiet courage. Her tender feelings for Uncas, though never revealed openly, are implied by her longing glances.

The survivors, led by Hawkeye, Chingachgook, and Uncas, finally reach Fort William Henry only to find that Colonel Munro and his men are under attack by French and Huron forces led by General Montcalm. When the militiamen, who are in the fort to support Colonel Munro's troops, learn that the settlements are also being attacked, they threaten to return to their homes. Munro forbids them to go, but with Hawkeye's aid, some manage to slip away. When Munro finds out that the militiamen have gone, he imprisons Hawkeye for sedition. The love between Cora and Hawkeye continues to bloom—to the chagrin of the priggish Heyward, who professes his love for her also.

Under continuous bombardment from Montcalm's forces, Munro seeks support from a nearby British garrison but learns that aid will not be sent. As the situation becomes hopeless for Munro, Montcalm delivers the terms of surrender. Under a cease-fire, Munro and his soldiers are allowed to leave the fort before it is sacked and destroyed.

Magua waits to attack Munro until his retreating troops are exposed and vulnerable. During the massacre that follows, Munro is killed and Hawkeye rescues Cora and Alice. Together with Heyward, Chingachgook, and Uncas, they escape and take refuge in a cave beneath a waterfall. When Magua and his warriors finally locate them, Hawkeye, Chingachgook, and Uncas leap through the falls to safety. Before leaving, Hawkeye vows to return for Cora. Heyward, Cora, and Alice are taken prisoner by Magua and his warriors.

Magua takes his captives to a Huron village, where he seeks the chief's permission to kill Munro's daughters and to ransom Heyward. Hawkeye and the Mohicans arrive, however, just in time to challenge Magua and plead for their release. The chief finally decides that Hawkeye and Heyward are to be set free. Alice will be given to Magua as his bride, and Cora will be burned at the stake. In an act of love only exceeded by his courage, Heyward offers to take Cora's place. As the fire consumes Heyward, Hawkeye ends his suffering with a bullet.

Magua takes the captive Alice and leads his party out of the Huron camp. As they travel a path that meanders high along the edge of a cliff, they are set upon by Uncas, who is determined to free Alice. While the members of his party look on, Magua and Uncas become locked in a fight to the death. After Magua throws the mortally wounded Uncas off the cliff, Alice stoically leaps after Uncas. Enraged at the death of his son, Chingachgook attacks and kills Magua. The film ends with Hawkeye, Chingachgook, and Cora standing together on the mountainside, gazing skyward in mourning for Uncas, the last of the Mohicans.

In his retelling of events from the French and Indian Wars and his descriptions of early American frontier settlements, novelist James Fenimore Cooper was able to create an America where mythical figures engaged one another in struggles that would determine the shape and character of a new country. Nevertheless, Michael Mann and Christopher Crowe, who cowrote the screenplay for *The Last of the Mohicans*, made several changes that departed from Cooper's novel. For example, Cooper's Natty Bumppo has been given the more dignified name of Nathaniel Poe (although both the novel and the film refer to him as Hawkeye). Hawkeye has also been given Cora as a love interest, which is a stretch from the original. In Cooper's tale, it is Uncas who is attracted to Cora. Hawkeye is merely a distant admirer. Daniel Day-Lewis' romantic image was no doubt a temptation to Mann in pairing him with Madeleine Stowe. In the book, when Cora is held prisoner by Magua, it is Hawkeye, not Heyward, who offers to take her place.

Other details of the story were adhered to more faithfully. An authentic replica of the wooden fort erected by the British in 1755 near Lake George, New York, was constructed in North Carolina. The Colonial village of Albany and other frontier settlements were re-created in North Carolina's old-growth forests, which double for mid-eighteenth century New York woodlands. Great care was taken by Mann to achieve the original look of the Northeastern tribes, down to haircuts and body paint. Mann said that it was his intention to portray Native Americans more faithfully and sympathetically in his film than Cooper did in his novel.

While the major scenes of violence in the film are of Native Americans fighting other tribes or whites, it is clear that their "savagery" was to a great extent a result of their encounters with the colonists. Magua, the most bloodthirsty Native American, kills Munro in revenge for the loss of his family and for the suffering that his people have endured. Chingachgook and Uncas symbolize the exploitation and near-extinction of the tribes during the Colonial wars. Hawkeye, the "white" Native American, is a combination of a cultured, sensitive colonist and a man who lives according to "natural" laws. He emerges as a mythic character who fuses the qualities of civilization (honor, gallantry, fair play) with the essential wisdom of earlier, more innocent times.

The Last of the Mohicans is beautifully filmed, with many scenes shot in wide angle to capture the sweeping panorama of the landscape. Mann, who is known for such stylish productions as the television series *Miami Vice* and the film *Manhunter* (1986), here strives for a lush, painterly look. The action sequences are so closely paced that it seems as though the camera is panting just to keep up. One comes away from this breathtaking epic not so much with a greater understanding of the historical period depicted or of the characters portrayed but rather with a sense of exhilaration and enthusiasm for the adventure.

Francis Poole

Reviews

Boxoffice. December, 1992, p. R-85.
Chicago Tribune. September 25, 1992, VII, p. 37.
Film Comment. XXVIII, November, 1992, p. 72.
The Hollywood Reporter. September 23, 1992, p. 5.
Los Angeles Times. September 25, 1992, p. F1.
The New York Times. September 25, 1992, p. B2.
Newsweek. September 28, 1992, p. 48.
Rolling Stone. October 29, 1992, p. 76.
Time. CXL, September 28, 1992, p. 72.
Variety. CCCXLVIII, August 27, 1992.

THE LAWNMOWER MAN

Production: Gimel Everett for Allied Vision/Lane Pringle, in association with Fuji Eight Co. Ltd.; released by New Line Cinema
Direction: Brett Leonard
Screenplay: Brett Leonard and Gimel Everett; based on the short story by Stephen King
Cinematography: Russell Carpenter
Editing: Alan Baumgarten
Production design: Alex McDowell
Art direction: Chris Farmer
Set decoration: Jacqueline Masson
Computer animation and design: Xaos
Computer animation and visual effects: Angel Studios
Special effects: Western Images
Sound: Russell Fager
Costume design: Mary Jane Fort
Music: Dan Wyman
MPAA rating: R
Running time: 105 minutes

Principal characters:

Jobe Smith	Jeff Fahey
Dr. Lawrence Angelo	Pierce Brosnan
Marnie Burke	Jenny Wright
Sebastian Timms	Mark Bringleson
Terry McKeen	Geoffrey Lewis
Father McKeen	Jeremy Slate
Director	Dean Norris

Dr. Lawrence Angelo (Pierce Brosnan) researches the educational possibilities of virtual reality—lifelike, computerized video simulations of reality experienced with the help of special goggles. With the help of neurotropic drugs and financial support from The Shop, his experiments on chimpanzees have yielded incredible results. His most recent subject made astounding progress until it went on a rampage, broke out of its cage, and shot security guards. The problem is that The Shop conducts covert operations and therefore funds Dr. Angelo to find ways to encourage aggressive and violent behaviors. Dr. Angelo has agreed to these conditions because his research matters above all else, but the ethics involved begin to nag at him uncomfortably. When he tells his partner, Sebastian Timms (Mark Bringleson), that he refuses to continue the aggression experiments, The Shop offers him a hiatus, during which he sits in his home laboratory playing virtual reality games and divorcing himself from the world around him, including his wife.

Dr. Angelo wants to advance his research to human subjects, and he wants to continue working on intelligence enhancement rather than on violence. He decides to begin experimenting on his gardener's assistant, Jobe Smith (Jeff Fahey). Jobe, a mentally handicapped young man, lives in a shed behind the church and earns his keep by doing groundskeeping and janitorial work. His guardian, Father McKeen (Jeremy Slate), takes great pleasure in punishing Jobe for his failures—such as not killing the ants on the floor in front of the altar—with a wide leather belt. When Dr. Angelo asks Jobe if he would like to become smarter by playing some games, Jobe seems delighted.

They start with simple exercises, such as matching shapes, but Angelo's experiments proceed at an astounding pace, surpassing his highest expectations. Jobe grows in intelligence by the minute, learning Latin in two hours. Angelo approaches The Shop and asks to return to work because he can go no further with Jobe at home. They welcome him back, but the audience knows that their only interest is in inducing extreme aggressive states.

Jobe mows the lawn of a widow who decides to seduce him, and he begins to enter adulthood not only intellectually but experientially as well. Marnie (Jenny Wright) teaches him about sexual pleasures. As his education continues, however, it becomes clear that Jobe is developing unexpected psychic powers, mind reading and telekinesis in particular. He "hears" Marnie's sexual fantasies and decides to fulfill them in virtual reality. He takes her to the laboratory and hooks her to the machines, placing himself in Dr. Angelo's usual control/participant configuration. At first, Marnie finds the experience pleasurable and fantastic, but as it continues, she becomes increasingly terror stricken. When they come out of virtual reality, Marnie has deteriorated to an essentially preverbal state, never to recover.

As time passes, Jobe surpasses Angelo even in his own field. When The Shop demands that Angelo return the experiments to the original aggressive drug formulations and virtual reality programs, Timms switches the vials of drugs and replaces the programs without informing Angelo. Jobe responds immediately, becoming hostile and pugnacious. He begins to take revenge on his enemies. One night, he sends Father McKeen into flames, gives the gas station attendant who had tortured him his original limited intellectual capacity, and decapitates his former best friend's father—who beat both mother and son regularly—with a lawn mower. He does all these things simply by using his newfound psychic powers.

Jobe decides to insert himself into a computer network in order to live out the rest of his life in an electronic environment. He has textbook delusions of grandeur, imagining himself as spread throughout the world's information systems and wielding unlimited power. He tells Dr. Angelo that people will know when his plan has succeeded because every telephone in the world will ring simultaneously. Angelo believes that he has managed to block Jobe's access to the network until all the telephones start to ring.

Despite the facts that its premise is wonderful and the possibilities of virtual reality are fascinating, *The Lawnmower Man* is simply not a good film. Its computer graphics, for example, which are beautiful and abundant, are neither state of the art nor, in this story's context, convincing. In order to believe that virtual reality is an extraordinary learning environment, one would have to believe that it appears to be reality. The virtual reality environments in this film are all geometric and gridded, their palette is almost exclusively primary colors, and their graphics are low resolution.

The filmmakers and computer animators chose to separate the worlds of reality and virtual reality in a heavy-handed manner rather than blur the distinction between them. *Total Recall* (1990), for example, dealt with confusion between real and simulated worlds in a more interesting way; viewers are kept uncertain as to whether they are watching the Arnold Schwarzenegger character's paid-for fantasy, reality, some combination of the two, or something else entirely. Its tense uncertainty depends on precisely what *The Lawnmower Man*'s director and computer artists chose not to do—make an alternate reality look real.

Screenwriters Brett Leonard and Gimel Everett manage to jam a tremendous number of science-fiction clichés into the film. The only developed character is Dr. Angelo, and Mary Shelley essentially created that character two centuries ago. The power of science seduces Dr. Angelo, making him forget the good of any one individual or of humankind in general. His only connection to the world is through his research, which obsesses him; his ethics haunt him but do not dissuade him. This is a familiar story.

When Dr. Angelo's wife leaves him because of his obsession, it reminds one of *Close Encounters of the Third Kind* (1977), as do scenes toward the end of the film when his next-door neighbor and her child join forces with him. Jeff Fahey spends the last twenty minutes of the film in a sort of wet suit with fluorescent stripes that glow when his powers surge; he is also frequently backlit in haze. The motel-room painting religious effect of this image connects directly with the Dr. Frankenstein theme and the dangers of attempting to cross the border between humanity and God.

Angelo and Jobe, rather obviously, have similar problems understanding the limits of their own powers, as does Father McKeen. Each of them in his own way takes on what the film seems to suggest rightly belongs to God: Angelo dispenses intelligence, Father McKeen dispenses penance and absolution, and Jobe dispenses retribution. These religious underpinnings are thin, however, and they do not bear up to examination. The themes—because they move precisely into the heart of everyone's fears about science run amok—already have been played out countless times in science fiction.

The banalities that Leonard and Everett seem to have thrown into the film are unearned and ineffective. The relationship between Jobe and Marnie is, in this sense, strikingly familiar. Since a film needs a love interest (or at least a sex interest), Leonard and Everett provide one, but it comes from nowhere and contributes nothing significant to the plot. One does not care about the characters or the relationship, largely because one is never told anything about their motivations or responses. The acting does little to relieve the problems with the film's clichéd plot and approach to effects. With the exception of Fahey's portrayal of the mentally handicapped Jobe, the cast seems more like cardboard replicas than actors.

Anahid Kassabian

Reviews

American Cinematographer. LXXIII, April, 1992, p. 58.
Cinéfantastique. XXII, April, 1992, p. 6.
The Hollywood Reporter. March 6, 1992, p. 12.
Los Angeles Times. March 6, 1992, p. F18.
New Statesman and Society. V, May 29, 1992, p. 34.
The New York Times. March 7, 1992, p. 12.
Omni. XIV, March, 1992, p. 31.
Sight and Sound. II, June, 1992, p. 43.
Variety. February 20, 1992, p. 2.
The Washington Post. September 6, 1992, p. G1.

A LEAGUE OF THEIR OWN

Production: Robert Greenhut and Elliot Abbott for Parkway; released by Columbia Pictures
Direction: Penny Marshall
Screenplay: Lowell Ganz and Babaloo Mandel; based on a story by Kim Wilson and Kelly Candaele
Cinematography: Miroslav Ondricek
Editing: George Bowers
Production design: Bill Groom
Art direction: Tim Galvin
Set decoration: George DeTitta, Jr.
Sound: Les Lazarowitz
Makeup: Bernadette Mazur
Costume design: Cynthia Flynt
Music: Hans Zimmer
MPAA rating: PG
Running time: 124 minutes

Principal characters:

Jimmy Dugan	Tom Hanks
Dottie Hinson	Geena Davis
Kit Keller	Lori Petty
Mae Mordabito	Madonna
Doris Murphy	Rosie O'Donnell
Marla Hooch	Megan Cavanagh
Ernie Capadino	Jon Lovitz
Ira Lowenstein	David Strathairn
Bob Hinson	Bill Pullman
Walter Harvey	Garry Marshall
Ellen Sue Gotlander	Freddie Simpson
Older Dottie	Lynn Cartwright

Several significant baseball films appeared during the 1980's, when Barry Levinson's *The Natural* (1984) and Phil Alden Robinson's *Field of Dreams* (1989) won critical acclaim for looking back in baseball history—the latter to the Chicago Black Sox scandal and the legendary "Shoeless" Joe Jackson—not to expose the corruption in sport, but to demonstrate the enduring triumph of the game over its detractors and its role in forging bonds between families. Both films, despite their realistic game footage, are fantasies with overlays of myth, symbolism, and the supernatural. Although it also concerns the myth and mystique of the game, Ron Shelton's *Bull Durham* (1988) is a more realistic film that stresses male camaraderie and the off-diamond lives of the players. *A League of Their Own* does concern baseball history—in this case the formation of the All American Girls Professional Baseball League—but it is marked by more realism than fantasy and plays off and against the male baseball mystique. It is a feminist film that depicts how baseball builds female character and bonds women to one another.

Based on a story by Kim Wilson and Kelly Candaele and scripted by Lowell Ganz and Babaloo Mandel, the film is also indebted to a television documentary entitled "A League of Their Own," which concerned the 1988 reunion of professional women baseball players in Cooperstown, New York, the site of the Baseball Hall of Fame. In fact, the story begins in 1992 as an older Dottie Hinson (Lynn Cartwright) wavers about attending the Cooperstown reunion game and the ceremony inaugurating the women's wing of the Baseball Hall of Fame. Before the flashback to the 1943 season, the film features a sequence involving Dottie's words to her two competitive basketball-playing grandsons: She advises the older one to let the younger one shoot and encourages the younger one to win. This sibling rivalry foreshadows the rivalry between the young Dottie (Geena Davis) and her sister Kit Keller (Lori Petty), and it is that rivalry which is foreground against the historical background.

When Dottie arrives in Cooperstown and sees her former teammates, she is reminded of her past, which is portrayed in flashback. The initial flashback sequence occurs in Oregon, where Dottie and Kit are working in a dairy and playing softball. After watching Kit strike out and Dottie get the winning base hit, raunchy and wisecracking Ernie Capadino (Jon Lovitz), a scout for the new women's baseball league, recruits Dottie and is persuaded to take Kit along. His subsequent stop is in Colorado, where he also picks up the hard-hitting but decidedly unattractive Marla Hooch (Megan Cavanagh), but only after Dottie and Kit threaten to quit—this episode sets the tone for the theme of female solidarity in the film. The competitive tryouts in Chicago feature Mae Mordabito (Madonna), a former dance hall hostess, and Doris Murphy (Rosie O'Donnell), the bouncer at the dance hall, but even they are impressed by Dottie's baseball skills. The tryouts culminate with the posting of the team rosters, and the solidarity theme is reiterated when one player helps a distraught, illiterate player find her name on the Rockford Peaches roster.

In the next sequence, the focus is on Walter Harvey (Garry Marshall), a candy bar magnate and major league team owner who founded the women's league in order to keep major league baseball, threatened by World War II, before the fans. He hires Jimmy Dugan (Tom Hanks), a home run king whose drinking has shortened his career, to manage the Rockford Peaches. Initially, Jimmy's loutish behavior, obscene speech, unkempt appearance, and demeaning attitude toward ballplayers who cry distance him from the game and his team. Nevertheless, the Rockford Peaches' performance and his love for baseball draw him into the game and into grudging respect for his players, particularly Dottie, who has taken charge in his unofficial absence. When low attendance threatens the league, the Peaches, led by Dottie, begin to play inspired "showboat" baseball, which gains for them headlines and banner crowds. Kit, however, who is playing in her sister's shadow, resents Dottie's success. The sibling rivalry climaxes when catcher Dottie tells Jimmy that Kit no longer has her stuff and Jimmy brings in a relief pitcher. The subsequent battle results in Kit being traded to the Racine Belles, the Peaches' World Series opponent.

When her husband, Bob (Bill Pullman), returns from the war, Dottie must choose between going home with him to Oregon or staying with the team through the World Series. The choice is somewhat complicated by the growing attraction between Dottie and Jimmy, who cannot understand her decision to give up baseball for domestic life. Without Dottie, the Peaches fall behind in the series but finally knot the series at three games each. In the last game, Dottie reappears, and her outstanding catching and base hit off Kit give the Peaches the lead. A despondent Kit foresees a replay of the Oregon softball game where Dottie starred, and the situation worsens when Kit must bat in the last inning. As in the Oregon game, she swings and misses two high pitches, but she drives home the tying run with a hit and then attempts to stretch it to a home run. Kit has a home-plate collision with Dottie, who had earlier held the ball in a similar situation. Dottie and Kit fall, and this time Dottie almost inexplicably releases the ball as her hand hits the ground.

Now Kit is the victor, the signer of autographs, and Dottie is in the literal shadows, almost out of the frame while she watches her younger sister. Kit has emerged as a star and gained a separate identity and the two are sentimentally reconciled as equals. Reconciliation, growth, and increased self-esteem are the subjects of this film, which slights the win-at-all-costs competitiveness associated with professional men's baseball (despite several shots of Doris Murphy's chatter and feistiness). In fact, one of the most touching moments in the film concerns the aggressive Doris, who in a bus conversation discusses her boyfriend-by-default—all the other men thought that she was strange because she did not fit the feminine ideal. She concludes that she is fine and literally says "goodbye" to the shreds of his picture, which she throws out the window. Further complicating gender stereotypes is Ellen Sue Gotlander (Freddie Simpson), a former Miss Georgia whose feminine appearance contrasts with her competitiveness as Kit's replacement on the Peaches.

Dowdy Marla Hooch epitomizes several of the gender concerns in the film. With her head-down posture, her masculine walk, and her short, straight haircut, she is the antithesis of the feminine ideal of the period, but her father reared her as he would a boy, not as a girl. He acknowledges his failings, as Marla is a dismal failure at the charm school in which the league enrolls its players. The turning point in her life occurs at a roadhouse, where her emotional but horrible singing wins the heart of a male patron who eventually marries her and takes her away from baseball. Her case raises some issues that detract somewhat from the feminist message the film seems determined to advance: Is the real place for women in sports or at home? Does a woman's self-esteem depend primarily on male approval?

The women's impractical uniforms—the women who protest wearing them are told that other women will wear them if they will not—reflect the male chauvinism of Walter Harvey, whose exploitation of the women will end when the "real" male ballplayers return. This exploitation, however, only mirrors the larger societal exploitation that Ira Lowenstein (David Strathairn) indicts when he questions the postwar roles of Rosie the Riveter and other working women. In another memorable sequence, the film addresses the issue of racism when an errant baseball is retrieved by an African American woman, who throws it with power some distance to Dottie—the exchange of looks between the two women speaks volumes about race, economic opportunity, and gender in 1940's America.

Despite the presence of Madonna, whose raunchiness and flamboyance are at once featured and muted in the film, *A League of Their Own* provides not only an entertaining look at women's baseball but also an incisive and sympathetic examination of gender issues. The cinematography of veteran Miroslav Ondricek contributes much to the success of the film. Moving from color to black and white as the film shifts from present to past, his simulated newsreel footage reminds the audience of the 1940's and mixes historical fact with historical fiction, including *Life* magazine covers. The past, even though filmed mostly in color, has a period feel that is reinforced by the costumes. The last sequence, which involves the veterans playing at Cooperstown, is filled with brilliant color, stressing the vitality and skill of the players and their continued enthusiasm for America's game.

Thomas L. Erskine

Reviews

Boxoffice. August/September, 1992, p. R-61.
Chicago Tribune. July 1, 1992, V, p. 1.
The Christian Science Monitor. July 3, 1992, p. 12.
Entertainment Weekly. July 10, 1992, p. 39.
The Hollywood Reporter. June 29, 1992, p. 5.
Los Angeles Times. July 1, 1992, p. F1.
The New Republic. CCVII, August 3, 1992, p. 28.
The New York Times. July 1, 1992, p. C13.
Time. CXL, July 6, 1992, p. 72.
Variety. June 29, 1992, p. 2.

LEAP OF FAITH

Production: Michael Manheim and David V. Picker; released by Paramount Pictures
Direction: Richard Pearce
Screenplay: Janus Cercone
Cinematography: Matthew F. Leonetti
Editing: Don Zimmerman, Mark Warner, and John F. Burnett
Production design: Patrizia Von Brandenstein
Art direction: Dennis Bradford
Set decoration: Gretchen Rau
Casting: Gretchen Rennell
Sound: Peter Hliddel
Costume design: Theadora Van Runkle
Music: Cliff Eidelman
MPAA rating: PG-13
Running time: 110 minutes

Principal characters:

Jonas Nightengale	Steve Martin
Jane Larson	Debra Winger
Marva	Lolita Davidovich
Will	Liam Neeson
Boyd	Lukas Haas
Hoover	Meat Loaf
Matt	Philip Seymour Hoffman
Tiny	M. C. Gainey
Georgette	La Chanze
Ornella	Delores Hall
Titus	John Toles-Bey
Lucille	Albertina Walker
Ricky	Ricky Dillard

Leap of Faith, starring Steve Martin, is not the lighthearted comedy typical of his work, but neither is it quite the departure that the darkly inventive, Depression-era tale *Pennies from Heaven* (1981) was. The film centers on Martin as a cynical revival preacher who eventually sees the error of his selfish ways; it might best be called a lighthearted drama. Despite creditable efforts from all concerned, the film ultimately misses its mark.

Jonas Nightengale (Martin) leads a revival show that cruises the Bible Belt with a motor home containing an electronic command center, a convoy of tractor trailers full of stage equipment, and a full gospel choir called the Angels of Mercy. His shows are performed in a tent filled with technological gadgets and elaborate lighting effects. As Jonas and his troupe are driving across Kansas, a truck engine fails and the crew is stuck in the small, depressed town of Rustwater. Jonas decides to pitch the revival tent right there and make the best of a bad situation.

Rustwater is a town in desperate straits; the townspeople and local farmers are reeling from recession and drought; if rain does not come soon, the year's crop will fail. Jonas and his manager, Jane Larson (Debra Winger), immediately encounter difficulties in securing the permits to hold their meetings. Will (Liam Neeson), the local sheriff, knowing a con artist when he sees one, only reluctantly allows Nightengale to do his show. Soon, however, the choir is rehearsing, the tent is raised, and the stage is set for collisions between cynical operators and just-plain-folks, with eventual revelations and changes of heart.

The opening night of the revival show is a tour de force. Film viewers see the rousing show that the audience in the tent sees, including the fine gospel music performances, but they also see Jane at the helm of a sophisticated electronic system that allows her to observe the audience via television monitors. She communicates by headset radio with members of the crew moving among the people and then relays the information they overhear to Jonas, who uses it to astound his audience.

As the story proceeds, scenes of the nightly revival shows alternate with glimpses of life in the outside world. There is an immediate attraction between Jane and Will, although Jane is at first reluctant to become involved with him. Living her life in the fast lane of the interstate, she seems to enjoy her superiority to the simple people who hand over their money to Jonas' revival extravaganza. Yet Will senses, as the audience does, that Jane is capable of much better things.

Jonas, meanwhile, becomes nominally involved in the lives of a local waitress, Marva (Lolita Davidovich), and her disabled younger brother, Boyd (Lukas Haas), who can walk only with the aid of a crutch. Jonas has sexual designs on Marva, but she is not interested. She hates phony evangelists, she tells him, because one had come through town a few years before and promised to heal her brother's leg; all he did was break Boyd's heart. Nevertheless, Boyd maintains a naïve faith that is the equal of Marva's cynicism.

Will interrupts the revival meeting one night by announcing that Jonas has a criminal past in New York. Jonas at first thinks that his days in Rainwater are through, but then he recovers triumphantly. Yes, he proclaims boldly to those gathered in the tent, he was a sinner—but who better than a former sinner to save others from sin? He keeps his audience enthralled, leaving Will dumbfounded both at Jonas' resourcefulness and at people's willingness to be deceived.

Jonas emphasizes faith healing in his performances. Inevitably, as he is at the peak of a showy "healing" frenzy one night, young Boyd approaches the stage, hoping that Jonas can heal his leg. Suddenly seeing him, Jonas is filled with dread (and perhaps remorse); he flees the stage. The crowd, however, demands that Jonas return to heal one more person—Boyd. At Jonas' touch, Boyd tentatively manages to walk again.

Boyd, convinced of Jonas' healing powers, wants to leave town with the revival company, but Jonas has been stunned by this turn of events. Early the next morning, he steals out of town alone. At film's end, he is riding away in the cab of a truck, the driver having picked him up hitchhiking. As Jonas looks out the truck window, the desperately needed rain begins to fall.

The primary flaw in *Leap of Faith* is the tonal shift between the majority of the film and its final twenty minutes. The first part of the film painstakingly portrays the array of tricks the revivalist crew uses to fool the gullible. It plays as an entertaining exposé of con artistry—a tradition reminiscent of such films as *The Sting* (1973) and *The Grifters* (1990). *Leap of Faith* even boasts a technical credit for a "cons and frauds" consultant. Because of the revival show's electronic gear and television monitors, the film's veiled comment on the sophisticated con game that is run by so many televangelists is unavoidable.

Unfortunately, this clear-eyed portrayal of master scam artists using religion to entertain and bilk the faithful is simply not reconcilable with the hokeyness of the film's ending. After establishing a certain direction and tone, the film veers off into another realm. By the end, there is not one conversion from cynicism to a kind of faith but two—Jonas' and Jane's. In addition, Boyd is able to walk again and the whole town is miraculously "cured" when the long-awaited rain begins to fall. The musical overkill in the final scenes exemplifies the problems with this closure; the music is pure Hollywood cliché, with gushing violins playing angelic chords.

Martin's performance is at the center of the film, and as much fun as he is to watch, he does not project the intensity and charisma that one associates with a successful revivalist. Even while preaching (in Jonas' case, "performing" would be a better word), he seems more genial than filled with evangelical fervor. Martin is light on his feet, but nimbleness is not enough for this role. Offstage, Jonas remains elusive; in his scenes with Marva and Boyd, viewers never find out whether he says certain things from his heart or as part of yet another act. Throughout, he somehow seems too much the "regular guy." One could argue that this very quality is what so often makes a successful con artist, but the film does not seem to be trying to make that point; neither does it attempt any philosophical comments on the banality of evil. It does point out a certain moral ambiguity in Jonas' line of work, however, when Jonas passionately insists that he is giving the people something valuable for their money: "a good show, plenty of music, worthwhile sentiments." For a moment, one wants to accept the rationalization; Jonas may even be persuading himself.

Jonas and Jane each have a scene in which to accuse the other of being the most cynical, heartless wretch on the face of the earth. Yet Jane gradually (and predictably) warms up to Neeson's easygoing, gently earnest Will. Her shift in loyalty—she arrives late for the show one night, temporarily stranding Jonas without her needed radio information—would carry more weight, however, if viewers had more information on the nature of Jonas and Jane's relationship. Has it ever been more than platonic, or have they always been only business partners?

The direction by Richard Pearce, whose work includes *Country* (1984) and *The Long Walk Home* (1990), is fine, as are the technical credits; particularly effective is the design of Jonas' revival tent—part cathedral, part circus tent. Location filming (actually done in Texas) creates the proper midwestern atmosphere.

The film's prominent use of rousing gospel music is noteworthy; the music is one of its unique and enjoyable features. Among the top-notch contributors are singers Albertina Walker and Delores Hall, choirmaster Edwin Hawkins, and producer George Duke. Yet there is an odd aspect to the Angels of Mercy's role in Jonas' entourage and in the film itself. The choir is never integrated into the action; occasionally its members comment bemusedly on Jonas' behavior in a way that sounds as though they have no idea that he is crooked. There is something a bit jarring in this, although the filmmakers certainly did not intend it. The choir members' seeming lack of comprehension brings them unsettlingly close to stereotypical portrayals of African Americans.

Leap of Faith was released in mid-December by a studio hoping for a holiday hit, but the film did not find enough of an audience to secure a successful run. One problem was simply that it was not a "typical" Steve Martin comedy, but another may have been that the film's two different tones managed to alienate its viewers. Many religious viewers would have been put off by the cynicism of the opening sections (particularly around Christmastime), whereas viewers appreciative of the debunking of phony revivalists would have felt cheated by the film's all-too-pat ending.

McCrea Adams

Reviews

Chicago Tribune. December 18, 1992, VII, p. 29.
The Christian Science Monitor. December 18, 1992, p. 12.
The Hollywood Reporter. December 15, 1992, p. 10.
Los Angeles Times. December 18, 1992, p. F1.
National Review. XLV, February, 1993, p. 60.
The New York Times. December 18, 1992, p. C14.
Newsweek. CXX, December 28, 1992, p. 58.
Time. CXL, December 28, 1992, p. 64.
Variety. December 15, 1992, p. 4.
The Washington Post. December 18, 1992, p. D1.

LETHAL WEAPON III

Production: Joel Silver and Richard Donner for Silver Pictures; released by Warner Bros.
Direction: Richard Donner
Screenplay: Jeffrey Boam and Robert Mark Kamen; based on a story by Boam and on characters created by Shane Black
Cinematography: Jan De Bont
Editing: Robert Brown and Battle Davis
Production design: James Spencer
Art direction: Greg Papalia
Set decoration: Richard Goddard
Casting: Marion Dougherty
Special effects supervision: Matt Sweeney
Sound: Thomas Causey
Costume design: Nick Scarano
Stunt coordination: Charlie Picerni and Mic Rodgers
Music: Michael Kamen, Eric Clapton, and David Sanborn
MPAA rating: R
Running time: 118 minutes

Principal characters:

Martin Riggs	Mel Gibson
Roger Murtaugh	Danny Glover
Leo Getz	Joe Pesci
Lorna Cole	Rene Russo
Jack Travis	Stuart Wilson
Captain Murphy	Steve Kahan
Trish Murtaugh	Darlene Love
Rianne Murtaugh	Traci Wolfe
Nick Murtaugh	Damon Hines
Carrie Murtaugh	Ebonie Smith
Tyrone	Gregory Millar
Dr. Stephanie Woods	Mary Ellen Trainor

In 1992, one of the big winners of the early summer film sweepstakes was *Lethal Weapon III*. According to *The Washington Post*, it had the biggest opening weekend since *Batman* (1989), three years before, earning $33.2 million and overwhelming all the competition in release before Memorial Day. This figure was eclipsed weeks later, however, with the release of *Batman Returns* (reviewed in this volume). It then continued to dominate the market; by the end of its second week, it had grossed more than $70 million. By year's end, the sequel made more than $144 million, surpassed only by *Batman Returns*.

If anyone had wondered why Hollywood continues to make sequels, *Lethal Weapon III* provided the rationale. The *Lethal Weapon* series has perfected the genre of the police buddy film, and Warner Bros. was smart enough to stay with Richard Donner, the director who first brought the Mel Gibson-Danny Glover white-black cop team to life on the screen. Not all film critics were enthusiastic about the film. For example, Gene Siskel did not find it sufficiently innovative. Yet, the film drew record numbers of viewers. This sequel follows the pattern of *Lethal Weapon II* (1989) and brings back many of the same characters: Darlene Love as Trish Murtaugh, Traci Wolfe as Rianne Murtaugh, and Joe Pesci as Leo Getz, for example. There is not much substance to the story, which is carried along by spasms of violence and star acting.

While the film has little more to offer than escapist entertainment, it starts off with a bang, as detectives Martin Riggs (Gibson) and Roger Murtaugh (Glover) are sent to investigate a bomb threat at an office building. They find the bomb, and Riggs undertakes to dismantle it. He cannot decide whether to cut the red wire or the blue one on the detonating device, and ultimately he makes the wrong choice. Riggs and Murtaugh manage to escape the building before it explodes, but they are demoted to work on the beat as a result of Riggs's mistake.

The spectacular bombing of the office building is merely a device to reintroduce the characters and their typical traits, the manic Riggs playing off the down-to-earth Murtaugh. The true plot begins about ten minutes later when, as cops on the beat, they come across an armored-truck robbery in progress. Riggs jumps on the truck as it is escaping, with Murtaugh in pursuit in a second armored truck. (This truck's woman driver immediately develops a huge crush on the married Murtaugh, setting up a situation that provides continuing comic relief.) This heroic exploit then reinstates Riggs and Murtaugh to detective status. It also provides an exciting chase sequence early in the film, to keep the thrill-seeking audience happy.

The script follows a definite path and offers a well-constructed machine of a film. Their investigation of the robbery puts Riggs and Murtaugh in pursuit of a ruthless renegade cop named Jack Travis (Stuart Wilson), who runs a construction company as a front. He is also a drug dealer who provides high-tech firearms and ammunition to local drug lords.

A new wrinkle in the plot is Murtaugh's plan to take advantage of early retirement. He changes his mind at the end of the motion picture, however, leaving open the door for a *Lethal Weapon IV*. The film also borrows shamelessly from *Boyz 'n the Hood* (1991), when Roger's son, Nick (Damon Hines), becomes friendly with a street gang that is involved in drug dealing. Murtaugh puts an end to this problem when he kills his son's best friend in a shoot-out after intercepting a drug deal. Murtaugh is racked with guilt, however, and he has further misgivings about continuing his police career.

More interesting is the introduction of a new character to the formula. After some antagonism, Riggs befriends a tough female cop named Lorna Cole (Rene Russo), who works for Internal Affairs. She turns out to be both his match and his female counterpart—tough, bold, brazen, and violent. The best scene in the film has the two of them becoming romantically involved after they inspect and admire each other's scars from wounds suffered in the line of duty. Ultimately, both are tracking down Travis, the renegade, so they have a reason to be working together. Their complementary teamwork has as much potential as the mismatched teamwork between Riggs and Murtaugh. Nevertheless, the filmmakers do not allow this new romantic team to eclipse the traditional buddy one.

Riggs is determined to stop smoking, and as a substitute for cigarettes, he munches on dog biscuits. When Riggs and Lorna encounter a ferocious guard dog, Riggs is able to win the animal over by sharing his treats—one of the most improbable and contrived scenes in the film but also one of the most amusing because of Gibson's comic acting. The weakest link in the motion picture is the Leo Getz character, carried over from the previous sequel and played by Pesci, who does the best that he can with an inferior character that is more irritating than comic. This time, the Getz character is a Beverly Hills real-estate entrepreneur trying to sell Murtaugh's house. He has no real function, however, in the plot.

The development of the *Lethal Weapon* formula demonstrates an interesting experiment in marketing. In the first *Lethal Weapon* (1987), Gibson's character was a suicidal manic-depressive who had served in the Vietnam War, who had recently lost his wife, and whose unpredictable outbursts made the film interesting. *Lethal Weapon II* shifted to physical comedy of the sort popularized by the Three Stooges, and this comedy served to improve the product—or at least to make it more popular. Therefore, the eye-poking humor of this sequel is effectively carried over to *Lethal Weapon III*. The screenplay, by Jeffrey Boam and Robert Mark Kamen, preserves the comic tone of the preceding sequel. The dialogue has some snappy moments, but it is more often self-consciously cute.

On the whole, this is paint-by-numbers filmmaking. *Variety* observed that the motion picture is "really more about moments—either comic or thrilling—than any sort of cohesive whole," but praised Michael Kamen, Eric Clapton, and David Sanborn for having produced an "admirable score." Jan De Bont's cinematography is faultless. If this formula blockbuster is satisfactory as a sequel, it is because the effective teamwork and the nonstop action and banter make it easier for Gibson and Glover to lope through a mediocre plot and past the inane foolishness of Pesci's character. As Jack Kroll noted in *Newsweek*, *Lethal Weapon III* offers "violence as pure farce." In this respect and others, it may be regarded as a perfect sequel.

James M. Welsh

Reviews

Chicago Tribune. May 15, 1992, VII, p. 25.
Entertainment Weekly. May 22, 1992, p. 50.
Films in Review. XLIII, July, 1992, p. 269.

The Hollywood Reporter. May 14, 1992, p. 5.
Los Angeles Times. May 15, 1992, p. F1.
The New York Times. May 15, 1992, p. B4.
Newsweek. CXIX, May 25, 1992, p. 91.
Rolling Stone. June 25, 1992, p. 49.
Variety. May 14, 1992, p. 4.
The Washington Post. May 15, 1992, p. B1.

LIGHT SLEEPER

Production: Linda Reisman; released by Fine Line Features
Direction: Paul Schrader
Screenplay: Paul Schrader
Cinematography: Ed Lachman
Editing: Kristina Boden
Production design: Richard Hornung
Casting: Ellen Chenoweth
Costume design: Giorgio Armani
Music: Michael Been
MPAA rating: R
Running time: 103 minutes

Principal characters:

John LeTour	Willem Dafoe
Ann	Susan Sarandon
Marianne	Dana Delany
Robert	David Clennon
Teresa	Mary Beth Hurt
Tis	Victor Garber
Randi	Jane Adams

Paul Schrader, along with his contemporary and sometime collaborator Martin Scorsese, came of age professionally in the 1970's. An era lost somewhere between the activism and youthful exuberance of the 1960's and the button-down yuppiedom of the 1980's, the 1970's was a period of transition for Americans. Scorsese and Schrader, among others, chronicled the dark, seamy underside of life during the decade of Vietnam and its angry aftermath. They told of the anxiety of a drug culture and the anger of a nation whose innocence had been lost.

Scorsese and Schrader teamed up in 1976 to create *Taxi Driver*, one of the most vivid and memorable films in modern American cinema. Written by Schrader and directed by Scorsese, *Taxi Driver* tells the tale of the angry and paranoid Travis Bickle (played by Robert De Niro), whose paranoia leads him on a self-righteous path of violence. Schrader then broke out on his own and directed *American Gigolo* (1980), another quirky film filled with characters who inhabit the outer edges of society. Julian Kay (played by Richard Gere) is a high-class hustler whose self-centered existence begins a downward spiral toward murder and scandal.

Schrader continued his panorama of lost souls in 1992 with *Light Sleeper*, starring Willem Dafoe, Susan Sarandon, and Dana Delany. The progression in characters from Travis Bickle to John LeTour, the protagonist in *Light Sleeper* (played by Dafoe), is complete. LeTour owns something that neither Travis Bickle nor Julian Kay possesses: a conscience.

LeTour works as a high-class drug delivery agent for Ann (Sarandon), New York's classiest dealer, a sexy but motherly figure who is looking to get out of the drug business. It is the 1990's and crack, the crude and hard-edged street variation of cocaine, has found its demand, leaving no room for uptown dealers like Ann. After a Columbia University student is killed in a drug-related incident, the police are coming down even harder on small-time dealers, and Ann and LeTour are feeling the heat. Ann and LeTour are too enmeshed in the upscale New York City drug life to break out. Like Julian Kay in *American Gigolo*, whose occupation becomes his identity, LeTour finds it impossible to consider life without dealing. Although he has been clean of drugs for years, dealing is his life and Ann is his only family. Forty years old and awakening to his lost sense of place in the world, LeTour wanders the streets on sleepless nights searching for meaning in his life. Schrader described how LeTour's character fits in with his previous characters: "In *Taxi Driver*, I wrote about this character when he was in his 20's and he was young and paranoid and angry, and he saw the city as his enemy. In *American Gigolo*, the character was examined in his 30's when he was very narcissistic, very self-involved, and he was a gigolo. Now he's 40 and he's anxious. He's looking at the back stretch of his life, wondering, 'What's the second half gonna be like? Is there a plan?' "

LeTour's life changes irrevocably when, one night during a drop, he spots Marianne (Delany), his former girlfriend and love of his life, who is back in New York to care for her dying mother. Thrilled to see Marianne again, LeTour tries to rekindle their love, hoping that she might be the inspiration that he needs to face the world without dealing drugs. Marianne, however, is sober now, after a long struggle, and sees LeTour as a bad habit that she cannot afford to take up again. Yet, as he persists, she eventually gives in to her feelings, and they share a night of passion. Marianne's mother passes away the next day, and Marianne blames LeTour for yet another tragedy in her life, ordering him never to see her again.

Days later, as he is making a delivery to Tis (Victor Garber), one of Ann's wealthy European clients, LeTour sees a drugged and grief-stricken Marianne stumble out of Tis's bedroom. Keeping his cool, LeTour leaves without incident. Shaken and devastated, he can barely navigate his way back to the street. Suddenly, he hears a scream as a body falls from the skyscraper to the concrete below. Sensing the worst, LeTour fights through the gathering crowd and sees that the crumpled body on the sidewalk is Marianne.

Tis, worried that LeTour will go to the police and accuse him of pushing Marianne to her death, phones Ann and requests that LeTour make a personal delivery that night. LeTour, having bought a gun, is suspicious of Tis's intentions and insists that Ann join him on the delivery. She does, although she senses that LeTour is on edge. Tis's bodyguards are armed and waiting for LeTour in the trap. Ann runs out into the hallway as LeTour shoots Tis and his bodyguards dead. LeTour is taken to jail without resistance.

LeTour's act is more than vengeance for Marianne's death. It is a way of finally freeing himself of the dead-end track from which he knew no escape. Because of the investigation, Ann is forced to quit the drug business once and for all. She is successful in her legitimate cosmetics business and continues to visit LeTour in jail, as they have forged a new, closer relationship away from the business. As LeTour is finally forced to face life without drugs, he realizes there is life after dealing. He is looking forward, not backward, for the first time in his life.

Willem Dafoe, Susan Sarandon, and Dana Delany are interesting choices for this film. Dafoe, a screen veteran and Academy Award nominee for *Platoon* (1986), had found great success in creating seedy characters such as the ones that he played in *Wild at Heart* (1990) and *Born on the Fourth of July* (1989), but he proved that he could play the straight man, as he did in *Mississippi Burning* (1988) and *Flight of the Intruder* (1991). He had worked with Schrader before in Martin Scorsese's *The Last Temptation of Christ* (1988), which Schrader wrote, and seemed the perfect choice to play John LeTour. LeTour is an obsessive character who has lost his passion—a difficult assignment for any actor—but Dafoe plays LeTour with quiet abandon, brilliantly making him his own.

Sarandon and Delany, however, seem to be almost surprising selections to play Ann and Marianne in this quiet and low-budget film. Sarandon, a big-name Hollywood star who had just come off a high-profile Academy Award nomination for *Thelma and Louise* (1991), takes a relatively minor character in *Light Sleeper* and infuses her with charm and grace. Delany found great success on television, winning awards for her portrayal of army nurse Colleen McMurphy in the highly acclaimed series *China Beach*, and ignited a film career by starring with Steve Martin in *Housesitter* (1992; reviewed in this volume). She takes a risk playing the doomed Marianne, a character who seems to be as far away from the angelic Colleen McMurphy as possible. Although a challenge for an actress, such a role at this point in a career could spell disaster, but time will show that Delany is a true talent and that her performance in *Light Sleeper* is worthy of distinction.

Paul Schrader seems to be more optimistic in this film, perhaps reflecting the mood of the 1990's as compared to the bleak 1970's. He had a goal in mind with *Light Sleeper*: He says that he was interested in showing "how people really aren't that dissimilar, and people who do things that are evil may not necessarily be evil themselves." This opinion is a far cry from that of Travis Bickle, who is considered to be one of the most paranoid and demonic characters in modern film history.

Catherine R. Springer

Reviews

Chicago Tribune. September 4, 1992, VII, p. 33.
The Christian Science Monitor. August 27, 1992, p. 13.
Entertainment Weekly. August 28, 1992, p. 40.
Film Comment. XXVIII, March, 1992, p. 50.
Los Angeles Times. September 4, 1992, p. F4.

National Review. XLIV, October 5, 1992, p. 62.
The New York Times. August 21, 1992, p. C12.
People Weekly. September 7, 1992, p. 14.
Sight and Sound. I, April, 1992, p. 54.
Variety. CCCXLVI, January 27, 1992.

LORENZO'S OIL

Production: Doug Mitchell and George Miller for Kennedy Miller; released by Universal Pictures
Direction: George Miller
Screenplay: George Miller and Nick Enright
Cinematography: John Seale
Editing: Richard Francis-Bruce, Marcus D'Arcy, and Lee Smith
Production design: Kristen Zea
Art direction: Dennis Bradford
Set decoration: Karen A. O'Hara
Casting: John Lyons
Sound: Ben Osmo
Sound design: Lee Smith
Costume design: Colleen Atwood
Music supervision: Christine Woodruff
MPAA rating: PG-13
Running time: 135 minutes

Principal characters:

Augusto Odone .... Nick Nolte
Michaela Odone .... Susan Sarandon
Lorenzo Odone .... Zack O'Malley Greenburg
Professor Nikolais .... Peter Ustinov
Deirdre Murphy .... Kathleen Wilhoite
Dr. Judalon .... Gerry Bamman
Wendy Gimble .... Margo Martindale
Ellard Muscatine .... James Rebhorn
Loretta Muscatine .... Ann Hearn
Omouri .... Maduka Steady
Comorian teacher .... Mary Wakio
Don Suddaby .... Himself

Director George Miller's drama *Lorenzo's Oil*, based on the true story of the Odone family, is a film that is extremely hard to enjoy; the experience of watching the Odones struggling to keep their dying child alive is not even remotely an entertaining one. In the film, Miller is relentless in his depiction of the family's great emotional despair and the horrific effects of disease on five-year-old Lorenzo Odone. One senses early in the film that Miller will offer no easy miracles, no respite from the family's pain, and ultimately, no chance of a full recovery. Despite this overwhelming pathos, however, *Lorenzo's Oil* is a film to be greatly admired because of the brutal honesty of the filmmaking and the sight of actors performing at the peak of their craft.

Miller, an Australian who began his feature career directing wild, futuristic action thrillers, employs his usual hyperkinetic directorial style to put a new spin on a trite genre. With frenetic editing and a camera that appears to be always on the move, Miller takes the tired medical drama and transforms it into something quite unique: a full-fledged medical thriller. In his early Australian films, *Mad Max* (1979) and *The Road Warrior* (1981), Miller, using the same breathless pacing and manic camera movements that he employs in *Lorenzo's Oil,* made a name for himself as one of the premier international action directors. Steven Spielberg soon tapped him to direct the "Nightmare at 20,000 Feet" segment of *Twilight Zone—The Movie* (1983). The episode was universally praised as the best in the film and successfully launched Miller's Hollywood career. After codirecting a disappointing third installment of the *Mad Max* trilogy, *Mad Max Beyond Thunderdome* (1985), and directing the disastrous *The Witches of Eastwick* (1987), however, Miller's career looked like a mere flash in the pan.

Lorenzo's Oil is considered by many to be quite a departure for the former action director. Yet the film seems like a logical next step for Miller. Before becoming a filmmaker, he graduated from the University of New South Wales medical school, and in 1972, he began a residency at Sydney's St. Vincent's Hospital. Making short subjects was Miller's hobby until his *Violence in the Cinema—Part One*, a satire on film violence codirected by the late Byron Kennedy, won several awards on the international film festival circuit. *Lorenzo's Oil,* therefore, takes a subject to which Miller is obviously close and blends it with his unique visual style, creating a film that pushes him back into the American film scene. Perhaps, his medical knowledge and his compassion for the victims of disease contributed to the critical success of the film; the film's screenplay, cowritten by Nick Enright, was nominated for Best Original Screenplay by the Academy of Motion Picture Arts and Sciences.

In 1984, Augusto (Nick Nolte) and Michaela (Susan Sarandon) Odone, an international banker from Italy and an Irish-American linguist, respectively, learn that their young son, Lorenzo (Zack O'Malley Greenburg), is a victim of adrenoleukodystrophy (ALD), a fatal disease that, because of its rarity, is generally ignored by the medical research community. The disease, by decreasing the body's ability to process saturated fat and allowing those saturated fats to attack the nervous system, causes dementia, blindness, paralysis, and eventually death. Michaela and Augusto, upon learning of their son's disease, are shocked that doctors are not searching diligently for a cure. Michaela also must deal with extreme guilt; the disease only affects young males and is passed on by a defective gene from the mother. While Michaela shuts off her emotions, alienating most of those around her, Lorenzo quickly falls victim to the initial ravages of the disease. His behavior becomes uncontrollable, his speech disintegrates, and his mobility is drastically diminished. Michaela and Augusto place Lorenzo on a special diet that eliminates most saturated fats and reluctantly join a support group headed by Ellard and Loretta Muscatine (James Rebhorn and Ann Hearn). The Odones are frustrated by the group's unconditional support for the doctors treating the stricken children and are shocked that no one has been trying to provoke the authorities into extensively researching ALD. Pledging to their son, who is now immobile and without speech, that they will do everything humanly possible to save him, the Odones begin their quest of finding a cure for the disease.

Discovering long-ignored research, Michaela determines that, through fatty-acid manipulation, saturated fats in animals have been found to decrease. The Odones believe, in direct opposition to the experts, that if they introduce saturated fats to Lorenzo's diet, his body will cease creating the fats that are deteriorating his myelin, the tissue that protects his nervous system. After securing an olive oil product with the proper fatty-acid composition, they take Lorenzo off the special diet diagnosed by their doctor, Professor Nikolais (Peter Ustinov), and begin feeding him their special oil. Immediately, Lorenzo's saturated fat count plummets. (His paralysis and dementia, however, are unaffected.) The Odones celebrate their success, but when they ask the Muscatines to alert the other parents in the support group, the Muscatines scold the Odones for their arrogance. The Muscatines trust only the doctors, and they tell the Odones that their supposed cure may be only prolonging their son's misery.

Lorenzo's saturated fat count soon levels off, and the Odones must face the fact that their olive oil may be only temporary treatment. Lorenzo, unable to swallow, begins to have convulsions that last through the night. Augusto questions his and Michaela's search for a cure; perhaps it would be best to let Lorenzo die rather than to continue his suffering. Michaela, though, refuses to give up and angrily throws her helpful sister, Deirdre (Kathleen Wilhoite), out of her house for questioning her ethics. During a horrendous day and night in which Lorenzo suffers his most harrowing convulsions, Michaela whispers to Lorenzo to stop fighting if he is in too much pain. Lorenzo survives the ordeal, and the Odones find renewed strength.

Augusto, after extensive research, formulates a new theory: By manipulating the saturated fats in the olive oil solution, the deadly saturated fats could be completely replaced with safer fats easily processed by Lorenzo's body. The Odones find an English biochemist, Don Suddaby (playing himself), who makes the new oil. Professor Nikolais lectures them about the possible toxicity of the olive oil solution and about the dangers of taking medical science into their own unprofessional hands. After testing the oil successfully on themselves, the Odones begin feeding it intravenously to Lorenzo. Within days, Lorenzo's saturated fat count is back to normal, and the progress of his debilitating disease is stopped. The Odones are ecstatic, but their success is bittersweet: Lorenzo's ravaged nervous system is beyond repair. The Odones have discovered a cure for ALD, but it is too late perhaps to save Lorenzo. They must now turn their efforts to finding a way to rebuild his destroyed myelin so that Lorenzo will someday be able to walk and speak. As the film ends, George Miller treats the viewer to scores of images of actual boys saved from ALD by their treatment with Lorenzo's oil.

Miller, by refusing to compromise by appealing to the lowest common denominator, is quite successful in differentiating *Lorenzo's Oil* from the average disease-of-the-week television film. He and cowriter Enright shove every medical fact they can into the film, and like the Odones themselves, a viewer is quickly overwhelmed. Miller and actor Nick Nolte give Augusto a much-criticized Italian accent in order to remain absolutely faithful to the dynamics of the actual story. Furthermore, Miller never allows the film to sink into sentimental melodrama. In only one scene, in which Augusto tells Michaela that their cure will not save Lorenzo, does Miller allow Susan Sarandon to let loose with tears of anguish.

Much credit for the honest emotions on display in *Lorenzo's Oil* must be given to veteran actress Susan Sarandon. With her brave portrayal of Michaela Odone, she gives what many critics called her finest performance. For her work in *Lorenzo's Oil*, Sarandon was nominated for a Golden Globe by the Hollywood Foreign Press and an Academy Award as Best Actress. The actress plays Michaela as a relentlessly protective mother, a woman who saves all of her love and compassion for her dying child. Sarandon risks offending a viewer's sympathy by her humorless performance, but by expertly depicting her character's strength and courage, she ultimately comes off as a full-fledged modern heroine. In the moment late in film when Michaela finally is allowed to mourn for her son, Sarandon is particularly effective. With her haggard face and exhausted eyes, she suggests not only the great emotional burden that she has been forced to carry but also the extreme guilt that her character harbors for transmitting the disease to her son. Neither she nor Miller shy away from what is required to make *Lorenzo's Oil* a truly inspiring film.

Greg Changnon

Reviews

Chicago Tribune. January 15, 1993, VII, p. 19.
Entertainment Weekly. CLIII, January 15, 1993, p. 34.
The Hollywood Reporter. CCCXXV, December 21, 1992, p. 6.
Los Angeles Times. December 30, 1992, p. F1.
The New York Times. December 30, 1992, CXLII, p. B1.
The New Yorker. LXVIII, January 11, 1993, p. 101.
Newsweek. CXXI, January 4, 1993, p. 50.
Time. CXLI, January 11, 1993, p. 53.
Variety. December 22, 1993, p. 10.
The Washington Post. January 15, 1993, p. B1.

LOVE FIELD

Production: Sarah Pillsbury and Midge Sanford; released by Orion Pictures
Direction: Jonathan Kaplan
Screenplay: Don Roos
Cinematography: Ralf Bode
Editing: Jane Kurson
Production design: Mark Freeborn
Art direction: David Willson and Lance King
Set decoration: Jim Erickson
Casting: Julie Selzer and Sally Dennison
Sound: Glen Anderson
Costume design: Peter Mitchell and Colleen Atwood
Music: Jerry Goldsmith
MPAA rating: PG-13
Running time: 104 minutes

Principal characters:

Lurene Hallett	Michelle Pfeiffer
Paul Cater	Dennis Haysbert
Jonell	Stephanie McFadden
Ray Hallett	Brian Kerwin
Mrs. Enright	Louise Latham
Mrs. Heisenbuttal	Peggy Rea
Hazel	Beth Grant

One of the most profound events in American history was the assassination of John F. Kennedy on November 22, 1963. It affected not only the political life of the country but also its heart and soul. Values and belief systems were violently uprooted and challenged by the immense tragedy. Minds that once were clear suddenly became clouded by doubt and suspicion. Human emotion was raw, and everyone felt vulnerable and afraid when assaulted with the horrific images coming across the airways. It was a shocking and unforgettable moment, and some said that it was literally the end of innocence.

This historic day was the backdrop that coproducer and screenwriter Don Roos chose for his story in *Love Field* because it served as a constant reminder of how rapidly people and events were changing during that chaotic upheaval. Director Jonathan Kaplan was intrigued by "the national tragedy which would change this country forever, and the experience of three people whose lives change simultaneously." The juxtaposition of these events makes for an interesting and compelling story about conflicting human emotions.

President Kennedy and the First Lady are arriving in Dallas. Everyone is excited, but no one more than Lurene Hallett (Michelle Pfeiffer). She believes that she has a deep kinship with Mrs. Kennedy: She is around the same age and, like Jackie, lost a baby through miscarriage. Often, she imagines that she is the First Lady and sometimes hears John Kennedy's voice when her husband (Brian Kerwin) speaks to her. She duplicates the First Lady's famous bouffant hairstyle, even though hers is more the color of another famous personality, Marilyn Monroe. At Love Field airport in Dallas, she waits nervously and anxiously to catch a glimpse of the famous couple, only to miss her chance to shake their hands when they do pass by the crowd. She leaves disappointed, but also delighted simply to have seen them up close. There they were, the king and queen of "Camelot," only a few feet from her own reality—a dream come true.

Suddenly, Kennedy is dead. The television repeatedly shows the film footage of Mrs. Kennedy climbing onto the back of the convertible in an attempt to retrieve part of her husband's brain. Lurene is devastated, as is everyone, and the dream becomes a nightmare. Horror replaces joy, smiles turn to tears, and an aura of surrealism takes over everything.

In Lurene's eyes, because of her special bond with Jackie, she believes that she must attend the funeral of her slain hero. In an attempt to find some sanity in a world gone mad, she heads toward Washington, D.C., by bus. On her quest, she encounters an African American man named Paul Johnson (Dennis Haysbert) and his small daughter, Jonell (Stephanie McFadden). Eventually, Lurene discovers that Paul Johnson is really Paul Cater and, through a series of events, finds out once again that things are not as they appear. Undaunted by the day's events and the mystery surrounding her traveling companions, Lurene is determined to get to Washington in time for the funeral.

"The road lends itself to film," says Jonathan Kaplan. "People tend to experience time more differently during a long trip. Film can communicate the dreamlike nature of a journey, compressing or expanding time in the same way the characters experience it." Usually, in road films, the main characters are running from something to something new and better. Their destination may be some geographic location, but ultimately it is self-discovery. In *Thelma and Louise* (1991), the two women were searching for their independence, escaping the shackles that the men in their lives had imposed on them. As they traveled down the road, the audience wondered if freedom was right around the bend for them. What would be the fate of these renegades who were fleeing from imprisoned lives? Would they find what they were searching for?

In many ways, the audience asks the same questions about Lurene and Paul in *Love Field*. It appears that they have little in common with each other on the surface. Lurene, a white woman who is somewhat fed up with her marriage, asks, "What do you do when you marry someone you grew up with, then discover you have nothing to talk about. There's always children." Paul Cater, an African American pharmacist, has worked hard to carve out some dignity for himself and has fought to overcome the extreme racism of the early 1960's. As he puts it, there is a difference between "being bored and being black."

As the bus rolls down the highway, more is revealed to Lurene about Paul and the little girl. She mistakenly believes that he is involved in foul play and, consequently, involves the Federal Bureau of Investigation (FBI). After realizing her error, she sides with Paul in his attempt to hold onto his child, Jonell. At this point in the story, they both become fugitives from justice. In their mutual determination, Lurene and Paul continue their journey, involving themselves in petty crimes along the way.

This is an American tale, and the locations used (North Carolina and Richmond, Virginia) capture the authentic sense of Americana that is required by the story. The openness of the terrain serves as a symbol of the vastness of experiences that awaits the three main characters. Much detail was also used to re-create the time period authentically. The film offers viewers a glimpse into the past, allowing them to experience life in the early 1960's, a simpler time about to become much more complicated by the events of November, 1963. The film is able to convey the impact of the assassination on the people's attitudes and belief systems. At one point, Lurene sighs, "Everything is so confusing all of a sudden." She speaks not only for herself but for the entire nation as well.

Michelle Pfeiffer's performance in *Love Field* did not go unnoticed, as she was nominated for a Golden Globe Award, a People's Choice Award, and an Academy Award. Her substantial talent is showcased well in the film. There is a commitment by Pfeiffer to the role that is unwavering, and the choices she makes as an actress are both affecting and surprising. Lurene is a well-crafted and believable character. In the beginning of the film, Lurene appears to be simple and somewhat silly. As the story progresses, however, the many different layers of this woman start to emerge. The audience begins to see not only her vulnerability and sensitivity but her vitality and strength as well. Viewers see a woman about to break free from old, restrictive ideas imposed on her by others. In some ways, Lurene represents the early emergence of the feminist movement in her efforts to become a free-thinking individual. In a dramatic confrontation with Paul, she proclaims, "We're both runnin'. We're both wantin' somethin' more." It is a performance of tremendous grace, warmth, beauty, and humor, which is a praiseworthy achievement for any actress.

Dennis Haysbert's restrained characterization of Paul offers a nice balance to the high energy of Lurene. At first, he looks upon her as somewhat spoiled and dim-witted, but he slowly begins to recognize her considerable strengths. He sees Lurene's compassion for his child and her willingness to tackle the issues that arise between them. It is to these actors' credit that both characters steadily evolve throughout the film, becoming more enlightened human beings.

Love Field also deals with the difficult issue of racism in the early 1960's. Throughout the film, Lurene and Paul are challenged by the tremendous prejudice at this time and by the lack of acceptance of interracial relationships. Even in their own minds, because of their upbringing and conditioning, their mutual attraction is difficult to accept. At one point, Lurene wakes up on the bus to find Paul leaning over her. She is startled and says, "Oh, I thought it was the bogeyman." It is said innocently enough but reveals how such racist feelings are ingrained in Lurene's psyche. In another, more powerful example, Paul is beaten by three rednecks as his daughter watches. The camera closes in on Jonell, and the pain, horror, and confusion register on the child's face. The scene creates a powerful impact.

While the film tackles some very difficult issues, it does so without being heavy-handed. It does not preach to the audience, but forces viewers to examine their own feelings and beliefs. The film also tells a love story between three people who manage to come together in spite of many obstacles. It gives a glimpse of another era, one that gave birth to many important ideas and values. *Love Field* embarks on a journey, and the destination may well be the viewer's own self-discovery.

Robert F. Chicatelli

Reviews

Chicago Tribune. February 12, 1993, VII, p. 24.
The Hollywood Reporter. December 9, 1992, p. 6.
Los Angeles Times. December 11, 1992, p. F14.
National Review. XLV, March 29, 1993, p. 70.
The New Republic. CCVIII, March 15, 1993, p. 24.
The New York Times. December 11, 1992, p. B8.
The New Yorker. LXVIII, December 14, 1992, p. 121.
Time. CXL, December 21, 1992, p. 79.
Variety. December 9, 1992, p. 2.
The Washington Post. February 12, 1993, p. C1.

THE LOVER

Origin: France and Great Britain
Released: 1992
Released in U.S.: 1992
Production: Claude Berri for Renn, Burrill, and Films A2; released by Metro-Goldwyn-Mayer
Direction: Jean-Jacques Annaud
Screenplay: Gérard Brach and Jean-Jacques Annaud; based on the novel by Marguerite Duras
Cinematography: Robert Fraisse
Editing: Noëlle Boisson
Production design: Thanh At Hoang
Sound: Laurent Quaglio
Costume design: Yvonne Sassinet de Nesle
Music: Gabriel Yared
MPAA rating: R
Running time: 103 minutes

Principal characters:

The young girl	Jane March
The Chinese man	Tony Leung
The mother	Frédérique Meininger
Narrator	Jeanne Moreau
The elder brother	Arnaud Giovaninetti
The younger brother	Melvil Poupaud
Hélène Lagonelle	Lisa Faulkner
Chinese man's father	Xiem Mang

Advertised as an erotic love story for sophisticated viewers, Jean-Jacques Annaud's *The Lover* is much more and considerably less. It is much more in its effective evocation of colonial Vietnam of the 1920's, and it is considerably less in that its sexual interest is more cerebral than emotional. The main characters are a poor eighteen-year-old French schoolgirl (Jane March) and a wealthy thirty-two-year-old Chinese gentleman (Tony Leung). Their story is told in linear time but is often interpreted by a voice-over narrator (Jeanne Moreau) who represents the girl writing her memoirs many decades later.

The French girl lives on a failed rubber plantation in the countryside. Details about the absent father and the family's decline are never given, but the mother (Frédérique Meininger) states that she has made every mistake a woman can make. One of these is that her elder son (Arnaud Giovaninetti), an opium addict, is totally undisciplined and is a tyrant to everyone. The younger son (Melvil Poupaud) is the quintessential wimp given to weeping when put upon, which is often. The young woman's only relief from this emotional swamp is the time she spends at a mediocre boarding school in Saigon.

The film begins when the young woman boards a rickety old bus to return to school. This and subsequent trips allow cinematographer Robert Fraisse to show a Vietnam unruined by modern war. His camera remains nonjudgmental, showing the beauty of the land and its people without prettifying poverty. Always the audience sees only exteriors; it is in—but not within—Vietnam. One never really knows what the indigenous people are thinking or doing. In this the audience is like the French and Chinese settlers who are the film's central subject.

At a picturesque ferry crossing, the girl leaves the bus for some fresh air. Pretty without being a great beauty, she wears a simple schoolgirl's frock, and her hair is gathered in two braids. Her only distinction is a man's fedora. The narrator informs us that this marks her as a rebel. While the girl leans on the ferry's railing, a white limousine boards.

The car's sole passenger is a Chinese male. Enchanted by the young woman, he makes her acquaintance and invites her to continue her trip in the comfort of his luxurious automobile. One wonders if he is charmed by her youth, her European background, her availability, or some personal aura. The girl may be responding because she is a lonely rebel, or this may be a prototypical sexual awakening. Many questions are suggested through glances and the touch of fingers. The dialogue throughout the film is spare, holding back as much as it reveals.

The young woman confides her adventure to Hélène (Lisa Faulkner), the only other French girl in the school. They gossip about a former European classmate who has been found prostituting herself, less for money than for the thrill. The heroine expresses empathy for that impulse, and Hélène says she would rather be a prostitute than do the kind of social work her family has prepared her to do. The prostitution theme will emerge as one of the film's major touchstones.

The romance which began on the road to Saigon develops in a surprisingly swift and nonchalant fashion. The gentleman simply waits in his car by the school, and the young woman goes with him. Thereafter, his car picks her up after school and takes her to the rooms he has rented in a dingy area in Chinatown. This love nest is separated from the street by flimsy wood shutters. The audience experiences the Chinese culture through the sound coming in from the street.

The sex scenes are central to the film, and the first are by far the longest. Rather than developed erotic realism based on individual motivation, they essentially follow the conventions of soft-core pornography, rushing to the physical experience without an emotional buildup. Various body parts, mostly the girl's, are blown up for tactile effect; at a certain point the two bodies become a series of pulsating shadows that move like the sea.

In many respects the film's approach is faithful to the style of the best-selling novel by Marguerite Duras upon which it is based. Duras's technique is to present surfaces and allow the reader to provide meaning. This would seem a viable approach for an erotic film, but in this case the film simply lacks emotion or urgency.

The woman seems insensitive to the racial and sexual taboos she violates. She takes money from the man and seems to enjoy knowing that he has made love with other European women, but all of her reactions are recorded with a minimum of depth and language. Even her own sexual awakening seems curiously irrelevant. The author does not even give her main characters names. This kind of abstraction soon wears thin.

The Chinese gentleman's motives also remain vague. He will later tell his father (Xiem Mang) that his lust is so strong he cannot control himself, but one never gets a sense of that passion when he is with his lover. He wants her to say that she is having sex for money, but he never seems to believe it. He understands even better than she that this is only an erotic interlude in their lives, but no aura of sexual adventure flows from this perception. His only emotional confession is his revelation that he never thought it would be possible to make love to a European woman in an Asian land.

Having forsaken character development or any serious probing of the erotic relationship, the film drifts into soap opera. The couple begins to go out in the Chinese part of town, and the young woman does not bother returning to the school at night. Viewers are told that society is outraged, but no scenes explore that reaction. When her family confronts the young woman, she says he is only a friend. In a strange sequence, the impoverished family agrees to be taken to dinner at an expensive restaurant. The two brothers eat as if on the brink of starvation. The elder brother only addresses his Chinese host to insult him, but the mother is impressed by the Chinese man's bankroll and aristocratic manners.

Following the dinner, the mother endorses the relationship. She has her daughter "borrow" a large sum of money to meet boarding school costs and other family debts. The mother brazenly tells the school administrator that her daughter is allowed to come and go as she pleases. The administrator accedes to the situation, as her school's reputation rests on having at least one or two "full-blooded" Europeans as students.

The Chinese man's family intervenes in a different and more decisive way. They are an incredibly rich clan, and the man has been betrothed to a woman from another wealthy Chinese family since the age of six. To put an end to scandal and finalize the union of the two families, the man's father insists the wedding must proceed at once. The son's pleas for a bit more time are brushed aside.

The Chinese gentleman tells his lover that he is totally dependent on his family for survival. Their affair must end. He will pay off her brother's opium debt and give her mother the money needed to return the family to France. The only consolation for the girl is that he agrees that they can meet one last time after his marriage.

On the day of the wedding, the girl observes the transfer of the veiled bride by boat. As always, everything is external: Opulent Chinese, poor Vietnamese, and déclassé French touch but do not interact. All emotion remains concealed. Some time later, when she goes to the post-marital rendezvous, she finds the love nest stripped of their belongings. She waits through the greater part of a day and night, but her lover does not appear.

The film's penultimate sequences occur in the port of Saigon. The girl stands by the rail of a steamer and looks for the Chinese man on the shore. Only as the boat pulls away does she catch sight of his limousine discreetly parked in a side street. Even though he never shows himself, she feels great comfort. Later that night she will cry out that she has indeed loved him all along. One assumes she speaks the truth at last, but the viewer feels little connection to a character so lifelessly drawn. A brief anticlimax informs the audience that the Chinese gentleman and his wife came to Paris after World War II and that he confessed he had loved her in Saigon and loved her still.

The emotional flatness of the film is largely attributable to its distancing techniques and arid ambiance. Not helping matters is the fact that the film is a French and British coproduction in which French culture was not allowed to dominate. American audiences may appreciate not having to read subtitles, but the film is heavily damaged by its cultural flatness and confusion. Except for the heavily accented narrator's voice, the characters give no hint of being French, and a few have prominent English accents. The mannerisms of the frumpy mother suggest the British raj in India rather than the French in Vietnam. Tony Leung's Chinese gentleman, in turn, could as easily have been a Hong Kong drug dealer as a Sorbonne graduate. The nameless characters remain ciphers. One does not know much more about them at the end of the film than at the beginning.

The film's lack of cultural identity has been widely commented on by critics, and the French film industry has ruled it ineligible as a French film in any of the Cesars competition, France's equivalent of the Oscars. Instead, *The Lover* was given the backhanded compliment of being nominated for competition in the best foreign film category.

Dan Georgakas

Reviews

Chicago Tribune. October 30, 1992, VII, p. 42.
The Christian Science Monitor. December 11, 1992, p. 12.
Entertainment Weekly. November 6, 1992, p. 44.
The Hollywood Reporter. September 16, 1992, p. 5.
Los Angeles Times. October 30, 1992, p. F1.
The New York Times. October 30, 1992, p. B1.
The New Yorker. LXVIII, November 16, 1992, p. 132.
Newsweek. CXX, November 23, 1992, p. 78.
Time. CXL, November 2, 1992, p. 70.
Variety. March 23, 1992, p. 2.

MALCOLM X

Production: Marvin Worth and Spike Lee for 40 Acres and a Mule Filmworks, in association with Largo International N.V.; released by Warner Bros.
Direction: Spike Lee
Screenplay: Arnold Perl and Spike Lee; based on the book *The Autobiography of Malcolm X* as told to Alex Haley
Cinematography: Ernest Dickerson
Editing: Barry Alexander Brown
Production design: Wynn Thomas
Art direction: Tom Warren
Set decoration: Ted Glass
Casting: Robi Reed
Sound: Rolf Pardula
Costume design: Ruth Carter
Choreography: Otis Sallid
Stunt coordination: Jeff Ward
Music: Terence Blanchard
MPAA rating: PG-13
Running time: 201 minutes

Principal characters:

Malcolm X	Denzel Washington
Betty Shabazz	Angela Bassett
Baines	Albert Hall
Elijah Muhammad	Al Freeman, Jr.
Shorty	Spike Lee
West Indian Archie	Delroy Lindo
Sophia	Kate Vernon
Laura	Theresa Randle
Louise Little	Lonette McKee
Earl Little	Tommy Hollis
Benjamin 2X	Jean LaMarre
Brother Earl	James McDaniel
Sidney	Ernest Thomas
Miss Dunne	Karen Allen
Mr. Ostrowski	David Patrick Kelly
Chaplain Gill	Christopher Plummer
Brother Johnson	Steve White
Nelson Mandela	Himself
Ossie Davis	Himself

In *Malcolm X*, Spike Lee created a fascinating and powerful biographical film, taking great pains to stay true to his source material, primarily the book *The Autobi-*

ography of Malcolm X (1965), as told to Alex Haley. Unlike many other Hollywood film biographies, such as *The Babe Ruth Story* (1948), Spike Lee's film does not rewrite history. Instead, he provides a lesson in history without boring his viewers or talking down to them. The fact that Lee's film not only holds the audience's interest for 201 minutes but actually keeps them riveted to their seats as well is a remarkable feat.

Like most of Lee's films, this one starts off with a bang. An American flag fills the screen, while images of the 1991 beating of black motorist Rodney King by four white Los Angeles police officers are intercut, signifying that not much changed in the twenty-six years after Malcolm's death. The flag then burns until all that remains is a red, white, and blue *X*. Lee is unequaled in his use of the opening credits to draw a viewer into his films, as he also did in *Do the Right Thing* (1989) and *Jungle Fever* (1991).

The film then cuts to the Roxbury section of Boston during World War II. Malcolm X (Denzel Washington), still known as Malcolm Little during this time, and his friend Shorty (Spike Lee) are shown parading around town in their outrageously flashy zoot suits. Shorty then prepares to give Malcolm his first conk, which will straighten Malcolm's hair in an effort to make it look like a white man's hair. The congolene mixture, which consists of lye, eggs, and potatoes, produces the desired effect but takes a painful toll as it burns Malcolm's scalp. This is a pivotal scene in the early part of the film, showing the lengths to which Malcolm will go in his efforts to appear more white.

Malcolm soon becomes involved with a white woman, Sophia (Kate Vernon), whom he has met at the Roseland Ballroom. Malcolm hurriedly takes his date, a sweet, virginal young African American woman named Laura (Theresa Randle), home and rushes back to the ballroom to meet Sophia. This action is another example of Malcolm's early desire to be white.

There are many flashbacks to Malcolm's childhood, with Denzel Washington's narration of these scenes uncannily reminiscent of the conversational tone from *The Autobiography of Malcolm X*. In these flashbacks, the audience is exposed to the painful influence of white people on Malcolm's life: the Ku Klux Klan burning down the house in which he lived as a child; the image of his father, Earl Little (Tommy Hollis), left on the trolley tracks to die; the insurance company refusing to pay off his father's life insurance policy, claiming that his death on the trolley tracks was a suicide; the welfare worker, Miss Dunne (Karen Allen), who shortly thereafter dismantles the family unit, sending the children into foster care; and one of Malcolm's teachers, Mr. Ostrowski (David Patrick Kelly), telling Malcolm that his goal of becoming a lawyer is unrealistic because of his race.

Malcolm and Sophia wind up in Harlem, where Malcolm begins working for West Indian Archie (Delroy Lindo), who heads a numbers racket. Malcolm becomes a runner for Archie, who takes Malcolm under his wing and, in the process, exposes him to the world of guns, cocaine, and high living. Archie gets Malcolm out of his zoot suits and into more elegant and expensive suits. A misunderstanding with

Archie, however, sends Malcolm and Sophia fleeing back to Boston, where they reunite with Shorty.

Malcolm and Shorty begin to rob houses and are soon caught and sentenced to ten years of hard labor. His time in prison is the first turning point of Malcolm's life. He meets a fellow inmate named Baines (Albert Hall), who introduces Malcolm to Islam and becomes his mentor. As he embraces Islam, Malcolm sees the folly of trying to emulate the whites. He finally gets rid of his conk hairstyle and begins to educate himself in prison.

Once out of prison, Malcolm is introduced to Elijah Muhammad (Al Freeman, Jr.), the founder and spiritual leader of the Nation of Islam. Soon Malcolm is preaching on the streets of New York, trying to convert black Christians coming out of church. The meetings at the Muslim temples begin to draw larger crowds as Malcolm's popularity soars. Elijah Muhammad eventually makes Malcolm the national minister, charged with building temples all across the United States.

Malcolm begins to use his newly acquired power when he and approximately fifty members of the Fruit of Islam descend on a police station, saving the life of a badly beaten Brother Johnson (Steve White), who had been arrested for no apparent reason. This scene perfectly illustrates what is probably the most important statement that Spike Lee makes in the film. He dispels the myth that Malcolm X advocated violence. Malcolm X never advocated random violence, but he would use whatever power he had for self-defense. Malcolm considered this approach intelligence, not violence.

Malcolm X was a passionate man who was true to his beliefs. He was fiercely intelligent and had an open mind. Spike Lee shows these traits through Malcolm's many transformations. Malcolm begins to become disillusioned with the Nation of Islam when he finds out about the sexual improprieties of Elijah Muhammad. Malcolm is devastated by this news. Adding to the strain is the fact that other ministers in the Nation of Islam have become jealous of his popularity, especially his former mentor, Baines.

Malcolm is eventually forced out of the Nation of Islam and begins receiving death threats. He forms his own organization, known as the Muslim Mosque, Inc. The second major turning point in Malcolm's life comes during his pilgrimage to the holy city of Mecca. Here he realizes that being a Muslim is not about skin color. He meets numerous devout Muslims of many races, including white Muslims, on his pilgrimage. It is a spiritual rebirth, as powerful as the one that he had in prison. He recants his hatred of white people and speaks against his earlier sweeping generalizations upon his return to the United States.

By the time that Malcolm X is assassinated, the audience truly feels the sadness and horror of this act. Spike Lee is careful not to turn this crucial moment of the film into another sentimental Hollywood tearjerker. Instead of manipulating his audience into passive sympathy, Lee instead encourages the action of thought, of outrage.

Lee overcame a number of well-publicized obstacles to make this film, which is so obviously a labor of love. He prevailed over financial conflicts with Warner Bros.

and criticism from segments of the African American community to produce a masterpiece of American cinema that is every bit the equal of his earlier masterpiece, *Do the Right Thing*.

Denzel Washington, who won the Academy Award for Best Supporting Actor for *Glory* (1989), turns in an amazing performance as Malcolm X. His speech patterns and body language are so perfect that it is a shock when black-and-white film footage and photographs of the real Malcolm X are shown following the assassination scene.

Most of the critical praise for this film centered on Washington's spectacular performance. He was selected as best actor by the New York Film Critics, the Boston Society of Film Critics, and the forty-third Berlinale Awards. He was runner-up in the best actor category as voted by the Los Angeles Film Critics. Washington also received best actor nominations from both the Academy Awards and the Golden Globe Awards.

The supporting performances are excellent as well, especially the portrayal of Malcolm's wife, Betty Shabazz, by Angela Bassett and the portrayal of Elijah Muhammad by Freeman. Lee himself was back in fine acting form after his disappointing performances in *Mo' Better Blues* (1990) and *Jungle Fever*.

As usual, Ernest Dickerson did a brilliant job as director of photography. While there are traces of his flashy signature cinematography in the early portion of the film, Dickerson and Lee settle down as the film progresses, not letting their technical wizardry get in the way of the story.

Costume designer Ruth Carter also deserves special mention, as she did a wonderful job of re-creating the look of each time period covered in the film. Carter received an Academy Award nomination for best costume design for her work in *Malcolm X*. Carter had worked with Lee on every one of his films, except for his first, *She's Gotta Have It* (1986). Together with Dickerson and production designer Wynn Thomas, both of whom had worked on all of Lee's films, they form a team whose collaboration greatly enhances the final product.

While *Malcolm X* failed to receive a best picture nomination from the Academy Awards, it was generally a favorite with the critics. In a consensus of 106 critics nationwide, as compiled by the *San Francisco Chronicle*, *Malcolm X* placed fourth, mentioned in fifty-eight Top Ten lists, including a number-one selection by *Chicago Sun-Times* critic Roger Ebert. *Malcolm X* placed higher than three of the Academy Award best picture nominees according to the consensus, coming in one place ahead of the *The Crying Game* (1992; reviewed in this volume), and far outdistancing *A Few Good Men* (1992; reviewed in this volume) and *Scent of a Woman* (1992; reviewed in this volume).

Lee stated that he was born to make this film, that this film was the reason that he became a filmmaker. Ironically, both Lee and Malcolm X had to endure the wrath of the press, who often either misquoted them or took their quotes out of context to make them appear to be racists, attempting to turn their outspokenness on the subject of racism against them. Yet, in *Malcolm X*, Lee created a historically accurate film that is accessible to people of all races, not only African Americans. Prior to this film, while Malcolm X had remained a well-known figure within the African American community, he was in danger of being written out of history. Most almanacs did not even list Malcolm X in their sections on famous people or even assassination attempts. With this film, Lee sought to ensure that Malcolm X would regain his rightful place in history. Because of this goal, and the fact that it is so well made, *Malcolm X* is one of the most important films in the history of American cinema.

George Delalis

Reviews

Chicago Tribune. November 18, 1992, V, p. 1.
The Christian Science Monitor. November 18, 1992, p. 14.
Entertainment Weekly. November 20, 1992, p. 68.
The Hollywood Reporter. November 10, 1992, p. 6.
Los Angeles Times. November 18, 1992, p. F1.
The New York Times. November 18, 1992, p. B1.
Newsweek. CXX, November 16, 1992, p. 74.
Time. CXL, November 23, 1992, p. 64.
Variety. November 10, 1992, p. 2.
The Washington Post. November 18, 1992, p. C1.

THE MAMBO KINGS

Production: Arnon Milchan and Arne Glimcher, in association with Le Studio Canal Plus, Regency Enterprises, and Alcor Films; released by Warner Bros.
Direction: Arne Glimcher
Screenplay: Cynthia Cidre; based on the novel *The Mambo Kings Play Songs of Love*, by Oscar Hijuelos
Cinematography: Michael Ballhaus
Editing: Claire Simpson
Production design: Stuart Wurtzel
Art direction: Steve Saklad
Set decoration: Kara Lindstrom
Casting: Billy Hopkins and Suzanne Smith
Sound: Susumu Tokunow
Costume design: Ann Roth, Gary Jones, and Bridget Kelly
Choreography: Michael Peters
Music: Robert Kraft and Carlos Franzetti
Mambo arrangements: Ray Santos
MPAA rating: R
Running time: 101 minutes

Principal characters:

Cesar Castillo .... Armand Assante
Nestor Castillo .... Antonio Banderas
Lanna Lake .... Cathy Moriarty
Desi Arnaz .... Desi Arnaz, Jr.
Delores Fuentes .... Maruschka Detmers
Evalina Montoya .... Celia Cruz
Fernando Perez .... Roscoe Lee Browne
Miguel Montoya .... Vondie Curtis-Hall
Tito Puente .... Himself
María Rivera .... Talisa Soto

Art gallery owner Arne Glimcher had a vision that became an obsession. Turning Oscar Hijuelos' Pulitzer Prize-winning novel, *The Mambo Kings Play Songs of Love* (1989), into a film was his vision; mambo was his obsession. Glimcher combines the two in a stunning, vibrant screen experience called *The Mambo Kings*—a seemingly odd stretch for the director and founder of the prestigious Pace Gallery in New York City. Yet Glimcher maintains a passionate love affair with the sound of the mambo, described as the child of the rumba and the cha-cha-cha, and transfers his vision-turned-obsession to the screen in this release from Warner Bros. *The Mambo Kings* marks Glimcher's directorial debut, although he has produced other feature films, notably Leonard Nimoy's *The Good Mother* (1988) and the highly acclaimed *Goril-*

las in the Mist (1988). Glimcher also produced *The Mambo Kings*, along with powerhouse producer Arnon Milchan, whose production credits include *The King of Comedy* (1983), *Brazil* (1985), *The War of the Roses* (1989), *Pretty Woman* (1990), and the award-winning *JFK* (1991).

Stars Armand Assante and Antonio Banderas share the spotlight in *The Mambo Kings* with the high-spirited and invigorating beat of the mambo. Legends Tito Puente and Celia Cruz lend brilliant mambo sounds with authentic help from Assante and Banderas, who make full use of the vocal and trumpet lessons that they took for the roles. Dedication to the project is evident all around; the actors took drastic pay cuts, Glimcher worked for scale, and he and Milchan received no compensation for their work as producers. *The Mambo Kings* exudes labor-of-love status, from the opening credits to the final fade to black. Their efforts were rewarded not only with critical acclaim for the film, but with an Academy Award nomination for best original song for "Beautiful Maria of My Soul."

Cesar (Assante) and Nestor Castillo (Banderas) emigrate from Havana to New York City in 1952 to pursue the American Dream, mambo-style. Cesar, the headstrong lover whose passion for women is surpassed only by his passion for success, is a brash troublemaker wearing his confidence like a tailored suit. Nestor, on the other hand, is the sensitive songwriter with a broken heart. María (Talisa Soto), his only true love, married another man in Cuba, so Cesar brings Nestor to the United States in hopes of beginning life anew and leaving their troubled past behind.

The Mambo Kings not only boasts an intoxicating blend of music and mood but also is driven by a broiling chemistry between the two loyal brothers. *The Mambo Kings* tells the tragic tale of passion, brotherly love, and the everlasting illusion of the American Dream. Although the music is enticing and captivating, the characterizations of Cesar and Nestor carry the film. In the spirit of the mambo, Cesar and Nestor exude sexuality as if they invented it. Although their personalities inevitably clash, the brothers share a common lust for beautiful women. Cesar falls in love with sensuous cigarette girl Lanna Lake (Cathy Moriarty), who seems to stand as a trophy to Cesar's American conquest. Nestor marries Delores Fuentes (Maruschka Detmers), a quiet, sensitive woman who has dreams of going to college and becoming a schoolteacher. The Castillo brothers love with the same intensity and abandon that they infuse into their music. Their loyalty as brothers is similarly shown with passion and energy, as blood proves thicker than water.

Assante was the final choice for the part of Cesar, after such actors as Jeremy Irons, Robert De Niro, and Kevin Kline were seriously considered for the role. Assante won the job to the great delight of Glimcher, who describes having Assante play Cesar as "the thrill of my life." Known for his intense performances in such films as *Private Benjamin* (1980), *Q & A* (1990), and *The Marrying Man* (1991), he turns on the heat in *The Mambo Kings*, playing Cesar with emotional strength and sex appeal. Banderas, Glimcher's first choice to play Nestor, is relatively unknown to American audiences. Banderas is notable for his roles in the highly regarded Spanish imports *Women on the Verge of a Nervous Breakdown* (1988) and *Tie Me*

Up! Tie Me Down! (1990), in which he starred for legendary Spanish director Pedro Almodóvar. Banderas, one of the most popular icons in Spain, brings his European style and sizzle to the American screen in portraying the haunted tragic lover. The actor, who spoke no English before shooting began, took English lessons during the day and trumpet lessons at night to play the part of Nestor.

Fresh off the bus, the brothers head to the mambo mecca of New York, the Palladium, where Tito Puente and his orchestra hold court. Cesar charms his way onstage and plays with Puente himself, catching the eye of everyone in the room. Singer Evalina Montoya (Celia Cruz) owns the nightclub Club Babalu and takes a personal interest in the brothers after hearing them play, offering them her spiritual advice and friendship.

Cesar and Nestor work by day in a meat-packing plant while putting together their band, the Mambo Kings. They land several nightclub gigs before mambo godfather Fernando Perez (Roscoe Lee Browne) approaches Cesar and Nestor with an offer. Perez rules the New York mambo scene with an iron fist, controlling most clubs, including the Palladium. To reach the top, Perez advises, the Mambo Kings need to sign on with him or suffer the consequences. The brash Cesar refuses to be bought, however, and snubs Perez's offer to send the Mambo Kings to the top, determined to make it on his own terms. The Castillo brothers represent "the last moment of innocence in America," according to Glimcher; they are innocent enough to believe that they can make it without Perez. Reality hits hard, however, as the band is unable to book a gig, and they are forced to play Bar Mitzvahs and weddings to make ends meet.

Cesar and Nestor must rely on the kindness of friends, specifically their friend Evalina, who lets them perform at her club. Nestor's love ballad, "Beautiful María of My Soul," catches the ear of mambo fan Desi Arnaz (Desi Arnaz, Jr.), who immediately falls in love with the tune and asks the brothers to perform the song on his show, *I Love Lucy*. Overwhelmed by the chance, the brothers head for Hollywood and prepare for stardom. Their appearance on the popular television show leads to a record deal with Desilu Productions, but New York is not as kind to the Castillo brothers, as they still cannot find a place to play in the town controlled by Perez.

Cesar refuses to accept that big-time success is unattainable, but Nestor is easily disillusioned, as he drowns himself in alcohol. Nestor cannot run from his past as easily as Cesar can, and he is constantly haunted by his memory of María. Her ghost follows him wherever he goes, even into his marriage with Delores. Although she loves him, Delores cannot continue giving herself to a man who is unable to give anything in return. Emotionally devastated, Nestor sees his marriage collapsing, his relationship with his brother straining, and his career failing. More than that, Nestor begins to feel like a pawn in Cesar's grand design for American success. From the beginning, Nestor was never interested in the spotlight of fame, as Cesar was. All Nestor wanted was to own a nightclub of his own, to write his songs, and to play the music that he loves. Desperate, Nestor strikes a deal with the devil. Feeling betrayed and used by Cesar, Nestor deals with Perez behind Cesar's back, agreeing to give control to Perez in exchange for getting the Mambo Kings back on top again.

The band plays to a sold-out house at the Palladium, and although Cesar revels in the sweet taste of success, Nestor cannot bear the guilt of having betrayed his brother. He pleads with Perez to cancel their agreement, but Perez promises to destroy the brothers if he does. Seeing no way out and unable to tell Cesar the truth of his disloyalty, Nestor loses control of the car while driving and fatally crashes into a tree. Nestor's death devastates Cesar, as he realizes that all he has ever done has been because of Nestor. In tribute to Nestor, Cesar opens a nightclub, but the magic is gone. He sings Nestor's ballad, "Beautiful María of My Soul" one last time, as if he finally, and for the first time, understands its meaning.

The family element is crucial to the significance of *The Mambo Kings*. Glimcher points out that "the film examines the family structure that kept people together and destroyed them as well." *The Mambo Kings* is a skillfully crafted, sizzling tale of love, music, and shattered dreams that blends elements of tragedy and drama with the foot-tapping, contagious rhythms of the mambo.

Catherine R. Springer

Reviews

Chicago Tribune. March 13, 1992, VII, p. 39.
The Christian Science Monitor. March 17, 1992, p. 11.
The Hollywood Reporter. February 19, 1992, p. 10.
Los Angeles Times. February 28, 1992, p. F1.
The New York Times. February 28, 1992, p. B5.
Newsweek. CXIX, March 9, 1992, p. 63.
People Weekly. XXXVII, March 9, 1992, p. 14.
Rolling Stone. March 19, 1992, p. 101.
Time. CXXXIX, March 9, 1992, p. 66.
Variety. February 10, 1992, p. 2.

MEDICINE MAN

Production: Andrew G. Vajna and Donna Dubrow for Hollywood Pictures and Cinergi Productions; released by Buena Vista
Direction: John McTiernan
Screenplay: Tom Schulman and Sally Robinson; based on a story by Schulman
Cinematography: Donald McAlpine
Editing: Michael R. Miller
Production design: John Krenz Reinhart, Jr.
Art direction: Don Diers, Jesus Buenrostro, and Marlisi Storchi
Set decoration: Enrique Estevez
Casting: Bonnie Timmermann
Sound: Douglas B. Arnold
Costume design: Marilyn Vance-Straker and Rita Murtimho
Brazilian Indian choreography: Maria Fatima Toledo
Special effects supervision: John Thomas and Laurencio Cordero "Chovy"
Music: Jerry Goldsmith
MPAA rating: PG-13
Running time: 106 minutes

Principal characters:

Dr. Robert Campbell .... Sean Connery
Dr. Rae Crane .... Lorraine Bracco
Dr. Miguel Ornega .... José Wilker
Tanaki .... Rodolfo de Alexandre
Jahausa .... Francisco Tsirene Tsere Rereme
Palala .... Elias Monteiro da Silva
Kalana .... Edinei Maria Serrio Dos Santos
Imana .... Bec-Kana-Re Dos Santos Kaiapo
Medicine Man .... Angelo Barra Moreira

All totaled, the talent assembled for *Medicine Man* has more than a dozen Academy Award, Golden Globe, and film critic awards and nominations. Tom Schulman, the author of the original story behind the film ("The Stand") and the coauthor of the screenplay, brought John McTiernan—the director of *Predator* (1987), *Die Hard* (1988), and *The Hunt for Red October* (1990)—to the project. Schulman, best known for his Academy Award-winning screenplay for *Dead Poets Society* (1989), wanted McTiernan because "he's a great storyteller with a powerful filmmaking technique." McTiernan brought in Sean Connery, the original James Bond, who brought in Lorraine Bracco, who starred in 1990's *GoodFellas*. With the leads in place, the director spent the fall and winter of 1990-1991 searching for a workable rain forest; the shooting of the "Brazilian" tale began in March, 1991, in the jungles of Catemaco, Mexico.

Biochemist Robert Campbell (Connery) has spent the last six years in a rain forest in Brazil researching the rare tropical vegetation and searching for a cure for cancer. He has "gone native" in the best Hollywood storytelling tradition: For example, Campbell wears a toucan headdress over his long gray ponytail and short pants as he joins in the ritual for the harvest of the peach palm. He is a man with a past, now a renegade, a loner, and possibly a scientific genius. He is also egomaniacal, opinionated, and quite impossible. As the film opens, Campbell has not only found the cure for cancer but also lost it.

Dr. Rae Crane (Bracco), on the other hand, has spent years as an award-winning biochemist, laboratory researcher, and administrator. She now heads the foundation that funds all of Campbell's research, and she has entered the heart of darkness to discover what has happened to the once-fabled Dr. Campbell. She enters the jungle out of control and out of place in her surroundings, a New Yorker in the wilds. The audience's first view of her is on the airplane, a close-up of manicured hands and a large engagement diamond as Crane is adjusting her formidable antisnake boots. As tourists deplane, the scientist continues to prepare for her journey, adding an oversized pack and the dehydrated food once popularized by astronauts.

As the credits roll, Crane and her native guides make their way by limousine, by helicopter, by burro, by foot, and by canoe, through dense vegetation, pouring rain, and darkest night to Campbell's camp. Quickly, Campbell and Crane work through many of the necessary conventions of romantic comedy: mistaken identity, open hostility, verbal jousting, cool cooperation, and, finally, romance. *Medicine Man* manages to combine (and create) disparate genres: environmental thriller, romantic comedy, mystical mystery. Much of the film works to echo and update the roles played by Katharine Hepburn and Humphrey Bogart in the 1951 film *The African Queen.*

In many ways, the film itself is a great success and a failure. The rain forest is the major force in the film and also the source of much of that success and failure. Because the much-sought-after herb with supposed curative powers grows only in the jungle canopy (the tree tops), the scientists must use ropes and counterbalances to harvest it more than one hundred feet above the ground. Both Connery and Bracco did most of their stunts—not only in the tree tops but also in the waterfalls, cliffs, and rivers—and the footage is breathtakingly foreign and beautiful. Donald McAlpine's cinematography captures toucans, spider monkeys, and brightly colored ants with *National Geographic* clarity. As much as the rain forest adds, however, it also takes away.

In *Medicine Man*, McTiernan worked with ambient sounds—rain, insects, the buzz of the forest. Yet what this sound adds in authenticity, which is a considerable amount, it more than takes away in clarity. As Campbell's laboratory is without walls, any sound within it, such as dialogue, reverberates off the ceiling and any sound without it, such as rain and insects, echoes through it. Thus, most of the interior dialogue is lost. A further problem is the extreme light and shadow of the jungle. Exterior scenes alternate between too-dark-to-see and too-light-to-see. For example, early in the film Campbell takes Crane above the canopy to perch godlike and survey the horizons and the far-reaching expanse of trees. Technically, however, when the characters burst through the upper reaches of limbs, the shot is bleached of color; instead of life and adventure, the viewer is reminded of old slides or largely forgotten dreams.

McTiernan is a master at blowing up buildings and portraying authentic gunfire. McTiernan-made violence has hair and teeth. (Yet McTiernan admits to being drawn to this film because it did not contain "a single machine gun.") Perhaps, then, it is no surprise that the most successful scene in the film is the attack of the "giant earthmovers," the machinery that destroys the rain forest faster than the scientists can research the invaluable natural resource. The scenes of violence convey real menace, relying on camera angles that are themselves an imposition, that create palpable discomfort in the viewer. Campbell and Crane are dwarfed by the scale of the destruction. Even the workers operating the machines seem larger than life, nothing but muscled, unreasoning arms operating cold, mindless steel. It is all very chilling.

In contrast, the scenes of quiet reflection and even playful antics fall flat. For example, in an effort to speed their research, the two scientists enlist the aid of the local tribe in preparing cultures for later enzyme tests. McTiernan works to explore the differences between the trained foreigners and what he portrays as happy-go-lucky Native Americans, another Hollywood convention. To capture this dichotomy, McTiernan selects a tracking shot that chronicles the assembled persons at first chest and then at posterior height. What McTiernan must see as visual humor—a long row of brown buttocks next to khaki L. L. Bean shorts—not only fails to amuse but also manages to offend. Even less happily, he does it twice.

Other portions of the film prove equally distressing. Crane is portrayed as a simpering prima donna: demanding a bath, carrying too much luggage, failing to maintain the pace set by others, and crying at the smallest pretext. Campbell treats her as a nuisance and an inferior, behavior that grates more than it entertains. The story introduces a variety of subplots that finally get lost in the shuffle: Crane's fiancé, Campbell's brush with swine-flu immortality, the ousting of the local medicine man—and, yes, even the romance arises out of nowhere.

Despite its technical flaws, however, *Medicine Man* is finally an engaging film, interesting enough to make viewers wish that they could hear what the actors are saying and see what the actors are doing. Despite a confused and patchy plot, the characters are interesting and likable, and regardless of whether the audience is ever clear on how the scientists managed to arrive at their last scene, nevertheless these same viewers will want Campbell and Crane to succeed. Plagued with mixed reviews and rumors of a stormy set, the film did well at the box office, beginning its first weekend with an estimated $8 million gross and ending the year with $45.5 million. Nevertheless, the film was listed on no fewer than five of 1992's Worst Films lists. *Medicine Man* deals seriously with some of the greatest concerns of the decade—the vanishing rain forest, the accountability of science and scientists, and the need for lifesaving, miracle cures—yet it manages to entertain audiences in the process. That success in itself is a minor miracle.

Roberta F. Green

Reviews

Chicago Tribune. February 7, 1992, V, p. 3.
The Christian Science Monitor. February 13, 1992, p. 13.
Films in Review. XLIII, March, 1992, p. 121.
The Hollywood Reporter. February 7, 1992, p. 5.
Los Angeles Times. February 7, 1992, p. F10.
The New York Times. February 7, 1992, p. B4.
Premiere. V, February 1, 1992, p. 58.
Sight and Sound. II, June, 1992, p. 47.
USA Today. February 11, 1992, p. 1D.
Variety. February 7, 1992, p. 2.

MEDITERRANEO

Origin: Italy
Released: 1991
Released in U.S.: 1992
Production: Gianni Minervini, Mario Cecchi Gori, and Vittorio Cecchi Gori for Penta Films; released by Miramax Films
Direction: Gabriele Salvatores
Screenplay: Vincenzo Monteleone
Cinematography: Italo Petriccione
Editing: Nino Baragali
Art direction: Thalia Istikopoulos
Music: Giancarlo Bigazzi
MPAA rating: no listing
Running time: 102 minutes

Principal characters:

Sergeant Lo Russo	Diego Abatantuono
Lieutenant Montini	Claudio Bigagli
Farina	Giuseppe Cederna
Noventa	Claudio Bisio
Strazzabosco	Gigio Alberti
Colosanti	Ugo Conti
Felice Munaron	Memo Dini
Libero Munaron	Vasco Mirandolo
Vasilissa	Vanna Barba
Shepherdess	Irene Grazioli
Priest	Luigi Montini

As the initial credits of *Mediterraneo* roll, one hears the languid lapping of ocean waves and enters the world of Lina Wertmüller's *Swept Away* (1974)—the beautiful, lost Greek island that epitomizes the absence of civilization and a loss of inhibitions. Since the success of *Swept Away* and its illustrious predecessor, Federico Fellini's *La Dolce Vita* (1960), Italian filmmakers have evoked perfect romantic settings for escape and reconsideration of the daily round of Italian life. Sent on an expeditionary mission to a remote, unimportant, seemingly deserted Greek island by the Italian high command during the early years of World War II, the small band of soldiers-misfits in *Mediterraneo* is immediately forgotten by the Italian military. With its chronic deserter, Noventa (Claudio Bisio); its Tyrolean mountaineers, the hilarious Munaron brothers (Memo Dini and Vasco Mirandolo), who are made ill at ease by the proximity of so much water; and the hapless, undereducated Farina (Giuseppe Cederna), who anticipates the thoughts of Lieutenant Montini (Claudio Bigagli), the small band of men is likable but ineffectual outside civilization. The lieutenant is the central character, narrator, and leader—the man to whom all the company of soldiers looks for both military and moral leadership. He guides and directs his band of soldiers, who are fearful, unwilling, and inept. Strazzabosco (Gigio Alberti), for example, loves his donkey above all else and is far more concerned about her than he is about their mission.

If *Swept Away*, which seems to be set on the same lost Aegean island, was a crazy, comic distopia, then this film is a crazy, comic utopia. Like all utopian films, this one offers a moral vision, yet it is anything but moralistic. It is a life-affirming, witty, deceptively quiet tale of what happens once the Roman conquerors invade Grecian soil. The fact that, prior to the Roman Empire, Greece was the dominant world power is gently alluded to by the lieutenant when he hands the bored Farina an Italian translation of Greek poetry. These poems transfix the younger man and may ultimately change his life. He is a man who, like the others on this expedition, has had scant time to reflect on his life. With Farina's opening of the book of erotic Greek poetry, however, the daily life of the soldiers becomes increasingly sensual and natural. Each in his own way opens himself to the raw sensuality endemic on the island, and their discovery of the joys of relaxation and eroticism parallels their discovery of the natives of the island as well. The Greek villagers are shrewder than at first the soldiers imagine: Although the Italians are allowed to believe that they are the conquerors, the "conquered" win them over to their philosophy of life.

A passionate shepherdess (Irene Grazioli), apparently straight out of Greek and Latin poetry, cavorts nude with the Munaron brothers in a hilltop idyll. They prove that they can be on guard duty and enjoy themselves at the same time, as they immediately spot an approaching boat. They are duly laughed at for identifying the interloper as a potential enemy, but hindsight proves them to have been right. The boatman who arrives sporting a battered Turkish flag on his dinghy looks harmless enough, but he has brought hashish and other drugs. The soldiers spend the whole night laughing and smoking. Whenever he is asked anything, the Turk repeatedly answers "dunno" until they decide that this must be his name. At dawn, when they are all asleep, he carries away all of their money, watches, and most significantly their guns. He takes everything, in fact, except the chronic deserter, who is foiled again. Only now does the local priest (Luigi Montini), whose church frescoes the lieutenant is painting, reveal that the villagers have harbored a large cache of weapons. It is indulgently suggested that, should they need them later, the soldiers are welcome to share these guns.

Afterward, Sergeant Lo Russo (Diego Abatantuono), the aggressive bull of the troop, ruefully observes that it would be satisfactory if thieves always stole the weapons and left the drugs. Lo Russo is the obligatory patriot without whom no war film can make sense, the man who is sure that he has a mission and that a kind of Manifest Destiny is directing his (and Italy's) course. He symbolizes the bellicose military-industrial establishment of Western nations, as even Italy needlessly stockpiles weapons of war, whose expense and service eclipses the human ability to relax and enjoy life.

From this point onward, the film is about soldiers with no weapons or discernible uniforms, thus questioning the identity of a soldier without these accoutrements. Contact with Italy had been destroyed at the outset when Strazzabosco threw their radio to the ground to protest the accidental shooting of his beloved pet donkey. Thus, the film also questions the nature of an army without communications and contact with a source of command. Subtly, the director presents the dream of peace, played out in real life and in living color. The film also reveals the harm that drugs can do, as the soldiers are sleepy at the very moment that they should be most vigilant. The soldiers lose their identity, and hence their only real *raison d'être* on the island, as a consequence of the drug dealer's theft.

Mediterraneo shows that the soldiers' other escape—sex with the local prostitute Vasilissa (Vanna Barba), seemingly the only professional in the entire village—is just as invalid and questionable a refuge from reality as drugs. Initially, the soldiers are happy to visit her in a precisely ordered sequence ordained by rank and age, a sequence arranged by Lo Russo. Yet the shy Farina is a virgin and, as the youngest, is last in line. At first, he tenderly pulls the covers up around her when he finds her exhausted and sleeping upon his arrival. In time, however, she questions why he never wants to make love. They begin to spend their free time together and gradually grow more and more fond of each other until at last they become lovers. Farina's character alters drastically with his newfound responsibility, and he and Vasilissa marry. By the time that the band of soldiers is "found" by the victorious British and conveyed back to Italy, the soldiers are merely relaxed civilians who have long since stopped judging anyone or anything. They dully participate in the treatment of other human beings as objects when they return ignominiously escorted by the conquering British troops. In *Mediterraneo*, the Italian "conquerors" must share the prostitute and even villagers first with the Germans and then with the men of the village, who return at the end of the war. Without batting an eye, the village maidens wave their Italian lovers off when the village men return. It is clearly the Italian former conquerors who are the losers. Only Farina flagrantly rebels, refusing to leave the island and his new wife. His scene played in an olive barrel is both farcical and unforgettably comic; it is certainly one of the best moments in the entire film.

The quality of the acting is generally superb. The film is about the finding of true values and authenticity in life, but it is also about the enduring character of the camaraderie between friends. Feminists may wish there were more women in the film, and gay rights activists may wish that the one gay man was taken more seriously, but the film's statement is a steady and sure affirmation of the deeper human values of love, loyalty, and friendship.

Every decade has its own classic antiwar film: *Dr. Strangelove* (1964) epitomized antiwar sentiments for the 1960's, and *M*A*S*H* (1970) and *The Deer Hunter* (1978) did so for the 1970's. *Mediterraneo* is the antiwar film for the 1990's. As a film about the ridiculousness, challenges, and limitations of the military, *Mediterraneo* constantly evokes *M*A*S*H*, Robert Altman's wacky film. The former is an avowedly antiwar film that shows the wartime occupation of a peaceful country from an exhausted soldier's perspective.

The film has a gentle, whimsical humor and spectacular views of the pristine Greek island. Moreover, it is original: It may be the only war film ever made that contains no violence against any human being. *Mediterraneo* won numerous awards, among them the 1992 Academy Award for best foreign-language film, the Italian David di Donatelo Award for best picture, and the 1992 Palm Springs Film Festival's award for best foreign-language film. Some critics charged that it is trite and sentimental, but most agreed that it deserved the awards that it reaped because of the strong stand that it takes on a controversial issue. Furthermore, it has the courage to laugh at itself and, in so doing, laugh at the pretensions of all who wage war on peaceful civilians instead of treating them like the potentially friendly human beings that they actually are.

Cher Langdell

Reviews

Chicago Tribune. April 24, 1992, VII, p. 46.
Films in Review. XLIII, May, 1992, p. 192.
The Hollywood Reporter. March 3, 1992, p. 11.
Los Angeles Times. March 27, 1992, p. F8.
The New York Times. March 22, 1992, p. 18.
Time. CXXXIX, April 27, 1992, p. 71.
Variety. March 27, 1992, p. 2.
The Wall Street Journal. March 26, 1992, p. A12.

A MIDNIGHT CLEAR

Production: Dale Pollock and Bill Borden for Beacon Communications and A&M Films; released by InterStar Releasing
Direction: Keith Gordon
Screenplay: Keith Gordon; based on the novel by William Wharton
Cinematography: Tom Richmond
Editing: Don Brochu
Production design: David Nichols
Art direction: David Lubin
Casting: Gary Zuckerbrod
Sound: John (Earl) Stein
Costume design: Barbara Tfank
Stunt coordination: Steve Davison
Music: Mark Isham
MPAA rating: R
Running time: 107 minutes

Principal characters:

Will Knott	Ethan Hawke
Bud Miller	Peter Berg
Mel Avakian	Kevin Dillon
Stan Shutzer	Arye Gross
Vince (Mother) Wilkins	Gary Sinise
Paul (Father) Mundy	Frank Whaley
Major Griffin	John C. McGinley
Lieutenant Ware	Larry Joshua
Sergeant	David Jensen
Old German soldier	Curt Lowens
Janice	Rachel Griffin
Morrie	Tim Shoemaker

A Midnight Clear is a clean, crystalline icicle of a film—all purity, sweeping snow scenes, and innocence betrayed. It aims at being devoid of sentiment and succeeds in being one of the blackest antiwar films ever made. It attempts to say something new about war and nearly succeeds. What is remarkable and intriguing about the film is the fact that the plot has more ironic twists than a corkscrew and that it coins a new kind of antiwar film. Taking all the clichés of antiwar films from *All Quiet on the Western Front* (1930), *The Virgin Soldiers* (1969), *Gallipolli* (1980), *Platoon* (1986), *Hamburger Hill* (1987), and *Full Metal Jacket* (1987), the creators of *A Midnight Clear* attempt to turn them all inside out, so as to display the bathos and stupidity of developing stereotypes around the antiwar genre; war itself presents the ultimate horror and thus cannot and should not be sentimentalized. The film offers a black humor that is extremely grotesque.

As the action commences, the audience watches one soldier, "Mother" (Gary Sinise), crashing down a snowy hillock in the Alps, chased by his colleague in the unit, who is also the narrator, Will Knott (Ethan Hawke). In December, 1944, having endured years of the mentally and physically gruelling World War II, he has gone berserk and is stripping off his clothes. Will Knott, alias "Won't," is determined to save him, or rather to preserve the façade of his sanity. It becomes clear throughout the course of the film that what has driven him mad is the thought that his baby daughter died before he could see her. He is also obsessed by the thought that no one cares about or loves anyone or anything in late 1944, at the moment of seeming Apocalypse or Armageddon. With the world gone mad and engaged in apparently wholly inexplicable mass slaughter, Mother too evinces only awe and mute horror, punctuated with occasional bouts of active madness in which he runs amok. Knott tells no one when these occur, as Mother would be discharged from the military on grounds of insanity.

The unit has been together so long and become so close that two members of the little family have been designated "Mother" and "Father." Naturally, when events are seen in this light, it becomes impossible to contemplate committing Mother to an institution. Paul Mundy (Frank Whaley), the unit's Father, is a soldier whose true calling is to the Catholic priesthood; it is his encouragement that has enabled each man to retain whatever shred of sanity that he still possesses. Stan Shutzer (Arye Gross) is the soldier designated to communicate with the Germans when the unit encounters them because, as a Jew, he speaks Yiddish. The fact that he is Jewish presents obvious problems for the Germans in particular and hence by extension for the Americans as well. The true soldier among them is Mel Avakian (Kevin Dillon). Major Griffin (John C. McGinley) is their commander, who sends the unit out to gather information on perilous, badly planned errands; in his eyes is exactly the right blend of the naïve assumption of authority and madness. It seems that Mother's madness reflects the major's. The sergeant, dourly played by David Jensen, and Lieutenant Ware (Larry Joshua) embody the faceless submission to authority, the tacit bending to a bully's will, that are the hallmarks of so many war films and that always usher in the end of innocence. The troop of soldiers is caught in the clutches of an egotistical, foolish major without tact or principles.

Knott, however, is the actual mother of this group. He is the one soon put into the position of leader when the unit, a reconnaissance team selected for the high intelligence of its members, is sent into the nearby mountains to gather information on the Germans' movements. The unit encamps at an elegant chateau, with cases of old wine and sardines. Despite the initial inevitable surprises, like the shock of finding a baby deer clambering around the dark recesses of the stately home, they quickly find that they are living like kings—or at least like civilians. This is good for them as human beings but bad for them as soldiers, as discipline becomes harder to maintain. Surveillance must proceed, however, and almost immediately something unusual is detected: They are led to believe that ghosts may inhabit the graveyard adjoining the house. Closer observation reveals that the supposed ghosts bid the Americans goodnight in German.

It becomes increasingly clear to the audience, and at last to the soldiers, that there are live Germans haunting this particular graveyard and that they have a mischievous sense of humor. For example, when one American drops his map, they arrange a clever means of returning it after keeping it overnight. By the time that the American unit actually verifies that there is a German unit living in close proximity to their house, they have also realized that these are apparently friendly foot soldiers, not the Schutzstaffel (SS). Staggered by this fact, they are mystified by the Germans' playful behavior. Once, in a panic, one of the Americans hurls a grenade at the Germans, who have been giggling at them and mocking them in German. Instead of throwing back a grenade, they return fire with a "grenade" snowball—a snowball with a stick thrust through it to emulate a German grenade. Soon, to the Americans' great surprise and joy, a snowball fight is in full swing. This scene is one of the highpoints of the film, a true mark of the quirky originality of its plot.

When a delegation of Germans arrives one day to ask for a chance to speak with them, Knott appoints a time for discussion. Shutzer acts as German interpreter. Because Knott does not have the appearance of an authoritative officer who is able to accept the surrender of this small contingent of Germans, Bud Miller (Peter Berg) impersonates the Americans' commanding officer. With his blond hair and tall Aryan good looks, Bud fulfills the Germans' expectations of what an American commanding officer might be. In this role, Berg does an excellent job of appearing to be an inept enlisted man humorously trying to act like an officer, taking sotto voce orders from Knott. A mutual plan for a peaceful surrender is developed. Yet, in a fatal oversight, everyone in the unit except Mother is taken into confidence in this plan. Mother has retired to an attic lair, in which he broods over the stately home's great masterpieces, which have been hidden there. In these works, he finds consolation that all human life has not been in vain. Simply gazing on a family portrait that has been beautifully rendered, he remarks that that artisan had a security born of faith in humankind and a reverence for life. He exists in a spiritual midnight of the soul, however, not a midnight clear.

After a meeting in which each side presents the other with simple Christmas presents, a peaceful capturing of the German troops is planned for the next day. All is going smoothly when Mother, summoned by the sound of firing in the air, shoots down one of the Germans, who then shoots the closest American soldier. A melee breaks out. The illusion of a simple, friendly, painless surrender is suddenly shattered, never to be recovered, as cleanly and instantly as their illusions of a noble war. Shutzer is wounded and Father is dead, as is another of the Americans; all the Germans have been killed.

Then, the most harrowing episode of the story ensues. The major and lieutenant arrive to scold the men for their unsoldierly conduct and disreputable, squalid quarters. They have transgressed the code of decorum and are punished by being deserted by the commanding officers, who hasten away with the wounded. They leave

Father behind for the men to tend to and take the only pair of chains for their jeep's tires. There ensues another of the goldlit ritual scenes, in which they communally bathe Father's body together and silently, mournfully bid him goodbye. Yet, instead of burying him, in a solemn echo of William Faulkner's novel *As I Lay Dying* (1930), they carry him with them. When they finally arrive back at the camp, having narrowly escaped the oncoming German offensive and traversed a dangerous no-man's-land, the regiment has departed. No word or message has been left for them.

At this point, *A Midnight Clear* challenges orthodox Christianity by presenting an array of Christian symbols, all seen perversely distorted. First, the unit itself resembles Christ's band of apostles, but by the time they are sent out on their present mission, only half remain. The Christian implication is that those who have died are martyrs and that these men are about to meet their martyrdom as well. On the other hand, subsequent events lead the viewer to question the intelligence and bravery of some of these would-be martyrs. Ritual plays a significant role in the film—first there is the ritual in which these initially virgin soldiers all set out to lose their virginity—which raises the issue of whether the film is anti-Christian.

The unit's survivors devise a nefarious plan to avoid being detected: They take fresh blood, squeezed out of Father (in an ironic echo of the Eucharist), and paint huge white sheets with red crosses to indicate a neutral Red Cross status. Father's "crucified" body, which they now carry upright as if hung on a cross, is a disturbing or grimly ironic Christian symbol inverted. Their crucified Christ, "Father," exists honestly to save them from capture by the German forces; he is used as a religious artifact in death even as his life was wholly self-sacrificial. His was the position of the unit's encourager, and his goodness had created the sense of solidarity and camaraderie needed to withstand the pressures of the war. The trick of employing the dead Father as a macabre disguise works. They finally rejoin their regiment and relate to the commanding officer a story of having been captured and having escaped. Consequently, they argue, they had to masquerade as Red Cross workers in order to gain immunity and safe passage to their regiment. The officers scold them unsympathetically, threatening punishment. The sergeant has not been fooled by the story that they have concocted to cover their unsoldierly conduct, but on the other hand, he indicates that they have succeeded in escaping detection by the top brass. Knott is in tears as the film ends. The message is wholly nihilistic.

After their discharge, Knott arranges for Mother to win the Medal of Honor. On ten successive New Year's Days, Knott receives a crisp new ten-dollar bill in payment of a bet that he had wanted to lose. The bills arrive in envelopes without return addresses, and after the debt has been paid, Mother never writes to him again. Indeed, this film itself is like a message from the dead at the Maginot Line. Although widely and well reviewed, as well as thought-provoking with its original plot, the film presents such a bleak vision that many viewers go away from it puzzled into the dark.

A Midnight Clear's setting is the stilly beautiful winter wonderland of Park City, Utah, meant to be the Alps. Yet the beauty of the scene stands in starkly ironic contrast to the ghastliness of the human cataclysm of World War II. Hence, the outer beauty of nature belies the ugliness of inner human nature. The audience sees how the genre of the antiwar film evolves toward a conscious omission of all but the grimmest humor. Whereas *M*A*S*H* (1970) and *Mediterraneo* (1992; reviewed in this volume) carry the antiwar genre in the direction of black comedy, mining a rich vein of humor, in *A Midnight Clear* the genre has soared into the outer blackness—a midnight that, if clear, is also evil and absolutely without stars, light, life, or insight. The acting, while competent, is not superior. In such a deflationary film, charisma would be entirely out of place.

If *A Midnight Clear* deprives the viewer of any illusions about the horrors of war and says most emphatically that war is not comic but evil, then one is merely left with a grotesque humor and some sympathy for the clear-eyed youths who try to emulate the peace on earth and goodwill toward humankind embodied in the Christian vision, while trapped in the utterly inhuman machine of war. The one final memorable, if gruesome, image is that of a dead American and a dead German soldier "dancing" together in a frozen, posed embrace. The unit had encountered the mawkish pair on the road to the chateau and after they had gazed in mute horror for some minutes, one had quipped, "Well, at least he finally got a date." *A Midnight Clear* illustrates how, once war is declared all bets and dates are off, all civilization is destroyed, and all religion and humanity are horribly nullified. The film's overriding moral purpose is to ensure that there will never be a World War III; for that reason, the film is highly recommended, although it is not for the immature or for the morally fainthearted.

Cher Langdell

Reviews

American Film: Magazine of the Film and Television Arts. XVII, January, 1992, p. 52.
Boxoffice. April, 1992, p. R-33.
Chicago Tribune. May 1, 1992, VII, p. 49.
The Christian Science Monitor. March 27, 1992, p. 16.
The Hollywood Reporter. April 23, 1992, p. 5.
Los Angeles Times. April 24, 1992, p. F6.
The New York Times. April 24, 1992, p. B1.
Newsweek. CXIX, May 11, 1992, p. 77.
Time. CXXXIX, May 11, 1992, p. 60.
Variety. March 30, 1992, p. 23.

MISSISSIPPI MASALA

Production: Michael Nozik and Mira Nair for Cinecom Entertainment Group, in association with Odyssey/Cinecom International, Film Four International, Mirabi Films, Movieworks, and Black River Productions; released by the Samuel Goldwyn Company
Direction: Mira Nair
Screenplay: Sooni Taraporevala
Cinematography: Ed Lachman
Editing: Roberto Silvi
Production design: Mitch Epstein
Art direction: Jefferson Sage
Set decoration: Jeannette Scott
Casting: Judy Claman, Dinaz Stafford, Susie Figgis, and Simon/Kumin Casting
Sound: Alex Griswold
Costume design: Ellen Lutter, Susan Lyall, and Kinnari Panikar
Music: L. Subramaniam
MPAA rating: R
Running time: 118 minutes

Principal characters:

Demetrius .... Denzel Washington
Mina .... Sarita Choudhury
Jay .... Roshan Seth
Kinnu .... Sharmila Tagore
Tyrone .... Charles S. Dutton
Williben .... Joe Seneca
Anil .... Ranjit Chowdhry
Okelo .... Konga Mbandu
Dexter .... Tico Wells
Alicia LeShay .... Natalie Oliver
Pontiac .... Mohan Gokhale
Kanti Napkin .... Mohan Agashe
Aunt Rose .... Yvette Hawkins
Jammubhai .... Anjan Srivastava
Chanda .... Dipti Suther
Kasumben .... Varsha Thaker
Harry Patel .... Ashok Lath
Young Mina .... Sahira Nair

Indian director Mira Nair's first feature film, the multiaward-winning *Salaam Bombay!* (1988), explored the world of young street orphans struggling to survive on the mean streets of Bombay. Nair dedicated the film to these young outcasts of society who, despite their squalid and harsh existence, still strove to maintain a sense of dignity. In *Mississippi Masala*, Nair explores the lives of another band of outcast Indians, who this time are struggling to make a living in a small town far removed from their homeland, and their dealings with the African American and white communities surrounding them. As in her previous film, Nair presents all of her characters as fallible, mixed-up mortals bound by strong cultural traditions, all of them capable of exhibiting deep-seated prejudices as well as profound compassion and love.

The film opens in Kampala, Uganda, in 1972. Jay (Roshan Seth), his wife, Kinnu (Sharmila Tagore), and their young daughter, Mina (Sahira Nair), are preparing to flee the country along with the rest of the nonblack African population, as ordered by the country's new fanatic leader, Idi Amin. Jay, whose heritage is Indian but who was born and reared in Uganda, is overwhelmed by the turn of events and lashes out in frustration at his lifelong friend, Okelo (Konga Mbandu), who is sympathetic to both Jay's feelings of outrage and his own black African heritage. After a hazardous journey across Uganda to the airport, Jay and his family first fly to England. Then, as the sound-track music segues from traditional Indian strains to blues, the family finally comes to rest in the Southern United States.

With a title card announcing a new setting and decade—Greenwood, Mississippi, 1990—Mina (Sarita Choudhury), now a beautiful and spirited young woman, zips around a Piggly Wiggly supermarket gathering supplies for her family and friends. Mina's father and mother own a local liquor store and live in a motel run by fellow Indians who have settled in the area. In fact, Indian-run motels dominate this part of the country, and their owners and relatives have formed a loose extended family over the years. Mina and the others are in the middle of preparing for a traditional Indian wedding. The groom, Anil (Ranjit Chowdhry), is the owner of the Monte Cristo Motel, where Mina and her family reside. On her way back to the motel with her supplies, the impetuous Mina gets into an accident with a van. The van's owner is Demetrius (Denzel Washington), an African American man who runs a local carpet-cleaning business.

The wedding is depicted as both solemnly traditional and irreverently goofy. As family and friends gather in one of the motel rooms to perform the ceremony, some of the guests fidget and yawn during the attending priest's talk of maintaining Indian traditions, and redneck neighbors complain about the racket and the weird music. More humor follows, as Anil and his new bride bed down in their tacky honeymoon suite and the blushing bride aggressively stifles her new husband's amorous advances with a look of boredom.

Mina, meanwhile, leaves the ceremony early and drives to a local nightclub with Harry Patel (Ashok Lath), a family friend who is strongly attracted to her. The club is a popular hangout for young African Americans, many of whom are Mina's friends. Demetrius is also present, as is his former girlfriend, Alicia LeShay (Natalie Oliver), who has arrived with her new record-producer boyfriend. Attempting to make Alicia jealous, Demetrius spots Mina and asks her to dance, upsetting Harry, who finally returns to the motel alone.

Demetrius later asks Mina over for Sunday dinner, an offer that she accepts. Demetrius lives with his aging father, Williben (Joe Seneca), and his younger brother, Dexter (Tico Wells). Also on hand for the homey and affectionate gathering is Aunt Rose (Yvette Hawkins) and Demetrius' business partner and best friend, Tyrone (Charles S. Dutton). The family is curious about Mina and intrigued when she tells them that, although she is Indian, she grew up in Africa. Dexter then comments about how ironic it is that all of them have never seen the land of their traditional heritage, then asks, "So what's Africa like? It isn't like *Shaka Zulu* is it?" Later, when Alicia makes a sudden appearance, Demetrius whisks Mina away and they have an affectionate interlude while walking along the banks of a gorgeously lush bayou.

While Demetrius and Mina pursue their growing affections for each other, Jay pursues his own passion, one that has obsessed him for nearly two decades—suing the Ugandan government. Jay hopes to reclaim his Ugandan property and, ultimately, to win the right to return to the country that he believes is his true homeland. When he receives a reply from Uganda recognizing his plea and requesting that he return to Uganda to argue his case in court, Jay thinks that he is on the verge of redeeming himself.

Demetrius and Mina, meanwhile, have become more enamored and sneak off to nearby Biloxi for a weekend. As they enjoy each other's company, however, they are spotted by some of Mina's Indian friends, who break into her and Demetrius' motel room and demand that Mina return to her family. A fight breaks out and the police are called, igniting a scandal that outrages the entire community. Both Mina's and Demetrius' families demand that the lovers remain true to their heritages and forget about seeing each other ever again. The white community is also outraged over the affair, and Demetrius' predominantly white customers begin to cancel their accounts with him, resulting in the president of the local bank threatening to repossess Demetrius' van if he misses any more payments on his loan. Demetrius confronts Jay, demanding that he be permitted to see Mina. When Jay refuses, Demetrius is appalled, pointing out that the only thing that really separates the two of them is a minuscule difference in the color of their skin, that they are both fighting discrimination in their own way. The confrontation leaves Jay shaken, and he thinks back to the time when he was ejected from Uganda even though he believed himself to be more of an African than an Indian.

The scandal and its repercussions finally upset Anil to the point where he asks Jay and his family to vacate the motel. Jay decides to return to Uganda with Kinnu and Mina, and the family begins packing. Mina, wanting to say goodbye to Demetrius, leaves in Anil's car to track him down. When she finally finds him, Demetrius tries to avoid her, believing that she is to blame for his business problems. Mina persuades him, however, that they must not let outside forces keep them apart, and the two decide to run off together.

As Mina and Demetrius make plans to start their own carpet-cleaning business in another state, Jay decides to return to Uganda alone, leaving Kinnu behind to manage the liquor store. When he arrives in Uganda, he finds the country totally changed, his estate in ruins, and his old friend Okelo dead. Realizing that he is now truly an outcast in the country of his birth, he makes plans to return to Mississippi and to his real love, his wife.

The most outstanding aspect of *Mississippi Masala* is that, despite its volatile subject matter—racial and ethnic prejudice—the film maintains a subtly humorous and warmly affectionate tone throughout most of the action. There are heated confrontations between the various family members and some extremely tense moments when it seems as if the screen will erupt in bloodshed. Nevertheless, director Nair and screenwriter Sooni Taraporevala always manage to avoid indulging in scenes of emotional hysteria and steer the action back to saner and more playful dramatic territory. Nair's ability to emphasize humor and compassion while dealing with such an emotionally charged subject is a refreshing change from other recent films that have dealt with the same topic, most specifically Spike Lee's *Jungle Fever* (1991), in which shrill emotional outbursts and pedantic moralizing dominated the screen and served to alienate the audience from the drama. Also, unlike Lee's film, which took many mean-spirited and sarcastic swipes at his narrow-minded minor characters—especially Italian Americans—Nair pokes fun at both African American and traditional Indian cultures without slighting the common humanity shared by all of her characters.

Along with the film's gentle, humorous tone, Nair creates a warm, sensual atmosphere by emphasizing the close-knit, small-town friendliness of the setting. She achieves this effect by cutting back and forth between the various cultural communities and then interweaving them by, for example, having traditional Indian music slowly segue into Southern blues and then complementing the aural interplay with the sight of an old African American man playing his harmonica inside the liquor store owned by Jay and Kinnu. Nair also adds to the film's sensual aura by dramatizing Demetrius and Mina's attraction for each other in a very sedate, slowly progressive manner. First, she shows the two enjoying their first kiss by having the characters take their time and truly enjoy the moment. She then subtly increases the slow-burning, erotic intensity in two later scenes when Demetrius and Mina talk on the phone and casually touch themselves—in traditionally nonerogenous zones. Then, in their motel love nest, Nair shows the two again slowly and playfully stroking each other in long, loving caresses. By avoiding any gratuitous, frenzied sex between the characters, Nair draws the audience closer to the couple and makes their mutual attraction a totally believable and deeply emotional experience.

With her insistence on a more levelheaded and playful examination of racial and ethnic prejudice, Nair elicits extremely sympathetic performances from all of her cast members. Washington and newcomer Choudhury are especially fine as the two lovers from different cultures who set off a community-wide scandal that ultimately brings them and their immediate families closer together. Although the actors are obliged to utter dialogue tinged with sermonistic phrases about remaining true to one's cultural heritage, the actors are able to emphasize their characters' unique personality quirks and remain fully believable, sympathetic beings.

At one point, Mina explains to Demetrius how she feels about her own ethnic makeup by describing herself as a masala, which she defines as a colorful, tasty mixture of hot spices. This definition is the film's underlying philosophy—that, by mixing up traditions and cultures and races, humanity will lose its compulsion to label one faction of itself superior to the other and thus avoid creating groups considered inferior outcasts. Humanity would be much "tastier" if the passions and traditions of each group were blended and spread evenly upon the planet in a thick, spicy glaze, a concoction that Nair most assuredly would help cook up and serve.

Jim Kline

Reviews

Boxoffice. March, 1992, p. R-24.
Chicago Tribune. February 14, 1992, VII, p. 24.
The Christian Science Monitor. March 24, 1992, p. 11.
The Hollywood Reporter. November 18, 1991, p. 8.
Los Angeles Times. February 14, 1992, p. F8.
The New York Times. February 5, 1992, p. B1.
Newsweek. CXIX, February 17, 1992, p. 65.
Sight and Sound. I, January, 1992, p. 50.
Time. CXXXIX, March 2, 1992, p. 67.
Variety. September 11, 1991, p. 2.

MR. BASEBALL

Production: Fred Schepisi, Doug Claybourne, and Robert Newmyer for Outlaw, in association with Pacific Artists; released by Universal Pictures
Direction: Fred Schepisi
Screenplay: Gary Ross, Kevin Wade, and Monte Merrick; based on the story by Theo Pelletier and John Junkerman
Cinematography: Ian Baker
Editing: Peter Honess
Production design: Ted Haworth
Art direction: Katsumi Nakazawa
Set decoration: Yuuki Sato and Hirohide Shibata
Casting: Dianne Crittenden
Visual effects supervision: Michael J. McAlister
Sound: David Kelson
Costume design: Bruce Finlayson
Music: Jerry Goldsmith
MPAA rating: PG-13
Running time: 109 minutes

Principal characters:
Jack Elliot . . . . Tom Selleck
Uchiyama . . . . Ken Takakura
Hiroko Uchiyama . . . . Aya Takanashi
Max "Hammer" Dubois . . . . Dennis Haysbert
Yoji Nishimura . . . . Toshi Shioya

Most baseball films of the 1980's were about much more than baseball as a sport. *The Natural* (1984) and *Field of Dreams* (1989) focus on redemption, the American Dream, and the mythical nature of baseball; *Eight Men Out* (1988) on the moral and economic sides of the game; and *Bull Durham* (1988) on baseball as religion and aphrodisiac. *Mr. Baseball* deals with the sport as a tool for cultural tolerance and international communication.

When Jack Elliot (Tom Selleck), the veteran first baseman for the New York Yankees, finds himself supplanted by a promising rookie, the team unceremoniously trades him to the Chunichi Dragons in Nagoya, Japan. (Such exchanges do not happen in the real world; players' contracts are sold to Japanese teams only at the request of the athletes.)

Jack arrives in Japan knowing little about the country and caring less, interested only in continuing his career to reestablish himself as a major leaguer in the United States. Jack also reeks of xenophobia, calling attention to the natives' short stature and impenetrable language at an airport press conference. Even his interpreter, Yoji Nishimura (Toshi Shioya), cannot prevent Jack from constantly doing the wrong thing, such as not removing his shoes before entering the locker room and not bathing before entering the whirlpool bath.

Japanese baseball emphasizes teamwork at the expense of the motivations of the individual, respect for the sacred honor of the sport and its attendant rituals, and practice, practice, practice. Japanese teams practice for hours each day, regardless of whether a game is scheduled. Jack rebels at the antiquated calisthenics that he is required to perform before being allowed to take batting practice.

Much of the dramatic tension in *Mr. Baseball* revolves around the conflicts between Jack, the representative of American selfishness, laziness, and arrogance, and his no-nonsense manager, Uchiyama (Ken Takakura). Uchiyama is a stern traditionalist who attempts to remake Jack to fit into the team while Jack, who persuades his teammates to show more enthusiasm on the bench, tries to make his humorless mentor become less rigid.

Jack's respite from the pressure of baseball comes from Hiroko (Aya Takanashi), the fashion designer who attaches herself to him as a sort of unofficial guide. When he begins to make an effort to understand the Japanese way, Jack and Hiroko start falling in love. When Jack discovers halfway through the film that she is his manager's daughter, a reversal takes place. His relationship with Hiroko becomes strained, while he and Uchiyama find themselves understanding each other.

Mr. Baseball received considerable prerelease publicity resulting from suspicions about its portrayal of the Japanese. After Matsushita Electric Industrial acquired Universal Pictures in 1991, rumors abounded that the film's tone would be softened to avoid offending the distributor's new owners, as well as Japanese audiences. At the other extreme, when *Mr. Baseball* was released, the American Broadcasting Company (ABC) refused to air television advertisements for the film because the network believed that the spots demeaned the Japanese characters.

These responses are peculiar because they assume that the film's premise has to be anti-Japanese and therefore racist. Instead, *Mr. Baseball* is clearly about how Jack Elliot overcomes not racial prejudice or jealousy over Japan's economic achievements but his unease with another culture. American players on other teams warn Jack about certain Japanese matters, but they are clearly foils used to indicate the typical American attitudes above which he must learn to rise. As for softening the tone, the film also shows how the Japanese can be so tied to their traditions that they blind themselves to other approaches to baseball and, by extension, to life. *Mr. Baseball* criticizes Japanese baseball for being too concerned with competition at the expense of fun—the important element that Jack introduces to his team through his individuality and leadership.

Fred Schepisi is the perfect director for such a film as *Mr. Baseball.* He is an Australian who has specialized in films dealing with clashes between cultures: white and aboriginal Australians in *The Chant of Jimmy Blacksmith* (1978), modern scientists and a Neanderthal in *Iceman* (1984), and British, American, and Soviet spies and citizens in *The Russia House* (1990). Schepisi focuses on the conflict between individuals and the society that regards them as strange or threatening in these films, as well as in *Roxanne* (1987) and *A Cry in the Dark* (1988).

Schepisi is adept at social comedy, as *Roxanne*, one of his best films, illustrates. *Mr. Baseball* could easily have resorted to easy stereotypes and clumsy slapstick to make its points, but Schepisi narrowly walks the fine line between the affectionately satirical and the foolish. He stages the baseball sequences well. The director always conveys the sense that real athletes are performing authentic feats in a real stadium with real spectators, a considerable deficiency in many other baseball films. Schepisi does not, however, handle the narrative aspects of the games as well, and it is often difficult to determine exactly what is occurring.

Tom Selleck has striven in his mostly unsuccessful film career to overcome his image as a pleasant television star. In the *Magnum, P.I.* series, he portrayed an extremely likable, trustworthy man with compassion and tolerance toward everyone except hardened criminals and those who opposed the American involvement in the Vietnam War. He then played variations on the Magnum character in his films, most notably in the highly successful *Three Men and a Baby* (1987) and its less commercially successful sequel, *Three Men and a Little Lady* (1990).

With *Mr. Baseball*, Selleck finally succeeds in creating a character with little resemblance to Thomas Magnum. Jack is obnoxious and self-absorbed in the innocent way of a child because, as a pampered American athlete, he has never had to grow up. Selleck presents Jack as a combination of Peter Pan and Andy Hardy, with the ego and attention span of the stereotypical rock star. Jack is nevertheless sympathetic because he demonstrates sufficient sensitivity—as an aging athlete unwilling to give up on the passion of his life—to indicate that he is capable of maturity. Like Robert Redford in *The Natural* and Kevin Costner in *Bull Durham*, Selleck is also convincing as a baseball player, looking awkward only when Jack is unable to perform as he did in the past. This achievement is remarkable for any actor, much less for one a decade older than his character.

Because Jack's ego is the center of *Mr. Baseball*, the other actors have little to do but play off him. The film is the two hundredth for Ken Takakura, who appeared in several other American films, notably *The Yakuza* (1975) and *Black Rain* (1989). While he has little opportunity to display more than taciturnity and bemusement, he makes the manager's slow development of tolerance for his American star believable. The beautiful Aya Takanashi displays so much intelligence as Hiroko that her falling for such a jerk as Jack initially appears to strain credibility.

Michael Adams

Reviews

Boxoffice. December, 1992, p. R-89.
Chicago Tribune. October 2, 1992, VII, p. 26.
The Hollywood Reporter. September 28, 1992, p. 6.
Los Angeles Times. October 2, 1992, p. F12.

The New York Times. October 2, 1992, p. B6.
San Francisco Chronicle. October 2, 1992, p. C3.
Sports Illustrated. LXXVII, October 5, 1992, p. 10.
USA Today. October 2, 1992, p. D4.
Variety. September 28, 1992, p. 2.
The Washington Post. October 2, 1992, p. C7.

MR. SATURDAY NIGHT

Production: Billy Crystal for Lowell Ganz, Babaloo Mandel, Face, and Castle Rock Entertainment, in association with New Line Cinema; released by Columbia Pictures
Direction: Billy Crystal
Screenplay: Billy Crystal, Lowell Ganz, and Babaloo Mandel
Cinematography: Don Peterman
Editing: Kent Beyda
Production design: Albert Brenner
Art direction: Carol Winstead Wood
Set design: Harold Fuhrman
Set decoration: Kathe Klopp
Casting: Pam Dixon
Sound: Jeff Wexler
Makeup: Peter Montagna, Bill Farley, and Steve LaPorte
Costume design: Ruth Myers
Choreography: Lester Wilson
Music: Marc Shaiman
MPAA rating: R
Running time: 119 minutes

Principal characters:

Buddy Young, Jr. .... Billy Crystal
Stan Yankelman .... David Paymer
Elaine .... Julie Warner
Annie .... Helen Hunt
Susan .... Mary Mara
Phil Gussman .... Jerry Orbach
Larry Meyerson .... Ron Silver
Mom .... Sage Allen
Abie Yankelman (at age fifteen) .... Jason Marsden
Stan Yankelman (at age eighteen) .... Michael Weiner
Gene .... Jackie Gayle
Freddie .... Carl Ballantine
Joey .... Slappy White
Jerry Lewis .... Himself

Mr. Saturday Night brings to the big screen a character that Billy Crystal created in the 1980's and fashions a life story of a comic who simply cannot give up performing. Inspired by the experiences of comedians from Jack Carter to Milton Berle to Sid Caesar, Crystal turns in what *Variety* called a "relentlessly jokey and shamelessly schmaltzy" film, functioning as producer, director, writer, and actor.

Mr. Saturday Night offers Jewish froth and pain, as comedian Buddy Young, Jr. (Crystal), looks back to the highs and lows that defined his career and family relations.

Intriguingly created in numerous flashbacks, *Mr. Saturday Night* explores the life and times of a quintessential Jewish comic who started "working" his family after dinner and ends up "playing" crowds in Florida condos. In spite of ever-rocky relationships with his daughter, Susan (Mary Mara), Buddy struggles to please audiences at amateur shows, in the Catskills, on live television, and in Las Vegas casinos. He never is able to make it big, and to him his life is a disappointment.

Mr. Saturday Night is surely autobiographical—in part. Like Buddy, Crystal has always worn a soft heart on his sleeve with imprudent but not mean-spirited jokes. Unlike Crystal, however, Buddy Young, Jr., is a cinematic jerk who chronically drowns his career in vitriol and belittles those, particularly his wife and daughter, who try to help him. Crystal undercuts the soft nostalgic side of a Brooklyn childhood, with its core family life and neighborhood amateur shows.

The heart of the film is this portrayal of ethnic Jewish life in New York City, as it is a defining experience for Buddy. Buddy and his brother never fully come to grips with their relationship growing up in Brooklyn. Buddy meets his wife at a Catskills resort in the early 1950's, and she remains his truest, most devoted fan. Ironically, Crystal, who grew up in the suburbs to which many Brooklynites fled, never experienced firsthand the environment that he so effectively portrays.

The actors in *Mr. Saturday Night* perform brilliantly, making the film memorable. Julie Warner is convincing as Buddy's long-suffering wife, Elaine. A wispy, radiant Helen Hunt plays Annie, a young, determined agent masterminding Buddy's comeback. Ron Silver skillfully gets to the heart of the ruthless Larry Meyerson, Hollywood's hottest director, who auditions Buddy for a film role of a lifetime.

Surely another one of the highlights of *Mr. Saturday Night* is its expert makeup. Peter Montagna, Bill Farley, and Steve LaPorte (plus Ruth Myers' costumes and Don Peterman's skilled camerawork) make the film a fascinating exploration of the pitfalls of aging. Montagna originally developed the makeup for the character of Buddy when Crystal was a regular on television's *Saturday Night Live*. In *Mr. Saturday Night*, the aging effects serve to remind the audience of the mortality that looms in the future.

Crystal's Buddy Young, Jr., feels like the genuine article, a Jewish New Yorker through and through. An entertainer since birth, he is a master of the insult who was weaned on vaudeville, burlesque, and Catskills humor. Through it all, Buddy reveals, through his flashbacks, that he was forever his own worst enemy, continually undercutting himself at key turning points during his life. Too often, his emotions and pride got the better of the situation, and thus he was never able to reach the acme of show business to which he aspired.

Buddy's only true close relationship was with his brother, Stan (David Paymer), a kind, gentle man who functioned as Buddy's second banana. Stan, as agent and gofer, endlessly put up with everything that Buddy dished out. Paymer is outstanding in this pivotal role, winning an Academy Award nomination for best supporting actor. Nevertheless, one can fault Crystal, as writer and director, for milking the fraternal relationship (and Paymer's considerable skills) a bit too often.

At its best, *Mr. Saturday Night* offers a genuine portrait of an old vaudevillian in his proper milieu. One-liners flow endlessly from Buddy's lips. Even at his mother's funeral, Buddy insists on telling jokes; this aspect of the character's nature is displayed in Crystal's expert timing. One of the best moments in the film comes when Buddy Young, Jr., the fictional character, meets Jerry Lewis, the real-life comedian, at a Friar's Club lunch.

Crystal looks at how his beloved Borscht Belt world was transformed by the very medium that made his own career—television. In one of the film's most effective scenes, a blend of black-and-white footage and color staging, Buddy hurls nasty insults on *The Ed Sullivan Show* when he must follow the Beatles: He cannot stand the competition.

As the producer and director of the film, Crystal went to some lengths for an authentic look. For example, an exact replica of New York City's famed Friar's Club was built on Columbia's Culver City lot, and Crystal sought and employed comedians such as Slappy White and Carl Ballantine to add a genuine flavor to the film.

Mr. Saturday Night explores numerous themes, from aging to obsession with one's career. Buddy Young, Jr., is obsessed with comedy and cannot retire. In a telling moment, he praises his mother by describing her as his best audience. In the end, however, he alienates his family for the sake of his lukewarm career. The audience only sees his son in infancy, and Buddy and his daughter never truly reconcile. Buddy is forever seeking the approval of others for his own value. He never is able to find peace within himself. His defining experience remains Jewish life in Brooklyn.

Mr. Saturday Night opened late in September, 1992, to modest business during a busy fall film season. Many critics noted that the film seemed to be too specialized, appealing to ethnic populations in big cities.

Douglas Gomery

Reviews

Boxoffice. December, 1992, p. R-87.
Chicago Tribune. September 23, 1992, V, p. 1.
Entertainment Weekly. October 2, 1992, p. 41.
The Hollywood Reporter. September 14, 1992, p. 6.
Los Angeles Times. September 23, 1992, p. F1.
The New York Times. September 23, 1992, p. B1.
Newsweek. CXX, October 5, 1992, p. 74.
Rolling Stone. October 29, 1992, p. 78.
Variety. September 14, 1992, p. 3.
The Washington Post. September 25, 1992, p. B1.

MO' MONEY

Production: Michael Rachmil for Wife N' Kids; released by Columbia Pictures
Direction: Peter Macdonald
Screenplay: Damon Wayans
Cinematography: Don Burgess
Editing: Hubert C. de La Bouillerie
Production design: William Arnold
Set decoration: Michael Claypool
Casting: Aleta Chappelle
Sound: Russell Williams II
Costume design: Michelle Cole
Music: Jay Gruska
Songs: Jimmy Jam and Terry Lewis
MPAA rating: R
Running time: 89 minutes

Principal characters:

Johnny Stewart	Damon Wayans
Seymour Stewart	Marlon Wayans
Amber Evans	Stacey Dash
Lieutenant Raymond Walsh	Joe Santos
Keith Heading	John Diehl
Tom Dilton	Harry J. Lennix
Chris Fields	Mark Beltzman
Charlotte	Almayvonne
Eddie	Quincy Wong
Lloyd	Kevin Casey
Reverend Pimp Daddy	Gordon McClure

Mo' Money opens with a credit sequence of a brutal car crash and murder of a Dynasty Credit Card Corporation messenger and the switching of a computer file in his possession. This mysterious night-time assassination acts as a preface to the main action of the film, foreshadowing the conspiracy of credit card theft to come. The audience then meets Johnny Stewart (Damon Wayans) and Seymour Stewart (Marlon Wayans), young brothers living on their own in Chicago. Since the death of their father, one of the finest police officers in the city, the brothers have been living by their wits. Small con games such as three-card monte and other illegal street pursuits are getting them nowhere. The film introduces them as a pair of connivers who lure a man to their apartment to buy a hot television set. When Johnny, pretending to be a crazed-out junkie, fakes a heroin overdose, the man flees in fear with an empty box. Johnny and Seymour happily divide the stolen money, run down an alley, and try to rob a drunk who happens to be a police officer in disguise. One chase leads to another, and Johnny ends up in a holding cell with some mean-looking and comic characters. It is an ignominious end for a streetwise wizard caught jumping a turnstile. In one of the most amusing scenes of the film, Johnny's lawyer, the Reverend Pimp Daddy (Gordon McClure), parodies a preacher and testifies a totally incomprehensible, zany defense to an outraged judge and amazed courtroom. Even more amazingly, Johnny is acquitted.

Lieutenant Raymond Walsh (Joe Santos), a friend of Johnny and Seymour's father, intercedes on behalf of Johnny. A typical doughnut-loving, hardheaded, disheveled Colombo-type detective, Walsh urges Johnny (in the name of his father) to go straight and get a job. Johnny refuses to change his life-style—until he meets the beautiful (but curiously wooden) Amber Evans (Stacey Dash) on the street. She rejects him but he pursues her into the labyrinthine corridors of the Dynasty Credit Card Corporation, where she works.

Unable to forget Amber and ignoring Seymour's plea to stay with him on the street, Johnny applies for and wins a job as a mailroom clerk at Dynasty. Soon, he is flirting with Amber in typical office-romance fashion while her uptight and insulting boyfriend, Tom Dilton (Harry J. Lennix), looks on and the sexually voracious Charlotte (Almayvonne) gleefully pursues Johnny.

As a mailroom clerk, Johnny is no competition for Tom, who lavishes the best, such as tickets to the opera, on Amber. Tom delivers the meanest line of the film when he confronts Johnny's friendly greeting of "Hey, brother" with the snobbish retort "What is that?" It is one of few moments in the film that takes the audience by surprise and suggests the depths of class warfare in African American society. Tom, as an upwardly mobile African American executive, seems to have the advantage over Johnny, but Johnny has something else going for him—he looks great in hats. All he lacks is the money to win Amber, or so he believes. Suddenly, Johnny receives inspiration and discovers a way to use deceased patrons' credit cards. What he does not realize is that the chief of security for Dynasty, Keith Heading (John Diehl), is running a major credit card scam involving the same con. The credit cards that Johnny steals are actually planted there by Keith. Once Johnny takes them, he is implicated in the conspiracy, and Keith strongarms him into his service.

Nevertheless, Johnny, Seymour, Amber, and Charlotte go on a gigantic spending spree that leads to some slightly amusing but mostly fanciful episodes into the din of a nightclub. Johnny is having second thoughts about his ultimate scam, however, and Amber fears that the money comes from drug sales—it is not money that she looks for in a man.

Johnny decides to go straight, and Amber thinks that she can get the computer files with the names that Keith has been using. Somehow, Seymour and Charlotte also end up in the dark corridors of Dynasty. Keith and his henchmen, looking suitably slick and tough with sharkskin suits and automatic rifles, capture Seymour and walk in on Johnny and Amber as they try to retrieve the information from the computer. Mayhem ensues for an interminable period of staccato gunfire, car chases, and shrieks. The amazing gymnastics and stamina of Johnny eventually leads to the death of the greedy Keith. Johnny, Lieutenant Walsh, and Amber are reconciled in a hospital room, where Johnny is recuperating from minor injuries. Even Seymour and Charlotte show up and seem to like each other.

Mo' Money is a film that cannot make up its mind: It starts as a comedy, bogs down in a deadpan romance, and ends with a cacophonous crescendo of violence that has little rhythm and no rhyme or reason. As the title suggests, the film is about the lack of money and what people will do to get it. Johnny and Seymour live for the moment, day to day, with little concern about their future. Suddenly offered as much money as he wants, Johnny spends it like a kid raiding the cookie jar. In the end, Johnny forsakes greed for love, but the message comes too late and is delivered too weakly, causing one to wonder at its authenticity. This moral message is so buried under cinematic clichés that it is barely recognizable. The film borrows heavily from three genres and pays little back in terms of innovation or depth of insight.

The film works best as a comedy. When the camera focuses on the two brothers and their episodic street life, the film has a certain raffish charm. Both Damon Wayans and Marlon Wayans are attractive, even radiant, on screen, and some minor character acting is superb. Once the film enters the sanitized interior of the Dynasty Corporation, however, it loses its manic street style and succumbs to blatant motivations and one-dimensional characters. This simplified program subverts the promising beginning of the film, as well as the prodigious acting talents of both Wayans brothers. The possibilities for the comic exploration of social relations between whites and blacks is lost once comedy gives way to lackluster romance and then explodes into gratuitous violence. Also lost is the opportunity to contrast working people's aspirations against corporate greed. These deeper themes are suggested but never fully explored as the film gives in to easy answers. Furthermore, once the film loses direction and lightness, it seems to perpetuate harmful stereotypes of African American men succumbing to crime and greed with nary a thought for the consequences.

With a running time of only eighty-nine minutes, the film signals its own lack of plot innovation and furthers its demise with an exaggerated and confusing climax. The final third of the film is simply too long and too much of a poor imitation of the brilliant subway and car chase in *The French Connection* (1971). For all its frenzied car crashes and its brutality, the climax remains unmoving because of its illogical editing and uneven pace. Moreover, what might be an interesting sound track always seems buried beneath the crunch of breaking glass.

Mo' Money never blends its contrasting elements of comedy, romance, and action together. It leaves its talented stars stranded for lack of plot motivation, and it breaks little new ground in genre situations and almost none in depicting social relations. The film seems particularly weak when compared to such contemporary African American satiric comedies as Spike Lee's *Do the Right Thing* (1989). The eclectic nature of this film might prove fascinating in a stronger director's hand, but in this film the genres simply clash, making a loud sound but no music.

The success of *Mo' Money* at the box office, with $40.2 million grossed by

December 31, 1992, proves the drawing strength of its main star, Damon Wayans, who is best known for his work in the Fox Network's successful television satire *In Living Color*. It also suggests that the growing number of African American-oriented films continues to establish large box-office draws.

Stephen Soitos

Reviews

Boxoffice. October, 1992, p. R-69.
Chicago Tribune. July 24, 1992, I, p. 16.
The Hollywood Reporter. July 27, 1992, p. 5.
Jet. LXXXII, July 27, 1992, p. 34.
Los Angeles Times. July 27, 1992, p. F6.
The New York Times. July 25, 1992, p. 13.
Rolling Stone. September 10, 1992, p. 49.
Sight and Sound. II, December, 1992, p. 44.
Variety. July 27, 1992, p. 3.
The Washington Post. July 25, 1992, p. B5.

MY COUSIN VINNY

Production: Dale Launer and Paul Schiff; released by Twentieth Century-Fox
Direction: Jonathan Lynn
Screenplay: Dale Launer
Cinematography: Peter Deming
Editing: Tony Lombardo
Production design: Victoria Paul
Art direction: Randall Schmook and Michael Rizzo
Set decoration: Michael Seirton
Costume design: Carol Wood
Music: Randy Edelman
MPAA rating: R
Running time: 119 minutes

Principal characters:
Vinny Gambini .... Joe Pesci
Bill Gambini .... Ralph Macchio
Mona Lisa Vito .... Marisa Tomei (AA)
Stan Rothenstein .... Mitchell Whitfield
Judge Chamberlain Haller .... Fred Gwynne
Jim Trotter III .... Lane Smith
John Gibbons .... Austin Pendleton

Bill Gambini (Ralph Macchio) and his friend Stan (Mitchell Whitfield) are driving through the South on vacation when the Wahzoo City, Alabama, police arrest them on murder charges. Since they have no money, Bill's mother gets his cousin Vinny (Joe Pesci) to drive down from New York to defend them. As a defense attorney, Vinny's credentials seem a bit slim—it took him six tries to pass the bar examination, and he has never argued a case before. He does not even own a suit, which hard-nosed Judge Chamberlain Haller (Fred Gwynne) requires in his courtroom. To top it all off, the evidence against Bill and Stan is pretty damaging: Three eyewitnesses saw them go into the store where the murder took place, then saw their rather distinctive 1960's convertible leave hurriedly. The tire tracks even match. Moreover, the prosecutor is slick, professional, and local.

Stan is so worried that he decides to choose the public defender over Vinny. Defender Gibbons (Austin Pendleton) seems collected and rational in comparison to the bumbling Vinny, but the operative word is "seems." In the courtroom, the professional, knowledgeable Gibbons begins stuttering and becomes completely ineffectual. As the trial proceeds, Stan realizes that Vinny is a world-class arguer, and he changes attorneys a second time.

Vinny struggles against great odds to learn Alabama case law, courtroom procedures, and Judge Haller's idiosyncracies. He stays up each night until 3 A.M. trying to study. He changes hotel rooms every night, because some noise at each location—a train, hogs, a dripping faucet—wakes him up before dawn. He slips in the mud and gets his one newly bought suit filthy. Unable to find a one-hour cleaner, he buys a second-hand rust-colored tuxedo, which infuriates Judge Haller even further. Vinny continuously lies to Haller about his experience and his name in order to get the judge's approval to serve as the boys' attorney. Each time Haller checks out Vinny's story and comes up empty-handed, Vinny has to invent a new excuse and a new story.

He has family history on his side, however; the Gambinis argue with one another constantly, as Bill tells Stan, and Vinny's skills stand him in good stead. Interviewing the prosecution's witnesses, he discovers fatal flaws in each of their stories. He pores over the photographs of the incriminating tire tracks until he finds the key to the case. His girlfriend Lisa (Marisa Tomei) surprisingly saves the day as the expert witness who proves that the tire tracks do not belong to the boys' car.

Dale Launer's screenplay raises some important issues through the characters of Vinny and Lisa. Vinny's victory depends on Lisa's comprehensive mechanical expertise, which catches everyone off guard. Mona Lisa Vito looks like a stereotypical gum-chewing Brooklyn bimbo: Her clothes could not be tighter nor her skirts shorter. She is beautiful but cheap-looking (no one is surprised when she testifies that she is an unemployed hairdresser). Her knowledge of car mechanics, however, is both unpredictable and undeniable. This plot twist reminds viewers that victories are not individual accomplishments, no matter how much they may seem to be. Vinny needs Lisa in order to win the case.

Vinny does not know anything about trial procedure. The reason, he says, is that law students are supposed to learn by observing trials. Since he worked two jobs while going to law school, he never had time to frequent courtrooms. His class background hindered him from learning all that he should have; it also makes him look and sound uneducated. Yet that does not mean that he may not have the makings of a good lawyer—or that he is not one already. It simply means that he has not had certain advantages that most law students, lawyers, judges, and clients take for granted.

Launer's screenplay also undermines traditional Northern and Southern stereotypes. Working-class Italians prove to be formidable courtroom opponents; Alabamans also thwart standard film expectations. For one thing, Judge Haller is a stickler for procedure. While he demands much from Vinny, and is suspicious of him, he certainly does not favor the local prosecutor in any way. In Haller's courtroom, procedure is procedure; there is no way around it. In addition, prosecuting attorney Jim Trotter III (Lane Smith) more resembles Atticus Finch of *To Kill a Mockingbird* (1962) than television's Southern defense attorney, Ben Matlock. Trotter's smooth, educated speech and manner meet motion-picture courtroom standards anywhere in the country.

Director Jonathan Lynn long ago proved himself a master of comedy. The British comedy series *Yes, Minister* and *Yes, Prime Minister*, which he cowrote, have won many awards and garnered a following in the United States. His experience in comedy, which also includes *Clue* (1985) and *Nuns on the Run* (1990), stands him in good stead in this film. The even, consistent, finely timed direction could serve as a model for filmmakers, scholars, and audiences who want to know what makes good comedy. Launer's credits are equally impressive, including *Ruthless People* (1986) and *Dirty Rotten Scoundrels* (1988), both of which contain some of the class and gender themes that reappear in *My Cousin Vinny.*

Carol Wood's costume designs deserve special mention. Costume design is often overlooked in film criticism unless a film is a period piece, but Wood's costumes for Marisa Tomei capture Lisa's personal history. Her outfits for Joe Pesci range from fun but out-of-place to outrageously funny. Vinny's second-hand tuxedo will be difficult for viewers to forget for a long time to come. The Southerners do not suffer for Vinny and Lisa's extravagant habiliments. While their clothes may not catch the eye, they provide a perfect backdrop for the New Yorkers' displays without resorting to monotony or stereotype.

In some ways, Joe Pesci's acting contradicts much of the work done by Launer, Lynn, Wood, and others. Pesci is arguably a one-note actor, playing the same character in every film he makes. Differences between his roles in *GoodFellas* (1990) and *My Cousin Vinny* cannot be denied, but the fact remains that Pesci's characters are invariably tough, Italian New Yorkers. No actor today portrays those characters better.

Marisa Tomei's portrayal of Lisa creates a very peculiar feminist role model. Tomei's Lisa is tough, as tough as Pesci's Vinny. The constant display of Tomei's body does not translate into a conflation of femininity with sexuality, as is frequently the case with women in films. Nor does her relationship with Vinny depend on sex at its core—the chemistry between Pesci and Tomei when they argue will stand up to comparison with Spencer Tracy and Katharine Hepburn any day. For her performance, Tomei won an Academy Award for best supporting actress.

As the judge, Fred Gwynne embodies the ingredients of a great character actor. Although viewers may recognize him from his past television work, there is no room on the screen for those memories, because Judge Chamberlain Haller takes up all the space. He pushes out those old time-worn identifications without pushing aside Pesci or Tomei or anyone else. Judge Haller is a character, neither stereotype nor caricature. Gwynne makes it seem as if Haller had existed before the film and will continue sitting on the bench for quite some time.

My Cousin Vinny excels at its comic project because it creates a reality that is based on one of its themes: Nothing happens through the efforts of one individual alone. Lynn, Launer, Pesci, Tomei, Gwynne, and a host of others turn this insight into a film that makes important points about gender, class, disability, North-South relations, and American individualism without missing a beat or a laugh.

Anahid Kassabian

Reviews

Chicago Tribune. March 13, 1992, VII, p. 39.
Films in Review. XLIII, May, 1992, p. 180.
The Hollywood Reporter. March 2, 1992, p. 8.
Los Angeles Times. March 13, 1992, p. F8.
New Statesman and Society. V, July 17, 1992, p. 44.
The New York Times. March 13, 1992, p. B9.
The New Yorker. LXVIII, April 20, 1992, p. 84.
Premiere. V, March, 1992, p. 84.
Time. CXXXIX, April 6, 1992, p. 69.
Variety. March 2, 1992, p. 4.

NIGHT AND THE CITY

Production: Jane Rosenthal and Irwin Winkler for Tribeca, in association with Penta Entertainment; released by Twentieth Century-Fox
Direction: Irwin Winkler
Screenplay: Richard Price; based on the novel by Gerald Kersh and on the 1950 film written by Jo Eisinger
Cinematography: Tak Fujimoto
Editing: David Brenner
Production design: Peter Larkin
Art direction: Charley Beale
Set decoration: Robert J. Franco
Casting: Todd Thaler
Sound: Tod Maitland
Costume design: Richard Bruno
Music: James Newton Howard
MPAA rating: R
Running time: 103 minutes

Principal characters:

Harry Fabian	Robert De Niro
Helen	Jessica Lange
Phil	Cliff Gorman
Boom Boom Grossman	Alan King
Al Grossman	Jack Warden
Peck	Eli Wallach

Robert De Niro is in a class of his own in Hollywood. He is the rare type of actor who has garnered enough respect and clout in the industry to be able to pick and choose with whom he works. Yet this characteristic is not a new one for De Niro, who is almost better known for his creative alliances, particularly with director Martin Scorsese, than for his performances. De Niro had starred for Scorsese in several films, from *Mean Streets* (1973) to *Cape Fear* (1991), so it came as no surprise to film audiences to find De Niro teamed up in 1992 with another longtime collaborator, Irwin Winkler, in the remake of Jules Dassin's 1950 *film noir Night and the City*. Winkler, a successful veteran producer, produced De Niro's films *New York, New York* (1977), *Raging Bull* (1980), and *GoodFellas* (1990) before first directing him in *Guilty by Suspicion* (1991). Winkler made his directorial debut with that film, which, coincidentally, also featured Scorsese in an acting role. Winkler, De Niro, and Scorsese are well known in Hollywood for bringing a certain style of filmmaking to the screen—a gritty, harsh, New York vision of the world. *Night and the City* is no exception.

Night and the City is set in New York City, and the flavor of the streets is tasted early in the film as the setting serves as a separate character altogether. De Niro plays small-time lawyer Harry Fabian, a stereotypical "ambulance chaser" who lives light on his feet and quick on his wits. Harry's very existence depends upon varying degrees of risk-taking, from talking his clients into fake whiplash to sleeping with the wife of a friend. A fast talker and big dreamer, Harry longs to hit the big time, to play with the big boys, but he lacks the resources or the inspiration to do so.

The theme of a hustler dreaming of making it big is one that is not uncommon in Hollywood. Winkler himself notes that one line of dialogue in the first scene of the original *Night and the City*, which starred Richard Widmark and Gene Tierney, was what drove him to remake the 1950 English film. The line "You know, I really want to be somebody" has been heard, in some form, in some of the most classic films of the modern era, including Elia Kazan's *On the Waterfront* (1954), John G. Avildsen's *Rocky* (1976), and Scorsese's *Raging Bull*. Countless films have been made about the small-time hero bucking the odds to chase a dream, but perhaps none have been made with such a seductively tragic feel as Winkler's *Night and the City*.

Harry stumbles across his calling to success as he becomes involved in a run-of-the-mill assault lawsuit that he brings against a top boxing champion. Although the case is a sham, Harry manages to kick up quite a bit of negative publicity along the way for the fighter, who is managed by notorious promoter Boom Boom Grossman (Alan King), a feat that lands Harry squarely on Boom Boom's bad side.

Meanwhile, oblivious to the resentment that he has stirred up in Boom Boom's camp, Harry is drawn to Boom Boom's profession: the power, the respect, and the money that is involved in boxing promotion. Harry feels inspired and sets out to raise the money needed to put on an event of his own.

The key to the setup of *Night and the City* is that it must and does clearly establish who Harry Fabian is. The film is driven solely by the motivations within Harry's character, and the audience has to understand that character in order for the plot line to advance. Winkler and De Niro waste no time in defining Harry: He is a low-rent hustler who lives by the seat of his pants, who makes it day by day, any way that he can. He is the kind of guy who always gets himself into situations that he cannot see coming and often cannot escape. One such situation is the seemingly trivial lawsuit that he pursues against Boom Boom's boxer. Although, through the lawsuit, he discovers the seductively intoxicating world of boxing promotion, he also gains the negative attention of Boom Boom, who has taken it upon himself to teach Harry a lesson.

Things are only made worse when Harry enlists Boom Boom's older brother Al (Jack Warden) to be his partner. Harry finds Al, a former champion and top manager, in a senior citizen's home resting his bad heart. Al is only too eager to get back into boxing again, but Boom Boom is fearful of the strain that it would put on his brother's heart. Boom Boom warns Harry that, if anything should happen to Al, then Boom Boom will hold Harry personally responsible.

Once Harry has Al in his corner, they round up a bunch of motley-looking, low-rated local boxers to fight for them and then set out on the tremendous task of raising the funds needed to make an event happen. Harry scours the streets of New York searching for investors but has little luck. He goes to Phil (Cliff Gorman), who owns the bar that both Harry and Boom Boom frequent. Phil is married to Helen (Jessica Lange) and is unaware that Helen and Harry are having an affair behind his back. Harry, confident that Phil will never find out, asks Phil to become his partner. Phil knows what a con artist Harry is, however, and declines to give him money, but Helen talks Phil into agreeing to match Harry's funds. Helen has money of her own that she will give to Harry, in exchange for a favor. Helen wants to leave Phil and open a bar of her own, but because of a police record, she cannot get a liquor license. Harry agrees to use his connections to get her a license, while she agrees to give him the money that he needs to get started in the boxing business.

Once Harry begins the process of putting the event together, however, the costs begin to pile up beyond his expectations. He begins to realize that he might be in over his head, but ever the optimist, he refuses to give up and is determined to get the money. Harry goes to Phil again, but by this time Boom Boom, in retaliation for the lawsuit, has told Phil about Harry's affair with Helen. Phil, already incensed about Helen's leaving him to open her own bar, recognizes Harry as the one to blame for losing her and decides to take revenge. Phil agrees verbally to loan Harry more money, telling him that he will have the money on fight night. Harry, unaware that Phil knows about him and Helen, takes Phil on his word and makes all the final arrangements for the fight, handing IOUs to everyone involved and promising to pay them later.

As the fight time approaches, Harry goes to Phil for the promised money, and Phil exacts his revenge by reneging on the deal, leaving Harry high and dry and in deep trouble. He frantically goes to a loan shark, who gives Harry the cash that he needs, but everything begins to unravel as the disasters begin to multiply. His boxers fail prefight physicals and drug tests, and Harry is forced to scramble to find replacement boxers. The final blow to Harry's dreams is struck when Al dies of a heart attack while setting up for the fight.

Unable to assemble any last-minute replacements and with Al dead, Harry is forced to call off the fight and face the music. Knowing that Boom Boom will be after him for Al's death and that the loan shark will be after him for the money, Harry finally realizes that he has dug himself into a hole out of which even he cannot climb. Helen urges him to go with her to California, but he declines, determined to stand his ground and face his fate.

Harry Fabian is a tragic figure, almost literary in his elements. He himself builds the house of cards that ends up crumbling around him. Harry is not a victim of anyone but himself. What makes him tragic is that, despite his snakelike surface, one can detect in Harry an inner innocence, an honest dreamer who trusts more than he should. What makes *Night and the City* work, however, is that Harry never loses faith in himself or his dreams, even as he barely escapes with his life. It is almost expected that Harry survives in the end, because, although it does seem his destiny to exist in anonymity, it is not in his optimistic nature ever to quit. Harry is a scrapper, vulnerable yet enduring.

Night and the City is certainly not the best work ever turned in by De Niro, Lange, or Winkler, but it navigates the complicated plot lines well. De Niro is superb, as usual, in portraying Harry as a likeable but not necessarily endearing Harry Fabian. The backdrop of New York City is amply used, with most scenes shot deep in the city itself. Just like 1991's *Cape Fear*, a remake that was brought up to modern standards and tastes, *Night and the City* shifts its location from London to New York City, and the effect is powerful.

Catherine R. Springer

Reviews

Chicago Tribune. October 23, 1992, VII, p. 33.
The Christian Science Monitor. October 27, 1992, p. 11.
Entertainment Weekly. October 23, 1992, p. 43.
The Hollywood Reporter. October 12, 1992, p. 5.
Los Angeles Times. October 23, 1992, p. F1.
The New York Times. October 10, 1992, p. 12.
The New Yorker. LXVIII, October 19, 1992, p. 106.
Newsweek. CXX, October 19, 1992, p. 67.
Variety. October 12, 1992, p. 2.
The Washington Post. October 23, 1992, p. C6.

NIGHT ON EARTH

Production: Jim Jarmusch for JVC, in association with Victor Corp. of Japan, Victor Musical Industries, Pyramide/Le Studio Canal Plus, Pandora Film, and Channel 4, and Locus Solus; released by Fine Line Features
Direction: Jim Jarmusch
Screenplay: Jim Jarmusch
Cinematography: Frederick Elmes
Editing: Jay Rabinowitz
Production management: Susan Shapiro (Los Angeles), Kathie Hersh (New York), Gilles Sacuto (Paris), and Manuela Pineski-Berger (Rome)
Sound: Drew Kunin
Music: Tom Waits
Songs: Tom Waits and Kathleen Brennan
MPAA rating: R
Running time: 130 minutes

Principal characters:

Corky	Winona Ryder
Victoria Snelling	Gena Rowlands
YoYo	Giancarlo Esposito
Helmut	Armin Mueller-Stahl
Angela	Rosie Perez
Paris cabdriver	Isaach De Bankolé
Blind passenger	Béatrice Dalle
Rome cabdriver	Roberto Benigni
Priest	Paolo Bonacelli
Helsinki cabdriver (Mika)	Matti Pellonpää
First passenger	Kari Väänänen
Second passenger	Sakari Kuosmanen
Third passenger	Tomi Salmela

Award-winning writer, director, former New York University student and cult hero Jim Jarmusch resists the convention of the ending—happy or otherwise. He maintains that life has no plot and that "the most important people in our lives we tend to meet by accident." Jarmusch explores this theory in *Night on Earth* as he creates five simultaneously occurring encounters in taxis in five different cities.

The first vignette takes place in Los Angeles. A teenage cabbie named Corky (Winona Ryder) drops off a band of intoxicated rock musicians at the airport, where she spies her next fare. Expensively dressed Victoria Snelling (Gena Rowlands) exits the baggage claim area struggling with several suitcases but never breaking the verbal stride with which she conducts business over her portable telephone. Though taken aback to find that this ninety-pound, grease-covered waif is really a taxi driver, Victoria gets into the cab, hesitating only long enough to instruct Corky on the proper handling of fine luggage.

The two get to know each other surprisingly well on their short trip from LAX to Beverly Hills. Corky is less interested in hearing about her passenger's career as a prominent casting director than she is in eavesdropping on Victoria's inquiries about the lover who may have left her while she was out of town. Victoria learns that Corky aspires to one day be a mechanic and a mother of sons.

As the impatient producer at the other end of Victoria's phone call presses her to find an ingenue for his film, Victoria has a brainstorm and hangs up after assuring the producer, "I'm sorry I sound calm; I assure you I'm hysterical." By the time they reach Victoria's circular driveway, Victoria makes Corky an offer she cannot imagine anyone refusing. To Victoria's amazement, however, Corky has not the least interest in being Hollywood's next great leading lady. Not unchanged by the encounter, Victoria ignores her ringing telephone as, baffled, she watches the contentedly self-assured girl drive off into the Los Angeles night.

Ryder is just the sort of star Victoria would have liked to make of Corky. Since her film debut at age thirteen in *Lucas* (1986), Ryder has starred in both mainstream and cult sensations, including *Beetlejuice* (1988), *Heathers* (1989), *Edward Scissorhands* (1990), and *Mermaids* (1990). Rowlands' distinguished career has brought her nominations for the Golden Globe, the Academy Award, and Berlin's Silver Bear Award. Among her films are *Gloria* (1980), *Another Woman* (1988), and *Once Around* (1991).

The second story takes place in New York, where a cold, tired, and frustrated young African American man named YoYo (Giancarlo Esposito) is trying unsuccessfully to hail a cab. Dozens of drivers ignore YoYo's promises of generous tips if they stop and his curses when they do not. Finally YoYo is saved by an Eastern Bloc immigrant named Helmut (Armin Mueller-Stahl); or perhaps it is the other way around. Helmut's grasp of the English language is only slightly better than his knowledge of the streets of New York, and his sense of direction is even less than his familiarity with the workings of an automobile. YoYo begins to wonder if he should walk to Brooklyn. Helmut, however, begs YoYo, apparently his first fare in the United States, to stay. YoYo agrees, but only on the condition that Helmut allow him to drive.

Between the two boroughs, the men exchange histories, philosophies, heartaches, and jokes. The irrepressibly optimistic Helmut (whose name amuses YoYo to no end, as YoYo's does him) was once a circus clown with a loving family. YoYo has yet to experience the joys Helmut has had and lost, though his family life becomes part of this long cab ride home when YoYo spots his sister-in-law Angela (Rosie Perez) on the way. Beautiful, energetic, foul-mouthed Angela does not want a ride home, but this does not stop YoYo from picking her up and tossing her into the back seat. Once there, she does not stop talking for an instant, alternately cursing YoYo for everything he says, does, or thinks and charming the intrigued if somewhat confused Helmut. Once home, YoYo teaches Helmut always to count his fee lest he be cheated, instructs him on how to get back to Manhattan, then watches Helmut drive off in the wrong direction, delighted at the success of his first night as a cabbie.

Although Perez's role is the smallest of the three, Jarmusch wrote the segment especially for her; the actress and choreographer has also been seen in *Do the Right Thing* (1989) and *White Men Can't Jump* (1992; reviewed in this volume). Esposito's career spans stage, television, film, and writing as well as acting. He too appeared in Spike Lee's *Do the Right Thing*. Mueller-Stahl, before being blacklisted for his political views by the government of his native East Germany, was a veteran of more than seventy-six motion pictures. After emigrating to West Germany in 1980, he appeared in several award-winning films directed by Rainer Werner Fassbinder and by István Szabó. In the United States, he has appeared in *Avalon* (1990) and *Kafka* (1991).

The film's third segment, which was the first written by Jarmusch, juxtaposes a fare's physical blindness with the less apparent, more insidious cultural blindness of her driver. Isaach De Bankolé portrays a cabbie from the Ivory Coast who, after angrily evicting two African diplomats for their assumption that he must be intellectually inferior to them because his skin is a shade darker than theirs, picks up a sexy young blind woman, played by Béatrice Dalle, because he assumes that she will give him no trouble. Through his incessant curiosity, the driver brings all the trouble on himself. The woman mistakes his questions about how blind people function in the world for pity, and she is prepared with an endless supply of well-rehearsed counterattacks. Dalle first appeared on the screen in *37-2 Le Matin* (1986), released in the United States as *Betty Blue* (1986), and De Bankolé has been honored in France for his work on both stage and screen.

The most comic installment by far takes place in Rome, where Roberto Benigni plays a high-strung cabbie with an overwhelming urge to confess years' worth of sins to a priest who needs a ride to the hospital. As the driver lists numerous events of lust, adultery, and bestiality, the priest, played skillfully and almost wordlessly by renowned Italian stage actor Paolo Bonacelli, suffers a heart attack. Realizing that he has a dead clergyman in his cab, Benigni's character panics and dumps the corpse on a convenient park bench. Benigni is a star of film, television, and stand-up comedy in Italy; his only prior appearance in an American motion picture was also for Jim Jarmusch, in *Down by Law* (1986).

The film's final and most poignant cab ride takes place just before dawn in Helsinki. Finland's leading actor, Matti Pellonpää, portrays Mika, a sadly quiet cabbie who becomes impatient with his three customers (Kari Väänänen, Sakari Kuosmanen, and Tomi Salmela), who are so drunk that they can barely remember their addresses. They explain that one of them lost his job and his car, and discovered that his sixteen-year-old daughter was pregnant, all on the same day. Though liquor has long since rendered this man unable to feel the pain, his faithful friends continue to console him, until Mika gives them a story really worth crying over. They learn that Mika and his wife had a baby girl, but when the doctors told them their daughter would not live, Mika decided not to love her. For weeks he mourned as the child fought for her life in the hospital. Finally Mika could stand the pain no more and opened his heart; the child died that night. When the taxi reaches its destination, the trio crawls out of the cab, sobbing for and blessing Mika and his wife. Mika drives off, leaving the man who had had the bad day just emerging from his stupor and wondering how he came to be sprawled out on the ice in front of his house as his neighbors bid him good morning on their way to work. The cast of this portion of *Night on Earth* are all highly respected and well known for their stage and screen work in Finland.

Gravel-voiced singer/songwriter Tom Waits supplies the songs and score, which, chameleon-like, change beautifully and subtly to complement each unusual, disparate, and exciting scene.

Eleah Horwitz

Reviews

Boxoffice. June, 1992, p. R-49.
Chicago Tribune. May 8, 1992, VII, p. 32.
The Christian Science Monitor. May 7, 1992, p. 13.
The Hollywood Reporter. October 4, 1991, p. 8.
Los Angeles Times. May 8, 1992, p. F8.
The New York Times. October 4, 1991, p. B1.
Newsweek. CXIX, May 18, 1992, p. 66.
Rolling Stone. May 14, 1992, p. 111.
Time. CXXXIX, May 18, 1992, p. 78.
Variety. October 4, 1991, p. 2.

OF MICE AND MEN

Production: Russ Smith and Gary Sinise; released by Metro-Goldwyn-Mayer
Direction: Gary Sinise
Screenplay: Horton Foote; based on the novel by John Steinbeck
Cinematography: Kenneth MacMillan
Editing: Robert L. Sinise
Production design: David Gropman
Art direction: Dan Davis
Set decoration: Karen Schulz and Joyce Anne Gilstrap
Set design: Cheryl T. Smith
Casting: Amanda Mackey and Cathy Sandrich
Sound: David Brownlow
Costume design: Shay Cunliffe
Music: Mark Isham
MPAA rating: PG-13
Running time: 110 minutes

Principal characters:

Lennie .... John Malkovich
George .... Gary Sinise
Candy .... Ray Walston
Curley .... Casey Siemaszko
Curley's wife .... Sherilyn Fenn
Slim .... John Terry
Carlson .... Richard Riehle
Whitt .... Alexis Arquette
Crooks .... Joe Morton
The boss .... Noble Willingham

The Nobel Prize-winning novelist John Steinbeck left the world two indisputable masterpieces: *The Grapes of Wrath* (1939), with John Ford's 1940 screen adaptation standing as a classic, and the exquisite short novel *Of Mice and Men* (1937). The novel's masterful first screen adaptation in 1939 starred Lon Chaney, Jr., as the big, dumb Lennie and Burgess Meredith as his shrewd protector, George.

Steinbeck's pair of itinerant ranch laborers are classic characters; they have been imitated, parodied, and reworked any number of times. In Gary Sinise's ambitious but only partly successful adaptation, John Malkovich gives Lennie a memorably high-pitched, thin voice. Sinise, of Chicago's Steppenwolf Theater Company, directed and starred as Tom Joad in a Tony Award-winning 1985 stage version of *The Grapes of Wrath*. As George, he offers glimpses of a depth and humanity in his character that even Steinbeck did not quite succeed in giving him.

After a clumsy, unhelpful opening scene—a young woman in a torn dress runs in terror from Lennie's inarticulate affection; Lennie and George jump in a box car and make yet another getaway—the viewer is treated to vintage Steinbeck dialogue. "I like beans with ketchup," announces Lennie. "We ain't got any," replies George wearily. "Whatever we ain't got, that's what you want." George goes on to ponder: "When I think of the swell time I could have without you . . ."

Yet he is devoted to Lennie, as to a child. George needs the helpless giant to give his own aimless, impoverished life meaning. "Do you want I should go away and leave you alone?" asks Lennie heartbreakingly, though not without native craftiness. "Where the hell would you go?" replies George. "George"—Malkovich's Lennie pronounces the name "Dord"—"Dord, if you don't want me, I'll go off and find a cave." "Jesus Christ, your Aunt Clara wouldn't like you runnin' off by yourself," George answers, weary but steadfast.

George and Lennie live day to day, but they cherish a dream of owning a little house of their very own. "Tell me about the rabbits, George," is Lennie's famous, unforgettable line. George obliges, beginning his oft-repeated reverie: "Guys like us, that work on ranches, are the loneliest guys in the world. They ain't got no family and they don't belong no place. They got nothing to look ahead to." Lennie excitedly replies, "But not us, Dord, because I got you to look after me and you got me to look after you." George goes on to tell of the little white house they will someday own, with a fence, and a few chickens, and—of course—rabbits.

The pair make their way to a ranch, finding work and bunks in a barrack. They meet Curley (Casey Siemaszko), the violent, arrogant son of the owner; the kind, gentle foreman Slim (well done by John Terry); Candy (Ray Walston), the old-timer who cannot resist wanting to share their dream of a little house; the bitter, ostracized African American Crooks (Joe Morton), who befriends Lennie; and, tragically, Curley's wife (Sherilyn Fenn). Curley's wife—she has no other name in the book or in the film—is a beautiful young woman, neglected and abused by Curley. She wanders around, looking not for sex but for friendship and company among the hired men. When Lennie and George first meet her, the foreshadowing is painfully heavy: "She's purty," notes Lennie. "Keep away from her," replies George curtly.

A dog on the ranch has just had puppies, and George allows Lennie to have one of them. The old man, Candy, has an ancient dog that he loves very much. The other hands use the occasion of the new litter to persuade Candy to let them shoot his old dog. "That dog ain't no good to you," says the gruff Carlson (Richard Riehle). "He ain't no good to his self." After Carlson shoots the dog offscreen (the characters in the bunkhouse hear the shot), Candy weeps and says, "I shoulda shot that dog myself. Shouldn't a let nobody else shoot my dog." The symbolism and foreshadowing are a bit heavy-handed, but one forgives some metaphorical clumsiness in a writer as sincere as Steinbeck. One does wish Sinise had done something here and elsewhere to give new life to the author's chronic earnestness, though.

Many viewers will have read the book as assigned reading in high school. The plot and its repeating, foreshadowing images are familiar: Lennie likes stroking soft, furry things. In an early scene, he has a dead mouse in his pocket. When George makes him throw it away, he protests that he found it dead. Later, he unwittingly kills his new puppy. When Curley's wife confronts him with her loneliness in a barn, it is inevitable that despite George's terrified warning, the story's ending will not be happy. Following the tragic encounter in the barn, a chase ensues, with Lennie hiding in the swamp where George had told him to go if ever he got into trouble. "I ain't gonna let 'em hurt Lennie," says George to Candy, and of course he keeps his word. The pair's encounter in the swamp is wrenching, but this time, George cannot protect Lennie.

Steinbeck's novel is so heavily driven by dialogue and by the characters' responses to and involvements with one another that it is really a play in novel form; indeed, Steinbeck himself adapted it for the stage. Sinise's faithful screen version cannot help but seem, like *Driving Miss Daisy* (1989), a bit cloyingly like a filmed play, with an almost perfunctory attempt to flesh out the setting. The sets and lighting are run-of-the-mill Hollywood, almost television quality, and as such are disappointing.

Moreover, there is something about this film that leaves the viewer rather flat. It is successful enough: The performances are very good, and the heartrending denouement is appropriately foreshadowed, sad and tragic. In the end, though, Sinise's screening is too faithful to Steinbeck, too reverent. John Steinbeck was an American novelist of historic stature who had great sympathy for ordinary people, and *Of Mice and Men* is without question one of his finest works. Yet he was a self-taught writer with little capacity for irony or subtlety. Sinise, by filming *Of Mice and Men* too faithfully, fails to improve on it, instead offering warmed-over Steinbeck. The dialogue is still exquisite, the plot is still well conceived and well crafted, and the acting is good enough; the film is to be recommended. The overall effect of Sinise's film, though, is to make the viewer want to read the book again. The book, though a masterpiece, could have benefited from a fresher interpretation that would have resonated for viewers in the 1990's.

Ethan Casey

Reviews

Chicago Tribune. October 2, 1992, VII, p. 21.
Entertainment Weekly. October 16, 1992, p. 53.
The Hollywood Reporter. May 21, 1992, p. 5.
Los Angeles Times. October 2, 1992, p. F12.
The New Republic. CCVII, November 2, 1992, p. 24.
The New York Times. October 2, 1992, p. B3.
The New Yorker. November 30, 1992, p. 37.
Sight and Sound. III, January, 1993, p. 50.
Time. CXL, October 19, 1992, p. 81.
Variety. May 18, 1992, p. 8.

PASSENGER 57

Production: Lee Rich, Dan Paulson, and Dylan Sellers; released by Warner Bros.
Direction: Kevin Hooks
Screenplay: David Loughery and Dan Gordon; based on a story by Stewart Raffill and Gordon
Cinematography: Mark Irwin
Editing: Richard Nord
Production design: Jaymes Hinkle
Art direction: Alan Muraoka
Set decoration: Don K. Ivey
Casting: Shari Rhodes
Sound: Robert Anderson, Jr.
Costume design: Brad Loman
Stunt coordination: Glenn Wilder and Jeff Ward
Music: Stanley Clarke
MPAA rating: R
Running time: 83 minutes

Principal characters:

John Cutter	Wesley Snipes
Charles Rane	Bruce Payne
Sly Delvecchio	Tom Sizemore
Marti Slayton	Alex Datcher
Stuart Ramsey	Bruce Greenwood
Dwight Henderson	Robert Hooks
Sabrina Ritchie	Elizabeth Hurley
Forget	Michael Horse
Vincent	Marc Macaulay
Chief Biggs	Ernie Lively

It seems the John McTiernan blockbuster *Die Hard* (1988) had more of an effect on Hollywood than anyone could have foreseen. In 1992, there was *Under Siege* (reviewed in this volume), a box-office hit starring action favorite Steven Seagal, which featured a story loosely based on the 1988 Bruce Willis smash and its sequel, *Die Hard II: Die Harder* (1990). Hollywood then produced *Passenger 57*, a rollicking good-vs.-evil action picture starring Wesley Snipes. *Passenger 57* tries to distance itself from the *Die Hard* connection by shifting locations, but, at heart, it is still the story of one man against a team of terrorists led by a psychotic and ruthless killer.

While *Die Hard* took place in a skyscraper and *Under Siege* was set on a battleship, *Passenger 57* offers the ultimate location of entrapment: an airplane. Snipes plays security expert John Cutter, a former airline security instructor who has just been selected to head a counterterrorism unit in Los Angeles. John is booked on a flight to Los Angeles at the same time that the Federal Bureau of Investigation (FBI) is planning to relocate convicted terrorist Charles Rane (Bruce Payne) to Los Angeles. Rane is an international terrorist who specializes in hijackings and bombings. A ruthless killer, Rane will eliminate anyone who gets in his way. Even more so, Rane is determined never to see the inside of a jail, let alone the electric chair, which is his destiny should he make it to California. Rane's plan is not to make it that far.

The FBI's first mistake is to transport Rane on a commercial passenger jet. Because Rane's crimes have been centered on international airline terrorism, it can be assumed that he has contacts and accomplices in every corner of the airline industry. Although the FBI is confident that their transport of Rane is top secret and that no one will be able to discover when and on which plane he will be transported, Rane's partners within the airlines are able to plant five of Rane's colleagues on his plane, including a flight attendant and an airline worker.

Once airborne, Rane's accomplices make their move, killing the FBI agents who are holding their boss. Rane then takes control of the cockpit crew members and demands their cooperation. As the terrorists seize the jumbo jet, Cutter is trapped in the bathroom in the rear of the plane. Unarmed, he attempts to phone his headquarters back in Miami to get their assistance but is discovered by one of Rane's men. Cutter easily disarms the terrorist, using his martial arts skills, and takes his gun. Cutter threatens to kill the man if Rane does not surrender, but Rane proves his ruthlessness by killing an innocent passenger in cold blood, claiming that he holds no value for human life and that it would be in Cutter's best interest, not to mention the hostages' interests, to drop his weapon. Cutter drops his gun but manages to elude Rane's men by escaping to the hold of the plane below the passenger area. He cuts the fuel lines, dumping the jet's fuel, which forces the pilot to land immediately. Rane realizes what Cutter has done but is unable to stop him before he jumps off the plane as it touches down.

Cutter is apprehended by local police, who think that he is one of the terrorists. Because he is unable to persuade the local sheriff of his innocence, Cutter knows that he must attempt to stop Rane on his own. When Rane negotiates with the local authorities to release half of the hostages in exchange for fuel, Cutter knows that it is a trick: Rane would not let half of his hostages go when they are his greatest bargaining tool. Cutter decides that Rane is planning to escape from the plane during the mass confusion that takes place as half of the hostages are released. Cutter eludes the local police, steals a motorcycle, and chases Rane and two of his accomplices to a local fairground. After a lengthy pursuit in the crowded carnival, Rane is finally taken into custody as the FBI arrives and is able to verify Cutter's legitimacy. Rane's partners are still holding half of the hostages on the plane, however, and Rane promises that, if he is not released and put back on the plane, his colleagues will begin killing the hostages. With no reason to doubt his promise, the FBI has no choice but to comply. Cutter has other plans, however, as he manages to grab the jet's landing gear as it taxis down the runway and climb back in the departing plane.

Cutter then eliminates Rane's partners one by one, until the final duel between Rane and Cutter takes place at thirty thousand feet.

Wesley Snipes earned the lead in *Passenger 57*. A well-respected actor, Snipes achieved his stardom with starring roles in Mario Van Peebles' *New Jack City* (1991), Spike Lee's *Jungle Fever* (1991), and Ron Shelton's *White Men Can't Jump* (1992; reviewed in this volume). He gained particular acclaim for his role in *The Waterdance* (1992; reviewed in this volume), proving the range of his abilities. Snipes is the sort of actor who manages to elicit critical praise for his performance no matter what the film. Such is the case with *Passenger 57*. Although critical acclaim for the film itself was less than overwhelming, Snipes's performance drew unanimous raves. Perhaps even more important, from a critical standpoint, is that *Passenger 57* was the first film of its kind: a major box-office action film that features an African American in the lead role—as the hero. It was truly a career move for Snipes, who finally received the recognition that he deserved as a mainstream star.

Bruce Payne, a relative newcomer to American film audiences, was a student of the prestigious Royal Academy of Dramatic Arts in London, and this background can be seen in his role as the psychotic Charles Rane. Payne is chilling as he portrays Rane with a sturdy sense of mission. Even though Rane is captured twice by the authorities, it seems that nothing and no one can stop him. Audiences are reminded of the relentless nature of Hannibal Lecter in 1991's Academy Award-winning *The Silence of the Lambs*. Payne shares Anthony Hopkins' cold-steel stare and self-assured approach, although Rane is much more action-oriented than Lecter. Rane, who possesses near-superhuman strength, is challenged by Cutter's formidable opposition, but good wins over evil in the end.

In 1992, with the climate of inner-city strife, environmental collapse, and economic hardship, Americans seemed to be searching for heroes. Bill Clinton was elected president largely because he offered youth and a new perspective to the White House—reminiscent of another great American hero, John F. Kennedy. It seems that this need for heroes is the best answer to why there have been and will continue to be so many *Die Hard* clones coming out of Hollywood. Americans have always been eager to embrace the notion of good winning over evil and the concept of one individual overcoming incredible obstacles to save lives by risking his or her own. Until this film, these great Hollywood heroes had consistently been white males. *Passenger 57* hoped to signal a trend changing the look of the Hollywood hero.

Catherine R. Springer

Reviews

Chicago Tribune. November 6, 1992, VII, p. 33.
Entertainment Weekly. November 20, 1992, p. 70.

The Hollywood Reporter. November 6, 1992, p. 6.
Jet. LXXXIII, November 9, 1992, p. 56.
Los Angeles Times. November 6, 1992, p. F1.
The New York Times. November 6, 1992, p. B3.
USA Today. November 6, 1992, p. D2.
Variety. November 6, 1992, p. 3.
The Village Voice. November 17, 1992, p. 102.
The Washington Post. November 6, 1992, p. D6.

PASSION FISH

Production: Sarah Green and Maggie Renzi for Atchafalaya Films; released by Miramax Films
Direction: John Sayles
Screenplay: John Sayles
Cinematography: Roger Deakins
Editing: John Sayles
Production design: Dan Bishop and Dianna Freas
Casting: Barbara Hewson Shapiro
Sound: John Sutton
Costume design: Cynthia Flynt
Music: Mason Daring
MPAA rating: R
Running time: 138 minutes

Principal characters:

May-Alice	Mary McDonnell
Chantelle	Alfre Woodard
Rennie	David Strathairn
Sugar	Vondie Curtis-Hall
Reeves	Leo Burmester
Ti-Marie	Nora Dunn
Precious	Mary Portser
Kim	Sheila Kelley
Dawn	Angela Bassett
Nina	Nancy Mette
Dr. Blades	John Henry

Writer and filmmaker John Sayles has spent his career crafting a vision of what his generation is looking for in life. Each of Sayles's films is concerned with discovering a better understanding of what adulthood means to those individuals whose values were shaped by the turbulent 1960's. *Passion Fish* offers Sayles the chance to explore the relationship between two very different women who have a common problem—self destruction. On her way to a beauty salon appointment to have her legs waxed, May-Alice (Mary McDonnell), a soap opera television star, is struck by a taxi. Recovering in the hospital, May-Alice is unable to come to terms with the fact that she is now paralyzed from the waist down.

In the wake of her misfortune, May-Alice leaves New York City and returns to her parents' home in Louisiana. Because May-Alice's parents died some years previously, the old house is in need of repair. Unable to do anything for herself, May-Alice hires a series of helpers who, each in her own way, cannot cope with the type of person that May-Alice has become. Much of her day is spent watching television and drinking. When the agency sends Chantelle (Alfre Woodard) as a replacement, May-Alice meets her match. Chantelle comes from another culture, background, and mind-set. The once-spoiled daytime television star is forced to accept her circumstances, or at the very least stop feeling sorry for herself.

While previous helpers pandered to May-Alice's every wish, the no-nonsense Chantelle has a different approach to home care. Both patient and caregiver realize that the arrangement must work: Chantelle needs the work, and May-Alice fears that the agency would not send another helper. These two strong-willed women resign themselves to making the best of their situation. Little by little, each woman reveals more of what she feels about life. Chantelle is a recovering cocaine addict. Because of her irresponsible behavior, her daughter is presently in the care of the girl's father. Both women seek some kind of romance in their life but believe that their present circumstances inhibit such a relationship.

On a shopping trip to the local town, Chantelle, driving the old family car, runs out of gas. Seeing Chantelle's plight, Sugar (Vondie Curtis-Hall), a local blacksmith, takes her into town. While Sugar would like to date Chantelle, Chantelle prefers some caution. Refusing a ride back to her car, Chantelle meets an old school friend of May-Alice, Rennie (David Strathairn), who offers to construct a ramp for May-Alice's wheelchair. On the morning that Rennie comes to the house, May-Alice is both surprised and delighted about the unexpected visitor.

While she was growing up, May-Alice had longed for the day that she could leave this corner of Louisiana. Coming back under such conditions is difficult for the proud actress. When two old school friends come for tea, May-Alice realizes the enormous culture gap that has developed since she left. Ti-Marie (Nora Dunn) and Precious (Mary Portser) are unsure of themselves around May-Alice, thinking that she will not remember anything about her former school life. For May-Alice, the entire visit is excruciatingly boring and irrelevant.

A certain acceptance by May-Alice of her disability and a respect for Chantelle relieve some of the tension around the house. Chantelle decides one day to remove all alcohol from the house. This action causes May-Alice to become very angry and starts an argument between the two women. Eventually, May-Alice realizes that her drinking has become a problem and, as Chantelle learned with her cocaine habit, that she must live without alcohol.

Breaking into the humdrum existence of Chantelle and May-Alice, Rennie invites them to a boat trip on the bayou. Reluctant at first, May-Alice finally agrees to go out into the waters of the Louisiana swamps. She is amazed at how adept Rennie is at finding his way around this swampland. The boating party takes a short break on one of the islands. With uncanny ease, Rennie lands a good-sized fish. Before the two women have time to object, Rennie guts the fish and produces two small fish from the larger one. A local custom describes these fish as "passion fish," and by wishing on them, the holder will find true romance.

When friends from her television series come to visit, May-Alice finds that she is strong enough emotionally to meet them. Kim (Sheila Kelley), Dawn (Angela Bassett), and Nina (Nancy Mette) are so fully involved in the story of the soap opera that fiction and fact are often mixed up for them. May-Alice begins to realize that her forced retirement from television means very little to her now. With Chantelle and the possibility of meeting with Rennie for more than the occasional boat trip, living in the old family home has become tolerable.

With *Passion Fish*, John Sayles enters the psyche of someone who has known success and fame, and who through a tragic turn of events then loses everything. Portraying any kind of disability in a dramatic setting has always been a difficult task. Films such as *The Elephant Man* (1980), with John Hurt, and *Rain Man* (1988), with Dustin Hoffman, attempted to explore the lives of disabled people. *Passion Fish* pulls in two directions. On the one hand, it is the story of a recovering paraplegic, and on the other, it is the story of a friendship that could only be formed under special circumstances. By the end of the film, the latter tale has won over the former.

This focus on relationships seems more important to Sayles than exploring the traumatic event of May-Alice's accident. Thus, the film emphasizes May-Alice's self-discovery through her confinement to a wheelchair, rather than the world of a paraplegic. May-Alice appears reluctant to speak about her former life as a well-known television star. Because the audience's sympathy for May-Alice is limited to the little that she says about herself, a vacuum exists within the story. What actually drives the film is not May-Alice's desire to better herself but rather the determination of the true heroine of the story, Chantelle, who does not allow May-Alice to become a bed-ridden alcoholic. May-Alice instead serves as the catalyst in *Passion Fish*.

Some critics argued that the film is too long and that Sayles should have edited out more of the dialogue. Such a criticism may be valid with many action-oriented films, but not in the context of a story that is principally driven by dialogue. Moreover, the extended length of the film—at more than two hours—creates a pace that imitates the life-style of the particular part of the South that it explores.

The character of May-Alice is gracefully portrayed by Mary McDonnell. McDonnell began her film career by starring as a boardinghouse owner in Sayles's period drama *Matewan* (1987), and the reunion created by *Passion Fish* was one that McDonnell gladly welcomed. While McDonnell manages to convey the loss experienced by May-Alice as a result of her accident, she never allows a sense of utter hopelessness to overwhelm her character. McDonnell merely touches on the anger that would have to be expected in such circumstances. Despite this sometimes two-dimensional approach to the character, McDonnell's spirited performance was good enough to earn for her an Academy Award nomination for best actress.

Alfre Woodard brings to the role of Chantelle a warmth and sympathy that adds dimension and texture to a film that so easily could have become two-dimensional. Chantelle slowly and uncertainly speaks about her own difficulties, which are in many ways no less tragic than those of May-Alice. Chantelle's grace and caring when confronted by the mean-spirited May-Alice are powerfully portrayed by Woodard. Both actresses appeared in *Grand Canyon* (1991), although ironically they never appeared in the same scene. *Passion Fish* brings together their divergent styles to create a relationship that overshadows the theme of disability.

Passion Fish succeeds in many more places than it fails. There is a definite sense of movement toward an objective—even when that objective is an ill-defined one. Very often, the story's subject matter seems to be limited more by budgetary constraints than by the limitations of the writer. Sayles proved in the 1980's his ability to delve into human affairs and come out with some definite answers. The main theme in *Passion Fish* seems to be the chance to look at life anew. Only when tragedy strikes is there sufficient opportunity and time to reexamine what one has achieved. May-Alice and Chantelle coincidentally arrive at the same point in their lives and permit themselves to stop for a moment of reflection. Sayles's films always carry a message, and in *Passion Fish*, he shows that human resilience is needed to find meaning in life.

Richard G. Cormack

Reviews

Chicago Tribune. January 29, 1993, VII, p. 20.
Entertainment Weekly. February 5, 1993, p. 36.
The Hollywood Reporter. September 21, 1992, p. 5.
Los Angeles Times. December 9, 1992, p. F3.
National Review. XLV, March 15, 1993, p. 61.
The New York Times. December 14, 1992, p. B3.
Newsweek. CXXI, January 11, 1993, p. 52.
Time. CXLI, January 25, 1993, p. 69.
Variety. September 23, 1992, p. 2.
The Washington Post. January 29, 1993, p. C7.

PATRIOT GAMES

Production: Mace Neufeld and Robert Rehme; released by Paramount Pictures
Direction: Phillip Noyce
Screenplay: W. Peter Iliff and Donald Stewart; based on the novel by Tom Clancy
Cinematography: Donald M. McAlpine
Editing: Neil Travis and William Hoy
Production design: Joseph Nemec III
Art direction: Joseph P. Lucky
Set design: Walter P. Martishius
Set decoration: John M. Dwyer
Casting: Amanda Mackey and Cathy Sandrich
Special effects production: Dale L. Martin
Special visual effects: Video Image
Sound: Jack Solomon
Costume design: Norma Moriceau
Stunt coordination: David R. Ellis and Steve Boyum
Music: James Horner
MPAA rating: R
Running time: 116 minutes

Principal characters:

Jack Ryan .... Harrison Ford
Cathy Ryan .... Anne Archer
Kevin O'Donnell .... Patrick Bergin
Sean Miller .... Sean Bean
Sally Ryan .... Thora Birch
Lord Holmes .... James Fox
Robby Jackson .... Samuel L. Jackson
Annette .... Polly Walker
Admiral James Greer .... James Earl Jones
Paddy O'Neil .... Richard Harris

In *Patriot Games*, Harrison Ford stars as Jack Ryan, a former Central Intelligence Agency (CIA) analyst who is vacationing in London with his wife, Cathy (Anne Archer), and daughter, Sally (Thora Birch). Happening on a terrorist attack by a radical offshoot group of the Irish Republican Army (IRA), Ryan kills one of the attackers. The dead man's older brother, Sean Miller (Sean Bean), escapes from police custody and vows revenge. The rest of the film presents a duel of techno-gamesmanship (echoing the title) in which Ryan does all that he can to protect his family. In an explosive finale—a well-edited boat chase recalling Martin Scorsese's *Cape Fear* (1991)—Ryan kills Miller.

Tom Clancy was paid one million dollars to have his best-selling novel made into this film. Unlike the process that transformed the first of his popular novels, *The Hunt for Red October*, into the 1990 film, Clancy publicly raised a number of objections to the filming of *Patriot Games*. In particular, he found it ludicrous that the producers cast forty-nine-year-old Harrison Ford to play the thirty-two-year-old Jack Ryan.

Certainly, this film represents no simple remake of a popular book. Prince Charles is the kidnapping target in the novel. In the film, the minister of state for Northern Ireland, Lord Holmes, is saved by Ryan. In the book, after Ryan foils the attackers, he becomes an instant celebrity in the British media; Queen Elizabeth II even visits Ryan in the hospital and then makes the Ryan family house guests in Buckingham Palace. Lord Holmes, a distant member of the royal family and a bit of a fool, stands in for his cousins Charles and Elizabeth.

Clancy applauded the efforts of the producers of *Patriot Games* to consult the best experts. During the film's four-month production schedule, producer Mace Neufeld and director Phillip Noyce received unprecedented assistance from the CIA, even being allowed to film exteriors of the actual Langley, Virginia, headquarters building and grounds.

Yet the filmmakers were not able to follow the book in all details. For example, they adapted various locations. The Royal Naval College at Greenwich, England, doubled as the vicinity around Buckingham Palace, where the initial terrorist attack sets the narrative in motion. The Mojave Desert doubled as Africa, and the exterior of the Ryans' Maryland home, which was supposed to be looking over the Chesapeake Bay, was built alongside the rocky cliffs of Palos Verdes, California. Production designer Joseph Nemec III and his associates transformed a seven-acre Pacific Ocean site into an eastern Maryland vision complete with apple orchards, a boat house, and a duck pond. He also had to re-create interior offices and high-tech CIA equipment on Stage 5 at Paramount Studios in Hollywood.

Patriot Games is a carefully paced, leisurely told story. It has a stately momentum that at times lacks expected character development and plot complication. The ending is predictable and presents a hollow finale. In addition, save computer images of the attack on the terrorist camp in the desert, there is little of the technology that one has come to expect in Tom Clancy thrillers. The blame might fall on director Phillip Noyce, an inexperienced filmmaker from Australia whose previous feature film credit consisted of a low-budget but critically acclaimed Australian film, *Dead Calm* (1989). Yet the beginning of *Patriot Games* represents skillful exposition, as Noyce uses elegiac music and the dappled, shadowed world of London to set up his world of terror. Noyce was helped in creating this striking opening by fellow Australian Donald McAlpine, the cinematographer for *Patriot Games*.

In the end, however, *Patriot Games* is a producer's film, a work of Mace Neufeld and Robert Rehme. Neufeld "directed" Noyce on all the locations and in the Paramount back lot in Hollywood while Rehme handled the financial details of the deal and planned the distribution and promotion.

A minor flap marred the release of *Patriot Games*. The week before the national opening, influential *Variety* reviewer Joseph McBride raised objections to what he deemed story bias toward the British and lack of sympathy toward the IRA. In an unusual step, Paramount Pictures' executives not only voiced a stern protest but also decided to halt Paramount's considerable paid advertising in *Variety*. *Variety* editor Peter Bart announced that McBride was forbidden from reviewing future Paramount films. Nevertheless, this intra-industry conflict had little effect on the critical or popular reception of *Patriot Games*.

Thematically, *Patriot Games* resonated with 1992 audiences because of its emphasis on the importance of family. Ryan is willing to do anything to protect his family; his wife urges him to go back to the CIA and get Sean Miller. Ryan had given up his job as an analyst for the CIA for the quiet life of a professor of history at the United States Naval Academy. Like his character in the Indiana Jones films, however, this Harrison Ford character quickly drops his mild-mannered professorial demeanor and slips back into the mode of the agent-action figure. Nothing will stop Ryan from doing all that is necessary to eliminate the threat to his family's safety.

Critics generally liked *Patriot Games*, particularly Harrison Ford's performance. *Patriot Games* accomplished its stated mission of offering gripping summer entertainment, and the public seemed to agree, making *Patriot Games* one of the top-grossing films of 1992. In the end, even Clancy declared the film a success, praising it to all who sought out his opinion. Clancy, like the filmgoing public, looked forward to the next two "Jack Ryan" films from Neufeld, Rehme, and Paramount Pictures.

Douglas Gomery

Reviews

Chicago Tribune. June 5, 1992, VII, p. 39.
The Christian Science Monitor. June 22, 1992, p. 13.
Entertainment Weekly. June 5, 1992, p. 36.
Film Comment. XXVIII, July, 1992, p. 72.
The Hollywood Reporter. June 3, 1992, p. 5.
Los Angeles Times. June 5, 1992, p. F1.
The New York Times. June 5, 1992, p. B1.
Newsweek. June 8, 1992, p. 59.
Variety. June 3, 1992, p. 2.
The Washington Post. June 5, 1992, p. C1.

PETER'S FRIENDS

Origin: Great Britain
Released: 1992
Released in U.S.: 1992
Production: Kenneth Branagh for Renaissance Films; released by the Samuel Goldwyn Company
Direction: Kenneth Branagh
Screenplay: Rita Rudner and Martin Bergman
Cinematography: Roger Lanser
Editing: Andrew Marcus
Production design: Tim Harvey
Art direction: Martin Childs
Sound: David Crozier
Costume design: Susan Coates and Stephanie Collie
MPAA rating: no listing
Running time: 100 minutes

Principal characters:

Peter	Stephen Fry
Maggie	Emma Thompson
Andrew	Kenneth Branagh
Carol	Rita Rudner
Roger	Hugh Laurie
Mary	Imelda Staunton
Sarah	Alphonsia Emmanuel
Brian	Tony Slattery
Vera	Phyllida Law
Paul	Alex Lowe

Kenneth Branagh made an usually auspicious debut as a film director with *Henry V* (1989). A young British stage actor/director who had appeared in only a few films, Branagh's accomplishment in this adaptation of the William Shakespeare play was remarkable in part because it was so unexpected. For someone who had never directed a film to attempt something on so large a scale, tackling material that had already been filmed by no less than Laurence Olivier and Orson Welles, showed nerve if nothing else. Fortunately, Branagh had plenty of cinematic talent to back up his brashness, for his *Henry V* is superior in every way, except perhaps in the use of color, to Olivier's 1944 film. Branagh eschews the Shakespearean pageantry to emphasize the humanity, even the ordinariness, of the characters. More significantly, he takes as his model for the film's central battle sequences those in Welles's *Chimes at Midnight* (1966), nearly matching that genius' majestic staging of the bloodshed.

Branagh proved that he could follow a tough act with *Dead Again* (1991), a less ambitious film but still a cinematic achievement. Copying the techniques of Welles again—in *Touch of Evil* (1958) this time—Branagh also openly invited comparisons with the greatest entertainer among film directors: Alfred Hitchcock. Borrowing elements from a half dozen or more of Hitchcock's films, Branagh created a hugely enjoyable *film noir* thriller that is both intelligent and proudly vulgar.

Branagh would eventually have to come down to earth, and, unfortunately, *Peter's Friends* is decidedly mundane when compared with his previous films. The director takes as his models not Hitchcock, Welles, or Olivier but such lesser lights as Lawrence Kasdan and Blake Edwards. Branagh is to be admired for not attempting to treat the same material or employ the same style in each of his films, for wanting to make something on a smaller scale, but the screenplay for *Peter's Friends* is altogether too modest for such a talented director.

Ten years after leaving college, six friends reunite for a New Year's celebration at the country estate that Peter (Stephen Fry) has recently inherited from his father. Each of the friends has one or more problems. Peter, insulated by his wealth, has never had the tenacity to accomplish any of his goals. Maggie (Emma Thompson) is happy working for a publisher but desperately unhappy over her unmarried state. Even her cat does not love her as much as she would like. Andrew (Branagh) has become a cliché of a Hollywood hack. Married to American actress Carol (Rita Rudner), the star of the popular situation comedy that he writes and despises, Andrew is a recovering alcoholic who has not made love to his wife in months.

Roger (Hugh Laurie) and Mary (Imelda Staunton) are married, write successful advertising jingles, and have a son, but the boy's twin has died recently. Every time the phone rings, Mary sprints for it, dreading bad news from the babysitter. Roger is annoyed and embarrassed by his wife's obsessive worry, and their marriage seems to be falling apart. Sarah (Alphonsia Emmanuel), a costume designer, is a sex addict afraid of a relationship becoming too serious. She is insatiable in her appetite for her companion, Brian (Tony Slattery), a boorish actor, until he decides to leave his wife. She criticizes him for his disloyalty and is turned off sexually. Sarah is, however, attracted anew to old flame Andrew because he seems unavailable.

Even the hangers-on have their burdens. Carol, also an alcoholic, is devoted to healthy food and exercise, but she binges on forbidden treats when the others are out of the way. Brian is a cretin who fancies himself a wit. After telling his wife he is leaving her, he turns into a crybaby.

Peter's Friends has been called a British version of Kasdan's *The Big Chill* (1983) for the close similarities in plot and character. Some viewers found *The Big Chill*, despite a talented director and cast, insufferable because its protagonists are consumed by their petty problems. The characters in *Peter's Friends* do not take themselves quite as seriously and are willing to laugh at one another and at themselves, but they are even less fully developed than Kasdan's crowd.

Peter's Friends, written by Rudner and Martin Bergman, her husband, resembles the kind of television comedy with which Andrew is ashamed to be associated. Trite witticisms, punch lines, and physical humor occur with a numbing predictability. The seriousness of the characters' problems, especially the death of the child, is typical of a television hack's unsubtle striving for poignancy. Too often, the refusal of the comic and dramatic elements to blend recalls the worst of Blake Edwards' films.

Branagh, to give him credit, seems uneasy with the pathos imposed on the film's comic elements. For example, the genuine pain of Mary and Roger is muted somewhat by their never having close-ups to draw the audience even further into their suffering. At the other extreme, however, is the climactic scene in which the genial Peter admits that he too is in a dreadfully bleak dilemma as the camera moves in ever closer on him. Cinematographer Roger Lanser lights *Peter's Friends* with dark corners to the frames, muted colors, and mist outside—all of which serves to emphasize the heavy-handedness at the expense of the comedy. The scene in which the protagonists gather around the piano to sing "The Way You Look Tonight" as a way to show that art is a needed escape from life's realities is moving in its own right, but it also provides the audience with a needed respite from the grim goings-on.

The main virtue of *Peter's Friends* is the performances. While Rudner and Slattery are unable to rise above the cartoonishness of their characters, the others succeed in instilling some life into their parts. Staunton, though given too little to do, effectively conveys both Mary's rage and her need for normalcy. Laurie, an outstanding farceur in British television's *Blackadder* and *Jeeves and Wooster*, displays an unexpected dramatic flair. Roger's plea that a father can care as deeply about the death of a child as its mother is the emotional high point of the film. Emmanuel bursts with the energy for which Sarah needs an outlet while showing the character's pathetic fear of the ordinary.

Branagh lets Andrew be a needed source of common sense until his predictable drunken scene. Thompson, one of those rare performers equally effective at drama and comedy, exhibits her range while risking letting Maggie appear to be foolish. Fry, another versatile performer, seems able to change his face and body language at will. His Peter is believable as both clumsy loser and compassionate friend.

Peter's Friends is more interesting if one knows that Thompson, Fry, Laurie, Slattery, and Bergman were friends who performed in revues much like the one that opens the film and that there are several other similar connections between the performers and their characters. *Peter's Friends* is a true reunion for these friends. It is too bad that the script, which could easily have been a dark comedy chiding the protagonists for their pettiness, is so banal.

Michael Adams

Reviews

Chicago Tribune. December 25, 1992, VII, p. 28.
The Christian Science Monitor. December 31, 1992, p. 13.

Entertainment Weekly. January 15, 1993, p. 36.
The Hollywood Reporter. September 18, 1992, p. 6.
Los Angeles Times. December 25, 1992, p. F8.
The New York Times. December 25, 1992, p. B4.
Newsweek. CXXI, January 4, 1993, p. 50.
Time. CXLI, January 11, 1993, p. 50.
Variety. September 11, 1992.
The Washington Post. December 25, 1992, p. B7.

THE PLAYBOYS

Production: William P. Cartlidge and Simon Perry for Green Umbrella Films; released by the Samuel Goldwyn Company
Direction: Gillies Mackinnon
Screenplay: Shane Connaughton and Kerry Crabbe
Cinematography: Jack Conroy
Editing: Humphrey Dixon
Production design: Andy Harris
Art direction: Arden Gantly
Casting: Irene Lamb and Pam Dixon
Costume design: Consolata Boyle
Music: Jean-Claude Petit
MPAA rating: PG-13
Running time: 108 minutes

Principal characters:

Hegarty .... Albert Finney
Tom .... Aidan Quinn
Tara .... Robin Wright
Freddie .... Milo O'Shea
Father Malone .... Alan Devlin
Brigid .... Niamh Cusack
Rachel .... Stella McCusker
Denzil .... Niall Buggy
Vonnie .... Anna Livia Ryan
Mick .... Adrian Dunbar
Ryan (John Joe) .... Lorcan Cranitch

In the late 1980's and early 1990's, Hollywood began to take notice of Irish films. In 1989, *My Left Foot* took the industry by storm when the film's two stars, Daniel Day-Lewis and Brenda Fricker, received Academy Awards for Best Actor and Best Supporting Actress, respectively. In 1991, another small Irish film, *The Commitments*, made more Hollywood waves and earned an Oscar nomination for Best Editing. In 1992, the Irish invasion continued with *The Playboys*, a tale of life in and around a small town in Ireland.

It certainly does not hurt the fate of *The Playboys* that it was coscripted by the Oscar-nominated writer of *My Left Foot*, Shane Connaughton. Connaughton, following the success of *My Left Foot*, chose to write on a subject a little closer to home. *The Playboys* is set in a small village near the Northern Ireland border, much like the town of Redhills, where Connaughton grew up. The fictional town strikes such a resemblance to the writer's birthplace, in fact, that first-time director Gillies Mackinnon, a longtime friend of Connaughton, decided to shoot *The Playboys* on location in Redhills, fulfilling a lifelong dream for Connaughton. Many townspeople play themselves, adding an authentic look and feel to the film.

Perhaps the most crucial element in achieving a successful and powerful final product, however, in addition to a genuine atmosphere, is the casting. Established actors Aidan Quinn, Robin Wright, and Albert Finney are the driving forces behind *The Playboys*, bringing the screenplay to life. Quinn made his mark in such critical successes as *An Early Frost* (1985), *Desperately Seeking Susan* (1985), *The Mission* (1986), *Avalon* (1990), and *At Play in the Fields of the Lord* (1991). A second-generation Irishman, Quinn spent several years of his youth in Ireland, a history that made him a cinch to play wandering actor Tom. Wright, who plays Tara, the headstrong heroine, is perhaps best known to film audiences as having played the title role in the Rob Reiner blockbuster *The Princess Bride* (1987).

It is veteran actor Finney who attracts the most attention in *The Playboys*, however, as he lends his legendary theatrical strength to the character of Sergeant Brendan Hegarty, infusing him with power and subtle rage. Finney, a native of England and world-renowned stage actor, made his film debut in 1960 as Laurence Olivier's son in *The Entertainer* (1960) and went on to earn Academy Award nominations for *Tom Jones* (1963), *Murder on the Orient Express* (1974), *The Dresser* (1983), and *Under the Volcano* (1984).

In contrast to Finney's extraordinary film and stage career, first-time director Gillies Mackinnon is a relative novice. Although Mackinnon has made two films for the British Broadcasting Company and won the Michael Powell Award at the Edinburgh Film Festival in 1991, *The Playboys* is his first foray into international cinema. Mackinnon's youth and fresh perspective serve as perfect complements to Connaughton's experience and knowledge.

The story, which takes place in 1957 in a small Irish village, centers on independent Tara Maguire (Wright), who gives birth in the opening scenes of the film. Unmarried and living with her sister, Tara is the talk of this small town, in which everybody knows everybody else's business. Tara refuses to divulge the identity of the baby's natural father, a scandal that heats to a boil once the baby is born. Tara also refuses to marry either of her two suitors, both of whom are madly in love with her, each in his own peculiar way. Mick (Adrian Dunbar), a poor farmer, pleads a proposal in the pouring rain and a drunken stupor late at night, claiming a desire to care for Tara and the baby, even if it is not his. Yet Tara is uninterested in Mick, just as she is unmoved by her other passionate suitor, Sergeant Hegarty (Finney), the village constable.

The two men vie for Tara's affections in the early scenes of the film, establishing her hold on the men in the village and illuminating her character as independent and determined to stay that way. When Mick, despondent over the unusual flooding that has destroyed his crops, commits suicide, the village erupts in an avalanche of moral preachings and pressures Tara to marry, marriage being the only path to respectability for both herself and her baby. Leading the religious and moral crusade is Father Malone (Alan Devlin), the town priest. Father Malone publicly castigates

Tara in church, suggesting that she must be held personally responsible for starting the moral decay that led to Mick's suicide. But Tara refuses to fall victim to public demands or religious scrutiny as she continues to deny Hegarty's proposals of marriage.

Hegarty, a grand figure and the only villager who is able to match Tara in passion and vigor, is obsessed with having her as his wife. Having been demoted and moved from Dublin to the tiny village several years earlier because of his alcoholism, Hegarty carries with him a bitterness and a silent rage that is only soothed by Tara's company; she makes him feel alive. Hegarty's drinking only adds to his depression over having been denied by the woman he loves, and he sinks deeper and deeper into a silent obsession with Tara.

In the midst of the moral turmoil and longings of the heart, the village is visited by a wandering band of actors called the Playboys, a theater troupe that travels from village to village performing all things theatrical, from vaudeville to Shakespeare. The troupe settles in on the village green in the center of town, where they park their trailers and stake their tent. Led by Freddie (Milo O'Shea), a seasoned veteran whose best years are far behind him, the eight-person troupe is a motley bunch, consisting of down-on-their-luck performers trying to earn a living. The most charismatic of the crew is Tom (Quinn), who immediately catches the eye of unsuspecting Tara. Tom is easily smitten by Tara's beauty, but romance is the furthest thought from Tara's mind. Tom, however, is persistent, and he gradually charms his way into her heart. Tom offers something to Tara for which she desperately hungers: a glimpse of life beyond her tiny village. Tom is the only man in town who is unafraid to match wits with her. She is intimidating to most men, but Tom sees Tara as a challenge rather than a threat. She, in turn, is enthused by his daring.

As Tom and Tara slowly fall in love with each other, Sergeant Hegarty's jealousy boils to a murderous rage. In a vengeful moment, he reveals to Tom that he is the father of Tara's baby. Although Tara reluctantly confirms this, Tom and Tara's bond is too strong to be broken. Tom welcomes the baby into his heart as Hegarty's fury becomes unbearable. In a desperate attempt to gain control of his Tara-centered world, Hegarty throws Tom in jail, accusing him of being a member of the Irish Republican Army. Tom is released, as he is found to be innocent, but Hegarty refuses to let go. In a drunken rage, he charges the stage where Tom is performing and attempts to rip the tent apart with his bare hands. Exhausted yet relentless, he then kidnaps Tara's baby and challenges Tom to a fistfight in the center of town. As Tom defends himself against Hegarty's poorly aimed blows, Hegarty suffers his most humiliating defeat yet, the final loss of dignity in front of his child and the woman he loves. Hegarty stumbles away, a broken man, as Tara and her baby join the Playboys to travel the world and be with Tom.

Despite the apparent simplicity of its story line, *The Playboys* plays more like a detailed and textured novel than it does a Hollywood screenplay. Besides the obviously authentic setting, the film captures the passion of the people and gives an honest glimpse of life in a rural Irish village. The town is neither mythologized nor demeaned. The simple fact is that a small village can have problems such as alcoholism and suicide just as the big city can.

Tara and Hegarty are rich characters with layers of subtext hidden beneath their sturdy surfaces. In the beginning, the film strikes a certain resemblance to Nathaniel Hawthorne's classic novel *The Scarlet Letter* (1850), a similar tale of a "marked" woman who must suffer the scorns of her society. Robin Wright is powerful, playing Tara with a feminist edge and keeping her lusty attraction intact as she drives all the men wild. The viewer is reminded of a young Jessica Lange, as Wright plays Tara with a passion that smolders just beneath the self-determined independence and strength.

Albert Finney has perhaps the toughest assignment of all with Hegarty—the film's "villain," for lack of a more accurate description. Finney plays Hegarty with subtle power, as the character battles against alcoholism, impending retirement, heartache, and loneliness. Hegarty remains a sympathetic character despite his inner rage and obsession, a true testament to Finney's talent.

The Playboys is, to a certain degree, about the need to escape the tiny, suffocating village, yet it is also a tale of passion and love and of realizing when one has lost. The most fascinating aspect of the story is that it refuses to become a typical Hollywood romance. Tom and Tara do live "happily ever after," but the audience is perfectly aware that the ending is bittersweet. Tom and Tara's love is accompanied by Hegarty's pain, which vetoes the audience's ability to feel overjoyed by the ending. *The Playboys* is about simple people with real passions, pains, and dreams. It serves as a fine directorial debut.

Catherine R. Springer

Reviews

Chicago Tribune. May 1, 1992, VII, p. 42.
Entertainment Weekly. May 15, 1992, p. 42.
The Hollywood Reporter. April 21, 1992, p. 10.
Los Angeles Times. April 29, 1992, p. F9.
The New York Times. April 23, 1992, p. B3.
Newsweek. CXIX, May 11, 1992, p. 77.
People Weekly. May 11, 1992, p. 18.
Rolling Stone. May 14, 1992, p. 114.
Variety. CCCXLVII, April 20, 1992, p. 46.
The Washington Post. May 1, 1992, p. C1.

THE PLAYER

Production: David Brown, Michael Tolkin, and Nick Wechsler for Avenue Pictures, in association with Spelling Entertainment; released by Fine Line Features
Direction: Robert Altman
Screenplay: Michael Tolkin; based on his novel
Cinematography: Jean Lepine
Editing: Geraldine Peroni
Production design: Stephen Altman
Art direction: Jerry Fleming
Set decoration: Susan Emshwiller
Sound: John Pritchett
Costume design: Alexander Julian
Music: Thomas Newman
MPAA rating: R
Running time: 123 minutes

Principal characters:

Griffin Mill	Tim Robbins
June Gudmundsdottir	Greta Scacchi
Walter Stuckel	Fred Ward
Detective Avery	Whoopi Goldberg
Larry Levy	Peter Gallagher
Joel Levison	Brion James
Bonnie Sherow	Cynthia Stevenson
David Kahane	Vincent D'Onofrio
Andy Civella	Dean Stockwell
Tom Oakley	Richard E. Grant
Dick Mellen	Sydney Pollack
Detective DeLongpre	Lyle Lovett
Celia	Dina Merrill

With *The Player*, a director who has been said to have a "problem" with endings delivers what may be the most perfect closure since *Sunset Boulevard* (1950) concluded with an out-of-luck screenwriter floating face-down in the swimming pool while the camera focused on a close-up of aging Norma Desmond. *The Player* marks what many Robert Altman enthusiasts are claiming to be the director's triumphant return to his legitimate place in modern American cinema. Though the script is by Michael Tolkin, based on his novel of the same name, there was little doubt—critics all but unanimously embraced the film—that the finished product represented a long overdue feather in Altman's cap.

The story commences with a long tracking shot that moves within the cloistered back lot of a motion picture studio while countless voices rattle off "pitches" of their story ideas for film projects. Walter Stuckel (Fred Ward), a security guard who detests all foreign films, is a walking symbol. The entire film, in fact, is filled with inside jokes. For example, Buck Henry, the author of *The Graduate* (1967), drones on about the possibility of a sequel concerning an ailing Mrs. Robinson living in Elaine and Ben's attic. There are many such brilliantly satirical moments, enjoyable in and of themselves. This is a very good thing, because the plot unfolds rather slowly.

The protagonist (the word "hero" would be problematic) is the young and well-dressed studio executive Griffin Mill (Tim Robbins), for whom these pitches represent his coveted position of power and allow him to make the payments on his Range Rover. No passionate lover of motion pictures, as were the moguls of yore, Griffin is rather a clichéd and emotionally bankrupt yuppie substitute; he cannot even communicate with his story editor girlfriend except by presenting his conflict in a third-person treatment format. Gradually the audience begins to see the world as Griffin does—as a long list of dull meetings and parties where greetings with the stars of the screen take on a bizarre dullness. The meeting and greeting of all the big-name stars who make cameo appearances become surprisingly tedious by the time the obligatory introductions have been made. Only Burt Reynolds jumps out in a memorable moment of playing himself as he loudly proclaims his negative opinion of Griffin.

The bitterness felt by all who are outsiders—most notably, screenwriters—is vividly portrayed: Griffin is receiving hate mail and death threats from a disgruntled writer to whom he failed to return a call. In a stroke of narrative brilliance, the writers in the story are quite obnoxious; they are hardly sacrificial lambs. In addition, Tolkin and Altman both possess enough skill to make their unlikely main character—for at least one shining moment—become much more interesting than his character sketch would ever intimate. In an attempt to resolve his problem, Griffin seeks out David Kahane (Vincent D'Onofrio), the writer he deduces is making the increasingly ominous threats. Seeking to make amends, Griffin instead plunges himself into a nightmarish second act that includes murder. His problems compound as he finds himself under investigation by police detective Avery (Whoopi Goldberg) while struggling to protect his job against the encroachments of newly hired executive Larry Levy (Peter Gallagher).

As Griffin finds his true nature, everything in *The Player* lines up perfectly—right down to Griffin's seduction of the dead writer's girlfriend, June Gudmundsdottir (Greta Scacchi), and a hilarious use of the film-within-a-film device. Griffin's studio produces a film that was originally intended to be a serious statement on the death penalty and social inequality; it was to feature no big-name stars. The shamelessly manipulative ending to the Bruce Willis and Julia Roberts film the studio finally makes is, ironically, exactly the ending that had to be filmed for *The Player* to maintain its own integrity. Yet the clincher, which makes the film's elements add up so perfectly, is in the subtle indication of the "bad guy" in the whole affair. The true antagonists of *The Player* are not the shallow studio executives who sit in a meeting and fantasize about how they can do away with the screenwriter as an element and simply select stories themselves from newspaper headlines. The villain, in the final analysis, is the audience.

The one individual for whom the audience is asked to feel sympathy by the end of the film is Griffin's scorned former girlfriend, Bonnie Sherow (Cynthia Stevenson). She is left sobbing inconsolably after every other character in the world of the film has sold out—including Tom Oakley (Richard E. Grant), the writer of the Bruce Willis travesty of what was to have been a socially responsible film. "But what about reality?" she asks Oakley, the very individual who had previously pontificated on the subject. In response, he immediately points to the extremely poor reception of the original version's screening for a test audience in Canoga Park, "now that's reality."

Altman seemed to burst onto the motion picture scene (though he had worked in television and industrial films for years) with *M*A*S*H* in 1970, a story no other director at the time appeared to want to film. Based on a blatantly antiauthoritarian book of episodes in the Korean War, this breakthrough film was a surprise hit and contains many of the unmistakable characteristics which have come to be associated with Altman's style. Primarily, he used an ensemble cast of virtual unknowns, almost in the manner of repertory theater, and shot on a low budget and on location, away from threats of studio interference. Stylistically, he has always been a director who uses technological developments such as overlapping sound to lend a particular sense of realism to his work.

From his first films, Altman has been concerned with dissecting the ideology and institutions where pomposity or authoritarianism exists, such as the military bureaucracy in *M*A*S*H* and the politics, framed by the sacred knee-jerk conservatism of grass-roots country music, of *Nashville* (1975). It is no wonder that Altman compares himself to documentary filmmaker Frederick Wiseman rather than to other mainstream fiction film directors. These two particular films—with their large egalitarian casts, chaotic, overlapping story lines, and clever reflexivity—are the most lauded of his work, even though the director has frequently offered audiences varied pictures of smaller scope. For whatever reasons an artist is recognized or connects somehow with the culture of a particular time, audiences and critics connected with and approved of *The Player* as an important chapter in the continuation of Altman's career.

Perhaps there is a certain rightness of form supporting content in this tale of the powerful "players" of Hollywood, where the creators of modern-day myth reside. After more than two decades of elongating the tension between naturalism and the stylized construction that necessarily accompanies the filmmaking process in genre pictures such as the revisionist western *McCabe and Mrs. Miller* (1971), nothing could be more appropriate than Altman taking a jab at the thinly veiled fascism of the motion-picture industry. The fun comes from the fact that he does this as he incorporates celebrity icons such as Cher, Nick Nolte, Elliott Gould, Susan Sarandon, and dozens more into the action. Yet *The Player* is not intended to please everybody. It is delicate, darkly unfolding, and difficult, especially as it denies certain audience expectations.

The sense of satisfaction in the flawless articulation of the resolution of *The Player* is something that was missing from *Nashville*. There, amid the competing stories of the twenty-four main characters, the viewer is kept distant from the final apocalyptic act. In the case of *The Player*, "we have seen the enemy, and he is us." Time may prove this to be Altman's most memorable signature piece.

Mary E. Belles

Reviews

Boxoffice. June, 1992, p. R-45.
Chicago Tribune. April 24, 1992, VII, p. 39.
The Christian Science Monitor. April 10, 1992, p. 14.
Film Comment. XXVIII, May, 1992, p. 20.
The Hollywood Reporter. March 16, 1992, p. 9.
Los Angeles Times. April 10, 1992, CXI, p. F1.
The New York Times. April 10, 1992, p. B1.
The New Yorker. LXVIII, April 20, 1992, p. 81.
Newsweek. March 2, 1992, p. 61.
Variety. March 16, 1992, p. 3.

PRELUDE TO A KISS

Production: Michael Gruskoff and Michael I. Levy; released by Twentieth Century-Fox
Direction: Norman René
Screenplay: Craig Lucas; based on his play
Cinematography: Stefan Czapsky
Editing: Stephen A. Rotter
Production design: Andrew Jackness
Art direction: W. Steven Graham, Maxine Walters, and Ray Kluga
Set decoration: Cindy Carr and Sue Raney
Set design: Karen Fletcher
Casting: Jason LaPadura and Natalie Hart
Sound: Les Lazarowitz and James Sabat
Costume design: Walker Hicklin
Music: Howard Shore
MPAA rating: PG-13
Running time: 106 minutes

Principal characters:

Peter Hoskins .... Alec Baldwin
Rita Boyle .... Meg Ryan
Old Man (Julius) .... Sydney Walker
Dr. Boyle .... Ned Beatty
Marion Boyle .... Patty Duke
Leah Blier .... Kathy Bates
Taylor .... Stanley Tucci
Tom .... Rocky Carroll
Jerry Blier .... Richard Riehle

When Chicagoans Peter Hoskins (Alec Baldwin) and Rita Boyle (Meg Ryan) are introduced at a party, they dance and drink together. They soon fall head-over-heels in love, and a fast-moving romance ensues. Rita takes Peter to meet her parents (played by Ned Beatty and Patty Duke); before long, Peter and Rita are getting married at her parents' Lake Forest home, in an idyllic backyard ceremony overlooking Lake Michigan. A strange old man (Sydney Walker) appears, however, seeming to have wandered to this house and this backyard by chance. As the hosts prepare to evict him, he asks to be allowed to kiss the bride; Rita acquiesces. What happens when they kiss sets the plot in motion: The souls of the old man and Rita change places.

When the newlyweds go to Jamaica for their honeymoon, Peter finds himself in the company of a Rita with radically different tastes and outlooks. She is no longer the socially conscious and lovably neurotic woman Peter thought he married. Moreover, she suddenly declares that she wants to have children; she had previously been afraid of the very idea. When the couple returns to Chicago, a distraught Peter seeks the advice of a friend, who simply tells him that people change when they get married. Eventually Peter deduces what has happened and confronts the stranger in Rita's body. "Rita" promptly flees to the safety of her parents' house and refuses to see him. When Peter goes to the bar where Rita worked and finds an old man sitting forlornly alone in a booth, he realizes that it is actually Rita, trapped in the old man's body. Reunited, Peter and Rita keep company and try to figure out a way to remedy their predicament.

They manage to find the house where the old man lived. Peter learns from his daughter, Leah Blier (Kathy Bates), that the old man, whose name is Julius, is dying of cancer. With the help of Rita's mother, Peter and Rita trick Julius into coming to Peter's apartment, whereupon Peter, Rita, and Julius sort things out and Julius agrees to return to his own body. Rita and Peter are at last reunited, with bodies, souls, and love intact.

Prelude to a Kiss, with its body-switching premise, belongs to the film genre that includes such comedy and fantasy films with supernatural elements as *Freaky Friday* (1977), *All of Me* (1984), *Starman* (1984), *Big* (1988), and *Ghost* (1990). These films generally wring humor and varying degrees of pathos from the situation while making passing commentary on gender or social roles. *Prelude to a Kiss* attempts to do all these things while including ruminations on disease, aging, and death, and the film ultimately becomes a somewhat disjointed combination of romance and downbeat fatalism. To its credit, the film eschews the standard comedic mistaken-identity confusions, but the conversations and soliloquies with which it replaces such high jinks slow the film's pace and confuse its direction.

The performances by Baldwin, Ryan, and Bates (in a small role) are fine, if unexceptional, and Duke and Beatty are entertainingly quirky. The film was scripted by Craig Lucas, who adapted his play for the screen (Baldwin starred in the play's New York premiere, and Walker appeared in a San Francisco production). Director Norman René had directed the premieres of all Lucas' stage works beginning in 1980; he also directed his and Lucas' first motion picture project, *Longtime Companion* (1990). The theatrical origins of *Prelude to a Kiss* are apparent in the length and reflective tone of many of its speeches and scenes. The film adaptation is generally effective in expanding the play's setting without overwhelming the action.

The body-switching gimmick is intended as a jumping-off point for an exploration of love. What is it, the film asks, that a person loves about someone else? After Peter and Rita giddily fall in love, his love is put to the test. The Rita he loves has vanished, and a stranger seems to inhabit her body. Although Peter initially was attracted to her physically, as well as spiritually and intellectually, her physical presence alone is not enough; it becomes unsettling, then increasingly aggravating. Even after the old man in Rita's body reads her diary and can painstakingly mimic her preferences and attitudes, Peter knows that it is not her. Later, when he is spending time with Rita (that is, Rita in the old man's body), this situation is frustrating as well. The soul of the person he loves is with him, but it is in a body that is all wrong—old, decrepit, and the wrong sex. "I miss Rita," a downcast Peter says simply. Yet his feelings of love are strong enough to compel him to kiss the old man/Rita tenderly on the mouth.

The film's title, in fact, although it may refer to the kiss at the wedding during which Rita and the old man switch souls, could as easily be referring to this second kiss. As romance and courtship were the prelude to Peter and Rita's wedding, so Peter's love for Rita, no matter what she looks like, is prelude to him kissing the old man. A third important kiss occurs when Peter, Rita, and the old man are finally together, and Rita and the old man attempt to switch back: They kiss, but nothing happens. There is no magic in a kiss itself, they discover. Magic—in this case, the switching—occurs when the desire for something is deep enough.

Prelude to a Kiss largely manages to avoid cinematic clichés. For example, the one scene that audiences have seen many times before—the awkwardness of a person first meeting his or her lover's parents—is somehow given new life. The scene also provides one of the few truly comedic moments (the Jamaica honeymoon being another). Yet the film does have some crucial problems. In particular, for a film that attempts to mix seriousness with its fantasy, it has too many weak points in its characterizations and philosophizing. For example, Ryan's Rita is supposed to be plagued with deep psychic fears, but beyond her words, the audience is given no sense of this fear. Rita seems so lively and effervescent, from when she is first seen dancing at the party, that the fear does not ring true. When, at film's end, she says that she is no longer "scared," the announcement carries no weight. Similarly, the idea (voiced by the old man) that magical things can happen if one only wants them badly enough is the stuff of cartoon fantasies; here, it seems out of place.

According to director René, the film is "life affirming." Yet, although Peter and Rita's love triumphs, the image of their happiness is no stronger than the sad face of the lonely, dying old man. Lucas and René were attempting a fantasy about love, a romantic comedy, but *Prelude to a Kiss* is ultimately too haunted by aging and death (perhaps even, as some reviewers have suggested, by underlying fears about love and sexuality in the age of AIDS, or acquired immune deficiency syndrome) to fit that description. Audiences did not respond well to the film's approach, and it did not remain long in theatrical release. Yet despite its weaknesses—and because of its willingness to look at uncomfortable aspects of life—the film presents its odd love story in a unique, understated way.

McCrea Adams

Reviews

Boxoffice. August/September, 1992, p. R-62.
Chicago Tribune. July 10, 1992, VII, p. 31.
Entertainment Weekly. July 17, 1992, p. 36.

Films in Review. XLIII, September, 1992, p. 340.
The Hollywood Reporter. July 10, 1992, p. 5.
Los Angeles Times. July 10, 1992, p. F14.
The New York Times. July 10, 1992, p. B5.
The New Yorker. LXVIII, July 27, 1992, p. 55.
Time. CXL, July 20, 1992, p. 78.
Variety. July 10, 1992, p. 4.

RAISE THE RED LANTERN

Origin: China, Hong Kong, and Taiwan
Released: 1991
Released in U.S.: 1992
Production: Chiu Fu-Sheng for ERA International Ltd., in association with China Film Co-Production Corporation; released by Orion Classics
Direction: Zhang Yimou
Screenplay: Ni Zhen; based on the novel *Wives and Concubines*, by Su Tong
Cinematography: Zhao Fei
Editing: Du Yuan
Art direction: Cao Jiuping and Dong Huamiao
Sound: Li Lanhua
Makeup: Sun Wei
Costume design: Huang Lihua
Music: Zhao Jiping
MPAA rating: PG
Running time: 125 minutes

Principal characters:

Songlian .... Gong Li
Chen Zuoqian .... Ma Jingwu
Meishan .... He Caifei
Zhuoyun .... Cao Cuifeng
Yuru .... Jin Shuyuan
Yan'er .... Kong Lin
Mother Song .... Ding Weimin
Dr. Gao .... Cui Zhihgang

Zhang Yimou's classically stark directing style entirely complements the simple plot of *Raise the Red Lantern*. The intriguing situation around which the story is spun is given close examination by cinematographer Zhao Fei's mostly slow-moving, or immobile, camera. The frame, more often than not, contains a picture of stunning composition and visual beauty that is all the more remarkable because it serves as counterpoint to the grimness, even the ugliness, of the tale. The result of this potent mix of elements is a film that the mind effortlessly grasps and retains; haunting moments linger in the memory long afterward.

Both this motion picture and the director's previous film *Ju Dou* (1990) deal with the imprisoning quality of certain customs. A nineteen-year-old woman, Songlian (Gong Li), dissatisfied by her relationship with her stepmother and by a lack of money, decides to marry a wealthy man, Chen Zuoqian (Ma Jingwu). She gives up her studies at the university and tearfully makes her way to her new home. One sees early the strong resistance of her personality to the bondage that she is choosing out of want of any better options. She becomes the fourth mistress of Chen and is soon apprised of the customs of his house. A lit red lantern is placed near the door of the wife that Chen has chosen as his partner for the night. Just before the announcement is to be made each day, the four wives stand outside their respective doorways, which surround a rectangular grey courtyard, and within sight of each other, are subjected to the possible humiliation of not being chosen. Jealousy between the wives grows fierce, exacerbated by the fact that the wife who is currently favored tends to win many benefits from the servants, including her choice of foods for that day's menu and a foot massage that becomes—perhaps more for its symbolic significance than for its physical benefits—almost addictive.

Songlian's fires of defiance make her an aggressive but not always wise rival. She often reveals her bad feelings to the master, making him testy, and is frequently outmaneuvered by two of the other wives. One of them, Meishan (He Caifei), a former professional opera singer, performs an exceptional coup on Songlian's first night: She sends word by servants that she is sick and needs the master's immediate attention. He abandons the bed of his new bride and spends the rest of the night with this third mistress. Lines of warfare are immediately drawn. As the story develops, however, all is not as it seems. Songlian comes to realize that Meishan has redeeming qualities and is far from being her worst enemy.

The introduction of each of the other three wives is a study in dissimilarity. On the second day, Songlian is taken to visit the first wife, Yuru (Jin Shuyuan), who seems ancient to the young woman. The mother of the master's grown son, she looks eminently sad, although she does and says the prescribed things. Clearly, she is too old to expect the master to choose her bed and seems resigned to the dreary remainder of her life. She does, however, demand some respect in the household by virtue of having borne a son. The second wife, Zhuoyun (Cao Cuifeng), is a happy contrast, cheerfully greeting Songlian like a future friend and mentor. She offers her tea and, later in the film, a gift of beautiful silk. The third wife snubs Songlian when she comes to pay the traditional visit, having her servants say that she is still not well. When they finally do meet, Meishan continues to spurn the younger woman's attempts to be conciliatory, and Songlian is forced to employ her own cunning.

One day, Songlian is passing time wandering along paths on the rooftops and comes to the door of a turret that is secured with a heavy chain and lock. She is able to pry the door open enough to see two pairs of women's slippers on a pile of ashes. The ominous sight makes her shudder, and later she asks about the room. Her questions are discouraged, but her persistence wins for her the information that two wives from an earlier generation had been executed there because of illicit relationships. This foreshadowing amply prepares the viewer to expect the worst, and when the story takes any turn toward the possibility of adultery, there is an increase in dramatic tension. At one point, when Songlian first sees her husband's grown son, whom she is drawn to because he plays an exquisitely alluring flute and is handsome besides, the expectation of catastrophe mounts. Each turn of the plot—even the most surprising—has the force of the inevitable.

Without being a didactically profeminist work, the film effectively dramatizes the double standard operative in northern China in the 1920's, a standard that, Zhang implies, while it is no longer acted out with the same brutality, nevertheless reflects the way that many people think. Chen's exploitation of each of his wives is unveiled one layer at a time; it becomes apparent that he has no strong affection for any of them. Talking to the fourth wife, he refers to the third as a bitch. He burns Songlian's flute, which had belonged to her father, without telling her, because he believes that a flute should only be played by men. Although each of the wives must be available for the master if selected, and may be killed if caught straying into other men's beds, the master is free to caress the fourth mistress' servant, Yan'er (Kong Lin), or presumably anyone else willing to be fondled. When he is caught by Songlian, there is not even a murmur of apology. Evidently, four wives are not quite enough for him, and Chen arrogantly assumes what custom says are his rights. The women's presence in his household serves his pleasure and comfort. Songlian senses these realities from the beginning; she is extremely somber on the night of her wedding, which seems more like a death.

Both *Ju Dou* and *Raise the Red Lantern* deal with infidelity and its ensuing violence, yet Zhang, veering away from common Western cinematic practices, is never graphic in his treatment of these elements: Neither the sex nor the violent contacts are explicitly shown. Sexual foreplay on Songlian's honeymoon night is seen from a distance and through the netted curtain that encloses the canopy bed. In addition, the viewer shares with Songlian, by means of a long shot over the snow-covered rooftop, the appalling sight of one of the wives being carried by a group of male servants into the little locked room, which had earlier been referred to as the house of death. The servants emerge from the room without their female prisoner and disperse. There is almost total quiet. Songlian approaches the turret, reeling with horror-filled anticipation, and the viewer approaches with her by means of a hand-held camera shot. Then there is a long shot of the room's exterior, again over the snow-covered rooftops. Songlian enters the room, and her scream rings out in the distance. Tension and horror are achieved without showing the actual execution, or even the remains of the victim. Zhang has found effective cinematic equivalents for the way violence is depicted on Eastern stages. Striking metaphorical representations of death, such as having a red ribbon fall from the victim's mouth, are part of the style of Chinese theater. Cinema, a medium that by its nature demands a greater degree of realism, cannot use such devices successfully, but Zhang has found ways to manipulate the medium so that offscreen acts acquire greater force than if they had been shown.

Zhang is one of China's new wave of directors, a graduate of the reopened Beijing Film Academy. His films, he claims, are made with a Chinese audience in mind. Therefore, it is ironic and sad that *Raise the Red Lantern* and *Ju Dou* were forbidden a release in China. Many Chinese critics who saw his first film, *Red Sorghum* (1988), objected to his portrayal of their country, claiming that he shows China in an unfavorable light to the rest of the world. Outside China, his reputation has grown since *Red Sorghum* was shown at the Berlin and New York film festivals. *Raise the Red Lantern* is evidence of artistic growth; with a greater economy of means, Zhang has achieved a film of even greater power. *Raise the Red Lantern* won the Silver Lion Award at the 1991 Venice Film Festival and was recognized as best foreign-language film by both the New York Film Critics Circle and the National Society of Film Critics. Viewers have good reason to anticipate his continued growth and a provocative and formidable body of work.

Cono Robert Marcazzo

Reviews

Boxoffice. March, 1992, p. R-27.
Chicago Tribune. March 27, 1992, VII, p. 42.
Films in Review. XLIII, May, 1992, p. 193.
The Hollywood Reporter. March 12, 1992, p. 10.
Los Angeles Times. March 13, 1992, p. F14.
The New York Times. March 20, 1992, p. B13.
Rolling Stone. March 19, 1992, p. 102.
Sight and Sound. I, February, 1992, p. 41.
Time. CXXXIX, April 6, 1992, p. 66.
Variety. September 6, 1991, p. 7.

RAISING CAIN

Production: Gale Anne Hurd for Pacific Western; released by Universal Pictures
Direction: Brian DePalma
Screenplay: Brian DePalma
Cinematography: Stephen H. Burum
Editing: Paul Hirsch, Bonnie Koehler, and Robert Dalva
Production design: Doug Kraner
Art direction: Mark Billerman
Set decoration: Barbara Munch
Casting: Pam Dixon
Sound: Nelson Stoll
Costume design: Bobbie Read
Music: Pino Donaggio
MPAA rating: R
Running time: 95 minutes

Principal characters:

Carter/Cain/Dr. Nix	John Lithgow
Jenny	Lolita Davidovich
Jack	Steven Bauer
Dr. Waldheim	Frances Sternhagen
Lieutenant Terri	Gregg Henry
Sergeant Cally	Tom Bower
Sarah	Mel Harris
Karen	Teri Austin
Nan	Gabrielle Carteris
Mack	Barton Heyman
Amy	Amanda Pombo
Emma	Kathleen Callan

Brian DePalma, the director of such audacious suspense films as *Dressed to Kill* (1980) and *Body Double* (1984) and such critically acclaimed action films as *The Untouchables* (1987) and *Casualties of War* (1989), returned to a familiar genre with the psychodrama *Raising Cain*. Following his disastrous experience with a messy adaptation of Tom Wolfe's novel *Bonfire of the Vanities* (1990), DePalma withdrew for two years to renew himself and to reevaluate the direction that he wanted to follow as a filmmaker. During his absence from Hollywood, he moved to Palo Alto, California, married *Terminator II* producer Gale Anne Hurd, and had a child. In *Raising Cain*, DePalma revisited the wacky world of his early thrillers such as *Carrie* (1976). Like *Carrie*, this film offers a special brand of terror and suspense, one with a definite sense of humor if not pure looniness.

The plot of *Raising Cain* was suggested to DePalma by the true story of a psychologist who became so obsessed with rearing his daughter that he quit his job to be with her full time. DePalma altered the character of the psychologist by giving him multiple personalities. In the film, the child psychologist, Carter (John Lithgow), takes time off from work to rear his young daughter. Yet he is soon plunged into an emotional abyss, as his own repressed upbringing resurfaces with bizarre and terrifying consequences. Outwardly, Carter seems the loving husband to his wife, Jenny (Lolita Davidovich), and a devoted father to daughter Amy (Amanda Pombo). The experience of parenthood, however, triggers the fragmentation of his personality, causing him to alternate Jekyll-and-Hyde-like between his normal self and an evil twin, Cain (John Lithgow).

As the film opens, the audience first sees Carter on a television monitor comforting his daughter as he tucks her into bed. The child's room is under the continuous gaze of a closed-circuit video camera so that Carter can maintain a watchful eye on his daughter even when he is elsewhere in the house. After this rather curious opening shot, there is a quick cut to a sunny playground where Carter is talking with a woman friend who is there with her two children. Because Carter's wife apparently has the car, his friend offers him a ride home. On the way, Carter mentions that his father runs a "visionary" clinic for gifted children. He tries to pressure her to consider allowing her children to be part of a control group in an experiment that his father is planning. The woman expresses skepticism, and they begin to argue about the soundness of such experimental child-rearing practices.

Suddenly, Carter reaches over and blows some powder in the woman's eyes, temporarily blinding her. When she pulls over and stops the car, Carter covers her mouth and nose with a chloroform-soaked rag, rendering her unconscious. This scene comes as a complete surprise and has the effect of pulling the rug out from under the viewer. Further confusion ensues when the soft-spoken, tweedy Carter, obviously upset with what he has just done, is joined curbside by Cain, a black-clad, wisecracking punk who begins giving orders to his flustered alter ego. At Cain's suggestions, Carter drives home, where he places the woman in the trunk of her car. He then proceeds to a nearby marsh, where he rolls the car into the water, submerging it in the ooze. Next, Carter drives to a seedy 1960's-vintage motel, where his father, Dr. Nix (John Lithgow), is staying. It seems that the wily doctor wants his son to provide him with the children he needs for his experiments.

In what serves as the first act of *Raising Cain*, DePalma does two things successfully. He establishes a sense of unpredictability and thus heightens the viewer's curiosity about who Carter and Cain are, and he introduces the prime cause of the ensuing mayhem, the demented Dr. Nix. What follows this sinister opening is a succession of episodes that lead violently, and at times disjointedly, toward an expansion and final exposition of plot. Part of the off-balance feel of *Raising Cain* is attributable to DePalma's use of dream sequences and flashbacks. While always visually gripping, these scenes are somewhat randomly intercut within the narrative, producing a multilayered story that is not always easy to follow.

For example, when Carter's wife has a chance encounter with her former lover,

Jack (Steven Bauer), in a clock shop, she impulsively buys an alarm clock for him as a present. After meeting later in the park, they make love in the nearby woods. Is this a dream? Or is that Cain watching the lovers embrace from behind a tree? Suddenly, Jenny bolts awake as if from a horrible nightmare. Hurrying to Jack's hotel, she slips into his room and spends the night in his bed.

When Jenny does not return home that night, Carter calls the police. In yet another dream sequence, Jenny has a grisly run-in with a lance held by a statue. Is this a premonition? Shocked to find herself waking up in Jack's bed, Jenny hurries home, where Carter has been waiting anxiously. Carter's feigned concern for her safety turns ugly, however, and he attacks Jenny. During this violent episode, Carter has a flashback to the lovemaking scene that he witnessed in the woods. As he watches from behind a tree, Cain approaches and tells Carter to go home. He explains that he, Cain, will be Carter for a while. Cain then proceeds to commit various acts of child-snatching and murder at the park.

Meanwhile, Carter disposes of Jenny's body and attempts to frame Jack for the disappearances in the park. While the police are trying to get a grip on developments, Mack (Barton Heyman), a former cop, remembers that Carter's father had been arrested years before in a case that involved child-buying. The police contact Dr. Waldheim (Frances Sternhagen), who was trained by Dr. Nix and who is an expert in the study of multiple personalities. Jack is arrested, and Carter is taken into custody for questoning by Dr. Waldheim.

As she questions Carter, Dr. Waldheim is able to regress him to his childhood. During the exploration, she discovers the existence and origin of Cain, Margo, and Josh, Carter's other personalities. The fragmentation of Carter's self was a result of his own father's bizarre methods of child rearing. Carter is the "normal" self, and Cain, his cynical twin, appears to take over whenever anything unpleasant happens. Dr. Waldheim also learns that it was Cain who did all the killing. Then, in a bit of rather heavy-handed melodrama, Jenny is found to be alive after all. When Carter escapes from custody by stealing Dr. Waldheim's wig and dressing as a woman (Margo), Jenny follows him to a climactic rendezvous with Dr. Nix.

Raising Cain is a psychodrama containing wicked humor throughout. The wittiness of Cain, the scenes in which a hapless Carter squirms before his look-alike father, and Lithgow dressed in drag as the oafish Margo all provide giggles. With Lithgow playing five characters, he could be accused of stealing scenes from himself. The actor, who was twice nominated for an Academy Award, for *The World According to Garp* (1982) and *Terms of Endearment* (1983), is adept at playing average characters who are slightly off center. In *Raising Cain*, he shows his tremendous range and versatility. The supporting cast of Davidovich, Bauer, and Sternhagen turn in fine perfomances as well. In the end, however, it is DePalma's wacky vision of the nail biter that gives this black comedy its demented sense of fun.

Francis Poole

Reviews

Boxoffice. October, 1992, p. R-70.
Chicago Tribune. August 7, 1992, I, p. 14.
The Christian Science Monitor. August 10, 1992, p. 11.
The Hollywood Reporter. August 3, 1992, p. 5.
Los Angeles Times. August 7, 1992, p. F14.
The New York Times. August 7, 1992, p. B3.
The New Yorker. August 24, 1992, p. 78.
Rolling Stone. August 6, 1992, p. 64.
Time. CXL, August 17, 1992, p. 63.
Variety. August 3, 1992, p. 2.

RESERVOIR DOGS

Production: Lawrence Bender for Live Entertainment, in association with Monte Hellman and Richard N. Gladstein; released by Miramax Films
Direction: Quentin Tarantino
Screenplay: Quentin Tarantino
Cinematography: Andrzej Sekula
Editing: Sally Menke
Production design: David Wasco
Costume design: Betsy Heimann
Music supervision: Karyn Rachtman
MPAA rating: R
Running time: 99 minutes

Principal characters:

Mr. White	Harvey Keitel
Mr. Orange	Tim Roth
Nice Guy Eddie	Chris Penn
Mr. Pink	Steve Buscemi
Joe Cabot	Lawrence Tierney
Mr. Blonde	Michael Madsen
Mr. Brown	Quentin Tarantino
Mr. Blue	Eddie Bunker
Hostage police officer	Kirk Baltz
Holdaway	Randy Brooks

Reservoir Dogs marks the exciting film debut of writer-director Quentin Tarantino. In his midtwenties and with no filmmaking training when he finished the script in October, 1990, Tarantino and his partner, producer Lawrence Bender, were able to secure financing for the film by circulating the script among their acting coaches. One of their teachers showed it to Harvey Keitel, who wanted to meet with Tarantino and who eventually coproduced and starred in the film. Tarantino's film illustrates well the attributes of a gifted apprentice stepping confidently into the ranks of the professionals. In such situations, enthusiasm usually wins out over self-control. In the case of *Reservoir Dogs*, some lapses appear, but on the whole the sheer love of filmmaking carries the motion picture along and compensates for the occasional thinness of thought.

The film almost seems to have been designed as a series of challenges. Can the formula caper film—in this case, a group of former convicts planning a robbery of a jewelry store—be enlivened? Can the traditional linear narrative of crime films be changed in interesting ways? Can the clichéd crook-torturing-cop scene be redeemed with originality? Can an effective film be made about a robbery without actually showing the robbery? The brashness implied by all these questions indicates Tarantino's self-confidence as a young filmmaker. That the answer to all the questions is yes indicates his talent.

The structure of the film blurs the cause-effect plotting of most motion pictures with some interesting transitions and departures. The precredit sequence shows the crooks, who know each other only by the false names assigned by the leader, Joe (Lawrence Tierney), eating breakfast before the heist. Their protracted conversations about minutiae such as the ethics of tipping recall the relaxed banter of Barry Levinson's *Diner* (1982). Though this small talk is played for comedy, Tarantino positions the camera low enough to emphasize the backs and shoulders of the black-suited men sitting on the near side of the table. This sinister foreground element, partly obscuring the faces of some of the speakers, adds a touch of menace and uncertainty to the scene. After the opening credits, the film fades in on two of the men speeding from the robbery in their getaway car: Mr. White (Harvey Keitel), driving and holding the hand of the badly wounded Mr. Orange (Tim Roth), who screams in fear and agony in the back seat. The sharp contrast between the leisurely breakfast, at which no subject is too trivial to be discussed in detail, and the high-speed, bloody car ride to the warehouse rendezvous jolts the audience at the film's outset.

Tarantino springs more surprises when the men gather at the warehouse after the botched robbery. The dialogue has been filled with the sort of profanities expected of convicts, but with the crisis of Mr. Orange's grave wounds, the warehouse scene begins with an odd and effective touch of humanity. Mr. White, still holding the hand of his companion, nurses him to a place on the floor and carefully combs his hair. Mr. White assures Mr. Orange in almost a motherly way that he will not die. "Bless your heart for what you're trying to do," Mr. Orange responds. The audience's reaction to this scene, as to so many in the film, is likely to be ambiguous. The glimpses of compassion revealed by the men add poignancy, but the feeling lingers that any film that changes moods so quickly will probably change again soon.

The next development does, in fact, swing the film from sympathy for the wounded to puzzling out a whodunit. Mr. White sees that, for the robbery to have miscarried and for Mr. Orange to have been shot, one of their accomplices has to be an undercover police officer. When joined at the warehouse by Mr. Pink (Steve Buscemi), Mr. White explains his suspicion. Another gang member, Mr. Blonde (Michael Madsen), arrives and adds more tension by interrupting Mr. White's fulminations: "Are you going to bark all day little doggie, or are you going to bite?" Mr. Pink, always the professional, defuses a fight between his two cronies and tries to focus them on uncovering the identity of the secret cop. Mr. Blonde, the man of action, returns to his car and brings in from his trunk a policeman (Kirk Baltz) he kidnapped after the robbery. He ties him to a chair and begins demanding that he name his secret accomplice.

This set piece—the torturing of the cop—is the film's turning point and its most notorious scene. Mr. White and Mr. Pink leave Mr. Blonde alone with the captive police officer and the wounded Mr. Orange. Mr. Blonde performs the punishments with the flair of a practiced hand. He steps up the volume on the radio, flicks open a straight razor, struts around a bit to the 1970's song "Stuck in the Middle with You," and, as the camera pans discreetly away for a few seconds, severs the police officer's right ear. But he is only starting. While still dancing to the music, he douses the screaming cop with gasoline, then brandishes a cigarette lighter. At this point, Mr. Blonde is shot by the undercover cop, who has been watching in secret. In language as profane as that of the crooks, the two cops shout recriminations at each other and wildly search for options. They hope that Joe, the ringleader, will eventually arrive at the warehouse.

The shock value of this scene brings to mind a number of literary analogues. Some reviewers have drawn parallels to the blinding of Gloucester in *King Lear* (c. 1605-1606). The Shakespearean play most like the film, however, would have to be *Titus Andronicus* (c. 1592-1594), Shakespeare's early revenge play that wallows in five acts of violence and features a severed tongue, severed limbs, and children baked into pies. Shakespeare's gory fun with the conventions of Senecan tragedy overcame his discipline as a young writer in the same way that Tarantino's exuberance as a first-time filmmaker fails to give *Reservoir Dogs* much depth of meaning below the stylistic excess. Other literary precursors include the Jacobean tragedies of John Webster, Antonin Artaud's theater of cruelty, and the pulp fiction of Jim Thompson. Tarantino may or may not be familiar with these supposed influences, but his film shares with these works the elements of horrific violence, decadence, and a point of view bordering on black comedy.

The remainder of the film alternates between waiting for Joe and his son Eddie (Chris Penn) to arrive at the warehouse and showing, in flashbacks, how the undercover cop earned the trust of the gang. The most effective of these involves the extended flashback of the cop learning "the commode story," a monologue made up by the police to convince the convicts that the cop has taken part in big-time robberies. Tarantino creates sympathy for this police officer by showing how he is coached like an actor on the importance of getting his speech perfect in every detail. A stationary camera pictures him rehearsing the story by pacing back and forth in and out of the frame. When the cop finally delivers the commode story to the crooks in a bar, Tarantino cuts into the speech with another flashback, one that dramatizes this fabricated story as the cop's voice continues on the soundtrack. He relates the uneasiness that he felt when he supposedly carried hidden drugs into a men's room only to find a group of police officers and a drug-sniffing dog already there. By crosscutting this flashback-that-never-happened with the expectant and sympathetic looks of the crooks hearing the story, Tarantino makes plausible the gang's accepting as one of their own someone who was really a police officer. The suspense of the concluding scenes centers on whether the undercover cop can keep his identity a secret from the criminals long enough for Joe and his son to arrive and be captured by the police.

In spite of the scene-by-scene effectiveness of *Reservoir Dogs*, Tarantino seems not fully to realize that eventually the question "so what?" may occur to his audience. The implication appears to be that because Tarantino clearly took such pleasure in writing and directing the film—he even appears in the small role of Mr. Brown, one of the crooks killed at the scene of the crime—the audience should therefore enjoy it in the same spirit. The limits of the film involve content more than style. The film is something like the homework of a prodigy who has mastered the rules and theories of a discipline but whose ability to see complexity has not yet caught up with his ingenuity. Such limits, however, are easy to overlook, especially since the film suggests that Tarantino may add maturity to the engaging audacity and style that he already possesses.

Glenn Hopp

Reviews

Boxoffice. December, 1992, p. R-89.
Chicago Tribune. October 23, 1992, VII, p. 38.
The Christian Science Monitor. October 5, 1992, p. 10.
Entertainment Weekly. October 30, 1992, p. 62.
Film Comment. XXVIII, November, 1992, p. 6.
The Hollywood Reporter. January 23, 1992, p. 9.
Los Angeles Times. October 23, 1992, p. F1.
The New York Times. October 23, 1992, p. B6.
The New Yorker. October 19, 1992, p. 105.
Variety. January 23, 1992, p. 2.

A RIVER RUNS THROUGH IT

Production: Robert Redford and Patrick Markey; released by Columbia Pictures
Direction: Robert Redford
Screenplay: Richard Friedenberg; based on the novella by Norman Maclean
Cinematography: Philippe Rousselot (AA)
Editing: Lynzee Klingman and Robert Estrin
Production design: Jon Hutman
Art direction: Walter Martishius
Set decoration: Gretchen Rau
Casting: Elisabeth Leustig
Consulting: Jean Maclean Snyder and Joel Snyder
Sound: Hans Roland
Costume design: Bernie Pollack and Kathy O'Rear
Music: Mark Isham
MPAA rating: PG
Running time: 123 minutes

Principal characters:

Norman Maclean	Craig Sheffer
Paul Maclean	Brad Pitt
Reverend Maclean	Tom Skerritt
Jessie Burns	Emily Lloyd
Mrs. Maclean	Brenda Blethyn
Mrs. Burns	Edie McClurg
Neal Burns	Stephen Shellen
Young Norman	Joseph Gordon-Levitt
Young Paul	Vann Gravage
Mabel	Nicole Burdette
Rawhide	Susan Traylor

"In our family, there was no clear line between religion and fly-fishing." Thus begins Norman Maclean's autobiographical tale of his youth in Montana with his strict, Presbyterian minister father and his beloved but ultimately doomed brother. It was with similar religious fervor that Maclean oversaw the evolution of what he considered "a love poem to my family" from award-winning 1976 novella to major motion picture.

For years, writer and professor Norman Maclean resisted Hollywood's pleas to turn his highly acclaimed work into a film. Many had tried to sway him. Academy Award-winning actor William Hurt went so far as to journey to Montana to fish with Maclean, hoping to impress the author into suggesting that he play Maclean's brother in a film version of the story. Maclean told Hurt, "Well, Bill, you're a pretty good fisherman but not good enough to be my brother."

Robert Redford had better luck with what he would refer to as "the elaborate dance": three meetings with Maclean, each two weeks apart, in Maclean's adopted hometown of Chicago. The two had met in the early 1980's when Redford invited Maclean to visit his Sundance Institute in Provo, Utah. This series of visits in Chicago, however, was the result of a promise from Redford that, unlike the previous producers who had brandished contracts that would strip Maclean of his right to story control, the two would just talk, each free to walk away at any point without explanation or apology. At the end of the third meeting, Maclean granted Redford an option, and after being allowed to approve Richard Friedenberg's finished script, Maclean stepped back to let Redford make the film.

Redford, narrating as the voice of the author, tells the story starting with the boys' childhood. Young Norman (Joseph Gordon-Levitt) and Paul (Vann Gravage) were educated at home by their father, the Reverend Maclean (Tom Skerritt). Mornings were reserved for the study of mathematics, history, and above all, the English language. In the afternoon, the boys were released into nature for the equally revered study of fly-fishing. The reverend's lessons on this art were strict and thorough. No one, he believed, who did not know how to fish properly should be allowed to disgrace a fish by catching it. He therefore drilled his sons daily, often with the aid of a metronome, in time casting, on a four-count stroke between the positions of ten o'clock and two o'clock. After a day's catch had been made, the boys would lie on the bank and watch the sky. Imagining their futures, Paul is dismayed to hear that there is no such thing as a professional fly fisherman.

Norman's memories of his brother are reverential. Even as the elder brother, Norman was always in awe of Paul: "Paul simply knew that he was tougher than any man alive." This awe is evidenced by scenes of the teenage Norman (Craig Sheffer) succumbing to a challenge of Paul (Brad Pitt) to join him on a perilous ride through white waters in a ramshackle rowboat, hearing Paul stand up to the proprietor of a saloon who would keep Paul's date Mabel (Nicole Burdette) from entering because she is half Cheyenne, and watching Paul pursue a trout so huge and fierce that it almost drowns him before it tires.

The brothers' paths begin to diverge when Norman goes away to college. As taken with teaching English literature as he is with fly-fishing, Norman is dubbed with the nickname "Professor" by his sibling who, in Norman's absence, has become a newspaper reporter in nearby Helena, Montana. Immediately upon his arrival home, Norman is summoned into his father's study and questioned about his plans for the future. Paul, having a rich history of defying his father, claims relief at having moved out long ago and thereby not falling prey to parental inquisition. In so doing, however, he has also missed out on the praise that Norman, degree in hand and job offers in the mail, is now receiving so abundantly. Paul's pride in his brother turns to jealousy in the presence of their appropriately enthusiastic parents.

Far enough away to do what he pleases but close enough to be spurred on by familial conflicts, Paul turns increasingly to drinking and gambling as a way of making himself feel larger than life and more in touch than his do-good brother. The police phone the family's home almost nightly asking Norman to fetch Paul from jail, warning that Paul is heading for disaster. Ashamed and embarrassed to see Paul bruised and dazed on a smelly cot in a dank cell, Norman offers him the money that it would take to pay his gambling debts. Paul ignores the offer, making clear in his silence that Norman is not to offer again.

While Paul sinks deeper and deeper into despair, Norman ascends to a new challenge: love. At a local cotillion, Norman sees and is instantly smitten by Jessie Burns (Emily Lloyd). Their first conversation is a rocky one, with Norman stumbling onto sensitive subjects and girlfriends pulling Jessie away. Thoughtful pursuit, however, wins Norman a date and several more until he and Jessie realize that they are in love.

The film's most comic sequence involves Norman's desire to endear himself to Jessie's family and the trouble that desire causes him. Mrs. Burns (Edie McClurg) has elicited a promise from Norman to take her visiting son, Neal (Stephen Shellen), fishing with him and Paul one Sunday morning. Having been unable to tear himself away from the local prostitute, picturesquely named Rawhide (Susan Traylor), Neal commits the cardinal sin of arriving late to the river, hungover and with Rawhide in tow. Upon Neal's formal introduction of Rawhide to the Maclean brothers, they reply in unison, "We've met," then turn quickly to stare at each other, taken aback by the social contacts that each has made without the other's knowledge. While Norman and Paul fish with the seriousness that their upbringing has bestowed on the art, Neal and Rawhide fall asleep, face down and naked in the sun, and receive deep burns. Though Rawhide, true to her name, claims not to feel a thing, Neal can neither sit in Norman's car nor don his trousers. Thus he is led wincing and limping home by Norman, in whose face Jessie slams the door for having allowed such a fate to befall her much overrated brother.

In the end, Norman and Jessie leave Montana to start a life together, knowing that the dreams they share, as well as those on which they differ, are only to be fulfilled elsewhere. Paul, though suffering from the same needs as his brother to live a larger, more adventurous life than their parents, cannot bring himself to leave the river, but is unable to live within its boundaries.

The carefully chosen cast interacts splendidly. Craig Sheffer manages to shine as credible and admirable in a role that is less active than reactive. Brad Pitt, who portrayed the fun-loving but devious hitchhiker in *Thelma and Louise* (1991), again skillfully balances the beautiful and the dangerous in a character who is charming but not charmed. Tom Skerritt's Reverend Maclean is realistically restrained while letting just enough love show through his tough veneer. Emily Lloyd, Brenda Blethyn, and Nicole Burdette are competent in underwritten roles that, though diverse in personality, share the quality of mystery. Edie McClurg and Susan Traylor are delightful as much-needed comic relief.

As producer and director, Redford perceived that the key to making the transition from page to screen lay in maintaining the strongest element in the book: Norman's voice. Who better to serve as narrator than the Academy Award-nominated veteran of more than thirty popular films—Redford himself. Like his directorial debut *Ordinary People* (1980), this film deals primarily with a family that, though loving, is hurt by its inability to adequately communicate feelings. In addition to family issues, Redford is also strongly moved by environmental causes. He and award-winning cinematographer Philippe Rousselot had to piece five rivers together on film in order to re-create the Big Blackfoot River of Montana as it appeared in the early part of the twentieth century—a sad commentary on the state of nature in the United States.

For their work on *A River Runs Through It*, Rousselot won an Academy Award for achievement in cinematography, Richard Friedenberg was nominated for best screenplay based on previously published material, Robert Redford received a Golden Globe nomination for best director, and Mark Isham was selected runner-up by the Los Angeles Film Critics Association for best score.

Maclean's children reported that, in the last year of their father's life, when he was ill, they asked if there was anything he wanted. Maclean replied, "I want to see my movie." Maclean would surely have approved of this faithful treatment of his story and of his life.

Eleah Horwitz

Reviews

Boxoffice. December, 1992, p. R-85.
Chicago Tribune. October 9, 1992, VII, p. 27.
The Christian Science Monitor. October 13, 1992, p. 11.
Entertainment Weekly. October 9, 1992, p. 42.
The Hollywood Reporter. September 14, 1992, p. 7.
Los Angeles Times. October 9, 1992, p. F1.
The New York Times. October 9, 1992, p. B1.
Smithsonian. XXIII, September, 1992, p. 120.
Variety. September 14, 1992, p. 8.
The Washington Post. October 16, 1992, p. D1.

SARAFINA!

Origin: South Africa
Released: 1992
Released in U.S.: 1992
Production: Anant Singh for Hollywood Pictures, Miramax Films, Distant Horizon, and Ideal Films, in association with Videovision Enterprises, Les Films Ariane, Vanguard Films, and the BBC; released by Buena Vista Pictures
Direction: Darrell James Roodt
Screenplay: William Nicholson and Mbongeni Ngema; based on the play by Ngema
Cinematography: Mark Vicente
Editing: Peter Hollywood, Sarah Thomas, and David Heitner
Production design: David Barkham
Sound: Henry Prentice
Costume design: Sylvia Van Heerden
Choreography: Michael Peters and Mbongeni Ngema
Music: Stanley Myers
Songs: Mbongeni Ngema and Hugh Masekela
MPAA rating: PG-13
Running time: 115 minutes

Principal characters:

Sarafina .... Leleti Khumalo
Mary Masembuko .... Whoopi Goldberg
Angelina .... Miriam Makeba
School principal .... John Kani
Crocodile .... Dumisani Dlamini
Guitar .... Sipho Kunene

The process of bringing *Sarafina!* to the screen began in 1985. The premise of the film can be found in the words of antiapartheid activist Nelson Mandela after his release from nearly twenty-eight years of imprisonment: "We have never lost hope because our cause was supported by the youth, and any cause that receives support from the youth can never fail." Specifically, the 1976 riots by schoolchildren in Soweto were the youth-led activity that became the subject of a musical by Mbongeni Ngema, South Africa's most famous playwright-composer. Encouraged by a talk with Mandela's wife, Winnie, Ngema had developed the idea of writing a musical to combine two subjects: the *mbaqanga* music of South Africa—which the film's production notes describe as "a pounding, hypnotic blend of indigenous African sounds with strains resembling blues and gospel"—and the fervor of children inspired by their teacher to oppose racial injustice. Ngema explained that "the musician side of me wanted to popularize South African music, and the writer side wanted to make the story of the children known."

Sarafina! debuted as a stage work in 1987 in Johannesburg, South Africa, and ran for ten weeks. Even this modest-sounding success came against sizable odds: The poverty of most South African townships and the scarcity of drama and music training usually prevented such luxuries as stage musicals. *Sarafina!*, however, caught the attention of Gregory Mosher, the artistic director of Lincoln Center, who brought the production to the United States, where it eventually played on Broadway and earned five Tony nominations. As the popularity of the show increased, Ngema undertook plans for a screen version.

Although Ngema based the character of the rebellious schoolteacher Mary Masembuko (Whoopi Goldberg) on a real person—Phumzile Mlambo, a teacher who defied the authorities in Durban, South Africa—the title character is his own creation. Young Sarafina (Leleti Khumalo) wants to sing the part of Nelson Mandela in her school concert, but she also yearns for a future as a Hollywood star. The first song in the film shows her ebullience by placing her and other dancers in front of a large Hollywood-like sign that spells out Soweto. The scraps and residue of the township's junkyard form a makeshift limousine, motion picture camera, and Academy Award as Sarafina indulges her fantasy of fame. Though her life-affirming nature never completely deserts her, Sarafina's surface optimism disappears and her inner resolve hardens when she experiences firsthand the injustices of apartheid. Ngema compares the character's temperament to that of Winnie Mandela: "Winnie is . . . very charming, but a very tough woman. The South African system has made her even tougher . . . . Those are the qualities I infused in Sarafina."

The first half of the film relies in many scenes on the setting of the classroom. Freedom of mind is the goal for Mary, Sarafina's teacher in Soweto. She rejects the orthodox curriculum advised by her principal and seeks to instill in her students an appreciation for the complexities of history, especially as they apply to blacks struggling under apartheid. Mary reminds her class that history does not even note the names of many significant blacks and that to early white explorers South Africa was merely "a gas station stop on the way somewhere else." She tells her pupils that they must know "the truth of what we got right and what we got wrong and learn from it." Another early song—a setting of the Lord's Prayer arranged by Ngema—dramatizes the powerful influence that Mary has over the children. Asked by the principal to pronounce the morning invocation, Mary launches into her passionate prayer, and soon she and the children dance and worship in the quadrangle. Ngema's music, especially the majestic "Freedom Is Coming Tomorrow," succeeds at conveying the visceral emotions of the characters' struggle.

As the film develops, teaching takes on thematic significance. Mary's personal drama of following or departing from the prescribed syllabus is given a larger dimension: It becomes a vehicle for nurturing or maiming a child's soul. Her principal warns her about supplementing the accepted readings with dangerous material about black pride. With military police patrolling school walkways, he calls such recklessness "playing with fire." One of Mary's students informs on her, and it is significant that, when the white police invade her classroom to take her away, she is debunking the traditional interpretation of Napoleon's 1812 defeat (that Napoleon's army could not endure the harsh winter) with her more seditious view (that the defeat occurred because people burned their houses rather than be conquered). Her replacement tries to restore order by dully resuming the lesson on Napoleon, but Mary's students will not tolerate his reading of history. The hapless substitute foolishly shouts about the severity of Russian winters. The students hoot him down. As foreshadowed by the principal's words, a fiery riot ensues. The same quadrangle that had earlier witnessed the celebratory rendition of the Lord's Prayer now becomes a stage for bloodshed as soldiers gun down students.

The second half of the film relies on the setting of the prison, which becomes a classroom of another sort. Liberation links these two memorable settings. Both school room and prison express the constricted, overcrowded need for breaking out of the limits that constrain the human spirit. Freedom of body becomes the goal for Sarafina and other students after they are interrogated and imprisoned. Some of the most effective scenes in the film feature characters listed in the credits only as "Testimony 1," "Testimony 2," and so on. These young blacks address the camera directly and describe prison atrocities in a cold, emotionless tone. The moody lyricism of the scenes fits perfectly with some of composer Ngema's musical laments. One girl reports of her incarceration in a room strewn with dead bodies, her matter-of-fact delivery eerily contrasting the horror that she recounts; another youth describes electric tortures as the shadows of prison bars cross her blank face. The emerging analogy is not lost on Sarafina. She sees that prison, like school, teaches blacks a lesson.

Two of the strongest scenes in the film take place in the affluent home of the whites for whom Sarafina's mother (Miriam Makeba) works as a housekeeper. The filmmakers design these matching scenes (one comes early in the film, the other after Sarafina's release from prison) to reflect the girl's change of attitude. In the first, Sarafina visits her mother and tries playfully to upset the sterile order of the household, with its blinding white walls, by pitching cushions on the floors and disarranging knickknacks. Her rhetoric at this point overmatches her experiences. Having learned from her teacher that the "schoolbooks are full of lies," she boastfully claims that she would rather die like her father fighting for freedom than live like her mother serving whites. After her numbing ordeal in prison, however, Sarafina returns to her mother for comfort. In this second scene, she passes the white family's lawn party, glancing at them warily on her way to the back door. Now she sees her mother as more of a hero and realizes sadly that the nature of apartheid ("they make us hate them") fosters confrontation.

Her prison lesson about hate, however, does not seem to have taken hold. Sarafina revisits the place where a black constable was burned to death by rioting students and then obeys her teacher's wishes by throwing away the rifle that had belonged to Mary's freedom-fighting husband. Encouraging her classmates to take part in the school concert, Sarafina herself sings the part of Nelson Mandela. She quotes Mandela's words of freedom just as a black preacher had earlier spoken them at the funeral of the children killed at the school riots.

Sarafina! presents its message powerfully. Though the filmmakers claimed that, for the screen version, they omitted some of the music and concentrated more on the character of Sarafina, it would be a mistake to expect from the film an in-depth character study. Instead, the message of freedom and the terrible human costs of racial injustice give the film its distinctive energy and passion.

Glenn Hopp

Reviews

Boxoffice. December, 1992, p. R-88.
Chicago Tribune. September 25, 1992, VII, p. 42.
The Hollywood Reporter. May 15, 1992, p. 7.
Jet. LXXXII, September 28, 1992, p. 54.
Los Angeles Times. September 18, 1992, p. F1.
New Statesman and Society. VI, January 15, 1993, p. 34.
The New York Times. September 18, 1992, p. B7.
The New Yorker. October 19, 1992, p. 34.
Variety. May 14, 1992, p. 17.
The Washington Post. September 25, 1992, p. B7.

SCENT OF A WOMAN

Production: Martin Brest for City Light Films; released by Universal Pictures
Direction: Martin Brest
Screenplay: Bo Goldman; suggested by a character from the film *Profumo di donna*, which was based on the novel *Il buio e il miele*, by Giovanni Arpino
Cinematography: Donald E. Thorin
Editing: William Steinkamp, Michael Tronick, and Harvey Rosenstock
Production design: Angelo Graham
Art direction: W. Steven Graham
Set decoration: George DeTitta, Jr.
Casting: Ellen Lewis
Sound: Danny Michael
Costume design: Aude Bronson-Howard
Music: Thomas Newman
MPAA rating: R
Running time: 157 minutes

Principal characters:

Lieutenant Colonel Frank Slade .... Al Pacino (AA)
Charlie Simms .... Chris O'Donnell
Mr. Trask .... James Rebhorn
Donna .... Gabrielle Anwar
George Willis, Jr. .... Philip Seymour Hoffman
W. R. Slade .... Richard Venture
Randy .... Bradley Whitford
Officer Gore .... Ron Eldard
Christine Downes .... Frances Conroy
Karen Rossi .... Sally Murphy
Harry Havemeyer .... Nicholas Sadler
Manny .... Gene Canfield
Gretchen .... Rochelle Oliver
Gail .... Margaret Eginton
Garry .... Tom Riis Farrell
Trent Potter .... Todd Louiso
Jimmy Jameson .... Matt Smith
Mrs. Hunsaker .... June Squibb

Perhaps the most surprising feature of *Scent of a Woman* is how little it has to do with women, or scents of women. Reviewers have speculated at some length about the title and its significance to the film. One anticipated a detective film in which a female criminal is hunted down by her scent. Others have found the title, and the few portions of the film that discuss related matters, objectionable and unnecessary.

Regardless of these observations, it is clear that the film has significant merit and deserves inquiry beyond its title.

Charlie Simms (Chris O'Donnell) is a scholarship student at a prestigious preparatory school. In order to earn money for a plane ticket home at Christmas break, Charlie answers a listing posted on the school's job board. It is an appealing position: care for a family member over the Thanksgiving weekend. Unfortunately, that family member turns out to be Lieutenant Colonel Frank Slade (Al Pacino), who is angry, often unkind, and even more often self-destructive. He is also blind. When Charlie arrives to begin his weekend of "babysitting," he finds Slade packed and ready to go—to Manhattan, for a weekend of the best of everything. Over that weekend, each of these characters tries to work through what seem to be insurmountable problems. Slade and Charlie learn to rely on each other and learn valuable life lessons in the process.

The character of Slade is the centerpiece of the film, and Pacino's performance is remarkably strong. Pacino adopts a foghorn of a voice, punctuated with a nasal "yee-haw" that is a memorable trademark even if it is not a pleasant sound. Furthermore, Pacino plays Slade broadly. His passions are larger than life: his fits of temper, his bouts with depression, his expressions of love and support. For Pacino's Slade, there is only one speed—full speed ahead. He drinks too much, smokes too much, yells too much, and causes too much trouble. He says exactly what he is thinking. For example, on the flight to New York, Slade bluntly instructs Charlie on what he sees as the pleasures of life, his voice blasting through the plane. Charlie squirms in his seat; whatever Slade does or says is a broadcast, even his discussions of intimacies. Slade's volume and velocity are both the strength and the weakness of Pacino's characterization.

For the role of Slade, Pacino carefully researched his part, devoting himself to capturing authentically each movement of his visually impaired character. Working through the Associated Blind and the Lighthouse, two New York-based organizations offering assistance to the blind, Pacino met with almost a dozen blind persons, learning not only how a blind person acts but also how it feels to be blind. At the Lighthouse, Pacino learned how to use a cane, how to walk with a sighted person, how to use other senses such as hearing and touch, how to locate the numbers on a telephone pad, and how to find a chair, seat himself, pour liquid from a bottle, and light a cigar. At one point in the film, Slade dances a tango with a young woman named Donna (Gabrielle Anwar). Remarkably, Pacino conveys the sense both of being blind and of being an expert dancer. It is one of the great and life-affirming scenes in the film.

O'Donnell's Charlie Simms, on the other hand, is meek, respectful, and obedient. He is undone by Slade's blustering, but he is a responsible young man who will care for his charge, as he has promised to do. In addition, Slade does seem to offer some wisdom. For example, before Charlie left school for the holiday, he witnessed a prank. The schoolmaster has tried to force Charlie to identify the culprits. It is a moral dilemma. From his position of experience, Slade offers advice that proves true, and Charlie, in his innocence, is impressed. An odd friendship and interdependence grows. While Pacino's portrayal of Slade received the majority of the press on the film, O'Donnell may actually give the finer performance. It is no mean feat to stay on screen with a fireball and continue to command attention believably.

The film was shot on location at the Waldorf-Astoria Hotel, the Plaza's Oak Room, the Pierre Hotel, and Park Avenue in New York City, which functions as the third main character in this film, with all of its glamour and its complications. Certainly many of Slade's and Simms's adventures and misadventures would lose their impact if the film had taken place anywhere else. Only in New York City can one tango at a moment's notice or test-drive a Ferrari in big-city traffic, zipping around skyscrapers. The city offers supreme tests—and rewards—for this innocent young man and his angry charge. For audiences who know and love New York, the film offers lovingly detailed shots of the city. For audiences who do not know New York, the film shows the Gotham City of everyone's daydreams and nightmares.

As confined by the story line, the action occurs over Thanksgiving weekend exclusively; much criticism of the film has dealt with the screen time devoted to resolving each character's dilemma. The film follows Slade and Charlie back to their respective venues and watches to see whether the new men are able to function better than the old. Moreover, their new alliance is confronted with an additional test. Many critics thought that the film should have left such resolutions to the audience's imagination rather than untying each of the knots. Yet screenwriter Bo Goldman has written memorable lines for Slade throughout, and audiences may find that they have made such an investment in the characters that they enjoy seeing these problems resolved. Perhaps it would be more realistic to leave the problems in place, but it is great entertainment and catharsis to see them dissolve.

Scent of a Woman was nominated for four Academy Awards (best picture, best director, best actor, and adapted screenplay) and four Golden Globes (best drama, best actor in a drama, best supporting actor—Chris O'Donnell, and best screenplay). Al Pacino won the Academy Award for best actor, commenting as he accepted the award that this win was a break in his streak—he had been nominated six times before, but this was his first Oscar. Additionally, Harvey Rosenstock, William Steinkamp, and Michael Tronick were nominated for American Cinema Editors' ACE Eddie for 1992 for their work in editing the film.

Scent of a Woman is a film about conformity and about coming of age—at any age. It offers moments to make audiences both cheer and squirm. There are gimmicks, such as a blind man driving a car and dancing a tango, but there is also real emotion.

Roberta F. Green

Reviews

Chicago Tribune. December 23, 1992, V, p. 3.
Entertainment Weekly. December 18, 1992, p. 42.

The Hollywood Reporter. December 17, 1992, p. 8.
Los Angeles Times. December 23, 1992, p. F1.
The New York Times. December 23, 1992, p. B1.
The New Yorker. LXVIII, December 28, 1992, p. 198.
Newsweek. CXX, December 28, 1992, p. 56.
Time. CXL, December 28, 1992, p. 64.
Variety. December 16, 1992, p. 2.
The Washington Post. December 23, 1992, p. C1.

SHADOWS AND FOG

Production: Robert Greenhut; released by Orion Pictures
Direction: Woody Allen
Screenplay: Woody Allen
Cinematography: Carlo Di Palma
Editing: Susan E. Morse
Production design: Santo Loquasto
Art direction: Speed Hopkins
Set decoration: George DeTitta, Jr., and Amy Marshall
Casting: Juliet Taylor
Sound: James Sabat
Costume design: Jeffrey Kurland
Music: Kurt Weill
MPAA rating: PG-13
Running time: 86 minutes

Principal characters:

Max Kleinman	Woody Allen
Irmy	Mia Farrow
Clown	John Malkovich
Marie	Madonna
Doctor	Donald Pleasence
Prostitutes	Lily Tomlin
	Jodie Foster
	Kathy Bates
	Anne Lange
Student Jack	John Cusack
Eve	Kate Nelligan
Hacker's follower	Fred Gwynne
Alma	Julie Kavner
Magician	Kenneth Mars
Hacker	David Ogden Stiers
Mr. Paulsen	Philip Bosco
Spiro	Charles Cragin
Killer	Michael Kirby

Shadows and Fog is a typically atypical Woody Allen film filled with strong Allenesque touches and themes presented in a unique format and setting. A period piece, set in an unnamed European locale in the 1920's, the film mixes brooding, existential angst with slapstick to create an engagingly mannered morality play about humanity's search for meaning and fulfillment in a universe filled with inhuman horrors and irreverent delights.

Beautifully photographed in moody black and white by master cinematographer Carlo Di Palma, the film quickly captures the ethereal essence of its title. Images of a dark, fog-enshrouded city street appear, and a man walking through the eerie urban setting is suddenly attacked and strangled to death by a hulking figure while lively orchestral music from Kurt Weill's *Die Dreigroschenoper* (1931; *The Threepenny Opera*) plays on the sound track. After this nightmarish opening scene, the action cuts quickly to the interior of a small room occupied by Max Kleinman (Allen), a meek clerical worker who is awakened from a night's sleep by a vigilante group organized to track down the killer responsible for a series of brutal murders in the neighborhood. When Max objects to being disturbed in the middle of the night, the rabid group accuses him of cowardice and hints that he might be responsible for the killings himself. Max, confused by their accusations and their obscure references to having a master plan to capture the killer, asks for more information but is only given vague answers. Before he is given any further instructions regarding his role in the plan to capture the killer, the vigilante group vanishes and he is left alone to wander the streets, mumbling to himself about the madness of the entire affair and worrying about being spotted by his boss in the middle of the night.

While Max stumbles around in the fog-drenched darkness, the scene shifts to the outskirts of the city, where a circus troupe is settling down after the evening's poorly attended performance. When the domestically inclined sword swallower, Irmy (Mia Farrow), finds her conceited clown husband (John Malkovich) in bed with the trapeze artist (Madonna), she runs away from the troupe and ventures into the city. She quickly encounters a seasoned prostitute (Lily Tomlin), who informs her about the maniac on the loose and invites her to spend the night out of harm's way at the local brothel. Irmy, reluctant at first to accompany the woman, finally accepts her offer and soon finds herself surrounded by a bevy of raucous whores (Jodie Foster and Anne Lange), led by the maternal madam (Kathy Bates). Later, the house is invaded by a group of students from the local university. One of the students, Jack (John Cusack), is immediately smitten by Irmy and tempts her with large sums of money to have sex with him. Irmy, who first strongly objects to his proposition, finally succumbs to his offer when his fee reaches seven hundred dollars.

While Irmy and Jack go off to one of the bedrooms, Max visits with a local doctor (Donald Pleasence), who is interested in catching the killer for scientific reasons, wanting to dissect the man in order to better understand the origins of evil. Later, after Max has departed, the killer (Michael Kirby) visits the doctor, who hardly has time to ask the maniac what compels him to do evil before he becomes the latest victim.

When Max learns later that the doctor has been murdered, he sneaks into the police station to retrieve a glass containing his fingerprints which the police have confiscated from the doctor's lab. While he is there, he runs into Irmy, who has been picked up as a prostitute. After she pays off the police, she and Max strike up a conversation and wander through the dark streets together. While they walk, they encounter various people: a starving young woman with a baby, whom they aid by giving her some of Irmy's money; a member of the vigilante group, who informs them that another murder has occurred (although this time the murder was the result of the vigilantes fighting among one another over the best way to catch the maniac); and finally Max's boss, whom they find peeping through a woman's window. Later, they encounter a mob of squabbling vigilantes that has enlisted the help of clairvoyant Spiro (Charles Cragin), whose specialty is sniffing out guilty individuals. When he sniffs Max, the group descends upon him and retrieves the incriminating glass that he stole from the police. In a panic, Max runs off and takes refuge in the house of his former fiancée, Alma (Julie Kavner), who is still holding a grudge against him for abandoning her at the altar. When she pulls out a gun and begins to load it, Max runs off again.

While Max is dodging the vigilantes and the killer, Irmy's husband tracks her down and tries to wrestle her back to the circus. As they fight in the street, they come across the starving young woman lying dead on the ground, the killer's latest victim. Irmy finds the woman's baby and insists that she and her husband rear it as their own. The husband is reluctant at first but finally agrees, and the two return to the circus.

Max's wanderings lead him to the circus, where he arrives just in time to rescue Irmy from the killer, who has been stalking her. When the killer runs off, Max encounters the circus' alcoholic magician (Kenneth Mars), who rigs up a magic box to capture the killer. The trick works when the killer returns and tries to attack Max. Just as the rest of the circus troupe arrives to hustle off the killer to jail, however, he mysteriously disappears.

Max, realizing that his life has radically altered during the long night, decides to abandon his dreary clerical job and accept the magician's offer to become his new assistant. With the killer still on the loose and the rabid vigilante group still warring among itself over what action to take against the maniac, the magician remarks, "Everybody needs my illusions, like they need the air," and the film ends.

Shadows and Fog is a skillful blending of radically disparate themes and cinematic styles. Allen mixes nightmarish, Kafkaesque motifs with stand-up comedy routines, filming the action in a brooding, German expressionistic style with touches of silent film slapstick thrown in for comedy relief. The result is an amazing and exciting comedy/drama filled with philosophical ponderings about evil, death, and the existence of God, as well as hilarious one-liners delivered in the classic, neurotic Woody Allen style.

In many of his films, Allen mixes serious and playful themes, comedy and drama, existential angst and looniness, in order to explore the many facets of the human condition. *Shadows and Fog* is his most radical mixture to date. Filmed entirely on an elaborate, claustrophobic set depicting an old European community, the film has the look of such dark, dreamy, German expressionist classics as *The Cabinet of Dr. Caligari* (1920), *Metropolis* (1927), and *M* (1931). The set design by Santo Loquasto and the cinematography by Di Palma are both extraordinary, creating an atmosphere of mystery and dread. Di Palma's camera work is especially effective, moving through the shadowy environment, panning back and forth between characters talking to one another, even stalking off by itself to capture the killer's shadow looming out of the darkness or slowly panning away from the killer as he strangles his latest victim to peer into the window of the brothel, where Irmy and Jack are making love. There is an extraordinary scene that takes place in the brothel where the camera turns slowly around and around, catching the faces of the prostitutes in gorgeous close up as they chatter on about some of their most unusual customers. The scene is reminiscent of another all-woman table discussion from *Hannah and Her Sisters* (1986), also filmed by Di Palma. This time, however, instead of circling around the actresses, the camera is positioned inside their circle, as if it were a bemused observer of these catty women reveling in their company, turning from one expressive face to another to catch the moment in its entirety. The effect is one of an intense, subjective intimacy that draws the audience more deeply into the action, making it an active participant in the events.

Although there are strong Kafkaesque themes to the film—individuals struggling to comprehend the absurd complexities of life, putting bureaucratic illogic ahead of human concerns while a larger evil threatens to annihilate them all—the overall plot is highly reminiscent of a film by one of Allen's favorite directors, Ingmar Bergman's *The Seventh Seal* (1956). Like the Bergman classic, the characters in *Shadows and Fog* deal with a plague of deaths perpetrated by a seemingly unstoppable force that some believe to be in league with a vengeful God. Also, like the earlier film, there is the circus troupe that represents the benign and compassionate spirit of humankind, a force that is potent enough to combat the evils of life. Along with these serious themes, Allen delivers some of his best witticisms to illustrate vividly another of his favorite themes: the power of—and the need for—humor in life. Also, as in all of his films, Allen effectively uses music to complement the overall mood of the action, this time using Weill's jaunty, cabaret-style songs to underscore the film's 1920's European setting.

The film does have its faults, which proved serious enough to damage its overall commercial and critical acceptance. The most serious fault is that Allen uses too many well-known actors in parts that give them little or no time to create any sort of well-defined character. Also, as usual, Allen gives his character the most three-dimensional shadings and all the best lines. Allen is basically playing his standard modern urban neurotic type, which at times clashes with the film's period setting and the mannered, highly theatrical dialogue that the other characters speak. Although this incongruity is responsible for some of the film's funniest one liners, it makes Allen's character appear too radically anachronistic and also blunts the effectiveness of the film's serious subtext. Overall, however, *Shadows and Fog* is another solid achievement from a master filmmaker still able to startle, challenge, aggravate, and delight his audiences after having done the same in twenty previous efforts.

Jim Kline

Reviews

Chicago Tribune. March 20, 1992, VII, p. 32.
Commonweal. CXIX, May 8, 1992, p. 19.
Films in Review. XLIII, July, 1992, p. 261.
The Hollywood Reporter. March 19, 1992, p. 8.
Los Angeles Times. March 20, 1992, p. F1.
The Nation. CCLIV, April 27, 1992, p. 570.
The New York Times. March 20, 1992, p. B1.
Newsweek. CXIX, March 23, 1992, p. 54.
Time. CXXXIX, March 23, 1992, p. 65.
Variety. February 12, 1992, p. 2.

SHINING THROUGH

Production: Howard Rosenman and Carol Baum, in association with Peter V. Miller Investment Corp. and Sandollar Productions; released by Twentieth Century-Fox
Direction: David Seltzer
Screenplay: David Seltzer; based on the novel by Susan Isaacs
Cinematography: Jan De Bont
Editing: Craig McKay
Production design: Anthony Pratt
Art direction: Desmond Crowe and Kevin Phipps
Set decoration: Peter Howitt
Casting: Simone Reynolds, Mary Gail Artz, and Barbara Cohen
Special effects supervision: Richard Conway
Sound: Ivan Sharrock
Costume design: Marit Allen
Music: Michael Kamen
MPAA rating: R
Running time: 132 minutes

Principal characters:

Ed Leland	Michael Douglas
Linda Voss	Melanie Griffith
Franze-Otto Dietrich	Liam Neeson
Margrete Von Eberstein	Joely Richardson
Sunflower	John Gielgud
Andrew Berringer	Francis Guinan
Fishmonger	Patrick Winczewski

Shining Through is a mostly unselfconscious throwback to old-fashioned filmmaking, offering equal measures of adventure and romance. The protagonist constantly refers to what she has learned about spying from motion pictures of the late 1930's, and *Shining Through* lovingly exploits clichés from espionage and World War II films from subsequent decades. The major difference between this film and such examples of the genre as Alfred Hitchcock's *Foreign Correspondent* (1940) and Billy Wilder's *Five Graves to Cairo* (1943) is that the naïve central character initiated into the dangers of spying and the horrors of warfare is a woman.

Linda Voss (Melanie Griffith), a working-class young woman from Queens, longs to lead an exciting life like those of the characters she sees in films, but she settles for being secretary to Ed Leland (Michael Douglas), a no-nonsense Manhattan lawyer. Leland hires Linda because she speaks fluent German. (Her father is a Jewish immigrant.) Because of the many foreign clients who come to Leland's office, her boss's frequent trips to Europe, and the letters that he dictates in obvious code, Linda quickly surmises that Leland is a spy. They become lovers, but Leland abandons her when the United States enters World War II. Moving to Washington, D.C., Linda meets Leland, now an Army officer, sometime later and forces him to hire her again.

When an important undercover agent in Berlin is killed, Linda convinces Leland, against his better judgment, to allow her to replace the spy. Posing as a chef inside the home of a high-ranking Nazi, Linda bungles the job by preparing an inedible meal. Another Nazi, Franze-Otto Dietrich (Liam Neeson), takes pity on Linda and hires her as nanny to his two motherless children.

While working for Dietrich, Linda attempts to keep in touch with her anti-Nazi contacts: an elderly diplomat known as Sunflower (John Gielgud), a beautiful aristocrat named Margrete Von Eberstein (Joely Richardson), and a fishmonger (Patrick Winczewski). She also tries to track down her Jewish relatives, whom she believes to be in hiding. The fishmonger learns their address, but when Linda arrives, they are gone and there are signs of a struggle.

Dietrich slowly becomes suspicious of Linda, initially thinking that she is spying on him for his superiors, who doubt his loyalty. With Dietrich on the verge of killing her, Linda finds and photographs plans for a secret weapon in his basement and escapes. Running to Margrete for assistance, she discovers that her friend is a double agent responsible for the deaths of Linda's Jewish relatives. Margrete wounds Linda, only to be killed herself. Leland arrives in time to carry the seriously injured Linda to the freedom of Switzerland, a bloody escape made all the more daring by Leland's posing as a Nazi officer without being able to speak German.

Shining Through, based on a best-selling novel by Susan Isaacs, is not concerned with historical accuracy regarding World War II or espionage but with romanticizing the clichés of films dealing with these subjects and having a female protagonist. Yet *Shining Through* is less interested in political correctness than in wish fulfillment. Linda has seen spy films and has told herself she could perform as ably as the characters on the big screen. Through her knowledge of German and her luck of being in the right place at the right time, she is given that chance. In going undercover in wartime Germany, Linda is a stand-in for those in the audience like her who say to themselves that they could be heroic if given the opportunity. One problem with *Shining Through*, however, is that once Linda goes undercover, she has little chance to be heroic, being much more preoccupied with survival and with avoiding discovery. Her finding and photographing the secret plans seems almost an afterthought by the filmmakers. Linda's actual spying is secondary to her taking risks almost for their own sake.

Writer-director David Seltzer, best known for his screenplay for *The Omen* (1976), had directed two previous films: *Lucas* (1986) and *Punchline* (1988). As a large-scale romantic adventure, *Shining Through* represents a considerable departure from these low-key comedy-dramas. Seltzer directs in a competent, unflashy style recalling that of the big studio films of the 1950's. Seltzer's directorial skills are displayed best in two particular scenes. In the first, Linda attempts to pass a message to the fishmonger by concealing it in the mouth of a fish in his shop only to knock this fish and dozens of others onto the floor. Panic-stricken, she scrambles to find the right fish, oblivious to the stares of the customers. The other standout scene is the showdown with Margrete. Linda must not only survive the shootout but also evade capture by the Nazis pouring into Margrete's apartment. Bleeding profusely, she has enough presence of mind to leave a false trail before hiding in a laundry chute. Contributing to the suspense of these scenes is the editing by Craig McKay, who also worked on *The Silence of the Lambs* (1991).

Melanie Griffith is a perfect choice to play Linda because she has both glamour and the limitations, such as her little-girl voice, that make her credible as an every-woman. Usually cast as a seductress, as in *Something Wild* (1986), or as a victim, as in *Stormy Monday* (1988), she is given a chance in *Shining Through* to create a smart and sexy character capable of a range of human frailties. Michael Douglas has progressed from a callow leading man to a mature star, helping him to coast through his underwritten role. Douglas is also to be admired, at this stage in his career, for playing a part secondary to the female lead.

John Gielgud, often much better on the screen in comic roles, is allowed only to display peevishness. Liam Neeson presents one of the most subtle Nazis in film history, making Dietrich believably human without being too sympathetic. Patrick Winczewski has presence as the quick-witted fishmonger. The best performance in *Shining Through* is that of Joely Richardson, the daughter of Vanessa Redgrave and director Tony Richardson and the younger sister of Natasha Richardson. Equally convincing as a German aristocrat, an apparent anti-Nazi, and a villain, Richardson endows Margrete with considerable old-style film-star panache, aided by Marit Allen's inventive period costumes.

Michael Adams

Reviews

Boxoffice. March, 1992, p. R-21.
Chicago Tribune. January 31, 1992, VII, p. 33.
The Christian Science Monitor. LXXXIV, January 31, 1992, p. 12.
Entertainment Weekly. February 7, 1992, p. 38.
The Hollywood Reporter. January 30, 1992, p. 10.
Los Angeles Times. January 31, 1992, p. F1.
The New York Times. January 31, 1992, p. B6.
Time. CXXXIX, February 10, 1992, p. 76.
Variety. CCCXLVI, January 30, 1992, p. 2.
The Washington Post. January 31, 1992, p. 34.

SINGLE WHITE FEMALE

Production: Barbet Schroeder; released by Columbia Pictures
Direction: Barbet Schroeder
Screenplay: Don Roos; based on the novel *SWF Seeks Same*, by John Lutz
Cinematography: Luciano Tovoli
Editing: Lee Percy
Production design: Milena Canonero
Art direction: P. Michael Johnston
Set decoration: Anne H. Ahrens
Casting: Howard Feuer
Costume design: Jacqueline de la Fontaine
Music: Howard Shore
MPAA rating: R
Running time: 107 minutes

Principal characters:

Allison Jones .... Bridget Fonda
Hedra Carlson .... Jennifer Jason Leigh
Sam Rawson .... Steven Weber
Graham Knox .... Peter Friedman
Mitchell Myerson .... Stephen Tobolowsky

As a thriller, *Single White Female* is a comedy. First, there are some intentional laughs. For example, new roommate Hedra Carlson (Jennifer Jason Leigh) has moved in with Allison Jones (Bridget Fonda). After Hedy has apparently murdered their upstairs neighbor, Graham (Peter Friedman), Allie is suspicious and suggests that Hedy move out. "I'll change, Allie. I can change," implores Hedy. To which Allie deadpans: "No. That's not it at all. You've been a good roommate." Then there are the embarrassingly hilarious attempts at Hitchcockian effects: vertical staircase shots, a puppy's grisly fate, and heavy-handed foreshadowing. Finally, there is the dialogue: too much, stilted, and seemingly lifted straight from a second- or third-rate novel.

As the tale unfolds, self-employed Manhattan software analyst Allie Jones learns via her answering machine that her hapless, unlikeable fiancé Sam (Steven Weber) has slept with his former wife. Distraught and bitter, she throws him out of their rent-controlled apartment. Even controlled rents being what they are in the Big Apple, she advertises for a roommate: "West Side SWF seeks female." She interviews the requisite motley crew of applicants, then spontaneously chooses Hedy, based on a rather nosy act of kindness and a giggly fun time spent repairing a kitchen faucet together. Hedy balks on learning about Sam, worried that he and Allie might reconcile; Sam's return would force her to move out. Allie assures her that will not happen. "When can you move in?" she asks impulsively. "No. Really?" sighs Hedy.

"Congratulations," replies Allie, condescendingly offering her hand, as she reclines elegantly on the sofa.

Hedy erases the persistently remorseful Sam's phone messages and intercepts his mail, but he forces his way into the flat and wins Allie back. Three turns out to be a crowd, and the plot turns on the need for Hedy to move out. When Hedy's puppy ignores her and becomes attached to Allie instead—"The poor dog doesn't know who's who anymore," says Allie irritably and rather too foreshadowingly—the viewer knows an ill fate awaits all concerned, beginning with the dog.

Hedy needs to feel needed, and she is when Allie's only client, Mitch Myerson (Stephen Tobolowsky), tries to rape Allie. Hedy phones Myerson late at night, pretending to be Allison, and threatens him. Then she treats Allie to a joint trip to the hairdresser, from which the two emerge coiffed and dressed exactly alike. Unnerved by Hedy's appearance, Allie rummages in Hedy's closet and finds a shoebox filled with old clippings and photographs. Hedy's real name, she learns, is Ellen Besch, and her twin sister died not at birth, as she had told Allie, but in a tragic accident.

After she trails Hedy to a sleazy all-night sex joint, where Hedy uses Allie's name, Allie confides in Graham, the gay white male upstairs (and the film's only likeable character). Graham urges her to get rid of Hedy and calls a psychiatrist friend for advice. As it happens, the air vents between the apartments carry sound. Hedy overhears, and while Allie tries to call Hedy's parents, Hedy is upstairs attacking Graham with a metal rod.

A sleepy Sam returns to his own room in another building late at night and is later awakened by a woman performing fellatio on him. Though her hair and coat are exactly like Allie's, the woman is Hedy, and she proceeds to murder Sam with one of her spiked heels. The audience is meant to believe that Hedy is "hypervigilant"; from this point on, she is nothing if not hyper-resourceful, frantically but carefully erasing fingerprints, burning incriminating clothing, pulling a revolver out of a leather boot. Just as the tension of the situation is established far too predictably in the film's first half, so at the end it is resolved with a spree of killings, desperate-killer clichés, and moldy plot twists—such as the "person who is dead but not really dead," here used twice.

Everything about this film is perfunctory, from the cloying opening scene to Hedy's predictable demise. The apartment building is old-fashioned and dark, and the air vents carry sound. In pursuit of Allie in the building's dank basement, Hedy smashes a mirror, overemphasizing the theme of identity and twins. This theme is too blatant and far too pat: Because the apartment is rent-controlled, Hedy's name cannot be on the lease. That is convenient, because she is not really Hedy anyway, and when she murders Sam, she is wearing a haircut and an overcoat exactly like Allie's. What director Barbet Schroeder, who also directed *Reversal of Fortune* (1990), might call a resonant motif is actually a too-handy plot hook. "I know you weren't yourself when you did this thing," Allie says. "I know," retorts Hedy. "I was you."

Nevertheless, the story's potential—tapped, by Leigh's strong acting and Fonda's competent if stilted portrayal (she somehow does not have the presence to convince the audience she is a self-employed software expert), just enough to break the surface and tease the viewer into regretting the film left unmade—can be found in this theme. "I never met anyone so scared of being alone," Hedy sneers to Allie. Neither did Allie: "Allie, come out now!" screams Hedy as she hunts her, meat hook in hand, in the basement. "I'm scared!" The film's intriguing but elusive subtext is an unrequited love affair between the two women. "Please," begs Allison, as Hedy holds a knife to her throat. They kiss. "Don't make me leave you, Ellen." This interesting, dark tale of loneliness in the big city, madness, and the consequences of intimacy is left largely untold in favor of a sloppy, second-rate thriller.

Single White Female invites comparisons to paranoid thrillers such as the hugely successful *Fatal Attraction* (1987) and the lesbian-icepick-murder film *Basic Instinct* (1992; reviewed in this volume), both starring Michael Douglas, as well as to *Pacific Heights* (1990), about the Tenant (as opposed to the Roommate) from Hell. These films seem to comment on modern American society—a fear of the "other," the "outsider." They may be instead indications of what Hollywood supposes American society to have become.

Some might argue that *Single White Female* displays the Hollywood hierarchy's fear of or distaste for women, that it is misogynist. All three of Hedy's victims are men; the only one who survives is Graham, who is homosexual. Hedy is defeated in the end, at the hands of the woman who but for Hedy would have been content to marry Sam, who had inexplicably regained her trust (Allie is offered as an "independent" career woman; one is given no cause to think of Sam as anything other than an ordinary, unexceptional creep). Moreover, Hedy's intention in giving Sam fellatio is to compromise his promise that he would not cheat on Allie again: "You knew it was me," she says to him, "—and you didn't care."

The studio's production information calls Hedy "the ultimate female who will do everything for others—as long as she feels secure" and claims that the conflict drives "both women to their most primal extremes from which only one can emerge." Both women certainly get primal before film's end (which takes too long to arrive), but at the cost of much credibility. Director Schroeder calls his film "a kind of modern fairy tale. Allie learns to be alone, to be a real person." One could and should ask of Schroeder a question many asked about *Thelma and Louise* (1991), another, better film made by men about women becoming primal: Must a woman kill in order to be independent?

In any case, no thriller should rely as heavily as this one does on clumsy dialogue and overwrought genre clichés. A much tighter, more original script, and less heavy-handed direction, would not have answered important questions about realism and the portrayal of women, but would have made *Single White Female* measurably more thrilling and less oddly comic.

Ethan Casey

Reviews

Boxoffice. October, 1992, p. R-72.
Chicago Tribune. August 14, 1992, VII, p. 21.
The Christian Science Monitor. August 19, 1992, p. 14.
Entertainment Weekly. August 14, 1992, p. 34.
The Hollywood Reporter. August 10, 1992, p. 5.
Los Angeles Times. August 14, 1992, p. F1.
The New York Times. August 14, 1992, p. C8.
The New Yorker. LXVIII, August 24, 1992, p. 77.
Newsweek. September 17, 1992, p. 56.
Variety. August 10, 1992, p. 4.

SINGLES

Production: Cameron Crowe and Richard Hashimoto for Atkinson/Knickerbocker Films; released by Warner Bros.
Direction: Cameron Crowe
Screenplay: Cameron Crowe
Cinematography: Ueli Steiger
Editing: Richard Chew
Production design: Stephen Lineweaver
Art direction: Mark Haack
Set design: Cosmas Demetriou
Set decoration: Clay Griffith
Casting: Marion Dougherty
Sound: Art Rochester
Costume design: Jane Ruhm
Music: Paul Westerberg
MPAA rating: PG-13
Running time: 99 minutes

Principal characters:

Janet Livermore	Bridget Fonda
Steve Dunne	Campbell Scott
Linda Powell	Kyra Sedgwick
Debbie Hunt	Sheila Kelley
Cliff Poncier	Matt Dillon
David Bailey	Jim True
Dr. Jamison	Bill Pullman

Romantic comedies are nothing new—each generation of filmmakers works at re-creating them. For example, Rock Hudson and Doris Day played corporate executives who bantered through *Pillow Talk* (1959), reaching true love simultaneously and at the last moment. The action then moved to the beach, with teenage romantic romps such as *Where the Boys Are* (1960), *Gidget Goes Hawaiian* (1961), and *Beach Blanket Bingo* (1965). By the mid-1980's, the playing field had been redefined: The true danger was commitment. Cynicism had entered the genre. In the 1990's, the genre exploded across television with Fox's *Beverly Hills 90210* and *Melrose Place*, after being blended with such television staples as *Thirtysomething*, which rose to fame highlighting Yuppie angst. This same genre then crept to the Pacific Northwest with Cameron Crowe's *Singles*.

Singles is a film of character rather than of action. It is the story of six friends, most of whom live in the same apartment building in Seattle and all of whom have a strong interest in Seattle's alternative rock scene. At the center of this film are two couples, one quite stable (young professionals), the other quite iconoclastic (colorful oddballs). Linda (Kyra Sedgwick), an environmentalist, always falls for the wrong men and so is sure that Steve (Campbell Scott), a city engineer, must be the wrong one, too. This indecision extends their courtship through the length of the film. In the other couple, Janet (Bridget Fonda), a happy-go-lucky waitress, believes that she is in love with Cliff (Matt Dillon), perhaps the one musician in Seattle not on his way to stardom. The two couples prove visually interesting foils for each other, as they work their way to love or through love.

Counterbalancing the centerpiece couples are two lone characters, each with a surefire way to meet people: Debbie (Sheila Kelley) tries a video dating service, and Bailey (Jim True) collects phone numbers that he will never be brave enough to call. These two remain the outriggers to this film—steadying, balancing, yet always outside the main action.

Director and writer Cameron Crowe built his career on translating the lives and interests of young people from real life to the screen. After writing *Fast Times at Ridgemont High*, a novel of high school misadventures that became a hit film in 1982, Crowe directed *Say Anything* (1989), a story of mismatched high schoolers hopelessly in love. While the characters in *Singles* are Crowe's oldest subjects to date, their concerns and their lives lack verisimilitude. For example, the sets are just that—sets. The apartments are reduced to a piece of furniture or two, the coffeehouse to one booth. Even the club scenes are reduced to the central characters lined up looking straight ahead at a band that the audience rarely sees. While the characters move their heads to the music, the viewer gets no feel for the music or the club; the characters seem to be literally performing some mating ritual, contorting and nodding at one another. The net result of these barren, cardboard surroundings is that the characters really are the film: There is nothing else, not even a plot. Unfortunately, the weight of the film proves too much for them, and *Singles* drones along without direction.

Nevertheless, the film contains some very clever scenes. Janet consults Dr. Jamison (Bill Pullman), a plastic surgeon, about receiving breast implants. (It seems that Cliff, a musician without clear standards, has rigorous standards when it comes to the build of his companions.) Some of the best moments of the film occur in Dr. Jamison's office, although the scenes are never really integrated into the film. For example, as Janet and Dr. Jamison negotiate the size of implants that she would receive, they play an odd type of duet on the computer, Janet typing in the coordinates for significantly larger breasts while Dr. Jamison urges moderation and restraint by typing in the coordinates for modest breasts. Even Dr. Jamison's office is an entertaining visual metaphor. On his wall are two large light fixtures in the shape of women's breasts. The characters seem not to notice them; they are a clever addition for the careful viewer.

Another high point of *Singles* is the character of Debbie, who adds to the film by re-creating herself as a caricature. She must shoot a videotape of herself to submit to the dating service. Through a series of odd coincidences, Debbie works with an unknown misfit director (played by Tim Burton, the director of the *Batman* films) to make her wonderfully individual video, a cross between *Superman* (1978) and *Blade Runner* (1982). Unafraid to play her role to the hilt, Kelley creates Debbie the man hunter, Debbie the triathelete of shopping, Debbie the overly neat and aggravating roommate. After selecting her video date, Debbie outfits herself to meet this Mr. Right. It would be unfair to spoil the surprise of this event, as Debbie's date provides one of the truly humorous scenes in the film.

Returning to the entertaining Dr. Jamison, he proves to be a fine match for Janet—the two of them lonely, wacky, and endearing. Yet even his character has scenes that lack meaning and focus. When Janet returns to receive the implants, Dr. Jamison confesses his love for her in one of the most real, most heartfelt, and most comic scenes of the film. The whole idea, however, is abandoned. So completely do the characters divorce themselves from this idea and this scene that it is almost as if it did not happen. Dr. Jamison is never spoken of again.

The fate of the love-struck Dr. Jamison is not the only time that the film introduces plot twists without laying groundwork for them and not the only time that the film introduces a plot twist and then drops it. Another example is Linda's pregnancy. Much is made in the film of buying the pregnancy test, planning a future, and fearing change. Then, through an unexplained accident, the child is lost. Audiences cannot help but wonder what these scenes were about. Also, there is the running joke of Cliff working on Janet's car stereo, a wasted series of scenes without meaning or humor.

Character development, plot, setting, theme, and all the other cinematic components should work in coordinated patterns, creating a particular view for the audience, a tapestry that in many ways resembles life. *Singles* is a tapestry with some of its threads pulled awry. Dr. Jamison's love cry and Linda's accident are pulled threads that extend substantially beyond the surface. Therefore, the portions that are out of sync with the rest of the film draw excessive attention to themselves, either positively (making the audience wish that the whole film was that way) or negatively (making the audience wish that the scenes had never appeared). Unfortunately, without these extremes the film's "tapestry" is flat. The solution would be to create a pattern of scenes that rise from the surface, or to add plot, so that even the flat portions have purpose.

Singles received almost exclusively positive reviews that cited the film as young and hip with a great sound track, noting the special appearances by Seattle rock groups such as Pearl Jam, Soundgarden, and Alice In Chains. Perhaps more interesting, however, were some of the criticisms of the film; one reviewer found that the characters "look willfully shell shocked without ever having been shelled." This is perhaps part of the problem. In the end, each of these characters is mostly happy and untouched by the misadventures of their lives. The characters are all smooth and forgettable.

Even in light of the unevenness of the film, *Singles* was exceedingly popular with twentysomething filmgoers. Part of this appeal was no doubt because of the lineup of popular young actors who played the lead roles, realistically portraying the trial-

and-error process of being a young adult. It is possible, however, that the film's popularity is attributable in even larger part to the subject matter of the film. Specifically, each of the scenes deals with at least one—if not several—aspects of life in "the real world": balancing dating, love, roommates, work, family, and friendships. While each of these offers opportunities, each also is a challenge and a stress. Each can be a great adventure or a major disappointment. For example, throughout the film, Steve balances the competing pressures of a budding-turned-rocky relationship with Linda, a friendship with the misfit Bailey, and a major, high-risk design project for work. These pressures very nearly capsize Steve, although by film's end, some prove to be his main supports. Arguably, then, it is this ability to portray the dreams and realities of being twentysomething in the 1990's that drew young people to *Singles*.

Also, beyond being a romantic comedy, *Singles* is an ensemble film, a genre of film recently experiencing a resurgence in popularity. While *The Big Chill* (1983) had a different plot structure (a group of long-separated friends from the 1960's gather in the 1980's for a weekend reunion), it is similar to *Singles* in that both films focus on the joys and stresses of friendship, on the way one plans life versus the way life works out. Also, both films have hit sound tracks. Another film of the same or similar genre, however, that perhaps even more closely parallels *Singles* is *St. Elmo's Fire* (1985). Both *Singles* and *St. Elmo's Fire* showed the perils of the transition from home or college into the real world, the benefits and costs of friendship, and the possibility of surviving it all happily. Once again, both films had hit sound tracks. *Singles*, therefore, follows in a line of hit films about change and friendship, all set to the music of the time.

Young people will no doubt want to watch these young "in love with love" people as they explore the dating scene in Seattle, but, without a sense of irony or a hint of passion and fire, *Singles* is a disappointment.

Roberta F. Green

Reviews

Boxoffice. December, 1992, p. R-90.
Chicago Tribune. September 18, 1992, VII, p. 38.
The Christian Science Monitor. October 5, 1992, p. 10.
Entertainment Weekly. September 18, 1992, p. 52.
The Hollywood Reporter. September 10, 1992, p. 5.
Los Angeles Times. September 18, 1992, p. F1.
The New York Times. September 18, 1992, p. B7.
Newsweek. CXX, September 21, 1992, p. 78.
Variety. September 9, 1992, p. 2.
The Washington Post. September 18, 1992, p. N48.

SISTER ACT

Production: Teri Schwartz for Scott Rudin, Touchstone Pictures, and Touchwood Pacific Partners I; released by Buena Vista
Direction: Emile Ardolino
Screenplay: Joseph Howard
Cinematography: Adam Greenberg
Editing: Richard Halsey
Production design: Jackson DeGovia
Set design: Robert M. Beall and Ann Harris
Set decoration: Thomas L. Roysden
Sound: Darin Knight
Costume design: Molly Maginnis
Music: Marc Shaiman
MPAA rating: PG
Running time: 100 minutes

Principal characters:

Deloris Van Cartier	Whoopi Goldberg
Mother Superior	Maggie Smith
Sister Mary Patrick	Kathy Najimy
Sister Mary Robert	Wendy Makkena
Sister Mary Lazarus	Mary Wickes
Vince LaRocca	Harvey Keitel
Eddie Souther	Bill Nunn
Joey	Robert Miranda
Willy	Richard Portnow
Bishop O'Hara	Joseph Maher
Little Deloris	Isis Carmen Jones
Connie LaRocca	Toni Kalem

Sister Act admittedly draws on the tradition of church as sanctuary, such as that well-known sanctuary provided to Quasimodo in Victor Hugo's early nineteenth century novel *The Hunchback of Notre Dame*. The makers of *Sister Act*, however, tried to update the convention by countering the solitude and solace of the church—here a convent—with the worldliness of the person seeking sanctuary. Director Emile Ardolino, who also directed *Dirty Dancing* (1987), *Chances Are* (1989), and *Three Men and a Little Lady* (1990), described his view of the production this way: "A brassy, streetwise, lusty lounge singer, in short, the opposite of a nun, is forced to hide in a convent to protect herself from gangsters. The surprise for the character is that she finds friendship, love and her own self-worth in a place she least expects it."

Sister Act begins in a schoolroom with a young Deloris (Isis Carmen Jones) flippantly responding that the four apostles were John, Paul, George, and Ringo (the members of the singing group the Beatles). While her response earns for her the chuckles of her peers, her stern teacher counters, "Have you any idea what girls like you become?" In answer, the film cuts to an adult Deloris Van Cartier (Whoopi Goldberg) performing as lead singer in a trio in a Reno casino. Performing a medley of girl-group Motown hits, Deloris' lounge act is overpowered by the din of slot machines and the ennui of the lounge regulars. Dissatisfied with the progress of her career and with her romance with her married mobster boss, Vince LaRocca (Harvey Keitel), Deloris vows to leave town and begin again elsewhere. Armed with the purple mink that Vince gave her—although it originally belonged to Mrs. LaRocca (Toni Kalem)—Deloris charges into Vince's office for a final showdown. Instead, she witnesses a murder.

After a rigorous chase scene, Deloris escapes to police headquarters, where Eddie Souther (Bill Nunn) offers her protection in return for her testimony against Vince, a mobster the police have repeatedly tried to catch and convict. Deloris hesitantly agrees and is hidden in a convent in a deteriorating neighborhood in San Francisco. The Mother Superior (Maggie Smith) begrudgingly allows Deloris to stay only after being offered ten thousand dollars to help the convent remain open in an era of shrinking church budgets. Although Deloris is horrified at the cuisine and accommodations, she finds her niche in leading the convent choir. What follows is perhaps best described by Goldberg in the production notes: "This story is about self-discovery, and discovering that when you're open to receiving help, it comes to you. Deloris thinks her life is all right, until she is forced to spend time learning what right really is. These nuns help to change her life."

In addition to being one of a series of sanctuary stories, *Sister Act* is also one in a long series of nun films, including *The Bell's of St. Mary's* (1945), *The Nun's Story* (1959), *The Sound of Music* (1965), *The Trouble with Angels* (1966), *The Singing Nun* (1966), *Where Angels Go, Trouble Follows* (1968), *Nuns on the Run* (1990), and the television series *The Flying Nun*. Certainly the reviews of *Sister Act* touched on some similarities between various lighthearted nun films. What was repeatedly cited as the main developmental technique in many of the nun films is also key in this one. Much of the humor arises from placing a sheltered nun in the more sophisticated world around her, or pitting a sheltered nun against a worldly foil. The nuns' surprise in encountering the world and/or the nun's adoption of worldly phrases (for example, a nun saying "far out") or abilities (such as a nun "rocking out" to "hip" music) creates the desired tension between what the audience expects of a nun and what an audience sees of this particular nun. *Sister Act* relies on such conventions. In one particularly telling scene, Sister Mary Robert (Wendy Makkena) comes to Deloris' cell and tells of her hopes that there is something inside her that is her gift, her individual ability, something that no one else can offer. Sister Mary Robert is the stereotypical nun, a meek person who is mouselike in her appearance and her demeanor. With Deloris' coaching, however, Sister Mary Robert becomes a real dynamo, belting out Motown solos, learning "cool" dance movements, finding her gift is song—a typically "sisterly" gift.

Such odd combinations also advance the film's action. At one point, Deloris can stand the convent no longer and sneaks out to a biker bar across the street. Unbeknown to Deloris, she is followed by the mouselike Sister Mary Robert and the robust and endlessly happy Sister Mary Patrick (Kathy Najimy), who also appeared with Goldberg in *Soapdish* (1991). The humor in this scene arises partly from the visual contrast of a nun seated at a bar next to a group of bikers and partly from the reactions of the bar's patrons as all three nuns circulate through the room. This episode also allows for a few clever lines. For example, when Sister Mary Patrick borrows a quarter for the jukebox, she happily tells the amazed lender, "Thank you. This will be returned to you tenfold," as she bubbles along to the dance floor.

Another vehicle for humor is a nun who totally fails to fit the mold of the stereotypical nun. Sister Mary Lazarus (Mary Wickes) is just such a nun. Wickes appeared as the bus-driving Sister Clarissa in both *The Trouble with Angels* and *Where Angels Go, Trouble Follows*, a role that also stretched the conventions for nunlike behavior. Here, Sister Mary Lazarus laments the passing of life in the convent that "was hell on Earth and I loved it." She proves herself the equal of any mobster, and her craggy face and voice emerging from the wimple alone provide comic entertainment.

Much of the success of *Sister Act* is attributable to casting. Goldberg adds much buoyancy to the film, with her trademark walk in what she dubs her "penguin" suit and her well-known double takes. While Bette Midler was originally slated to play Deloris, her work on *For the Boys* (1991) made her involvement impossible. The change from Midler to Goldberg led to some happy surprises, such as the revelation that Goldberg has a good strong singing voice (she did her own singing in the film after approximately thirty hours of training with a vocal consultant). Said Goldberg in the production notes, "My character, Deloris, isn't as bad a singer as we initially thought she was going to be, but she's no Patti Labelle, either. And I have a special affection for the '60s songs we did. I don't have a set of pipes like Martha Reeves or Mary Wells, but we managed to put a little bit of our own flavor into the songs."

Reviewers were quick to point out, however, that the change in personnel resulted in some awkward moments. For example, Deloris is the only African American woman in the convent, a point that is never overtly recognized. Yet when the Mother Superior objects to a person such as Deloris in her convent—a reaction no doubt meant to signal snobbery—several reviewers found the subtext to be offensively racist. A scene of Deloris nonchalantly tossing a basketball over her shoulder and making the shot was cut when Goldberg reportedly objected to its stereotypical representation of African Americans. Another scene that sparked similar controversy on the already-stormy set is one in which a hungry Deloris steals a tomato from the convent's garden. This scene, however, remains in the final verison of the film.

The screenplay for this film received much press because it is the result of the troubled labors of no less than seven screenwriters, represented by the pseudonym

"Joseph Howard." Among those reported to be contributors to the final product are Carrie Fisher, who also wrote the screenplay for the film of her novel *Postcards from the Edge* (1990); Robert Harling, who wrote *Soapdish* and *Steel Magnolias* (1989); and Nancy Meyers, the scriptwriter for *Father of the Bride* (1991). While there are admittedly few surprises in plot, the screenplay does offer some pleasing one-liners. After Deloris' first encounter with convent cuisine, she quips, "What are you—the Pritikin order?" During the nuns' escape to the biker bar, one patron says to another, "If this turns into a nuns' bar, I'm out of here." When Mother Superior is reminded that she has taken a vow of hospitality, she responds, "I lied." While these lines may appear flat in isolation, their artful delivery, combined with the momentum from pleasing but stereotypical characters and a sound track filled with memorable 1960's songs, produces a happy hodgepodge of summer fun.

As for Ardolino's direction, it is best described as a "no surprises" approach. For the sequences showing Deloris having a significant effect on the choir and the community, Ardolino uses a very typical and serviceable convention: a montage sequence. While this is a respectable choice, it is hardly innovative. In addition, the camera records action without giving clues to any underlying tensions or meanings, perhaps because the film itself is rather straightforward. For example, when the night-time escape of Deloris, Sister Mary Robert, and Sister Mary Patrick is detected by the Mother Superior, the confrontation between Deloris and the Mother Superior is recorded by a stationary camera recording a series of flat medium shots and close-ups. Clearly, the life in the film does not come from its direction or cinematography; perhaps it comes from the music, the acting, and the screenplay.

After its summer release, *Sister Act* continued to draw attention and awards. Although the film was not an Oscar contender, it was nominated for a Golden Globe for best comedy or musical, with Goldberg also nominated for best actress in a comedy or musical. Both the film—tying for first place honors with *Home Alone II: Lost in New York* (1992; reviewed in this volume)—and Goldberg also received recognition in the People's Choice Awards. Further, Goldberg and Kathy Najimy won as best actress and supporting actress, respectively, in the American Comedy Awards. Finally, the film itself was given a Hubie Award nomination, based on audience approval ratings.

So popular was *Sister Act* that plans began in early 1993 for *Sister Act II*, for which Goldberg was to have earned an amount reported to be anywhere from $7 million to $12 million, to date the largest salary paid a woman performer for a single role.

Reviewers labeled *Sister Act* everything from "predictable," "gooey," and "sugary" to "unpretentiously amusing" and "endearingly upbeat," yet it opened in second place with a strong $11.9 million opening weekend, earning $139.5 million by year's end (making *Sister Act* one of the top-grossing pictures for 1992 in the United States and Canada). Three hundred New York nuns attending a special premiere reportedly gave *Sister Act* six hundred "thumbs up." Most aptly, Sister Maureen Blauvelt of the Dominican order gave *Sister Act* rave reviews: "It was pure delight."

For all of its flaws and shortcomings, *Sister Act* is irresistably—although predictably—good entertainment.

Roberta F. Green

Reviews

Boxoffice. July, 1992, p. R-53.
Chicago Tribune. May 29, 1992, VII, p. 33.
Entertainment Weekly. May 29, 1992, p. 46.
The Hollywood Reporter. May 18, 1992, p. 5.
Jet. LXXXII, June 1, 1992, p. 34.
Los Angeles Times. May 29, 1992, p. F1.
The New York Times. May 29, 1992, p. B3.
Newsweek. CXIX, June 8, 1992, p. 59.
Time. CXXXIX, June 1, 1992, p. 81.
Variety. May 18, 1992, p. 3.

SNEAKERS

Production: Walter F. Parkes and Lawrence Lasker; released by Universal Pictures
Direction: Phil Alden Robinson
Screenplay: Phil Alden Robinson, Lawrence Lasker, and Walter F. Parkes
Cinematography: John Lindley
Editing: Tom Rolf
Production design: Patrizia von Brandenstein
Art direction: Dianne Wager
Set decoration: Samara Schaffer
Set design: James J. Murakami, Keith B. Burns, and James Tocci
Casting: Risa Bramon Garcia and Juel Bestrop
Sound: Willie D. Burton
Special effects coordination: Kenneth Pepiot
Computer effects supervision: Steve Grumette
Costume design: Bernie Pollack
Stunt coordination: Glenn H. Randall, Jr.
Music: James Horner
MPAA rating: PG-13
Running time: 121 minutes

Principal characters:

Bishop . . . . Robert Redford
Crease . . . . Sidney Poitier
Cosmo . . . . Ben Kingsley
Mother . . . . Dan Aykroyd
Whistler . . . . David Strathairn
Carl . . . . River Phoenix
Liz . . . . Mary McDonnell
Gregor . . . . George Hearn
Dick Gordon . . . . Timothy Busfield
Werner Brandes . . . . Stephen Tobolowsky
Young Bishop . . . . Gary Hershberger
Young Cosmo . . . . Jojo Marr

It all began as an accident. In the process of doing research for their screenplay for *WarGames* (1983), producers Lawrence Lasker and Walter F. Parkes attended a variety of computer conventions, gathering basic background on computer hackers. At a fateful convention in Chicago, at the Atari booth, Lasker and Parkes asked for information on "sneakers," a term that they thought referred to "kids who were hackers." What they learned, however, was enough to sustain them and collaborator Phil Alden Robinson, the director of *Field of Dreams* (1989), through ten long years of rewrites. Sneakers, they learned, are high-tech security renegades who break into secured installations and information databases. The three screenwriters were hooked: They pitched their idea as the "high tech *Dirty Dozen*" (1967), and, years later, *Sneakers* emerged as a self-proclaimed cross between "Three Days of the Hacker" (*Three Days of the Condor*, 1975) and "Raiders of the Lost Computer" (*Raiders of the Lost Ark*, 1981).

Sneakers begins in the 1960's, with two young computer Robin Hoods—Bishop (Gary Hershberger) and Cosmo (Jojo Marr)—breaking into computer systems to steal from the rich and give to the poor. Years later, the older Bishop (Robert Redford), now a fugitive, nevertheless continues his computer exploits professionally. He leads a band of merry pranksters: Crease (Sidney Poitier), formerly of the Central Intelligence Agency (CIA); Carl (River Phoenix), a teenage computer hacker; Mother (Dan Ackroyd), a gadgeteer and conspiracy enthusiast; and Whistler (David Strathairn), a blind audio wizard with perfect pitch. Bound as much by their strengths as by their weaknesses, the group lightheartedly sets about their day-to-day capers, until one arrives at their doorstep that they cannot pass up, no matter how hard they try.

One aspect of *Sneakers* remains largely uncredited: the technological background itself. The writers spent years meeting with technological wizards (many of whom still live underground), learning the setup of the work and of the caper, pushing for authenticity. For example, Robinson, Lasker, and Parkes met with the president of just such a security consulting firm, learning a few tricks of the trade, as well as with such underground figures as the notorious "Captain Crunch." The Captain, who served in part as inspiration for the character of Cosmo, rose to notoriety in the 1970's when he discovered that a whistle he received as a prize in a cereal box gave him access to free phone service and to the "blue box" that guides nearly all telephone transmission equipment. The writers were getting a feel for the sort of boldness, ego, and creativity necessary for the lives that these characters were going to live.

Finally, the writers' search led them to a renowned mathematician, who told them of the high-priced data scrambling or encryption devices that protect the security of information for the government and corporations. The writers were hooked when they discovered cryptology and with it, their thesis—what if there were a "black box" somewhere that could potentially decode any computer data in the world? The rest is *Sneakers*.

The success of *Sneakers* is also attributable to its sleek and confident style. The film knows it is good, well made, and commercial (in the best understanding of that word), from its whimsical cryptological title sequence to its mischievous final frames. Some of that credit should go to production designer Patrizia von Brandenstein and set decorator Samara Schaffer, who have "used the complex world of high-tech surveillance as a visual backdrop." Viewers feel as if they are on the edge of something new, something vaguely dangerous, and conversely, something not all that foreign after all. For example, Brandenstein and Schaffer created the Sneakers' office, a loft like any other at first glance. Yet, when set alive by the hum and clatter of electronic processing and hacker banter, when the giant computers and screens move to the fore, the space is transformed into a teenager's war room, a clubhouse where even the secret handshake is electronically encoded. Here anything is possible; here one wrong key, one wrong operator, and all is lost. This effect is achieved visually, through set design and through sound. Audiences will not soon forget what they learn in "hearing" the world through Whistler's eyes, or the cold, lifeless chatter of Whistler's braille computer at work.

Added to the technical precision is a remarkable ensemble cast. Redford, who had been largely unseen since the less-than-successful *Havana* (1990), gives a fine performance and carries much of the weight of the film. Not unlike Cary Grant's character in *To Catch a Thief* (1955), Redford's Bishop is somewhere between honest and dishonest, yet clearly on the mark with sophistication and charm. Redford is settling into his age with less strain than in some of his other recent films, and while the camera clearly reveals wrinkles and gray hairs, Redford handles his role with authority. It is pleasant to see Redford play something other than a romantic lead, and he shows great facility with comedy and action. Ben Kingsley's misguided genius, the grown-up Cosmo, is eerie in his isolation, while the other characters build such camaraderie that it is virtually impossible to see them as individuals. In sum, there is not a bad performance in the film, although there is perhaps a wasted one. Mary McDonnell, who plays Liz, a piano teacher, old acquaintance, and unwilling accomplice, is largely unused. While the production notes specify that Liz should be attractive and intelligent, McDonnell has much more to offer than the role's occasional walk-throughs and grimaces.

As for possible themes, this film presents several possibilities. Some viewers may come away from the film convinced of the dangers inherent in information. For example, the notorious black box that advances the plot in MacGuffin-like style breaks any code and allows entry to any computer system: air traffic control, defense, financial records. The film makes frighteningly clear the reliance that society places on computers, machines, and databases—all of which are open to tampering. In the film, even supersecret installations allow easy access once the sneakers find the electronic key. Other possible themes are the failure of idealism and the dangers of zealotry. Bishop and Cosmo, both products of the 1960's, both burning with beliefs in change, end up quite differently. In one, that fire serves as fuel; in the other, it consumes completely.

As several critics remarked, the film reprises some of Redford's earlier roles, such as those he played in the 1970's: *Three Days of the Condor*, *The Sting* (1973), and *All the President's Men* (1976). *Sneakers* may also remind audiences of such television classics as *Mission Impossible* and *I Spy*. What is perhaps most reminiscent of these earlier works is the quick pacing and the detailed plot, both features often missing from many more modern films. If this is the cinema of the 1970's, filtered through the philosophy of the 1960's and projected onto the technological buildup of the 1990's, it never looked so good. *Sneakers* is the kind of film that has something to offer each member of the audience. It is whimsical and frightening—

and perhaps even prophetic. Whether viewers consider it a story of distorted idealism or of the power of information, *Sneakers* remains great entertainment.

Roberta F. Green

Reviews

Boxoffice. November, 1992, p. R-77.
Chicago Tribune. September 9, 1992, V, p. 1.
The Christian Science Monitor. September 14, 1992, p. 11.
Entertainment Weekly. September 11, 1992, p. 72.
The Hollywood Reporter. September 8, 1992, p. 10.
Los Angeles Times. September 9, 1992, p. F1.
The New York Times. September 9, 1992, p. C18.
Newsweek. CXX, September 21, 1992, p. 78.
Time. CXL, September 14, 1992, p. 72.
Variety. September 8, 1992, p. 4.

SOUTH CENTRAL

Production: Janet Yang and William B. Steakley for Oliver Stone and Ixtlan Productions, in association with Monument Pictures and Enchantment Films; released by Warner Bros.
Direction: Steve Anderson
Screenplay: Steve Anderson; based on the novel *Crips*, by Donald Bakeer
Cinematography: Charlie Lieberman
Editing: Steve Nevius
Production design: David Brian Miller and Marina Kieser
Art direction: Andrew D. Brothers
Set decoration: Caroline Stover
Casting: Jaki Brown
Costume design: Mary Law Weir
Music: Tim Truman
MPAA rating: R
Running time: 99 minutes

Principal characters:

Bobby	Glenn Plummer
Ray Ray	Byron Keith Minns
Bear	Lexie D. Bigham
Loco	Vincent Craig Dupree
Carole	LaRita Shelby
Genie Lamp	Kevin Best
Henchman	"Big Daddy" Wayne
Buddha	Tim DeZarn
Nurse Shelly	Starletta Dupois
Ali	Carl Lumbly
Jimmie	Christian Coleman
Willie Manchester	Ivory Ocean

Based on the novel *Crips*, by Los Angeles high school teacher Donald Bakeer, *South Central* is about Bobby (Glenn Plummer), a young man in the "Deuce" gang in South Central Los Angeles. Upon getting out of jail after serving a one-year sentence, Bobby revives his participation in the Deuce and learns that he has become a father. At first shocked by this knowledge, and resentful at not having been told earlier, he quickly grows to love his handsome baby son and to value fatherhood as he confronts the challenges presented by his membership in the gang. He had not yet attained manhood himself when he became a father; the film is about both how he grows up and how he learns to be a father to his son.

Baby Jimmie (Allan and Alvin Hatcher) steals the scene from the moment he is introduced to his surprised father, and Carole (LaRita Shelby), Jimmie's young mother, does her best to reignite her and Bobby's love. Bobby, however, is pressured by Ray Ray (Byron Keith Minns), the gang leader, to perform acts of violence to prove his loyalty and earn his Deuce tattoo. Goaded on by Ray Ray, Bobby confronts and combats rival gang leader Genie Lamp (Kevin Best), who is encroaching on Deuce territory. Although Genie Lamp's gang is introducing harder drugs into the neighborhood, the Deuce gang members do not perceive the issue morally. It is merely a question of power on their home ground. This lust for power eclipses Bobby's relationship with Carole to the point that there is no possible life for them together, especially after Bobby actually kills Genie Lamp, shooting through a potato to silence the gun.

Craftily trapped by an undercover police officer posing as a prostitute, Bobby and his cronies are arrested. In a devilish ploy, the interrogators allow Bobby to see and hold baby Jimmie, who had been with him in a joyriding car at the time of the arrest, one last time; they try to entice him into betraying the other gang members in exchange for his own freedom. He remains silent but pays a high price: He is sent to jail for murder, effectively a life sentence. He seems finally to have lost his son, who is left in the custody of his mother, a drug addict.

In prison, Bobby gets into a scrape with the Aryan gang. In a hair-raising scene, he is rescued by Ali (Carl Lumbly), a Black Muslim. Ali essentially forces him to begin learning about modern black sociocultural thought and revolutionary political theory. Bobby then finally reads the history of his people willingly. Ali tests him along the way, ensuring that he absorbs all the most important aspects of black thought and politics. Ali's politics are the progressive, nonviolent politics of radical social change; he is totally opposed to gangs and the generational perpetuation of violence they bring about. Bobby is convinced that he will be an utter failure if he allows the cycle of crime, drugs, violence, and death to triumph in his own family. He faces the fact that gangs have meant the undoing of the black family and the degeneration of whole communities in South Central Los Angeles. Perhaps his own life has not been an unmitigated success, but Bobby sees that Jimmie's can be saved if his father can help him. Ali removes the Deuce tattoo from Bobby's face and coaches him in the way he must act when he comes up for review by the parole board. Ali himself was the father of a son killed in gang warfare; a devout Black Muslim, he is clearly atoning for his own failure as a father in impelling Bobby to find and reform Jimmie. These scenes, enhanced by the camera work, are some of the most intimate in *South Central*.

In the meantime, ten-year-old Jimmie (Christian Coleman) has recently been manipulated by Ray Ray into entering a life of crime: Ray Ray offers the nearly starving and virtually parentless child tempting sums of money to steal BMW stereos. The boy meets his match when one car owner, Willie Manchester (Ivory Ocean), alerted to the theft, shoots the boy in the back with a shotgun, almost killing him. Both are black, which makes the point—perhaps too obviously—that blacks die as often at the hands of other blacks than as a result of interracial violence. Jimmie is rushed to the hospital, tenuously clinging to life. Nurse Shelly (Starletta

Dupois) makes him her special charge and gently restores him to health. Dupois plays her part with all the loving care of the ideal nurse, and Shelly acts like the mother Jimmie never truly had. When Jimmie's own mother comes to visit him, Shelly confronts her like a lioness guarding a cub. Carole's whorish red dress and almost casual attitude betray her indifference to her responsibilities to the child—or perhaps her inability to cope with the burden of rearing the boy alone.

Around this time the newly matured and morally conscious Bobby is released from prison and sets out to find his boy. Jimmie has grown up without knowing his father, and he is not exactly eager to rush into his arms once he learns that Bobby has rejected the Deuce. A poignant scene of rejection ensues in the foster juvenile home in which Jimmie lives; Bobby is told that he cannot see his son for months and will be blocked at every turn because he has been in prison. Jimmie escapes from the home, however, and a dramatic turning point and climax occur when Bobby goes to Ray Ray's headquarters to wrest Jimmie from the clutches of Ray Ray, who is expertly guarded by their longtime mutual friend Bear (Lexie D. Bigham). Ray Ray has captured the vicious middle-class shooter Willie Manchester and placed a gun in Jimmie's hands—he is pushing him to kill his attacker the same way Ray Ray had earlier convinced Bobby to kill an enemy. In a very real sense, in this final scene the good father and the evil gang members are struggling for the soul of this bright, attractive boy.

The acting, in both large and small roles, is superior. Bigham, for example, is the quintessential bodyguard. Thirteen-year-old Christian Coleman makes a stunning debut as Jimmie: He looks very much as though he might be ready to kill at the drop of a hat. Moreover, Dupois's performance shows that nurse Shelly's silent strength and persistent love for the boy are the forces that restore his life and health, enabling his father to guide him toward a more ethical manhood. Even more important, at the correct time, Shelly is a true professional with the strength to let go of Jimmie.

The fiercely maintained male code by which the film's inner-city gang members operate, confirmed here by the hard-driving music that dramatically underscores the film's major moments, dictates that they are gang members first and family members second. Ali has instilled in the mature Bobby the ability to question and challenge this hierarchy of values without lowering himself to violence. Ultimately, Ali and Bobby make others aware of his child's need for a father's guiding presence and love. Bobby reclaims all that he has left on earth—his own son. Even though the more real and rounded of the film's characters are male, some of the best acting is done by a woman, Dupois, as well as by Lumbly and Plummer, playing men who are courageous enough to show their softer, more tender sides.

The father and son in this inspiring, poignant film are ennobled by the struggles they confront with not a whiff of self-pity or imagined helplessness in the face of the odds against them. Although *South Central* appears at first to be a film about gang violence and its self-perpetuation in South Central Los Angeles, the film is in fact a visceral cry to the entire population of the United States to wake up and take notice. First it portrays how a boy unwittingly descends from innocently joining a gang to forced participation in drug use and dealing, to committing a murder under peer pressure, to going to prison, and finally to continuing the cycle of hatred and oppression. *South Central,* however, presents a solution to the problem of the sundering of the inner-city family by poverty-engendered hatred, violence, and gang warfare. Steve Anderson is a visionary, as is his mentor, Oliver Stone. Anderson's dream of a unified family as the cornerstone of a peaceful, harmonious community is central to the film, which appears to begin where *Boyz 'n the Hood* (1991) leaves off. Instead of capitalizing on the bizarre drama of violence, however, *South Central* sets itself the challenge of breaking the vicious generational cycle of poverty, violence, and crime. Anderson's solution is the reunification of the black family. If the father can remain in the home rather than escaping into gang violence leading to prison, he argues, the future of the black communities in South Central, and the future of the African American family in general, will be assured.

This film explores, without the interracial orientation, some of the same terrain covered by *Grand Canyon* (1991), but it takes a harder, more intense look at the roots of the family's disintegration in gang violence. It seeks not only to point the finger at gangs but also to offer an incentive to black fathers everywhere to re-forge their bonds with their children and with their families as a whole. No one can take issue with the validity and humanity of Anderson's vision, and what the film says is equally applicable to families of any race. As reviewer Joseph McBride remarked at the opening of the film's run, "It's not often that a film comes along with the power to save lives—*South Central* is one . . . [and it] deserves the widest possible release."

Cher Langdell

Reviews

Chicago Tribune. September 18, 1992, VII, p. 42.
Entertainment Weekly. October 30, 1992, p. 64.
The Hollywood Reporter. October 14, 1992, p. 6.
Jet. LXXXII, October 5, 1992, p. 60.
Los Angeles Times. October 16, 1992, p. F1.
The New York Times. October 16, 1992, p. B8.
The New Yorker. LXVIII, November 2, 1992, p. 102.
Time. CXL, November 30, 1992, p. 79.
Variety. September 18, 1992, p. 24.
The Washington Post. September 21, 1992, p. D7.

A STRANGER AMONG US

Production: Steve Golin, Sigurjon Sighvatsson, and Howard Rosenman for Hollywood Pictures, in association with Touchwood Pacific Partners I, Propaganda Films, and Sandollar/Isis; released by Buena Vista
Direction: Sidney Lumet
Screenplay: Robert J. Avrech
Cinematography: Andrzej Bartkowiak
Editing: Andrew Mondshein
Production design: Philip Rosenberg
Art direction: Steve Graham
Set decoration: Gary Brink
Casting: Joy Todd
Costume design: Gary Jones and Ann Roth
Music: Jerry Bock
MPAA rating: PG-13
Running time: 109 minutes

Principal characters:

Emily Eden	Melanie Griffith
Ariel	Eric Thal
Leah	Mia Sara
Levine	John Pankow
Rebbe	Lee Richardson
Nick	Jamey Sheridan
Yaakov Klausman	Jake Weber
Emily's father	Burtt Harris
Tony Baldessari	James Gandolfini
Chris Baldessari	Chris Collins

The lonely policeman has been a standard character in crime fiction since the police procedural genre was developed by Lawrence Treat in 1945 with his novel *V as in Victim* and has inevitably made his way into motion pictures. A good example is Andy Kilvinsky (George C. Scott) in *The New Centurions* (1972), adapted from the Joseph Wambaugh novel of the same title. Many women would not want to marry a police officer because his occupation would make them feel chronically insecure. The most debilitating feature of the work, however, is its psychological effect: Some officers begin to see the whole world in a different light, with everyone they meet a potential criminal. The character Martin Riggs (Mel Gibson) in *Lethal Weapon* (1987) and its two successful sequels, *Lethal Weapon II* (1989) and *Lethal Weapon III* (1992; reviewed in this volume), is a rather zany variation of the same kind of socially maladjusted character: Riggs uses his partner, Roger Murtaugh (Danny Glover), and Murtaugh's wife and children as his surrogate family because he is unable to sustain any intimate relationships of his own.

Before *A Stranger Among Us*, the lonely police officers in films had all been men. This film introduces a new variation on an old theme in the person of Emily Eden (Melanie Griffith), a lonely New York City policewoman—or "police-person," as she sometimes describes herself, indicating that she is a little uncertain about her gender identity. In one effective scene, she visits her divorced father (Burtt Harris), the quintessential retired police officer, who is sitting alone watching television and drinking himself into oblivion. While he shares her interest in police work and has obviously inspired her to follow in his footsteps, it is painfully evident that he has never been able to treat her with the tender affection she craves and that he probably wishes she had been born a boy.

Emily is what her fellow officers call a "cowboy." Like Martin Riggs, she enjoys taking risks. She wants to prove she is as tough as any man. In an early scene, she drags her male partner into a drug bust that goes awry because she refuses to wait for reinforcements. Her partner is wounded, and Emily finds it hard to obtain a new assignment because the other male officers are understandably reluctant to work with her. Finally, to get rid of her, her supervisor assigns Emily to a missing persons case in a community of Hassidic Jews.

Right away, Emily senses that she has not only stepped into a different world but into a different century. The men all dress in severe, black, three-piece suits, and the women wear dresses that conceal everything from their chins to the tips of their old-fashioned shoes. They are strongly reminiscent of the unworldly Pennsylvania Amish farmers encountered by another lonely police officer: narcotics detective John Book (Harrison Ford) in *Witness* (1985), a film that was nominated for eight Academy Awards and evidently inspired the makers of *A Stranger Among Us*.

Emily arrives in her usual plainclothes outfit, featuring a miniskirt and a low-cut blouse, with a huge automatic pistol concealed under her jacket. The culture clash represented by Emily and her clients is a major theme of the film. Fortunately, it is not done to death: Emily begins appearing in more conservative attire after she realizes what a spectacle she is making of herself, and she also begins to modify her coarse language.

The case itself is elementary. Most members of this Hassidic community are involved in cutting and merchandising diamonds. One young Jew named Yaakov Klausman (Jake Weber) has disappeared from a locked room where he was cutting and polishing $700,000 worth of diamonds. Emily quickly discovers that he was murdered and his body stuffed inside the false ceiling, where his blood soaked through an acoustical panel. She deduces that the murderers must have been personally known to him; otherwise, they could never have gotten through the tight security system.

Acting on this assumption, Emily merges into the community, sharing a room with the virginal daughter of the head of the community, Leah (Mia Sara), and eating her meals with the whole extended family. She meets Leah's brother Ariel (Eric Thal), who is deeply engrossed in rabbinical studies and destined to become the

Rebbe, the head of the community. There is an immediate chemical reaction between these two mismatched young people. Ariel, who has taken vows not even to think about sex before marriage, is deeply troubled by his interest in Emily, whereas she thinks it might be fun to go to bed with him. The love affair between the shy, chaste Ariel and the aggressive, streetwise Emily is another major theme of the film.

Emily, with the curiosity of a good detective, is fascinated by her new acquaintances and asks many questions. What particularly impresses her is the love shared by all the members. There are colorful scenes involving communal singing and dancing and the sharing of lavish meals. The viewer, like Emily, is led to believe that something important is missing from many modern people's lives with the loss of the basic values the Hassidim still revere.

The excellent color photography enhances the theme of the beauty of traditional values by focusing on the simple interiors, with their lovingly polished furniture and woodwork. The rich glow of the wood is reminiscent of the beautiful old interiors photographed in *The Verdict* (1982) and *Driving Miss Daisy* (1989). Yet the photography is not mere art for art's sake; it visually symbolizes the feelings of warmth, security, purpose, and sense of belonging experienced vicariously by Emily, who has not known these feelings in her own life.

While Emily is working with Ariel at a counter in the diamond mart, two thugs appear, brimming with malice and self-confidence. They are the notorious Baldessari brothers (James Gandolfini and Chris Collins). They demand protection money, intimating that they are responsible for the murder of the young diamond-cutter and are fully capable of further violence if their demands are not met.

Emily sets up an electronic trap, so that the extortionists will be videotaped when they return for their payoff. Later, she behaves with her customary "cowboy" bravado and arrests the two enormous men singlehandedly. Going through their pockets, she discovers an empty velvet jewelry bag that is identified as one taken by the thieves who murdered Klausman.

Even though they are handcuffed together, the two desperate men make a break, commandeer a taxicab, and nearly escape through the congested streets of the diamond district. This is one of those car-crashing, window-smashing, guns-blazing scenes that Hollywood does so well. The intrepid Emily stands in front of the onrushing taxicab and fires through its windshield, killing one of the brothers and fatally wounding the other. The dying man solemnly assures her that they were not responsible for Klausman's murder but were only trying to capitalize on it.

Emily believes him because he is obviously in terror of death and is making what amounts to a deathbed confession. When she discusses the matter with Ariel, they agree that the real murderer must be someone inside the Hassidic community. Now they believe the murderer was one of the persons present when Emily arrested the Baldessari brothers, because the jewelry bag must have been planted on one of the extortionists during the confusion following their arrest.

This is sufficient evidence for Emily and Ariel to guess the murderer's true identity. Only one outsider, besides Emily herself, has been living in the Hassidic community. This individual is apprehended while trying to leave with the cash obtained from the stolen diamonds concealed in a suitcase, along with the murder weapon.

By this time, Emily and Ariel have fallen in love and have come perilously close to expressing their feelings in intimate physical terms. For Ariel, this act would be catastrophic, as it would represent a betrayal of his religious principles. Furthermore, his father has already chosen a bride for him who is, of course, also a member of their supremely orthodox branch of Judaism. Emily at last comes to understand that the best way for her to express her love for Ariel is to give him up, just as John Book finally gave up Rachel (Kelly McGillis) in *Witness*.

Melanie Griffith is a small, slender young woman and might not be anyone's idea of a tough New York cop; however, she provides an excellent performance that allows the viewer to overlook this incongruity. Emily has come to understand that sex without love is frustrating and degrading. She fends off the crude sexual advances of a male colleague by telling him that she has decided to wait, in accordance with Hassidic tradition, until her one predestined soulmate appears. Among the other things she has gained from the Hassidic community is at least a glimmer of religious faith.

A Stranger Among Us holds audience interest but does not measure up to its prototype, *Witness*, because it fails to deliver a gripping crime story. Instead, it uses the criminal investigation as an transparent device to place the protagonist into an setting where the main elements of interest are the Hassidic customs, the tormented relationship of the mismatched lovers, and the problems of being a woman in a male-dominated profession.

Bill Delaney

Reviews

Chicago Tribune. July 17, 1992, VII, p. 36.
The Christian Science Monitor. July 23, 1992, p. 13.
Entertainment Weekly. July 24, 1992, p. 40.
Films in Review. XLIII, November, 1992, p. 408.
The Hollywood Reporter. May 15, 1992, p. 7.
Los Angeles Times. July 17, 1992, p. F4.
The New York Times. July 17, 1992, p. B2.
The New Yorker. LXVIII, July 27, 1992, p. 55.
Time. CXL, July 27, 1992, p. 73.
Variety. May 15, 1992, p. 21.

A TALE OF SPRINGTIME (CONTE DE PRINTEMPS)

Origin: France
Released: 1992
Released in U.S.: 1992
Production: Margaret Menegoz for Les Films du Losange and Soficas Investimage; released by Orion Classics
Direction: Eric Rohmer
Screenplay: Eric Rohmer
Cinematography: Luc Pagès and Philippe Renaut
Editing: Maria-Luisa Garcia and Françoise Combès
Production design: no listing
Production management: Françoise Etchegaray
Sound: Pascal Ribier, Ludovic Hénault, and Jean-Pierre Laforce
MPAA rating: PG
Running time: 107 minutes

Principal characters:

Jeanne	Anne Teyssèdre
Natacha	Florence Darel
Igor	Hugues Quester
Eve	Eloïse Bennett
Gaëlle	Sophie Robin

French filmmaker Eric Rohmer is considered the quintessential director of French art films. Throughout his long and varied lifetime within the industry, Rohmer has often been described as someone who makes films without any message. To some extent, this is true. Rohmer's style is to produce not a predictable film but rather something that will provoke audiences to talk about what they have experienced. In a time that has seen the cost of producing commercial films soar, Rohmer still manages to bring a unique style to the screen.

A Tale of Springtime exhibits the very mold and style of Rohmer's best-known films. Such films as *La Collectionneuse* (1967), *Le Genou de Claire* (1970; *Claire's Knee*, 1971), *Pauline à la plage* (1982; *Pauline at the Beach*, 1983), *Les Nuits de la pleine lune* (1984; *Full Moon in Paris*, 1984), and *Le Rayon vert* (1986; *Summer*, 1986) all reflect the need for Rohmer to explore life from a unique perspective.

An almost cinema verité approach is employed by Rohmer in *A Tale of Springtime*. Jeanne (Anne Teyssèdre) is a teacher of philosophy who is living with her boyfriend in a small Parisian apartment. There is uncertainty in her relationship with her boyfriend. Without knowing the full reason, Jeanne decides that she really wants some time on her own. Returning to her own apartment, Jeanne assures her cousin Gaëlle (Sophie Robin) that she can stay a little longer.

An old school friend invites Jeanne to a class reunion. While sitting alone on a couch waiting for her friend to return to the party, she strikes up a conversation with a guest. Natacha (Florence Darel) also feels lonely, not only because she does not know anybody but also because she lives alone in her father's home. Almost on a whim, Natacha invites Jeanne to come and stay with her at least for a few days. Jeanne surprises herself and accepts the invitation. Natacha's father, Igor (Hugues Quester), only rarely comes to the apartment, so Jeanne should not think that she would be putting him to any inconvenience by using his room.

While Jeanne is having a shower, Igor returns to the apartment to pick up some clothing. When the two meet in the hallway, they are rather embarrassed. Jeanne is dripping wet and wrapped only in a towel. When Natacha returns, she apologizes that she had forgotten to mention that her father needed to drop by the apartment. This brings up the subject of Igor's latest girlfriend. Natacha disapproves of Eve (Eloïse Bennett). This is partly out of jealousy but much more because Eve is in her early twenties and therefore too young for her father.

In fact, it is Natacha's belief that Eve stole a necklace that was to be given to Natacha as a birthday present. Jeanne tries to reason with Natacha that her allegations are only founded on speculation. Natacha agrees that there may be a logical explanation, yet somehow she wants to believe the worst about Eve.

Jeanne and Eve eventually meet at a dinner party given by Natacha. The atmosphere is strained, with Natacha and Eve continually criticizing each other. Igor tries to remain neutral throughout the debates. Jeanne, however, finds Eve interesting, and they have a nice conversation despite the animosity that is evident between Natacha and Eve. There is some talk about visiting the family home in Fontainebleau. Igor wants to work on the garden, and he suggests that Natacha might enjoy helping him. Natacha explains that she cannot come down and help with the garden, and she suggests that Igor and Eve could go instead. Between all the various suggestions, it is unclear what everyone will do, and the dinner party ends on a note of confusion.

Natacha, despite what she had said, decides to spend the weekend at the family house. When Eve sees Natacha and Jeanne arriving, she immediately storms off to the train station and leaves Igor wondering what to do next. Natacha's boyfriend also arrives unannounced, and they leave Igor and Jeanne to work in the garden for the rest of the weekend. After dinner, Igor and Jeanne talk to each other in the sitting room. Igor asks Jeanne if he can kiss her; she allows him to without any reservations. After the kiss, there is a tense moment when Jeanne wants to leave. Igor tries to persuade her to stay, but Jeanne insists, and will not be persuaded to stay any longer.

On returning to Paris, Jeanne all but accuses Natacha of creating the situation where she was left alone with her father. Natacha denies that this was ever her intention, even though she had been more than interested in Jeanne and her father getting together. Jeanne decides that nothing more can be achieved from speaking with Natacha and starts to pack her suitcase. As Jeanne gathers together her clothes from the top shelf of an armoire, a shoebox falls to the ground. Out of the box, a beautiful necklace appears, the one that Natacha's father had bought for her and that has been lost all this time. Somehow the finding of the necklace restores the friendship between Natacha and Jeanne, and they part on good terms.

A Tale of Springtime allows this already controversial director another opportunity to explore relationships. Enduring the pacing of Rohmer's films has been compared with watching paint dry. Such criticism is an accurate assessment of how Rohmer's films are perceived.

A Tale of Springtime endeavors to explore a simple theme beginning with the simplest of premises. In fact, the strength of the film comes from the very fact that there is very little manipulation of the story line. This simplicity is why Rohmer's works are viewed with a certain skepticism. Much of Rohmer's work attempts to film life as it is happening. There is a documentary quality to *A Tale of Springtime* that borders on cinema verité, yet does not quite cross that border.

Despite the obvious criticisms, *A Tale of Springtime* proves to be an exceptionally well-made film, given the very narrow plot. Anne Teyssèdre brings a warmth and understanding to her role as Jeanne. Although Jeanne appears somewhat indecisive about her life and life in general, there is a realism about the character. The friendship that occurs rather like spontaneous combustion between Jeanne and Natacha is intriguing only because of how simply the friendship occurs.

The character of Natacha, as played by Florence Darel, begins strongly but tends to become less defined as the story progresses. This effect is attributable entirely to the development of the story line. Natacha shows herself at the beginning to be strong and forthright. Although lonely, her music studies give her the necessary impetus for life. As Natacha thinks more about her relationship with her father and what she really wants out of life, however, a certain gloom sets in over her character. This does not adversely affect the film, but there is a tendency for the focus to move from Natacha to Jeanne.

Throughout the film, the most dramatic character is Natacha, and when she becomes involved in self reflection, the whole pace of the narrative slows down. Along with this aspect of the story is the long build to Jeanne and Igor's encounter. From the first encounter between the two, the direction of the plot becomes inevitable. Yet Rohmer allows too much time to elapse between the first introduction and the scene in which they actually speak to each other alone. Even when they do finally get a chance to talk, there is nothing significantly revealed about their characters: Igor knows no more about himself and his relationship with Eve, and Jeanne does not discover what she seems to be missing in life.

Rohmer, in many respects, redefines the accepted view of what a "slice-of-life" picture is able to achieve. By focusing exclusively on just two or three characters, Rohmer is able to introduce new ways of telling a story. This method of writing and directing has left many within the film industry a little confused. Some believe that this style of filmmaking is really a deviation from the accepted practices of story telling. Others believe that Rohmer continues to explore new approaches to the genre film. Whatever decision is finally made, Rohmer's films still attract sufficient attention to make his work a necessary part of any film school course on film theory.

Richard G. Cormack

Reviews

Boxoffice. August/September, 1992, p. R-66.
Chicago Tribune. November 6, 1992, VII, p. 37.
Entertainment Weekly. August 31, 1992, p. 40.
Films in Review. XLIII, September, 1992, p. 342.
Los Angeles Times. August 19, 1992, p. F4.
The New Republic. CCVII, August 31, 1992, p. 32.
The New York Times. September 25, 1992, p. C14.
San Francisco Chronicle. September 4, 1992, p. C3.
Variety. CCCXXXVIII, February 28, 1992, p. 25.
The Village Voice. August 21, 1992, p. 58.

THIS IS MY LIFE

Production: Lynda Obst; released by Twentieth Century-Fox
Direction: Nora Ephron
Screenplay: Nora Ephron and Delia Ephron; based on the novel *This Is Your Life*, by Meg Wolitzer
Cinematography: Bobby Byrne
Editing: Robert Reitano
Production design: David Chapman
Art direction: Barbra Matis
Set decoration: Hilton Rosemarin and Jaro Dick
Casting: Juliet Taylor
Sound: Doug Ganton
Costume design: Jeffrey Kurland
Music: Carly Simon
MPAA rating: PG-13
Running time: 105 minutes

Principal characters:

Dottie Ingels .... Julie Kavner
Erica Ingels .... Samantha Mathis
Opal Ingels .... Gaby Hoffmann
Claudia Curtis .... Carrie Fisher
Arnold Moss .... Dan Aykroyd
Jordan Strang .... Danny Zorn
Aunt Harriet .... Estelle Harris

Screenwriter Nora Ephron secured the reputation as one of Hollywood's most bankable and critically acclaimed writers after she received Academy Award nominations for Best Original Screenplay with *Silkwood* (1983) and *When Harry Met Sally*. . . (1989). Three more years would elapse, however, before Ephron would take center stage as director. Ephron wanted a subject that had some personal interest for her, and reading Meg Wolitzer's 1988 novel *This Is Your Life*, Ephron knew it was the ideal project for her directorial debut. Ephron had first attained fame for penning the best-selling autobiography *Heartburn*, based on her life with famous political reporter Carl Bernstein, which was made into a feature film starring Meryl Streep and Jack Nicholson in 1986. She brought this project even closer to home by cowriting the *This Is My Life* screenplay with her sister, Delia Ephron, a best-selling novelist in her own right. Lynda Obst, who produced the award-winning *The Fisher King* (1991), and songwriter and popular singer Carly Simon round out the collective female power package. Simon's original compositions add a lyrical and upbeat dimension to the film. A story of dreams, family, and love, *This Is My Life* is an affecting and realistic portrayal of a working mother desperately seeking to balance her dual aspirations of stand-up comedy and motherhood.

Dottie Ingels (Julie Kavner) is a bubbly single mother whose imagination propels her into the comedy limelight. In real life, she settles for fluorescent by earning laughs at the cosmetics counter in Macy's department store, flooring her customers with gags about everything from the cosmetic benefits of sheep's placenta to dark tans. At home, she finds emotional support from her two girls, sixteen-year-old Erica (Samantha Mathis) and ten-year-old Opal (Gaby Hoffmann). They are Dottie's biggest fans and share her dream of the comedy big time, but they also must content themselves with nightly spoofs of *The Tonight Show* and wait patiently for Johnny Carson to call.

Ephron guided the film in a new direction by casting Kavner in the role of Dottie after Hollywood star Bette Midler turned it down. Kavner lends a particular anonymity to the role, as she is a relatively unknown but highly respected character actress best recognized for her television work on *Rhoda* and *The Tracey Ullman Show* and for the familiar voice of Marge Simpson on the animated series *The Simpsons*. Her film work ranges from top supporting roles in Penny Marshall's *Awakenings* (1990) to a collection of Woody Allen productions. Mathis made her big-screen debut in the sleeper hit *Pump Up the Volume* (1990), opposite Christian Slater, and Hoffmann turns in her third starring role of her career at the ripe age of ten.

Simon's energetic sound track breathes first life into the film, as her song "The Show Must Go On" establishes the lighthearted tone and colorful animation of Dottie's character. Dottie and Erica introduce themselves in a voice-over during the opening credits, revealing the dual-perspective narrative method through which the story unfolds. *This Is My Life* opens with warmth and vigor, capturing the spirit of Dottie Ingels and her grand vision of comic fame, yet the film confidently settles into a simple tale of love and obligation.

Dottie divorced Erica and Opal's father when the girls were young and moved them into the house of her Aunt Harriet (Estelle Harris) in Queens. When Harriet dies suddenly and leaves Dottie the house, she seizes the opportunity to sell it and buy an apartment in Manhattan. Dottie invests some of the money in her girls and finally invests the remainder in igniting her career. She quits her job and throws herself into the late-night comedy scene, where she immediately carves her comic niche, including occasional spots on local talk shows. She hires an agent, Claudia Curtis (Carrie Fisher), who works for mega-agent Arnold Moss (Dan Aykroyd). Moss takes a personal interest in Dottie and insists that she travel to Los Angeles to gain exposure and professional experience. Dottie finally tastes the potential for stardom, but performing in Los Angeles means leaving the girls for weeks at a time, which is what Dottie wants least and what Erica and Opal fear most. All three recognize the opportunity at hand, however, so Erica and Opal reluctantly send their mother off with good wishes and crossed fingers.

The two points of view of the narrative, Dottie and Erica, begin to diverge once Dottie hits comedy stardom in Los Angeles. Dottie uses an anecdote from Erica's personal life in her public routine and Erica is mortified. Previously flattered to be a part of their mother's onstage performance, the girls feel used and abandoned. Weeks pass, and Erica and Opal see more of their mother on television than in person. Life goes on for the girls, however, as Erica makes the major decision of her young life: to have sex with her boyfriend, Jordan Strang (Danny Zorn). As if life were not traumatic enough, Erica is further humiliated as Jordan's mother unexpectedly walks in on the two neophytes.

Timing is everything, both in stand-up and in life, and Dottie's absence comes at the worst time for Erica, who needs her mother more than ever. For Erica, talking to her ten-year-old sister is out of the question. Like an emotional time bomb, Erica shuts herself in her room, finding escape from her embarrassment and adolescent pain in solitude. The void that Dottie has left in her daughters' lives induces only bitterness in Erica, who is no longer blinded by the romantic vision of her mom's stardom. The pain tugs at Opal too, who idealizes Dottie yet begins to sense her distance as she watches Erica's sadness turn to hostility. Opal, once dependent on both Dottie and Erica, must fend for herself because she has, for all practical purposes, lost both a sister and a mother. Confused and hurt, she tries her best to bridge the gap between them, but only Dottie's physical presence can mend the wounds.

Dottie, meanwhile, stands oblivious to her children's concerns, taking for granted that they are still supportive of her. The passion on both sides finally ignites when Dottie becomes romantically involved with Moss and the conflicting points of view set off fireworks within the Ingels trio. Erica and Opal have a hard enough time battling the spotlight for their mother's attention and affection, but now they have to battle a man as well. Dottie walks in as Erica performs a blistering parody of her mother and Moss, which finally brings Erica's real emotions to light for Dottie. Hurt and angry, Dottie puts her foot down and lets it be known that she will not sacrifice her happiness for her children. Erica angrily accuses Dottie of abandoning them and caring more about her career then her children. Emotions run hot as the argument heats to a boil and doors slam, cutting mother off from child, sister from sister.

Dottie works through her anger during the night and offers breakfast and a fresh start the following morning, only to find Erica and Opal gone. They intend to live with their father in Albany, as they search for a regular life with an attentive parent—something that they think they have lost with their mother. They find only confused indifference from their father, however, who insults his former wife and shows only apathy when they suggest that they live with him. As their father criticizes Dottie while they sit in a strange living room staring at a man neither of them remembers, Erica and Opal instantly recognize their mistake and hurry back to Dottie, whom they need, despite everything.

This Is My Life is a classic tale of the major dilemma facing most working mothers in the United States in the 1990's. For children, success is measured not by fame or fortune but by how much attention they receive from their parents. For parents, especially parents with big dreams, the pursuit of happiness does not necessarily stop once children are in the picture. The classic conflict that is played out between individual needs and parental obligation is an age-old one and is handled with candor and vision by Nora Ephron and company. Many people cited Ephron's screenplay for *When Harry Met Sally . . .* as the most romantic film in recent cinema history because of its realistic approach to relationships. *This Is My Life* is yet another example of Ephron's ability to give sincere treatment to real issues and to handle them with sensitivity and honesty.

Catherine R. Springer

Reviews

Chicago Tribune. March 6, 1992, VII, p. 35.
The Christian Science Monitor. February 25, 1992, p. 11.
Films in Review. XLIII, May, 1992, p. 191.
The Hollywood Reporter. January 20, 1992, p. 11.
Los Angeles Times. February 21, 1992, p. F8.
The New York Times. February 21, 1992, p. B2.
The New Yorker. LXVIII, March 9, 1992, p. 82.
Rolling Stone. March 5, 1992, p. 75.
Time. CXXXIX, February 24, 1992, p. 68.
Variety. January 20, 1992, p. 2.

THUNDERHEART

Production: Robert De Niro, Jane Rosenthal, and John Fusco for Tribeca/Waterhorse; released by TriStar Pictures
Direction: Michael Apted
Screenplay: John Fusco
Cinematography: Roger Deakins
Editing: Ian Crafford
Production design: Dan Bishop
Art direction: Bill Ballou
Set decoration: Dianna Freas
Casting: Lisa Clarkson
Sound: Chris Newman
Costume design: Susan Lyall
Music: James Horner
MPAA rating: R
Running time: 118 minutes

Principal characters:

Ray Levoi .... Val Kilmer
Frank Coutelle .... Sam Shepard
Walter Crow Horse .... Graham Greene
Jack Milton .... Fred Ward
Maggie Eagle Bear .... Sheila Tousey
Grandpa Sam Reaches .... Chief Ted Thin Elk
Jimmy Looks Twice .... John Trudell

Despite an unfortunate muddle of elements and incoherent editing in the film's middle segments, *Thunderheart* makes powerful statements on several significant themes: the violation of human rights, the need to fight cruel and unjust authority whatever the cost, the inner turmoil that one man undergoes when he is caught between two cultures, his eventual reconcilement with the ghosts of his past, his acceptance of his true identity.

The film's success is attributable in great part to Val Kilmer's deeply felt portrayal of Ray Levoi, a Federal Bureau of Investigation (FBI) agent who, because he is part Sioux, is sent to investigate a murder on a reservation in South Dakota. Kilmer, with this performance and his portrayal of Jim Morrison in *The Doors* (1991), seems to be leaping to higher and higher planes of acting accomplishment. Levoi, at first glance, is the converse of Morrison; he seems about as conventional in his dark suit and appropriate short haircut as Morrison was nonconformist. Kilmer probably has not looked so well-groomed in a role since his Broadway stage appearance in *Slab Boys* (1983), in which he played the pampered relative of a factory owner.

Also outstanding is Graham Greene's portrayal of Walter Crow Horse, a reservation police officer who utilizes Native American methods of investigation and serves as a foil to Levoi, who believes in modern, scientific techniques. Their conflict springs also from the fact that Levoi does not want to be thought of as Sioux, but rather as American. Their verbal sparring provides delightful entertainment in the film's early segments.

The film invites comparison with Kevin Costner's *Dances with Wolves* (1990), partly because of the presence of Oneida tribal member Greene—although the wisecracking, obscenely gesturing character that he plays in *Thunderheart* is radically different from the holy man that he portrayed in Costner's film. The two films are thematically linked because each deals with one man's spiritual rebirth and is set primarily among the Sioux, who are victimized by authorities. *Dances with Wolves*, however, takes place at the time of the Civil War, and *Thunderheart* is based on incidents that took place in the 1970's.

Nevertheless, director Michael Apted's film does not purport to be anything but fiction and belongs more to the genre of criminal investigation films in its intrigue and complexity of plot. Even the conventional, climactic car chase, which leaves a trail of wrecked vehicles in its wake, is included once it is clear who are the heroes and who are the villains. In many ways, a more apt comparison would be with films such as *No Way Out* (1987), in which director Roger Donaldson takes the viewer through a tangle of double agents, cover-ups, abuses of power, and conspiracies but somehow manages to keep the story line as clear as it should be at any given moment. Even though Apted is not as successful in this regard, he succeeds with more important matters and gives his film a depth of seriousness that the other motion picture cannot claim.

Apted transcends the criminal investigation genre by looking more than fleetingly at Levoi's struggle to reconcile the conflict between his habitual self and his newly discovered self. Levoi's intentions are very clear early in the story: He is a team player, striving for advancement. When he is assigned as a partner to veteran Frank Coutelle (Sam Shepard) in investigating the murder, he thinks it perversely amusing that he is being sent for public relations reasons because he is part Sioux, as he does not believe that he has anything in common with Native Americans. Unwilling, however, to contradict his boss, he voices no objections, although inwardly he resists the role that he is being asked to play. Shortly after this segment, Apted cuts to a striking profile shot of Levoi standing in his suit and tie but looking nevertheless very Native American. (Kilmer is part Cherokee.)

When the two agents arrive at the reservation, Levoi does what he can to distance himself from any identity with the Sioux. He comments with distaste about the shabby lives that they are living, in trailers surrounded by litter and with children playing in the dirt, and he uses more than required force when they catch Walter Crow Horse attempting to remove the murdered man's body. Coutelle has to warn Levoi to stop trying to prove that the Sioux are not his people.

Yet Levoi's perceptions and allegiances alter. Step by step, he grows aware that there is something rotten on the reservation and that the smell is not coming from the expected places. He becomes caught between two worlds, and his inner conflict greatly intensifies. His habit is to obey; his inclination becomes more and more to flail out and destroy injustice. Excitement builds in the film as he takes progressively greater risks and jeopardizes his bright future as a federal agent.

The distance that Levoi has to travel from obstinate resistance to fierce embracement of his roots is vast, and such a change, when credibly executed, can be the stuff of great drama. The miracle of Kilmer's performance is that he is never less than convincing, despite the extent of the character's turnabout and such tricky devices of plot as mystical, drug-induced visions and implications of reincarnation.

Grandpa Sam Reaches (Chief Ted Thin Elk), an old medicine man to whom Levoi goes for information, serves as a catalyst in causing these mystical experiences to take place. Apted effectively employs almost imperceptibly slow zoom shots of Levoi listening in a sweat to the old man's words, which dredge up images from the deep recesses of his memory—images from both his childhood and some previous life. Trusted to the skills of a less inspired actor, this dalliance with mysticism could become incredible, if not laughable. As Kilmer plays it, there are compelling moments. Thin Elk, making his professional acting debut, speaks at length in one of these sequences; Apted wisely manages to keep the viewer's attention on Levoi's responses to what the old man says, thereby camouflaging the great discrepancy between his acting skills and Kilmer's.

An additional threat to credibility is the fact that characters around Levoi do not always behave in an understandable manner. One example is Maggie Eagle Bear (Sheila Tousey), a Dartmouth graduate who is using her education and spunk on behalf of her people in their fight against corrupt authority. She is, at first, opposed to Levoi's intrusion into their lives; he is, after all, with the FBI, which is siding with those who she believes are the problem. She becomes aware, however, of Levoi's emerging commitment to finding the truth. While he is visiting her home, men in two vehicles fire volleys of ammunition from high-powered weapons into the house, injuring her young son. In a rousing sequence, Levoi rushes the bloodied child to a clinic, presumably saving his life and then, when he sees the shooters drive into town bragging about the damage that they have caused, attacks them in an explosion of rage, even though they are theoretically the FBI's allies.

Maggie witnesses these events, but the next time that Levoi encounters her, she is inexplicably cool toward him, never mentioning his efforts on her child's behalf. When they meet yet another time, he asks how the boy is and she thanks him for his actions. One cannot help but wonder why there is an intervening episode involving her and Levoi before she acknowledges their most significant shared event. The strange sequence is most likely the result of an editing choice, one of several that cause confusion when the thickening plot, woven of several developing strands, needs to be kept clear.

The desire for authenticity led Apted, who is well known for his documentary filmmaking, to cast all the Native American roles with performers who are at least part Native American. Apted was fortunate to have Kilmer, Greene, and Tousey (a Menominee and Stockbridge-Munsee tribal member), who are all fine professionals. The rebellious Jimmy Looks Twice (John Trudell) is a suspect for the murder under investigation. Trudell, whose father was a Santee, is convincing and intense in his professional acting debut. After a protest, the actor lost his wife and three children in a suspicious fire that was officially ruled an accident. He has been an impassioned fighter for Native American causes, and his real-life convictions have evidently informed his performance.

Apted's *Incident at Oglala* (1992), a documentary, was released shortly before *Thunderheart*. The director's interest in the subject and his distress over the suffering and grievances of a wronged people led him to devote a large amount of creative energy to these two full-length works and to infuse the fictional one with the profundity and genuine passion demanded by the very real issues that it treats.

Cono Robert Marcazzo

Reviews

Chicago Tribune. April 3, 1992, VII, p. 32.
Films in Review. XLIII, May, 1992, p. 186.
The Hollywood Reporter. March 25, 1992, p. 5.
Los Angeles Times. April 3, 1992, p. F1.
National Review. XLIV, June 8, 1992, p. 53.
The New York Times. April 3, 1992, p. B1.
Newsweek. CXIX, April 13, 1992, p. 68.
Sight and Sound. II, October, 1992, p. 57.
Time. CXXXIX, May 4, 1992, p. 77.
Variety. March 24, 1992, p. 2.

TOTO THE HERO
(TOTO LE HÉROS)

Origin: Belgium, France, and Germany
Released: 1991
Released in U.S.: 1992
Production: Pierre Drouot and Dany Geys for Jacqueline Pierreux, Iblis Films, Les Productions Philippe Dussart, Metropolis Filmproduktion, RTBF, FR3 Films Production, ZDF, and Canal Plus; released by Triton Pictures
Direction: Jaco van Dormael
Screenplay: Jaco van Dormael
Cinematography: Walther van den Ende
Editing: Susana Rossberg
Art direction: Hubert Pouille
Sound: Dominique Warnier and Jean-Paul Loublier
Costume design: An D'Huys and Anne van Bree
Music: Pierre van Dormael
MPAA rating: PG-13
Running time: 90 minutes

Principal characters:

Thomas van Hasebroeck .... Michel Bouquet
Thomas (as a young man) .... Jo de Backer
Thomas (as a child) .... Thomas Godet
Evelyne .... Gisela Uhlen
Evelyne (as a young woman) .... Mireille Perrier
Alice .... Sandrine Blancke
Alfred .... Peter Böhlke
Alfred (as a young man) .... Didier Ferney
Alfred (as a child) .... Hugo Harold Harrisson
Thomas' mother .... Fabienne Loriaux
Thomas' father .... Klaus Schindler
Célestin (as a young man) .... Pascal Duquenne
Célestin (as a child) .... Karim Moussati
Mr. Kant .... Didier de Neck
Mrs. Kant .... Christine Smeysters

Jaco van Dormael's background as a clown in Belgium's Big Flying Circus prepared him well for the creation of *Toto the Hero*. Directing from his own screenplay, van Dormael brings fantasy, danger, and exhaustingly great fun to his characters and their audiences.

In this, his motion picture debut, van Dormael garnered two Felix (European Film Award) awards, for best film and best screenplay, and the Camera d'Or at

Cannes for best first film. Although *Toto the Hero* is van Dormael's first full-length feature, he has written, directed, and received many awards for his various short films, such as *L'Imitateur* (1982) and *De Boot* (1985), as well as his thesis film, *Maedli la breche*, which in 1981 won an Academy Award for the best film by a foreign student. A Belgian film in French, presented in the United States with English subtitles, *Toto the Hero* represents a coproduction of Belgium, France, and Germany, with nationalities being split almost equally among the actors, producers, technicians, and financiers.

In the spirit of *Cinema Paradiso* (1989), *Toto the Hero* reveals an old man's use of selective memory to examine the events of his life, especially in his youth, that led him to the woeful state that he finds himself in near death. Like Jimmy Stewart's character in Frank Capra's classic *It's a Wonderful Life* (1946), van Dormael's hero relives his life after failing to see all the wonderful events and feelings that it contained and how important he was to others.

From his tiny, dimly lit room in a senior citizen's home, Thomas van Hasebroeck (Michel Bouquet—winner of the Felix for best actor) half fantasizes, half plots to murder Alfred Kant (Peter Böhlke). Disjointed shots of a murder, an investigation, and an autopsy flash across the screen, but are they glimpses of what has already happened, what is about to happen, or what happens repeatedly but only in Thomas' mind?

Thomas believes that a fire in the hospital where he was born caused him to be confused with Alfred. Thus, he was accidentally sent to live with the van Hasebroecks, while the wealthy and prestigious Mr. and Mrs. Kant (Didier de Neck and Christine Smeysters), who should have been his parents, reared Alfred. That is why Alfred's life has been so charmed and his own so bereft—or so Thomas insists.

Thomas' family is remembered as idyllically as the television sitcom families of the 1950's. Home is a virtual playground where loved ones arrive via parachutes into the backyard, babies seem to come from washing machines, and the world ends outside his front door. When his father (Klaus Schindler) entertains young Thomas (Thomas Godet) by playing the piano and singing Charles Trenet's 1938 nonsense song "Boum," often accompanied by Thomas' exquisitely beautiful sister, Alice (Sandrine Blancke), even the tulips in the garden sway in time.

Thomas' idyllic vision is shattered when his pilot father's plane goes missing in a storm while transporting a cargo of marmalade for Mr. Kant's grocery store. Kant accepts no responsibility for the widowed mother of three, forcing Thomas' mother to steal to feed her family and Thomas to invent the fantasy of himself as Toto, a private investigator action hero whose mission is to murder the foul Alfred, who stole his rightful life.

Thomas confronts Alfred with his theory about the error in the burning nursery; Alfred punches Thomas in the stomach. Thomas ingeniously saves his brother, Célestin (Karim Moussati), who has Down's syndrome, from Alfred's dare to jump off a bridge; Alfred generates a humiliating nickname with which he and the other boys taunt Thomas. The final, and most unforgivable blow, comes when Alfred courts Alice and wins her love.

A call comes from France, where remnants of Thomas' father's airplane were found. Thomas' mother takes Célestin and goes there to search for her husband, leaving Alice to get herself and Thomas off to camp, where they will be cared for until she returns. Alice, however, easily persuades Thomas to stay with her and live alone in their house, hiding their lack of supervision from those outside. Together and alone against the world, Alice and Thomas form a bond of trust and love that borders on incest. Clearly, Thomas worships his beautiful, talented, and inventive sister.

As Alice begins to be aware of her changing body, she elicits Thomas' opinion about the various parts of it. Unable to answer her questions directly, Thomas simply states that the Egyptian queen Nefertiti married her brother. Yet Alice soon abandons their secret home, under the guise of attending a trumpet lesson, to rendezvous with Alfred. When Thomas learns that Alice has revealed their secret to Alfred and has endangered their precious arrangement, even Toto the Hero is not strong enough to counter the attack. Thomas tells Alice that she must choose between himself and Alfred, and that if she really loves him, then she will burn down the Kants' house as she threatened to do after they murdered Alice and Thomas' father. Before Thomas can take back his ultimatum, Alice marches into the Kants' barn with a can of gasoline. Thomas' screams are drowned out by those of Alfred as they see the barn explode and burn to the ground with Alice inside.

Years later, Thomas (Jo de Backer) is a young man with a boring job in a big city, where he seemingly has no friends and certainly no love life. Several times a day, he looks at and touches the photograph of Alice that sits on his desk. One day, Thomas spots Evelyne (Mireille Perrier), a woman who looks astoundingly like a grown-up version of Alice. He pursues her and they eventually fall in love, despite the fact that she is married and that the affair is further frustrated by Thomas' need to pretend that she is the reincarnation of his dead sister. They plan to run away together, but when Thomas goes to Evelyne's home to pick her up, he meets her husband—Alfred. Devastated, Thomas boards the first train out of town and does not return for some forty or fifty years, when he intends to murder Alfred.

The newscasts report that there have been attempts to assassinate the wealthy and powerful Alfred Kant, moving Thomas to act quickly if he is to get there first. Thomas skillfully escapes from the home and travels to his old neighborhood, where he guesses that Alfred is hiding from his would-be killers. Old Alfred is glad to see Thomas, whom he thinks of as an old friend. He knows all about Thomas and Evelyne and bears him no grudge, having himself remarried long ago. Evelyne left him years before, remarried, and still keeps in touch. Everyone except Thomas, it seems, was able to move on with his or her life.

Thomas locks Alfred in the bathroom, steals a suit of his clothes, and hitchhikes back to the city, imagining along the way that he sees his father and little Alice performing "Boum" in the back of the truck in front of him. In a first and final act of forgiveness, Thomas masquerades as Alfred, luring the assassin to himself instead of the one on whom Thomas has blamed every misery in his long, miserable life. The body that has flashed across the screen so many times was not Alfred's, nor was it Thomas' fantasy: it was Thomas'.

Yet this revelation is not the end of the story. As Thomas' body is cremated—ironically, or perhaps symmetrically, ending his life in the flames that he believed he began it in—he laughs. As his ashes are scattered from an airplane, his spirit travels to tell Alfred what he did for him, to chase the chickens in Alfred's garden, and to soar joyfully through the sky, finally free of the oppressive bitterness that he allowed to isolate him from any happiness in his life. Toto's bitterness is transformed into a thrilling adventure, promising joy and fulfillment in death and beyond.

With the help of cinematographer Walther van den Ende, who won the Felix for his work on *Toto the Hero*, van Dormael does a masterful job of paralleling the way in which the human mind works: not in a chronological or any logical order, but leaping from thought to thought, moment to moment, and decade to decade as the pieces of one's life are psychologically and emotionally tied together. Unafraid to deal honestly and even sensually with childhood sexuality, van Dormael explains Thomas' obsession with Alice, which caused him to waste his long life.

One must pay close attention not only to follow the feverishly paced and sometimes choppy cuts between the various eras of Thomas' life and between his memories and fantasies but also so as not to miss a single one of the touching, smile-provoking, laugh-inducing moments that emerge from within the tragedies to make life bearable, and this motion picture delightful.

Eleah Horwitz

Reviews

Chicago Tribune. March 27, 1992, VII, p. 34.
The Christian Science Monitor. May 14, 1992, p. 13.
The Hollywood Reporter. September 23, 1991, p. 5.
Los Angeles Times. March 12, 1992, p. F1.
The New York Times. September 21, 1991, p. 10.
Newsweek. CXIX, April 6, 1992, p. 64.
Rolling Stone. March 5, 1992, p. 78.
Time. CXXXIX, March 30, 1992, p. 71.
Variety. September 9, 1991, p. 13.
The Village Voice. March 10, 1992, p. 56.

TOYS

Production: Mark Johnson and Barry Levinson for Baltimore Pictures; distributed by Twentieth Century-Fox
Direction: Barry Levinson
Screenplay: Valerie Curtin and Barry Levinson
Cinematography: Adam Greenberg
Editing: Stu Linder
Production design: Ferdinando Scarfiotti
Art direction: Edward Richardson
Set decoration: Linda De Scenna
Casting: Ellen Chenoweth
Special effects coordination: Clayton Pinney
Visual effects supervision: Mat Beck
Special visual effects: Dream Quest Images
Sound: Ron Judkins
Sound design: Richard Beggs
Costume design: Albert Wolsky
Choreography: Anthony Thomas
Music: Hans Zimmer and Trevor Horn
MPAA rating: PG-13
Running time: 122 minutes

Principal characters:

Leslie Zevo	Robin Williams
The General	Michael Gambon
Alsatia Zevo	Joan Cusack
Gwen	Robin Wright
Patrick	L.L. Cool J.
Kenneth Zevo	Donald O'Connor
Owens Owens	Arthur Malet
Zevo, Sr.	Jack Warden
Nurse Debbie	Debi Mazar
Choir soloist	Wendy Melvoin
Cortez	Julio Oscar Mechoso
Baker	Jamie Foxx
Shimera	Shelly Desai

When toy factory owner Kenneth Zevo (Donald O'Connor) realizes that he is nearing the end of his life, he must decide who will carry on for him after he is gone. His most obvious choice would be his son, Leslie (Robin Williams), but Leslie is a bit too innocent to cope with such responsibility. Kenneth's daughter, Alsatia (Joan Cusack), works designing doll clothes. Wearing human-sized versions of flat-surfaced, tabbed, paper doll apparel, she is even less in touch with reality than her brother is. As a consequence, Kenneth asks his brother, the General (Michael Gambon), who has followed in their father's military footsteps, to step in and help.

The General is a soldier with no war to fight and no hope for a war in the future. At first, he is not interested in managing a toy factory, but at the mention of industrial espionage, his interest is piqued. When Kenneth dies—his twirling beanie cap is connected to his pacemaker—the General takes over the factory. One of his first goals is to turn the toys into military weapons and the children who play his video games into high-technology warriors. To help him in these plans, he enlists the help of his son, Patrick (L.L. Cool J.), an expert in covert operations.

Meanwhile, Leslie has become preoccupied with Gwen (Robin Wright), the Southern belle who runs the copy machine. He soon realizes that his father hired this young woman in the hopes that just such a romance would develop. Reality begins to intrude on the blissful Leslie, however, when formerly happy workers start leaving in droves because of the General's policies. It is only a matter of time before Leslie is forced to stop inventing and playing with the company's "fun" toys in order to thwart the General's "war" toys. The result is an all-out battle between "good" dolls and stuffed animals and "bad" military gadgets. The choice is between innocence and destruction. The winner of this war is never in doubt, as the film's whimsical message is clear from the very set-up of the plot. Because of this one-note story line, the only things that can make *Toys* of interest are the acting and the sets.

It is difficult to believe that director Barry Levinson, who used Robin Williams' comedic talents so well in *Good Morning, Vietnam* (1987), could ask the actor to be so cloying here. Williams plays Leslie like a monotonous, innocent fool. Only once does Williams show a spark of his comic genius: when Leslie gives the toys a pep talk before they go into battle with the General's machines. Williams plays the scene as if his character were part Abraham Lincoln, part Winston Churchill, part George S. Patton, and part John F. Kennedy. It is the only truly appealing moment in his time on the screen.

Michael Gambon, best known for his role in the television series *The Singing Detective*, shown in the United States on the Public Broadcasting System (PBS), tries hard. Even his performance, however, is tedious. In fact, the only standout, and the only surprise in the film, is Joan Cusack. Her Alsatia is so far off the scale that she is at least interesting.

If there are any winners in this film, they are those people responsible for the sets and costumes. Especially noteworthy is production designer Ferdinando Scarfiotti, who won an Academy Award for his work on *The Last Emperor* (1987) and was nominated for another Oscar for his work on *Toys*, but lost to *Howards End* (reviewed in this volume). The toy factory is set amid a golden field of wheat that stretches to the horizon, and the Zevo house appears to be nothing more than a pop-up-book illustration. The sets and settings that decorate the film are far more intriguing than what goes on in it. Also nominated for an Oscar was Albert Wolsky, whose costumes (especially the tab "paper" dresses worn by Alsatia) were just as imaginative as Scarfiotti's sets. Unfortunately, just as in the other nomination, the award for costume design went to another film, *Bram Stoker's Dracula* (reviewed in this volume).

Toys attempts to be a whimsical, contemporary fable that seems to be aimed more at adults than at children. The result, however, is a lethally slow and lackluster motion picture that fabricates emotions for the audience to grab hold of because it cannot elicit them honestly.

Beverley Bare Buehrer

Reviews

Boxoffice. February, 1993, p. R-10.
Chicago Tribune. December 18, 1992, VII, p. 27.
The Christian Science Monitor. December 24, 1992, p. 12.
Entertainment Weekly. January 8, 1993, p. 35.
The Hollywood Reporter. December 18, 1992, p. 6.
Los Angeles Times. December 18, 1992, p. F1.
The New York Times. December 18, 1992, p. B1.
Time. CXL, December 28, 1992, p. 64.
Variety. December 18, 1992, p. 4.
The Washington Post. December 18, 1992, p. D1.

TWIN PEAKS
Fire Walk with Me

Production: Gregg Fienberg for Francis Bouygues and CIBY Pictures; released by New Line Cinema
Direction: David Lynch
Screenplay: David Lynch and Robert Engels
Cinematography: Ron Garcia
Editing: Mary Sweeney
Production design: Patricia Norris
Set decoration: Leslie Morales
Casting: Johanna Ray
Sound: Jon Huck
Costume design: Patricia Norris
Music: Angelo Badalamenti
MPAA rating: R
Running time: 135 minutes

Principal characters:

Laura Palmer .... Sheryl Lee
Leland Palmer .... Ray Wise
Special Agent Dale Cooper .... Kyle MacLachlan
Donna Hayward .... Moira Kelly
Gordon Cole .... David Lynch
Special Agent Chester Desmond .... Chris Isaak
Phillip Jeffries .... David Bowie
Carl Rodd .... Harry Dean Stanton
Bobby Briggs .... Dana Ashbrook
Sam Stanley .... Kiefer Sutherland
Norma Jennings .... Peggy Lipton
James Hurley .... James Marshall
Sarah Palmer .... Grace Zabriskie
Shelly Johnson .... Mädchen Amick
Albert Rosenfeld .... Miguel Ferrer
Teresa Banks .... Pamela Gidley
Bob .... Frank Silva
Leo Johnson .... Eric DaRe
Annie Blackburn .... Heather Graham
Harold Smith .... Lenny Von Dohlen
Ronette Pulaski .... Phoebe Augustine
Woodman .... Jurgen Prochnow
Sheriff Cable .... Gary Bullock
Man from Another Planet .... Michael J. Anderson

When Leland Palmer (Ray Wise) smashes a television at the beginning of *Twin Peaks: Fire Walk with Me*, he does more than begin a film based on one of television's most cultish, popular, and critically confused series, *Twin Peaks*. He also sets the stage for the fact that this film will symbolically and realistically smash the boundaries that reigned in director David Lynch's vision. On the television, viewers wanted to know "who killed Laura Palmer." In the film, Lynch wants to tell who Laura Palmer (Sheryl Lee) was and why she died, and he does it in what would have been an unshowable R-rated television episode.

Laura Palmer was only a specter in the television series. When her plastic-wrapped, dead body washed up on the shore in the first episode, she started the innovative and quirky television series, which set out to identify her killer. Many viewers believed that this discovery took too long to make, that the process became too supernatural and pained to be worth the wait. Viewers and critics began abandoning the series, but when the series was canceled, "Peakers" wanted more. Lynch obliged by making this "prequel," which delves into the murder and the weeks preceding Laura's death.

The film begins with a half-hour introduction into the FBI's investigation into the murder of Teresa Banks (Pamela Gidley), whose death was alluded to in the series and which happened one year before Laura's demise. On the case are Special Agent Chester Desmond (Chris Isaak) and Sam Stanley (Kiefer Sutherland). Just as Desmond seems to find a substantial clue at the Fat Trout Trailer Park, run by Harry Dean Stanton's Carl Rodd, he mysteriously disappears.

From there, the film moves forward a year to focus on Laura Palmer's story and the week before her death. She is seen falling into the depths of depravity: consuming cocaine provided by the high-school dealer and general bad boy Bobby Briggs (Dana Ashbrook), spurning the attentions of tortured boyfriend James Hurley (James Marshall), attending orgies at a seedy club across the Canadian border, and being tortured by the evil presence of Bob (Frank Silva), who sneaks into her window at night and does unspeakable things to the "innocent" young teenager. The deeper that Laura plunges, the more she allows herself to fall.

Home life is no better for Laura. Besides fighting Bob's unwanted advances, her chain-smoking mother (Grace Zabriskie) seems ineffectual against the rantings of Laura's father, Leland, who is obsessed with his daughter's dirty fingernails and his own dirty and incestuous thoughts and actions. Even in sleep there is no respite, for there Laura enters the surreal and unsettling red-curtained room frequented by the backward-speaking dwarf (Michael J. Anderson).

By the time that Laura's descent has reached its lowest point in an abandoned Pullman car in the woods, she is murdered, her body wrapped in plastic and set afloat in the river. The film ends exactly where the television series began.

When *Twin Peaks: Fire Walk with Me* was screened at the Cannes Film Festival, it was greeted with boos from the audience. When the film actually premiered, it was not in the United States but in Japan, where the series was currently running and where the fad was at its height. When it was finally time to appear on American screens, the film was not given any advance screenings for critics; usually, this ploy suggests a film in which the studio has little faith. Yet *Twin Peaks* is not that bad. Of course, it is not good either.

Lynch's films are known for their examinations of the undersides of life. From *Eraserhead* (1978) through *Wild at Heart* (1990), and especially in *Blue Velvet* (1986), Lynch seemed to delight in lifting up the skirts of the normal world to see what kind of underwear it was wearing. In *Twin Peaks*, he may have outdone himself. It is a sleazy film, reveling in Laura's debauchery and filling the screen with drugs, alcohol, sex, and violence.

While all this was alluded to in the television series, on the big screen Lynch indulges every idea that he must have suppressed on the small one. Yet what made the television show so quirky—its whimsy, its offbeat style, its kookiness—is missing in the film. Special Agent Dale Cooper (Kyle MacLachlan) lent a kind of sincere goodness to contrast with the mayhem that he encountered, but in the film, he is relegated to a mere cameo. His loss is greatly felt.

He is not the only character exiled to brief screen time. Some, such as Peggy Lipton's Norma Jennings and Mädchen Amick's Shelly Johnson, seem to be inserted into the film for no apparent reason other than familiarity. On the other hand, other familiar faces are completely missing (including Sherilyn Fenn, Joan Chen, and Richard Beymer), and the Donna with whom audiences were familiar, Lara Flynn Boyle, has been replaced by Moira Kelly.

One element that remained is the haunting music of Angelo Badalamenti. Added to the familiar strains of the *Twin Peaks* theme, which won a Grammy for the composer, is pounding bar music which is so loud that the characters must communicate to the audience via subtitles.

Occasionally, audiences may wish that other sections of the film had subtitles. Instead of indicating what the actors are saying, such subtitles would explain Lynch's oblique symbolism (what does the long-nosed, white-masked little boy really mean?) and obscure dialogue ("I am the Great Went"?). Is that dwarf the gatekeeper to the netherworld? No answers are provided to these questions.

What audiences probably hoped for in a *Twin Peaks* film are further quirky adventures and insights into the surreal world that ended up driving many viewers and critics away from the television series. Lynch, who appears early in the film reprising his role as the almost-deaf FBI Bureau Chief Gordon Cole, seems to have instead sacrificed those goals in favor of indulging in the R-rated scenes that he could not show in prime time.

There is no real mystery in *Twin Peaks: Fire Walk with Me*, as Laura's murderer had already been identified as her father. Lynch argued that the film can stand on its own without a viewer having seen the television series, but in reality, although it is a chronological prequel, the film is the culmination of the series. Like the television version, it is a presentation of mood more than plot, but unfortunately the goofiness is gone, replaced in large part by kinkiness. The good humor has given way to unpleasantness and the mystery exchanged for voyeurism.

Twin Peaks: Fire Walk with Me is not a great film, but it does give a feeling of completion to a fascinating television series. Despite everything, Lynch's films are always intriguing. By Hollywood standards, that is innovative.

Beverley Bare Buehrer

Reviews

Boxoffice. November, 1992, p. R-82.
Chicago Tribune. August 28, 1992, VII, p. 33.
The Christian Science Monitor. September 1, 1992, p. 11.
Entertainment Weekly. September 11, 1992, p. 74.
The Hollywood Reporter. May 18, 1992, p. 5.
Los Angeles Times. September 1, 1992, Calendar, p. 3.
The New York Times. August 29, 1992, p. 13.
Time. September 7, 1992, p. 69.
USA Today. August 31, 1992, p. 4D.
Variety. May 18, 1992, p. 2.

UNDER SIEGE

Production: Arnon Milchan, Steven Seagal, and Steven Reuther, in association with Regency Enterprises, Le Studio Canal Plus, and Alcor Films; released by Warner Bros.
Direction: Andrew Davis
Screenplay: J. F. Lawton
Cinematography: Frank Tidy
Editing: Robert A. Ferretti, Dennis Virkler, Don Brochu, and Dov Hoenig
Production design: Bill Kenney
Art direction: Bill Hiney
Set decoration: Rick Gentz
Set design: Al Manzer
Casting: Pamela Basker
Sound: Scott Smith
Costume design: Richard Bruno
Stunt coordination: Conrad E. Palmisano
Music: Gary Chang
MPAA rating: R
Running time: 102 minutes

Principal characters:

Casey Ryback	Steven Seagal
William Strannix	Tommy Lee Jones
Commander Krill	Gary Busey
Jordan Tate	Erika Eleniak
Captain Adams	Patrick O'Neal

With the fall of the Berlin Wall in 1990 and the opening of the borders in Eastern Europe came the unofficial end to what had been known as the Cold War. An undeclared war between the two superpowers, the United States and the Soviet Union, the Cold War centered a planet's fear on nuclear war, as arsenals grew and nations became less and less trusting of one another. The United States found the need to establish two certain weapons in order to keep up: nuclear armed battleships and the Central Intelligence Agency (CIA). With the Cold War over, however, the need for these two weapons decreases.

This brief historical perspective serves as the backdrop to the mainstream action/adventure film *Under Siege*, starring Steven Seagal. Seagal first made his film and box-office splash in *Above the Law* (1988), which he cowrote and produced. An unknown at the time, Seagal soared to stardom as he brought a curious mix to American film audiences. Armed with Chuck Norris' martial arts talents and Arnold Schwarzenegger's low-key manner, Seagal carved his own niche in Hollywood and continued to gain popularity. *Under Siege* broke box-office records during its first weekend of release and went on to become yet another smash success. It even garnered two Academy Award nominations, for best sound and best sound effects editing. Seagal's other films, *Hard to Kill* (1990), *Marked for Death* (1990), and *Out for Justice* (1991), were also box-office winners, giving him a level of Hollywood bankability in the early 1990's equaled only by the likes of Tom Cruise and Kevin Costner.

What makes Seagal successful is his low-key approach to modern male machismo. Seagal's soft-spoken characters possess a dry wit and a straightforward method of violence and revenge. Although Seagal portrays characters who will not turn their backs on automatic weapons, they prefer to use their hands and feet to inflict their pain, which results in an intensity that audiences seem to enjoy.

In *Under Siege*, Seagal does again what he does best, although this time the film shamelessly steals its basic premise from the hugely successful Bruce Willis action/adventure film *Die Hard* (1988), which was directed by John McTiernan. *Die Hard* pits one man alone in a skyscraper against a group of armed terrorists who hold several hostages and attempt to steal an unspeakable amount of money. In *Under Siege*, Seagal stars as a cook on a decommissioned Naval nuclear battleship who finds himself alone against a group of armed terrorists who are seeking to sell the ship's cargo of nuclear warheads to foreign "investors."

Once the viewer gets past the obvious *Die Hard* parallels, the setting is almost enough to carry *Under Siege*. Set on the decommissioned USS *Missouri* (and actually filmed on the permanently moored USS *Alabama* in Mobile, Alabama), *Under Siege* works because audiences recognize the realistic setting within which it maneuvers. Director Andrew Davis, who also directed Seagal in *Above the Law*, attempts to invoke realism at every possible turn in the film, even to the extent of using real footage of the actual decommissioning ceremonies of the USS *Missouri* at Pearl Harbor. President George Bush even makes an appearance in the film, providing an eerie, almost awkward moment for the audience, which had come to be entertained by escapist amusement, not to be reminded of the political atmosphere of the United States at the time of the film's release.

The band of terrorists who take over the naval battleship is led by former CIA operative William Strannix (Tommy Lee Jones), who is out for revenge against his former employers: They had ordered him assassinated when his top-secret operation was no longer essential to the agency. Fresh from an Academy Award nomination for Best Supporting Actor in Oliver Stone's *JFK* (1991), Jones seems to steal some of the spotlight from Seagal in *Under Siege*, a rare occurrence for the action star, whose films usually feature unknowns in the supporting roles. Jones employs his characteristic sardonic wit as he plays Strannix with an intriguing blend of cunning and psychotic recklessness. A veteran actor, Jones finally broke free from the middle ranks of Hollywood actors with *JFK* and achieved well-deserved mainstream success with *Under Siege*.

Pitted against Strannix is Seagal's character, Casey Ryback, a low-ranking cook with a colorful military history. A former Navy SEAL and top-level combat operative in Vietnam, Ryback was demoted to cook after striking an officer. Although he has gained a reputation as a troublemaker, Ryback is popular with the sailors as he dishes out one-liners with his stew. Ryback also has an ally in Captain Adams (Patrick O'Neal), the ship's commander, who appreciates Ryback's military accomplishments and keeps him on as his personal cook.

Strannix is joined in his diabolical plot to take over the battleship and sell off the ship's nuclear arsenal by crooked *Missouri* officer Commander Krill (Gary Busey), whose involvement enables Strannix and his band of terrorists to bypass normal procedure and land on the ship. Busey, like Jones, is also a veteran screen actor who relished the opportunity to costar in a mainstream hit. Best known for his Oscar-nominated portrayal of the late Buddy Holly in *The Buddy Holly Story* (1978) and for his widely publicized motorcycle accident that fueled debate about California's mandatory helmet law, Busey is well known in Hollywood and is a familiar face to audiences.

The power-hungry and opportunistic Krill sees the final voyage of the USS *Missouri* as the perfect chance to get revenge on the commanders who never gave him enough respect, as well as to earn a little extra cash on the side. Recently decommissioned and sailing with a skeleton crew, the *Missouri* is vulnerable to Krill's betrayal, as suspicions are low and the sailors and commanders are unprepared. Krill arranges for a "surprise" birthday celebration for Captain Adams as he sidesteps normal procedure and allows a helicopter of entertainers and caterers to land on the battleship. The only surprise that these entertainers have planned, however, is terror. Strannix and his followers execute the commanding officers and lock the rest of the crew in the hold of the ship. Strannix and Krill, having carried out what they believe to be a flawless operation, continue on to the second stage of their plan, unaware that Ryback, confined in a meat locker by Krill before the helicopter landed, has escaped and is plotting a one-man assault on their orchestrated plot. As Krill and Strannix head for their rendezvous with an Italian submarine that will carry off the payload of missiles, Ryback contacts the Pentagon crisis center and proceeds on his mission of retaking the ship and its cargo. He is aided along the way by Jordan Tate (Erika Eleniak), a Playboy centerfold brought along by the terrorists as part of their cover, and a group of sailors that eluded Strannix when he took over the ship. Together, they take on the terrorists and rescue the missiles before they get into the wrong hands.

Although *Under Siege* is a formula big-name action film, there is an interesting psychological aspect that deserves discussion. The characters of Strannix and Ryback are more than worthwhile adversaries; they are two sides of the same coin. Both characters were trained to be top operatives, Strannix with the CIA and Ryback with the Navy. Both Strannix and Ryback were given the kind of top-level training that is crucial to the maintaining of the United States' self-image as an international political and military force. The difference between them is a simple difference in faith—Ryback has some and Strannix does not. The film makes no mistake in pointing out that, although the benefits of having such highly trained personnel are tangible, the dangers are serious as well. In the end, the film is eager to show that the only thing that separates Strannix and Ryback is patriotism, which must always win out in the end. Although the portrayals in this film are obviously aimed at endorsing pride in the American military, *Under Siege* still raised the issue of how much power the CIA continued to have in the immediate post-Cold War age and of whether the world still needed to have floating nuclear arsenals on the high seas.

Under Siege is, in the end, a Steven Seagal vehicle for violence, male ego boosting, and box-office dollars. Yet, in 1992, it served as a disturbing yet fascinating reflection of what the United States had become and reminded American viewers that history cannot be simply forgotten because the dangers did not seem to be as prevalent after the end of the Cold War.

Catherine R. Springer

Reviews

Boxoffice. December, 1992, p. R-88.
Chicago Tribune. October 9, 1992, VII, p. 32.
Entertainment Weekly. October 23, 1992, p. 44.
The Hollywood Reporter. October 9, 1992, p. 6.
Los Angeles Times. October 9, 1992, p. F4.
The New York Times. October 9, 1992, p. B9.
The New Yorker. LXVIII, November 16, 1992, p. 130.
San Francisco Chronicle. October 9, 1992, p. C3.
Variety. October 9, 1992, p. 2.
The Washington Post. October 9, 1992, p. B7.

UNFORGIVEN

Production: Clint Eastwood (AA) for Malpaso; released by Warner Bros.
Direction: Clint Eastwood (AA)
Screenplay: David Webb Peoples
Cinematography: Jack N. Green
Editing: Joel Cox (AA)
Production design: Henry Bumstead
Art direction: Rick Roberts and Adrian Gorton
Set design: James J. Murakami
Set decoration: Janice Blackie-Goodine
Casting: Phyllis Huffman and Stuart Aikins
Sound: Rob Young
Men's wardrobe supervision: Carla Hetland
Women's wardrobe supervision: Joanne Hansen
Music: Lennie Niehaus
MPAA rating: R
Running time: 130 minutes

Principal characters:

William Munny .... Clint Eastwood
Little Bill Daggett .... Gene Hackman (AA)
Ned Logan .... Morgan Freeman
English Bob .... Richard Harris
The "Schofield Kid" .... Jaimz Woolvett
W. W. Beauchamp .... Saul Rubinek
Strawberry Alice .... Frances Fisher
Delilah Fitzgerald .... Anna Thomson
Quick Mike .... David Mucci
Davey Bunting .... Rob Campbell
Skinny Dubois .... Anthony James
Little Sue .... Tara Dawn Frederick
Silky .... Beverley Elliott
Faith .... Liisa Repo-Martell
Crow Creek Kate .... Josie Smith
Will Munny .... Shane Meier
Penny Munny .... Aline Levasseur

When *Unforgiven* was released in the summer of 1992, it was met with critical acclaim and popular success. In the months following, it was accorded the kind of wide recognition rarely given to a reflective genre work before the passage of years provides the proper context for rediscovery. By the end of April, 1993, it had grossed more than $92,000,000 and received awards from almost every critics group, the

Golden Globes, and the Directors Guild (with Clint Eastwood's direction and Gene Hackman's supporting role winning most frequently), culminating in four Academy Awards (Best Picture, Director, Supporting Actor, and Editing) and nominations for Original Screenplay, Cinematography, Art Direction and Set Decoration, Sound, and Eastwood as Actor. As Eastwood observed, this was a rare occasion when the Academy agreed with Cahiers du Cinema in its choice of best film of the year, and many would agree that it was a rare deserving winner in that category.

The greatest glory of *Unforgiven*, however, may lie in the years ahead. There are strong intimations within the work that this single film at once closes one phase and opens another in the career of Clint Eastwood. More startlingly, it restores classical grace and moral beauty to the Western, a genre which was once cinema's most eloquent and enlightened but which has been abused for decades by coarsening, facetiousness, and revisionism. Contemporary audiences who do not know the Westerns of earlier years may be surprised at the intelligence and seriousness of *Unforgiven*, but the film is within a long and rich tradition. Such notable works as *The Gunfighter* (1950), *Shane* (1953), and *Man of the West* (1958), for example, all show that the hero, cast in a certain light or pushed by circumstance, can be a cold-blooded killer who is pulled by conflicting impulses to turn away from violence or back to it. The mature Western is not about good guys in white hats and bad guys in black hats, it does not romanticize violence, and it does not consist of one action scene after another. Traditionally (though this is not a given), a dramatic situation develops which is finally resolved in a shoot-out, but this confrontation is not one from which the characters move away easily after it is over; these resolutions tend to be very cathartic, much more so than the climaxes of most films. Further, women are far more central to the classical Western's intention than is generally realized. The iconography and conventions of the genre may seem simple and limited, but if respected, they are marvelously flexible and afford great freedom to the artist. *Unforgiven*, which presents especially challenging and provocative variations on its archetypes, proves all of this once again.

On its face, the story in David Webb Peoples' screenplay is admirably lean and straightforward. In Big Whiskey, Wyoming, in 1880, prostitute Delilah Fitzgerald (Anna Thomson) is violently attacked by a cowboy, cut up, and left with scars. The local sheriff, Little Bill Daggett (Gene Hackman), a pragmatist with much harsh frontier experience, decides that an appropriate punishment for the cowboy, Quick Mike (David Mucci), and his more innocent though culpable partner Davey (Rob Campbell) will be a payment of horses to the owner of the brothel-saloon, Skinny Dubois (Anthony James). This enrages the woman's fellow prostitutes, who, led by strong-willed Strawberry Alice (Frances Fisher), raise a one-thousand-dollar bounty on the lives of the two cowboys. Among those drawn by the prospect of this money is the Schofield Kid (Jaimz Woolvett), whose youthful bravado conceals the fact that he is very nearsighted and could not do the job alone. He solicits the help of William Munny (Eastwood), a former outlaw who is now a struggling Kansas hog farmer. Redeemed by the love of his late wife Claudia, Munny had promised her not to take up his guns again, but the prospect of a better life for their two children overcomes his reluctance. He enlists Ned Logan (Morgan Freeman), his old partner who has also turned to a peaceful life, and the three men ride out for Big Whiskey.

Also pursuing the bounty is the flamboyant gunman English Bob (Richard Harris), who arrives in town accompanied by his biographer, W. W. Beauchamp (Saul Rubinek). The sheriff, who enforces a no-firearms-in-town policy and knows Bob from other times and other towns, gets the drop on him with the help of his deputies and brutally beats him. Later, Daggett learns of the arrival of Munny, Logan, and the Kid. Munny has become gravely ill on the journey and sits alone in the saloon while his partners go up to see the prostitutes. Weak, confused, and uncertain, he handles a confrontation with Daggett badly and the sheriff beats him also, then lets him crawl out into the street, where his companions help him leave town. Will believes that he is close to death, but he recovers and the three men go after the cowboys. Ned finds himself unable to go through with the killings, but Munny kills Davey and the Kid kills Mike. Afterward, they learn that Ned has been captured and that the sheriff has killed him. Sending the Kid on to Kansas with the money, Will rides back to town in a nocturnal rainstorm, walks into the saloon, murders Skinny Dubois in cold blood, and kills the sheriff and four deputies in a shoot-out. Riding out, he threatens further retaliation on the town if Ned is not buried properly, if any prostitutes are further harmed, or if there are attempted reprisals against him.

Plainly, *Unforgiven* is centrally about killing and violence, subjects which it treats with great insight as well as effective realism. Characters do not always die quickly or easily here, and the film sanctions no killing—not for vengeance or bounty, not by sheriff or outlaw, not by man or woman. The first actual death takes place late in the film and is very significant, for it involves the protracted killing of Davey, who is ambushed and slowly bleeds to death. The sequence interweaves a number of interesting elements. Davey, who had held Delilah while Mike cut her but then tried to stop his partner once he saw what was happening, is one of the film's most sympathetic characters: Regretful of the incident, he had tried to give a pony to the girl in an early, poignant scene. (In a beautiful irony, Delilah herself, clearly sorry for Davey in that scene, is never as anxious for revenge as her protective fellow prostitutes.) Additionally, self-possessed Ned, on whom Will always leaned, finds himself unable to shoot in a beautifully projected moment of self-revelation. Finally, Will, who has just been seen at his most tender and sensitive in the previous scene with Delilah, begins to regain his self-assurance by executing the messy killing. Therefore, the context is rich with challenging ambiguities that make an easy response impossible.

This kind of treatment extends to the other killings as well, and to the relationship of the characters to their violent acts. The Schofield Kid, for example, is a wonderful variation on a familiar type. His boasts of five earlier killings are, unsurprisingly, not true, but everything else about him is fresh, beginning with his myopia. He does not find himself unable to kill Mike, as might be expected, nor does this first killing make him become more violent than the protagonist, as often happens. Instead, he realizes the seriousness of taking a life and decides never to do so again. Even more fascinating is the villain Little Bill Daggett, powerfully incarnated by Gene Hackman in a much-honored performance which captures all the conviction that ambivalences of personal and social morality can have. Some of the character's actions, such as prohibiting firearms in town, are consistent with being a sheriff and evoke the heroes of other films, and he is absolutely right in seeking to prevent the killings of the cowboys for bounty. At the same time, his lack of justice in the opening sequence sets in motion all the action that follows, even though his motive seems to be a rejection of further violence ("Haven't you seen enough blood for one night?" he asks Alice with fierce sincerity). Moreover, his excessively brutal treatment of the bounty hunters plays intriguingly against his affability and completely contradicts his expressed sense of fairness and his status as a lawman.

The most interesting character, however, is William Munny. In a starkly beautiful climax, all trace of sentiment is removed from the presentation of the character. The audience learns—and he himself affirms it—that in the old days he killed women and children as well as other men. Executing the wounded and helpless Daggett, he is remorseless. Strangely, while the idea of becoming a killer again reminds him of his past deeds and is clearly the thing that makes him sick, his return to killing makes him whole again—capable, confident, physically sound. It would be comforting to believe that, even as he recovers, he is destroyed spiritually, but Eastwood's realization of the film and portrayal of the character—who resonates so strongly with the screen persona that he had been developing since his films with directors Sergio Leone and Don Siegel, to whom the film is dedicated—do not encourage such an untroubling response. Rather, the character seems to be a divided soul, a genuine tragic hero (rare in twentieth century art) whose moment of catharsis—the stunningly staged, filmed, and edited saloon shoot-out—brings him in a circle to what he was before Claudia. The man who leaves Big Whiskey at the end is cold, pitiless, and ruthless—a murderer. Still, he is also the man seen before: a man who could suffer guilt, try bravely not to begin drinking again, be touchingly loyal to the memory of his wife, be concerned for the future of his children, be comforting and kind to the cut whore, sit shivering in the saloon in lonely illness, be heartbreakingly vulnerable in his closeness to his own death, and articulate a self-aware understanding of what it means to take a life. He has won deep empathy, and what he becomes as the circle closes cannot, and should not, take away this empathy. For if life is sacred, as the cruel action of *Unforgiven* suggests, then the inseparability of Munny's light and dark sides is emblematic of this sacredness.

This idea suggests a key to the film's profound concern, alluded to almost poetically in a written prologue and epilogue, with the relationship between Will and Claudia, which, more than that between Will and the antagonist Daggett or Will and his friend Ned, is the story's central one. In Westerns, women give balance to men and are given balance in return. (The extent to which this is and is not true in the relationships of the various prostitutes with the various men in the story enriches that part of the text.) Nevertheless, what Will had once been, as well as the better man he could be, was part of what drew Claudia in the first place. So it is not simply for women to show what goodness is—they have their own dark mysteries to unravel and their own stories to be told. One feels that Eastwood could tell them, too, in his films yet to be made, for Claudia's absence shadows the action with a haunting presence.

Like other great Westerns, *Unforgiven* carries its ideas in an unpretentious frame which harmonizes physical beauty and a narrative of mounting tension. Superbly cast and played, with evocative locations and an especially fine job of production design by the great Henry Bumstead, it boasts many magical moments of *mise-en-scène* enhanced by the painterly moodiness of Jack N. Green's cinematography (such as Munny's final ride into town—filmed subjectively but with the camera finally appearing to liberate from his point of view as in a Kenji Mizoguchi film), wonderful inflections in dialogue delivery (especially in the tense first meeting of Munny and Daggett), rich humor (such as Munny's initial attempt to mount his horse), and an appreciation of contrasts in mood (the reflective interludes which weave in close to the killings). One sequence that shows the film's qualities especially well—notably Eastwood's thoughtful direction and Joel Cox's graceful editing—involves the wait beneath a tree on an open plain as one of the prostitutes, Little Sue (Tara Dawn Frederick), rides from town to bring the bounty to Munny and the Kid. The images concisely establish the relationship of the tree to the town and oncoming rider, then gradually, after establishing a rhythm between long shots and closer ones of the two waiting men, begin to shift focus subtly to a more intimate exchange between the two men. This exchange is composed mostly in alternating shots as the Kid drinks and slumps on the ground, his bravado dissolving before our eyes (in a remarkable piece of acting by Jaimz Woolvett which allows the audience to witness the stages of a transformation almost line by line), while the more outwardly composed Munny eloquently echoes with a heartbreaking reflectiveness the other's thoughts about taking a life.

In the past, Eastwood as a director has sometimes seemed more at ease with casual or discursive narratives such as *Bronco Billy* (1980), *Honkytonk Man* (1982), or *Bird* (1988) than with the action films that fans of the actor have wanted from him. In the maturity which this Western displays, however, he confidently embraces both the personal aspect of those films, which had been his best, and the majesty of a classical cinema which few other American directors still practice at creating. *Unforgiven* is the apotheosis of Eastwood, forever deepening one's sense of the action hero that he has been while initiating a journey into the high country of new artistic challenges.

Blake Lucas

Reviews

Boxoffice. October, 1992, p. R-68.

Chicago Tribune. August 7, 1992, VII, p. 27.

Entertainment Weekly. August 14, 1992, p. 38.
Film Comment. XXVIII, September, 1992, p. 12.
The Hollywood Reporter. July 31, 1992, p. 7.
Los Angeles Times. August 7, 1992, p. F1.
The New York Times. August 7, 1992, p. B1.
Newsweek. August 10, 1992, p. 52.
Variety. July 31, 1992, p. 2.
The Washington Post. August 7, 1992, p. C1.

UNLAWFUL ENTRY

Production: Charles Gordon for Largo Entertainment, in association with JVC Entertainment; released by Twentieth Century-Fox
Direction: Jonathan Kaplan
Screenplay: Lewis Colick; based on a story by George D. Putnam, John Katchmer, and Colick
Cinematography: Jamie Anderson
Editing: Curtiss Clayton
Production design: Lawrence G. Paull
Art direction: Bruce Crone
Set decoration: Rick Simpson
Set design: Dawn Snyder
Casting: Jackie Burch
Sound: Glenn Anderson
Costume design: April Ferry
Music: James Horner
MPAA rating: R
Running time: 111 minutes

Principal characters:

Michael Carr .... Kurt Russell
Officer Pete Davis .... Ray Liotta
Karen Carr .... Madeleine Stowe
Officer Roy Cole .... Roger E. Mosley
Roger Graham .... Ken Lerner
Penny .... Deborah Offner
Jerome Lurie .... Carmen Argenziano
Captain Hayes .... Andy Romano
Ernie Pike .... Johnny Ray McGhee
Leon .... Dino Anello

Early in Jonathan Kaplan's *Unlawful Entry*, Officer Pete Davis (Ray Liotta) tells the woman (Madeleine Stowe) he has befriended that life as a Los Angeles police officer is unimaginably violent. In a brutally honest voice, he says, "It's not a TV show out there, Mrs. Carr. Reality would scare a lot of people." If this highly derivative urban thriller is to be believed, then equally frightening are the dispositions of the police officers who "serve and protect."

The filmgoers of 1992 hardly needed a motion picture to tell them about the fragile psyches of the Los Angeles Police Department (LAPD). One needed only to watch the nightly news or an astute neighbor's home videotape. Fortunately for its producers, *Unlawful Entry* was released a mere six weeks after the Los Angeles riots, a nationally covered tragedy sparked by the acquittal of the officers who beat motorist Rodney King. Consequently, the film, drawing on headlines, was ultimately more enticing than it actually deserved to be. Even the usually reliable Kaplan, who always seems to add something fresh to all varieties of genre films, could not prevent the film from becoming another member of the psycho-on-the-loose genre.

The box-office success of Adrian Lyne's *Fatal Attraction* (1987) sparked new life into a type of narrative that follows the terrifying transformation of a trusted acquaintance into a deranged killer. By preying on filmgoers' fear that their secure and stable world can be torn apart by someone as innocuous as the local police officer, these films are safe bets to be not only viscerally chilling but highly commercial as well. Filmmakers were working with the genre as early as 1963, when director Joseph Losey made *The Servant*. That film is based on a Harold Pinter screenplay in which a butler (Dirk Bogarde) gained the upper hand on his employer by taking advantage of that man's sexual weaknesses. Despite the early experimentation, this narrative type only became popular in the 1980's, as American filmmakers have increasingly turned to the genre in order to reflect their country's changing political and economic mood.

In the waning years of the Reagan era, Joseph Ruben directed Terry O'Quinn in *The Stepfather* (1987), which took a lethal stab at the American family so proudly reestablished by Ronald Reagan and his administration. O'Quinn played the perfect new husband for a widow (Shelley Hack) and an ideal stepfather to her teenage daughter. A real estate man who sold family values as well as suburban dwellings, O'Quinn's character showed his true colors when his new family was beset by ordinary domestic tensions; the man was really a serial killer with a history of slaughtering fatherless families. In later years, as Reagan's policies crumbled, more films were released that took the pure American family and revealed it to be a feeding ground for malignant souls who were more adept with knives than with spatulas. Yuppie life-styles were attacked in American films by lunatics who made it clear that no one—not even the happiest, wealthiest, most stable family—was safe from evil. Director John Schlesinger unleashed a deranged tenant (Michael Keaton) on new homeowners (Matthew Modine and Melanie Griffith) in *Pacific Heights* (1990), forever making landlords suspicious of their tenants. The wealthy family in Curtis Hansen's *The Hand That Rocks the Cradle* (1992; reviewed in this volume) falls under siege from a revenge-crazed nanny (Rebecca De Mornay) who plots to steal away the brood of a new mother (Annabella Sciorra).

Unlawful Entry, in which the happy home of Michael and Karen Carr (Kurt Russell and Madeleine Stowe) is ravaged by a police officer, is another initiate in the genre. Michael Carr, a businessperson who searches for investors for nightclubs, and his wife, Karen, a schoolteacher, are alone one evening when an intruder (Johnny Ray McGhee) enters their unsecured and heavily mortgaged Los Angeles home. The man attacks Michael and escapes after threatening Karen with a knife. Officer Pete Davis (Liotta) and his partner, Officer Roy Cole (Roger E. Mosley), soon arrive on the scene and recommend the installation of an alarm system. Davis becomes friendly with the Carrs and helps them to select such a system. Davis tells the Carrs about the brutality of police work and asks an interested Michael to accompany him on a midnight patrol.

The next evening, Michael rides with Davis and Cole. After dropping off his partner, Davis takes Michael to the tenement where he has tracked down Ernie Pike, the intruder that broke into the Carr home. Davis offers to let Michael beat the man up. When Michael refuses, Davis tries to goad him into doing it, suggesting Michael is deficient in protecting his wife. Finally, Davis severely beats Pike himself. Later, an unnerved Michael describes the incident to an unsympathetic Karen, who is glad that Davis has brought the criminal to justice. When Davis comes the next day to apologize to Karen, he continues to gather her sympathies by revealing his physical and emotional wounds from police work.

Michael, still spooked by Davis' show of brutality the previous evening, becomes upset when the off-duty officer attends a party for Michael's new dance club. Michael demands that he leave and stay away from both him and his wife. Davis appears at Karen's school the next day, and the two go to a bar, where Davis mines for information about Karen's marriage. A flattered Karen confides in Davis, who becomes further enamored.

Later, at a business dinner, Michael discovers that his credit cards have all been canceled and that a boot has been placed on his car for outstanding traffic tickets. Michael fears that Davis is trying to sabotage him. When he hears that his investors have been scared away by Davis, acting as a security expert, Michael's lawyer (Ken Lerner) advises his client to bribe the officer. Davis refuses, and when Cole tells Davis to leave the Carrs alone or he will recommend him for a psychiatric exam, Davis kills Cole, contriving to make the murder look like a botched drug bust.

When narcotics agents invade the Carrs' home and discover cocaine, Michael is thrown in jail for drug trafficking. A prior conviction leads to an unusually high bail, and Karen is left alone and vulnerable. Davis, after visiting Michael in jail and claiming that Karen is now his, goes to the desperate Karen, but she refuses to see him. He murders Karen's schoolteacher friend (Deborah Offner) and finds his way into the house. Davis tries to seduce Karen; when she fights back, he begins to rape her. Michael, released from jail by his lawyer, arrives just in time to do violent battle with Davis. As Karen watches, Michael kills Davis with almost a dozen gunshots, and the couple waits for sane officers to arrive.

The lackadaisical script for *Unlawful Entry* was created by three television veterans: George D. Putnam, John Katchmer, and Lewis Colick. Based on the implausibilities sprinkled throughout the film, they seem unable to create an effective narrative for a longer piece of material. The cracked psyche of Officer Davis is never given a cause in the film, except for the broad explanation that the brutality of police work has driven him to violence. This does not explain, however, why his psychological breakdown comes with his exposure to the Carrs. Surely, as a police veteran, he has dealt previously with home invasions and come in contact with other beautiful, vulnerable women. The success of the narrative is based on the assumption that the Carrs, who enjoy an apparently healthy marriage, do not discuss with each other their solo meetings with Davis. This assumption stretches credibility and, consequently, severely weakens the film.

Director Kaplan works hard to imbue the film with immediacy; his pace is quick and forceful and his camera, cutting frantically between actors, attempts to weed out underlying tensions. Unfortunately, his actors are not up for the challenge. Kaplan, who guided Jodie Foster to an Academy Award for *The Accused* (1988) and coaxed critically acclaimed performances out of Bonnie Bedelia and Mary Stuart Masterson in *Heart Like a Wheel* (1983) and *Immediate Family* (1989), respectively, fails to solicit anything surprising here. Liotta, so effective as the violent husband in Jonathan Demme's *Something Wild* (1986) and as the crazed mobster in Martin Scorsese's *GoodFellas* (1990), makes Davis a bland, one-dimensional villain; his blue eyes flash with evil but little else. Stowe, forever playing the prize for two competitive men (the 1987 release *Stakeout* and 1990's *Revenge*), provides her usual wispy theatrics, and Russell is merely serviceable in the modest role of hero. Perhaps Kaplan's greatest sin in a film that attempts to criticize the brutality of contemporary society, however, is providing a resolution so gratuitously violent that it renders his message meaningless.

Greg Changnon

Reviews

Boxoffice. August/September, 1992, p. R-65.
Chicago Tribune. June 26, 1992, VII, p. 27.
The Christian Science Monitor. July 14, 1992, p. 11.
Entertainment Weekly. July 10, 1992, CXXVI, p. 41.
The Hollywood Reporter. CCCXXII, June 22, 1992, p. 8.
Los Angeles Times. June 26, 1992, p. F1.
The New York Times. June 26, 1992, CXLI, p. B4.
The New Yorker. July 13, 1992, p. 67.
Time. CXL, July 13, 1992, p. 81.
Variety. CCXXXVI, June 22, 1992, p. 4.

USED PEOPLE

Production: Peggy Rajski for Lawrence Gordon and Largo Entertainment, in association with JVC Entertainment; released by Twentieth Century-Fox
Direction: Beeban Kidron
Screenplay: Todd Graff; based on material from his stage work *The Grandma Plays*
Cinematography: David Watkin
Editing: John Tintori
Production design: Stuart Wurtzel
Art direction: Gregory Paul Keen
Set decoration: Hilton Rosemarin
Sound: Douglas Ganton
Costume design: Marilyn Vance-Straker
Music: Rachel Portman
MPAA rating: PG-13
Running time: 116 minutes

Principal characters:

Pearl	Shirley MacLaine
Joe	Marcello Mastroianni
Bibby	Kathy Bates
Norma	Marcia Gay Harden
Freida	Jessica Tandy
Becky	Sylvia Sidney
Jack	Bob Dishy
Paolo	Charles Cioffi
Swee' Pea	Matthew Branton
Frank	Joe Pantoliano

With the traditional family of father, mother, and children becoming less the norm in American society, *Used People* seeks to examine how a family manages to stay together despite the often harsh words that can be said. *Used People* offers a glimpse of the Berman family and shows how they survive as a family in Queens, New York, in 1969.

The film actually begins in an apartment in 1946. Just as Pearl (Shirley MacLaine) has given up hope of keeping her husband's dinner from getting ruined, Jack (Bob Dishy) finally arrives home late. A man of few words who cannot express his feelings, Jack asks his wife to dance with him right there in the kitchen. Pearl finds this request unusual but goes along with the moment. After a few rounds of the kitchen, Jack rather clumsily lets her slip. Embarrassed, he sits and eats his meal in silence.

In 1969, with the sudden death of Jack, Pearl is left alone and confused. The entire family—including Pearl's daughters, Bibby (Kathy Bates) and Norma (Marcia Gay Harden), and her mother, Freida (Jessica Tandy)—comes to her apartment after the funeral. Such a large gathering suffocates Pearl, who retires to her room. Later that day, a stranger presents himself at the apartment door asking for Pearl, saying that he is a friend of Jack. She allows Joe Meledandri (Marcello Mastroianni) into her bedroom. Joe explains his circumstances and then shocks the entire family, most of whom are in the bedroom with them, by asking Pearl out for coffee.

Joe takes Pearl across Queens to his brother-in-law's restaurant. There Joe explains that Jack came to the bar one night back in 1946 and explained that he was going to leave Pearl. Joe was to have delivered a note and some money to Pearl after Jack's departure. Pearl listens in disbelief while Joe retells the story of that night. Joe suggested that Jack dance with his wife when he returned home. When Joe followed him home and watched Pearl and Jack dance, however, he unexpectedly fell in love with Pearl. With little formality, Joe now expresses his enduring passion for Pearl, who begins to see him as a threat to her security.

Pearl rushes out of the restaurant, as this sudden revelation is more than she is able to handle. Busying herself in looking after her family and keeping house, Pearl tries to deny what has happened in her life. Joe attempts to speak to her on many occasions. First, he waits outside her apartment, but she refuses to speak to him. Then he offers to teach her grandson, Swee' Pea (Matthew Branton), how to play the accordion.

Joe invites Pearl and her family to a meal at the family restaurant. During the evening, Joe's brother-in-law Frank (Joe Pantoliano), who is married with one daughter, tries to arrange a meeting with Norma at some bar on a Friday night. Norma shows minimal interest. Swee' Pea, finding out that Frank is a psychiatrist, wants to show him that his dead grandfather Jack protects him from everything and that the young boy is like Superman. Frank is taken to a railway track, where Swee' Pea places his hand on the electrified third rail but is not hurt.

Unfortunately, the dinner offers Bibby and Norma an opportunity to start a battle of words. Norma accuses Bibby of being fat, and Bibby accuses Norma of playing roles as if she were in a motion picture. When Norma swears, Joe becomes extremely angry and chastises her for using such language, while Pearl interjects that her daughter can say what she likes. At this point, everyone gets up and leaves.

Distressed by the events of the previous evening, Joe sends a gift of an air conditioner to Pearl. Begrudgingly, Pearl accepts the gift, but the motor runs dead a few minutes after the unit is installed. Joe volunteers to fix the air conditioner, and he mentions to Pearl that Swee' Pea is spending time with Frank. Shocked at this news, Pearl begins to believe that her family is disintegrating around her because of her involvement with Joe.

One hot afternoon while playing in the park, Pearl wades into a small pool to retrieve Swee' Pea's ball. Without warning, Joe picks up the ball, exchanges a few pleasantries, and then kisses Pearl. From that moment on, Pearl is a different woman. Norma discovers that Swee' Pea is meeting with Frank and forbids her son from going to see him again. Swee' Pea tries to commit suicide by jumping off the roof of an apartment building across from Joe's. Joe, alerted by the neighbors, grabs the boy a moment before Swee' Pea jumps.

This event causes Norma and Swee' Pea to discuss the pain that they have both experienced since Norma's baby died and her husband abandoned them. Pearl thanks Joe for his heroic deed and accepts his proposal of marriage. Seeing her mother create a new life out of her old one, Bibby decides to go to California and seek a new life of her own there, much to her mother's astonishment.

Twenty-three years earlier, Joe had seen Pearl dance with her husband, Jack. Joe both saved the marriage and fell in love with Pearl. This enduring love eventually causes the entire Berman family to examine their own values and relationships. In the end, Joe serves as a catalyst for helping these individuals to find themselves and thus construct a stronger, more loving family.

Used People manages to convey the essence of this typical New York family, bordered on one side by religion and on the other by family feuds. While the Bermans' common bond is their Jewish background, this closeness tends to cause a certain claustrophobia within the family. The Berman family is used to talking about everything but feelings, and such a family is often kept together through guilt and manipulation. Pearl's daughters both love and despise their mother. When Joe does the unthinkable and asks Pearl to go out for a coffee on the day of her husband's funeral, the close family ties, both good and bad, are immediately challenged.

Used People is ultimately about resolution. Pearl needs to resolve her feelings about a marriage that denied her most of her dreams. Norma and Bibby, whose marriages have both ended in divorce, seek some kind of help and guidance from their mother but meet only indifference and hostility. Into this complex and seemingly unresolvable situation comes a stranger who can work miracles. From the moment that Joe enters the funeral party and asks for Pearl, Marcello Mastroianni's performance galvanizes the film in the same way that his character eventually galvanizes the family through love and determination.

Todd Graff's screenplay, which was adapted from his stage work *The Grandma Plays* about his Grandmother Pearl, fully explores the complex relationships that exist within this family. What makes *Used People* a more poignant family drama than most is the way in which Graff incorporates all the minor relationships into one theme. One notable relationship is that between Freida and her best friend, Becky (Sylvia Sidney). These octogenarians have been lifelong friends, and they enjoy the sparring and repartee that comes with knowing each other so well. (Jessica Tandy played the character of Idgie Threadgoode in 1991's *Fried Green Tomatoes*, and there are clear similarities between that role and her portrayal of Freida.) In contrast, Pearl and Joe are beginning a new relationship that is being built along the same lines. The message of both relationships is that close personal friendship is a worthwhile human pursuit.

A more tragic side of the Berman family is symbolized by the figure of Swee' Pea, who, because of his mother's bizarre habit of dressing like film stars, experiences immense emotional strain. Joe is the first to mention Swee' Pea's problem to

Pearl, who immediately denies that any member of her family could be in such a condition. The Bermans are plagued by misunderstanding, anger, unspoken resentment, and bitterness, yet they find a way to express themselves through Pearl's relationship with Joe.

Bringing the fictional Berman and the Meledandri families together required an unusual cast of actors. Director Beeban Kidron was able to gather together such international stars as Kathy Bates, Jessica Tandy, Marcello Mastroianni, Shirley MacLaine, and Sylvia Sidney. As a first-time director of a major motion picture, Kidron shows an unusual understanding of the chemistry that exists between these actors. It is this sensitivity that makes *Used People* such a success.

The uniqueness of *Used People* rests in the singular character of Joe Meledandri, a character that seems tailor-made for the sophisticated Mastroianni, who plays the best English-speaking role of his career. He is the one who brings true love back into Pearl's life, inspires Bibby to seek her fortune through traveling to California, and allows Norma to see how much her son Swee' Pea needs her love and attention. Joe stands for change, forgiveness, and hope.

Richard G. Cormack

Reviews

Chicago Tribune. December 25, 1992, VII, p. 16.
Entertainment Weekly. January 15, 1993, p. 36.
The Hollywood Reporter. December 11, 1992, p. 8.
Los Angeles Times. December 16, 1992, p. F7.
The New York Times. December 16, 1992.
Newsweek. CXX, December 21, 1992, p. 67.
Time. CXL, December 28, 1992, p. 65.
USA Today. December 16, 1992, p. D1.
Variety. December 11, 1992, p. 5.
The Washington Post. December 25, 1992, p. B1.

THE WATERDANCE

Production: Gale Anne Hurd and Marie Cantin for No Frills Films; released by the Samuel Goldwyn Company
Direction: Neal Jimenez and Michael Steinberg
Screenplay: Neal Jimenez
Cinematography: Mark Plummer
Editing: Jeff Freeman
Production design: Robert Ziembicki
Art direction: Ted Berner
Set decoration: Julie M. Anderson
Casting: Pam Dixon
Sound: Steve Nelson
Costume design: Isis Mussenden
Music: Michael Convertino
MPAA rating: R
Running time: 106 minutes

Principal characters:

Joel Garcia .... Eric Stoltz
Anna .... Helen Hunt
Raymond Hill .... Wesley Snipes
Bloss .... William Forsythe
Rosa .... Elizabeth Peña
Les .... William Allen Young
Pat .... Grace Zabriskie
Vernon .... Casey Stengal

It is the artist's compulsion, and sometimes the artist's curse, to want to turn every life experience into a story. In screenwriter Neal Jimenez's case, the result is the exquisitely compelling motion picture *The Waterdance*. On a camping trip in 1984, Jimenez fell and broke his neck, causing him to be paralyzed from the waist down. The five months that he spent in rehabilitation—his observations, thoughts, and feelings about the people he met there, his own future, and the relationships in his life—were the framework for his semiautobiographical screenplay. The author of *River's Edge* (1987) and *For the Boys* (1991), Jimenez aspired to direct as well as to write, and he invited his former University of California at Los Angeles film school classmate Michael Steinberg to help him with *The Waterdance*. Their original intention was that Steinberg would handle the technical aspects of film direction while Jimenez concentrated on the actors, but shortly after filming began, and with reportedly few clashes of will, the first-time codirectors found themselves sharing responsibilities rather than dividing them. Their joint efforts produced a seamless exploration of one man's ascent from fear, pain, and bitterness to eventual strength, courage, and acceptance.

The startling opening scene is a close-up of Joel Garcia (Eric Stoltz) awaking in the hospital to find himself restrained by a medieval-looking device called a "halo" and silently weeping at the morphine-clouded realization that he has broken his neck. From Joel's point of view, the standard sights and sounds of a hospital are considerably more disturbing than usual. Wheeled into the room where he will live for the next six months, Joel is greeted by his ward mate and self-appointed welcome wagon Raymond Hill (Wesley Snipes).

Raymond is a fast-talking, hard-drinking character who is trying to persuade himself that the accident which caused his paralysis was God's way of telling him to slow down and spend more time with his wife and daughter. Unfortunately, Ray will be forced to accept that his family lost interest in him long ago while he was too intoxicated to notice.

Another resident of the spinal injury ward is Bloss (William Forsythe), a loudmouthed and bigoted motorcyclist who is constantly frustrated, first by the delay of his mother, Pat (Grace Zabriskie), in securing an attorney to sue the driver who Bloss believes is responsible for his accident and then by what he is certain are racially motivated disputes over what programs should be watched on the ward's one television set. Rosa (Elizabeth Peña) and Les (William Allen Young) are the nurses who struggle to keep their patients including Vernon (Casey Stengal), who cannot speak except to call their names, as comfortable as possible given their acute physical and emotional pain.

Perhaps the most important person in Joel's life—before, during, and hopefully after his accident—is his married girlfriend, Anna (Helen Hunt). At his side from the opening shot when she reaches through the halo to stroke Joel's face, Anna does her best to help Joel deal with his loss, which is a loss for her as well. Anna smiles and reassures Joel when he comments that she seems to be "taking all this rather well," then weeps as soon as she steps outside the hospital and thus out of Joel's earshot.

Prior to the accident, Joel had been working to persuade Anna to leave her husband. Although still in love with Anna, as she is with him, Joel unhappily finds himself jealous of Anna for her ability to walk. As they struggle to resolve their differences as if everything were the same as before, they are repeatedly confronted with the unavoidable consequences of Joel's physical change.

Desperately afraid to face his own pain and sense of loss, Joel clings first to his wit. Stating emphatically that, as a writer, he does not need his legs and therefore his life should not change, Joel attempts to distance himself from the other patients with humor. When that approach wears thin, Joel turns to anger, which is most easily unleashed on those closest to him—namely Anna. When he finds that even the patient and faithful Anna can be pushed too far, Joel further jeopardizes his recovery with a dependence on painkillers.

After one of many fights, Anna does not visit for three weeks. During that time, Joel becomes more acquainted with the other patients, the procedures that he must learn to get along without the use of his legs, and his own feelings. When interviewed by a physiologist, Joel jokes that, although he has not yet begun to acknowledge his loss, he does have an emotional crash penciled into his calendar.

Among the most delicate issues that *The Waterdance* handles with honesty and seeming ease is that of sexuality. Joel attends a class taught by a paraplegic who explains frankly but sensitively and with humor that, contrary to popular assumption, enjoyable sexual relationships are still possible if one is willing to make the necessary adjustments in emotional and psychological approach, as well as in physical technique and expectations.

A touching letter from Joel brings Anna back to try to work out their problems. They spend a day away from the hospital, trying to recapture the comfort and excitement on which they so recently relied, only to be brutally reminded of and frustrated by their new limitations. Meanwhile, Ray and Bloss find themselves an unlikely team when they sneak out of the hospital to enjoy an off-limits bottle of liquor in the night air and, in an effort to slap palms, fall out of their wheelchairs and onto the lawn. Lying there, staring up at the stars, Ray reveals the source of the film's title when he tells Bloss about his recurring dream in which he can move again under water.

Eventually, these men from different backgrounds and of disparate temperaments come to work together and, if not actually to like one another, at least to respect one another and the common ground they share. Each must face his own aloneness: Bloss, when he realizes that he himself may have been at fault in the accident that paralyzed him; Ray, when he is discharged from the hospital with nowhere to go; and finally Joel, who brings himself to confess his grief tearfully only to the silent and incoherent Vernon.

Many actors were considered for the part of Joel Garcia, but Eric Stoltz won it when he arrived at a Los Angeles restaurant in a wheelchair for a meeting with Jimenez and Steinberg. Stoltz reportedly remained in the wheelchair throughout the eight-week production schedule. He was so adept at portraying Jimenez that both directors expressed surprise when they saw Stoltz out of the chair for the first time during postproduction. This was not the first time that Stoltz had portrayed a character whose spirit was challenged by his own body. He won a Golden Globe nomination for his portrayal of a teenager suffering from a disfiguring disease in *Mask* (1985). Among his other films are *Fast Times at Ridgemont High* (1982), *Some Kind of Wonderful* (1987), and *Memphis Belle* (1990).

Helen Hunt's career spans the large and small screens as well as the stage. She appeared on Broadway along with Stoltz in a production of Thornton Wilder's *Our Town*. Among Hunt's previous films are *Peggy Sue Got Married* (1986), *Project X* (1987), and *Miles from Home* (1988). In addition to the acclaim that he has received for his work on television and the Broadway stage, Wesley Snipes earned widespread attention and praise for his work in Spike Lee's *Mo' Better Blues* (1990) and the controversial *Jungle Fever* (1991). Snipes has enjoyed much variety in the roles he has played in such films as *Wildcats* (1986), *Major League* (1989), *New Jack City* (1991), and *White Men Can't Jump* (1992; reviewed in this volume). William Forsythe's film credits include *Once Upon a Time in America* (1984), *Raising Ari-*

zona (1987), *Dick Tracy* (1990), and *American Me* (1992; reviewed in this volume). Elizabeth Peña comes from a family that was involved in theater and motion pictures throughout her childhood. In addition to her many television credits, she has appeared in such diverse films as *Down and Out in Beverly Hills* (1986), *La Bamba* (1987), *Batteries Not Included* (1987), and *Jacob's Ladder* (1990).

Winner of the audience and screenwriting awards at the 1992 Sundance Film Festival, *The Waterdance* was rescued by producer Gale Anne Hurd from a maze of studio politics that could have kept it unproduced forever. Known more for action/adventure box-office smashes such as *Alien* (1979) and *The Terminator* (1984) and its sequel *Terminator II: Judgment Day* (1991), Hurd designed the company No Frills Films to promote first-time writers and directors.

Like *My Left Foot* (1989)—which even Jimenez admits to taking months to see then, upon finally seeing it, wondering why he stayed away so long—*The Waterdance*'s subject matter may be daunting, but its execution is a masterpiece of laughter, pain, and sensuality that should not be missed.

Eleah Horwitz

Reviews

Boxoffice. June, 1992, p. R-47.
Chicago Tribune. May 15, 1992, VII, p. 31.
Entertainment Weekly. May 22, 1992, p. 53.
The Hollywood Reporter. January 22, 1992, p. 5.
Los Angeles Times. May 13, 1992, p. F1.
The New York Times. May 13, 1992, p. B3.
Newsweek. CXIX, May 18, 1992, p. 66.
Rolling Stone. May 28, 1992, p. 60.
Time. CXXXIX, May 18, 1992, p. 81.
Variety. January 23, 1992, p. 2.

WAYNE'S WORLD

Production: Lorne Michaels; released by Paramount Pictures
Direction: Penelope Spheeris
Screenplay: Mike Myers, Bonnie Turner, and Terry Turner; based on characters created by Myers
Cinematography: Theo Van de Sande
Editing: Malcolm Campbell
Production design: Gregg Fonseca
Art direction: Bruce Miller
Set decoration: Jay R. Hart
Casting: Glenn Daniels
Sound: Thomas Nelson
Stunt coordination: Allan Graf
Music: J. Peter Robinson
MPAA rating: PG-13
Running time: 95 minutes

Principal characters:

Wayne Campbell .... Mike Myers
Garth Algar .... Dana Carvey
Benjamin Oliver .... Rob Lowe
Cassandra .... Tia Carrere
Noah Vanderhoff .... Brian Doyle-Murray
Stacy .... Lara Flynn Boyle
Russell .... Kurt Fuller
Mrs. Vanderhoff .... Colleen Camp
Alan .... Michael DeLuise
Neil .... Dan Bell
Alice Cooper .... Himself
Garth's dream woman .... Donna Dixon
Tiny .... Meat Loaf
Doughnut shop owner .... Ed O'Neill
Benjamin Oliver's girlfriend .... Ione Skye
Police officer .... Robert Patrick

Wayne's World is based on the hilarious *Saturday Night Live* television sketches featuring Mike Myers as Wayne Campbell and Dana Carvey as his buddy Garth Algar. Wayne and Garth are the stars of a public-access cable television show that is broadcast from Wayne's basement in Aurora, Illinois. Their low-budget, unpretentious program usually has Wayne and Garth talking excitedly about their first love (classic heavy-metal bands) and their second love (babes). Both Wayne and Garth appear dressed in faded, torn jeans (and ridiculously fake long hair wigs), with Garth usually sporting an old Aerosmith rock band T-shirt as he bangs away on nonexistent drums while Wayne strums on his unplugged electric guitar, both singing the simplistic *Wayne's World* theme song ("Wayne's world! Party time! Excellent! WrrrrrWrrrr!"). Their language is thick with outrageous teenage slang as they ramble about whatever irrelevant subject happens to pop into their heads, hurling playful insults at each other, lusting after actresses and fashion models, and speaking reverently about a current favorite heavy-metal band before signing off with a reprise of the show's theme song. As a five-minute television sketch, *Wayne's World* is indeed excellent. As a ninety-five-minute, big-budget feature film, however, it is somewhat less than that.

The film essentially picks up where the cable-access television show would normally end. Wayne and Garth wrap up another successful broadcast of their show; then, with Wayne addressing the film audience, he and Garth and three other buddies hop into Wayne's "Mirthmobile" and drive off in search of quality party time. Eventually, they arrive at a local heavy-metal club, and Wayne immediately falls in love with the lead singer of the band performing that night, Cassandra (Tia Carrere), a beautiful and spirited young Asian woman.

While Wayne and his pals party into the night, evil and corrupting forces scheme to exploit them. Benjamin Oliver (Rob Lowe), a slimy television executive, has just finished watching Wayne and Garth's show for the first time while lounging in bed with a pizza delivery girl (Ione Skye). Noticing the enthusiastic response that the program has elicited from his newfound love, Benjamin begins to plot how to steal the show away from Wayne and turn it into a big-budget network program. Soon afterward, Benjamin and his slimy business partner, Russell (Kurt Fuller), trick the equally slimy and very wealthy owner of a chain of video arcades into sponsoring the new *Wayne's World*. Then, the unscrupulous Benjamin begins to seek Wayne and Garth.

Benjamin finds the two at one of their favorite hangouts and tempts them with a contract, promising them complete control over the program plus a hefty salary. Wayne, who has always dreamed of being paid to do his show, agrees to the contract, ignoring Garth's aside to the camera regarding Benjamin's too-good-to-be-true offer. Wayne is ecstatic: His dreams of success are approaching fruition, his dream girl is responding to his loopy but very sincere advances, and his best buddy is still very loyal to his philosophy of life, which, in a nutshell, is "Party 'till you hurl."

To celebrate the signing of the contract, Benjamin invites Wayne, Garth, and Cassandra up to his high-rise apartment. While Garth snoops around in Benjamin's bedroom and Wayne admires the view from the balcony, Benjamin makes advances toward Cassandra, ultimately making points with her by offering to feature her and her band in a big-budget music video.

When the time comes for the first official broadcast of the new *Wayne's World*, Wayne and Garth are stunned by the flashy, commercially crass approach to the show. Neon lights, a big band theme song introduction, and unauthorized guests undermine the show's originally unrehearsed and unpretentious appeal. When

Benjamin demands that Wayne interview the show's sponsor, Noah Vanderhoff (Brian Doyle-Murray), as the show's first guest, Wayne slyly insults Vanderhoff on the air. An infuriated Benjamin fires Wayne on the spot, then announces that he, not Wayne, owns the rights to the show. Wayne immediately storms out of the television studio, leaving a tongue-tied Garth alone in front of the television cameras to finish the show.

Afterward, Garth yells at Wayne for abandoning him, and the two best friends part as enemies. Then Wayne picks a fight with Cassandra, accusing her of sleeping with Benjamin in order to land a music video deal. Realizing that he might have overreacted, however, Wayne makes up with Garth and later confronts Cassandra while she is in the middle of filming her music video, ultimately winning her away from the nefarious Benjamin. Wayne and Garth then arrange a special impromptu—and illegal—television broadcast for Cassandra and her band, which is picked up by a record producer passing through town in his television-equipped stretch limo. The film ends with three wildly alternative finales—one with totally disastrous repercussions for Wayne and Garth, the other two totally redemptive, and all three totally wacky.

Wayne's World, which proved to be the fifth highest grossing film of the year, is extremely likable with much to recommend it and nearly as much to condemn it. By far, the film's biggest assets are its two main characters, played with a sweet, loopy innocence by Myers and Carvey. Myers emphasizes Wayne's mischievous, irreverent party boy attributes, an aging teenager in love with the basics of life: loud music, brainless friends, mindless fun, and beautiful women. Carvey's Garth is a dopey, wide-eyed innocent addicted to video games, electronics, and Wayne's philosophy of life. With the exception of Carrere's strong, sexy, and very convincingly talented Cassandra, however, the other characters, along with the script itself, are extremely underdeveloped.

Much of the film has an unrehearsed feel to it, as if director Penelope Spheeris encouraged her cast to improvise after placing them in key settings. Sometimes this comedy verité approach works, as it does in the scene involving Wayne and Cassandra in her bedroom, with Wayne trying to make her laugh by striking goofy poses and strutting around her room dressed only in his underwear. It also works in the scene with Garth talking to Wayne about being sexually attracted to Bugs Bunny while the two of them lie on the hood of the Mirthmobile near an airport runway. Yet many scenes appear as if Spheeris were waiting to yell "Cut!" after something amusing happens, and, in many cases, nothing does.

In other instances, a scene's punch line is a weak variation of a standard joke. For example, when Wayne and Garth visit a friend who works at a car repair shop, Garth innocently picks up an electric bolt gun and scars the side of a car when he loses control of the instrument. The scene is totally superfluous and seems to have been conceived merely to give Carvey an excuse to play with the bolt gun, which he does with no real comic inventiveness. Another similar and equally superfluous scene has Wayne and Garth playing street hockey, a setting that is actually an excuse to stage an old gag involving Wayne's former girlfriend, Stacy (Lara Flynn Boyle), riding by on a bike trying to catch Wayne's eye and crashing into a parked car. Many other scenes suffer from this type of approach to comedy, where too much time is wasted setting up gags that are tired variations of slapstick comedy routines.

Other attempts at comedy involving parodies of well-known commercials, television shows, and films also have varying degrees of effectiveness. Such shows as *Mission Impossible*, *The Twilight Zone*, and *Laverne and Shirley*, and such films as *Terminator II: Judgment Day* (1991) and the James Bond series, are satirized, along with several blatantly gratuitous plugs for Pepsi, Pizza Hut, and Reebok. In these scenes, the filmmakers seem to be trying to capture the irreverent spirit of such other silly, successful television/film-reference satires as *Airplane!* (1980) and the two *Naked Gun* films (1988 and 1991). The setups for these satirical jabs are too laborious, however, although the *Laverne and Shirley* scene works quite well, re-creating the opening segment of the show with an exact and hilarious preciseness. Of course, if the viewer is unfamiliar with this old television sitcom—and any of the film's other in-joke references for that matter—the comedy effect is reduced to nil. Overall, the film seems more of a backhanded homage to the two successful *Bill and Ted* films (1989 and 1991) than anything else, with Wayne and Garth attempting to imitate the airheaded, party-obsessed spirit of those earlier efforts.

Director Spheeris, whose most successful previous films were two documentaries chronicling the decadent, intensely anarchic spirit of punk rock and heavy-metal bands and their fans—*The Decline of Western Civilization* (1981) and *The Decline of Western Civilization Part II: The Metal Years* (1988)—is more successful at staging the film's many musical interludes. Carrere's numbers are especially well executed and benefit immensely from the fact that Carrere sings her numbers live. The film's two best scenes are also musical numbers, the first featuring Wayne, Garth, and their buddies thrashing around in the Mirthmobile while lip-synching to Queen's "Bohemian Rhapsody" and the second a hilarious fantasy interlude involving Garth dancing provocatively in front of his doughnut shop dream girl (Donna Dixon) while lip-synching to Jimi Hendrix's "Foxy Lady."

Ultimately, *Wayne's World* attempts to satirize itself as it tells the story of a successful, low-budget public-access television show being turned into a big-budget fiasco by greedy corporate exploiters. Yet this in-joke approach to the comedy only serves to stifle the development of the two main characters, who nevertheless manage to remain extremely likable throughout the action despite the wildly uneven attempts at humor. If only the filmmakers had given their extremely talented main actors the chance to develop their charming and irreverent characters more fully, then *Wayne's World* could have been successful in all ways. Instead, the film is infected with the same overblown pretensions and underdeveloped material that sabotaged the success of another film—*Strange Brew* (1983)—based on a recurring skit from a satirical television show—*SCTV*—which featured two lunkheaded nitwits—the beer-guzzling McKenzie Brothers (Rick Moranis and Dave Thomas). Both of these films wanted to be goofy, nonstop party fests, but their small-screen, one-dimensional origins and satirical compulsions proved to be party wreckers when transferred to the big screen.

Jim Kline

Reviews

Chicago Tribune. February 14, 1992, VII, p. 25.
Films in Review. XLIII, May, 1992, p. 181.
The Hollywood Reporter. February 14, 1992, p. 8.
Los Angeles Times. February 14, 1992, p. F1.
The New York Times. February 14, 1992, p. B6.
Newsweek. CXIX, March 2, 1992, p. 62.
People Weekly. February 24, 1992, p. 15.
Rolling Stone. March 19, 1992, p. 34.
Time. CXXXIX, March 2, 1992, p. 68.
Variety. February 14, 1992, p. 2.

WHERE ANGELS FEAR TO TREAD

Origin: Great Britain
Released: 1992
Released in U.S.: 1992
Production: Derek Granger for Sovereign Pictures, in association with LWT, Jeffrey Taylor, and Stagescreen Productions; released by Fine Line Features
Direction: Charles Sturridge
Screenplay: Tim Sullivan, Derek Granger, and Charles Sturridge; based on the novel by E. M. Forster
Cinematography: Michael Coulter
Editing: Peter Coulson
Production design: Simon Holland
Casting: Joyce Gallie and Rita Forzano
Costume design: Monica Howe
Music: Rachel Portman
MPAA rating: PG
Running time: 113 minutes

Principal characters:

Caroline Abbott .... Helena Bonham Carter
Harriet Herriton .... Judy Davis
Phillip Herriton .... Rupert Graves
Lilia Herriton .... Helen Mirren
Gino Carella .... Giovanni Guidelli
Mrs. Herriton .... Barbara Jefford

In an age when many films are designed to bombard the senses like a roller coaster and there seems to be a fascination with the bizarre and the extreme, some viewers hope that motion pictures will go back to the basics. They want to be told a story about human beings with real problems who are seeking a solution, to watch an ensemble group of talented actors who reveal the truth with the simplicity of their performances, and perhaps to be influenced regarding the way in which they look at their own lives. *Where Angels Fear to Tread* contains the above-mentioned qualities. The film, an adaptation of an E. M. Forster novel, is intelligently directed by Charles Sturridge and is able to create a little magic without any special effects. It introduces the audience to a group of original and fascinating people and attempts to show the sharp contrasts between the two divergent cultures of England and Italy. The film may not offer vicarious thrills, but it is rewarding in many other areas. It enriches, informs, and gives deep insight into the behavior of the people of two intriguing cultures. *Where Angels Fear to Tread* requires the modern audience to slow down a bit and allow the events to unfold and build at their own pace, much the same as life. People who are accustomed to being catapulted through a film may have difficulty making the adjustment. A certain degree of patience is required, and it is well worth the wait.

The opening scene of Sturridge's film depicts two women embarking on a journey. It shows Lilia Herriton (Helen Mirren) and her chaperon, Caroline Abbott (Helena Bonham Carter), exchanging their good-byes, loading their luggage onto the carriage (the story is set at the beginning of the twentieth century), and engaging in the usual farewell conversation. The scene sets up a sense of anticipation of what lies ahead for these characters and creates an immediate involvement. The audience is invited to go along on the trip.

As time passes, it is revealed that Lilia, a recent widow, has met and fallen in love with a man who is half her age and Italian, a dangerous combination. When news of these events reaches Lilia's in-laws back home, through letters from Caroline, there is unanimous disapproval. It is decided that Lilia's brother-in-law, Phillip (Rupert Graves), must go to Italy to talk some English sense into Lilia. No one considers that meddling in another's affairs might be inappropriate; it simply must be done. This attitude illustrates the English trait of "correctness," about which Forster seems to be commenting.

En route to the hotel in Italy where Lilia has been staying, the somewhat rowdy Hotel Montecartino, Caroline proceeds to inform Phillip about what has been taking place. On the carriage ride, they seem oblivious to the magical countryside through which they are traveling. (Michael Coulter, the film's director of photography, captures Italy in all of its intoxicating beauty and creates a magical setting for the plot to unfold.)

It appears that Phillip's protests to Lilia are to no avail, as the marriage has already taken place. Naturally, Lilia's young husband, Gino (Giovanni Guidelli), is charming and handsome but possesses a philandering nature apparent to all but Lilia; once again, love is blind.

Doggedly, Phillip returns to England, where he is greeted by an extremely angry and disappointed family. His mother, Mrs. Herriton (Barbara Jefford), and sister, Harriet (Judy Davis), are appalled by the events in Italy. Their scenes at the drawing room table, reminiscent of Oscar Wilde's brand of dry English humor, coupled with the deft comic timing of the actors provide some of the most enjoyable moments in the film. It is to Forster's credit that he allows the English to make fun of themselves, and it is to the actors' credit that they carry it off so well. Judy Davis, cited for Woody Allen's *Husbands and Wives* (1992; reviewed in this volume) and *Where Angels Fear to Tread*, was picked as best supporting actress by the Boston Society of Film Critics, as she was by the Los Angeles Film Critics. She was also nominated for an Academy Award for best supporting actress for her role in *Husbands and Wives*.

Meanwhile, back in Italy, Lilia's marriage is beginning to unravel. Gradually, she sees that her young lover is not the Prince Charming that she had originally thought him to be. He is immature and jealous, chauvinistic and unfaithful. He expects her to stay at home and be at his beck and call. This painful revelation reaches a peak when Gino slaps her down to the ground when she tries to stand up for herself. The recognition that she is trapped is registered on Lilia's face as she slowly sinks to the floor. It is a poignant moment and is the beginning of her surrender to her husband's will. Her struggle comes to an end when she suddenly dies during childbirth.

At this point, the film shifts focus to the battle that ensues for the custody of the child. Phillip and Harriet believe that they should take the boy and rear him with traditional English values, Caroline Abbott thinks that it is she who should rescue him from Gino, and Gino has no intention of giving him up. On the surface, the child is the issue. Upon closer examination, however, Forster is analyzing the complexity of conflicting values and the process of self-revelation. The characters are not only fighting for the child but also searching for some meaning and purpose to their own empty existence. It becomes a clash of individual wills and a clash of cultures. When self-will takes over and turns to obsession, disaster may occur. The film argues that there is a time to fight and a time to let go; in order to experience the joy in life, there must be a willingness to accept the pain.

What makes *Where Angels Fear to Tread* such a rewarding experience is that it tells a story and challenges the audience to make up its own mind about different belief systems. In a scene in church, Caroline provokes Phillip by saying, "You're dead, dead, dead! Why aren't you angry. You're so splendid. I can't bear to see you wasted!" It is as if she is looking out into the dark theater and reminding everyone watching to participate fully in life or else it will be wasted. She challenges viewers to live with passion and fervor. This film is a much more fulfilling experience than a ride on a roller coaster.

Robert F. Chicatelli

Reviews

Chicago Tribune. March 20, 1992, VII, p. 38.
The Christian Science Monitor. April 21, 1992, p. 11.
Films in Review. XLIII, May, 1992, p. 184.
The Hollywood Reporter. February 28, 1992, p. 14.
Los Angeles Times. March 11, 1992, p. F3.
The New York Times. February 28, 1992, p. B3.
Newsweek. CXIX, March 16, 1992, p. 66.
Rolling Stone. March 5, 1992, p. 78.
Time. CXXXIX, March 16, 1992, p. 72.
Variety. CCCXLIV, July 15, 1992, p. 38.

WHITE MEN CAN'T JUMP

Production: Don Miller and David Lester; released by Twentieth Century-Fox
Direction: Ron Shelton
Screenplay: Ron Shelton
Cinematography: Russell Boyd
Editing: Paul Seydor
Production design: Dennis Washington
Art direction: Roger Fortune
Set decoration: Robert Benton
Casting: Victoria Thomas
Sound: Kirk Francis
Costume design: Francine Jamison-Tanchuck
Music: Bennie Wallace
MPAA rating: R
Running time: 125 minutes

Principal characters:

Sidney Deane	Wesley Snipes
Billy Hoyle	Woody Harrelson
Gloria Clemente	Rosie Perez
Rhonda Deane	Tyra Ferrell

White Men Can't Jump is a lighthearted comedy of manners, full of snide remarks, ridicule, and reverse elitism. A white basketball player, Billy Hoyle (Woody Harrelson), dares to enter the courts and outwit African American players who are overconfident in estimating their game. Because they seriously believe that no white man who dresses the way that Billy does could possibly beat them in basketball, they are hustled in an entertaining series of increasingly challenging and lucrative games for money. As the stakes become higher and higher, camaraderie and finally grudging friendship grows between the African American star player, Sidney Deane (Wesley Snipes), and Billy.

As soon as Billy wins the first bet in the first game, however, Sidney identifies him as the hustler that he is and arranges to team up with him in a series of setups to swindle the African American basketball players of the Crenshaw district, Watts, and other African American neighborhoods in Los Angeles. Sidney is working a number of different jobs and is not by nature someone who would cheat his own people, but his wife, Rhonda (Tyra Ferrell), is a pushy, opinionated young mother of a year-old son. She is more than ready to move out of the Vista View Apartments, where there is neither vista, nor view, nor space enough for their family. Rhonda is able to persuade her husband to do anything that she desires. Thus, Sidney needs money, and his plan for tricking his own people into relinquishing it is partially justified by his situation as a married man under pressure from his wife.

In forming an alliance with Billy, Sidney is merely being an opportunist. He knows that they can trick the local players into falling for the game, and indeed they do, at first. Then Sidney fakes having an off game and they lose, contrary to their plan. All that Billy has is gone, so he returns home to tell his fiery Puerto Rican girlfriend, Gloria Clemente (Rosie Perez), about this experience. Gloria studies constantly in anticipation of her call to appear on the game show *Jeopardy*. Because Gloria is more intelligent and better with money than Billy is, she quickly sees through this ruse and climbs onto the bus with Billy to recover his half of the winnings. After Sidney blusters a bit about their not having had a partnership in the first place, Gloria persuades Rhonda to strike a deal in which Billy can recover most of what Sidney has taken from him.

They decide to mount a larger wager in a tougher contest, the Black-White Community Unity Two-on-Two Tournament, apparently sponsored by a local politician. In this contest, there is so much fighting between the players that the politician is heard to remark that he hopes he will not lose his backing as a result of this seedy game, which exemplifies, if anything, community discord. As Billy and Sidney play, they insult the other players in the hope of making them so angry that they will not play effectively. In addition, Billy rails at Sidney continuously because he believes that Sidney plays better when he is furious. Yet this match, although it ends successfully, leaves Billy penniless as before because, on their way home, Sidney and he wage all of their earnings on a free-throw contest. Billy insists that he can slam dunk the ball, but he is proved wrong. He slinks back home to Gloria, and upon learning of his new loss, she leaves him. Immediately, two mobsters, who have been pursuing the couple throughout the film over a botched car purchase and their failure to pay the debt, appear. Within a matter of minutes, Billy has lost his girlfriend and has nearly lost his life.

Given a week to find the cash, Billy seeks out Sidney to plead for help because he is broke, being chased by gangsters, and desperate. Sidney agrees to help and introduces Billy to a security guard on the *Jeopardy* show. After undergoing further trials by basketball, Billy wins Rosie an appearance on the game show, where she promptly triumphs, much to Billy's delight. Therefore, the film ends with an affirmation both of Billy and Rosie's relationship (and their ability to pay off the gangsters) and of the strong bond between Billy and Sidney.

White Men Can't Jump is an extremely popular film that cheerfully accepts racial stereotypes, differences, and prejudice as contemporary realities, yet manages to treat these topics without taking itself or anything else too seriously. The sparring language of the playground, with its insults, its profanity, and its crazy non sequiturs and put-downs, is as important a tool as basketball skills. Although the film is an easygoing comedy, with basketball-playing sequences full of finesse and absurdity, the emerging black-white friendship—and Sidney's growth from a person who would betray a white man just because he is white into someone who stands by his friends whatever their color—is its true subject. In its portrayal of the evolution of a close-knit friendship between men who have their differences but who are pulled together through their common commitment to a con game, the film resembles *The Sting* (1973). As in *The Sting*, *White Men Can't Jump* keeps the audience in suspense until the very last moment as to whether one partner will betray the other. In each film, one con man is the proverbial fish out of water, and the viewer is frequently led to wonder if this odd man out will prove too unreliable or insubstantial to carry out his part of the bargain and maintain the alliance.

Although there have been many buddy films about friendships that develop between apparently ill-matched types, relatively few have been made about a pair in which one person was white and one black. The film shows that, because the African American players initially misjudge Billy as a result of his appearance, blacks are no more immune to prejudice than whites. Billy is equally prejudiced because he is reluctant to get out of the bus at night in the Crenshaw district, believing that it is unsafe for any white man to enter an African American neighborhood after dark. It is only through verbal sparring and confrontations on the basketball court that the men draw out the best in each other. Thus, each comes naturally to respect the other. The final stereotype—the belief that white men cannot jump—is debunked as false in Billy's brilliant jump at the end of the last game.

These are characters who value themselves highly and arrogantly assert their rights. Perhaps a product of too much consciousness raising, Gloria maligns Billy for simply remedying the problem when she says that her mouth is dry, charging him to be more sympathetic and to express his understanding of her plight rather than simply eradicating the problem by getting her a glass of water. The women are liberated and just as aggressive in their own way as the men. If the basketball game is always street theater, then each exchange between characters is a sort of ritual combat. Male friendship wins out over sexual love as a prime motivator of men; the wild, imaginative reach of the players' crazy humor is finally far more intriguing than the steamy, erotic scenes.

Finally, although screenwriter and director Ron Shelton is himself white, the film affords keen insights into the prejudices and misconceptions that some African Americans have about whites and how they are overturned in real life. Unlike *Grand Canyon* (1991), in which an African American family and a white family are balanced against one another, first as individuals and then as crafters of a solid friendship between the two unorthodox family units, ultimately *White Men Can't Jump* is narrower in scope, less ambitious, and altogether a safer, more amusing film. Its tackling of the topic of racial prejudice through puncturing the stereotypes that whites and African Americans hold about one another as basketball players is a clever ploy, as good basketball and witty dialogue are highly watchable and pleasurable in and of themselves. Some critics derided Sidney's cocky elitism and Billy's seeming ignorance, claiming that the tables are turned too sharply in favor of an overly prejudiced view of whites.

In the first part of the film, Sidney forces Billy to stop playing Jimi Hendrix's "Purple Haze" because he believes that no white man can truly "hear" Hendrix. Billy points out, however, that most of the guitarist's band at that point was white and that he likes to listen to him. Over the course of the rest of the film, Sidney is forced to face his own racism and concedes at last, grudgingly, that a white man can both listen to and "hear" Hendrix. This film subtly, wittily, and gently promotes interracial harmony and understanding in Los Angeles and throughout the world as the most intelligent mode of behavior. This is a message that needs to be heard, and audiences made *White Men Can't Jump* one of the most popular films of 1992.

Cher Langdell

Reviews

Chicago Tribune. March 27, 1992, VII, p. 35.
Films in Review. XLIII, July, 1992, p. 263.
The Hollywood Reporter. March 27, 1992, p. 6.
Jet. LXXXI, March 30, 1992, p. 62.
Los Angeles Times. March 27, 1992, p. F1.
The New York Times. March 27, 1992, p. B2.
Newsweek. CXIX, April 6, 1992, p. 64.
Sight and Sound. II, October, 1992, p. 59.
Time. CXXXIX, April 6, 1992, p. 69.
Variety. March 27, 1992, p. 2.

MORE FILMS OF 1992

Abbreviations: *Pro.* = Production *Dir.* = Direction *Scr.* = Screenplay *Cine.* = Cinematography *Ed.* = Editing *P.d.* = Production design *A.d.* = Art direction *S.d.* = Set decoration *Mu.* = Music *MPAA* = MPAA rating *R.t.* = Running time

ACES: IRON EAGLE III
Pro. Ron Samuels for Carolco Pictures; New Line Cinema *Dir.* John Glen *Scr.* Kevin Elders; based on characters created by Elders and Sidney J. Furie *Cine.* Alec Mills *Ed.* Bernard Gribble *P.d.* Robb Wilson King *Mu.* Harry Manfredini *MPAA* R *R.t.* 98 min. *Cast:* Louis Gossett, Jr., Rachel McLish, Paul Freeman, Horst Buchholz, Christopher Cazenove, Sonny Chiba, Fred Dalton Thompson, Mitchell Ryan, Phill Lewis, Rob Estes, J. E. Freeman, Tom Bower, Juan Fernandez, Ray Mancini, Inez Perez, Branscombe Richmond.

In this ludicrously poor action/adventure, Louis Gossett, Jr., stars as a former World War II fighter pilot who teams up with three war buddies to fight a Peruvian drug cartel.

ADAM'S RIB (Russia, 1992)
Pro. Mosfilm; October Films *Dir.* Vyacheslav Krishtofovich *Scr.* Vladimir Kunin; based on the novel *House of Young Women*, by Anatoly Kurchatkin *Cine.* Pavel Lebedev *Ed.* Inna Brozhovskaya *P.d.* Sergei Khotimsky and Aleksandr Samulekin *Mu.* Vadim Khrapachev *R.t.* 75 min. *Cast:* Inna Churikova, Svetlana Ryabova, Masha Golubkina, Elena Bogdanova, Andrei Tolubeyev.

Forty-nine-year-old Nina (Inna Churikova), her mute and bedridden mother (Elena Bogdanova), and her two grown daughters, Lida (Svetlana Ryabova) and Nastya (Masha Golubkina), each from a different marriage, share a tiny apartment in an unnamed city in Russia, where they daily fight claustrophobia, loneliness, the limitations of their society, and sometimes each other in this tragicomic slice of Russian life.

THE ADJUSTER
Pro. Camelia Frieberg for Alliance Communications Corporation and Ego Film Arts; Orion Classics *Dir.* Atom Egoyan *Scr.* Atom Egoyan *Cine.* Paul Sarossy *Ed.* Susan Shipton *P.d.* Linda Del Rosario and Richard Paris *Mu.* Mychael Danna *MPAA* R *R.t.* 102 min. *Cast:* Elias Koteas, Arsinee Khanjian, Maury Chaykin, Gabrielle Rose, Jennifer Dale, David Hemblen, Patricia Collins.

An insurance claims adjuster, Noah (Elias Koteas), takes his work very personally as he not only puts clients up in a motel when they lose their homes to fire but also attempts to help them return to a normal life. Noah is so obsessed with his job, however, that he neglects his own personal life.

AFFENGEIL (Germany, 1992)
Pro. Rosa von Praunheim; First Run Features *Dir.* Rosa von Praunheim *Scr.* Rosa von Praunheim *Cine.* Klaus Janschewskj and Mike Kuchar *Ed.* Mike Shepard *Mu.* Maran Gosov and Thomas Marquard *R.t.* 87 min. *Cast:* Lotti Huber, Rosa von Praunheim, Helga Sloop, Gertrud Mischwitzky, Thomas Woischnig, Hans Peter Schwade, Frank Schafer.

Aging German actress and dancer Lotti Huber is the subject of this documentary by experimental filmmaker Rosa von Praunheim. In her seventies at the time of filming, Huber was a flamboyant personality, a woman who survived the Nazi concentration camps of World War II to become an exotic dancer in Palestine, a restaurateur in Cyprus, and an actress in her native Germany.

AFRAID OF THE DARK (Great Britain, 1992)

Pro. Simon Bosanquet for Telescope Films, Les Films Ariane, and Cine Cino, in association with Sovereign Pictures; Fine Line Features *Dir.* Mark Peploe *Scr.* Mark Peploe and Frederick Seidel *Cine.* Bruno de Keyzer *Ed.* Scott Thomas *P.d.* Caroline Amies *Mu.* Jason Osborn *MPAA* R *R.t.* 92 min. *Cast:* Ben Keyworth, James Fox, Fanny Ardant, Clare Holman, Paul McGann, Robert Stephens, Susan Woolridge, Jeremy Flynn.

Reality and fantasy blur in the mind of a little boy whose fear of going blind distorts his perception of the world.

ALAN AND NAOMI

Pro. David Anderson and Mark Balsam for Leucadia Film Corp. and Maltese Cos., Inc.; Triton Pictures *Dir.* Sterling VanWagenen *Scr.* Jordan Horowitz; based on the novel by Myron Levoy *Cine.* Paul Ryan *Ed.* Cari Coughlin *P.d.* George Goodridge *A.d.* Barbara Kahn Kretschmer *Mu.* Dick Hyman *MPAA* PG *R.t.* 95 min. *Cast:* Lukas Haas, Vanessa Zaoui, Michael Gross, Amy Aquino, Kevin Connolly, Zohra Lampert, Victoria Christian, Charlie Dow.

Lukas Haas stars as a fourteen-year-old Jewish boy, Alan, living in Brooklyn in the 1940's, who befriends a severely troubled neighbor girl, Naomi (Vanessa Zaoui). Naomi is a European refugee who witnessed her father's murder by the Nazis. Although initially reluctant to visit her, Alan strives patiently to bring her out of her shell.

ALBERTO EXPRESS (France, 1992)

Pro. Maurice Bernart; MK2 *Dir.* Arthur Joffe *Scr.* Arthur Joffe, Jean-Louis Benoit, and Christian Billette *Cine.* Philippe Welt *Ed.* Marie Castro-Brechignac *S.d.* Bernard Vezat *Mu.* Angelique Nachon and Jean-Claude Nachon *R.t.* 90 min. *Cast:* Sergio Castellitto, Nino Manfredi, Marie Trintignant, Marco Messeri, Jeanne Moreau, Eugenia Marruzzo.

When a young man, Alberto, prepares to leave home and strike out on his own, his father (Nino Manfredi) informs him that Alberto must repay his father for rearing him, and before Alberto himself becomes a father. Many years later, Alberto (Sergio Castellitto), broke and with a pregnant wife, takes a train to visit his father—attempting to raise the money by any means possible along the way.

AMERICAN FABULOUS

Pro. Rene Dakota for Dead Jesse Productions *Dir.* Rene Dakota *Scr.* Jeffrey Strouth *Cine.* Travis Ruse and Rene Dakota *Ed.* Rene Dakota *R.t.* 105 min. *Cast:* Jeffrey Strouth.

Jeffrey Strouth, storyteller extraordinaire, relates firsthand his life story from the inside of a vintage Cadillac as it tours Columbus, Ohio. With wit and humor, Strouth tells of a childhood with an alcoholic father, a near-fatal encounter with a truck driver, hitchhiking to Los Angeles, and many other colorful reminiscences.

ANTARCTICA

Pro. John Weiley and David Flatman for Heliograph Film, with the assistance of the Australian Film Commission and the Australian Film Finance Corp., Pty. Ltd., Museum of Science and Industry, Chicago *Dir.* John Weiley *Scr.* Les A. Murray, John Weiley, and Michael Parfit *Cine.* Tom Cowan, Malcolm Ludgate, and Hans Heldrich *Ed.* Nicholas Holmes *Mu.* Nigel Westlake *R.t.* 43 min. *Cast:* John Mills, Reginald Beckwith, Alex Scott.

This visually breathtaking documentary centers on Antarctica—both underwater and above ground. The film depicts a harsh environment teeming with wildlife and dotted with scientists who wish to explore it.

THE ARCHITECTURE OF DOOM (Sweden, 1991)

Pro. Peter Cohen; First Run Features *Dir.* Peter Cohen *Scr.* Peter Cohen *Cine.* Michael

Cohen, Gerhard Fromm, and Peter Ostlun *Ed.* Peter Cohen *Mu.* Richard Wagner and Hector Berlioz *R.t.* 119 min. *Cast:* Bruno Ganz.

Another slant on Adolf Hitler and the Holocaust is presented in this documentary by Swedish filmmaker Peter Cohen, who links Hitler's artistic sensibility with his need to achieve beauty and perfection through violence.

ARTICLE 99

Pro. Michael Gruskoff and Michael I. Levy; Orion Pictures *Dir.* Howard Deutch *Scr.* Ron Cutler *Cine.* Richard Bowen *Ed.* Richard Halsey *P.d.* Virginia L. Randolph *A.d.* Marc Fisichella *S.d.* Tom Stiller and Sarah Stone *Mu.* Danny Elfman *MPAA* R *R.t.* 99 min. *Cast:* Ray Liotta, Kiefer Sutherland, Forest Whitaker, Lea Thompson, John C. McGinley, John Mahoney, Keith David, Kathy Baker, Eli Wallach, Julie Bovasso, Troy Evans, Lynn Thigpen.

Doctors battle hospital bureaucracy in this comedy/drama set in a Veterans Administration hospital. Ray Liotta, Kiefer Sutherland, Forest Whitaker, and Lea Thompson star as doctors who are forced to circumvent what they interpret as ridiculous regulations imposed by the hospital's hard-boiled director (John Mahoney), in order to provide ailing veterans with the care that they need.

BASKET CASE III: THE PROGENY

Pro. Edgar Ievins for Ievins and Henenlotter; Shapiro Glickenhaus Entertainment *Dir.* Frank Henenlotter *Scr.* Frank Henenlotter and Robert Martin *Cine.* Bob Paone *Ed.* Greg Sheldon *P.d.* William Barclay *A.d.* Caty Maxey *Mu.* Joe Renzetti *MPAA* R *R.t.* 90 min. *Cast:* Annie Ross, Kevin Van Hentenryck, Dan Biggers, Gil Roper, Tina Louise Hilbert, James O'Doherty, Carla Morrell, Carmen Morrell, Berl Boykin, Denise Coop, James Derrick, Donna Hall, Dean Hines, Larry Hurd, Cedric Maurice, Diane Oxford, Beverly Bonner.

This horror film centers on Siamese twin brothers Duane (Kevin Van Hentenryck) and Belial—a deformed monster consisting of a head and arms. In this sequel, Belial has impregnated another monster, Eve, and Granny Ruth (Annie Ross) takes them all to a small Georgian town to stay with Uncle Hal (Dan Biggers), a doctor.

A BEATING HEART (*Un Coeur qui bat*; France, 1992)

Pro. Rene Cleitman for Hachette Premiere et Cie, U.C.G., Avril S.A., and FR3 Films, with the participation of the Centre National de la Cinematographie, Soficas Investimage 2, Investimage 3, and Canal +; MK2 *Dir.* Francois Dupeyron *Scr.* Francois Dupeyron *Cine.* Yves Angelo *Ed.* Francoise Collin *S.d.* Carlos Conti *Mu.* Jean-Pierre Drouet *R.t.* 100 min. *Cast:* Dominique Faysse, Thierry Fortineau, Jean-Marie Winling, Christophe Pichon.

An adulterous and spontaneous one-night stand with a younger man, Yves (Thierry Fortineau), leads a forty-something woman, Mado (Dominique Faysse), to reexamine her marriage and her life.

BEBE'S KIDS

Pro. Willard Carroll and Thomas L. Wilhite for Hudlin Bros./Hyperion Studio; Paramount Pictures *Dir.* Bruce Smith *Scr.* Reginald Hudlin; based on characters created by Robin Harris *Ed.* Lynne Southerland *P.d.* Fred Cline *A.d.* Doug Walker *Mu.* John Barnes *MPAA* PG-13 *R.t.* 73 min. *Voices:* Faizon Love, Vanessa Bell Calloway, Wayne Collins, Jonell Green, Marques Houston, Tone-Loc, Myra J., Nell Carter.

Based on a comedy routine by the late African American comic Robin Harris, this animated feature centers on a middle-aged, divorced man, Harris (voice of Faizon Love), who takes a beautiful woman, Jamika (voice of Vanessa Bell Calloway), and her well-behaved son to an amusement park. Unfortunately, Jamika also brings the three children of her friend Bebe, who are little terrors.

BECOMING COLETTE (USA and Germany, 1992)
Pro. Heinz Bibo and Peer Oppenheimer for Bibo Filmproduktions Gmbh, BC Productions Ltd., and Les Films Ariane, S.A.; Castle Hill Productions, Inc. *Dir.* Danny Huston *Scr.* Ruth Graham *Cine.* Wolfgang Treu *Ed.* Peter Taylor and Roberto Silvi *P.d.* Jan Schlubach and Berge Douy *Mu.* John Scott *MPAA* R *R.t.* 97 min. *Cast:* Klaus Maria Brandauer, Mathilda May, Virginia Madsen, Paul Rhys, John van Dreelen, Jean Pierre Aumont, Lucienne Hamon, Georg Tryphon.

This slight drama centers on real-life French author Colette (Mathilda May) and her unsatisfactory marriage to her publisher husband, Henri Gauthier-Villars (Klaus Maria Brandauer), her evolving literary career, and her racy life-style in early twentieth century Paris.

BED AND BREAKFAST
Pro. Jack Schwartzman; Hemdale Pictures *Dir.* Robert Ellis Miller *Scr.* Cindy Myers *Cine.* Peter Sova *Ed.* John F. Burnett *P.d.* Suzanne Cavedon *A.d.* Ron Wilson *S.d.* Tracey Doyle *Mu.* David Shire *MPAA* PG-13 *R.t.* 97 min. *Cast:* Roger Moore, Talia Shire, Colleen Dewhurst, Nina Siemaszko, Ford Rainey, Stephen Root, Jamie Walters.

When a debonair man with a shady past, Adam (Roger Moore), appears at an isolated Maine bed and breakfast, he charms his way into the lives of its three occupants: Ruth (Colleen Dewhurst), her daughter-in-law Claire (Talia Shire), and Claire's teenage daughter, Cassie (Nina Siemaszko).

BIG GIRLS DON'T CRY, THEY GET EVEN
Pro. Laurie Perlman and Gerald T. Olson, in association with Perlman Productions and MG Entertainment, Inc.; New Line Cinema *Dir.* Joan Micklin Silver *Scr.* Frank Mugavero; based on a story by Melissa Goddard, Mark Goddard, and Frank Mugavero *Cine.* Theo Van de Sande *Ed.* Janice Hampton *P.d.* Victoria Paul *A.d.* Brad Ricker *S.d.* Maya Shimoguchi and Joyce Anne Gilstrap *Mu.* Patrick Williams *MPAA* PG *R.t.* 96 min. *Cast:* Hillary Wolf, David Strathairn, Margaret Whitton, Griffin Dunne, Patricia Kalember, Adrienne Shelly, Dan Futterman, Jenny Lewis, Ben Savage, Trenton Teigen, Jessica Seely, Jim Haynie, Googy Gress, Meagan Fay.

In this cliché-ridden comedy, a teenage girl (Hillary Wolf) runs away from her fractured family to a lakeshore resort. When her father (Griffin Dunne), mother (Margaret Whitton), stepfather (David Strathairn), and various siblings and stepsiblings follow her there, the ad hoc trip becomes the catalyst for resolving their problems.

BLAME IT ON THE BELLBOY (Great Britain and USA, 1992)
Pro. Steve Abbott and Jennie Howarth for Hollywood Pictures, in association with Silver Screen Partners IV; Buena Vista *Dir.* Mark Herman *Scr.* Mark Herman *Cine.* Andrew Dunn *Ed.* Michael Ellis *P.d.* Gemma Jackson *A.d.* Peter Russell *S.d.* Peter Walpole *Mu.* Trevor Jones *MPAA* PG-13 *R.t.* 78 min. *Cast:* Dudley Moore, Bryan Brown, Richard Griffiths, Andreas Katsulas, Patsy Kensit, Alison Steadman, Penelope Wilton, Bronson Pinchot, Lindsay Anderson (voice), Jim Carter, Alex Norton.

In this comedy of mistaken identities, an Italian hotel bellboy (Bronson Pinchot) who does not speak much English confuses the mail of three very different guests with very similar last names—Orton (Dudley Moore), Lawton (Bryan Brown), and Horton (Richard Griffiths). The resulting comedic mix-up involves the switched itineraries of the real-estate agent, hit man, and philanderer, respectively, as the three men attempt to straighten out the misunderstanding.

BRAIN DONORS
Pro. Gil Netter and James D. Brubaker for Zucker Brothers and Paramount Pictures *Dir.* Dennis Dugan *Scr.* Pat Proft *Cine.* David M. Walsh *Ed.* Malcolm Campbell *P.d.* William J.

Cassidy *Mu.* Ira Newborn *MPAA* PG *R.t.* 90 min. *Cast:* John Turturro, Mel Smith, Bob Nelson, Nancy Marchand, John Savident, George de la Pena, Juli Donald, Spike Alexander.

In this Marx Brothers'-style comedy, an ambulance-chasing lawyer (John Turturro), a cabdriver (Mel Smith), and a jack-of-all-trades (Bob Nelson) team up in order to help a wealthy widow (Nancy Marchand) found a ballet company.

BREAKING THE RULES

Pro. Jonathan D. Krane and Kent Bateman for Sterling Entertainment; Miramax Films *Dir.* Neal Israel *Scr.* Paul W. Shapiro *Cine.* James Hayman *Ed.* Tom Walls *P.d.* Donald Light-Harris *Mu.* David Kitay *MPAA* PG-13 *R.t.* 100 min. *Cast:* Jason Bateman, C. Thomas Howell, Jonathan Silverman, Annie Potts, Kent Bateman, Shawn Phelan, Jackey Vinson, Marty Belafsky.

Jason Bateman stars in this formulaic tearjerker as a young man, Phil, who is stricken with cancer. Phil convinces two childhood buddies (C. Thomas Howell and Jonathan Silverman) to travel with him cross-country to Los Angeles so that he can fulfill his dream of auditioning for the television game show *Jeopardy!*

BRENDA STARR

Pro. Myron A. Hyman for AM/PM, in association with Tribune Entertainment Company; Triumph *Dir.* Robert Ellis Miller *Scr.* Jenny Wolkind, Noreen Stone, and James David Buchanan; based on the comic strip by Dale Messick *Cine.* Freddie Francis *Ed.* Mark Melnick *P.d.* John J. Lloyd *Mu.* Johnny Mandel *MPAA* PG *R.t.* 94 min. *Cast:* Brooke Shields, Timothy Dalton, Tony Peck, Diana Scarwid, Charles Durning, Eddie Albert, Jeffrey Tambor, June Gable, Henry Gibson, Ed Nelson.

Brooke Shields stars as ace reporter Brenda Starr when the 1940's comic-strip heroine comes to life to track down a German scientist with a secret formula in this flimsy action film. Timothy Dalton serves as her romantic interest, Basil St. John, and Tony Peck plays the strip's illustrator, who is also smitten by his well-dressed creation.

BUFFY THE VAMPIRE SLAYER

Pro. Kaz Kuzui and Howard Rosenman for Sandollar/Kuzui Enterprises; Twentieth Century-Fox *Dir.* Fran Rubel Kuzui *Scr.* Joss Whedon *Cine.* James Hayman *Ed.* Camilla Toniolo and Jill Savitt *P.d.* Lawrence Miller *A.d.* James Barrows and Randy Moore *S.d.* Claire Bowin *Mu.* Carter Burwell *MPAA* PG-13 *R.t.* 85 min. *Cast:* Kristy Swanson, Donald Sutherland, Paul Reubens, Rutger Hauer, Luke Perry, Michele Abrams, Hilary Swank, Paris Vaughan, David Arquette, Randall Batinkoff, Andrew Lowery, Sasha Jenson, Stephen Root, Candy Clark, Natasha Gregson Wagner, Mark DeCarlo.

When vampires invade Los Angeles, Merrick (Donald Sutherland) must find "the slayer" and tell her of her birthright. This champion turns out to be a frivolous and vacuous high school Valley girl named Buffy (Kristy Swanson). With the help of loner Pike (Luke Perry), Buffy turns her attention from shopping to vampire slaying.

CABEZA DE VACA (Mexico, 1992)

Pro. Concorde *Dir.* Nicolas Echevarria *Scr.* Guillermo Sheridan and Nicolas Echevarria *Cine.* Guillermo Navarro *Ed.* Rafael Castanedo *Mu.* Mario Lavista *R.t.* 111 min. *Cast:* Juan Diego, Daniel Gimenez Cacho, Roberto Sosa, Carlos Castanon, Gerardo Villarreal, Roberto Cobo, Jose Flores.

Based on real events, this film centers on a sixteenth century Spanish explorer, Alvar Nunez de Vaca (Juan Diego), who was shipwrecked off the coast of Florida in 1528. Accompanied by three other survivors, he embarks on a memorable eight-year voyage overland to the Pacific coast.

CANDYMAN

Pro. Steve Golin, Sigurjon Sighvatsson, and Alan Poul, in association with PolyGram Filmed Entertainment and Propaganda Films; TriStar Pictures *Dir.* Bernard Rose *Scr.* Bernard Rose; based on the short story "The Forbidden," by Clive Barker *Cine.* Anthony B. Richmond *Ed.* Dan Rae *P.d.* Jane Ann Stewart *A.d.* David Lazan *S.d.* Kathryn Peters *Mu.* Philip Glass *MPAA* R *R.t.* 101 min. *Cast:* Virginia Madsen, Tony Todd, Xander Berkeley, Kasi Lemmons, Vanessa Williams, DeJuan Guy, Michael Culkin, Stanley DeSantis, Gilbert Lewis, Bernard Rose.

The studies of a doctoral student, Helen Lyle (Virginia Madsen), lead her to a legendary, hook-handed killer, Candyman (Tony Todd), said to be seeking revenge for his own gruesome death a century ago.

CAPTAIN RON

Pro. David Permut and Paige Simpson for Touchstone Pictures, in association with Touchwood Pacific Partners I; Buena Vista Pictures *Dir.* Thom Eberhardt *Scr.* John Dwyer and Thom Eberhardt; based on a story by Dwyer *Cine.* Daryn Okada *Ed.* Tina Hirsch *P.d.* William F. Matthews *A.d.* James F. Truesdale *S.d.* Glenn Williams, Jeff Haley, and Irvin E. Jim Duffy, Jr. *Mu.* Nicholas Pike *MPAA* PG-13 *R.t.* 100 min. *Cast:* Kurt Russell, Martin Short, Mary Kay Place, Benjamin Salisbury, Meadow Sisto.

Ordinary Chicagoan Martin Harvey (Martin Short) inherits a once-grand celebrity boat, and involves his family in a wild Caribbean adventure as they attempt to sail back to Florida on the now-decrepit ship under the dubious stewardship of Captain Ron (Kurt Russell).

CENTER OF THE WEB

Pro. Ruta K. Aras for A.I.P. Home Video and Winters Group, in association with Sovereign Investment Group; Pyramid Distribution *Dir.* David A. Prior *Scr.* David A. Prior *Cine.* Andrew Parke *Ed.* Tony Malanowski *A.d.* Linda Lewis *Mu.* Greg Turner *MPAA* R *R.t.* 91 min. *Cast:* Robert Davi, Charlene Tilton, Ted Prior, Bo Hopkins, William Zipp, Tony Curtis, Charles Napier.

When a drama teacher (Ted Prior) is mistaken by two men for an assassin they hired, he is asked to maintain the deception by a Justice Department official (Robert Davi) in order to capture the persons masterminding the murder of a governor, in this low-budget tale of intrigue.

CHRISTOPHER COLUMBUS: THE DISCOVERY

Pro. Ilya Salkind for Alexander Salkind; Warner Bros. *Dir.* John Glen *Scr.* John Briley, Cary Bates, and Mario Puzo; based on a story by Puzo *Cine.* Alec Mills *Ed.* Matthew Glen *P.d.* Gil Parrondo *A.d.* Terry Pritchard, Luis Koldo, and Jose Maria Alarcon *Mu.* Cliff Eidelman *MPAA* PG-13 *R.t.* 120 min. *Cast:* Marlon Brando, Tom Selleck, George Corraface, Rachel Ward, Robert Davi, Catherine Zeta Jones, Oliver Cotton, Benicio Del Torro, Mathieu Carriere, Manuel de Blas, Glyn Grain, Peter Guinness, Nigel Terry.

The five-hundredth anniversary of Columbus' discovery of the New World inspired this historical drama starring George Corraface as the eponymous hero, Marlon Brando as Grand Inquisitor Torquemada, Tom Selleck as King Ferdinand, and Rachel Ward as Queen Isabella. More closely resembling a television docudrama, this fictionalized account of Columbus emphasizes the man's spirit of adventure in a tale filled with swordplay and sabotage.

CLASS ACT

Pro. Todd Black and Maynell Thomas for Wizan Black/Gordy de Passe; Warner Bros. *Dir.* Randall Millar *Scr.* John Semper and Cynthia Friedlob; based on a story by Michael Swerdlick, Wayne Rice, and Richard Brenne *Cine.* Francis Kenny *Ed.* John F. Burnett *P.d.*

David L. Snyder *A.d.* Sarah Knowles *S.d.* Robin Peyton *Mu.* Vassal Benford *MPAA* PG-13 *R.t.* 98 min. *Cast:* Christopher (Kid) Reid, Christopher (Play) Martin, Karyn Parsons, Alysia Rogers, Meshach Taylor, Doug E. Doug, Rick Ducommun, Raye Birk, Lamont Johnson, Pauly Shore, Mariann Aalda, Loretta Devine, Thomas Mikal Ford, Rhea Perlman.

Rap team Kid 'n Play (Christopher Reid and Christopher Martin) return to the big screen as two high school transfer students, nerdy intellectual Duncan (Reid) and dangerous trouble-maker Blade (Martin). They wreak havoc when their school records are switched and they pretend to be each other.

CLEARCUT (Canada, 1992)

Pro. Stephen J. Roth and Ian McDougal; Northern Arts Entertainment *Dir.* Richard Bugajski *Scr.* Rob Forsyth; based on the novel *A Dream Like Mine*, by M. T. Kelly *Cine.* Francois Protat *Ed.* Michael Rea *P.d.* Perri Gorrar *Mu.* Shane Harvey *MPAA* R *R.t.* 98 min. *Cast:* Graham Greene, Ron Lea, Michael Hogan, Floyd Red Crow Westerman, Raoul Trujillo, Rebecca Jenkins.

Excessively violent and unsatisfying, this drama centers on a Native American, Arthur (Graham Greene), a cruel and violent man with mystical powers, who exacts revenge for the destruction of the forests by white loggers. Following an unsuccessful court case against the local lumber company, Arthur kidnaps the nearby paper mill's manager (Michael Hogan) and the big-city lawyer (Ron Lea) sent to represent the Native Americans, and takes them on a brutal odyssey through the wilderness.

CLOSE TO EDEN (Russia, 1992)

Pro. Michel Seydoux for Camera One/Hachette premiere et Compagnie (France) and Studio Trite (URSS), in association with Rene Cleitman; Miramax Films *Dir.* Nikita Mikhalkov *Scr.* Roustam Ibraguimbekov; based on story by Nikita Mikhalkov and Ibraguimbekov *Cine.* Villenn Kaluta *Ed.* Joelle Hache *P.d.* Aleksei Levtchenko *Mu.* Eduard Artemiev *R.t.* 106 min. *Cast:* Bayaertu, Badema, Vladimir Gostukhin, Babushka, Bao Yongyan, Larisa Kuznetsova.

Set in China's Inner Mongolia in the late twentieth century, this pleasing drama centers on a nomad family man, Gombo (Bayaertu), and his struggle to maintain his family's traditional life-style against the inevitable encroachment of the modern world. By accident he meets and befriends a Russian road worker, Sergei (Vladimir Gostukhin), with whom he is encouraged to go to town by his beautiful wife, Pagma (Badema), who wants condoms—because they have already reached the limit on children set by Chinese law—and a television set.

COLD HEAVEN

Pro. Allan Scott and Jonathan D. Krane; Hemdale Pictures Corporation *Dir.* Nicolas Roeg *Scr.* Allan Scott; based on the novel by Brian Moore *Cine.* Francis Kenny *Ed.* Tony Lawson *P.d.* Steven Legler *A.d.* Nina Ruscio *S.d.* Cliff Cunningham *Mu.* Stanley Myers *MPAA* R *R.t.* 105 min. *Cast:* Theresa Russell, Mark Harmon, James Russo, Talia Shire, Will Patton, Richard Bradford, Julie Carmen.

Before an adulterous woman, Marie (Theresa Russell), can tell her husband, Dr. Alex Davenport (Mark Harmon), that she is leaving him for another man, her husband is killed while they are on vacation in Acapulco. Guilt-ridden Marie is then plagued both by a recurring religious vision and by the fact that her husband may not be completely dead.

CONSENTING ADULTS

Pro. Alan J. Pakula and David Permut, in association with Touchwood Pacific Partners I; Hollywood Pictures *Dir.* Alan J. Pakula *Scr.* Matthew Chapman *Cine.* Stephen Goldblatt *Ed.* Sam O'Steen *P.d.* Carol Spier *A.d.* Alicia Keywan *S.d.* Thomas Minton, Kathleen

Sullivan, and Gretchen Rau *Mu.* Michael Small *MPAA* R *R.t.* 100 min. *Cast:* Kevin Kline, Mary Elizabeth Mastrantonio, Kevin Spacey, Rebecca Miller, Forest Whitaker, E. G. Marshall, Kimberly McCullough.

Kevin Kline and Mary Elizabeth Mastrantonio star as Richard and Priscilla Parker, whose lives are forever changed by the arrival of their flamboyant new neighbors, Eddy and Kay Otis (Kevin Spacey and Rebecca Miller). Richard becomes trapped in Eddy's nefarious scheme of insurance fraud when he agrees to swap wives and Kay is found murdered the next morning.

COOL WORLD

Pro. Frank Mancuso, Jr.; Paramount Pictures *Dir.* Ralph Bakshi *Scr.* Michael Grais and Mark Victor *Cine.* John A. Alonzo *Ed.* Steve Mirkovich and Annamaria Szanto *A.d.* David James Bomba *S.d.* Lori Rowbotham, Mitchell Lee Simmons, and Merideth Boswell *Mu.* Mark Isham *MPAA* PG-13 *R.t.* 102 min. *Cast:* Kim Basinger, Gabriel Byrne, Brad Pitt, Michele Abrams, Deirdre O'Connell, Carrie Hamilton, Frank Sinatra, Jr., Charles Adler (voice), Maurice LaMarche (voice), Candi Milo (voice), Michael David Lally (voice), Joey Camen (voice), Gregory Snegoff (voice).

In this mix of animation and live action, a sexy cartoon character named Holli Would (Kim Basinger) tries to seduce her creator, Jack Deebs (Gabriel Byrne), in order to become human.

COUSIN BOBBY

Pro. Edward Saxon for Tesauro; Cinevista *Dir.* Jonathan Demme *Cine.* Ernest Dickerson, Craig Haagensen, Tony Jannelli, Jacek Laskus, and Declan Quinn *Ed.* David Greenwald *Mu.* Anton Sanko *R.t.* 70 min. *Cast:* Reverend Robert Castle, Jonathan Demme.

Jonathan Demme, Academy Award-winning director of *The Silence of the Lambs* (1991), directs this documentary that centers on his cousin, the Reverend Robert Castle. A priest in Harlem, cousin Bobby has been a militant civil rights activist for more than forty years, and Demme's film serves as a paean to this dedicated individual.

CRISSCROSS

Pro. Anthea Sylbert and Robin Forman for Hawn/Sylbert Movie Company; Metro-Goldwyn-Mayer *Dir.* Chris Menges *Scr.* Scott Sommer; based on his novella *Cine.* Ivan Strasburg *Ed.* Tony Lawson *P.d.* Crispian Sallis *Mu.* Trevor Jones *MPAA* R *R.t.* 100 min. *Cast:* Goldie Hawn, Arliss Howard, James Gammon, David Arnott, Keith Carradine, J. C. Quinn, Steve Buscemi, Paul Calderon, Cathryn dePrume, Nada Despotovich, David Anthony Marshall, Deirdre O'Connell, Anna Levine Thomson, Neil Giuntoli, Christy Martin, Damian Vantriglia, Derrick Velez, Frank Military, John Nesci.

Set in 1969 in Florida, this drama centers on a twelve-year-old boy, Chris Cross (David Arnott), and his single mother, Tracy (Goldie Hawn), who struggles as a waitress to provide for her son. Trouble ensues when Chris discovers a stash of cocaine and Tracy accepts a job as a stripper without her son's knowledge.

CROSSING THE BRIDGE

Pro. Jeffrey Silver and Robert Newmyer for Touchstone Pictures and Outlaw; Buena Vista *Dir.* Mike Binder *Scr.* Mike Binder *Cine.* Tom Sigel *Ed.* Adam Weiss *P.d.* Craig Stearns *A.d.* Jack D. L. Ballance *S.d.* Ellen Totleben *Mu.* Peter Himmelman *MPAA* R *R.t.* 103 min. *Cast:* Josh Charles, Jason Gedrick, Stephen Baldwin, Cheryl Pollak, Rita Taggart, Hy Anzell, Richard Edson, Ken Jenkins, Abraham Benrubi, David Schwimmer, Bob Nickman, James Krag, Rana Haugen, Jeffrey Tambor.

Set in 1975 in Detroit, this comic nostalgic drama centers on three young men (Josh Charles, Stephen Baldwin, and Jason Gedrick) who suffer from post-high school ennui. On a whim, the three accept a proposal to smuggle a load of drugs from Canada, then develop second thoughts.

CUP FINAL (Israel, 1992)

Pro. Michael Sharfshtein for Local Production Ltd. and Israel Broadcasting Authority; First Run Features *Dir.* Eran Riklis *Scr.* Eyal Halfon; based on the story by Eran Riklis *Cine.* Amnon Salomon *Ed.* Anal Lubarsky *Mu.* Raviv Gazil *R.t.* 107 min. *Cast:* Moshe Ivgi, Muhamad Bacri, Suheil Haddad, Sailm Dau, Basam Zuamut, Yuseff Abu Warda, Gasan Abbss, Sharon Alexander, Johnny Arbid.

Drawing parallels between sports and warfare, this drama is set in June, 1982, during the Israeli invasion of Lebanon and the World Cup soccer finals in Spain. The film centers on an Israeli soldier, Cohen (Moshe Ivgi), who is captured by Palestinians and forced to make the arduous journey to Beirut with them. Despite the war, Cohen and the Palestinian group's leader, Ziad (Muhamad Bacri), develop a tentative friendship based on their mutual love of soccer.

THE CUTTING EDGE

Pro. Ted Field, Karen Murphy, and Robert W. Cort for Interscope Communications; Metro-Goldwyn-Mayer *Dir.* Paul M. Glaser *Scr.* Tony Gilroy *Cine.* Elliot Davis *Ed.* Michael E. Polakow *P.d.* David Gropman *A.d.* Dan Davis *S.d.* Steve Shewchuk *Mu.* Patrick Williams *MPAA* PG *R.t.* 101 min. *Cast:* D. B. Sweeney, Moira Kelly, Roy Dotrice, Terry O'Quinn, Dwier Brown, Chris Benson.

In this romantic comedy, a beautiful but egotistical figure skater, Kate (Moira Kelly), pairs with a hockey player, Doug (D. B. Sweeney), in order to compete at the 1992 Winter Olympic Games. Good-natured Doug, who has left hockey because of an injury, melts Kate's frosty exterior while attempting this major career change in order to be able to continue skating.

DAMNED IN THE U.S.A. (Great Britain, 1991)

Pro. Paul Yule for Berwick Universal Pictures; Diusa Films *Dir.* Paul Yule *Cine.* Mark Benjamin, Robert Achs, and Luke Sacher *Ed.* John Street *R.t.* 68 min. *Cast:* Judge David Albanese, Dennis Barrie, Luther Campbell, Senator Alfonse M. D'Amato, Representative Thomas J. Downey, James Ford, Charles Freeman, Christie Hefner, Senator Jesse Helms, Senator Gordon Humphrey, Harry Lunn, Norma Ramos, Peter Reed, Joe Reilly, Andres Serrano, Jimmy Tingle, Reverend Donald Wildmon, Philip Yenawine.

Addressing the issue of censorship in the United States, this documentary centers on certain controversial events, such as the Cincinnati obscenity trial concerning a photography exhibit by Robert Mapplethorpe and the extreme tactics of the Reverend Donald Wildmon to suppress what he defines as pornography, in order to make a statement on the fine line between art and pornography.

DANZÓN (Mexico, 1992)

Pro. Jorge Sanchez for Instituto Mexicano de Cinematografia, Macondo Cine Video, Fondo de Fomento a la Calidad Cinematografica, Television Espanola, Tabasco Films, and Gobierno del Estado de Veracruz; Sony Pictures Classics *Dir.* María Novaro *Scr.* Beatriz Novaro and María Novaro *Cine.* Rodrigo García *Ed.* Nelson Rodriguez and María Novaro *MPAA* PG-13 *R.t.* 103 min. *Cast:* María Rojo, Carmen Salinas, Blanca Guerra, Tito Vasconcelos, Victor Vasconcelos, Margarita Isabel, Daniel Rergis.

A telephone operator, Julia (María Rojo), escapes the dull tedium of her life through ballroom dancing in the evenings. When her longtime partner, Carmelo (Daniel Rergis), of whom she knows very little, fails to arrive one night, Julia sets out on a journey to find him and, in the process, finds herself.

DAUGHTERS OF THE DUST

Pro. Julie Dash and Arthur Jafa for Geechee Girls and American Playhouse, in association with WMG; Kino International *Dir.* Julie Dash *Scr.* Julie Dash *Cine.* Arthur Jafa *Ed.* Amy Carey and Joseph Burton *P.d.* Kerry Marshall *A.d.* Michael Kelly Williams *Mu.* John Barnes *R.t.* 110 min. *Cast:* Cora Lee Day, Cheryl Lynn Bruce, Barbara-O, Tommy Hicks, Alva Rogers, Adisa Anderson, Kaycee Moore, Eartha D. Robinson, Bahni Turpin, Trula Hoosier, Kai-Lynn Warren (voice).

Set in 1902, this drama depicts the culture of the Gullahs, descendants of African slaves who inhabit the Sea Islands off the coast of South Carolina and Georgia. When two members of the Peazant family (Cheryl Lynn Bruce and Barbara-O) return from the mainland United States, the family prepares to emigrate in order to take advantage of the greater economic opportunities there.

A DAY IN OCTOBER (Denmark, 1992)

Pro. Just Betzer and Philippe Rivier for Kenmad/Panorama Film International; Castle Hill Productions, Inc. *Dir.* Kenneth Madsen *Scr.* Damian F. Slattery *Cine.* Henning Kristiansen *Ed.* Nicolas Gaster *P.d.* Sven Wichmann *S.d.* Torben Baekmark Pedersen *Mu.* Jens Lysdal and Adam Gorgoni *MPAA* PG-13 *R.t.* 103 min. *Cast:* D. B. Sweeney, Kelly Wolf, Tovah Feldshuh, Daniel Benzali, Ole Lemmeke, Kim Romer.

Set in Denmark during World War II, this drama centers on a fictional Jewish family that shelters a wounded Danish resistance fighter, Niels Jensen (D. B. Sweeney), who later helps them escape to Sweden along with many other Danish Jews. The film is based on actual events in 1943 when Danes helped 7,200 of their Jewish countrymen—almost their entire Jewish population—escape the Nazis.

DEEP COVER

Pro. Pierre David and Henry Bean; New Line Cinema *Dir.* Bill Duke *Scr.* Michael Tolkin and Henry Bean; based on a story by Tolkin *Cine.* Bojan Bazelli *Ed.* John Carter *P.d.* Pam Warner *A.d.* Daniel W. Bickel *S.d.* Donald Elmblad *Mu.* Michel Colombier *MPAA* R *R.t.* 122 min. *Cast:* Larry Fishburne, Jeff Goldblum, Victoria Dillard, Charles Martin Smith, Gregory Sierra, Clarence Williams III, Rene Assa, Arthur Mendoza, Alex Colon, Roger Guenveur Smith, Sydney Lassick, Kamala Lopez, Julio Oscar Mechoso, Glynn Turman.

A police officer (Larry Fishburne) is recruited by a Drug Enforcement Agency operative (Charles Martin Smith) to go undercover in order to expose a big Los Angeles drug dealer (Arthur Mendoza). With the help of dealer Jason (Jeff Goldblum), he slowly succumbs to the lures of drugs and money until he risks the tragic fate of his addict-criminal father.

DELICATESSEN (France, 1991)

Pro. Claude Ossard; Miramax Films *Dir.* Jean-Pierre Jeunet and Marc Caro *Scr.* Gilles Adrien *Cine.* Darius Khondji *Ed.* Herve Schneid *P.d.* Jean-Philippe Carp and Kreka Kjnakovic *Mu.* Carlos D'Alessio *R.t.* 95 min. *Cast:* Marie-Laure Dougnac, Dominique Pinon, Karin Viard, Jean-Claude Dreyfus, Ticky Holgado, Anne-Marie Pisani.

Set in a postapocalyptic future, this black comedy centers on a butcher (Jean-Claude Dreyfus) who carves up his assistants in order to maintain a supply of fresh meat for his customers. The butcher's problems mount when his nearsighted cellist daughter (Marie-Laure Dougnac) falls in love with his latest employee (Dominique Pinon), and when terrorist vegetarians arise from the sewers to try to put him out of business.

DESIRE AND HELL AT SUNSET MOTEL

Pro. Donald P. Borchers for Heron Communications and Image Organization; Two Moon Releasing *Dir.* Alien Castle *Scr.* Alien Castle *Cine.* Jamie Thompson *Ed.* James Gavin

Bedford *P.d.* Michael Clausen *S.d.* Jacquelyn Lemmon *Mu.* Alien Castle and Doug Walter *MPAA* PG-13 *R.t.* 90 min. *Cast:* Sherilyn Fenn, Whip Hubley, David Hewlett, David Johansen, Paul Bartel, Kenneth Toby.

Set in the 1950's, this black comedy centers on toy salesman Chester DeSoto (Whip Hubley) and his wife, Bridey (Sherilyn Fenn), who check into the Sunset Motel in Anaheim, where they become enmeshed in a web of murder and intrigue.

DIARY OF A HITMAN

Pro. Amin Q. Chaudhri for Vision International and Continental Film Group *Dir.* Roy London *Scr.* Kenneth Pressman; based on his play "Insider's Price" *Cine.* Yuri Sokol *Ed.* Brian Smedley-Aston *P.d.* Stephen Hendrickson *A.d.* Rusty Smith *Mu.* Michel Colombier *MPAA* R *R.t.* 91 min. *Cast:* Forest Whitaker, Sherilyn Fenn, Sharon Stone, Seymour Cassel, James Belushi, Lewis Smith, Lois Chiles, John Bedford Lloyd.

A professional hitman, Dekker (Forest Whitaker), begins to doubt his profession when a man (Lewis Smith) hires Dekker to kill his wife (Sherilyn Fenn) and baby. Dekker breaches professional ethics by not only meeting her but also developing sympathy for her.

DIGGSTOWN

Pro. Robert Schaffel for Schaffel/Eclectic Films; Metro-Goldwyn-Mayer *Dir.* Michael Ritchie *Scr.* Steven McKay; based on the novel *The Diggstown Ringers*, by Leonard Wise *Cine.* Gerry Fisher *Ed.* Don Zimmerman *P.d.* Steve Hendrickson *A.d.* Okowita *S.d.* Gregory Van Horn, Michael Devine, and Barbara Drake *Mu.* James Newton Howard *MPAA* R *R.t.* 97 min. *Cast:* James Woods, Louis Gossett, Jr., Bruce Dern, Oliver Platt, Heather Graham, Randall "Tex" Cobb, Thomas Wilson Brown, Duane Davis, Willie Green, Orestes Matacena.

Upon his release from prison, consummate con man Gabriel Caine (James Woods) returns to Diggstown for the ultimate con. Enlisting the aid of friend and aging boxer "Honey" Roy Palmer (Louis Gossett, Jr.), Caine bets the cruel and greedy owner of Diggstown, John Gillon (Bruce Dern), that Palmer can outbox ten men in twenty-four hours. The stakes are money, the freedom of the townspeople, and, ultimately, Caine's and Palmer's lives.

LA DISCRETE (France, 1992)

Pro. Alain Rocca for Les Productions Lazennec, in association with FR3 Films and Sara Films; MK2 Productions *Dir.* Christian Vincent *Scr.* Christian Vincent and Jean-Pierre Ronssin *Cine.* Romain Winding *Ed.* François Ceppi *S.d.* Sylvie Olivé *Mu.* Jay Gottlieb *R.t.* 95 min. *Cast:* Fabrice Luchini, Judith Henry, Maurice Garrel, Marie Bunel, François Toumarkine.

When French writer Antoine's (Fabrice Luchini) girlfriend leaves him, he seeks revenge by accepting the wager of a friend and editor (Maurice Garrel): Antoine will seduce a young woman chosen at random and then abandon her—and he will publish his experiences. The bet goes wrong when Antoine seduces and falls in love with Catherine (Judith Henry).

DR. GIGGLES

Pro. Stuart M. Besser for Largo Entertainment, in association with JVC Entertainment and Dark Horse; Universal Pictures *Dir.* Manny Coto *Scr.* Manny Coto and Graeme Whifler *Cine.* Robert Draper *Ed.* Debra Neil *P.d.* Bill Malley *A.d.* Alan Locke *S.d.* C. C. Rodarte *Mu.* Brian May *MPAA* R *R.t.* 95 min. *Cast:* Larry Drake, Holly Marie Combs, Cliff De Young, Glenn Quinn, Keith Diamond, Richard Bradford, Michelle Johnson, John Vickery, Nancy Fish, Sara Melson, Zoe Trilling, Darin Heames, Deborah Tucker, Doug E. Doug, Denise Barnes.

Larry Drake stars as the title character, otherwise known as Dr. Evan Rendell, the mentally ill son of a doctor with questionable ethics. Seeking revenge for his father's death, Rendell escapes from a mental institution and returns to his hometown where he proceeds to murder people left and right.

DOLLY DEAREST

Pro. Daniel Cady for Patriot Pictures, in association with Channeler Enterprises; Trimark *Dir.* Maria Lease *Scr.* Maria Lease; based on a story by Lease, Peter Sutcliffe, and Rod Nave *Cine.* Eric D. Andersen *Ed.* Geoffrey Rowland *P.d.* W. Brooke Wheeler *Mu.* Mark Snow *MPAA* R *R.t.* 93 min. *Cast:* Denise Crosby, Sam Bottoms, Chris Demetral, Candy Hutson, Lupe Ontiveros, Will Gotay, Alma Martinez, Enrique Renaldo, Rip Torn, Ed Gale.

In this low-budget version of *Child's Play* (1988), a couple with two children moves to Mexico where they start a doll factory. Unfortunately for them, a nearby archaeologist has unwittingly released evil spirits from an ancient mass grave that come to possess their daughter's doll.

DOUBLE EDGE

Pro. Amos Kollek and Rafi Reibenbach; Castle Hill Productions, Inc. *Dir.* Amos Kollek *Scr.* Amos Kollek *Cine.* Amnon Salomon *Ed.* David Tour and Vicki Hiatt *S.d.* Zvika Aloni *Mu.* Mira J. Spektor *MPAA* PG-13 *R.t.* 86 min. *Cast:* Faye Dunaway, Amos Kollek, Mohammad Bakri, Makram Khouri, Michael Schneider, Shmuel Shiloh, Anat Atzmon, Ann Belkin, Teddy Kollek, Abba Eban, Rabbi Meir Kahane, Hanan Ashrawi, Ziad Abu Zayad, Naomi Altaraz.

Faye Dunaway stars as a New York reporter, Faye Milano, sent to Israel for three weeks to cover the Palestinian-Israeli conflict. Unfortunately, Milano understands little of the issues and unwittingly becomes involved in the turmoil. Although the film features interviews with real-life political figures, such as former Israeli Foreign Minister Abba Eban and filmmaker Amos Kollek's father—Jerusalem mayor Teddy Kollek—both Dunaway and writer/director Kollek turn in poor performances in a decidedly weak film.

DOUBLE TROUBLE

Pro. Brad Krevoy and Steve Stabler; Motion Picture Corporation of America *Dir.* John Paragon *Scr.* Jeffrey Kerns, Kurt Wimmer, and Chuck Osbourne; based on a story by Wimmer and Osbourne *Cine.* Richard Michalak *Ed.* Jonas Thaler *P.d.* Johan Letenoux and Gilbert Mercier *S.d.* Marisol Jimenez *MPAA* R *R.t.* 90 min. *Cast:* Peter Paul, David Paul, Roddy McDowall, David Carradine, Steve Kanaly, James Doohan, A. J. Johnson, Bill Mumy, Troy Donahue.

In this weak action/adventure, a detective (David Paul) teams with his long-lost twin brother (Peter Paul), who is a thief, in order to catch a group of international jewel smugglers and their wealthy boss (Roddy McDowell).

DRIVE

Pro. Gregory D. Levy and Jefery Levy; Megagiant Entertainment, Inc. *Dir.* Jefery Levy *Scr.* Colin MacLeod and Jefery Levy *Cine.* Steven Wacks *Ed.* Lauren Zuckerman *Mu.* Charles Bisharat and Dr. Lee *R.t.* 87 min. *Cast:* David Warner, Steve Antin, Dedee Pfeiffer.

Set entirely inside an automobile on a Los Angeles freeway, *Drive* features two men—the Driver (David Warner) and the Passenger (Steve Antin)—who are making the daily ninety-minute commute to their downtown computer jobs. As the Driver rants over the current state of American society, the Passenger laments a lost love.

EDWARD II (Great Britain, 1992)

Pro. Steve Clark-Hall and Antony Root for British Screen, BBC Films, and Working Title; Fine Line Features *Dir.* Derek Jarman *Scr.* Derek Jarman, Stephen McBride, and Ken Butler; based on the play by Christopher Marlowe *Cine.* Ian Wilson *Ed.* George Akers *P.d.* Christopher Hobbs *A.d.* Rick Eyres *Mu.* Simon Fisher Turner *MPAA* R *R.t.* 90 min. *Cast:* Steven Waddington, Andrew Tiernan, Tilda Swinton, Nigel Terry, Kevin Collins, Jerome Flynn, John Lynch, Dudley Sutton, Jody Graber, Annie Lennox.

In this modern version of Christopher Marlowe's Elizabethan tragedy, the court of Edward II (Steven Waddington)—including his spurned queen, Isabella (Tilda Swinton)—revolts against its homosexual king and his power-hungry lover, Gaveston (Andrew Tiernan). The film contains explicit sex and graphic violence.

THE EFFICIENCY EXPERT (Australia, 1992)

Pro. Richard Brennan and Timothy White for Meridian Films, in association with Smiley Films; Miramax Films *Dir.* Mark Joffe *Scr.* Max Dann and Andrew Knight *Cine.* Ellery Ryan *Ed.* Nicholas Beauman *P.d.* Chris Kennedy *MPAA* PG *R.t.* 89 min. *Cast:* Anthony Hopkins, Ben Mendelsohn, Toni Collette, Alwyn Kurts, Dan Wyllie, Bruno Lawrence, Rebecca Rigg, Russell Crowe, Angela Punch McGregor.

Anthony Hopkins stars in this pleasant comedy as Wallace, a no-nonsense efficiency expert who has been hired by a family-owned moccasin business to streamline the company, but who, in turn, is won over by the friendly and eccentric people he may be putting out of business.

L'ELEGANT CRIMINEL (France, 1992)

Pro. Ariel Zeitoun; RKO Pictures *Dir.* Francis Girod *Scr.* Georges Conchon and Francis Girod *Cine.* Bruno de Keyzer *Mu.* Laurent Petitgirard *R.t.* 120 min. *Cast:* Daniel Auteuil, Jean Poiret, Marie-Armelle DeGuy, Maiwenn Le Besco, Jacques Weber, Patrick Pineau, Samuel Labarthe, François Perier, Genevìeve Casile.

Based on real events, this drama centers on Pierre Lacenaire (Daniel Auteuil), a nineteenth century French dandy and rogue who pleaded guilty to murder and was subsequently guillotined. Told in flashback, the narrative begins with Lacenaire in prison—an elegant young man visited by aristocrats and artists—then jumps back in time to his childhood and the beginning of his life in crime.

THE END OF OLD TIMES (Czechoslovakia, 1992)

Pro. Barrandov Film Studios; IFEX International *Dir.* Jiri Menzel *Scr.* Jiri Menzel and Jiri Blazek; based on a novel by Vladislav Vancura *Cine.* Jaromir Sofr *A.d.* Zbynek Hloch *Mu.* Jiri Sust *R.t.* 97 min. *Cast:* Josef Abrham, Marian Labuda, Jaromir Hanzlik, Rudolf Hrusinsky, Jan Hrusinsky, Jan Hartl, Barbora Leichnorova, Chantal Poullain-Polikova.

Set in Bohemia following the 1918 Czech revolution, this comedy centers on a wealthy and ambitious businessman (Marian Labuda) who seeks favor with the government in order to buy the large country estate that he currently runs. To this end, he throws a weekend-long party for his powerful neighbors and receives an unexpected guest—a man who claims to be royalty (Josef Abrham)—who becomes the life of the party.

FALLING FROM GRACE

Pro. Harry Sandler for Little b Pictures; Columbia Pictures *Dir.* John Mellencamp *Scr.* Larry McMurtry *Cine.* Victor Hammer *Ed.* Dennis Virkler *P.d.* George Corsillo *A.d.* Todd Hatfield *S.d.* Sandi Cook *MPAA* PG-13 *R.t.* 100 min. *Cast:* John Mellencamp, Mariel Hemingway, Claude Akins, Dub Taylor, Kay Lenz, Larry Crane, Kate Noonan, Dierdre O'Connell, John Prine, Brent Huff.

Musician John Mellencamp directs and stars in this drama about a successful musician, Bud Parks, who returns to his small Indiana hometown for the birthday celebration of his eighty-year-old grandfather (Dub Taylor). Once there, he becomes enmeshed in his family's problems and has an affair with an old girlfriend (Kay Lenz).

THE FAMINE WITHIN
Pro. Katherine Gilday for Panorama Entertainment Corp. and Kandor Prod., in association with Telefilm Canada, the Ontario Film Development Corp., National Film Board of Canada, and TVOntario; Direct Cinema Ltd. *Dir.* Katherine Gilday *Scr.* Katherine Gilday *Cine.* Joan Hutton *Ed.* Petra Valier *Mu.* Russell Walker *R.t.* 90 min. *Cast:* Rebecca Jenkins.

Women and dieting is the subject of this sobering documentary that examines the 1990's ideal of feminine beauty and women's sometimes life-and-death struggles to achieve it. The filmmakers contend that for many American women dieting has become an obsession which has led to life-threatening problems such as anorexia and bulimia.

FATHERS AND SONS
Pro. Jon Kilik for Addis/Wechsler; Pacific Pictures *Dir.* Paul Mones *Scr.* Paul Mones *Cine.* Ron Fortunato *Ed.* Janice Keuhnelian *P.d.* Eve Cauley *Mu.* Mason Daring *MPAA* R *R.t.* 99 min. *Cast:* Jeff Goldblum, Rory Cochrane, Natasha Gregson Wagner, Mitchell Marchand, Paul Hipp, Ellen Greene, Famke Janssen, Rosanna Arquette, Samuel L. Jackson, Joie Lee, Michael Disend.

Jeff Goldblum stars as widowed father Max Fish, who is struggling to rear his adolescent and moody son, Ed (Rory Cochrane). The drama tries to emphasize the similarities in the father's and son's lives despite the distance between the two, but a subplot involving a psychopathic serial murderer distracts from the main theme.

THE FAVOUR, THE WATCH, AND THE VERY BIG FISH (France and Great Britain, 1992)
Pro. Michelle de Broca for Les Films Ariane/Fildebroc/Umbrella Films Ltd., in association with Sovereign Pictures; Trimark Pictures *Dir.* Ben Lewin *Scr.* Ben Lewin; based on the short story "Rue Saint-Sulpice," by Marcel Aymé *Cine.* Bernard Zitzermann *Ed.* John Grover *P.d.* Carlos Conti *Mu.* Vladimir Cosma *MPAA* R *R.t.* 89 min. *Cast:* Bob Hoskins, Jeff Goldblum, Natasha Richardson, Michel Blanc, Jacques Villeret, Angela Pleasence, Jean-Pierre Cassel, Samuel Chaimovitch.

A shy Parisian photographer (Bob Hoskins), a beautiful woman (Natasha Richardson)—who dubs the moaning for pornographic films—and a pianist (Jeff Goldblum) with a Christ fixation form an unlikely triangle in this romantic comedy.

FEED
Pro. Kevin Rafferty and James Ridgeway for Video Democracy; Original Cinema *Dir.* Kevin Rafferty and James Ridgeway *Cine.* Kevin Rafferty *Ed.* Sarah Durham and Kevin Rafferty *R.t.* 76 min. *Cast:* George Bush, Bill Clinton, Paul Tsongas, Jerry Brown, Ross Perot, Bob Kerrey, Patrick Buchanan, Hillary Clinton, Sam Donaldson, Gennifer Flowers, Arnold Schwarzenegger.

Centering on the 1992 presidential campaign, this documentary is composed of candid video clips of the various presidential candidates as they wait to go on the air prior to the New Hampshire primary. From George Bush to Bill Clinton to Paul Tsongas and so on, these untelevised moments were captured by the satellite dish of Brian Springer, and are combined with other footage that includes such famous names and faces as Arnold Schwarzenegger, Gennifer Flowers, and Sam Donaldson for a revealing, and sometimes cruel, look at 1990's politics and politicians.

FERNGULLY: THE LAST RAINFOREST
Pro. Wayne Young and Peter Faiman for FAI Films, in association with Youngheart Productions; Twentieth Century-Fox *Dir.* Bill Kroyer *Scr.* Jim Cox; based on stories by Diana Young *Ed.* Gillian Hutshing *A.d.* Susan Kroyer, Ralph Eggleston (color stylist), and Victoria

Jenson (layout design) *Mu.* Alan Silvestri *MPAA* G *R.t.* 76 min. *Voices:* Tim Curry, Samantha Mathis, Jonathan Ward, Robin Williams, Christian Slater, Grace Zabriskie, Geoffrey Blake, Robert Pastorelli, Cheech Marin, Tommy Chong, Tone-Loc.

In this animated musical adventure, an Australian rainforest is threatened by loggers who awaken a malevolent spirit, Hexxus (voice of Tim Curry). When a fairy, Crysta (voice of Samantha Mathis), accidentally shrinks one of the loggers, Zak (voice of Jonathan Ward), down to her size, he joins forces with the inhabitants of FernGully to protect their home.

A FINE ROMANCE (Italy, 1992)

Pro. Arturo La Pegna and Massimiliano La Pegna; Castle Hill Productions, Inc. *Dir.* Gene Saks *Scr.* Ronald Harwood; based on *Tchin Tchin*, by Francois Billetdoux *Cine.* Franco Di Giacomo *Ed.* Richard Nord and Anna Poscetti *A.d.* Jean Michel Hugon and Michel Albournac *Mu.* Pino Donaggio *MPAA* PG-13 *R.t.* 83 min. *Cast:* Julie Andrews, Marcello Mastroianni, Ian Fitzgibbon, Jean-Pierre Castaldi.

Julie Andrews and Marcello Mastroianni star in this stale romantic comedy as a couple who become lovers when their respective spouses have an affair.

FLIRTING (Australia, 1991)

Pro. George Miller, Doug Mitchell, and Terry Hayes for Kennedy Miller; the Samuel Goldwyn Company *Dir.* John Duigan *Scr.* John Duigan *Cine.* Geoff Burton *Ed.* Robert Gibson *P.d.* Roger Ford *A.d.* Laurie Faen *S.d.* Kerrie Brown and Glen Johnson *Mu.* Christine Woodruff *R.t.* 99 min. *Cast:* Noah Taylor, Thandie Newton, Nicole Kidman, Bartholomew Rose, Felix Nobis, Jeff Truman, Marshall Napier, John Dicks, Fiona Press, Maggie Blinco, Jane Harders, Malcolm Robertson, Judi Farr, Freddie Paris, Femi Taylor, Harry Lawrence, Kurt Frey.

A lonely, thoughtful teenager (Noah Taylor) at a strict boarding school in rural Australia meets and falls in love with the only black student (Thandie Newton) at the sister school across the lake. The two defy convention, prejudice, and the rules of the schools, developing a relationship that they hope will withstand geographical and political separation.

FOLKS

Pro. Victor Drai and Malcolm R. Harding for Penta Pictures; Twentieth Century-Fox *Dir.* Ted Kotcheff *Scr.* Robert Klane *Cine.* Larry Pizer *Ed.* Joan E. Chapman *P.d.* William J. Creber *Mu.* Michel Colombier *MPAA* PG-13 *R.t.* 108 min. *Cast:* Tom Selleck, Don Ameche, Anne Jackson, Christine Ebersole, Wendy Crewson, Robert Pastorelli, Michael Murphy.

When hardworking and honest Chicago businessman Jon Aldrich (Tom Selleck) flies to Florida to see his mother (Anne Jackson), who is in the hospital, he discovers that his father (Don Ameche) is going senile. Although he has avoided his parents for the past eight years, Jon brings them home to his wife (Wendy Crewson) and children, where, amid problems at Jon's business, his parents slowly drive him insane. When Mom suggests that he kill them for the insurance money, Jon's comic attempts literally hurt him more than his parents.

FOR SASHA (France, 1992)

Pro. Alexandre Arcady and Diane Kurys; MK2 Productions U.S.A. *Dir.* Alexandre Arcady *Scr.* Alexandre Arcady and Daniel Saint Hamont *Cine.* Robert Alazraki *Ed.* Martine Barraque *P.d.* Tony Egry *Mu.* Philippe Sarde *R.t.* 110 min. *Cast:* Sophie Marceau, Richard Berry, Fabien Orcier, Niels Dubost, Jean-Claude De Goros.

Set in 1967 on the eve of the Six-Day War in Israel, this drama centers on a young French woman, Laura (Sophie Marceau), who lives on an Israeli kibbutz with her former philosophy teacher, Sasha (Richard Berry), who is twice her age. Three former classmates (Fabien Orcier, Niels Dubost, and Jean-Claude De Goros) who were all smitten with Laura arrive from

France in order to celebrate her twentieth birthday, awakening old emotions.

1492: CONQUEST OF PARADISE (Great Britain, France, and Spain, 1992)

Pro. Ridley Scott and Alain Goldman for Percy Main/Legende; Paramount Pictures *Dir.* Ridley Scott *Scr.* Roselyne Bosch *Cine.* Adrian Biddle *Ed.* William Anderson and Françoise Bonnot *P.d.* Norris Spencer *A.d.* Benjamin Fernandez and Leslie Tomkins *S.d.* Ann Mollo *Mu.* Vangelis *MPAA* PG-13 *R.t.* 150 min. *Cast:* Gérard Depardieu, Armand Assante, Sigourney Weaver, Loren Dean, Angela Molina, Fernando Rey, Michael Wincott, Tcheky Karyo, Kevin Dunn, Frank Langella, Mark Margolis, Kario Salem, Billy Sullivan, John Heffernan, Steven Waddington, Fernando Guillen, Bercelio Moya.

Renowned French actor Gérard Depardieu stars as Christopher Columbus, and Sigourney Weaver is Queen Isabel, in this overblown historical drama commemorating the five-hundredth anniversary of Columbus' discovery of the New World.

FREDDIE AS F.R.O.7 (Great Britain, 1992)

Pro. Norman Priggen and Jon Acevski for Hollywood Road Film Productions, Ltd., and J & M Entertainment, in association with Motion Pictures Investments; Miramax Films *Dir.* Jon Acevski *Scr.* Jon Acevski and David Ashton *Cine.* Rex Neville *Ed.* Alex Rayment and Mick Manning *A.d.* Paul Shardlow *Mu.* David Dundas and Rick Wentworth *MPAA* PG *R.t.* 90 min. *Voices:* Ben Kingsley, Jenny Agutter, Billie Whitelaw, Brian Blessed, Nigel Hawthorne, Michael Hordern, Edmund Kingsley, Phyllis Logan, Victor Maddern, Jonathan Pryce, Prunella Scales, John Sessions.

This superficial animated adventure centers on Freddie (voice of Ben Kingsley), who is a human-sized frog as the result of a spell cast by his wicked aunt Messina (voice of Billie Whitelaw) some years prior. Renowned as a French secret agent, Freddie is called to England to thwart the plan of Messina and the evil El Supremo (voice of Brian Blessed) to take over the world. The story is convoluted and improbable, and tries, unsuccessfully, to incorporate elements of fairy tale, pop culture, and science fiction.

FREEJACK

Pro. Ronald Shusett and Stuart Oken for James G. Robinson and Morgan Creek; Warner Bros. *Dir.* Geoff Murphy *Scr.* Steven Pressfield, Ronald Shusett, and Dan Gilroy; based on a story by Pressfield and Shusett and on the novel *Immortality, Inc.*, by Robert Sheckley *Cine.* Amir Mokri *Ed.* Dennis Virkler *P.d.* Joe Alves *A.d.* James A. Taylor *S.d.* Bruce A. Gibeson *Mu.* Trevor Jones *MPAA* R *R.t.* 108 min. *Cast:* Emilio Estevez, Mick Jagger, Rene Russo, Anthony Hopkins, Jonathan Banks, David Johansen, Amanda Plummer, Grand L. Bush, Frankie Faison, John Shea, Esai Morales.

In this science-fiction action film, a race car driver, Alex Furlong (Emilio Estevez), suffers a fatal collision in the year 1991 and is plucked from death and transported to the grim future of the year 2009, where his healthy body is wanted for a brain transplant. When Alex manages to escape, he is pursued by a bounty hunter (Mick Jagger).

FROZEN ASSETS

Pro. Don Klein for George Miller; RKO Pictures *Dir.* George Miller *Scr.* Don Klein and Tom Kartozian *Cine.* Ron Lautore and Geza Sinkovics *Ed.* Larry Bock *P.d.* Deborah Raymond and Dorian Vernacchio *Mu.* Michael Tavera *MPAA* PG-13 *R.t.* 96 min. *Cast:* Shelley Long, Corbin Bernsen, Larry Miller, Dody Goodman, Matt Clark, Jeanne Cooper, Paul Sand, Gloria Camden, Teri Copley.

Shelley Long and Corbin Bernsen star in this weak romantic comedy. Bernsen plays an executive, Zach Shepard, sent from Los Angeles to small-town Oregon to save a failing bank run by Long's character, Dr. Grace Murdock. Momentarily daunted that it is, in fact, a sperm bank, Shepard develops a contest with a prize for the entrant with the highest sperm count, and in the process, he and Murdock fall in love.

GATE II

Pro. Andras Hamori for Vision p.d.g. and Alliance Entertainment; Triumph *Dir.* Tibor Takacs *Scr.* Michael Nankin *Cine.* Bryan England *Ed.* Ronald Sanders *P.d.* William Beeton *S.d.* Nick White and Joe Verreault *Mu.* George Blondheim *MPAA* R *R.t.* 93 min. *Cast:* Louis Tripp, Pamela Segall, James Villemaire, Simon Reynolds, Neil Munro, James Kidnie, Andrea Ladanyi.

In this sequel to *The Gate* (1987), Terry (Louis Tripp), now a teenager, once more summons demons from beyond "The Gate," with the help of three other teens (Pamela Segall, James Villemaire, and Simon Reynolds), in order to help his widowed, alcoholic father (Neil Munro). Although the teens succeed in getting certain wishes granted, they live to regret it.

THE GIVING

Pro. Cevin Cathell, Tim Disney, and Eames Demetrios for Three Cats, Inc., in association with Jeremiah Pollock Associates; Northern Arts Entertainment *Dir.* Eames Demetrios *Scr.* Eames Demetrios *Cine.* Antonio Soriano *Ed.* Bruce Barrow and Nancy Richardson *P.d.* Diane Romine Clark and Lee Shane *Mu.* Stephen James Taylor *R.t.* 100 min. *Cast:* Kevin Kildow, Lee Hampton, Stephen Hornyak, James Asher Salt, Russell Smith, Satya Cyprian, Gail Green, Kellie A. McKuen, Joel (Wolf) Parker, Paul Boesing, Oliver Patterson, Michael McGee, Southern Comfort, Eleanor Alpert, Lois Yaroshefsky, Lionel Stoneham, Marilyn Stoneham, Gina Elten, Martha Kincare, Jacklin Townson, Paul H. Rosas, Rick Wolf, Gentle Culpepper.

A well-to-do bank executive/computer genius, Jeremiah Pollock (Kevin Kildow), becomes obsessed with aiding the homeless in Los Angeles: He donates money, goes on a hunger strike, lives on the street, and rigs his bank's instant cash machines so the homeless can use them.

GLADIATOR: (also known as *Bare Knuckles*)

Pro. Frank Price and Steve Roth for Price Entertainment; Columbia Pictures *Dir.* Rowdy Herrington *Scr.* Lyle Kessler and Robert Mark Kamen; based on a story by Djordje Milicevic and Kamen *Cine.* Tak Fujimoto *Ed.* Peter Zinner and Harry B. Miller III *P.d.* Gregg Fonseca *A.d.* Bruce Miller *S.d.* Jay R. Hart *Mu.* Brad Fiedel *MPAA* R *R.t.* 99 min. *Cast:* James Marshall, Cuba Gooding, Jr., Brian Dennehy, Robert Loggia, Ossie Davis, Cara Buono, John Heard, John Seda, Lance Slaughter, T. E. Russell, Francesca P. Roberts, Debra Sandlund.

In this mediocre action/adventure, a teenage Chicago boy, Tommy (James Marshall), is forced into illegal boxing matches in order to pay his father's gambling debts. When white Tommy is pitted against his black friend Lincoln (Cuba Gooding, Jr.), they discover who the real enemy is—unscrupulous white businessman Horn (Brian Dennehy), who stages the illegal fights.

THE GOOD WOMAN OF BANGKOK (Australia, 1992)

Pro. Dennis O'Rourke; Roxie Releasing *Dir.* Dennis O'Rourke *Scr.* Dennis O'Rourke *Cine.* Dennis O'Rourke *Ed.* Tim Litchfield *Mu.* Wolfgang Amadeus Mozart *R.t.* 82 min. *Cast:* Yaiwalak Chonchanakun (Aoi).

Painfully explicit, this documentary centers on a young Bangkok prostitute, Aoi, who is forced to sell herself in the big city in order to support her mother and daughters.

GUILTY AS CHARGED

Pro. Randolph Gale; I.R.S. Media *Dir.* Sam Irvin *Scr.* Charles Gale *Cine.* Richard Michalak *Ed.* Kevin Tent *P.d.* Byrnadette di Santo *A.d.* Ian Hardy *S.d.* Pascale Vaquette *Mu.* Steve

Bartek *MPAA* R *R.t.* 95 min. *Cast:* Rod Steiger, Heather Graham, Lyman Ward, Lauren Hutton, Isaac Hayes, Zelda Rubinstein.

In this black comedy, a vigilante meat packer (Rod Steiger) takes the law into his own hands when he begins executing murderers in his basement whom he considers to have escaped proper punishment.

THE GUN IN BETTY LOU'S HANDBAG

Pro. Scott Kroopf for Touchstone Pictures and Interscope Communications, in association with Nomura Babcock & Brown; Buena Vista *Dir.* Allan Moyle *Scr.* Grace Cary Bickley *Cine.* Charles Minsky *Ed.* Janice Hampton and Erica Huggins *P.d.* Michael Corenblith *A.d.* David J. Bomba *S.d.* Lori Rowbotham and Merideth Boswell Charbonnet *Mu.* Richard Gibbs *MPAA* PG-13 *R.t.* 89 min. *Cast:* Penelope Ann Miller, Eric Thal, Alfre Woodard, Julianne Moore, Andy Romano, Ray McKinnon, William Forsythe, Xander Berkeley, Michael O'Neill, Christopher John Fields, Cathy Moriarty.

When a neglected wife (Penelope Ann Miller) discovers the gun used in a local murder, she confesses to the crime in order to get the attention of her preoccupied police-officer husband (Eric Thal), only to discover that she gets more trouble than she bargained for.

HADESAE: THE FINAL INCIDENT (Iran, 1992)

Pro. Jack Kaprielian; Scoplin Pictures *Dir.* Kayvon Derakhshanian *Scr.* Ali Emami; based on a story by Kayvon Derakhshanian *Cine.* Del Chouia *Ed.* Kayvon Derakhshanian and Jack Kaprielian *Mu.* Kam Nejad *R.t.* 90 min. *Cast:* Bahman Mofid, Soraya Mofid, Babak Habibifar, Andy Bagheri, Sohaila Rahmaney, Sepideh Mashiah.

Set in Southern California, this drama centers on an Iranian man (Bahman Mofid) and woman (Soraya Mofid) who have kidnapped their daughter (Sepideh Mashiah) from a mental hospital after having escaped to the United States following the downfall of the shah. Their secret is threatened by the arrival of a group of Iranian tourists, who have car trouble on the family's ural Southern California property and come to them for help.

HARD PROMISES

Pro. Cindy Chvatal and William Petersen for Stone Group Pictures and High Horse Films; Columbia Pictures *Dir.* Martin Davidson *Scr.* Jule Selbo *Cine.* Andrzej Bartkowiak *Ed.* Bonnie Koehler *P.d.* Dan Leigh *Mu.* George S. Clinton *MPAA* PG *R.t.* 95 min. *Cast:* Sissy Spacek, William Petersen, Brian Kerwin, Mare Winningham, Jeff Perry, Olivia Burnette, Peter MacNicol, Ann Wedgeworth, Lois Smith, Amy Wright.

An invitation to his former wife's wedding brings a good-natured drifter, Joey (William Petersen), back home to a small town in Texas. Chris (Sissy Spacek), tired of Joey's prolonged absences, has divorced him without his knowledge and is within a day of marrying another man, Walter (Brian Kerwin). Repenting their lost years of marriage, Joey hopes to win Chris back.

HEARTS OF DARKNESS: A FILMMAKER'S APOCALYPSE

Pro. George Zaloom and Les Mayfield for Showtime and ZM, in association with Zoetrope Studios; Triton Pictures *Dir.* Fax Bahr and George Hickenlooper; documentary footage director Eleanor Coppola *Scr.* Fax Bahr and George Hickenlooper *Cine.* Vittorio Storaro *Ed.* Michael Greer and Jay Miracle *P.d.* Dean Tavoularis *Mu.* Todd Boekelheide *MPAA* R *R.t.* 96 min. *Cast:* Francis Ford Coppola, Eleanor Coppola, John Milius, Martin Sheen, George Lucas, Frederic Forrest, Larry Fishburne, Robert Duvall, Dennis Hopper.

This documentary—composed of film footage shot by Eleanor Coppola, director Francis Ford Coppola's wife, during the filming of her husband's *Apocalypse Now* (1979) and of interviews with the principals twelve years later—centers on the numerous difficulties that plagued the project. While on location in the Philippines, the crew witnessed tropical storms, civil war, and the firing and last-minute hiring of principals before achieving an acclaimed interpretation of Joseph Conrad's *Heart of Darkness*.

HELLRAISER III: HELL ON EARTH

Pro. Lawrence Mortorff for Fifth Avenue Entertainment; Dimension Pictures *Dir.* Anthony Hickox *Scr.* Peter Atkins; based on a story by Atkins and Tony Randel, and on characters created by Clive Barker *Cine.* Gerry Lively *Ed.* Christopher Cibelli *P.d.* Steve Hardie *A.d.* Tim Eckel *S.d.* Carey Meyer and David Allen Koneff *Mu.* Randy Miller *MPAA* R *R.t.* 92 min. *Cast:* Terry Farrell, Doug Bradley, Paula Marshall, Kevin Bernhardt, Ken Carpenter, Peter Boynton, Ashley Laurence, Aimee Leigh, Lawrence Mortorff.

The third in the *Hellraiser* series, this horror film centers on the evil Pinhead (Doug Bradley), a demon from Hell whose name describes his physical appearance, and an ambitious reporter, Joey Summerskill (Terry Farrell). When horror and mayhem break out at a local rock club, Summerskill goes to investigate.

HIGHWAY 61 (Canada, 1992)

Pro. Bruce McDonald and Colin Brunton for Shadow Shows Entertainment Corporation, in association with Film Four International; Skouras Pictures *Dir.* Bruce McDonald *Scr.* Don McKellar; based on a story by Bruce McDonald, McKellar, and Allan Magee *Cine.* Miroslaw Baszak *Ed.* Michael Pacek and Steve Munro *A.d.* Ian Brock *Mu.* Nash the Slash *MPAA* R *R.t.* 102 min. *Cast:* Don McKellar, Valerie Buhagiar, Earl Pastko, Jello Biafra, Hadley Obodiac, Peter Breck, Art Bergmann.

In this quirky road film, a small-town Canadian trumpeter, Pokey Jones (Don McKellar), with big-time dreams agrees to drive a young woman, Jackie (Valerie Buhagiar), to New Orleans to bury a body that Pokey found in his backyard and that Jackie claims was her brother. Jackie hides a stash of drugs in the dead man's mouth without Pokey's knowledge, and the two begin their trip pursued by no less than Satan himself (Earl Pastko), who wants the dead body.

HIGHWAY TO HELL

Pro. Mary Anne Page and John Byers for John Daly, Derek Gibson, and Goodman-Rosen/Josa/High Street Pictures; Hemdale *Dir.* Ate De Jong *Scr.* Brian Helgeland *Cine.* Robin Vidgeon *Ed.* Todd Ramsay and Randy Thornton *P.d.* Phillip Dean Foreman *Mu.* Hidden Faces *MPAA* R *R.t.* 95 min. *Cast:* Chad Lowe, Kristy Swanson, Patrick Bergin, Richard Farnsworth, Adam Storke, Pamela Gidley, Jarrett Lennon, C. J. Graham, Lita Ford, Gilbert Gottfried, Kevin Peter Hall, Anne Meara, Jerry Stiller, Amy Stiller, Ben Stiller.

In this version of the Orpheus myth, a young couple—Charlie (Chad Lowe) and Rachel (Kristy Swanson)—are driving through the desert to Las Vegas to get married when Rachel is kidnapped by a Hellcop (C. J. Graham). Charlie pursues them into Hell where he encounters Satan (Patrick Bergin).

THE HOURS AND TIMES

Pro. Christopher Münch for Good Machine, Inc.; Antarctic Pictures *Dir.* Christopher Münch *Scr.* Christopher Münch *Cine.* Christopher Münch *Cine.* Juan Carlos Valls *Ed.* Christopher Münch *Mu.* Carlos Calvo and David Loeb *R.t.* 60 min. *Cast:* David Angus, Ian Hart, Stephanie Pack, Robin McDonald, Sergio Moreno, Unity Grimwood.

This controversial film is based upon a real-life excursion to Barcelona made in 1963 by John Lennon and the Beatles' manager Brian Epstein. Münch suggests that Epstein (David Angus) and Lennon (Ian Hart) may have entered into a brief homosexual affair during that time.

HUGH HEFNER: ONCE UPON A TIME

Pro. Gary H. Grossman and Robert Heath for Lynch/Frost Prods.; I.R.S. *Dir.* Robert Heath *Scr.* Gary H. Grossman, Michael Gross, and Robert Heath *Cine.* Van Carlson, Dustin Teel, and Tony Zapata *Ed.* Michael Gross *Mu.* Charlotte Lansberg, Reeves Gabrels, and Tom Dube *R.t.* 91 min. *Cast:* James Coburn, Hugh Hefner.

Centering on Hugh Hefner, the creator of *Playboy* magazine, this eulogistic documentary chronicles Hefner's life story—from his repressed boyhood in the Midwest to the success of his *Playboy* empire.

THE HUMAN SHIELD

Pro. Christopher Pearce and Elie Cohn; Cannon Pictures *Dir.* Ted Post *Scr.* Mann Rubin; based on the story by Rubin and Mike Werb *Cine.* Yossi Wein *Ed.* Daniel Cahn and Matthew Booth *P.d.* Itzik Albalak *A.d.* Yehuda Ako *Mu.* Stephen Barber *MPAA* R *R.t.* 90 min. *Cast:* Michael Dudikoff, Tommy Hinkley, Hana Azoulay-Hasfari, Steve Inwood, Uri Gavriel, Avi Keidar, Geula Levy, Gil Dagon, Michael Shillo.

When a U.S. Marine instructor, Doug Matthews (Michael Dudikoff), earns the enmity of an evil Iraqi general, Ali (Steve Inwood), the general swears revenge. Five years later, Ali kidnaps and holds hostage Matthews' brother (Tommy Hinkley), forcing Matthews to return to Iraq and mount a one-man task force to rescue his brother.

I DON'T BUY KISSES ANYMORE

Pro. Mitchel Matovich for Web-Marc Pictures, Inc.; Skouras Pictures *Dir.* Robert Marcarelli *Scr.* Jonnie Lindsell *Cine.* Michael Ferris *Ed.* Joanne D'Antonio *P.d.* Byrnadette di Santo *S.d.* Katherine Orrison *Mu.* Cobb Bussinger *MPAA* PG *R.t.* 112 min. *Cast:* Jason Alexander, Nia Peeples, Lainie Kazan, Lou Jacobi, Eileen Brennan, David Bowe, Michele Scarabelli, Hilary Shepard, Marlena Giovi, Ralph Monaco, Arleen Sorkin, Cassie Yates, Al Ruscio, Lela Ivey, Matthias Hues, Larry Storch, Michael Laskin, Barbara Pilavin, Janna Levenstein.

When nice, overweight, Jewish Bernie Fishbine (Jason Alexander) falls in love with a beautiful Italian-American psychology graduate student, Theresa (Nia Peeples), he joins her aerobics class and gives up his nightly treat of chocolate candy kisses in an effort to lose weight. Theresa, on the other hand, initially uninterested in his romantic overtures, gradually falls in love with Bernie only to risk losing him when he discovers that she has used him as the subject of her thesis on obesity.

IN THE HEAT OF PASSION

Pro. Rodman Flender; Concorde Pictures *Dir.* Rodman Flender *Scr.* Rodman Flender *Cine.* Wally Pfister *Ed.* Patrick Rand *P.d.* Hector Velez *A.d.* Patrick Lees *Mu.* Art Wood and Ken Rarick *MPAA* R *R.t.* 82 min. *Cast:* Sally Kirkland, Nick Corri, Jack Carter, Michael Greene, Gloria Le Roy, Carl Franklin, Carlos Carrasco.

A small-time actor (Nick Corri), who portrays a rapist on a television show, becomes involved in real-life crime when he has a steamy affair with a wealthy psychiatrist (Sally Kirkland) and accidentally kills her husband (Michael Greene).

IN THE SHADOW OF THE STARS

Pro. Irving Saraf and Allie Light; First Run Features *Dir.* Irving Saraf and Allie Light *Cine.* Michael Chin *Ed.* Irving Saraf and Allie Light *Mu.* Wolfgang Amadeus Mozart, Giacomo Puccini, Gioacchino Rossini, Igor Stravinsky, Giuseppe Verdi, and Richard Wagner *R.t.* 93 min. *Cast:* Christine Lundquist, Frederick Matthews, David Burnakus, Ruth Ann Swensen, Shelly Seitz, Karl Saarni.

The ability to maintain one's individuality while forming part of a group is the subject of this lighthearted documentary that revolves around the chorus of the San Francisco Opera company. Focusing on several of its members, this film depicts their personal as well as professional lives in an upbeat look at the world of professional opera.

INCIDENT AT OGLALA

Pro. Arthur Chobanian and Robert Redford for Seven Arts/Wildwood and Spanish Fork Motion Picture Company; Miramax *Dir.* Michael Apted *Cine.* Maryse Alberti *Ed.* Susanne Rostock *Mu.* John Trudell and Jackson Browne *MPAA* PG *R.t.* 90 min. *Cast:* Robert Redford.

In this documentary reminiscent of *The Thin Blue Line* (1988), executive producer Robert Redford provides the narration for a film that reexamines the evidence in the 1975 murder case of two FBI agents on the Pine Ridge Reservation of South Dakota. In what appears to be a travesty of justice, Native American Leonard Peltier was convicted of the crime and sentenced to two consecutive terms in prison.

INNOCENT BLOOD

Pro. Lee Rich and Leslie Belzberg; Warner Bros. *Dir.* John Landis *Scr.* Michael Wolk *Cine.* Mac Ahlberg *Ed.* Dale Beldin *P.d.* Richard Sawyer *S.d.* Carl Stensel and Peg Cummings *Mu.* Ira Newborn *MPAA* R *R.t.* 112 min. *Cast:* Anne Parillaud, Robert Loggia, Anthony LaPaglia, Don Rickles, David Proval, Chazz Palminteri, Rocco Sisto, Tony Sirico, Tony Lip, Kim Coates, Elaine Kagan.

French actress Anne Parillaud makes her American film debut in this comic horror film as a morally correct vampire, Marie, who only attacks bad people. When Marie feasts on a cruel Mafia boss, Sal "The Shark" Macelli (Robert Loggia), but fails to kill him, Sal becomes a vampire as well. Marie then teams up with a police officer, Joe (Anthony LaPaglia), in order to capture Sal; Marie and Joe become romantically involved in the process.

INNOCENTS ABROAD

Pro. Vikram Jayanti for Dox Deluxe and Flower Films, in association with BBC/Centre de l'Audio-Visuel a Bruxelles/La Sept, Paris/Thirteen WNET/WDR/Miel Van Hoogenbemt *Dir.* Les Blank *Cine.* Les Blank *Ed.* Chris Simon *R.t.* 84 min. *Cast:* Mark Tinney.

This amusing documentary centers on a bus tour group of forty Americans traveling for two weeks through Europe. Attempting to be insightful rather than cynical, the filmmakers examine the larger issues of why tourists choose to travel this way and why Europeans put up with this seasonal onslaught.

INTO THE SUN

Pro. Kevin M. Kallberg and Oliver G. Hess; Trimark Pictures *Dir.* Fritz Kiersch *Scr.* John Brancato and Michael Ferris *Cine.* Steve Grass *Ed.* Barry Zetlin *P.d.* Gary T. New *A.d.* Dana Torrey *S.d.* A. Rosalind Crew *Mu.* Randy Miller *MPAA* R *R.t.* 100 min. *Cast:* Anthony Michael Hall, Michael Pare, Deborah Maria Moore, Terry Kiser, Brian Haley, Michael St. Gerard, Linden Ashby, Jack Heller, Ted Davis, Hunter Von Leer, Melissa Moore.

In a plot similar to 1991's *The Hard Way*, Anthony Michael Hall stars as an egotistical Hollywood actor, Tom Slade, who is assigned to a very reluctant Air Force pilot (Michael Pare) in order to prepare for a film role. The two must join forces when they are shot down over an Arab country during the Persian Gulf War and are taken hostage.

JENNIFER EIGHT

Pro. Gary Lucchesi and David Wimbury for Scott Rudin; Paramount Pictures *Dir.* Bruce Robinson *Scr.* Bruce Robinson *Cine.* Conrad L. Hall *Ed.* Conrad Buff *P.d.* Richard MacDonald *A.d.* William Durell, Jr. *S.d.* Jim Bayliss, Louis M. Mann, Cosmos A. Demetriou, Casey C. Hallenbeck, and Elizabeth Wilcox *Mu.* Christopher Young *MPAA* R *R.t.* 124 min. *Cast:* Andy Garcia, Uma Thurman, Lance Henriksen, Kathy Baker, Graham Beckel, Kevin

Conway, John Malkovich, Lenny Von Dohlen.

When Los Angeles police officer John Berlin (Andy Garcia) relocates to a small town in Northern California, he finds himself on the trail of a grisly serial murderer when a severed hand is discovered in the local dump. Berlin tries to protect a blind woman, Helena (Uma Thurman), who he believes may be the killer's next victim but instead falls in love with her and becomes a suspect in the police investigation.

JOHNNY STECCHINO (Italy, 1991)

Pro. Mario Cecchi Gori and Vittorio Cecchi Gori for C.G. Group Tiger Cinematografica/Penta Film; New Line Cinema *Dir.* Roberto Benigni *Scr.* Vincenzo Cerami and Roberto Benigni *Cine.* Giuseppe Lanci *Ed.* Nino Baragli *A.d.* Paolo Biagetti *Mu.* Evan Lurie *MPAA* R *R.t.* 100 min. *Cast:* Roberto Benigni, Nicoletta Braschi, Paolo Bonacelli, Ignazio Pappalardo, Franco Volpi, Alessandro de Santis.

The biggest box-office hit ever at its release in its country of origin, Italy, this romantic comedy stars director/coscreenwriter Roberto Benigni as a good-natured bus driver, Dante, who happens to be a dead ringer for a gangster, Johnny Stecchino (also played by Benigni). Dante's life is turned upside down when Johnny's wife, Maria (Nicoletta Braschi), sets up the innocent Dante in order to protect Johnny from his fellow gangsters.

JOHNNY SUEDE

Pro. Yoram Mandel and Ruth Waldburger for Vega Films, in association with Balthazar Pictures, Arena Films, and Starr Pictures; Miramax Films *Dir.* Tom DiCillo *Scr.* Tom DiCillo *Cine.* Joe DeSalvo *Ed.* Geraldine Peroni *P.d.* Patricia Woodbridge *A.d.* Laura Brock *Mu.* Jim Farmer and Link Wray *MPAA* R *R.t.* 95 min. *Cast:* Brad Pitt, Calvin Levels, Alison Moir, Catherine Keener, Tina Louise, Nick Cave, Wilfredo Giovanni Clark, Peter McRobbie, Michael Mulheren.

Brad Pitt stars as Johnny Suede, an idealistic young man who idolizes the late singer Ricky Nelson and aspires to be a musician. Although Johnny looks the part, with his elaborate clothes and pompadour hairstyle, he lacks the talent and ambition to succeed.

JUMPIN AT THE BONEYARD

Pro. Nina R. Sadowsky and Lloyd Goldfine for Kasdan Pictures and Boneyard; Twentieth Century-Fox *Dir.* Jeff Stanzler *Scr.* Jeff Stanzler *Cine.* Lloyd Goldfine *Ed.* Christopher Tellefsen *P.d.* Caroline Wallner *Mu.* Steve Postel *MPAA* R *R.t.* 107 min. *Cast:* Tim Roth, Alexis Arquette, Danitra Vance, Kathleen Chalfant, Samuel L. Jackson, Luiz Guzman, Elizabeth Bracco, Jeffrey Wright.

Tim Roth and Alexis Arquette star as estranged brothers Manny and Dan. When drug addict Dan breaks into recently divorced Manny's apartment to steal money, Manny overcomes his initial anger and decides to try to help Dan break his drug habit.

KILLER IMAGE (Canada, 1992)

Pro. David Winning, Rudy Barichello, and Bruce Harvey for Malofilm Group, Groundstar Entertainment, and Storia Films; Paramount Home Video *Dir.* David Winning *Scr.* David Winning, Stan Edmonds, and Jaron Summers; based on a story by Edmonds *Cine.* Dean Bennett *Ed.* Alan Collins *A.d.* Bruce Sinski *S.d.* Catherine Green *Mu.* Stephen Foster *MPAA* R *R.t.* 96 min. *Cast:* M. Emmet Walsh, John Pyper-Ferguson, Krista Errickson, Michael Ironside, Barbra Gajewskia, Paul Austin, Chantelle Jenkins, Kristie Baker.

In this routine thriller, a photographer (Paul Austin) is murdered after he takes photos of a corrupt senator (M. Emmet Walsh) with a prostitute and later witnesses the prostitute's murder at the hands of the senator's evil brother (Michael Ironside). When the photographer's brother (John Pyper-Ferguson) seeks revenge, he instead finds himself framed for murder.

K2 (Great Britain, 1992)
Pro. Jonathan Taplin, Marilyn Weiner, and Tim Van Rellim for Trans Pacific Films, in association with Miramax Films; Paramount Pictures *Dir.* Franc Roddam *Scr.* Patrick Meyers and Scott Roberts; based on the play by Meyers *Cine.* Gabriel Beristain *Ed.* Sean Barton *P.d.* Andrew Sanders *A.d.* Richard Hudolin *S.d.* Ted Kuchera *Mu.* Chaz Jankel *MPAA* R *R.t.* 104 min. *Cast:* Michael Biehn, Matt Craven, Raymond J. Barry, Luca Bercovici, Patricia Charbonneau, Julia Nickson-Soul, Hiroshi Fujioka, Jamal Shah.

Two friends with a passion for mountain climbing, Taylor Brooks (Michael Biehn) and Harold Jamison (Matt Craven), join a team that proposes to climb K2, the second-highest mountain in the world—and reputedly the most dangerous. The hardship and deprivation prove their friendship, amid the film's breathtaking cinematography.

KUFFS
Pro. Raynold Gideon for Dino De Laurentiis and Evans-Gideon; Universal Pictures *Dir.* Bruce A. Evans *Scr.* Bruce A. Evans and Raynold Gideon *Cine.* Thomas Del Ruth *Ed.* Stephen Semel *P.d.* Victoria Paul and Armin Ganz *A.d.* Tom Davick *S.d.* Claire Bowin and Diana Williams *Mu.* Harold Faltermeyer *MPAA* PG-13 *R.t.* 101 min. *Cast:* Christian Slater, Tony Goldwyn, Milla Jovovich, Bruce Boxleitner, Troy Evans, George de la Pena, Leon Rippy, Joshua Cadman, Mary Ellen Trainor, Lu Leonard, Kim Robillard, Scott Williamson, Aki Aleong, Henry G. Sanders, Stephen Park.

Christian Slater stars as an endearing but irresponsible high school dropout, George Kuffs, who leaves his pregnant girlfriend (Milla Jovovich) in Sacramento and heads for San Francisco to ask his brother, Brad (Bruce Boxleitner), for money. When Brad is shot and killed, George inherits Brad's business—a Patrol Special, which is like a branch of the city police force—and sets out to avenge his brother's death.

LADYBUGS
Pro. Albert S. Ruddy and Andre E. Morgan; Paramount Pictures *Dir.* Sidney J. Furie *Scr.* Curtis Burch *Cine.* Dan Burstall *Ed.* John W. Wheeler and Timothy N. Board *P.d.* Robb Wilson King *S.d.* Penny Stames *Mu.* Richard Gibbs *MPAA* PG-13 *R.t.* 90 min. *Cast:* Rodney Dangerfield, Jackée, Jonathan Brandis, Ilene Graff, Vinessa Shaw, Tom Parks, Jeanetta Arnett, Nancy Parsons, Blake Clark, Tommy Lasorda.

Rodney Dangerfield stars in this lukewarm comedy as a bootlicking salesman who takes on the job of coach of the company-sponsored girls soccer team. In order to improve the team, he persuades his fiancée's son (Jonathan Brandis) to dress like a girl and join the team.

THE LAST ACT (*Parde-ye akhar*; Iran, 1992)
Pro. Majid Modarresi and Mohammad Mehdi Dadgu for Cadre Film *Dir.* Varuzh Karim-Masihi *Scr.* Varuzh Karim-Masihi *Cine.* Asghar Rafiee Jam *Ed.* Varuzh Karim-Masihi *S.d.* Hassan Farsi *Mu.* Babak Bayat *R.t.* 113 min. *Cast:* Farimah Farjami, Darioush Arjmand, Nikou Kheradmand, Jamshid Hashempour, Saeed Poursamini.

Set in 1930's Tehran, this mystery/drama centers on a brother (Darioush Arjmand) and sister (Nikou Kheradmand) of an aristocratic family who plot an elaborate scheme in order to drive their older brother's wife (Farimah Farjami) to suicide and thus inherit the family fortune.

LAWS OF GRAVITY
Pro. Bob Gosse and Larry Meistrich; RKO Pictures Distribution *Dir.* Nick Gomez *Scr.* Nick Gomez *Cine.* Jean de Segonzac *Ed.* Tom McArdle *P.d.* Monica Bretherton *MPAA* R *R.t.* 100 min. *Cast:* Peter Greene, Edie Falco, Adam Trese, Arabella Field, Paul Schulzie, Tony Fernandez, James McCauley, Anibal Lierras, Miguel Sierra, Saul Stien, Larry Meistrich.

In this gritty and hard-edged film, two friends and small-time Brooklyn criminals, Jimmy (Peter Greene) and Jon (Adam Trese), are tempted by an acquaintance, Frankie (Paul Schulzie), to sell guns he brought from Florida, which triggers tragic results.

LEAVING NORMAL

Pro. Lindsay Doran for Mirage; Universal Pictures *Dir.* Edward Zwick *Scr.* Edward Solomon *Cine.* Ralf Bode *Ed.* Victor Du Bois *P.d.* Patricia Norris *Mu.* W. G. Snuffy Walden *MPAA* R *R.t.* 110 min. *Cast:* Meg Tilly, Christine Lahti, Patrika Darbo, Lenny Von Dohlen, Maury Chaykin, Brett Cullen, James Gammon.

Two women trying to find themselves is the theme of this female-buddy film: Christine Lahti plays a hard-boiled waitress and Meg Tilly a wife on-the-run. When the two meet at a bus stop in Normal, Wyoming, they start out on a road trip that takes them from the American West through Canada and on to Alaska.

LIFE ON A STRING (Germany, Great Britain, Japan, and China, 1992)

Pro. Don Ranvaud for Pandora Film, Serene Productions, Beijing Film Studio, and China Film Co-Production Corp., in association with Herald Ace, Channel Four, Berlin Filmforderung, and Diva Film; Kino International *Dir.* Chen Kaige *Scr.* Chen Kaige; based on a short story by Shi Tiesheng *Cine.* Gu Changwei *Ed.* Pei Xiaonan *P.d.* Shao Ruigang *Mu.* Qu Xiaosong *R.t.* 120 min. *Cast:* Liu Zhongyuan, Huang Lei, Xu Qing, Ma Ling, Zhang Zhenguan, Yao Jingou.

Set in China, this drama centers on two blind traveling banjo players: the elderly Saint (Liu Zhongyuan) and his younger apprentice, Shitou (Huang Lei). The blind Saint, who through the decades has become a learned and respected man, able to halt warring men with his music and songs, anxiously awaits the fulfillment of a prophecy that when he breaks the thousandth string on his banjo he will gain his sight.

THE LINGUINI INCIDENT

Pro. Arnold Orgolini for Rank Film Distributors and Isolar Enterprises; Academy Entertainment *Dir.* Richard Shepard *Scr.* Richard Shepard and Tamar Brott *Cine.* Robert Yeoman *Ed.* Sonya Polonsky *P.d.* Marcia Hinds-Johnson *A.d.* Bo Johnson *S.d.* Doug Sieck and Brian Polk *Mu.* Thomas Newman *MPAA* R *R.t.* 98 min. *Cast:* Rosanna Arquette, David Bowie, Eszter Balint, André Gregory, Buck Henry, Viveca Lindfors, Marlee Matlin, Eloy Casados, Michael Bonnabel, Maura Tierney, Lewis Arquette, Iman, Julian Lennon.

Set in a trendy New York restaurant, this screwball comedy centers on an oddball waitress, Lucy (Rosanna Arquette), who is obsessed with becoming the next Houdini. Desperate for money to launch her new career, she teams with fellow waitress Vivian (Eszter Balint) and the new English bartender, Monte (David Bowie)—who is apparently so anxious to get his green card that he proposes marriage to all the waitresses—in order to rob the restaurant's eccentric owners (André Gregory and Buck Henry).

LIQUID DREAMS

Pro. Zane W. Levitt and Diane Firestone for Zeta Entertainment and Fox/Elwes Corp.; Northern Arts Entertainment *Dir.* Mark Manos *Scr.* Zack Davis and Mark Manos *Cine.* Sven Kirsten *Ed.* Karen Joseph *P.d.* Pam Moffat *Mu.* Ed Tomney *R.t.* 91 min. *Cast:* Richard Steinmetz, Candice Daly, Barry Dennen, Juan Fernandez, Tracey Walter, Frankie Thorn, James Oseland, Mink Stole, Marilyn Tokuda, John Doe.

In this dark futuristic thriller, a woman (Candice Daly) seeks her sister's murderer in a sinister nightclub where the female dancers fall victim to strange sexual experiments.

LITTLE NEMO: ADVENTURES IN SLUMBERLAND (Japan, 1992)

Pro. Yutaka Fujioka for Tokyo Movie Shinsha Co., Ltd.; Hemdale Pictures Corporation *Dir.*

Masami Hata and William T. Hurtz *Scr.* Chris Columbus and Richard Outten; based on a story by Jean Mobius Giraud and Yutaka Fujioka, on characters by Winsor McCay, and on a screen concept by Ray Bradbury *Cine.* Hajime Hasegawa, Kenichi Kobayashi, Moriyuki Terashita, Takahisa Ogawa, Kazushige Ichinozuka, Atsuko Ito, Koji Asai, Takashi Nomura, Jin Nishiyama, Kiyoshi Kobayashi, Atsushi Yoshino, Kyoko Oosaki, Akio Saitoh, Hiroshi Kanai, Hitoshi Shirao, Hironori Yoshino, Mika Sakai, Rie Takeuchi, Kazushi Torigoe *Ed.* Takeshi Seyama *Mu.* Thomas Chase and Steve Rucker *MPAA* G *R.t.* 85 min. *Voices:* Gabriel Damon, Mickey Rooney, Rene Auberjonois, Danny Mann, Laura Mooney, Bernard Erhard, William E. Martin.

Based on a turn-of-the-century cartoon strip, this film centers on a young boy, Nemo (voice of Gabriel Damon), who enters the fantasy world of Slumberland and inadvertently betrays the trust of its king (voice of Bernard Erhard). When the king is kidnapped, Nemo embarks on a rescue mission accompanied by his trusty entourage.

LITTLE NOISES

Pro. Michael Spielberg and Brad M. Gilbert for Prism Entertainment; Monument Pictures *Dir.* Jane Spencer *Scr.* Jane Spencer and Jon Zeiderman; based on a story by Spencer and Anthony Brito *Cine.* Makoto Watanabe *Ed.* Ernie Fritz *P.d.* Charles Lagola *A.d.* Allison Cornyn *S.d.* Catie Dehaan *Mu.* Kurt Hoffman and Fritz Van Orden *R.t.* 80 min. *Cast:* Crispin Glover, Steven Schub, Tatum O'Neal, Rik Mayall, John McGinley, Tate Donovan, Nina Siemaszko, Matthew Hutton, Carole Shelley.

A discouraged young man, Joey (Crispin Glover), who has pretensions of being a writer, fulfills his dreams of success when he claims authorship of some brilliant poems written by a young deaf-mute, Marty (Matthew Hutton). Joey's gain is Marty's loss, as the young orphan loses everything including his home, and Joey must confront the reality of what he has done.

THE LIVING END

Pro. Marcus Hu and Jon Gerrans for October Films and Desperate Pictures, Ltd.; Strand *Dir.* Gregg Araki *Scr.* Gregg Araki *Cine.* Gregg Araki *Ed.* Gregg Araki *Mu.* Cole Coonce *R.t.* 92 min. *Cast:* Mike Dytri, Craig Gilmore, Darcy Marta, Scott Goetz, Mary Woronov, Johanna Went, Mark Finch, Bretton Vail, Nicole Dillenberg, Paul Bartel.

With a plot reminiscent of *Thelma and Louise* (1991), this film centers on two gay men with AIDS who take to the road. Jon (Craig Gilmore), a quiet, retiring writer, and Luke (Mike Dytri), his violent and rebellious lover, convinced they have nothing to lose, decide to throw caution to the wind, in this sexually explicit, violent drama.

LONDON KILLS ME (Great Britain, 1992)

Pro. Tim Bevan for Polygram and Working Title Films, in association with Film Four International; Fine Line Features *Dir.* Hanif Kureishi *Scr.* Hanif Kureishi *Cine.* Ed Lachman *Ed.* John Gregory *P.d.* Stuart Walker *A.d.* Diane Dancklefsen and Colin Blaymires *Mu.* Mark Springer and Sarah Sarhandi *MPAA* R *R.t.* 107 min. *Cast:* Justin Chadwick, Steven Mackintosh, Emer McCourt, Roshan Seth, Fiona Shaw, Brad Dourif, Tony Haygarth, Stevan Rimkus, Eleanor David, Alun Armstrong, Nick Dunning, Naveen Andrews, Garry Cooper.

A young, broke London drug dealer, Clint (Justin Chadwick), seeks a better life by applying for a waiter job at a restaurant, only to discover that he must first get a decent pair of shoes. In his effort to get the shoes, Clint finds himself pulled back into the drug world by his friend, Muffdiver (Steven Mackintosh), and girlfriend, Sylvie (Emer McCourt).

LOVE CRIMES

Pro. Rudy Langlais and Lizzie Borden for Sovereign Pictures; Millimeter Films *Dir.* Lizzie Borden *Scr.* Allan Moyle and Laurie Frank; based on a story by Moyle *Cine.* Jack N. Green

Ed. Nicholas C. Smith and Mike Jackson *P.d.* Armin Ganz *A.d.* John E. (Jack) Marty *S.d.* Rondey L. Leach *Mu.* Graeme Revell *MPAA* R *R.t.* 91 min. *Cast:* Sean Young, Patrick Bergin, Arnetia Walker, James Read, Ron Orbach, Fern Dorsey, Tina Hightower, Donna Biscoe.

In this suspense/thriller, a district attorney, Dana Greenway (Sean Young), tracks a man, David Hanover (Patrick Bergin), who poses as a photographer in order to seduce women. Greenway then falls prey to Hanover's charms as he prepares to make her his next victim.

LOVE POTION #9

Pro. Dale Launer; Twentieth Century-Fox *Dir.* Dale Launer *Scr.* Dale Launer; inspired by the song by Jerry Leiber and Mike Stoller *Cine.* William Wages *Ed.* Suzanne Pettit *P.d.* Linda Pearl *A.d.* Thomas Minton *S.d.* Sally Nicolaou *Mu.* Jed Leiber *MPAA* PG-13 *R.t.* 97 min. *Cast:* Tate Donovan, Sandra Bullock, Mary Mara, Dale Midkiff, Hillary Bailey Smith, Dylan Baker, Adrian Paul, Blake Clark, Anne Bancroft.

In this silly film adaptation of the 1959 hit song, two lonely and nerdy scientists—Paul Matthews (Tate Donovan) and Diane Farrow (Sandra Bullock)—experiment with a "love" potion, only to discover for themselves its rather potent effects.

LOVERS (*Amantes.* Spain, 1992)

Pro. Pedro Costa-Muste; Aries Film *Dir.* Vicente Aranda *Scr.* Alvaro del Amo, Carlos Perez Merinero, and Vicente Aranda *Cine.* Jose Luis Alcaine *Ed.* Teresa Font *A.d.* Josep Rosell *Mu.* Jose Nieto *R.t.* 103 min. *Cast:* Victoria Abril, Jorge Sanz, Maribel Verdu.

Set in 1950's Madrid, this drama centers on Paco (Jorge Sanz) and his fiancée, Trini (Maribel Verdu), whose contented relationship is disrupted when Paco becomes involved with a lascivious young widow, Luisa (Victoria Abril). Paco becomes so obsessed with the sexy Luisa, in fact, that he plots Trini's murder in order to steal her money and help Luisa.

THE LUNATIC (Jamaica, 1992)

Pro. Paul Heller and John Pringle for Island Pictures; Triton Pictures *Dir.* Lol Creme *Scr.* Anthony C. Winkler; based on his novel *Cine.* Richard Greatrex *Ed.* Michael Connell *A.d.* Giorgio Ferrari *Mu.* Wally Badarou *MPAA* R *R.t.* 93 min. *Cast:* Julie T. Wallace, Paul Campbell, Reggie Carter, Carl Bradshaw, Winston Stona, Linda Gambrill, Rosemary Murray, Lloyd Reckord.

A strange but endearing Jamaican man, Aloysius (Paul Campbell)—who talks to plants and animals and whose best friend is a tree (voice of Reggie Carter)—becomes the love slave of a corpulent and domineering German tourist, Inga (Julie T. Wallace). When Inga persuades him, along with another of her lovers, to rob a local landowner, Aloysius gets caught and goes to trial.

LUNATICS: A LOVE STORY

Pro. Bruce Campbell for Sam Raimi-Robert Tapert; Renaissance Pictures *Dir.* Josh Becker *Scr.* Josh Becker *Cine.* Jeff Dougherty *Ed.* Kaye Davis *P.d.* Peter Gurski *A.d.* Michele Poulik *S.d.* Michele Poulik *Mu.* Joseph Lo Duca *R.t.* 87 min. *Cast:* Theodore Raimi, Deborah Foreman, Bruce Campbell, George Aguilar, Brian McCree.

When a paranoid agoraphobic, Hank (Theodore Raimi), living in Los Angeles accidentally dials the wrong number, he meets a bewildered young Iowan woman, Nancy (Deborah Foreman), with a low self-esteem. After he persuades her to come to his aluminum-foil-lined apartment, the two discover true love.

MAN TROUBLE

Pro. Bruce Gilbert and Carole Eastman for Mario and Vittorio Cecchi Gori, Silvio Berlusconi, Penta Pictures, and American Filmworks/Budding Grove; Twentieth Century-Fox

Dir. Bob Rafelson *Scr.* Carole Eastman *Cine.* Stephen H. Burum *Ed.* William Steinkamp *P.d.* Mel Bourne *S.d.* Samara Schaffer *Mu.* Georges Delerue *MPAA* PG-13 *R.t.* 100 min. *Cast:* Jack Nicholson, Ellen Barkin, Harry Dean Stanton, Beverly D'Angelo, Michael McKean, Saul Rubinek, Viveka Davis, Veronica Cartwright, David Clennon, John Kapelos, Lauren Tom, Paul Mazursky, Gary Graham, Betty Carvalho, Mary Robin Redd.

Jack Nicholson and Ellen Barkin star in this weak comedy about a guard-dog trainer and an opera singer who, although leery about romance, gingerly enter into an affair when he is hired to protect her.

THE MAN WITHOUT A WORLD

Pro. Eleanor Antin; Milestone Films *Dir.* Eleanor Antin *Scr.* Eleanor Antin *Cine.* Richard Wargo *Ed.* Lynn Burnstan *A.d.* Sabato Fiorello *S.d.* Roger Sherman *Mu.* Lee Erwin and Charles Morrow *R.t.* 98 min. *Cast:* Pier Marton, Christine Berry, Anna Henriques, George Leonard, Don Sommese, Marcia Goodman, Sergun A. Tont, Luyba Talpalatsky, Eleanor Antin, Nicolai Lennox, Lisa Welti, Bennet Berger, Ellen Zweig, James Scott Kerwin, Sabato Fiorello.

Filmed in black and white, and claiming to be a rediscovered Yiddish silent film by a controversial Soviet director, this period comedy centers on a Yiddish poet (Pier Marton) who falls in love with a beautiful Jewish woman (Christine Berry).

MEATBALLS IV

Pro. Donald P. Borchers; Moviestore Entertainment *Dir.* Bob Logan *Scr.* Bob Logan *Cine.* Vance Burberry *Ed.* Peter H. Verity *P.d.* Dorian Vernacchio and Deborah Raymond *Mu.* Steve Hunter *MPAA* R *R.t.* 87 min. *Cast:* Corey Feldman, Jack Nance, Sarah Douglas, Bojesse Christopher, Johnny Cocktails, J. Trevor Edmond, Paige French, John Mendoza, Bentley Mitchum, Christy Thom, Deborah Tucker, Frank Walton, Kristi Ducati, Monique de Lacy, Wendy Nichols.

In this screwball comedy, a shiftless water-skier (Corey Feldman) is hired as director of a water-ski camp only to find that his efforts in a competition are threatened by a rival camp's insidious owner (Sarah Douglas).

MEMOIRS OF A RIVER (Hungary, 1992)

Pro. Gábor Hanák and Hubert Niogret for Studio Budapest-Kerszi, MOKEP, Kerszi-Felling, in association with the Minister of Culture and Communications/Paris; Quartet Films, Inc. *Dir.* Judit Elek *Scr.* Judit Elek *Cine.* Gábor Halász *Ed.* Katalin Kabdebó *P.d.* Andras Ozoraí *A.d.* Tamás Banovich *Mu.* Péter Eötvös *R.t.* 147 min. *Cast:* Sándor Gáspár, Pál Hetényi, Franciszek Pieczka, Andras Stohl, János Acs, Tamas Fodor.

In this dramatization of an actual event, a Jewish lumberman (Sándor Gáspár) is arrested and tortured in nineteenth century Hungary for the murder of a Catholic woman.

MEMOIRS OF AN INVISIBLE MAN

Pro. Bruce Bodner and Dan Kolsrud, in association with Le Studio Canal Plus, Regency Enterprises, and Alcor Films; Warner Bros. *Dir.* John Carpenter *Scr.* Robert Collector, Dana Olsen, and William Goldman; based on the novel by H. F. Saint *Cine.* William A. Fraker *Ed.* Marion Rothman *P.d.* Lawrence G. Paull *A.d.* Bruce Crone *S.d.* Elizabeth Lapp, Lauren Polizzi, Gerald Sigmon, and Rick Simpson *Mu.* Shirley Walker *MPAA* PG-13 *R.t.* 99 min. *Cast:* Chevy Chase, Daryl Hannah, Sam Neill, Michael McKean, Stephen Tobolowsky, Jim Norton.

Chevy Chase stars as Nick Halloway, a stock analyst, who is rendered invisible in a freak accident. Fighting the loneliness and isolation inherent in being invisible, Nick must outmaneuver a corrupt CIA agent (Sam Neill) who wants Nick to spy for the government, as well as maintain his newfound romance with beautiful documentary filmmaker Alice Monroe (Daryl Hannah).

THE MIGHTY DUCKS

Pro. Jordan Kerner and Jon Avnet for Walt Disney Pictures, in association with Touchwood Pacific Partners I; Buena Vista *Dir.* Stephen Herek *Scr.* Steven Brill *Cine.* Thomas Del Ruth *Ed.* Larry Bock and John F. Link *P.d.* Randy Ser *A.d.* Tony Fanning *S.d.* Jack Ballance and Julie Kaye Fanton *Mu.* David Newman *MPAA* PG *R.t.* 100 min. *Cast:* Emilio Estevez, Joss Ackland, Lane Smith, Heidi Kling, Josef Sommer, Joshua Jackson, Elden Ratliff, Shaun Weiss, Marguerite Moreau.

In this predictable, politically correct comic drama, Emilio Estevez stars as a pretentious yuppie lawyer, Gordon Bombay, who is forced to coach a pee-wee hockey team as community service following a drunk driving charge. In the process, Bombay learns humility, pulls his ragtag, streetwise team together, and finds romance.

MISTRESS

Pro. Meir Teper and Robert De Niro for J&M Entertainment; Rainbow/Tribeca *Dir.* Barry Primus *Scr.* Barry Primus and J. F. Lawton; based on a story by Primus *Cine.* Sven Kirsten *Ed.* Steven Weisberg *P.d.* Phil Peters *A.d.* Randy Eriksen *S.d.* Colin De Rouin and K. O. Fox *Mu.* Galt MacDermot *MPAA* R *R.t.* 108 min. *Cast:* Robert Wuhl, Martin Landau, Robert De Niro, Danny Aiello, Eli Wallach, Jace Alexander, Tuesday Knight, Sheryl Lee Ralph, Christopher Walken, Ernest Borgnine, Vasek C. Simek, Tomas R. Voth, Mary Mercier, Laurie Metcalf, Jean Smart.

In this mediocre satire of Hollywood filmmaking, a has-been producer, Jack Roth (Martin Landau), offers to produce the screenplay of a discouraged writer, Marvin Landisman (Robert Wuhl). As Marvin finds that he is forced to make one compromise after another in order to see his art brought to the big screen, three of the film's backers (Eli Wallach, Danny Aiello, and Robert De Niro) vie to see that their mistresses (Tuesday Knight, Jean Smart, and Sheryl Lee Ralph) get a part in the picture.

MOM AND DAD SAVE THE WORLD

Pro. Michael Phillips for HBO, in association with Cinema Plus L.P and Mercury/Douglas Films; Warner Bros. *Dir.* Greg Beeman *Scr.* Chris Matheson and Ed Solomon *Cine.* Jacques Haitkin *Ed.* W. O. Garret *P.d.* Craig Stearns *A.d.* Randy Moore *S.d.* Bill Rea and Dorree Cooper *Mu.* Jerry Goldsmith *MPAA* PG *R.t.* 88 min. *Cast:* Teri Garr, Jeffrey Jones, Jon Lovitz, Thalmus Rasulala, Wallace Shawn, Eric Idle, Dwier Brown, Kathy Ireland.

A middle-aged, middle-class married couple, Marge (Teri Garr) and Dick Nelson (Jeffrey Jones), are kidnapped and taken to the planet Spengo by its evil dictator (Jon Lovitz), who has become smitten with Marge. His plans to destroy the earth are then put on hold as he attempts to woo and win Marge, in this weak comedy adventure.

THE MONEY TREE

Pro. Christopher Dienstag; Black Sheep Films *Dir.* Alan Dienstag *Scr.* Christopher Dienstag and Alan Dienstag *Cine.* Donatello Bonato *Ed.* Susan Crutcher *Mu.* Lorin Rowan *R.t.* 92 min. *Cast:* Christopher Dienstag, Monica T. Caldwell, Malcolm Cohen, Nik Martin.

A young man, David (Christopher Dienstag), raises his first crop of marijuana, despite opposition from his ambitious and materialistic girlfriend, Erica (Monica T. Caldwell), who urges him to take up a more conventional, not to mention safer, occupation.

MONSTER IN A BOX (*Spalding Gray's Monster in a Box*; Great Britain, 1991)

Pro. Jon Blair, in association with Channel Four; Fine Line Features *Dir.* Nick Broomfield *Scr.* Spalding Gray *Cine.* Michael Coulter *Ed.* Graham Hutchings *P.d.* Ray Oxley *Mu.*

Laurie Anderson *MPAA* PG-13 *R.t.* 88 min. *Cast:* Spalding Gray.

Monologuist Spalding Gray continues to detail his life's adventures as he did in a previous one-man film, *Swimming to Cambodia* (1987). Here, his comic delivery revolves around a nineteen-hundred-page autobiographical novel—his "monster in a box"—that he is struggling to complete.

MONTANA RUN

Pro. Randy Thompson; Greycat Films *Dir.* Randy Thompson *Scr.* Randy Thompson, Ron Reid, and Dan Lishner *Cine.* William Brooks Baum *Ed.* Randy Thompson and Tim Maffia *Mu.* Randy Thompson *R.t.* 97 min. *Cast:* Randy Thompson, Dan Lishner, Ron Reid, Mayme Paul-Thompson.

Three stand-up comedians (Randy Thompson, Dan Lishner, and Mayme Paul-Thompson) and their promoter (Ron Reid) tour Montana by car, performing in small-town bars. The film, however, focuses on their off- rather than onstage lives.

THE MUPPET CHRISTMAS CAROL

Pro. Brian Henson and Martin G. Baker for Walt Disney Pictures and Jim Henson Productions; Buena Vista *Dir.* Brian Henson *Scr.* Jerry Juhl; based on "A Christmas Carol," by Charles Dickens *Cine.* John Fenner *Ed.* Michael Jablow *P.d.* Val Strazovec *A.d.* Alan Cassie and Dennis Bosher *S.d.* Michael Ford *Mu.* Miles Goodman *MPAA* G *R.t.* 85 min. *Voices:* Michael Caine, Dave Goelz, Steve Whitmire, Frank Oz, Jerry Nelson.

The Muppets give a delightful rendition of Charles Dickens' classic "A Christmas Carol," with Kermit the Frog playing Bob Cratchit, and Miss Piggy as his wife, and the Great Gonzo as Dickens himself. Veteran actor Michael Caine provides a heartfelt rendition of miserly Ebenezer Scrooge who undergoes a change for the better, and Paul Williams provides the lively song score.

MY FATHER IS COMING (USA and Germany, 1992)

Pro. Monika Treut for Hyena Films and Bluehorse Films; Tara Releasing *Dir.* Monika Treut *Scr.* Monika Treut and Bruce Benderson *Cine.* Elfi Mikesch *Ed.* Steve Brown *A.d.* Robin Ford *Mu.* David van Tieghem *R.t.* 82 min. *Cast:* Alfred Edel, Shelley Kästner, Annie Sprinkle, Michael Massee, Mary Lou Graulau, David Bronstein.

In this lukewarm comedy, a young German actress (Shelley Kästner), who is struggling to find work in New York City, panics when her domineering and protective father (Alfred Edel) decides to come from Germany for a visit. Comic mishaps occur when she tries to hide not only her professional failures but also the fact that she is a lesbian.

MY NEW GUN

Pro. Michael Flynn; I.R.S. Media, Inc. *Dir.* Stacy Cochran *Scr.* Stacy Cochran *Cine.* Ed Lachman *Ed.* Camilla Toniolo *P.d.* Toby Corbett *S.d.* Catherine Davis *Mu.* Pat Irwin *MPAA* R *R.t.* 99 min. *Cast:* Diane Lane, James Le Gros, Stephen Collins, Tess Harper, Bill Raymond, Bruce Altman, Maddie Corman.

When a self-important suburban husband, Gerald (Stephen Collins), forces the gift of a handgun on his reluctant wife, Debbie (Diane Lane), his misguided efforts to protect her backfire. A quirky neighbor, Skippy (James LeGros), who is smitten with Debbie, takes the gun without permission, leading to Gerald's misbegotten effort to retrieve it and a romance between his wife and Skippy.

NEWSIES

Pro. Michael Finnell for Walt Disney Pictures, in association with Touchwood Pacific Partners I; Buena Vista *Dir.* Kenny Ortega *Scr.* Bob Tzudiker and Noni White *Cine.* Andrew Laszlo *Ed.* William Reynolds *P.d.* William Sandell *A.d.* Nancy Patton *S.d.* Brad Ricker,

Carl J. Stensel, and Robert Gould *Mu.* Alan Menken *MPAA* PG *R.t.* 121 min. *Cast:* Christian Bale, David Moscow, Robert Duvall, Bill Pullman, Luke Edwards, Max Casella, Marty Belafsky, Arvie Lowe, Jr., Aaron Lohr, Ann-Margret, Ele Keats, Michael Lerner, Kevin Tighe.

Set in 1899 and based on a true story, this musical—with music by Academy Award-winning composer Alan Menken—centers on a New York City newsboys' strike. Led by a teenage orphan, Jack Kelly (Christian Bale), and his strategist friend, David Jacobs (David Moscow), the poverty-stricken newsboys refuse to sell the papers of publisher Joseph Pulitzer (Robert Duvall) when he decides to increase his profit at their expense.

NOISES OFF

Pro. Frank Marshall for Touchstone Pictures and Amblin Entertainment, in association with Touchwood Pacific Partners I; Buena Vista *Dir.* Peter Bogdanovich *Scr.* Marty Kaplan; based on the play by Michael Frayn *Cine.* Tim Suhrstedt *Ed.* Lisa Day *P.d.* Norman Newberry *A.d.* Daniel E. Maltese *Mu.* Phil Marshall *MPAA* PG-13 *R.t.* 102 min. *Cast:* Carol Burnett, Michael Caine, Denholm Elliott, Julie Hagerty, Marilu Henner, Mark Linn-Baker, Christopher Reeve, John Ritter, Nicollette Sheridan.

A band of eccentric, paranoid, and not-too-bright actors, two multitalented stagehands, and one frustrated director try to get a British sex farce from its obscure opening in Des Moines, Iowa, to Broadway.

NOTEBOOK ON CITIES AND CLOTHES

Pro. Road Movies Filmproduktion GMBH; Milestone from the Connoisseur Collection *Dir.* Wim Wenders *Scr.* Wim Wenders; based on a proposal by Francois Burkhardt *Cine.* Robbie Muller, Muriel Edelstein, Uli Kudicke, Wim Wenders, Masatoshi Nakajima, and Masahi Chikamori *Ed.* Dominique Auvray, Lenie Savietto, and Anne Schnee *Mu.* Laurent Petitgand *R.t.* 80 min. *Cast:* Yohji Yamamoto.

Pretentious and dull, this documentary centers on Japanese clothing designer Yohji Yamamoto. Filmmaker Wim Wenders features Yamamoto's personal philosophy, however, rather than his art.

ONCE UPON A CRIME

Pro. Dino De Laurentiis; Metro-Goldwyn-Mayer *Dir.* Eugene Levy *Scr.* Charles Shyer, Nancy Meyers, and Steve Kluger *Cine.* Giuseppe Rotunno *Ed.* Patrick Kennedy *P.d.* Pier Luigi Basile *S.d.* Gianfranco Fumagalli *Mu.* Richard Gibbs *MPAA* PG *R.t.* 94 min. *Cast:* John Candy, James Belushi, Cybill Shepherd, Sean Young, Richard Lewis, Ornella Muti, Giancarlo Giannini, George Hamilton, Roberto Sbaratto, Joss Ackland.

In this tepid comedy, an out-of-work actor (Richard Lewis) and a jilted woman (Sean Young) pair up in Rome to return a missing Dachshund to its owner in Monte Carlo and collect the reward. When the owner is murdered, they, along with a gambler (John Candy) and a married American couple (James Belushi and Cybill Shepherd), are implicated in the crime.

ONE FALSE MOVE

Pro. Jesse Beaton and Ben Myron for I.R.S. Media; I.R.S. Releasing *Dir.* Carl Franklin *Scr.* Billy Bob Thornton and Tom Epperson *Cine.* James L. Carter *Ed.* Carole Kravetz *P.d.* Gary T. New *A.d.* Dana Torrey *S.d.* Troy Myers *Mu.* Peter Haycock and Derek Holt *MPAA* R *R.t.* 105 min. *Cast:* Bill Paxton, Cynda Williams, Billy Bob Thornton, Michael Beach, Jim Metzler, Earl Billings, Natalie Canerday.

Three vicious criminals (Billy Bob Thornton, Michael Beach, and Cynda Williams) flee Los Angeles after murdering two families in order to attain a cache of drugs. They are trailed by two Los Angeles police officers (Jim Metzler and Earl Billings) as the three head to a small town in Arkansas, where the local sheriff (Bill Paxton) has been alerted and eagerly awaits them.

OUT ON A LIMB

Pro. Michael Hertzberg for Interscope Communications; Universal Pictures *Dir.* Francis Veber *Scr.* Daniel Goldin and Joshua Goldin *Cine.* Donald E. Thorin *Ed.* Glenn Farr *P.d.* Stephen Marsh *S.d.* Peg Cummings *Mu.* Van Dyke Parks *MPAA* PG *R.t.* 82 min. *Cast:* Matthew Broderick, Jeffrey Jones, Heidi Kling, John C. Reilly, Marian Mercer, Larry Hankin, David Margulies, Courtney Peldon, Michael Monks, Shawn Schepps.

In this very weak comedy, a young girl (Courtney Peldon) relates to her fellow schoolmates a fantastic story about how she spent her summer vacation. She tells of her brother (Matthew Broderick) being robbed of his clothes and car by a mysterious woman (Heidi Kling) and the murder of her evil stepfather (Jeffrey Jones).

THE OX (Sweden, 1991)

Pro. Jean Doumanian for Sandrew Film, SVT-1, Nordisk Film, and Sweetland Films AB; Castle Hill Productions and First Run Features *Dir.* Sven Nykvist *Scr.* Sven Nykvist and Lasse Summanen *Cine.* Sven Nykvist *Ed.* Lasse Summanen *P.d.* Peter Höimark *S.d.* Magnus Magnusson *Mu.* Thomas Drescher *MPAA* no listing *R.t.* 91 min. *Cast:* Stellan Skarsgard, Ewa Fröling, Max Von Sydow, Lennart Hjulström, Liv Ullmann, Björn Granath, Erland Josephson, Rikard Wollf, Helge Jordal, Agneta Prytz, Bjorn Gustafson, Jaqui Safra.

Set in nineteenth century Sweden, this critically acclaimed drama centers on a starving rural family in the 1860's. Stellan Skarsgard plays a family man who kills his boss's ox in order to feed his wife (Ewa Fröling) and baby—and who is then sentenced to life imprisonment.

THE PANAMA DECEPTION

Pro. Barbara Trent, Joanne Doroshow, Nico Panigutti, and David Kasper, in association with Channel 4; Empowerment Project *Dir.* Barbara Trent *Scr.* David Kasper *Cine.* Michael Dobo and Manuel Becker *Ed.* David Kasper *Mu.* Chuck Wild, Sting, Jorge Strunz, Jackson Browne, Ismael Rivera, and Ricky Barnes *R.t.* 91 min. *Cast:* Elizabeth Montgomery.

In this Academy Award-winning documentary, director Barbara Trent delivers a stinging indictment of the United States government and the media by examining their role in the 1989 U.S. invasion of Panama.

PASSED AWAY

Pro. Larry Brezner and Timothy Marx for Hollywood Pictures, in association with Touchwood Pacific Partners I and Morra/Brezner/Steinberg; Buena Vista *Dir.* Charlie Peters *Scr.* Charlie Peters *Cine.* Arthur Albert *Ed.* Harry Keramidas *P.d.* Catherine Hardwicke *A.d.* Gilbert Mercier *S.d.* Gene Serdena *Mu.* Richard Gibbs *MPAA* PG-13 *R.t.* 96 min. *Cast:* Bob Hoskins, Jack Warden, William Petersen, Helen Lloyd Breed, Maureen Stapleton, Pamela Reed, Tim Curry, Peter Riegert, Blair Brown, Patrick Breen, Nancy Travis, Teri Polo, Frances McDormand.

During the wake of family patriarch Jack Scanlan (Jack Warden), his four grown children search their own lives for meaning. Eldest son Johnny (Bob Hoskins) rebels when he is expected to take charge, prodigal daughter Terry (Pamela Reed) finds romance, son Frank (William Petersen) faces both parental and business troubles, and daughter Nora (Frances McDormand) reveals her newfound radical politics.

PEPI, LUCI, BOM (Spain, 1980)

Pro. Pepon Corominas for Figaro Films; Cinevista *Dir.* Pedro Almodóvar *Scr.* Pedro Almodóvar *Cine.* Paco Femenia *Ed.* Pepe Salcedo *R.t.* 80 min. *Cast:* Carmen Maura, Félix

Rotaeta, Olvido Gara "Alaska," Eva Siva.

The first feature film by Spanish director Pedro Almodóvar, *Pepi, Luci, Bom* is a low-budget loser featuring sexuality, perversion, and violence. This tasteless drama centers on a wealthy woman, Pepi (Carmen Maura), who seeks revenge against the police officer (Félix Rotaeta) who raped her.

PERHAPS SOME OTHER TIME (Iran, 1992)

Pro. Mohammad-Ali Farajollahi, Hushang Nurollahi, Reza Allpur Motealem, and Asad Delshad Ershadi for Mahtab Co. and Novin Film *Dir.* Bahram Beyzaie *Scr.* Bahram Beyzaie *Cine.* Asghar Rafi'i-Jam *Ed.* Bahram Beyzaie *A.d.* Iraj Raminfar *Mu.* Babak Bayat *R.t.* 120 min. *Cast:* Sussan Taslimi, Daryush Farhang, Ali-Reza Mojallal, Sirus Nasiri.

An Iranian documentary narrator (Daryush Farhang) becomes intensely jealous when, while viewing some film footage of a Tehran traffic jam, he catches a glimpse of his wife (Sussan Taslimi) in a car with another man.

PET SEMATARY II

Pro. Ralph S. Singleton for Columbus Circle Films; Paramount Pictures *Dir.* Mary Lambert *Scr.* Richard Outten *Cine.* Russell Carpenter *Ed.* Tom Finan *P.d.* Michelle Minch *A.d.* Karen Steward *S.d.* Jonathan Short, Gina Cranham, and Susan Benjamin *Mu.* Mark Governor *MPAA* R *R.t.* 102 min. *Cast:* Edward Furlong, Jason McGuire, Clancy Brown, Anthony Edwards, Darlanne Fluegel, Jared Rushton, Lisa Waltz, Sarah Trigger.

Set in small-town Maine, this horror film centers on two teenage boys—Jeff (Edward Furlong) and Drew (Jason McGuire)—who unleash the dark powers of a local graveyard when they bury Drew's beloved pet dog in an ancient Indian burial ground.

PIANO PIANO KID (Turkey, 1992)

Pro. Arif Keskiner; United Cinema Network *Dir.* Tunc Basaran *Scr.* Tunc Basaran, Umit Unal, and Kemal Demirel; based on the book by Demirel *Cine.* Colin Mounier *A.d.* Jale Basaran *Mu.* Can Kozlu *R.t.* 84 min. *Cast:* Rutkay Aziz, Emin Sivas.

An Istanbul native reminisces on his childhood growing up during World War II. Through the eyes of nine-year-old Kemal (Emin Sivas), the audience sees the poverty and hunger, but also the camaraderie and solidarity, of a people caught in the middle of war.

POISON IVY

Pro. Andy Ruben for MG Entertainment, Inc.; New Line Cinema *Dir.* Katt Shea Ruben *Scr.* Katt Shea Ruben and Andy Ruben *Cine.* Phedon Papamichael *Ed.* Gina Mittleman *P.d.* Virginia Lee *A.d.* Hayden Yates *S.d.* Michele Munoz *Mu.* Aaron Davies *MPAA* R *R.t.* 92 min. *Cast:* Sara Gilbert, Drew Barrymore, Tom Skerritt, Cheryl Ladd, Alan Stock, Jeanne Sakata, E. J. Moore, J. B. Quon, Leonardo Dicaprio, Michael Goldner, Charley Hayward, Tim Winters, Billy Charles Kane, Tony Ervolina.

Drew Barrymore stars as the eponymous Ivy, an orphaned teenager who adopts the wealthy parents of her new friend, Cooper (Sara Gilbert), as her own. Ivy proves to have sinister motives, however, when she methodically endears herself to the family in order to destroy it.

THE POWER OF ONE

Pro. Arnon Milchan for Regency Enterprises, Le Studio Canal Plus, and Alcor Films, with the participation of Village Roadshow Pictures; Warner Bros. *Dir.* John G. Avildsen *Scr.* Robert Mark Kamen; based on the novel by Bryce Courtenay *Cine.* Dean Semler *Ed.* John G. Avildsen *P.d.* Roger Hall *A.d.* Les Tomkins, Martin Hitchcock, and Kevin Phipps *S.d.* Karen Brookes *Mu.* Hans Zimmer *MPAA* PG-13 *R.t.* 126 min. *Cast:* Stephen Dorff, Armin Mueller-Stahl, Morgan Freeman, John Gielgud, Guy Witcher, Simon Fenton, Dominic

Walker, Fay Masterson, Alois Moyo, Clive Russell, Faith Edwards, Tracy Brooks Swope.

In South Africa, just prior to World War II, the English boy P. K. (Stephen Dorff) learns boxing from the black prison inmate Geel Piet (Morgan Freeman) and music from Doc (Armin Mueller-Stahl), who both act as his mentors. Geel Piet spreads the rumor among African tribes that P. K., whom he suspects will become a champion, is the mythic Rainmaker, the savior of a united Africa.

PROOF (Australia, 1991)

Pro. Lynda House for House and Moorhouse Films; Fine Line Features *Dir.* Jocelyn Moorhouse *Scr.* Jocelyn Moorhouse *Cine.* Martin McGrath *Ed.* Ken Sallows *P.d.* Patrick Reardon *S.d.* Dimity Huntington *Mu.* Not Drowning, Waving *MPAA* R *R.t.* 86 min. *Cast:* Hugo Weaving, Genevieve Picot, Russell Crowe, Heather Mitchell, Jeffrey Walker, Frank Gallacher, Frankie J. Holden, Daniel Pollock, Saskia Post, Cliff Ellen.

Martin (Hugo Weaving), a blind photographer, befriends Andy (Russell Crowe), a dishwasher in a café. Martin depends on Andy to describe his photographs, which are his only verification that the world he hears, touches, and smells is the same as the one that others see. Martin's housekeeper, Celia (Genevieve Picot), who has a strange love-hate relationship with the photographer, is threatened by the new friendship, and her vengeful acts severely test Martin's newfound trust of the sighted.

THE PUBLIC EYE

Pro. Sue Baden-Powell for Robert Zemeckis; Universal Pictures *Dir.* Howard Franklin *Scr.* Howard Franklin *Cine.* Peter Suschitzky *Ed.* Evan Lottman *P.d.* Marcia Hinds-Johnson *A.d.* Bo Johnson *S.d.* Jan Bergstrom *Mu.* Mark Isham *MPAA* R *R.t.* 99 min. *Cast:* Joe Pesci, Barbara Hershey, Stanley Tucci, Jared Harris, Jerry Adler, Dominic Chianese, Richard Foronjy, Richard Riehle, Gerry Becker, David Gianopoulos, Del Close, Bob Gunton.

Tabloid photographer Leon "Bernzy" Bernstein (Joe Pesci) prowls the streets of New York City in 1942, photographing the seamy side of life. In the course of his work, Bernzy becomes involved with a wealthy socialite and some local gangsters.

PURE COUNTRY

Pro. Jerry Weintraub; Warner Bros. *Dir.* Christopher Cain *Scr.* Rex McGee *Cine.* Richard Bowen *Ed.* Jack Hofstra *P.d.* Jeffrey Howard *S.d.* Derek R. Hill *Mu.* Steve Dorff *MPAA* PG *R.t.* 112 min. *Cast:* George Strait, Lesley Ann Warren, Isabel Glasser, Kyle Chandler, John Doe, Rory Calhoun, Molly McClure.

Country singer George Strait stars as a famous country singer, Dusty, who has grown tired of his glitzy Las Vegas life-style. When he returns to Texas to rediscover his roots, Dusty falls in love with a woman (Isabel Glasser) who is working to save the family ranch.

THE QUARREL (Canada, 1992)

Pro. David Brandes and Kim Todd for American Playhouse Theatrical Films, Atlantis Films Limited, and Apple & Honey, in association with Comweb Productions, the Ontario Film Development Corp., and Super Ecran; Apple & Honey Film Corp. *Dir.* Eli Cohen *Scr.* David Brandes; based on the short story "My Quarrel with Hersh Rasseyner," by Chaim Grade *Cine.* John Berrie *Ed.* Havelock Gradidge *P.d.* Michael Joy *Mu.* William Goldstein *R.t.* 88 min. *Cast:* Saul Rubinek, R. H. Thomson, Robert Haiat, Ellen Cohen, Ari Snyder.

Two estranged childhood Jewish friends (Saul Rubinek and R. H. Thomson), both survivors of the Holocaust, meet as adults and reprise philosophical and religious arguments that drove them apart years ago.

RADIO FLYER

Pro. Lauren Shuler-Donner for Stonebridge Entertainment, in association with Donner/Shuler-Donner Productions; Columbia Pictures *Dir.* Richard Donner *Scr.* David Mickey Evans *Cine.* Laszlo Kovacs *Ed.* Stuart Baird *P.d.* J. Michael Riva *A.d.* David Frederick Klassen *S.d.* Michael Taylor *Mu.* Hans Zimmer *MPAA* PG-13 *R.t.* 120 min. *Cast:* Lorraine Bracco, John Heard, Adam Baldwin, Elijah Wood, Joseph Mazzello, Ben Johnson, Sean Baca, Robert Munic, Tom Hanks (uncredited).

In this drama set in the 1960's, two brothers, Mike (Elijah Wood) and Bobby (Joseph Mazzello), move to California with their mother (Lorraine Bracco), where she soon remarries. Their new stepfather is a child abuser, and the two boys hide the younger one's beatings from their overworked mother while planning a fantastic escape in their "magic" Radio Flyer toy wagon.

RAMPAGE

Pro. David Salven; Miramax Films *Dir.* William Friedkin *Scr.* William Friedkin; based on the novel by William P. Wood *Cine.* Robert D. Yeoman *Ed.* Jere Huggins *P.d.* Buddy Cone *A.d.* Carol Clements *S.d.* Nancy Nye *Mu.* Ennio Morricone *MPAA* R *R.t.* 97 min. *Cast:* Michael Biehn, Alex McArthur, Nicholas Campbell, Deborah Van Valkenburgh, John Harkins, Art Lafleur, Billy Greenbush, Royce D. Applegate.

A mix of violence and propaganda, this thriller cum courtroom drama centers on a gruesome mass murderer, Charles Reece (Alex McArthur), and his ensuing trial that explores the controversial issue of capital punishment.

RAPID FIRE

Pro. Robert Lawrence; Twentieth Century-Fox *Dir.* Dwight H. Little *Scr.* Alan McElroy; based on a story by Cindy Cirile and McElroy *Cine.* Ric Waite *Ed.* Gib Jaffe *P.d.* Ron Foreman *A.d.* Charles Butcher *S.d.* Natalie Richards and Leslie Frankenheimer *Mu.* Christopher Young *MPAA* R *R.t.* 95 min. *Cast:* Brandon Lee, Powers Boothe, Nick Mancuso, Raymond J. Barry, Kate Hodge, Tzi Ma, Tony Longo, Michael Paul Chan.

Brandon Lee, son of martial arts legend Bruce Lee, stars as a pacifist college student who turns action hero when he inadvertently witnesses a murder and is compelled to team with a Chicago police officer (Powers Boothe) in order to crack a vicious drug cartel.

RASPAD (USSR, 1992)

Pro. Mikhail Kostiukovsky for Dovzhenko Studios/Lavra Studios, in association with Peter O. Almond and the Pacific Film Fund; MK2 Productions USA *Dir.* Mikhail Belikov *Scr.* Mikhail Belikov and Oleg Prihodko *Cine.* Vasily Trushkovsky and Aleksandr Shagaev *Ed.* Tatyana Magalias *P.d.* Inna Bichenkova *A.d.* Vacily Zaruba *Mu.* Igor Stentcuk *R.t.* 103 min. *Cast:* Sergei Shakurov, Tatyana Kochemasova, Stanislav Stankevich, Georgi Drozd, Aleksei Cerebriakov, Marina Mogilevskaya, Aleksei Gorbunov, Anatoly Groshevoy, Nikita Buldovsky, Natalya Plohotniuk, Nikolai Docenko, Valery Sheptekita, Valentina Masenko, Taracik Mikitenko, Valdimir Olekceenko, Olga Kuznetcova.

The 1986 nuclear disaster at the Chernobyl nuclear plant is the subject of this riveting drama. By focusing on the loss of trust between a Russian husband and wife (Sergei Shakurov and Tatyana Kochemasova), the filmmakers have succeeded in drawing parallels to the larger deception of the Soviet government in its handling of the Chernobyl accident and its aftermath.

RESIDENT ALIEN: QUENTIN CRISP IN AMERICA

Pro. Jonathan Nossiter for Crisp City; Greycat Films *Dir.* Jonathan Nossiter *Scr.* Jonathan Nossiter *Cine.* John R. Foster *Ed.* Jonathan Nossiter *A.d.* Chris Wise *R.t.* 85 min. *Cast:* Quentin Crisp, John Hurt, Fran Lebowitz, Sting, Robert Patrick, Michael Musto, Holly Woodlawn, Felicity Mason.

This pseudo-documentary centers on the eccentric octogenarian Quentin Crisp, "resident alien" of Manhattan. Originally from Great Britain, Crisp, a self-proclaimed homosexual, emigrated to the United States in 1976, where he has since maintained his unique life-style, as evidenced by his own words as well as those of his friends and acquaintances.

ROADSIDE PROPHETS

Pro. Peter McCarthy and David Swinson; Fine Line Features *Dir.* Abbe Wool *Scr.* Abbe Wool *Cine.* Tom Richmond *Ed.* Nancy Richardson *P.d.* J. Rae Fox *Mu.* Pray for Rain *MPAA* R *R.t.* 96 min. *Cast:* John Doe, Adam Horovitz, David Carradine, Timothy Leary, Arlo Guthrie, Barton Heyman, Jennifer Balgobin, John Cusack, Bill Cobbs, Lin Shaye.

A second-rate *Easy Rider* (1969), this drama centers on a biker, Joe (John Doe), who is seeking El Dorado—not the myth, but a Nevada casino—in order to scatter the ashes of a deceased acquaintance. Joe is soon joined by Sam (Adam Horovitz), and the two meet various strange individuals (played by such stars as John Cusack, Arlo Guthrie, and David Carradine) while on the road.

ROCK-A-DOODLE

Pro. Don Bluth, Gary Goldman, and John Pomeroy for Goldcrest and Sullivan Bluth Studios Ireland Ltd.; The Samuel Goldwyn Company *Dir.* Don Bluth *Scr.* David N. Weiss *Mu.* Robert Folk *MPAA* G *R.t.* 74 min. *Voices:* Glen Campbell, Ellen Greene, Christopher Plummer, Charles Nelson Reilly, Eddie Deezen, Phil Harris, Sandy Duncan, Sorrell Booke, Toby Scott Granger.

Mixing live action and animation, this musical adventure revolves around a rooster named Chanticleer (voice of Glen Campbell), who once believed that his crowing made the sun rise, but was then disillusioned by an evil owl, the Grand Duke (voice of Christopher Plummer), and ran away from the farm. When floods threaten the family farm of a real boy (Toby Scott Granger), he determines to seek Chanticleer's help and is subsequently changed into an animated kitten by the Grand Duke. He joins some other animated farm animals to go to the city to seek Chanticleer, who is now a rock singer nicknamed the King.

ROMEO AND JULIA

Pro. Kevin Kaufman; Kaufman Films *Dir.* Kevin Kaufman *Scr.* Kevin Kaufman *Cine.* Patrick Darrin *Ed.* Peter Hammer *R.t.* 92 min. *Cast:* Bob Koherr, Ivana Kane, Patrick McGuinness, Willard Morgan, Karen Porter White, Max Brandt.

Romeo (Bob Koherr) and Julia (Ivana Kane) are modern-day star-crossed lovers who meet on a bridge as each contemplates suicide, and soon fall in love, in this low-budget, uneven romance.

RUBIN AND ED

Pro. Paul Webster for Working Title Films; I.R.S. Releasing Corporation *Dir.* Trent Harris *Scr.* Trent Harris *Cine.* Bryan Duggan *Ed.* Brent Schoenfeld *P.d.* Clark Hunter *Mu.* Fredric Myrow *MPAA* PG-13 *R.t.* 82 min. *Cast:* Crispin Glover, Howard Hesseman, Karen Black, Michael Greene, Anna Louise Daniels, Brittaney Lewis.

Two alienated eccentrics—Rubin (Crispin Glover) and Ed (Howard Hesseman)—form a tenuous friendship in this lukewarm comedy. Ed is a loser salesman and Rubin is a recluse whom Ed has targeted for a seminar. Before the seminar, the two agree to travel together to the Utah desert to bury Rubin's dead cat.

RUBY

Pro. Sigurjon Sighvatsson and Steve Golin for Polygram and Propaganda Films; Triumph Releasing Corporation *Dir.* John Mackenzie *Scr.* Stephen Davis; based on his play *Love Field* *Cine.* Phil Meheux *Ed.* Richard Trevor *P.d.* David Brisbin *A.d.* Kenneth A. Hardy

S.d. Annie Mei-Ling Tien and Lauri Gaffin *Mu.* John Scott *MPAA* R *R.t.* 110 min. *Cast:* Danny Aiello, Sherilyn Fenn, Arliss Howard, Tobin Bell, David Duchovny, Richard Sarafian, Joe Cortese, Marc Lawrence, Willie Garson, Joe Viterelli, Carmine Caridi, Frank Orsatti, Jeffrey Nordling, Jane Hamilton, Maurice Benard, Robert S. Telford, Gerard David, Kevin Wiggins.

Released within months of Oliver Stone's Academy Award-nominated *JFK* (1991), this version of the events surrounding the assassinations of John F. Kennedy and Lee Harvey Oswald centers on Oswald's killer, Jack Ruby. As portrayed here by Danny Aiello, Ruby is a Dallas nightclub owner with mob connections who shoots Oswald in a desperate attempt to put forth his version of who shot Kennedy.

THE RUNESTONE

Pro. Harry E. Gould, Jr., and Thomas L. Wilhite; Hyperion Pictures/Signature Communications *Dir.* Willard Carroll *Scr.* Willard Carroll; based on the novella by Mark E. Rogers *Cine.* Misha Suslov *Ed.* Lynne Southerland *P.d.* Jon Gary Steele *A.d.* Stella Wang *S.d.* Nancy Arnold *Mu.* David Newman *MPAA* R *R.t.* 101 min. *Cast:* Peter Riegert, Joan Severance, William Hickey, Tim Ryan, Mitchell Laurance, Lawrence Tierney, Chris Young, Alexander Godunov.

An ancient Norse runestone discovered in a Pennsylvania mine wreaks havoc on New York City in the form of a murderous hairy monster, which is hunted down by Detective Gregory Fanducci (Peter Riegert).

SCHOOL TIES

Pro. Stanley R. Jaffe and Sherry Lansing; Paramount Pictures *Dir.* Robert Mandel *Scr.* Dick Wolf and Darryl Ponicsan; based on a story by Wolf *Cine.* Freddie Francis *Ed.* Jerry Greenberg and Jacqueline Cambas *P.d.* Jeannine Claudia Oppewall *A.d.* Steven Wolff *S.d.* Marc Fisichella and Rosemary Brandenburg *Mu.* Maurice Jarre *MPAA* PG-13 *R.t.* 107 min. *Cast:* Brendan Fraser, Matt Damon, Chris O'Donnell, Randall Batinkoff, Andrew Lowery, Cole Hauser, Ben Affleck, Anthony Rapp, Amy Locane, Peter Donat, Zeljko Ivanek, Kevin Tighe, Michael Higgins, Ed Lauter.

Set in the 1950's, this drama stars Brendan Fraser as a young high school student who wins a football scholarship to a snobbish New England prep school and hides his Jewish identity in order to fit in.

SHAKES THE CLOWN

Pro. Ann Luly and Paul Colichman for I.R.S. Media; I.R.S. Releasing *Dir.* Bobcat Goldthwait *Scr.* Bobcat Goldthwait *Cine.* Elliot Davis and Bobby Bukowski *Ed.* J. Kathleen Gibson *P.d.* Pamela Woodbridge *A.d.* Christopher B. Neeley *Mu.* Tom Scott *MPAA* R *R.t.* 86 min. *Cast:* Bobcat Goldthwait, Julie Brown, Paul Dooley, Robin Williams, Adam Sandler, Blake Clark, Florence Henderson, Tom Kenny.

Bobcat Goldthwait wrote, directed, and stars in this comic drama about the tensions and rivalry among circus clowns, rodeo clowns, and mimes. In this treacherous society, an alcoholic clown, Shakes (Goldthwait)—whose cheery exterior masks his troubled interior—is framed for the murder of his boss, Owen Cheese (Paul Dooley).

SHAKING THE TREE

Pro. Robert J. Wilson for U.S./Blue Ridge Filmtrust; Castle Hill Productions, Inc. *Dir.* Duane Clark *Scr.* Duane Clark and Steven Wilde *Cine.* Ronn Schmidt *Ed.* Martin L. Bernstein *P.d.* Sean Mannion *Mu.* David E. Russo *MPAA* R *R.t.* 107 min. *Cast:* Arye Gross, Gale Hansen, Doug Savant, Steven Wilde, Courteney Cox, Christina Haag, Michael Arabian, Nathan Davis, Ron Dean, Brittney Hansen.

This drama centers on four former high school buddies—Barry (Arye Gross), Sully (Gale Hansen), Michael (Doug Savant), and Duke (Steven Wilde)—who continue to maintain their close friendship ten years after graduation.

THE SILK ROAD (Japan, 1992)

Pro. Yoshiro Yuki, Masahiro Sato, and Mu Wanliang for Daiei Co., Ltd., Dentsu, Inc., and Marubeni; Trimark Pictures *Dir.* Junya Sato *Scr.* Tsuyoshi Yoshida and Junya Sato *Cine.* Akira Shizuka *Ed.* Akira Suzuki *A.d.* Hiroshi Tokuda and Kou Honglie *Mu.* Masaru Sato *MPAA* PG-13 *R.t.* 146 min. *Cast:* Koichi Sato, Toshiyuki Nishida, Tsunehiko Watase, Daijiro Harada, Takahiro Tamada, Anna Nakagawa, Yoshiko Mita.

In this sweeping historical epic set in eleventh century China, a young scholar, Zhao Xingde (Koichi Sato), becomes both a soldier for and trusted friend of a powerful general (Toshiyuki Nishida) during a time of political and military turmoil. This friendship is tested when both men fall in love with the same woman, a beautiful princess (Anna Nakagawa) whose homeland they have conquered.

SIMPLE MEN

Pro. Ted Hope and Hal Hartley for Zenith and American Playhouse Theatrical Films, in association with Fine Line Features, Film Four International, BIM Distribution, and True Fiction; Fine Line Features *Dir.* Hal Hartley *Scr.* Hal Hartley *Cine.* Michael Spiller *Ed.* Steve Hamilton *P.d.* Dan Ouellette *A.d.* Theresa DePrez *S.d.* Jeff Hartmann *Mu.* Ned Rifle *MPAA* R *R.t.* 106 min. *Cast:* Robert Burke, William Sage, Karen Sillas, Elina Lowensohn, Damian Young, Vivian Lanko, Martin Donovan, Mark Chandler Bailey, Chris Cooke, Jeffrey Howard, Holly Marie Combs, Joe Stevens, Marietta Marich, John Alexander MacKay, Bethany Wright.

In this film replete with quirky characters, two brothers, Bill (Robert Burke) and Dennis (William Sage), set out on a quest to find their estranged father, a fugitive from the law for having bombed the Pentagon in the 1960's, who is believed to be hiding on Long Island.

SOCIETY

Pro. Keith Walley for Wild Street Pictures and Keith Walley/Paul White; Zecca Corp. *Dir.* Brian Yuzna *Scr.* Woody Keith and Rick Fry *Cine.* Rick Fichter *Ed.* Peter Teschner *A.d.* Kelle DeForrest *Mu.* Mark Ryder and Phil Davies *MPAA* R *R.t.* 99 min. *Cast:* Billy Warlock, Devin DeVasquez, Evan Richards, Ben Meyerson, Ben Slack, Tim Bartell.

In this horror film, a Beverly Hills teenager, Bill Whitney (Billy Warlock), suspects that his wealthy family are aliens who feed on human flesh. Fantastic special effects are the film's major feature, designed by Japanese artist Screaming Mad George.

SPLIT SECOND (Great Britain, 1992)

Pro. Laura Gregory for Muse Productions B. V., Chris Hanley, and Challenge; InterStar Releasing *Dir.* Tony Maylam *Scr.* Gary Scott Thompson *Cine.* Clive Tickner *Ed.* Dan Rae *P.d.* Chris Edwards *Mu.* Stephen Parsons and Francis Haines *MPAA* R *R.t.* 90 min. *Cast:* Rutger Hauer, Kim Cattrall, Neil Duncan, Michael J. Pollard, Alun Armstrong, Pete Postlethwaite, Stewart Harvey-Wilson, Paul Grayson, Ian Dury, Roberta Eaton, Tony Steedman, Steven Hartley, Sarah Stockbridge, Colin Skeaping.

In this mediocre thriller, Rutger Hauer stars as a maverick London police officer in the year 2008. With his newly assigned and nerdy partner (Neil Duncan), he seeks a vicious monster who murders people in this ecologically devastated future.

THE STATION (Italy, 1992)

Pro. Domenico Procacci for Fandango S.r.1.; Aries Film *Dir.* Sergio Rubini *Scr.* Umberto Marino, Gianfilippo Ascione, and Sergio Rubini; based on a play by Marino *Cine.* Alessio

Gelsini *Ed.* Angelo Nicolini *S.d.* Carolina Ferrara and Luca Gobbi *R.t.* 92 min. *Cast:* Sergio Rubini, Margherita Buy, Ennio Fantastichini.

The quiet, well-ordered life of a small-town Italian stationmaster, Domenico (Sergio Rubini), is disrupted one night by the arrival of a stunning woman (Margherita Buy) who has quarreled with her violent, abusive boyfriend (Ennio Fantastichini) and must wait overnight for the next train to Rome.

STAY TUNED

Pro. James G. Robinson for Morgan Creek; Warner Bros. *Dir.* Peter Hyams *Scr.* Tom S. Parker and Jim Jennewein; based on a story by Parker, Jennewein, and Richard Siegel *Cine.* Peter Hyams *Ed.* Peter E. Berger *P.d.* Philip Harrison *A.d.* Richard Hudolin and David Willson *S.d.* Rose Marie McSherry, Daniel Bradette, Lin MacDonald, and Annmarie Corbett *Mu.* Bruce Broughton *MPAA* PG *R.t.* 87 min. *Cast:* John Ritter, Pam Dawber, Jeffrey Jones, David Tom, Heather McComb, Bob Dishy, Joyce Gordon, Eugene Levy, Erik King, Salt-n-Pepa.

John Ritter stars in this tepid comedy as a depressed family man and couch potato, Roy Knable, who makes a deal with the devil (Jeffrey Jones) when he is tempted by a 666-channel television on a trial basis. Roy and wife, Helen (Pam Dawber), then find themselves trapped in the television, where they must survive twenty-four hours of persecution on the system's perverse programming.

STEAL AMERICA

Pro. Liz Gazzanno for Seamless Pictures and Pacific Fund Film; Tara Releasing *Dir.* Lucy Phillips *Scr.* Lucy Phillips and Glen Scantlebury *Cine.* Jim Barett and Glen Scantlebury *Ed.* Glen Scantlebury *Mu.* Gregory Jones *R.t.* 84 min. *Cast:* Clara Bellino, Charlie Homo, Diviana Ingravallo, Kevin Haley, Liza Monjauze, Christopher Fisher.

Three European immigrants—Swiss Stella (Clara Bellino), French Christophe (Charlie Homo), and Italian Maria (Diviana Ingravallo)—settle in San Francisco and enmesh themselves in various romantic entanglements with each other and with an American, Jack (Kevin Haley), as they struggle to find purpose in their lives.

STEPHEN KING'S SLEEPWALKERS

Pro. Mark Victor, Michael Grais, and Nabeel Zahid for Ion Pictures; Columbia Pictures *Dir.* Mick Garris *Scr.* Stephen King *Cine.* Rodney Charters *Ed.* O. Nicholas Brown *P.d.* John DeCuir, Jr. *A.d.* Sig Tinglof *S.d.* Peter J. Kelly and Bruce A. Gibeson *Mu.* Nicholas Pike *MPAA* R *R.t.* 92 min. *Cast:* Brian Krause, Mädchen Amick, Alice Krige, Jim Haynie, Cindy Pickett, Ron Perlman, Lyman Ward, Dan Martin, Glenn Shadix, Cynthia Garris, Monty Bane, John Landis, Joe Dante, Stephen King, Clive Barker, Tobe Hooper.

In this horror film, Mary and Charles Brady (Alice Krige and Brian Krause) are mother and son sleepwalkers—shapeshifters who rob human virgins of their life force in order to survive.

STOP! OR MY MOM WILL SHOOT

Pro. Ivan Reitman, Joe Medjuck, and Michael C. Gross for Northern Lights; Universal Pictures *Dir.* Roger Spottiswoode *Scr.* Blake Snyder, William Osborne, and William Davies *Cine.* Frank Tidy *Ed.* Mark Conte and Lois Freeman-Fox *P.d.* Charles Rosen *A.d.* Diane Yates *S.d.* Robert Maddy and Don Remacle *Mu.* Alan Silvestri *MPAA* PG-13 *R.t.* 87 min. *Cast:* Sylvester Stallone, Estelle Getty, JoBeth Williams, Roger Rees, Martin Ferrero, Gailard Sartain, Dennis Burkley, J. Kenneth Campbell, Al Fann, Ella Joyce, John Wesley.

When the overbearing but loving mother (Estelle Getty) of a Los Angeles police officer, Joe Bomowski (Sylvester Stallone), comes for a short visit from the East Coast, Joe suffers her unwanted interferences in his personal and professional life. Problems come to a head when Joe learns that "Mom" will be his new partner after she witnesses a murder.

STORYVILLE

Pro. David Roe and Edward R. Pressman for Davis Entertainment Company; Twentieth Century-Fox *Dir.* Mark Frost *Scr.* Mark Frost and Lee Reynolds; based on the novel *Juryman*, by Frank Galbally and Robert Macklin *Cine.* Ron Garcia *Ed.* B. J. Sears *P.d.* Richard Hoover *A.d.* Kathleen M. McKernin *S.d.* Brian Kasch *Mu.* Carter Burwell *MPAA* R *R.t.* 110 min. *Cast:* James Spader, Joanne Whalley-Kilmer, Jason Robards, Piper Laurie, Charlotte Lewis, Michael Warren, Michael Parks, Chuck McCann, Charlie Haid, Chino Fats Williams, Woody Strode, Jeff Perry, Galyn Gorg, Justine Arlin.

In this tale of intrigue and deception in the Deep South, a wealthy and corrupt New Orleans political candidate, Cray Fowler (James Spader), is blackmailed when he is videotaped making love to a young Asian woman, Lee (Charlotte Lewis). When Lee is charged with the murder of her father, Cray represents Lee in court, where the assistant district attorney happens to be his former girlfriend (Joanne Whalley-Kilmer).

STRAIGHT TALK

Pro. Robert Chartoff and Fred Berner for Hollywood Pictures, in association with Touchwood Pacific Partners I and Sandollar Prods.; Buena Vista *Dir.* Barnet Kellman *Scr.* Craig Bolotin and Patricia Resnick; based on a story by Bolotin *Cine.* Peter Sova *Ed.* Michael Tronick *P.d.* Jeffrey Townsend *A.d.* Michael T. Perry *S.d.* Suzan Wexler and Daniel L. May *Mu.* Brad Fiedel *MPAA* PG *R.t.* 91 min. *Cast:* Dolly Parton, James Woods, Griffin Dunne, Michael Madsen, Deirdre O'Connell, John Sayles, Teri Hatcher, Spalding Gray, Jerry Orbach, Philip Bosco, Charles Fleischer, Keith MacKechnie, Jay Thomas, Amy Morton.

Tired of small-town life in Arkansas, Shirlee (Dolly Parton), a dance instructor, packs up and heads for Chicago. Soon after arriving, Shirlee rises to stardom as a talk-radio psychologist through a fortuitous case of mistaken identity. Newspaper reporter Jack (James Woods), however, believes Shirlee is not the "doctor" she claims to be and starts an investigation into her past.

SWOON

Pro. Christine Vachon for Intolerance, in association with American Playhouse Theatrical Films; Fine Line Features *Dir.* Tom Kalin *Scr.* Tom Kalin and Hilton Als *Cine.* Ellen Kuras *Ed.* Tom Kalin *P.d.* Therese Déprèz *A.d.* Stacey Jones *Mu.* James Bennett *MPAA* R *R.t.* 90 min. *Cast:* Daniel Schlachet, Craig Chester, Ron Vawter, Michael Kirby, Michael Stumm, Valda Z. Crabla, Natalie Stanford.

Based on real-life events, this drama revolves around two gay adolescents, Richard Loeb (Daniel Schlachet) and Nathan Leopold, Jr. (Craig Chester), from wealthy Jewish families who were convicted of kidnapping and murdering a young boy in the 1920's.

TERMINAL BLISS

Pro. Brian Cox for Cannon Pictures, in association with Distant Horizon *Dir.* Jordan Alan *Scr.* Jordan Alan *Cine.* Gregory Smith *Ed.* Bruce Sinofsky *P.d.* Catherine Tirr *Mu.* Frank W. Becker *MPAA* R *R.t.* 91 min. *Cast:* Timothy Owen, Luke Perry, Estee Chandler, Sonia Curtis, Micah Grant, Alexis Arquette.

Two teenagers, Alex (Timothy Owen) and John (Luke Perry), maintain a turbulent friendship in a film that depicts the life-styles of the rich and bored. Lacking parental guidance and direction, these two turn to sex and drugs to while away the time.

TETSUO: THE IRON MAN (Japan, 1992)

Pro. Shinya Tsukamoto for Kaiju Theater, in association with Japan Home Video/K2

Spirit/SEN; Original Cinema *Dir.* Shinya Tsukamoto *Scr.* Shinya Tsukamoto *Cine.* Shinya Tsukamoto and Kei Fujiwara *Ed.* Shinya Tsukamoto *A.d.* Shinya Tsukamoto *Mu.* Chu Ishikawa *R.t.* 67 min. *Cast:* Tomoroh Taguchi, Kei Fujiwara, Nobu Kanaoko, Shinya Tsukamoto, Naomasa Musaka, Renji Ishibashi.

In this kinky Japanese horror film, a man (Tomoroh Taguchi) realizes his worst nightmares as he slowly turns into a machine.

THANK YOU AND GOOD NIGHT!

Pro. Jan Oxenberg for American Playhouse Theatrical Films, POV Theatrical Films, and Red Wagon Films; Aries Film *Dir.* Jan Oxenberg *Scr.* Jan Oxenberg *Cine.* John Hazard *Ed.* Lucy Winer *P.d.* Pamela Woodbridge *A.d.* Kelly Reichert *S.d.* Catie deHaan *Mu.* Mark Suozzo *R.t.* 77 min. *Cast:* Mae Joffe, Jan Oxenberg.

This documentary-style drama centers on Mae Joffe, the grandmother of the filmmaker, Jan Oxenberg, and Mae's prolonged illness and death as a result of cancer. In a series of scenes featuring Oxenberg's grandmother, mother, and brother, as well as a cardboard cutout of herself as a five-year-old, Oxenberg evokes the pain and emotions of that difficult time, and yet maintains an upbeat outlook on life and death.

THERE'S NOTHING OUT THERE

Pro. Victor Kanefsky for Grandmaster; Valkhn Film *Dir.* Rolfe Kanefsky *Scr.* Rolfe Kanefsky *Cine.* Ed Hershberger *Ed.* Victor Kanefsky *S.d.* Virginia Dare *Mu.* Christopher Thomas *R.t.* 90 min. *Cast:* Craig Peck, Wendy Bednarz, Mark Collver, Bonnie Bowers, John Carhart III, Claudia Flores, Jeff Dachis.

In this parody of horror films by writer-director Rolfe Kanefsky, a group of teenagers goes to a cabin in the woods where the fears of one young man (Craig Peck)—a horror film fan—are realized when the group is threatened by a space alien in the woods.

THIRTY-FIVE UP (Great Britain, 1992)

Pro. Michael Apted for Granada Film; Samuel Goldwyn Company *Dir.* Michael Apted *Scr.* Michael Apted *Cine.* George Jesse Turner *Ed.* Claire Lewis *Ed.* Kim Horton *R.t.* 128 min. *Cast:* Charles, Andrew, John, Peter, Neil, Suzy, Paul, Symon, Tony, Jackie, Lynn, Susan, Bruce, Nicholas.

This documentary is part of a series that began in 1963 when fourteen seven-year-old children representing the various social classes in then-contemporary England were interviewed regarding their life aspirations. The filmmakers then proceeded to produce a sequel every seven years, tracking the lives and progress of these same individuals. Very sobering, this sequel, showing the participants at age thirty-five, presents the once-hopeful children as now world-weary adults, many of whom regret not having made the most of what they were given.

THREE NINJAS

Pro. Martha Chang for Touchstone Pictures and Global Venture Hollywood; Buena Vista *Dir.* Jon Turteltaub *Scr.* Edward Emanuel; based on a story by Kenny Kim *Cine.* Richard Michalak *Ed.* David Rennie *P.d.* Kirk Petruccelli *A.d.* Ken Kirchener and Greg Grande *S.d.* Carol Pressman *Mu.* Rick Marvin *MPAA* PG *R.t.* 84 min. *Cast:* Victor Wong, Michael Treanor, Max Elliott Slade, Chad Power, Rand Kingsley, Alan McRae, Margarita Franco, Toru Tanaka, Patrick Labyorteaux, Race Nelson, D. J. Harder.

In this weak action/adventure combining elements of *Home Alone* (1990) and *The Karate Kid* (1984), three brothers (Michael Treanor, Max Elliott Slade, and Chad Power) are trained in the martial arts by their grandfather (Victor Wong). They put their skills to use when a ruthless arms dealer (Rand Kingsley) kidnaps them.

TIME WILL TELL (*Bob Marley: Time Will Tell*; Great Britain, 1992)
Pro. Rocky Oldham for Island Visual Arts, PolyGram Video International, and Initial Film and Television; I.R.S. *Dir.* Declan Lowney *Ed.* Peter Bensimon and Tim Thornton-Allan *Mu.* Bob Marley Music, Inc. *R.t.* 85 min. *Cast:* Bob Marley.

This documentary centers on Jamaican reggae star Bob Marley and his brilliant career, which was cut short by his death at age thirty-six in 1981.

TIMEBOMB
Pro. Raffaella De Laurentiis; MGM/UA *Dir.* Avi Nesher *Scr.* Avi Nesher *Cine.* Anthony B. Richmond *Ed.* Isaac Sehayek *P.d.* Greg Pruss and Curtis A. Schnell *A.d.* Robert E. Lee *Mu.* Patrick Leonard *MPAA* R *R.t.* 96 min. *Cast:* Michael Biehn, Patsy Kensit, Tracy Scoggins, Robert Culp, Richard Jordan, Raymond St. Jacques, Billy Blanks, Jim Maniaci, Steven J. Oliver, Ray Mancini, Carlos Palomino, Harvey Fisher, Kate Mitchell, Sheila Young.

In this thriller, a former soldier, Eddy Kay (Michael Biehn), who served in Vietnam suffers hallucinations as the result of an insidious CIA experiment run by the evil Colonel Taylor (Richard Jordan). When Eddy seeks the help of a psychiatrist (Patsy Kensit), both of their lives are threatened by Taylor and his minions.

TOUS LES MATINS DU MONDE (France, 1991)
Pro. Jean-Louis Livi; October Films *Dir.* Alain Corneau *Scr.* Pascal Quignard; based on his novel *Cine.* Yves Angelo *Ed.* Marie-Josèphe Yoyotte *A.d.* Bernard Vezat *Mu.* Jordi Savall *R.t.* 114 min. *Cast:* Jean-Pierre Marielle, Gérard Depardieu, Anne Brochet, Guillaume Depardieu, Caroline Sihol, Carole Richert, Violaine Lacroix, Nadège Téron, Myriam Boyer, Jean-Claude Dreyfus, Yves Lambrecht, Michel Bouquet, Jean-Marie Poirer.

Gérard Depardieu stars in this award-winning historical drama as seventeenth century composer and musician Marin Marais, who reflects in his embittered old age on his youth when he was a student of Monsieur de Sainte Colombe (Jean-Pierre Marielle), a brilliant and reclusive artist whom he rejected in favor of the glamour of court life.

TRACES OF RED
Pro. David V. Picker and Mark Gordon; Samuel Goldwyn Company *Dir.* Andy Wolk *Scr.* Jim Piddock *Cine.* Tim Suhrstedt *Ed.* Trudy Ship *P.d.* Dan Bishop and Dianna Freas *A.d.* Richard Fojo *Mu.* Graeme Revell *MPAA* R *R.t.* 100 min. *Cast:* James Belushi, Lorraine Bracco, Tony Goldwyn, William Russ, Faye Grant, Michelle Joyner, Joe Lisi, Victoria Bass.

James Belushi and Tony Goldwyn star as two Palm Beach police officers who investigate the serial murders of three women, and Lorraine Bracco stars as a sexy widow who seduces them both. Although the acting is poor, the film features a number of plot twists.

TRESPASS
Pro. Neil Canton for Canton/Zemeckis/Gale; Universal Pictures *Dir.* Walter Hill *Scr.* Bob Gale and Robert Zemeckis *Cine.* Lloyd Ahern *Ed.* Freeman Davies *P.d.* Jon Hutman *A.d.* Charles Breen *S.d.* Kathleen Sullivan and Beth Rubino *Mu.* Ry Cooder *MPAA* R *R.t.* 101 min. *Cast:* Bill Paxton, Ice-T, William Sadler, Ice Cube, Art Evans, De'voreaux White, Bruce A. Young, Glenn Plummer, Stoney Jackson, T. E. Russell, Tiny Lister, John Toles-Bey, Byron Minns, Tico Wells.

In this action-packed drama, Bill Paxton and William Sadler star as two white fire fighters who track a secret cache of gold to an abandoned East St. Louis factory. When they arrive to collect it, however, they witness a gang killing led by the vicious King James (Ice-T), and are trapped in the building, using King James' brother (De'voreaux White) as a hostage.

TROPICAL RAINFOREST
Pro. Marian White and Ben Shedd for the Science Museum of Minnesota *Dir.* Ben Shedd

Scr. Simon Campbell-Jones *Cine.* Timothy C. Housel *Ed.* Vincent Stenerson *R.t.* 38 min. *Cast:* Geoffrey Holder.

This beautifully photographed and riveting documentary focuses on the grandeur of the 400-million-year-old rainforest and its rapid and large-scale destruction by humankind in the late twentieth century.

THE TUNE

Pro. Bill Plympton *Dir.* Bill Plympton *Scr.* Bill Plympton, Maureen McElheron, and P. C. Vey *Cine.* John Donnelly *Ed.* Merril Stern *Mu.* Maureen McElheron *R.t.* 69 min. *Voices:* Daniel Neiden, Maureen McElheron, Marty Nelson, Emily Bindiger, Chris Hoffman, Jimmy Ceribello, Ned Reynolds, Jeff Knight, Jennifer Senko.

In this animated fantasy, a would-be songwriter, Del (voice of Daniel Neiden), is ordered by his boss, Mr. Mega (voice of Marty Nelson), to write a hit song in forty-seven minutes. Panicked, Del wanders into the land of Flooby Nooby, where myriad strange characters croon tunes that parody popular musical genres. The first feature-length film by animator Bill Plympton, this musical comedy is, at times, irreverent and of questionable taste.

UNDER SUSPICION (Great Britain, 1992)

Pro. Brian Eastman for Rank Film Distributors, LWT, and Carnival; Columbia Pictures *Dir.* Simon Moore *Scr.* Simon Moore *Cine.* Vernon Layton and Ivan Strasburg *Ed.* Tariq Anwar *P.d.* Tim Hutchinson *A.d.* Tony Reading *S.d.* Stephenie McMillan and Joel Washnetz *Mu.* Christopher Gunning *MPAA* R *R.t.* 99 min. *Cast:* Liam Neeson, Laura San Giacomo, Kenneth Cranham, Alphonsia Emmanuel, Stephen Moore, Maggie O'Neill, Malcolm Storry, Alan Talbot, Martin Grace, Kevin Moore, Alex Norton, Michael Almaz.

Set in 1950's England, this *film noir* centers on a seedy detective, Tony Aaron (Liam Neeson), who specializes in divorce cases—he takes photographs of clients in bed with his wife, Hazel (Maggie O'Neill), to "prove" adultery. Tony has a mystery to solve when he arrives at a routine appointment and discovers that Hazel and a client have been murdered in bed. A suspect himself, Tony further complicates matters when he begins an affair with another suspect, femme fatale and mistress of his former client, Angeline (Laura San Giacomo).

UNIVERSAL SOLDIER

Pro. Allen Shapiro, Craig Baumgarten, and Joel B. Michaels for Mario Kassar and Indieprod, in association with Centropolis Film Productions; TriStar Pictures *Dir.* Roland Emmerich *Scr.* Richard Rothstein, Christopher Leitch, and Dean Devlin *Cine.* Karl Walter Lindenlaub *Ed.* Michael J. Duthie *A.d.* Nelson Coates *S.d.* Alex Carle *Mu.* Christopher Franke *MPAA* R *R.t.* 104 min. *Cast:* Jean-Claude Van Damme, Dolph Lundgren, Ally Walker, Ed O'Ross, Jerry Orbach, Leon Rippy, Tico Wells, Ralph Moeller, Robert Trebor, Rance Howard, Lilyan Chauvin.

This is a science-fiction thriller about dead Vietnam veterans secretly brought back to life. Rewired as cyborg super-soldiers, they are initially obedient, impervious to pain, and represent the United States' top secret antiterrorist weapon. A curious television news reporter discovers the secret and triggers the human memories of two soldiers (Jean-Claude Van Damme and Dolph Lundgren) with devastating consequences.

VAN GOGH (France, 1992)

Pro. Daniel Toscan du Plantier; Sony Pictures Classics *Dir.* Maurice Pialat *Scr.* Maurice Pialat *Cine.* Emmanuel Machuel, Gilles Henri, and Jacques Loiseleux *Ed.* Yann Dedet and Nathalie Hubert *P.d.* Edith Vesperini *MPAA* R *R.t.* 155 min. *Cast:* Jacques Dutronc, Alexandra London, Gérard Sety, Bernard Le Coq, Corinne Bourdon, Elsa Zylberstein, Leslie

Azzoula, Jacques Vida, Lisa Lametrie, Chantal Barbarit, Claudine Ducret.

This version of painter Vincent van Gogh's life centers on the artist (played by Jacques Dutronc) and his final two very productive months in Auvers-sur-Oise, at the home of Dr. Gachet (Gérard Sety) and his daughter, Marguerite (Alexandra London).

VENICE/VENICE

Pro. Judith Wolinsky for International Rainbow Pictures; Rainbow *Dir.* Henry Jaglom *Scr.* Henry Jaglom *Cine.* Hanania Baer *Ed.* Henry Jaglom *Mu.* Marshall Barer and David Colin Ross *R.t.* 108 min. *Cast:* Nelly Alard, Henry Jaglom, Melissa Leo, Suzanne Bertish, Daphna Kastner, David Duchovny.

Henry Jaglom directed, wrote, edited, and stars in this comic romantic drama as American independent filmmaker Dean who attends the Venice Film Festival in Italy. His romance with a French journalist, Jeanne (Nelly Alard), and clips of women discussing how films influenced their notions of romance point up the conflict between love in the cinema and in real life.

VOLERE, VOLARE (Italy, 1992)

Pro. Ernesto Di Sarro; Fine Line Features *Dir.* Maurizio Nichetti and Guido Manuli *Scr.* Maurizio Nichetti and Guido Manuli *Cine.* Mario Battistoni *Ed.* Rita Rossi and Anna Missoni *P.d.* Maria Pia Angelini *Mu.* Manuel de Sica *MPAA* R *R.t.* 92 min. *Cast:* Maurizio Nichetti, Angela Finocchiaro, Mariella Valentini, Patrizio Roversi, Remo Remotti, Mario Gravier, Luigi Gravier, Renato Scarpa, Massimo Sarchielli, Osavaldo Salvi, Lidia Biondi.

When a shy film sound technician (Maurizio Nichetti) falls in love with a beautiful and erotic young woman (Angela Finocchiaro), he is appalled to find himself slowly turning into an animated cartoon like those in the films he dubs.

VOYAGER (Germany, France, and Greece, 1992)

Pro. Eberhard Junkersdorf for Bioskop Film and Action Films, in association with STEFI II/Hellas Video; Castle Hill Productions, Inc. *Dir.* Volker Schlondorff *Scr.* Volker Schlondorff and Rudy Wurlitzer; based on the novel *Homo Faber*, by Max Frisch *Cine.* Yorgos Arvanitis and Pierre L'Homme *Ed.* Dagmar Hirtz *P.d.* Nicos Perakis *S.d.* Benedikt Herforth *Mu.* Stanley Myers *MPAA* PG-13 *R.t.* 117 min. *Cast:* Sam Shepard, Julie Delpy, Barbara Sukowa, Dieter Kirchlechner, Traci Lind, Deborah-Lee Furness, August Zirner, Thomas Heinze.

Sam Shepard stars as Walter Faber, an American engineer and world traveler, who, despite his scientific worldview, falls victim to fate. Years earlier he had fathered a child in Switzerland and left the country—leaving the woman with his best friend and plans for an abortion. Many years later, he meets and falls in love with an attractive young woman (Julie Delpy) while on an ocean cruise, only to find out too late that she is his daughter.

WATERLAND (Great Britain and USA, 1992)

Pro. Katy McGuinness and Patrick Cassavetti for Palace and Fine Line Features, in association with Pandora Cinema, Channel Four Films, and British Screen; Fine Line Features *Dir.* Stephen Gyllenhaal *Scr.* Peter Prince; based on the novel by Graham Swift *Cine.* Robert Elswit *Ed.* Lesley Walker *P.d.* Hugo Luczyc-Wyhowski *A.d.* Helen Rayner *Mu.* Carter Burwell *MPAA* R *R.t.* 95 min. *Cast:* Jeremy Irons, Sinead Cusack, Lena Headey, Grant Warnock, David Morrissey, Ethan Hawke, John Heard, Peter Postlethwaite, Siri Neal, Callum Dixon.

Pittsburgh history teacher Tom Crick (Jeremy Irons) tries to show his bored students the relevance of the past to the present by recounting his adolescence in the fen country of East Anglia. In exploring the past, he uncovers the darkest secrets of his wife, Mary (Sinead

Cusack), his mother, and his retarded brother. Mary's despair over her life drives her away from Tom.

WE'RE TALKIN' SERIOUS MONEY

Pro. Paul Hertzberg; Cinetel Films, Inc. *Dir.* James Lemmo *Scr.* James Lemmo and Leo Rossi *Cine.* Jacques Haitkin *Ed.* Steve Nevius *P.d.* Dins Danielson *A.d.* Susan Benjamin *S.d.* Rob Scolari *Mu.* Scott Grusin *MPAA* PG-13 *R.t.* 104 min. *Cast:* Dennis Farina, Leo Rossi, Fran Drescher.

Two New York con men (Dennis Farina and Leo Rossi) escape the mob and flee to the West Coast. These two fish-out-of-water try to work their get-rich-quick schemes in Los Angeles.

WHERE SLEEPING DOGS LIE

Pro. Mario Sotela for Sotela Pictures; August Entertainment *Dir.* Charles Finch *Scr.* Yolande Turner and Charles Finch *Cine.* Monty Rowan *Ed.* B. J. Sears and Gene M. Gemaine *P.d.* Eve Cauley *A.d.* Lisa Snyder *Mu.* Hans Zimmer and Mark Mancina *MPAA* R *R.t.* 89 min. *Cast:* Dylan McDermott, Tom Sizemore, Sharon Stone, Mary Woronov, David Combs, Shawne Rowe, Jillian McWhirter, Brett Cullen, Richard Zavaglia, Ron Karabatsos.

An unsuccessful writer (Dylan McDermott) takes up residence in a creepy mansion, where he is joined by an equally creepy boarder (Tom Sizemore). The writer then sets out to investigate a brutal murder that took place there, in order to write a novel.

WHERE THE DAY TAKES YOU

Pro. Paul Hertzberg for Cinetel Films, Inc.; New Line Cinema *Dir.* Marc Rocco *Scr.* Michael Hitchcock, Kurt Voss, and Marc Rocco *Cine.* King Baggot *Ed.* Russell Livingstone *P.d.* Kirk Petruccelli *S.d.* Greg Grande *Mu.* Mark Morgan *MPAA* R *R.t.* 105 min. *Cast:* Dermot Mulroney, Lara Flynn Boyle, Balthazar Getty, Sean Astin, James Le Gros, Ricki Lake, Kyle MacLachlan, Peter Dobson, Stephen Tobolowsky, Will Smith, Adam Baldwin, Laura San Giacomo, Christian Slater, Nancy McKeon, Alyssa Milano, Rachel Ticotin.

This sobering drama centers on a group of homeless adolescents (Dermot Mulroney, Lara Flynn Boyle, Balthazar Getty, Sean Astin, James Le Gros, and Ricki Lake) who inhabit Hollywood Boulevard, stealing, begging, and drug dealing in order to survive.

WHISPERS IN THE DARK

Pro. Martin Bregman and Michael S. Bregman; Paramount Pictures *Dir.* Christopher Crowe *Scr.* Christopher Crowe *Cine.* Michael Chapman *Ed.* Bill Pankow *P.d.* John Jay Moore *S.d.* Justin Scoppa, Jr. *Mu.* Thomas Newman *MPAA* R *R.t.* 102 min. *Cast:* Annabella Sciorra, Jamey Sheridan, Anthony LaPaglia, Jill Clayburgh, John Leguizamo, Deborah Unger, Alan Alda, Anthony Heald, Jacqueline Brookes, Gene Canfield.

A troubled psychiatrist, Dr. Ann Hecker (Annabella Sciorra), seeks professional help when she finds herself growing increasingly titillated by the sadomasochistic sexual encounters related to her by a patient, Eve (Deborah Unger). When Eve is found brutally murdered, two of the men in Ann's life become prime suspects: her new mild-mannered boyfriend (Jamey Sheridan), who is shown to have also been Eve's sexual partner; and one of her patients, Fast Johnny C (John Leguizamo), who is an artist with a violent streak.

WHITE SANDS

Pro. William Sackheim and Scott Rudin for James G. Robinson and Morgan Creek; Warner Bros. *Dir.* Roger Donaldson *Scr.* Daniel Pyne *Cine.* Peter Menzies, Jr. *Ed.* Nicholas Beauman *P.d.* John Graysmark *A.d.* Michael Rizzo *S.d.* Michael Seirton *Mu.* Patrick O'Hearn *MPAA* R *R.t.* 101 min. *Cast:* Willem Dafoe, Mary Elizabeth Mastrantonio, Mickey Rourke, Samuel L. Jackson, M. Emmet Walsh, James Rebhorn, Maura Tierney, Beth Grant, Mimi

Rogers, Alexander Nicksay, Fredrick Lopez, Miguel Sandoval, John Lafayette, Ken Thorley, Jack Kehler.

While attempting to learn the identity of a suicide victim, small-town deputy Ray Dolezal (Willem Dafoe) is forced undercover in an FBI sting operation, bluffing his way into a partnership with a dangerous arms dealer (Mickey Rourke) and the mysterious woman (Mary Elizabeth Mastrantonio) who brings them together.

WHITE TRASH

Pro. Fred Baker; Fred Baker Film & Video Company *Dir.* Fred Baker *Scr.* Mel Clay; based on his play *Cine.* Fred Baker *Ed.* Robert Simpson *P.d.* Mary Jane Bell *A.d.* Steve Nelson *Mu.* Fred Baker and Mariano Rocca *R.t.* 85 min. *Cast:* John Hartman, Sean Christiansen, Periel Marr, Wheaton James, Jack Betts, Winnie Thexton, Brian Patrick.

Set on the day of the funeral of a young Los Angeles prostitute (Brian Patrick) who has died of AIDS, this drama centers on his surviving friends—all fellow prostitutes—and his wealthy father (Jack Betts) and sister (Winnie Thexton), who have arrived from the East Coast.

WHO SHOT PAT?

Pro. Halle Brooks; Castle Hill *Dir.* Robert Brooks *Scr.* Robert Brooks and Halle Brooks *Cine.* Robert Brooks *Ed.* Robert Brooks and Halle Brooks *S.d.* Lionel Driskill *MPAA* R *R.t.* 102 min. *Cast:* David Knight, Sandra Bullock, Brad Randall, Kevin Otto, Aaron Ingram, Clint Jordan, Damon Chandler, Phil Rosenthal.

In this nostalgic look at 1950's Brooklyn, a group of high school students discovers growing racial prejudice and class conflict. *Who Shot Pat?* is a classic coming-of-age story and the first feature film by Halle and Robert Brooks.

WILD ORCHID II: TWO SHADES OF BLUE

Pro. David Saunders and Rafael Eisenman; Vision International *Dir.* Zalman King *Scr.* Zalman King *Cine.* Mark Reshovsky *Ed.* Marc Grossman and James Gavin *P.d.* Richard Amend *A.d.* Randy Eriksen *S.d.* Chance Rearden *Mu.* George S. Clinton *MPAA* R *R.t.* 107 min. *Cast:* Nina Siemaszko, Wendy Hughes, Brent Fraser, Robert Davi, Tom Skerritt, Joe Dallesandro, Christopher McDonald, Liane Curtis, Stafford Morgan, Bridgit Ryan, Lydie Denier, Gloria Rueben, Victoria Mahoney.

An orphaned teenage girl, Blue (Nina Siemaszko), becomes a prostitute in this drama set in 1958. Secretly yearning after a local high school boy (Brent Fraser), Blue attempts to leave the profession and be a normal high school student.

WIND

Pro. Mata Yamamoto and Tom Luddy for Francis Ford Coppola, Fred Fuchs, and Filmlink International and American Zoetrope; TriStar Pictures *Dir.* Carroll Ballard *Scr.* Rudy Wurlitzer and Mac Gudgeon; based on a story by Jeff Benjamin, Roger Vaughan, and Kimball Livingston *Cine.* John Toll *Ed.* Michael Chandler *P.d.* Laurence Eastwood *Mu.* Basil Poledouris *MPAA* PG-13 *R.t.* 125 min. *Cast:* Matthew Modine, Jennifer Grey, Cliff Robertson, Jack Thompson, Stellan Skarsgard, Rebecca Miller, Ned Vaughan.

A mistake by helmsman Will Parker (Matthew Modine) during the sailing final for the America's Cup leads to an unprecedented loss for the United States. Will then spends months working with his former girlfriend and sailing partner, Kate Bass (Jennifer Grey), to design a craft to sail against Australia and reclaim the trophy for the United States.

WISECRACKS (Canada, 1992)

Pro. Gail Singer and Signe Johansson for Zinger Films, in association with National Film Board of Canada's Studio D; Alliance *Dir.* Gail Singer *Cine.* Zoe Dirse and Bob Fresco *Ed.*

Gordon McClellan *Mu.* Maribeth Solomon *R.t.* 93 min. *Cast:* Phyllis Diller, Whoopi Goldberg, Sandra Shamas, Jenny Lecoat, The Clichettes, Faking It Three, Geri Jewell, Jenny Jones, Ellen DeGeneres, Paula Poundstone, Kim Wayans, Deborah Theaker, Joy Behar, Maxine Lapiduss, Pam Stone.

The difficulty of being a woman in the world of stand-up comedy is the theme of filmmaker Gail Singer's documentary *Wisecracks*. Singer combines old film footage of stars such as Mae West and Lucille Ball with contemporary footage of comediennes such as Ellen DeGeneres and Whoopi Goldberg to present an amusing perspective on the world of female comedy.

A WOMAN, HER MEN, AND HER FUTON

Pro. Dale Rosenbloom and Mussef Sibay for Interpersonal Films, in association with First Look Pictures; Overseas Film Group *Dir.* Mussef Sibay *Scr.* Mussef Sibay *Cine.* Michael Davis *Ed.* Howard Heard *P.d.* Peter Paul Raubertas *A.d.* Florina Roberts *Mu.* Joel Goldsmith *MPAA* R *R.t.* 90 min. *Cast:* Jennifer Rubin, Lance Edwards, Grant Show, Michael Cerveris, Robert Lipton, Delaune Michel, Richard Gordon, Jennifer Zuniga, Kathryn Atwood, Gary Cusano, Kirsten Hall.

Set in Los Angeles, this drama centers on a divorced young screenwriter, Helen (Jennifer Rubin), who maintains sexual relationships with several men, but remains unfulfilled. Even her liaison with a fellow would-be screenwriter, Donald (Lance Edwards), ends in disappointment. Ironically, both Helen's and Donald's scripts-in-progress mirror their real-life dilemmas.

YEAR OF THE COMET

Pro. Peter Yates and Nigel Wooll for Castle Rock Entertainment, in association with New Line Cinema; Columbia Pictures *Dir.* Peter Yates *Scr.* William Goldman *Cine.* Roger Pratt *Ed.* Ray Lovejoy *P.d.* Anthony Pratt *A.d.* Desmond Crowe and Chris Seagers *S.d.* Stephenie McMillan *Mu.* Hummie Mann *MPAA* PG-13 *R.t.* 89 min. *Cast:* Penelope Ann Miller, Tim Daly, Louis Jourdan, Art Malik, Ian Richardson, Ian McNeice, Timothy Bentinck, Julia McCarthy, Jacques Mathou, Arturo Venegas, Chapman Roberts, Nick Brimble, Andrew Robertson, Shane Rimmer, David Bamber, Nicholas Ward Jackson, Wilfred Bowman.

The discovery of a bottle of wine from 1811—the year of the comet—sends a wine auctioneer's daughter (Penelope Ann Miller) and a millionaire's rakish troubleshooter (Timothy Daly) on a chase from Scotland to southern France. Also involved in the chase is an evil scientist (Louis Jourdan) who wants a secret formula.

ZEBRAHEAD

Pro. Jeff Dowd, Charles Mitchell, and William Willett for Oliver Stone and Ixtlan; Triumph Releasing *Dir.* Anthony Drazan *Scr.* Anthony Drazan *Cine.* Maryse Alberti *Ed.* Elizabeth Kling *P.d.* Naomi Shohan *A.d.* Dan Whifler *S.d.* Penny Barrett *Mu.* Taj Mahal *MPAA* R *R.t.* 100 min. *Cast:* Michael Rapaport, N'Bushe Wright, DeShonn Castle, Ron Johnson, Paul Butler, Candy Ann Brown, Luke Reilly, Dan Ziskie, Kevin Corrigan, Martin Priest, Ray Sharkey, Helen Shaver, Marsha Florence.

In this contemporary Romeo-and-Juliet story, white teenager Zack (Michael Rapaport) falls in love with Nikki (N'Bushe Wright), the cousin of his African-American best friend, Dee (DeShonn Castle), to the consternation of Nikki's mother and their fellow schoolmates.

ZENTROPA (Germany, 1992)

Pro. Peter Aalbaek Jensen and Bo Christensen for Prestige Films; Miramax Films *Dir.* Lars von Trier *Scr.* Lars von Trier and Niels Vorsel *Cine.* Henning Bendtsen, Jean-Paul Meurisse, and Edward Klosinsky *Ed.* Herve Schneid *S.d.* Henning Bahs *Mu.* Joakim Holbek *R.t.* 107

min. *Cast:* Max von Sydow, Jean-Marc Barr, Barbara Sukowa, Udo Kier, Ernst-Hugo Jaregard, Erik Mork, Jorgen Reenberg, Henning Jensen, Eddie Constantin.

In this period drama, an American of German descent, Leopold Kessler (Jean-Marc Barr), travels to Germany following World War II and finds a job with a large railroad company—Zentropa. When Leopold becomes romantically entangled with the daughter (Barbara Sukowa) of Zentropa's owner, he also becomes enmeshed in a larger intrigue involving pro-Nazi terrorists.

OBITUARIES

Stella Adler (1901-December 21, 1992). Adler was a stage actress best known for her skills as an acting teacher. She was an adherent of the Stanislavsky method, which emphasized the actors' attempt to inhabit the emotions of the characters they portrayed. Marlon Brando, Shelley Winters, and Robert De Niro were among her students. She made a few film appearances, as in *Love on Toast* (1937) and *Shadow of the Thin Man* (1941).

Luis Alcoriza (1920-December 3, 1992). Alcoriza was a screenwriter and director. Born in Spain, he moved to Mexico during the Spanish Civil War. He became best known for his work with surrealist filmmaker Luis Buñuel, for whom he wrote ten scripts, including *Los olvidados* (1950; *The Young and the Damned*) and *El angel exterminador* (1962; *The Exterminating Angel*). His additional screenwriting credits include *El gran calavera* (1949; *The Great Madcap*) and *Él* (1952; *This Strange Passion*). He directed *Tlayucan* (1962; *The Pearly Tlayucan*), *Tarahumara* (1965), and *Las fuerzas vivas* (1975).

Peter Allen (1943-June 18, 1992). Allen was a singer and songwriter who received an Academy Award, along with collaborators Burt Bacharach, Carole Bayer Sager, and Christopher Cross, for his song "Arthur's Theme: Best That You Can Do" from *Arthur* (1981). Allen was married for a time to actress Liza Minnelli.

Nestor Almendros (1930-March 4, 1992). Almendros was a cinematographer who collaborated successfully with both American and French directors throughout his career. Born in Spain, he moved with his family to Cuba as a teenager, where he began making documentary films. After Fidel Castro's revolution, Almendros found his early work in disfavor with the new regime and fled to France, where he began a long and productive association with New Wave filmmakers Eric Rohmer, for whom he shot *Ma nuit chez Maud* (1969; *My Night at Maud's*, 1970) and *Le Genou de Claire* (1970; *Claire's Knee*, 1971), and François Truffaut, for whom he shot *L'Enfant sauvage* (1970; *The Wild Child*) and *L'Histoire d'Adèle H.* (1975; *The Story of Adèle H.*, 1976). He was known to avoid gimmicks in his photography and was a master of natural lighting. His work on *Days of Heaven* (1978) earned him an Academy Award nomination, even though contractual commitments forced him to abandon the film prior to its completion (Haskell Wexler finished his work). Almendros was also nominated for Academy Awards for *Kramer vs. Kramer* (1979), *The Blue Lagoon* (1980), and *Sophie's Choice* (1982). His additional film credits include *L'Amour l'après-midi* (1972; *Chloé in the Afternoon*), *The Marquise of O . . . (1976), Le Dernier Métro* (1980; *The Last Métro*), and *Billy Bathgate* (1991).

Dame Judith Anderson (February 10, 1898-January 3, 1992). Born Frances Margaret Anderson in Australia, Anderson was an actress best known for her sinister portrayals of evil women such as Mrs. Danvers in Hitchcock's *Rebecca* (1940), which earned her an Academy Award nomination as Best Supporting Actress. She also worked extensively on stage, where she portrayed a memorable Lady Macbeth both in England and in the United States. Her stage work was rewarded with the honorary British title of "Dame" in 1960. Anderson's film credits include *Laura* (1944), *The Ten Commandments* (1956), *Cat on a Hot Tin Roof* (1958), *Cinderfella* (1960), *A Man Called Horse* (1970), and *Star Trek III—The Search for Spock* (1984).

Dana Andrews (January 1, 1909-December 17, 1992). Andrews was an actor whose career peaked in the mid-1940's, when he was featured in *The Ox-Bow Incident* (1942), *Laura* (1944), and *The Best Years of Our Lives* (1946). Though never a marquee name, his talent and versatility won for him a wide variety of roles in films for more than thirty years.

His additional film credits include *The Westerner* (1940), *Tobacco Road* (1941), *Belle Star* (1941), *State Fair* (1945), *A Walk in the Sun* (1945), *Boomerang* (1947), *Elephant Walk* (1954), *The Crowded Sky* (1960), *The Loved One* (1965), *Airport 1975* (1974), and *The Last Tycoon* (1976).

Arletty (May 15, 1898-July 24, 1992). Born Leonie Bathiat, Arletty was a French actress who worked extensively throughout the 1930's and early 1940's. Her best-known role was in *Les Enfants du paradis* (1945; *Children of Paradise*, 1946). In the aftermath of World War II, she was accused of being a Nazi collaborator, which significantly damaged her career. Her additional film credits include *Un Chien qui rapporte* (1931), *Hôtel du nord* (1938), *Le Jour se lève* (1939; *Daybreak*), and *Les Visiteurs du soir* (1942; *The Devil's Own Envoy*).

Jack Arnold (October 14, 1916-March 17, 1992). Arnold was a director who made several classic 1950's science-fiction films. His film career began during World War II, when he worked in the Signal Corps with documentary filmmaker Robert Flaherty. Out of the service, he signed with Universal and made the film with which he is most often associated, *Creature from the Black Lagoon* (1954), which was shot in 3-D. He also made the classic troubled youth saga *High School Confidential!* (1958), whose title song was recorded by Jerry Lee Lewis. Arnold's additional film credits include *It Came from Outer Space* (1953), *Revenge of the Creature* (1955), *Tarantula* (1955), *The Incredible Shrinking Man* (1957), *The Mouse That Roared* (1959), and *The Lively Set* (1964).

Art Babbitt (1906-March 4, 1992). Babbitt was an animator who worked with Walt Disney on many of his classic features and shorts. He is credited with having developed the character of Goofy, and he worked on the Academy Award-winning short subject "The Three Little Pigs" (1933). His additional film credits include *Snow White and the Seven Dwarfs* (1937), *Fantasia* (1940), *Pinocchio* (1940), and *Dumbo* (1941).

Vilma Banky (January 9, 1898-March 18, 1992). Born Vilma Lonchit in Hungary, Banky was discovered by Samuel Goldwyn and became a star in the silent era. She appeared opposite Rudolph Valentino in *The Son of the Sheik* (1926) and married actor Rod La Rocque in 1927. She retired shortly after the advent of sound films. Banky's additional screen credits include the silent films *The Dark Angel* (1925), *The Awakening* (1928), and *This Is Heaven* (1929), as well as the sound production *The Rebel* (1933).

Freddie Bartholomew (March 28, 1924-January 23, 1992). Born Frederick Llewellyn, Bartholomew was a British-born child actor who was featured in several American hits in the 1930's. At the peak of his career, he ranked second only to Shirley Temple in popularity as a child performer. He made his stage debut at the age of three, and after appearing in two British films, he was chosen for the title role in the American production of *David Copperfield* (1935), which quickly made him a star. His niche was confirmed in *Little Lord Fauntleroy* (1936), the role with which he was most closely identified. He continued to appear as juvenile leads throughout the decade, in films such as *Captains Courageous* (1937), *Kidnapped* (1938), and *Lord Jeff* (1938), but as he grew older, his popularity waned. Bartholomew's film work continued sporadically until the early 1950's; *St. Benny the Dip* (1951) was his last screen appearance. His additional acting credits include *Fascination* (1931), *Anna Karenina* (1935), *The Devil Is a Sissy* (1936), *Lloyds of London* (1936), *The Swiss Family Robinson* (1940), *A Yank at Eton* (1942), and *The Town Went Wild* (1944).

Clem Beauchamp (1898-November 14, 1992). Beauchamp was a stuntman, production manager, and assistant director. He won an Academy Award for *Lives of a Bengal Lancer* (1935) during the period from 1932 to 1937 when there was an award for assistant directors.

Laslo Benedek (March 5, 1907-March 11, 1992). Born in Hungary, Benedek was a director who broke into film in Europe with producer Joe Pasternak, for whom he served as cameraman and assistant producer. He moved to the United States in 1937, finding work in Hollywood as an editor. His first directorial effort was the Frank Sinatra musical *The Kissing Bandit* (1948). Benedek's career was uneven, consisting largely of potboilers and B pictures. His reputation rests largely on the strength of two films, both made for producer Stanley Kramer. He directed the screen adaptation of Arthur Miller's play *Death of a Salesman* (1952) and *The Wild One* (1954), which starred Marlon Brando as an outlaw motorcyclist. The latter film continued to grow in popularity over the years, achieving something of a cult status by the end of the 1960's. Benedek's additional film credits include *Port of New York* (1949), *Bengal Brigade* (1954), *Affair in Havana* (1957), *Namu, the Killer Whale* (1966), and *The Night Visitor* (1970).

Shirley Booth (August 30, 1907-October 16, 1992). Born Thelma Booth Ford, Booth was a character actress who turned in award-winning performances in films, on the stage, and on television. Her most prominent film role was that of Lola Delaney in *Come Back, Little Sheba* (1952), for which she won an Academy Award as Best Actress. She is perhaps best known for her portrayal of the title character in the long-running television show *Hazel*, for which she won two Emmy Awards. Her additional film credits include *Main Street to Broadway* (1953), *About Mrs. Leslie* (1954), and *The Matchmaker* (1958).

Neville Brand (August 13, 1921-April 16, 1992). Brand was an actor who specialized in playing villains in films and on television. He is perhaps best known for his portrayals of mobster Al Capone in *The George Raft Story* (1961) and *The Scarface Mob* (1962), as well as on the 1960's television show *The Untouchables*. His additional screen credits include *D.O.A.* (1949), *Stalag 17* (1953), *Riot in Cell Block 11* (1954), *Love Me Tender* (1956), *Birdman of Alcatraz* (1962), *Tora! Tora! Tora!* (1970), and *The Return* (1980).

Steve Brodie (November 25, 1919-January 9, 1992). Born John Stevens, Brodie was an actor who specialized in action films and Westerns. His screen credits include *Thirty Seconds over Tokyo* (1944), *The Arizona Ranger* (1948), *Winchester '73* (1950), *Donovan's Brain* (1953), and *Roustabout* (1964).

Richard Brooks (May 18, 1912-March 11, 1992). Brooks was a screenwriter and director who was nominated for eight Academy Awards (winning one) over the course of his career. He began his film career as a writer for Universal, contributing to scripts for such B films as the serial *Don Winslow of the Coast Guard* (1943) and *Cobra Woman* (1944). His first break came when he collaborated with John Huston on the screenplay for *Key Largo* (1948), an experience which inspired him to direct. His first important film as a director was *Blackboard Jungle* (1955), which introduced the Bill Haley and the Comets' song "Rock Around the Clock" to a large audience and earned for Brooks his first Academy Award nomination for the screenplay. He was nominated for two Academy Awards for writing and directing the adaptation of Tennessee Williams' steamy play *Cat on a Hot Tin Roof* (1958). Perhaps the peak of his career came with the controversial and much-honored *Elmer Gantry* (1960), which he wrote and directed. He won an Academy Award for his screenplay, and he married actress Jean Simmons, one of the film's stars. Brooks continued to work extensively, mixing such successes as *The Professionals* (1966) and *In Cold Blood* (1967)—both of which earned for him Academy Award nominations for writing and directing—with such misfires as *Lord Jim* (1965) and *Bite the Bullet* (1975). His last important film was *Looking for Mr. Goodbar* (1977). His additional credits as writer-director include *Deadline U.S.A.* (1952), *The Brothers Karamazov* (1958), *Sweet Bird of Youth* (1962), and *$ (Dollars)* (1972).

Morris Carnovsky (September 5, 1898-September 1, 1992). Carnovsky was a character actor who had a distinguished Broadway career in addition to his numerous film appearances. His film career was interrupted in 1951 when he was blacklisted after refusing to testify before a congressional committee about his alleged membership in the Communist Party. His screen credits include *The Life of Émile Zola* (1937), *Rhapsody in Blue* (1945), *Dishonored Lady* (1947), and *The Second Woman* (1951).

Regina Carrol (1943-November 4, 1992). Born Regina Gelfan, Carrol was an actress who appeared in starlet roles early in her career. After marrying director Al Adamson, she was featured in many of his exploitation films, including *Satan's Sadists* (1970) and *Dracula vs. Frankenstein* (1971). Her additional film credits include *The Beat Generation* (1959), *Two Rode Together* (1961), and *Viva Las Vegas* (1964).

Mae Clarke (August 16, 1907-April 29, 1992). Born Mary Klotz, Clarke was an actress who had leading roles in numerous important films of the 1930's. She is best remembered for her role as the gang moll in *The Public Enemy* (1931), in which James Cagney pushed a grapefruit in her face. Her career declined rapidly by the end of the decade, and her roles thereafter were confined to cameos and B pictures. Her additional film credits include *Big Time* (1929), *Waterloo Bridge* (1931), *Frankenstein* (1931), *Reckless Living* (1931), *Nana* (1934), *Women in War* (1940), *Singin' in the Rain* (1952), and *Thoroughly Modern Millie* (1967).

Anita Colby (August 5, 1915-March 27, 1992). Colby was a prominent fashion model who acted in several Hollywood films. Her screen credits include *Mary of Scotland* (1936), *The Bride Walks Out* (1936), *Cover Girl* (1944), and *Brute Force* (1947).

Chuck Connors (April 10, 1921-November 10, 1992). Born Kevin Joseph Connors, Connors was an actor who was a tall leading man in films and on television. Prior to becoming an actor, he played both baseball and basketball professionally. He is best known for his starring role in the long-running television series *The Rifleman.* His film credits include *Pat and Mike* (1952), *Hold Back the Night* (1956), *The Hired Gun* (1957), *The Big Country* (1958), *Flipper* (1963), *Soylent Green* (1973), and *Tourist Trap* (1979).

Rita Corday (1924-November 23, 1992). Corday was an actress who used several names during the course of her career, including Paule Croset and Paula Corday. She married producer Harold Nebenzal in 1954 and retired from acting. Her film credits include *The Falcon Strikes Back* (1943), *The Body Snatcher* (1945), *Dick Tracy vs. Cueball* (1946), and *The Sword of Monte Cristo* (1951).

Franco Cristaldi (October 3, 1924-July 1, 1992). Cristaldi was an Italian producer whose films won three Academy Awards: *Divorzio all'italiana* (1961; *Divorce—Italian Style*), *Amarcord* (1973), and *Cinema Paradiso* (1989) all were named Best Foreign Film. He was married for a time to actress Claudia Cardinale. His additional film credits include *Le notti bianche* (1957; *White Nights*), *L'assassino* (1961; *The Ladykiller of Rome*), *La Cina è vicina* (1967; *China Is Near*), and *Wifemistress* (1977).

Cesare Danova (1926-March 19, 1992). Danova was an Italian actor who played supporting roles in American films after a career as a leading man in his native country. His screen credits include *La figlia del capitano* (1947; *The Captain's Daughter*), *Don Giovanni* (1955; *Don Juan*), *Cleopatra* (1963), *Viva Las Vegas* (1964), *Mean Streets* (1973), and *National Lampoon's Animal House* (1978).

Ray Danton (September 19, 1931-February 11, 1992). Danton was an actor and director. As an actor, he was a leading man who specialized in tough-guy roles, but by the mid-1960's, his acting appearances were restricted primarily to European films. In the 1970's, he directed a few low-budget horror films, including *The Deathmaster* (1972), *Crypt of the Living Dead*

(1973), and *Psychic Killer* (1975). His most prominent acting role was that of gangster Legs Diamond in *The Rise and Fall of Legs Diamond* (1960). He was married to actress Julie Adams. His additional acting credits include *I'll Cry Tomorrow* (1955), *Too Much, Too Soon* (1958), *The Beat Generation* (1959), *Portrait of a Mobster* (1961), *The George Raft Story* (1961), *The Longest Day* (1962), and *The Chapman Report* (1962).

Ken Darby (1909-January 24, 1992). Darby was a composer who won three Academy Awards with two different collaborators. Darby and Alfred Newman won the award for *The King and I* (1956) and *Camelot* (1967), and he and André Previn won for *Porgy and Bess* (1959). Darby and Newman were also nominated for their work on *South Pacific* (1958), *Flower Drum Song* (1961), and *How the West Was Won* (1962).

John Dehner (1915-February 4, 1992). Dehner was an actor who began his career as an animator on Walt Disney's *Fantasia* (1940) and *Bambi* (1942). As an actor, he specialized in playing villains in Westerns and action films. His film credits include *Barbary Pirate* (1949), *Scaramouche* (1952), *Apache* (1954), *The Left-Handed Gun* (1958), *Youngblood Hawke* (1964), *Slaughterhouse Five* (1972), *The Boys from Brazil* (1978), and *The Right Stuff* (1983).

Georges Delerue (March 12, 1925-March 20, 1992). Delerue was a French composer who scored more than 150 feature films. He is most closely associated with director François Truffaut, for whom he supplied the scores to *Tirez sur le pianiste* (1960; *Shoot the Piano Player*, 1962) and *Jules et Jim* (1962; *Jules and Jim*), and with Philippe de Broca, for whom he worked on sixteen films, including the cult classic *Le Roi de cœur* (1966; *King of Hearts*, 1967). He was nominated for four Academy Awards for his work on *Anne of the Thousand Days* (1969), *The Day of the Dolphin* (1973), *Julia* (1977), and *A Little Romance* (1979); he won the award for the latter film. His additional film credits include *Hiroshima mon amour* (1959), *The Pumpkin Eater* (1964), *A Man for All Seasons* (1966), *Il conformista* (1970; *The Conformist*), *La Nuit américaine* (1973; *Day for Night*), *Préparez vos mouchoirs* (1978; *Get Out Your Handkerchiefs*), *Platoon* (1986), and *Steel Magnolias* (1989).

Sandy Dennis (April 27, 1937-March 2, 1992). Dennis, an actress who starred both on Broadway and in films, had a halting delivery that communicated fragility to her audiences. She made her film debut in *Splendor in the Grass* (1961) in a supporting role. Shortly thereafter, she won two consecutive Tony Awards for her stage work, in *A Thousand Clowns* and *Any Wednesday*. Her next film role, as the young faculty wife with Elizabeth Taylor, Richard Burton, and George Segal in *Who's Afraid of Virginia Woolf?* (1966), earned for her an Academy Award as Best Supporting Actress. Her additional film credits include *Up the Down Staircase* (1967), *The Fox* (1968), *Sweet November* (1968), *The Out-of-Towners* (1970), *The Three Sisters* (1977, filmed at a 1966 stage production), *Come Back to the 5 & Dime Jimmy Dean, Jimmy Dean* (1982), and *Another Woman* (1988).

Richard Derr (1917-May 8, 1992). Derr was an actor best known for his lead role in *When Worlds Collide* (1951). His additional film credits include *Luxury Liner* (1948), *The Bride Goes Wild* (1948), *Something to Live For* (1952), and *The Drowning Pool* (1976).

Helen Deutsch (1906-March 15, 1992). Deutsch was a screenwriter who earned an Academy Award nomination for her screenplay for *Lili* (1953). Her additional film credits include *National Velvet* (1944), *King Solomon's Mines* (1950), *I'll Cry Tomorrow* (1955), *The Unsinkable Molly Brown* (1964), and *Valley of the Dolls* (1967).

Marlene Dietrich (December 27, 1901-May 6, 1992). Born Maria Magdalena Dietrich, Dietrich was a German actress who was one of the top international film stars of the 1930's. She brought an air of sometimes baroque sensuality to the screen that distinguished her from the other actresses of the day, bringing her notoriety as well as fame. She appeared in several

German films in the silent era, but it was not until she teamed up with director Josef von Sternberg that she reached her potential. Her role as the amoral Lola-Lola in *Der blaue Engel* (1930; *The Blue Angel*, 1931) made her an instant star. She and Sternberg continued to work together for five years, producing such hits as *Morocco* (1930), *Dishonored* (1931), *Shanghai Express* (1932), and *Blonde Venus* (1932). Her career, and Sternberg's, peaked with *The Scarlet Empress* (1934), a luxurious and exotic portrayal of the lustful Russian empress Catherine the Great. Ironically, some of the qualities that made her early work with Sternberg so successful eventually caused audiences to lose interest, as the films became more and more ornate and divorced from everyday reality. The pair's last film together was *The Devil Is a Woman* (1935). Her only other important film before World War II was the Western *Destry Rides Again* (1939), in which she played a rowdy saloon proprietress.

Dietrich dedicated the war years to providing moral support for the Allied cause, rejecting Adolf Hitler's demand that she return to Germany. She became an American citizen, selling war bonds and touring the battle zones with the USO; "Lili Marlene" became her signature song, supplanting *The Blue Angel*'s "Falling in Love Again." After the war, she made relatively few films, among them Alfred Hitchcock's *Stage Fright* (1950), Fritz Lang's Western *Rancho Notorious* (1952), and Stanley Kramer's *Judgment at Nuremberg* (1961), her last major film role. In the 1950's, she had a successful concert career as a cabaret-style singer. Her additional film credits include *Der kleine Napoleon* (1923; *Tragedy of Love*), *Die freudlose Gasse* (1925; *The Street of Sorrow*), *Song of Songs* (1933), *The Garden of Allah* (1936), *The Flame of New Orleans* (1941), *A Foreign Affair* (1948), *Witness for the Prosecution* (1957), and *Schöner Gigolo—Armer Gigolo* (1978; *Just a Gigolo*).

Philip Dunne (February 11, 1908-May 2, 1992). Dunne was a screenwriter, producer, and director who was one of the founders of the Screen Writers Guild. Best known as a writer, he was nominated for an Academy Award for his work on *How Green Was My Valley* (1941) and *David and Bathsheba* (1951). In 1955, he began to direct films, mostly from his own screenplays. These include *Prince of Players* (1955, which he also produced), *Ten North Frederick* (1958), and *Wild in the Country* (1961). Dunne was active politically in liberal causes, helping to found Americans for Democratic Action and writing speeches for John F. Kennedy during the 1960 presidential campaign. His additional screenwriting credits include *The Count of Monte Cristo* (1934), *The Last of the Mohicans* (1936), *The Ghost and Mrs. Muir* (1947), *The Robe* (1953), and *The Agony and the Ecstasy* (1965).

Denholm Elliott (May 31, 1922-October 6, 1992). Elliott was a British actor whose career peaked in the 1980's, when he was nominated for an Academy Award as Best Supporting Actor for his role in *A Room with a View* (1986). Primarily a character actor, he won three British Film Awards for supporting roles in *Trading Places* (1983), *A Private Function* (1984), and *Defence of the Realm* (1985). He was married for a time to actress Virginia McKenna. His additional film credits include *The Sound Barrier* (1952), *The Heart of the Matter* (1954), *King Rat* (1965), *Alfie* (1966), *Robin and Marian* (1976), *Saint Jack* (1979), *Raiders of the Lost Ark* (1981), and *Indiana Jones and the Last Crusade* (1989).

Henry Ephron (May 26, 1912-September 6, 1992). Ephron was a screenwriter and playwright who worked in collaboration with his wife, Phoebe Ephron. They specialized in comedy and shared an Academy Award nomination with Richard L. Breen for the Gregory Peck vehicle *Captain Newman, M.D.* (1963). Ephron was the father of writer Nora Ephron. His additional film credits include *Bride by Mistake* (1944), *Look for the Silver Lining* (1949), *There's No Business Like Show Business* (1954), *Daddy Long Legs* (1955), *Carousel* (1956), and *Desk Set* (1957), the latter two also produced by Henry.

José Ferrer (January 8, 1912-January 26, 1992). Born José Vincente Ferrer de Otero y Cintron, Ferrer was a Puerto Rican actor who won respect for a variety of performances on stage and in films. He earned an Academy Award nomination as Best Supporting Actor for his first film role in *Joan of Arc* (1948), and he won an Academy Award as Best Actor for his portrayal of the title character in *Cyrano de Bergerac* (1950), a role for which he had previously won a Tony Award on Broadway in 1947. Although the stage was the primary focus of his career—he won two Tony Awards for acting and a third for directing—he continued to make films of consistently high quality. He earned his third Academy Award nomination in the role of Henri de Toulouse-Lautrec in *Moulin Rouge* (1952). In addition to his acting credits, Ferrer also directed occasionally, including *The Shrike* (1955), one of his stage hits, and *The Great Man* (1956). His additional acting credits include *Miss Sadie Thompson* (1953), *The Caine Mutiny* (1954), *Lawrence of Arabia* (1962), *Ship of Fools* (1965), *Voyage of the Damned* (1976), *The Fifth Musketeer* (1979), *A Midsummer Night's Sex Comedy* (1982), and *Dune* (1984).

Mike J. Frankovich (September 29, 1910-January 1, 1992). Frankovich was a producer best known for his work for Columbia Pictures. His film credits include *Bob and Carol and Ted and Alice* (1969), *Cactus Flower* (1969), *Marooned* (1969), *There's a Girl in My Soup* (1970), *Butterflies Are Free* (1972), and *The Shootist* (1976).

Vincent Gardenia (January 7, 1922-December 9, 1992). Born Vincente Scognamiglio in Naples, Gardenia was an actor who specialized in character roles. He earned two Academy Award nominations (both for Best Supporting Actor) for *Bang the Drum Slowly* (1973) and *Moonstruck* (1987) in a career that spanned over three decades. His additional acting credits include *Cop Hater* (1958), *The Hustler* (1961), *Where's Poppa?* (1970), *The Front Page* (1974), *Heaven Can Wait* (1978), and *Little Shop of Horrors* (1986).

Paul Henreid (January 10, 1908-March 29, 1992). Born in Trieste, Italy, Henreid was an actor who specialized in playing suave, aristocratic Europeans. An ardent opponent of Nazism, he moved to the United States in 1940. Of his many roles, two stand out in the public mind. He starred opposite Bette Davis in *Now Voyager* (1942), in which he put two cigarettes in his mouth, lit them simultaneously, and passed one to Davis, a gesture that became widely imitated. He also played Victor Laszlo, Humphrey Bogart's rival for Ingrid Bergman's affections in *Casablanca* (1942). Later in his career, he produced and directed films as well as acting in them. He produced and acted in *So Young, So Bad* (1950); and he produced, directed, and acted in *For Men Only* (1952). By the 1960's, he cut back on his film work; *Exorcist II—The Heretic* (1977) marked his last screen appearance. His additional acting credits include *Goodbye, Mr. Chips* (1939), *In Our Time* (1944), *Of Human Bondage* (1946), *Pirates of Tripoli* (1955), *The Four Horsemen of the Apocalypse* (1961), and *The Madwoman of Chaillot* (1969).

Benny Hill (1924-April 20, 1992). Hill was a British actor and comedian best known for his risqué television show. He had a brief film career, and his screen credits include *Who Done It?* (1956), *Light Up the Sky* (1960), *Those Magnificent Men in Their Flying Machines* (1965), *Chitty Chitty Bang Bang* (1968), and *The Italian Job* (1969).

Sterling Holloway (January 14, 1905-November 22, 1992). Holloway was a character actor who specialized in playing hillbillies and other simple types. In addition to acting, Holloway also supplied voices for some of Walt Disney's animated feature films, including *Dumbo* (1941), *Bambi* (1942), *Alice in Wonderland* (1951), and *The Jungle Book* (1967). His acting credits include the silent film *Casey at the Bat* (1927), *Gold Diggers of 1933* (1933), *Maid of Salem* (1937), *Meet John Doe* (1941), *It's a Mad Mad Mad Mad World* (1963), and

Live a Little, Love a Little (1968).

Frankie Howerd (March 6, 1921-April 19, 1992). Born Francis Howard, Howerd was a British comic actor whose career included stage, music hall, radio, and television acting as well as his film appearances. His screen credits include *The Runaway Bus* (1954), *The Cool Mikado* (1963), *Carry on Doctor* (1968), and *Sgt. Pepper's Lonely Hearts Club Band* (1978).

John Ireland (January 30, 1914-March 21, 1992). Ireland was a Canadian-born actor who moved from lead to character roles in a career that included more than 150 films. His second wife, actress Joanne Dru, appeared in several films with Ireland, including *All the King's Men* (1949), in which his work earned for him an Academy Award nomination as Best Supporting Actor. By the late 1960's, his career was in decline, and he worked overseas or in such domestic exploitation films as *Satan's Cheerleaders* (1977). His additional film credits include *A Walk in the Sun* (1945), *My Darling Clementine* (1946), *I Shot Jesse James* (1949), *Gunfight at the O.K. Corral* (1957), *Spartacus* (1960), *Wild in the Country* (1961), *55 Days at Peking* (1963), and *I Saw What You Did* (1965).

Rudolf Ising (1903-July 18, 1992). Ising was an animator who helped start the Looney Tunes and Merrie Melodies series of cartoons. He began his film career in the silent era, working with Walt Disney on the Oswald the Rabbit series. Disney replaced Oswald with Mickey Mouse, and Ising struck out on his own. Ising, Hugh Harmon, and Leon Schlesinger created a character called Bosko, who was featured in Warner Bros.' first Looney Tunes cartoon. Ising and Harmon moved to Metro-Goldwyn-Mayer in 1934. Ising won an Academy Award for his cartoon short "The Milky Way" (1940).

Paul Jabara (1948-September 29, 1992). Jabara was an actor and songwriter whose greatest claim to fame was his Academy Award-winning song "Last Dance" from *Thank God, It's Friday* (1978). As an actor, Jabara appeared in *Midnight Cowboy* (1969), *The Lords of Flatbush* (1974), *Day of the Locust* (1975), and *Star 80* (1983).

Anna Johnstone (1913-October 16, 1992). Johnstone was a costume designer who worked on numerous important Hollywood films; her career was capped with two Academy Award nominations, for *The Godfather* (1972) and *Ragtime* (1981). Her additional film credits include *On the Waterfront* (1954), *East of Eden* (1955), *A Face in the Crowd* (1957), *Serpico* (1973), and *Dog Day Afternoon* (1975).

Jack Kelly (September 16, 1927-November 7, 1992). Kelly was an actor who appeared extensively on television as well as in films. His most memorable role was that of Bart Maverick opposite James Garner in the popular comedy-Western television series *Maverick*. His film credits include *Submarine Command* (1951), *To Hell and Back* (1955), *Forbidden Planet* (1956), *Love and Kisses* (1965), and *Young Billy Young* (1969).

Jack Kinney (1911-February 9, 1992). Kinney was an animator who had a long association with Walt Disney. He worked on the classic animated features *Pinocchio* (1940) and *Dumbo* (1941) and was responsible for most of the cartoons featuring the character Goofy. His animated short "Der Fuehrer's Face" (1942) earned for him an Academy Award. After leaving Disney in 1959, he produced Popeye cartoons and directed the animated feature *1,001 Arabian Nights* (1959), built around the character of "The Nearsighted Mr. Magoo."

Hans F. Koenekamp (1892-September 12, 1992). Koenekamp was a cinematographer who specialized in shooting miniature air battles in such films as *Captains of the Clouds* (1942), *Air Force* (1943), and *God Is My Co-Pilot* (1945). His additional credits include the mostly silent film *Noah's Ark* (1928), *Moby Dick* (1930), *High Sierra* (1941), and *Strangers on a Train* (1951).

Gracie Lantz (1903-March 17, 1992). Lantz was an actress who was married to animator

Walter Lantz, the producer of the Woody Woodpecker cartoons. Gracie Lantz provided the woodpecker's voice and famous laugh. Under her maiden name, Grace Stafford, she acted in such films as *Dr. Socrates* (1935), *Anthony Adverse* (1936), *Confessions of a Nazi Spy* (1939), *Indianapolis Speedway* (1939), and *Flight Angels* (1940).

Ginette Leclerc (February 9, 1912-January 1, 1992). Born Geneviève Manut, Leclerc was a French actress who specialized in playing vamps and seductresses in lightweight French films. Her screen credits include *Ciboulette* (1933), *L'Homme de nulle part* (1937; *The Late Mathias Pascal*), *Le Val d'enfer* (1943), *Le Plaisir* (1952), and *Tropic of Cancer* (1970).

Cleavon Little (1939-October 22, 1992). Little was an African-American actor best known for his role as the sheriff in Mel Brooks's *Blazing Saddles* (1974). He also worked extensively on stage and on television, winning a Tony and an Emmy Award for his work in those mediums. His additional film credits include *What's So Bad About Feeling Good?* (1968), *Cotton Comes to Harlem* (1970), *Vanishing Point* (1971), *FM* (1978), and *Arthur 2: On the Rocks* (1988).

Pare Lorentz (December 11, 1905-March 4, 1992). Lorentz was a director of documentaries whose work was so admired by President Franklin D. Roosevelt that he was appointed to head the U.S. Film Service in 1939. Lorentz's first film was *The Plow That Broke the Plains* (1936), concerning New Deal efforts to improve the lot of farmers in Oklahoma's Dust Bowl. *The River* (1937) dealt with flooding on the Mississippi River. His third film, *The Fight for Life* (1940), examined infant mortality among poor Americans. His final full-length documentary was *The Nuremberg Trials* (1946). During World War II, Lorentz made training films for the Air Force; after the war, he wrote and lectured extensively on the art of documentary filmmaking. He published an autobiography, *FDR's Moviemaker*, in 1992.

Michael A. Luciano (1910-September 15, 1992). Luciano was a film editor who worked extensively with director Robert Aldrich. He earned four Academy Award nominations for his work on Aldrich films, including *What Ever Happened to Baby Jane?* (1962), *Hush . . . Hush, Sweet Charlotte* (1965), *Flight of the Phoenix* (1966), and *The Dirty Dozen* (1967).

John Lund (February 6, 1913-May 10, 1992). Lund was an actor who specialized in romantic leads in the heyday of his career, the late 1940's. His acting credits include *To Each His Own* (1946), *A Foreign Affair* (1948), *Night Has a Thousand Eyes* (1948), *My Friend Irma* (1949), *High Society* (1956), and *The Wackiest Ship in the Army* (1960).

Ben Maddow (1910-October 9, 1992). Maddow was a screenwriter who worked in both documentary and feature films. In 1936, he was one of the founders of "The World Today," a newsreel with a liberal political viewpoint. He wrote and directed such documentaries as *The Stairs* (1953) and *The Savage Eye* (1960). His Hollywood film work included *Framed* (1947), *The Asphalt Jungle* (1950), *Johnny Guitar* (1954), and *The Way West* (1967).

Robert R. Martin (1916-January 16, 1992). Martin was a sound mixer who worked extensively with director Billy Wilder. He earned an Academy Award nomination with collaborator Clem Portman for his work on *Gaily, Gaily* (1969). His additional film credits include *Marty* (1955), *Some Like It Hot* (1959), *The Apartment* (1960), *West Side Story* (1961), *Irma La Douce* (1963), *The Fortune Cookie* (1966), and *The Front Page* (1974).

Andrew Marton (January 26, 1904-January 7, 1992). Born Endre Marton in Hungary, Marton was a director who broke into film as an editor for Ernst Lubitsch. His best work was done as a second-unit director in such films as *Mrs. Miniver* (1942), *Cleopatra* (1963), and *Catch-22* (1970), as well as *Ben-Hur* (1959), for which he designed the famous chariot race sequence. As a director, he made *Wolf's Clothing* (1936), *Gentle Annie* (1944), and *Clarence,* *the Cross-Eyed Lion* (1965). He codirected *King Solomon's Mines* (1950) and *The Longest Day* (1962).

Samuel Marx (1901-March 2, 1992). Marx was a writer and producer who worked extensively for Metro-Goldwyn-Mayer and Columbia in the 1930's and 1940's. He started the Andy Hardy series with *A Family Affair* (1937) and its early sequels, and he produced *Lassie Come Home* (1943). With newspaper columnist Walter Winchell, Marx coauthored *Unholy Partners* (1941), which starred Edward G. Robinson. He was also known for his books on Hollywood history. His additional film credits include *Society Doctor* (1935) and *Son of Lassie* (1945).

Wendell Mays (1921-March 28, 1992). Mays was a screenwriter best known for his work with director Otto Preminger. He received an Academy Award nomination for his work on Preminger's *Anatomy of a Murder* (1959). His additional film credits include *The Spirit of St. Louis* (1957), *Advise and Consent* (1962), *In Harm's Way* (1965), *Von Ryan's Express* (1965), and *The Poseidon Adventure* (1972).

David Miller (November 28, 1909-April 14, 1992). Miller was a director who directed the Academy Award-winning Documentary Short Subject *Seeds of Destiny* (1946) for the U.S. War Department. As a feature director, his best films were *Sudden Fear* (1952), *Midnight Lace* (1960), and *Lonely Are the Brave* (1962). His additional film credits include *Billy the Kid* (1941), *Flying Tigers* (1942), *The Story of Esther Costello* (1957), *Captain Newman, M.D.* (1963), and *Executive Action* (1973).

Robert Morley (May 25, 1908-June 3, 1992). Morley was a British character actor known for his shaggy eyebrows and his corpulent physique. He specialized in comedy, though his performance as King Louis XVI in *Marie Antoinette* (1938) earned for him an Academy Award nomination as Best Supporting Actor. His additional film credits include *Major Barbara* (1941), *Outcast of the Islands* (1951), *The African Queen* (1951), *Around the World in 80 Days* (1956), *Topkapi* (1964), *Those Magnificent Men in Their Flying Machines* (1965), *The Loved One* (1965), and *Who Is Killing the Great Chefs of Europe?* (1978).

William A. Mueller (1901-May 12, 1992). Mueller was a sound engineer and sound director who helped develop the Vitaphone sound system that Warner Bros. used on *The Jazz Singer* (1927). He earned two Academy Award nominations, for his work on *Calamity Jane* (1953) and *Mister Roberts* (1955).

George Murphy (July 4, 1902-May 3, 1992). Murphy was an actor and dancer who specialized in musicals and light comedy in the 1930's and 1940's. Though he was a popular performer and worked extensively, his film appearances were relatively bland. It is, rather, for his political career that he is best remembered. He was a strongly anticommunist head of the Screen Actors Guild, and he became active in Republican politics in Hollywood. In 1964, he was elected to the U.S. Senate from California for a single six-year term. His acting credits include *Kid Millions* (1934), *After the Dance* (1935), *Broadway Melody of 1938* (1937), *Hold That Co-Ed* (1938), *For Me and My Gal* (1942), *This Is the Army* (1943), *Broadway Rhythm* (1944), and *It's a Big Country* (1951).

Lawrence Naismith (1908-June 5, 1992). Born Lawrence Johnson, Naismith was a British character actor who appeared in more than fifty films as well as numerous Broadway plays. His film credits include *Mogambo* (1953), *Lust for Life* (1956), *Boy on a Dolphin* (1957), *Sink the Bismarck!* (1960), *Camelot* (1967), and *Young Winston* (1972).

Bill Naughton (1910-January 9, 1992). Naughton was a novelist and screenwriter whose screenplay for *Alfie* (1966), based on his own novel, received an Academy Award nomination.

Anthony Perkins (April 4, 1932-September 12, 1992). Perkins was an actor with numerous films to his credit but whose career was inevitably associated with the role of Norman Bates in Alfred Hitchcock's thriller *Psycho* (1960) and its sequels. The son of actor Osgood Perkins, Perkins made his film debut opposite Jean Simmons in *The Actress* (1953). He earned an Academy Award nomination as Best Supporting Actor for his role as a gentle Quaker boy in *Friendly Persuasion* (1956). His other significant pre-Hitchcock films included *Fear Strikes Out* (1957), based on the career of an emotionally tormented baseball player; *Desire Under the Elms* (1958); and *Tall Story* (1960), in which he starred opposite Jane Fonda in her film debut. Yet it was the role of Norman Bates, the sympathetic psychopath, that propelled him into the forefront of his audience's attention. Ironically, it also made it difficult for him to find good roles, at least in American films, because he was so identified with the Bates character. Frustrated, he went to Europe, where he made several films in the 1960's, including *Aimez-vous Brahms?* (1961; *Goodbye Again*) and *Paris brûle-t-il?* (1966; *Is Paris Burning?*).

When he returned to the United States, Perkins won critical accolades for his performance opposite Tuesday Weld in *Pretty Poison* (1968), and he continued to find work. He was never able to disassociate himself completely from the character of Norman Bates, however, and returned to the role toward the end of his career in *Psycho II* (1983) and *Psycho III* (1986), the latter of which he also directed. He also directed *Lucky Stiff* (1988). The final years of his life were marked by increasing debilitation from acquired immune deficiency syndrome (AIDS), to which he finally succumbed. His additional acting credits include *The Lonely Man* (1957), *The Matchmaker* (1958), *Green Mansions* (1959), *On the Beach* (1959), *Catch-22* (1970), *Play It As It Lays* (1972), *The Black Hole* (1979), and *Winter Kills* (1979).

Jean Poiret (1926-March 14, 1992). Poiret was an actor and writer best known for *La Cage aux folles* (1978), which he wrote initially as a play and for which he collaborated on the screenplay. As an actor, he appeared in *Le Dernier Métro* (1980; *The Last Métro*), *Poulet au vinaigre* (1984), and *Inspecteur Lavardin* (1985). His additional screenwriting credits include *La Cage aux folles II* (1980) and *La Cage aux folles III: The Wedding* (1985).

Satyajit Ray (May 2, 1921-April 23, 1992). Ray was an Indian director whose Apu trilogy in the 1950's first introduced Indian cinema to the rest of the world. His first film, *Pather panchali* (1955), was a naturalistic study of an impoverished Bengali family; it introduced the character of the young Apu (played by Subir Banerjee) and won a special jury prize at the Cannes Film Festival. He made two sequels, *Aparajito* (1956) and *Apu sansar* (1958; *The World of Apu*, 1959), tracing the growth of Apu to maturity. All but one of his films were made in Bengali (a minor language in India), which lessened their impact in his home country. *Shatranj ke khilarai* (1977; *The Chess Players*, 1978) was filmed in the majority language, Hindi. Ray wrote the screenplays to all of his films, and he became increasingly involved in the scoring and costume design as well. Shortly before his death, he was given an honorary Academy Award for his contributions to film. His additional films include *Devi* (1960; *The Goddess*, 1962), *Mahanagar* (1963; *The Big City*), *Aranyer din ratri* (1970; *Days and Nights in the Forest*), *Ashani sanket* (1973; *Distant Thunder*), and *The Stranger* (1991).

Renie (1901-June 23, 1992). Born Irene Brouillet, Renie was a costume designer who won an Academy Award for her work (along with Irene Sharaff and Vittorio Nino Novarese) on *Cleopatra* (1963). She and collaborator Charles LeMaire also received Academy Award nominations for *The Model and the Marriage Broker* (1951), *The President's Lady* (1953), and *The Big Fisherman* (1959). Her additional film credits include *Kitty Foyle* (1940), *Cat People* (1942), *Mr. Lucky* (1943), *The Sand Pebbles* (1966), and *Body Heat* (1981).

Frederic I. Rinaldo (1913-June 22, 1992). Rinaldo was a screenwriter who, with collaborator Robert Lees, wrote extensively for the comedy team of Bud Abbott and Lou Costello. These films included *Hold That Ghost* (1941), *Buck Privates Come Home* (1947), *Abbott and Costello Meet Frankenstein* (1948), and *Abbott and Costello Meet the Invisible Man* (1951). Rinaldo's additional screenwriting credits include *Street of Memories* (1940), *The Invisible Woman* (1941), and *Jumping Jacks* (1952).

Hal Roach (January 14, 1892-November 2, 1992). Roach was a producer, director, and screenwriter best known for his comedies in the silent and early sound eras. He broke into film in 1915, making shorts with his friend, comic actor Harold Lloyd. Roach's comedies were known for their plots, rather than relying solely on visual gags as did the films of his chief rival, Mack Sennett. Roach's formula proved to be successful, and he produced films starring Will Rogers, Harry "Snub" Pollard, Charlie Chase, and the comedy team of Stan Laurel and Oliver Hardy. While he directed some of the films, he left most of them in the hands of other filmmakers, particularly Leo McCarey. He also introduced the Our Gang comedies, featuring an ensemble of child actors; these shorts proved enduringly popular and enjoyed a revival on television (where they were renamed "Little Rascals") in the 1950's. Roach made the transition to sound smoothly, and he anticipated the decline of the one- and two-reel short as well. Working with his son, Hal Roach, Jr., he produced successful feature films during the 1940's. In the 1950's, he moved into television, where one of his productions was *Amos 'n'Andy*. His productions of Laurel and Hardy's *The Music Box* (1932) and the Our Gang's *Bored of Education* (1936) won Academy Awards for comedy short subjects. As producer-director, Roach's additional film credits include the silent shorts *Lonesome Luke* (1915), *Fireman, Save My Child* (1918), and *Number Please* (1920). As producer, his credits include the silent shorts *Our Gang* (1922), *Putting Pants on Philip* (1927), and *Another Fine Mess* (1930), as well as the sound features *Sons of the Desert* (1933), *Babes in Toyland* (1934), *Topper* (1937), *Of Mice and Men* (1939), *One Million B.C.* (1940), and *One Million Years B.C.* (1966).

Bill Rowe (?-September 29, 1992). Rowe was a sound man and director of postproduction at England's Elstree Studios. He won an Academy Award for his work on *The Last Emperor* (1987). His additional film credits include *Alien* (1979), *The French Lieutenant's Woman* (1981), and *The Killing Fields* (1984).

Robert W. Russell (1912-February 11, 1992). Russell was a screenwriter who, along with collaborator Frank Ross, earned an Academy Award nomination for *The More the Merrier* (1943). His additional screen credits include *The Well-Groomed Bride* (1946), *The Lady Says No* (1951), *Come September* (1961), and *Walk, Don't Run* (1966).

Chester W. Schaeffer (1902-January 5, 1992). Schaeffer was an editor whose work on *The Well* (1951) earned for him an Academy Award nomination. His additional film credits include *Dinner at Eight* (1933), *The Canterville Ghost* (1944), *Pillow Talk* (1959), and *The Oscar* (1966).

Robert Shayne (1910-November 29, 1992). Born Robert Shaen Dawe, Shayne was an actor who played a variety of lead and supporting roles, primarily in B pictures. His screen credits include *Mr. Skeffington* (1944), *Nobody Lives Forever* (1946), *Murder Is My Beat* (1955), *North by Northwest* (1959), and *Son of Flubber* (1963).

Herbert Spencer (1905-September 18, 1992). Born in Chile, Spencer was a composer and arranger whose work on *Scrooge* (1970) and *Jesus Christ Superstar* (1973) earned for him Academy Award nominations. He worked under Alfred Newman at Twentieth Century-Fox on such films as *Gentlemen Prefer Blondes* (1953), *The King and I* (1956), and *Hello,*

Dolly! (1969). In the 1970's, he began working with composer John Williams on such films as *Jaws* (1975), *Star Wars* (1977), *Close Encounters of the Third Kind* (1977), *Superman* (1978), and *E. T.: The Extra-Terrestrial* (1982).

June Storey (1919-December 18, 1992). Storey was an actress best known for her work in ten of Gene Autry's most famous Republic Westerns. These films included *South of the Border* (1939), *Blue Montana Skies* (1939), and *Rancho Grande* (1940). Her additional screen credits include *Girls' Dormitory* (1936), *In Old Chicago* (1938), *Island in the Sky* (1938), and *The Snake Pit* (1948).

John Sturges (January 3, 1911-August 18, 1992). Sturges was a director best known for his mature Westerns and other action films from the 1950's into the 1970's. A production designer and editor at RKO prior to World War II, Sturges made training films for the Army Air Corps, and after the war worked at Columbia making B pictures such as *The Man Who Dared* (1946) and *Keeper of the Bees* (1947). His breakthrough film was *Bad Day at Black Rock* (1954), dubbed a "psychological Western" by film critics. His *Gunfight at the O.K. Corral* (1957) was followed a decade later by another, darker look at the legend of Wyatt Earp in *Hour of the Gun* (1967). His most memorable film was *The Magnificent Seven* (1960), a reworking of Akira Kurosawa's *Seven Samurai* (1954) as a Western. Sturges continued his commitment to action pictures with *The Great Escape* (1963), featuring Steve McQueen; *Joe Kidd* (1972), which starred Clint Eastwood; and *McQ* (1974), one of John Wayne's last films. His additional film credits include *Escape from Fort Bravo* (1953), *Sergeants 3* (1962), *The Hallelujah Trail* (1965), *Ice Station Zebra* (1968), *Marooned* (1969), and *The Eagle Has Landed* (1977).

Marshall Thompson (November 27, 1925-May 18, 1992). Thompson was an actor who broke into films at Metro-Goldwyn-Mayer, where he played juvenile leads in such films as *Reckless Age* (1944) and *They Were Expendable* (1945). In the 1950's, he graduated to adult roles. He also appeared extensively on television, starring in *Daktari*, which was based on the film *Clarence, the Cross-Eyed Lion* (1965) in which he appeared and which he cowrote. His additional acting credits include *Command Decision* (1948), *To Hell and Back* (1955), *The First Man into Space* (1959), *A Yank in Viet-Nam* (1964, which he also directed), and *The Turning Point* (1977).

Dorothy Tree (May 21, 1909-February 12, 1992). Born Dorothy Triebitz, Tree was an actress who began her film career with *Just Imagine* (1930). She appeared opposite Edward G. Robinson in *Confessions of a Nazi Spy* (1939), which led to a succession of German parts. Her career was effectively ended in the early 1950's when she and her husband, screenwriter Michael Uris, ran afoul of the McCarthy-era blacklist. Her additional film credits include *The Three Godfathers* (1936), *Abe Lincoln in Illinois* (1940), *Nazi Agent* (1942), *Hitler: Dead or Alive* (1943), *The Asphalt Jungle* (1950), and *The Men* (1950).

Karl Tunberg (March 11, 1907-April 4, 1992). Tunberg was a screenwriter who had a lengthy career writing Hollywood features. He received an Academy Award nomination for his screenplay of *Ben-Hur* (1959). His additional screenwriting credits include *Rebecca of Sunnybrook Farm* (1938), *Down Argentine Way* (1940), *A Yank in the R.A.F.* (1941), *Beau Brummel* (1954), *Taras Bulba* (1962), and *Harlow* (1965).

Diane Varsi (1937-November 19, 1992). Varsi was an actress whose first role, as Lana Turner's troubled daughter in *Peyton Place* (1957), earned for her an Academy Award nomination as Best Supporting Actress. She appeared in several films shortly thereafter before deciding impulsively in 1959 to retire from films. She came to regret her decision a few years later but found it difficult to get work. Her additional screen credits include *Ten North*

Frederick (1958), *From Hell to Texas* (1958), *Wild in the Streets* (1968), *Bloody Mama* (1970), *Johnny Got His Gun* (1971), and *I Never Promised You a Rose Garden* (1977).

Bill Walker (1896-January 27, 1992). Walker was an African-American actor who was a leader in pressing for realistic, nonstereotypical film roles for black performers. His film credits include *The Long, Hot Summer* (1958), *Porgy and Bess* (1959), *To Kill a Mockingbird* (1962), and *The Great White Hope* (1970).

Nancy Walker (1922-March 25, 1992). Walker was an actress best known for her 1970's television work in such popular series as *The Mary Tyler Moore Show*, *Rhoda*, and *The Nancy Walker Show*. She specialized in comedy, and early in her career she appeared in musical comedies such as *Best Foot Forward* (1943), *Girl Crazy* (1943), and *Broadway Rhythm* (1944). After directing for television, she directed the disco musical *Can't Stop the Music* (1980).

Bill Williams (1916-September 21, 1992). Born William Katt, Williams was an actor who specialized in leading-man roles in action films as well as on television, where he starred in *The Adventures of Kit Carson*. He married his frequent costar, Barbara Hale; their son is actor William Katt. Williams' screen credits include *Thirty Seconds over Tokyo* (1944), *Till the End of Time* (1946), *A Likely Story* (1947), *Son of Paleface* (1952), *Oklahoma Territory* (1960), *The Hallelujah Trail* (1965), and *Rio Lobo* (1970).

Ian Wolfe (1896-January 23, 1992). Wolfe was a character actor who appeared in more than 150 films, specializing in the role of villains. His film credits include *The Barretts of Wimpole Street* (1934), *Mutiny on the Bounty* (1935), *Clive of India* (1935), *Johnny Belinda* (1948), *Julius Caesar* (1953), *Rebel Without a Cause* (1956), *The Lost World* (1960), and *THX-1138* (1971).

LIST OF AWARDS

Academy Awards

Best Picture: Unforgiven
Direction: Clint Eastwood (*Unforgiven*)
Actor: Al Pacino (*Scent of a Woman*)
Actress: Emma Thompson (*Howards End*)
Supporting Actor: Gene Hackman (*Unforgiven*)
Supporting Actress: Marisa Tomei (*My Cousin Vinny*)
Original Screenplay: Neil Jordan (*The Crying Game*)
Adapted Screenplay: Ruth Prawer Jhabvala (*Howards End*)
Cinematography: Philippe Rousselot (*A River Runs Through It*)
Editing: Joel Cox (*Unforgiven*)
Art Direction: Luciana Arrighi and Ian Whittaker (*Howards End*)
Visual Effects: Ken Ralston, Doug Chiang, Doug Smythe, and Tom Woodruff (*Death Becomes Her*)
Sound Effects Editing: Tom C. McCarthy and David E. Stone (*Bram Stoker's Dracula*)
Sound: Chris Jenkins, Doug Hemphill, Mark Smith, and Simon Kaye (*The Last of the Mohicans*)
Makeup: Greg Cannom, Michele Burke, and Matthew W. Mungle (*Bram Stoker's Dracula*)
Costume Design: Eiko Ishioka (*Bram Stoker's Dracula*)
Original Score: Alan Menken (*Aladdin*)
Original Song: "Whole New World" (*Aladdin*: music, Alan Menken; lyrics, Tim Rice)
Foreign-Language Film: Indochine (France)
Short Film, Animated: Mona Lisa Descending a Staircase (Joan C. Gratz)
Short Film, Live Action: Omnibus (Sam Karmann)
Documentary, Feature: The Panama Deception (Barbara Trent and David Kasper)
Documentary, Short Subject: Educating Peter (Thomas C. Goodwin and Gerardine Wurzburg)
Honorary Oscar: Federico Fellini
Gordon E. Sawyer Award: Erich Kaestner
Jean Hersholt Humanitarian Award: Audrey Hepburn and Elizabeth Taylor

Directors Guild of America Award

Director: Clint Eastwood (*Unforgiven*)

Writers Guild Awards

Original Screenplay: Neil Jordan (*The Crying Game*)
Adapted Screenplay: Michael Tolkin (*The Player*)

New York Film Critics Awards
Best Picture: The Player
Direction: Robert Altman (*The Player*)
Actor: Denzel Washington (*Malcolm X*)
Actress: Emma Thompson (*Howards End*)
Supporting Actor: Gene Hackman (*Unforgiven*)
Supporting Actress: Miranda Richardson (*The Crying Game*)
Screenplay: Neil Jordan (*The Crying Game*)
Cinematography: Jean Lapine (*The Player*)
Foreign-Language Film: Raise the Red Lantern (China)
New Director: Allison Anders (*Gas Food Lodging*)

Los Angeles Film Critics Awards
Best Picture: Unforgiven
Best Animated Film: Aladdin
Direction: Clint Eastwood (*Unforgiven*)
Actor: Clint Eastwood (*Unforgiven*)
Actress: Emma Thompson (*Howards End*)
Supporting Actor: Gene Hackman (*Unforgiven*)
Supporting Actress: Judy Davis (*Husbands and Wives*)
Screenplay: David Webb Peoples (*Unforgiven*)
Cinematography: Zhao Fei (*Raise the Red Lantern*)
Original Score: Zbigniew Preisner (*Damage*)
Foreign Film: The Crying Game (Great Britain and Ireland)
Outstanding Documentary: Black Harvest (Kevin Connolly and Robin Anderson) and *Threat* (Stefan Jarl), tie
Independent/Experimental: It Wasn't Love (Sadie Benning)
Career Achievement: Budd Boetticher
New Generation: Carl Franklin (*One False Move*)

National Society of Film Critics Awards
Best Picture: Unforgiven
Direction: Clint Eastwood (*Unforgiven*)
Actor: Stephen Rea (*The Crying Game*)
Actress: Emma Thompson (*Howards End*)
Supporting Actor: Gene Hackman (*Unforgiven*)
Supporting Actress: Judy Davis (*Husbands and Wives*)
Screenplay: David Webb Peoples (*Unforgiven*)
Cinematography: Zhao Fei (*Raise the Red Lantern*)
Documentary: American Dream (Barbara Kopple and Arthur Cohn)
Foreign-Language Film: Raise the Red Lantern (China)
Experimental Citation: Another Girl, Another Planet (Michael Almereyda)

National Board of Review Awards
Best English-Language Film: Howards End
Direction: James Ivory (*Howards End*)
Actor: Jack Lemmon (*Glengary Glen Ross*)
Actress: Emma Thompson (*Howards End*)
Supporting Actor: Jack Nicholson (*A Few Good Men*)
Supporting Actress: Judy Davis (*Husbands and Wives*)
Foreign-Language Film: Indochine (France)
Documentary: Brother's Keeper (Joe Berlinger and Bruce Sinofsky)
The D. W. Griffith Career Achievement Award: Shirley Temple

Golden Globe Awards
Best Picture, Drama: Scent of a Woman
Best Picture, Comedy or Musical: The Player
Direction: Clint Eastwood (*Unforgiven*)
Actor, Drama: Al Pacino (*Scent of a Woman*)
Actress, Drama: Emma Thompson (*Howards End*)
Actor, Comedy or Musical: Tim Robbins (*The Player*)
Actress, Comedy or Musical: Miranda Richardson (*Enchanted April*)
Supporting Actor: Gene Hackman (*Unforgiven*)
Supporting Actress: Joan Plowright (*Enchanted April)*
Screenplay: Bo Goldman (*Scent of a Woman*)
Original Score: Alan Menken (*Aladdin*)
Original Song: "A Whole New World" (*Aladdin:* music, Alan Menken; lyrics, Tim Rice)
Foreign-Language Film: Indochine (France)

Golden Palm Awards (Cannes International Film Festival)
Palme d'Or: The Best Intentions (Bille August)
Grand Jury Prize: The Stolen Children (Gianno Amelio)
Forty-fifth Anniversary Prize: Howards End (James Ivory)
Actor: Tim Robbins (*The Player*)
Actress: Pernilla August (*The Best Intentions*)
Direction: Robert Altman (*The Player*)
Jury Prize: El Sol Del Membrillo (Victor Erice) and *An Independent Life* (Vitali Kanevski), tie
Grand Technical Prize: Fernando Solanas (*The Voyage*)
Camera d'Or: John Turturro (*Mac*)
Palme d'Or, Short Film: Omnibus (Sam Karmann)
Special Jury Prize, Short Film: La Sensation (Manuel Poutte)

British Academy Awards
Best Picture: Howards End

Direction: Robert Altman (*The Player*)
Actor: Robert Downey, Jr. (*Chaplin*)
Actress: Emma Thompson (*Howards End*)
Supporting Actor: Gene Hackman (*Unforgiven*)
Supporting Actress: Miranda Richardson (*Damage*)
Original Screenplay: Woody Allen (*Husbands and Wives*)
Adapted Screenplay: Michael Tolkin (*The Player*)
Original Score: David Hirschfelder (*Strictly Ballroom*)
Best Foreign-Language Film: Raise the Red Lantern (China)
Short Film, Live Action: Omnibus (Anne Bennett and Sam Karmann)
Short Film, Animated: Daumier's Law (Ginger Gibbons and Geoff Dunbar)
Alexander Korda Award for Best British Film: The Crying Game (Steven Wooley and Neil Jordan)
Michael Balcon Award for Outstanding Contribution to Cinema: Kenneth Branagh

MAGILL'S CINEMA ANNUAL

TITLE INDEX

DIRECTOR INDEX

DIRECTOR INDEX

SCREENWRITER INDEX

SCREENWRITER INDEX

SCREENWRITER INDEX

CINEMATOGRAPHER INDEX

CINEMATOGRAPHER INDEX

EDITOR INDEX

EDITOR INDEX

EDITOR INDEX

ART DIRECTOR INDEX

ART DIRECTOR INDEX

ART DIRECTOR INDEX

ART DIRECTOR INDEX

MUSIC INDEX

MUSIC INDEX

MUSIC INDEX

PERFORMER INDEX

PERFORMER INDEX

PERFORMER INDEX

PERFORMER INDEX

PERFORMER INDEX

PERFORMER INDEX

PERFORMER INDEX

PERFORMER INDEX

PERFORMER INDEX

SUBJECT INDEX

The selection of subject headings combines standard Library of Congress Subject Headings and common usage in order to aid the film researcher. Cross references, listed as *See* and *See also*, are provided when appropriate. While all major themes, locales, and time periods have been indexed, some minor subjects covered in a particular film have not been included.

SUBJECT INDEX

SUBJECT INDEX